From Chains to Bonds

From Chains to Bonds

The Slave Trade Revisited

Edited by

Doudou Diène

Berghahn Books

NEW YORK • OXFORD

UNESCO Publishing

PARIS

Published in 2001 jointly by the **United Nations Educational, Scientific and Cultural Organization** and **Berghahn Books**

Library of Congress Cataloging-in-Publication Data

From chains to bonds : The slave trade revisited / edited by Doudou Diène.
     p. cm.
    Includes bibliographical references.
    ISBN 1-57181-265-2 (alk. paper)
    1. Slave trade–Africa–Congresses. 2. Slave trade–America–Congresses.
  3. Slave trade–Europe–Congresses. I. Diène, Doudou.

  HT1322 .F79 2001
  380.1'44'096–dc21   2001035400

  ISBN UNESCO: 92-3-103439-1

British Library Cataloguing in Publication Data

A catalogue record for this book is available from the British Library.

Printed in the United States on acid-free paper.

Contents

Part III Abolition of the Slave Trade and Slavery, and Changing Mentalities

List of Tables

Preface

IN HOSTING THE LAUNCHING CONFERENCE for the Slave Route project, Ouidah's ambition was to be the meeting place of memory – accepted and acknowledged – and the founding act of a dialogue based on solidarity around a common heritage. The Slave Route project in fact constitutes, on the ethical plane, a determination to acknowledge a major historical reality that has long been glossed over: the triangular commerce of the slave trade. The symbol of all forms of violence, this trade has been, generally speaking, either passed over in silence or dealt with furtively in history curricula as an episode in the relations between Europe and Africa.

In his address to the UNESCO General Conference at its 27th session, Mr Nicéphore Soglo, the former President of Benin, aptly situated the historical and moral significance of that process of concealment by quoting Nobel Peace Prize winner Elie Wiesel: 'The executioner always kills twice, the second time by silence.' Silence, the absence or virtual absence of the slave trade issue in most history textbooks in the majority of the world's countries. Silence, too, the failure to recognise the specificity of the phenomenon of the slave trade. It is precisely the urgent need to return to this key question that the UNESCO General Conference sought to assert, first and foremost, when it voted unanimously to launch the Slave Route project. In so doing, it established a framework for a process of reflection, at once global, multidisciplinary and international, designed to elucidate the underlying causes and mechanisms of the slave trade. This approach has been facilitated by corresponding initiatives – three of them exemplary – on the part of different member states.

- The Gorée-Almadies Memorial project, in Senegal, which highlights the deeper significance of the Island of Gorée, a site of memory that has been tenaciously preserved because it is a testimony to suffering and uprooting
- The exhibition 'Les anneaux de la mémoire', in the city of Nantes, which in many respects constitutes an ethical act of recognition inasmuch as it emanates from one of the major slave trading ports, which wished thereby to acknowledge the memory of the trade
- The 'Our third root' programme in Mexico, which gives substance to the many-sided nature of an identity long denied by highlighting, after the Amerindian and European roots, the African root of the cultures and civilisations of the Americas and the West Indies

This convergence of initiatives marked by the concern for historical truth and ethical rigour – representing a fresh look at the consequences of the slave trade – illuminates the other goal that the UNESCO General Conference wished to pursue through the Slave Route project. In a paradoxical way – but one that is both richly instructive and holds out great hope for the future – the initial barbarity of the slave trade was the act that founded new civilisations. In its primary sense, the slave trade was, it must be remembered, a movement: the movement – deportation, true, but none the less movement – of men and women who carried with them ideas, values, religions and traditions. It was precisely this culture in movement that maintained the strength to survive, to resist, to adapt and, finally, to ensure the rebirth of those men and women torn from the land of their forebears. Thus absolute violence produced, through the creative will of individual human beings and the life-force working through them, encounters and cross-fertilisations that, in the mysterious alchemy whereby identities are created, spawned new forms of culture and protean identities.

It is because it aims to apprehend, here and now, the reality of the birth and evolution of these new forms of life born of a death-fixated enterprise that the Slave Route project is truly focused on the future. Its essential ambition is to give substance, vitality and prominence to the fertile concept of 'links' adopted by the city of Nantes. For at the historical level, the link is at one and the same time part of the chain that held the slave fast and, looking to the future, the tie by which peoples whom history has thrown together into the storm are united at the deepest level. Bringing to light these links, promoting their different expressions, fostering proximities and solidarities, and highlighting the common core of a living heritage alike in its material and immaterial forms – these are all issues that make the Slave Route project and the Ouidah Conference central to, on the one hand, the United Nations Year for Tolerance and, on the other, the culture of peace, whose establishment UNESCO is seeking to promote. Peace, solidarity and development thus lie at the very heart of the project.

The Slave Route – so much conspired, so many connived to make it happen. Today, we reap the tangled legacy. What a moral debt for all those who took part, who gave their consent, who held their peace! And how great the ethical duty we have today to repeat, each morning, 'never again'!

And yet, in the twentieth century, what wars and violence, what barbarities! The Nazi atrocities, the sectarianism – once incomprehensible, and still intolerable – in Cambodia, the ethnic cleansing at the heart of Europe, the pitiless intercultural confrontations in Rwanda ...

We must therefore, looking our children straight in the eye, make the solemn pledge: Never again! We must make a reality of that *never again*, that *never more*, through preventive action, thanks to early warning systems – while realising that, in matters of prevention, success cannot be seen – and thanks to the rapid sharing of resources of every kind, a process that is crucial if we wish to root out intolerance.

History will record that it was in Benin, and more particularly at Ouidah, at once a memorial to and the living expression of the multiple consequences of the slave trade, that the international community decided to embark upon the fruitful enterprise of what I call its memory of the future. May our 'never again' of 1 September 1994, proclaimed at Ouidah, be heard and taken to heart in every corner of the globe, above all through this project of truly worldwide scope!

Let us hope that poets will never again write verse so bitter as the magnificent lines penned by Gratien Zoussou in 'I, once a slave, always a slave / I, always and ever, the slave':

> ... with all the fibres of my being
> Embroidered at all the trading-posts of Barbary.

Foreword

FOLLOWING THE 'OUIDAH 92' FESTIVAL, an event of worldwide impact which was attended by many distinguished intellectuals, a new meeting was held in this same historic city of Ouidah, so fraught with memories, on the occasion of the launching of UNESCO's international Slave Route project. Its purpose was to consider ways and means of enabling black peoples, formerly oppressed and reduced to slavery, to rise together, with the support of all the nations of the world, to the challenge of development.

The worst for black peoples is not that for centuries they were the victims of the greatest deportation in human history, the slave trade. The worst is that they themselves did, to a certain extent, internalise the racist discourse developed by that practice, and came finally to believe themselves to be inferior; that they lent a credulous and sometimes conniving ear to the sirens who sang in every tone the message of their congenital inferiority. Such sirens have been of every kind, from the most outrageous to the most ingenuous, from the 'big guns' represented by such aberrant works as Gobineau's *Essai sur l'inégalité des races humaines* and Hitler's *Mein Kampf* to the insidious statements of certain contemporary politicians. Otherwise serious, intelligent and efficacious men and women, these politicians, at the start of the twenty-first century, still believe that they can assert that Africa is not ripe for democracy, and are not above publishing sensationalist articles such as the one that appeared in a French weekly under the provocative title: 'A taboo question: should Africa be recolonised?'

That a project such as the Slave Route study can actually be launched is due to the fact that there are many who do not believe in such alleged racial flaws any more than they believe in the intrinsic superiority of some 'master race'. We know that the accidents of history must be explained in historical terms, that the atrocities which have occurred in Rwanda and in former Yugoslavia, just as much as those in Bosnia, are rooted in harsh realities and a tragic chain of circumstances. What is needed is concerted, lucid, intelligent action on the part of men and women of goodwill, and of the international community as a whole, rather than the sneering comments of some superficial analyst.

We can readily understand the sense of revolt voiced by the poet who wrote: 'Europe has for centuries crammed us full of lies and pumped us full of pestilence.' Europe? Césaire would be the first to reply: no, but rather a *certain* Europe, the Europe to which American and Caribbean blacks owe their deportation. But Europe was not alone. There was also the Middle East. We cannot pass over in silence the scale of the Middle Eastern slave trade. Many authors have highlighted this in their writings and publications, among them the late, lamented Ibrahima Baba Kaké, the highly gifted Guinean historian who died tragically in July 1994 and to whom I here pay heartfelt tribute for his irreplaceable contribution to African historical research.

All in all, whatever the origins of the slave trade and the itinerary that it followed, the results are in some respects the same: the same self-contempt, the same tragic internalisation of a sense of inferiority. That is where the true destitution lies. And in order to break out of it, we must dare to cast off the heap of lies that have been wrought over the centuries, to regain confidence in ourselves and come to understand that, as Césaire has so aptly written, 'man's work has only just begun'.

Benin is situated on that part of the Atlantic Coast that geographers until quite recently still called the 'Slave Coast'. In this country steeped in history we could not, even if we wished to, remain oblivious to the slave trade. Everything brings it to mind, from the ancient Portuguese fort and the vestiges of French and British forts at Ouidah to the sites which, in Porto-Novo, Calavi and else-where, are still today referred to in local languages as 'slave markets'. Other reminders include the ruins of the royal palace of Allada, the dwelling of the grandfather of Toussaint L'Ouverture, the famous general from Dahomey who played what is regarded as the key role in the liberation of Haiti during the French Revolution, as well as the Brazilian architecture of the old buildings erected in Porto-Novo and Ouidah by the freed slaves who had returned from Brazil, and the numerous families that still today bear Portuguese names: De Souza, Da Silva, D'Oliveira, Freitas, Vieira, D'Assomption, Da Conceição, D'Almeida, Paraiso or Garcia, to mention but a few. Everything in Benin reminds us of the shameful trafficking in slave labour and the heavy price our peoples had to pay, quite against their will, for the development and enrich-ment of today's industrialised countries – as I had occasion to point out in Nantes in November 1993 during a visit to the exhibition so appropriately enti-tled 'Les anneaux de la mémoire' (Links in memory's chain).

With its focus on these permanent cultural ties, and more particularly on the remarkable religious continuum that stretches from one Atlantic seaboard to the other, the 'Ouidah 92' Festival reminded anyone who might have been tempted to forget that Haitian voodoo is a later manifestation of the *vodun* cult still celebrated today in Aja-Fon country in southern Benin and southern Togo; that Brazilian candomblé is heir to the cult of the Orisha, still practised today throughout the Yoruba cultural area in southern Benin and southern Nigeria; that Fon, Mahi and Yoruba, spoken by us as vernacular languages, continue today to serve as sacred languages across the Atlantic; that the city of Kétou in the department of Ouémé in Benin in the heart of Yoruba country, with its magic gate built in the seventeenth or eighteenth century, is today, in the imagination of the followers of candomblé, a holy city.

That is why Benin began very early on to take an active interest in the Slave Route project, with its starting point in Haiti – a project about which a group of our intellectuals learned in December 1989 in Abomey, on the occasion of the commemoration of the death of King Glélé. Benin welcomed the opportunity to take part, in August 1991, in the first international meeting of experts organised on the project in Port-au-Prince, Haiti, and was happy to take the lead, as one of the meeting's recommendations urged it to do, until this major project could actually be included in UNESCO's regular programme and its financing underwritten by the organisation. Benin nevertheless will continue to do its utmost to support the project.

In doing so, however, we Africans cannot allow ourselves to become locked into a sterile attachment to the past, and even less to indulge complacently in the facile rhetoric of recrimination.

It is in a spirit of love, remote from all suspicion of hatred, and with a profound sense of the unity of the human race, that we must endeavour, transcending the falsifications and other lies designed to promote particular interests, to put history back on its feet.

Nor is there anything to be gained by concealing our own responsibilities in the disasters which have plagued and continue to plague us. Our collective complicity in the slave trade is well established, and our absurd divisions, our erring ways, and slavery as an endogenous institution have all been thoroughly explored by historians and anthropologists such as Claude Meillassoux and the Ivorian Harris Mémél-Foté, not forgetting one of the first Dahomeyan essayists writing in French, Louis Hounkanrin; nor can we ignore the cases of government mismanagement and even the predatory conduct of certain leaders. And that absurd will for power, that blind pursuit of power for power's sake, which inflicts so much suffering upon our peoples, is a reality that today stares us in the face.

What, finally, is to be said about Rwanda, Liberia, Somalia – about that immense tragedy that, from east to west, daily ravages our continent? Old demons that we believed had gone forever have been awakened, widening ancient divides and exacerbating tensions which were in some cases, it is true, created out of nothing by colonialism, but which should have been handled since the end of that system with greater skill and a greater sense of responsibility.

Such tragedies are, alas, also part of our history, and would preclude our continuing indefinitely to lay upon others the blame for our misfortunes, even if we were tempted to do so.

The fact nevertheless remains, stubborn and overwhelming, that we understand nothing about the underdevelopment or the extreme destitution of sub-Saharan Africa if we turn a blind eye to the historical scourges it has suffered for over four centuries: first, the slave trade, which was to empty it of its substance, then colonisation, which would in its own way – despite certain positive contributions that were, more often than not, purely fortuitous – complete, when all is said and done, this diabolical work, notably by causing increasingly large sections of our populations to lose the self-confidence and sense of initiative of which they were in ever greater need.

That is why the Slave Route project is of the greatest importance. Whole chapters of the history of the black peoples and of humankind are waiting to be illuminated or clarified, dynamic schemes are urgently in demand, and new prospects for South-South and South-North cooperation are crying out to be defined or redefined in all sectors.

The launching of this project is a great moment in history. It could mark a fresh start in many respects. It can provide an opportunity to pay tribute, once again, to all those, living and dead, who have helped to restore to black peoples, both in Africa and outside Africa, the necessary confidence in themselves, the awareness of their historical roots and of their continuity in time.

The destiny of the black peoples is inseparable from that of humankind. Conversely, humankind will never be truly itself if it still harbours within it a race that is downtrodden or peoples that are oppressed, crushed and without prospects. The major challenge today is to reinvent hope. Together, we can. Together, we must.

Nicéphore Soglo
President of the Republic of Benin, 1991–96

'The Body of Memory'

by Mohammed Kacimi

To Tchicaya U Tam'si, who said to me one day: "The future will be black";
and we chuckled together over the ambiguity of the remark.
(Asilah, 1988)

Like a storyteller in the days of my childhood haunted by the fear
of forgetting I come from the North of this divided continent
Many not knowing my name have even said that I am
an anonymous teller of tales
I am called Bambara
I open the book of memory of pitch-dark nights and of blood
fraught with moans with erasures with absent words
with the seepage of brown inks and of nostalgia
I have made the dumb birds sing the hollow wood
sculpt infinity's rites
I have thought to scan time as absolute unity
The Body free
Then …
The voice still red
the deep forest
The storm-tossed coasts
A few words glow
In the body
I have known the shores
whence
boats set sail for
night
From coast to coast

The wind rises on the black sand
My name is Bambara
I have known the breeze of the chilly isles
castration

the secrets of chaos
the mystery of pain
the ocean's gales
The crack of the white whip
of starless nights
My name is Bambara
They will tell me: it's ancient Bambara history
and I open wide my eyes
so as not to lose
the pain of the unknown
the resonance of drawn skins
on sculpted trunks
The intertwining of tales
the transmission of breath
On this continent that yields gold and flesh
liquid pleasures
so precious
It was at Ouidah on Gorée Island
through a door open upon the ocean
that I listened for the first time to the sounds of chains

My name is Bambara
I have known all the scum
of the earth
They'll tell me, that's not poetry
I'll say … what is poetry?
And back I come
to the tale
I paint my nerves
On unknown lands
I have traced out furrows
with my phallus
with my toes
scarred by dint of dreaming
of circles of fire of ebony songs
of forests like infinity
of the breasts of the uncles' daughters
of the hollow of their backs
all blood-soaked. Of the falling lines that trace the body's
crazy vertigo
The slave trader
stares at me
his eyes death-glazed
stinking of alcohol and sweat
the blood of black virgins
and tobacco

Outside
the wind
the lapping of the waves against the hull
and death
Does the wind have a soul?
Sinuous invisible
devilish ...
it makes the reeds rustle and the waves

bodies and sails and masts ...
          My name is Bambara
with my Sperm
you have sugared your coffee
on mild mornings
His Highness' tea
served at five each afternoon
the chocolate of princes and princesses
of tyrants of merchants of gunpowder
of flesh vicious brigands
and other merchants

of death ...
          Shelters made with my black skin
my brown or white skin
the body returns
in the breath of a saxophone
          of a trumpet
          or a piano
my body dwells in
the burns of the 'white summers'
loss transposes the voice

Like a return
          My name is Bambara
I am the secret Soil
of mysteries
From coast to coast
I have fed the fantasies
of kings and queens
Sometimes as a Eunuch
with deft teasing hands with white teeth
I have brought a shudder nightlong to the corridors
the secret passages of the palaces
and the honeycomb of the blind arcades
I have been the witness of vice
of adultery of plots of murders

of the son's conspiracy against the father
and the brother's against his brother

Up to the present day
        You can look at the Orientalist paintings
in which I am the secret object of a furtively peeping
and servile desire
        I know all the shapes of keyholes
the divisions of the odalisques' bodies the curves
of the buttocks of my masters and mistresses their warts
I can even facilitate their breeding or
improve their offspring
I am part of All the mysteries
of Every Age
I work my way back through Time
so as not to be long

I Bambara
        I say: nothing has changed
        the world penetrated by satellites by spies of
        all kinds unknown missiles
        cold wars and hot
        From Hiroshima to the ends of the desert
        where the oases die
        from tar and ultrasound and waste
and other poisons
that I know nothing of

        Ever still in the depths of the impenetrable nights
Tyrants bring down other Tyrants armies bring down
other armies
blood spills the same blood
My name is Bambara I am a teller of tales
my eyes glaze over my veins
open a white light
flows in my body
in that dark part of truth
events will be but
the splintering of the unexpected

From the Slave Trade to the Challenge of Development: Reflections on the Conditions for World Peace

Doudou Diène
Director of the Division for Intercultural Projects, UNESCO

The title of the launching conference for the international Slave Route project encapsulates the key concepts of 'slave trade, development and world peace', thereby signposting the intellectual itinerary of the intercultural dialogue that UNESCO plans to institute. The first concern, for UNESCO and for the international community, is purposely to revisit a historical occurrence that the French historian Jean-Michel Deveau has described, in his work *La France au temps des négriers*, as 'by virtue of its duration and scale, the greatest tragedy of human history'.

Due to the universal silence that has shrouded it, the extreme violence that attended it, the troubling light that it casts on the scale of values of the societies that spawned it and the immense transformations and interactions to which it gave rise, the transatlantic slave trade may be compared, in the historical dimension, to the invisible matter that, according to astrophysicists, occupies the greater part of the universe and whose imperceptible presence explains the movement of all the heavenly bodies. Development, human rights, cultural pluralism, these major issues of today's world are in fact deeply marked by a 'black hole' in the history of humanity: the transatlantic slave trade. Africa's state of development cannot be explained without reference to the radical destructuring of African societies and the terrible blood-letting to which Africa was subjected on a systematic, lasting and organized basis during the centuries of the trans-Saharan and transatlantic slave trade.

The current scale and persistence of violations of human rights are undoubtedly linked to the silence and oblivion in which the slave trade was cloaked because the championing of human rights is a combat waged by memory, one in which the tragedies that have remained hidden, unexplained and unacknowledged inevitably return to haunt us, and are repeated in time and space. The transatlantic slave trade, the most massive displacement of population in history, also constituted a clash of cultures that transformed the vast geocultural area of the Americas and the Caribbean into a living theatre in which the fundamental issue of today's world – cultural pluralism – continues to hold the stage. The construction of the ideology of the inequality of the races, the cornerstone of racism, is directly linked to the slave trade because it was essential to appease contemporary consciences and to justify the transformation of human beings into merchandise. It is therefore the whole set of basic preconditions for building 'the defences of peace [in] the minds of men', as prescribed by UNESCO's Constitution – development, human rights, intercultural dialogue, etc. – that the slave trade has marked so deeply with its stamp.

It was on these essential issues that several hundred intellectuals from Africa, Europe, the Americas, the Caribbean and Europe sought to shed light, to promote new thinking and to exchange the results of their research when they met in September 1994 at Ouidah (Benin) on the occasion of the launching conference for UNESCO's international Slave Route project. A number of artists and performers who also attended the meeting devoted their talents to expressing, through painting, sculpture and music, the extreme violence done to bodies and minds by the slave trade. Psychologists presented their findings concerning its impact upon the deeper strata of the subconscious, the memory and the imagination – these being the ultimate, unsoundable refuges against depersonalization, but also fertile soil for the renewals, encounters and interactions to come beyond the Middle Passage, as well as for new departures. But it was above all the vigilant, imperative concern to respect strict historical truth, in the face of the ignorance and revisionism which have clouded understanding of the slave trade, that marked the work of the Ouidah Conference and guaranteed the high scientific calibre of the communications presented in this volume. These communications confirm hypotheses and provide new facts but, above all, map out the future lines of inquiry concerning the slave trade and its consequences. Bringing together all relevant disciplines, the Ouidah Conference constituted, at a deep level, the meeting of men and women of every race whom the issue of the slave trade has literally haunted for many years – an issue which they have explored in the solitude of academic institutions where the mere fact of making it their special area of study frequently represented a risk for their careers.

The Conference also paid a moving tribute to the memory of Ibrahima Baba Kaké, one of the pioneers of historical research on the slave trade, who, having done sterling work to help prepare for the Conference, was felled by a heart attack at the very moment when he was about to pick up his tickets in order to attend. UNESCO wishes to honour his memory by publishing, as part of the introduction to this volume, the communication which he had prepared for the Conference – 'Popularisation of the History of the Slave Trade'.

The attendance at the Conference by Mr Nicéphore Soglo, President of the Republic of Benin from 1991 to 1996, and the former Director-General of UNESCO, symbolised the end of the silence which has surrounded the question of the slave trade and signified that, henceforth, the underlying causes, the practices involved and the consequences of the triangular trade constitute an issue of universal importance. The way is thus reopened for an approach which – in its study of the initial tragedy to the cultural cross-fertilization to which it has given rise – represents a sort of historical 'big bang' by which Africa's 'second exodus', after that of *Homo sapiens*, is transforming servitude into a new life-force.

Popularisation of the History of the Slave Trade

Ibrahima Baba Kaké

POPULARISATION WAS LONG CONSIDERED bad form by certain Western academics, most of whom were loath to drag science down to street level, considering it the preserve of an élite with its own jargon. For years African academics, adopting the same attitude, followed in their footsteps.

Fortunately, things have changed since then. Many scholars today understand the need to transmit their knowledge to the general public. What would be the use of a purely confidential science that had no outlet? Nothing is more off-putting than a science clothed in an esoteric language. Our scientists and other researchers should write primarily for the uninitiated.

The idea of popularising the black slave trade is certainly a very well-chosen theme. Of all the chapters of African history, it is without doubt the most important and, curiously, the one least known to the general public and even to African intellectuals. It is an important chapter for two reasons: first, because it lasted for the exceptionally long time of no less than 2000 years, if antiquity is taken into account, and second, because of its political, economic and socio-cultural impact on the African continent. There is, however, no dearth of documents concerning the slave trade. A lifetime would hardly suffice to inventory all the archives on the subject that are tucked away in American, Asian and European libraries and in the memory of African peoples. And there must be hundreds of thousands of books on the subject that deserve to be studied. There is no need to use all this material to bring home to the peoples of Africa the tragedy that the trade has been for the African continent. There are now some good synoptic works that should be popularised. We consider this all the more necessary because revisionists have flocked to the history of the slave trade in recent years. They minimise both its scale and its consequences. For instance, the American historian Philip D. Curtin, who is regarded as one of the leading experts on the transatlantic slave trade, has written unhesitatingly that it is possible and even likely that the rise in population following the introduction of new plants exceeded losses sustained owing to the black slave trade, and that transatlantic migrations therefore resulted in a net population increase rather than a population decrease (Curtin, 1969, p. 270). However, every historian is aware that the slave trade, owing to the diseases that it helped to propagate and the civil wars that it caused, was the primary cause of the decline in the African population. Some 10,000 to 15,000 slaves left for the New World from Western ports each year in the sixteenth and seventeenth centuries, and up to 100,000 (with peaks of 150,000) in the eighteenth century.

Another aspect that revisionists have deliberately muddled is the responsibility of African kings and princes for having sold their fellows out of greed, thus exculpating European slave traders. While it has been established that, as in all countries and at all times, a certain élite keen to safeguard its interests did join forces with the invader, the fact does remain that the Africans, starting with many of their chiefs, fought the European and Arab slave traders. An example is the desperate struggle waged by King Alfonso I of the Congo against the Portuguese slave traders: his letters of protest to the king of Portugal and to the Pope can be found in the archives in Lisbon and the Vatican. Another example is the resistance of Sundiata, founder of the empire of Mali, to the institution of slavery. Then there was the famous *fatwa* (consultation) of Ahmed Baba, the great scholar of Timbuktu, held under the Songhai empire: he not only refuted the idea of a curse called down by Shem, ancestor of the blacks, but also condemned the slave trade being carried on across the Sahara by North African Arabs. In addition, there was Shaka's refusal to give free rein to slave traders in Zulu country. It would be quite absurd to blame the African chiefs and exculpate European and Arab slave traders. Pope John Paul II was not wrong when he solemnly made apologies to Africa on behalf of the West during his visit to Gorée in 1990. He acknowledged that the slave trade was the holocaust of the African peoples.

The question now is whether the West owes reparation to Africa for the slave trade and colonisation. As early as the 1950s, the famous doctor Albert Schweitzer started to answer this question in his book *A l'orée de la forêt vierge*:

> How have Whites of all nations acted towards the natives since the discovery of the new lands? What is the significance of the mere fact that so many peoples have already disappeared from places reached by Europeans flaunting the name of Jesus?... Who can describe the injustices and acts of cruelty committed for centuries by the peoples of Europe? Who can ever assess the ills wrought by the spirits and diseases that we have brought them?... We are heavily in debt. The good we are doing them is an act not of charity but of reparation. And when we have done all in our power, we shall have made reparation for only a small part of the sins committed.

In 1993 the Nigerian Mosshood Olawale Abiola demanded that black peoples be compensated for the damage suffered by the continent because of the slave trade. The historian Ali A. Mazrui fully agrees when he writes, 'The State of Israel did not exist when the Nazis perpetrated their crimes against the Jews, but the State of Israel is one of the beneficiaries of the damages paid by the Federal Republic of Germany for the holocaust. Twelve years of hell for the Jews, against several centuries of servitude for the Blacks.' Towards the end of the 1980s most Americans were of the view that compensation should be paid to surviving Americans of Japanese origin who had been interned in camps during the Second World War, following a decision by the Roosevelt administration, out of fear that they would form a fifth column in favour of Japan (yet another example of years of injustice – seven in all – compared with several centuries of servitude for the blacks). The principle of reparation, indisputable for the peoples mentioned above, is considered ludicrous by many when raised in connection with blacks. The fight to secure the reparations owed to blacks is based not on the West's guilt but on its responsibility for having, despite the abolition of slavery, perpetuated hereditary racism from generation to generation. The aim therefore is to make whites aware of the need to pass on moral capital from parents to children.

Some people believe that Africa should forget the torments of the past – slavery and colonisation – and instead look to the future. Unfortunately, however, the ills wrought by slavery and colonisation are still apparent. This is why the popularisation of the history of the slave trade is of the utmost importance to Africans and the survivors of the Middle Passage, the Africans of the diaspora scattered to the four corners of the earth. The primary object is to make them aware of the scale of the slave trade and its effect on the continent's development. The findings of work done by our researchers, whether historians, economists, sociologists or other writers, should therefore be widely disseminated to the public through all existing channels.

The history of the slave trade should be a compulsory subject on the syllabus for examinations at every level in schools and universities. Students studying for a bachelor's or master's degree should also be expected to write papers on specific aspects of the slave trade. Slave trade experts too should prepare publications for schoolchildren (textbooks) and the general public (essays). Audiovisual materials (in particular, slide photographs) should be used to add substance to extramural courses and lectures on the black slave trade.

Short and long films should be made by African film-makers with the advice of specialists on the slave trade for regular showing in cinemas and schools. Everyone remembers the tremendous success of the television serial based on Alex Haley's book *Roots* several years ago: it helped black and white Americans to understand the tragedy suffered by black people at the time of the slave trade.

Radio and television discussions grouping teachers, students and the general public could do much to inform people about the slave trade. A general atlas of the trade should be prepared by an interdisciplinary team of geographers, historians, economists and so forth. Such an atlas should be on the bookshelves of every decision-maker, intellectual and political leader in the African states.

Frequent exhibitions on the slave trade should be organised, particularly along the lines of 'The Chains of Memory' exhibition held by the city of Nantes in 1993. They should cover the mechanisms of the trade, the conditions under which the slaves travelled, sea and land routes, revolts and the treatment of slaves on arrival. Iconographic material, to be found mainly in European and American libraries, is needed for such exhibitions. Certain important documents – for instance, portraits of famous slaves – could be used for post-cards and stamps as an effective means of instruction and popularisation.

An inventory of former slave markets – both on the coast and in the interior of the continent – could be drawn up and certain places of remembrance, such as Gorée, duly restored. Our streets and main squares could be renamed in memory of the leaders of slave uprisings such as Toussaint L'Ouverture and Nat Turner Karnou.

A biennial prize could be instituted to reward the author or institution that has contributed most to spreading knowledge of the history of the slave trade. There could also be a competition for pupils in the fourth to sixth years of secondary education: the writers of the best ten essays on the slave trade would win a trip to the West Indies or America.

The follow-up to these proposals depends very much on the determination and political will of African governments. The black slave trade in a sense is the Sho'ah of the black peoples. Like the Jews, they are duty bound not to hide this past; such forgetfulness would be a further crime against humankind. We should not forget that memory is the guarantor of the future. If only for that reason, it deserves to be kept alive.

Bibliography

ALFORD, T. 1977. *Prince among Slaves*. Marrickville (Australia), Harcourt Brace Jovanovich.

CURTIN, P.D. 1969. *The Atlantic Slave Trade: A Census*. Madison, University of Wisconsin Press.

DAVIDSON, B. 1961. *The African Slave Trade*. Atlanta, Little, Brown.

DESCHAMPS, H. 1971. *Histoire de la traite des noirs de l'Antiquité à nos jours*. Paris, Fayard.

DEVEAU, J.-M. 1990. *La traite rochelaise*. Paris, Karthala.

EVERETT, S. 1979. *Les esclaves*. Paris, Nathan.

FISHER, A.G.B., and FISHER, H.J. 1970. *Slavery and Muslim Society in Africa*. London, Hurst & Co. Publishers Ltd.

GENOVESE, E.D. 1968. *Economie politique de l'esclavage*. Paris, Maspero.

GORDON, M. 1987. *L'esclavage dans le monde arabe du VIIe au XXe siècle*. Paris, Robert Laffont.

HENNESSY, J.P. 1969. *La traite des noirs à travers l'Atlantique*. Paris, Fayard.

KAKE, I.B. 1988. *La traite négrière*. Paris, Présence africaine.

KAY, G. 1968. *La traite des noirs*. Paris, Robert Laffont.

KILSON, M.L., and ROTBERG, R.I. 1976. *The African Diaspora*. Cambridge, Mass., Harvard University Press.

MAZRUI, A.A. 'Le monde noir mérite-t-il des réparations?' Afrique 2000 (Brussels), Nov.–Dec. 1993.

MEILLASSOUX, C. (dir. publ.). 1975. *L'esclavage en Afrique précoloniale*. Paris, Maspéro.

NICHOLS, C.H. 1972. *Black Men in Chains*. New York, Laurence Hill & Co.

PLIMMER, C., and PLIMMER, D. 1973. *Slavery: The Anglo-American Involvement*. New York, David & Charles Barnes & Noble.

POPOVIC, A. 1976. *La révolte des esclaves en Irak du IIIe au IXe siècle*. Paris, Geuthner.

RENAULT, F., and DAGET, S. 1985. *Les Traites négrières en Afrique*. Paris, Karthala.

SCHOELCHER, V. 1948. *Esclavage et colonisation*. Paris, Presse Universitaires de France.

SCHWEITZER, A. 1953. *A l'orée de la forêt vierge*. Paris, Club français du livre.

UNESCO. 1979. *The African Slave Trade from the Fifteenth to the Nineteenth Century*. Paris, UNESCO.

VERGER, P. 1968. *Flux et reflux de la traite des nègres entre le golfe du Bénin et Bahia de Todos os Santos du XVIIe au XIXe siècle*. The Hague, Mouton.

WILLIAMS, E. 1968. *Capitalism and Slavery*. Paris, Présence africaine.

Part I

History, Memory and Archives of the Slave Trade

Chapter 1

Women, Marriage and Slavery in Nineteenth-Century Black Africa during the Precolonial Period

Catherine Coquery-Vidrovitch

THIS CHAPTER, based on the attentive reading of sources and sundry case-studies – a partial résumé of which is provided in the notes – constitutes an initial approach to a study on the history of women in black Africa.[1] The complex process of marriage, as practised in a whole range of black African societies, has frequently been described. In rural societies, where such monetary customs and practices as existed were little developed, and were reserved above all for purposes of interregional and international trade, or so-called long-distance commerce (which remained under the control of the chiefs and sovereigns), matrimonial alliances were at the core of the economic, social and even political systems of balance of the peasant world. They involved circuits developed by the leaders of the group – the elders, heads of family and chiefs of lineage – between families with whom an alliance was sought, or between families in which there existed a relationship of debt or dependency. The husband brought to the marriage agricultural and status-enhancing goods such as heads of cattle, copper bracelets and items of apparel. The fact that livestock featured so frequently in these agreements is indeed the sign that the family giving the bride away had as much opportunity to add to its wealth as the family which took her in. As the husband-to-be, customarily a young man, did not himself possess such goods, he was dependent in this matter upon his own group, that is, his chief of lineage. It also happened that his contribution might take the form essentially of work, particularly in Central and Southern Africa, or in forest areas, such as Ibo country, to the southeast of present-day Nigeria. The young man would himself take part in various tasks or activities, which constituted part or all of his debt to his future family by marriage. He could be reduced to a state of virtual serfdom by his future mother-in-law.[2]

As for the wife, she was expected first and foremost to be a good breeder. To be sure, in the Western Sahel, a young unmarried mother was treated as a figure of shame, and might well be expelled from her village.[3] But in certain societies, such as the maritime Ogooué (Gabon), the bride was required to give proof of her fertility by becoming pregnant before she married. If the child was male, the family of the bridegroom would take charge of the boy, but nevertheless waited for a daughter to be born before endorsing the marriage through the payment of the dowry; it was only then that it could be sure of the 'good quality' of the bride. This was proof at the very least that (contrary to what still happens today in India and China) although the birth of a girl, the guarantee of the transmission of the work force, may not have been glorified, neither was it considered to bring dishonour.[4]

Marriage was thus at one and the same time an economic, social and political matter, the negotiations concerning which were the prerogative of the elders, who alone had power to negotiate and exercise control over the group's wealth. However, if for one reason or another the wife left the marital home and went back to her own family, it had to return the gifts received, since the marriage contract had in essence been broken and the family had thereby recovered – and was frequently ready to renegotiate by means of another marriage – the working capacity represented by the wife. This custom was not, properly speaking, a mercantile act (any more, in any case, than was, in most instances, the provision of a dowry in the West), particularly inasmuch as the payment could represent a value that was more symbolic than real – even if, as will be seen below, the wife was truly regarded in such exchanges as a chattel to be exploited. But it was a social and political commitment, one that developed into outright mercantilism only with the expansion of the market economy.[5]

This matrimonial pattern operated in the case of women of free status, whether or not the society was endogamic, that is, between people belonging to the same lineage or clan. However, certain societies engaged at the same time in the taking or purchase of slaves for marriage. A remarkable study has been made of this issue, among others, in the ancient lineage-based southern societies of present-day Côte d'Ivoire. These were groups of limited size (Ani, Gouro, Alladian, etc.), ranging from a few thousand to some tens of thousands of individuals, living in or on the immediate edge of the forest, or else scattered along the coastal lagoons in fishing communities.[6] These small populations suffered, at least since the nineteenth century (the situation in regard to earlier periods can only be sensed), from real demographic problems resulting from the high death rates which made the chances of survival of the group and, even more, its productive capacity highly uncertain from one generation to the next. This is perceptible in terms of the genealogical memory of the dominant lineages, whereby succession became problematical on several occasions owing to the absence of lineal descendants.

Seeking slave wives elsewhere – acquired by combat or purchase – held a twofold interest: on the one hand, the hope of increasing reproductive capacities – a hope that, as we shall see, frequently proved vain; on the other, and even more so in the case of matrilineal but patrilocal systems, that of strengthening – vis-à-vis his rivals – the lineage of the husband, since the children of a slave wife did not follow the customary rules but belonged automatically and definitively to the family of the father. As regards the slave mother, unlike free women she did not have the right to break the marriage or to have extramarital relations. Similar customs have sometimes survived for a long time in restricted societies whose commitment to the lineage system remained strong. Such is the case, for example, in central Nigeria (Cross River Basin) where in the 1930s, and perhaps then more than formerly, the practice of carrying off children and the purchase of slaves were still being reported among the Obubra, in the customary form of early marriages. The fiction of matrimonial compensation made it possible to escape prosecution for buying slaves: in 1944, the price of a girl was approximately £30 (as compared with £25 for a boy), and the children came from large and poor families living in the neighbouring districts of Okigwe and Bende. The custom was encouraged by the traditional authorities, who saw in it on the one hand a means of combating a dwindling of the local population, accelerated by occupational migrations, and on the other, the instability of marriages contracted with women enjoying free status in matrilineal regimes.[7] It should nevertheless be noted that other forest-dwelling societies practising slavery, such as the Ibo in Nigeria, had on the contrary outlawed marriages between free men and slaves,[8] probably because the dynamic population growth of this society enabled it to forgo resorting to such expedients.

As regards the aristocratic societies of the Sahel, they were wholly hostile to 'mixed marriages': there, the slave was at best a concubine. Moreover, the reproductive capacity of slaves was manifestly lower than that of free women, their slave status militating against it on two counts: in material terms, the reality of family life was denied slaves as a result of their being looked upon as mere chattels, a factor which hardly encouraged women to procreate; moreover, the incidence of infanticide and the practice of abandoning children was higher than elsewhere in such communities.[9] It was therefore not so much for their reproductive potential as for their productive capacity that slave women were sought after.

Nevertheless, most women slaves – whether wives or not – played a considerable role in the countryside. The practice whereby a child was placed by its family as a security in order to wipe out a debt or to offer reparation for breaching a particular custom was common everywhere. Very young girls were particularly targeted, doubtless because they performed a subordinate function in the original lineage, which was therefore less affected by losing them, and also because they represented, for the host family, the promise of a greater volume of domestic work. Failure by the girl's family to take her back meant that, ultimately, she became the source of a line of dependants or slaves in the family of her new protector.

The Islamised regions of West Africa, which were extremely hierarchised, boasted several categories of slave women: for example, in Soninke country (present-day Mali), a distinction was made between women who served the crown and ordinary slaves. The former, who were relatively well integrated into the front-ranking families, and tended to be employed more in domestic tasks of spinning, child-minding, water-fetching and so on, or even as professional storytellers, might enjoy certain privileges.[10] Just as in the emirates of North Nigeria, they were virtually alone in being entitled to secure their freedom – that is, to recover all the social and political prerogatives of a free person, a privilege normally granted to concubines who had borne children to their masters. However, only very rarely has this indelible stain attached to their origins not been preserved, more or less as a secret, right up to the present day: a free man still envisages only with revulsion the marriage of his daughter to a slave, regardless of his status, whereas the reverse situation raises fewer objections. Marriage between a free woman and a slave was therefore a rare occurrence. But it was not necessarily forbidden: indeed, Baba de Karo, who was born in the emirates of North Nigeria, points out that in such cases the children were born free 'because they had sucked the milk of a free woman'.[11]

By and large, women were rather less frequently sold, offered as gifts or killed than men, and for two primary reasons: their value as labour, and the necessary role they performed in the reproduction of slave 'livestock'. But even if the slave woman was put in the care of a male slave, she was not properly speaking married to him inasmuch as the man had no paternity rights over his offspring, except if he had the means to buy back his 'spouse' and children. This happened but seldom, for the price was high: it amounted to virtually the entire agricultural production of all the working members, of both sexes, of his family. Otherwise, as in the case of livestock, the offspring of the females belonged to their owner. In Senoufo country, the children of slaves were in principle inalienable. They were circumcised around the age of 12 or 13, at their owner's expense, and became privileged slaves (or *worono*), sometimes closely associated with the family: *Komo-yugo ni kawadi si i* [The male slave is a stud],[12] and the children 'followed the milk', i.e. the mother.[13]

The master or his dependants were free to have sexual relations with slave women. Likewise the free young man who was placed in the care of a privileged slave in order to learn to work at the same time served his sexual apprenticeship with the daughters or wives of his host. If the latter happened to catch him with one of them, the slave had the right only to strike the young master symbolically with his fist.[14] Finally, the perpetuation from one generation to another of the status of slave women was a common phenomenon, but one that varied from society to society. In particular, the memory thereof was far more lasting in matrilineal societies – where the mother transmitted her status to her daughters – than in patrilineal societies, where filiation depended upon the (free) man who bought his (slave) wife.

In such societies, free young women of good families lived surrounded by slaves. This was still the situation described by Baba de Karo, born around 1890, whose mother was a cloistered wife and who was herself raised by a slave nanny. Each of the men of her family possessed at least 20 slaves; the price paid for one woman was two male slaves.

Slave women were undoubtedly more numerous in Africa than slave men. The notion that the Atlantic slave trade contributed largely to this situation should be handled with some caution. In point of fact, the widespread claim that the Atlantic market was above all a consumer of male slaves calls for review. A recent study would seem to demonstrate that the sex ratio was more balanced than has hitherto been supposed, because work on the American plantations, above all in its initial phases, made little or no distinction between the sexes.[15] It is nevertheless true that, even in those areas of Africa where agricultural work was undertaken above all by men, as in Hausa country, the wealthiest families might well possess several hundred slaves who were employed on a large scale in the fields, regardless of their sex.

In the nineteenth century, central and above all south-central Africa formed the centre of an unprecedented expansion of the slave trade towards the Indian Ocean, which was balanced by a growing demand for firearms and Western manufactured products imported through Islamised Arab and Swahili traders. The insecurity created by the razzias was even greater there than the very real insecurity that prevailed in the Sahel, in Hausa country, where Baba de Karo describes how the raiders targeted their razzias preferably on women and young girls. In order to buy back his wives and daughters, the husband was obliged – when, that is, he was able to track them down – to pay very high sums in ransom: in the case she quotes, 400,000 cowries[16] for the wife, 400,000 for each of the three children, 400,000 for the child yet to be born. Baba de Karo does not report the price paid for the ten slaves who were carried off at the same time, or even whether they were recovered.

Prey to intensive slave trafficking, central Africa also became the locus of an increasing use of slave labour for national purposes – even if such a situation doubtless already existed in earlier times – and of the hunt for slave wives. This was in particular the case in Bemba country (the border area of present-day Tanzania and southern Zaire): the matrilineal ideology and the meagreness of matrimonial compensation help to explain the relative absence of structural sanctions designed to prevent the conjugal mobility of women of free status. The reluctance of the region's first colonial judges to approve the emancipation of women, whose 'excessive freedoms' had to be restricted, is instructive in this regard: 'Lately Chief Mporokoso, after a visit to his villages, told me that the women of the country were becoming increasingly unruly, and that the result was an evident decline in the birth rate. We should bear in mind the character of the Wemba woman … which has always been particularly independent – more or less that of a shrew – and, as the "elders" are the first to acknowledge, inclined to infidelity.'[17]

The use of slaves as wives was therefore, in principle, a guarantee of stability inasmuch as the women could not be reclaimed, not having given rise to any matrimonial compensation. However, the uncertainties of their status, which allowed them to be sold in case of need – and such occasions were common in those times of intensive trafficking – might lead to these women being transformed into veritable working tools on legs, their protectors being paid each time at the top rate.

Such was the life story of Bwanika, who was sold and married ten times over between 1886 and 1911. Her tribulations occurred in three phases: the first in the reign of Msiri, a great slave trader who died in 1891, the second during a period of turbulence and insecurity when male protection came to be seen as a vital necessity, and the third when she was taken in by a religious mission. Bwanika was born some time in the early 1870s in Luba country, where she was sold by her father, a polygamist who possessed 12 wives. As was the custom, her father had been obliged to pay the price of three slaves to the family of his wife, in compensation for the death of the mother and in order to secure, in exchange, the right to marry one of her younger sisters in order to guarantee the inheritance. As he was able to find only two slaves, he sold one of his daughters to secure the third. He had promised to take her back, but could not put together the necessary sum. Resold for a bag of gunpowder, Bwanika passed from hand to hand, for she was still too young to serve as a wife (or to work in the fields), before ending up in the capital, Bunkeya, as the wife of a slave trader who kept her for himself (she was apparently a great beauty). Msiri's death led to the disintegration of the empire and to the city's ruin. Bwanika's old master fled to Kazembe, where the chief, Mukoka, took a fancy to her; however, as a result of the rivalry between the two men, her old master finally got rid of her by selling her to a gang of slavers from the west coast. Bwanika managed to escape, and was once again protected by a man who took her as his wife. This man worked as a mason for missionaries who were setting up on the shore of Lake Mweru; however, having reached British territory, he negotiated Bwanika's sale on the sly to Arab merchants. After escaping yet again, she found refuge with one of Msiri's former officials, a convert who had entered the service of the Mission and who bought her back for the price of a rifle. From then on, having been taken on by the missionaries and having become the trusted servant of the wife of one of them, her constant concern was to buy her own freedom. She acquired it by trading on a small scale in pottery and chicken-raising, which provided the cash needed to redeem the rifle. The missionary noted the change that followed in the couple's relationship: as a free woman, she from then on went to the fields in the company of her husband (who previously had never failed to remind her of her price) and ate together with him: 'They sat and spoke together under the veranda of their house and, when one happened to mention the other to strangers, they spoke in tones of deference and respect that previously had been lacking.'[18]

In short, Bwanika, a woman endowed with great energy and, it seems, remarkable intelligence, whose status had for some 20 years caused her more suffering than was reasonable, and who was fully involved in her community and upheld its customs, acknowledged herself – and was recognised by others – to be free only once she had personally won the means of buying her own freedom. This situation was quite common at that time in the region, according to the fairly large number of testimonies from British missionaries and police and law officers present at the turn of the century. The most disturbing case was doubtless that of the woman who sought tirelessly to persuade the British authorities to allow her to pay for herself a ransom that no one was demanding from her! This was indeed doubtless an exceptional circumstance, for what emerges from the few accounts of slave women's lives collected at the time by the missionaries is, on the contrary, the degree to which, despite the turbulent events of that period, the community and kinship networks passed their information on women to one another. For example, in the strips of land stretching from Lake Nyassa to Lake Tanganyika (in east-central Africa), we see how such women were eventually taken back into their community of origin, despite all the breaks in their lives resulting from sales, abductions and escapes, sometimes over distances of more than 100 kilometers. Because they were exchanged at least as frequently as cattle, ivory or firearms, they represented a real value that very few were willing to allow to escape.

Narwimba, Chisi and Meli were three women who had been abducted as young girls from their family environment and who had known a series of masters and husbands before ending up at the Mission. They were all nevertheless tracked down by their first protectors, in whose homes more than one ended her days – and indeed of their own free will, so keenly did they feel the need to remain integrated in their community of origin, where they returned to the agricultural and domestic tasks which they knew to be their lot. Ultimately, they submitted, despite the vigour with which they had battled against adversity, yielding with a certain fatalism to the demands of social conformism. The fact is that, in that troubled era, young uprooted men could make ends meet by seeking out new work opportunities in the world of colonisation that was opening up for them, or, quite simply because they were less subject to group pressure, since they had the power to found new lineages, even if these lineages were inferior ones. But such could not be the lot of women since, whether slaves or not, they always belonged to someone: to their own lineage or to that of their husband or their master.

The fact is particularly patent in the case of Narwimba, born in mid-century to a family of chiefs: her aristocratic status did not help her to escape the common lot of the women of her region. In fact, she probably had a more chequered existence, since she began her life quite normally as a chief's daughter, lawfully married to a man to whom she bore six children, of whom only one survived. It was then that, as a young widow, she passed to her husband's nephew, Mirambo. In the following decades, Mirambo was destined to become one of the main leaders of the groups carrying out slave raids throughout the region. To him also, Narwimba bore six children (of which two survived); but when she began to grow old (she was then turning 40), he started to lose interest in her. She formed part of the booty captured in the course of a raid by a neighbouring chief, who sought unsuccessfully to sell her. After further ups and downs during which she passed from hand to hand, she was eventually returned to Mirambo, but without her children, who remained in slavery. Her status as a neglected old woman became increasingly precarious; she was able to marry her daughter only to a slave, and had the greatest difficulty in ensuring that her granddaughter was not, in her turn, given away as security by Mirambo in order to settle a dispute between farmers. In desperation, she found refuge in her home village, where she was merely tolerated since she had no husband capable of clearing a plot of land which she herself might then cultivate. It was for this reason that, at the end of her life, she finally settled at the Mission.

Chisi, born around 1870, had an even more difficult life. Captured by slavers, together with her elder sister, when only a child, she was sold several times, passing from hand to hand as and when the Swahili caravans criss-cross-ing Nanwanga country happened upon her. She escaped and was hidden and taken in by a chief, who placed her in the care of a sort of adoptive father, who eventually married her. However, as the other wives mistreated her, she refused to follow the family when it went off to settle under the protection of a neigh-bouring chief. She was of course obliged to abandon to their care her children, whom she managed to recover later, for she appears to have had a particular knack of extricating herself from the most difficult situations. On the death of her former husband, she married a pedlar and, as a result of the long periods he spent away from home, led a life that, though relatively independent, was a difficult one, for she was without protection. Sentenced to pay a large fine, she had no alternative but to seek the protection of her second husband's family, and ended her days partly at the Mission and partly in the home of one or the other of her children.

As for Meli, who belonged to the following generation, she became a slave at the age of five, on the occasion of a Bemba reprisal raid against her father, a minor local chief. Captured with a group of women, she was abandoned by them when they managed to escape, leaving behind the children. Placed in a household, she experienced the hard lot of a domestic slave girl, and was even-tually sold to a Swahili elephant hunter for the price of four pieces of ivory. Resold several times for pieces of ivory or lengths of cloth, she moved from caravan to caravan, despite the fact that the area was just beginning to be colonised. Around the age of 10, she was freed by whites and brought to the Mission, where a slow process of identification was started when a woman who happened to be passing through and heard her name re-established con-tact with men from her family. Married at the turn of the century through the good offices of the missionaries – who received the corresponding matrimonial compensation – then baptised in 1910, she was finally reintegrated, doubly, into her community of origin, both recognised by her father's family and adopted by that of her husband, who nevertheless intended to reap some ben-efit therefrom. She was in fact following custom: at the death of her husband, who himself worked as a carpenter at the Mission, she passed successively into the hands of two of the latter's relatives, the second of whom was polyga-mous, and with whom she lived for nearly 10 years until he died. His death occurred in 1934, that is, right in the middle of the colonial era.[19]

It is clear that, in practice, the distinction between the tasks and duties of a free woman and those of a slave was slight, so slight indeed that the first travellers, missionaries or explorers almost always defined the slave as being male: 'true slavery' – servile work and the absence of rights of succession – was a status that pertained to men.[20] The fact was that without 'free' ances-tors, wives and children, the male slave was hence unable to found a lineage of his own, and was not regarded as a member of society. He was not, in fact, recognised as having either sex or age, socially speaking; it was in this sense that he could be obliged to undertake women's tasks, such as water-bearing. The male slave was therefore someone who was 'obliged to do work that a woman would otherwise have had to perform':[21] a more lapidary summary of the status of women, whether slaves or not, at the dawn of the colonial era, could not be formulated.

The status of the slave woman was defined rather as being that of a domestic servant, more fully integrated or, at least, more easily integrable on account of the ambiguity of her functions, and was therefore regarded as less irksome than that of the male slave. All in all, as has been pointed out in regard to the Nuer of Sudan,[22] the man had to assert his superiority and his independence by maintaining a certain distance between his role as the master of production and the actual need he had of slave women in order to satisfy his needs. For example, the fact that he was in charge of the livestock but that women and children were assigned the task of milking enabled him to maintain his prestige. It was the women, obliged to knuckle down by virtue of their function as food providers, who served as intermediaries between the men and the livestock, between man and nature and, finally, between social dignity and physical necessities.

Whatever may have been written to the contrary – for historians still tend to idealise women's status in precolonial times, claiming that it deteriorated only with colonisation[23] – the lot of African women was thus a hard one in the nineteenth century, perhaps even harder than previously as a result of domestic political and social disruptions. In the West, the gradual shutting down of the Atlantic slave trade triggered an accumulation of slaves on the domestic market. These were used throughout Western Sudan by the armies raised by new empires created through conquest, but also as production tools in a veritable slave-based system then being developed, both in the Sahel, for the hand-weaving of fabrics, and in forest areas, for the processing and transportation of the new export products – essentially, palm nuts. A similar trend occurred in East Africa with the agricultural colonisation that the Arab and Swahili landowners, encouraged by the sultanate of Zanzibar, instituted in the island in the form of clove plantations and, on the African coasts of present-day Kenya and Tanzania, in the form of cotton and even sugar-cane plantations. We know from the first administrative surveys carried out, on the eve of the end-of-the-century colonial conquest, that slaves accounted for at least a quarter of the population of western Africa, and probably more in eastern and central Africa. Undoubtedly, many of these, if not the majority, were women, despite the scant interest shown in them by the first Western observers and the relative silence of the traditions – traditions that, truth to tell, have seldom been analysed by researchers in this field. Until lately (prior to the work of Meillassoux and Foté), the tendency was in fact to minimise the slavery, internal to Africa, of the 'house slaves', in relation to international slave trafficking.

The purpose of this chapter has been precisely to demonstrate that, when the focus is concentrated on women slaves, we find that considerably more information exists than might at first have been supposed, and that received ideas must at all costs be distrusted.

Firstly, at a time when virtually all specialists were continuing to speak of African 'peasants',[24] without necessarily being aware of the trap of mistaking the term to refer exclusively to 'peasant men', Meillassoux published in 1975 an all but revolutionary work on the topic. In it, he highlights the pre-eminent role played by women in African agriculture, and develops the argument that they had been exploited twice over – both as producers and reproducer – whereas throughout the colonial era the West, particularly the Victorianised, middle-class West, was on the contrary dreaming , without in fact coming very near to achieving that dream, except at the ideological level, of restricting women to their reproductive function by confining them to the home. In France, historical works on African women have remained to date relatively few and far between, particularly if the literature is compared to that produced by feminists writing in English, as has proliferated in the past decade. However, these writings owe a good deal to the early translation into English of Meillassoux's *Femmes, greniers et capitaux.*

Secondly, breaking once again with the prevailing spirit of caution and conformism, Meillassoux has pursued one of the rare truly innovatory research projects written in French on the history not of the black slave trade but of slavery in Africa (and elsewhere). Once again, we find echoes of his other lines of enquiry: the opposition between slavery and kinship, the way it meshes into the structures of power, its links with trade – inseparable from war, but which is also at odds therewith – and the constant presence of women. His knowledge of the Sahelian area has enabled him to confirm what he unhesitatingly terms the slave-driven mode of production, a mode that the Ivorian sociologist Foté was demonstrating at the same time (1988) in relation to forest-dwelling communities: namely, that in the nineteenth century all those in power, and African societies as a whole, had not only integrated slavery into the system but had also turned it into a dominant tool of productive work. Here again, Meillassoux was able to build on earlier observations in order to show in what respect slavery was, even more than a men's affair, a women's affair: the male slave was someone condemned to do what free men regarded as women's work. As for women slaves, they were, all in all, sexless, inasmuch as they were maids of all work, including tasks that free women were sometimes not authorised to perform (such as working in the fields, in Hausa country, under the influence of a form of Islam that favoured the confinement of spouses). Even more than male slaves, slave women were useful for purposes of production, even if, as Meillassoux has demonstrated,[25] a whole range of factors serve to explain why they were only moderately useful, by contrast, for reproduction. This observation is indeed truer in the case of the Sahel than of forest areas, where the deficit – and hence the demographic justification – could, as has been shown by Terray (1969) and Perrot (1982), be significant. It is to this debate that the present chapter will, it is hoped, make a useful contribution.

Notes

1. C. Coquery-Vidrovitch, 1994.
2. M. Wright, 1983.
3. On this subject, see *Hyènes*, the film by the Senegalese director Djibril Diop Mambety, 1992.
4. This is the outcome of a personal survey.
5. C. Meillassoux, 1960.
6. E. Terray, 1969; C. Meillassoux, 1975; C.H. Perrot, 1982; H.M. Foté, 1988.
7. B.B. Naanen, 1991.
8. G. Thomas-Emeagwili, 1985.
9. C. Meillassoux (1986) casts serious doubt, in the light of specific quantitative examples, on the demographic contribution of slave women. Slave couples, who enjoyed little or no recognition, lived under the threat of very great instability.
10. M. Diawara, 1989.
11. M. Smith, 1969.
12. C. Meillassoux, 1973.
13. M. Smith, 1969.
14. Ibid.
15. D. Eltis and S. Engerman, 1992, 1993.
16. The cowry was a small shell native to the Maldive Islands in the Indian Ocean, and was used as currency. At the time in question, 400,000 cowries were roughly equivalent to £10 sterling.
17. Marshall (1910), quoted by M. Wright (1983) (translated from the French, the original being unavailable).
18. D. Campbell (1916), quoted by M. Wright (1983) (translated from the French, the original being unavailable).
19. M. Wright, 1975 (pp. 800–819), 1983, 1988.
20. M. Wright, 1975.
21. Niebor, 1910.
22. S. Hutchinson (1980).
23. The works dealing with this subject, generally written in English, in which the literature is far more abundant than that available in French, are too numerous to mention here. Suffice it to recall that the most common topic covered is that of the deterioration in the status of women during the colonial era as a result of a process of differential monetarisation, which allegedly tended to be monopolised by men, while women, doomed to combine their ancestral tasks in the countryside with those abandoned by migrant workers, were squeezed out into the 'informal' sector. This claim is, overall, correct. However, certain wives left as de facto mistresses of family smallholdings also succeeded in acquiring independence and deriving a number of benefits therefrom.
24. Following the example of the then path-breaking work by Henri Labouret, *Paysans d'Afrique occidentale*, 1941.
25. C. Meillassoux, 1975, 1986.

Bibliography

BOHANNAN, P., and DALTON, G. 1962. *Markets in Africa*. Evanston (Illinois), Northwestern University Press.

CAMPBELL, D. 1916 (1983). 'Ten times a slave but free at last: The thrilling story of Bwanika, a central African heroine'. Quoted by Marcia Wright.

COQUERY-VIDROVITCH, C. 1994. *Histoire des femmes en Afrique noire*. Paris, Desjonquères.

DIAWARA, M. 1989. Femmes, servitude et histoire: les traditions orales'. *History in Africa* (Atlanta), No. 16, pp. 71–96.

ELTIS, D, and ENGERMAN, S. 1992. 'Was the slave trade dominated by men?' *Journal of Interdisciplinary History* (Cambridge), Vol. 23, No. 2, pp. 237–257, MIT Press.

———. 1993. 'Fluctuations in sex and age ratios in the transatlantic slave trade, 1663–1864'. *Economic History Review* (Oxford), Basil Blackwell Ltd.

FOTÉ, H.M. 1988. *L'esclavage dans les sociétés lignagères d'Afrique noire. Exemple de la Côte d'Ivoire précoloniale, 1700–1920*. Paris, Université Paris V/EHESS (Ph.D. thesis).

HUTCHINSON, S. 1980. 'Relations between the sexes among the Nuer, 1930'. *Africa* (São Paulo), Vol. 50, No. 4, pp. 371–388, University of São Paulo.

LABOURET, H. 1941. *Paysans d'Afrique occidentale*. Paris, Gallimard.

MEILLASSOUX, C. 1960. 'Essai d'interprétation du phénomène économique dans les sociétés traditionnelles d'auto-subsistance'. *Cahiers d'études africaines* (Paris), Vol. I, No. 4, pp. 38–67, Editions de l'Ecole des Hautes Etudes en Sciences Sociales.

———. 1973. 'Etat et conditions des esclaves à Gumbu (Mali)'. *Journal of African History* (Cambridge), Vol. 14, No. 3, Cambridge University Press.

———. 1975. *Femmes, greniers et capitaux*. Paris, Maspero.

———. 1986. *Anthropologie de l'esclavage. Le ventre de fer et d'argent*. Paris, Maspero.

NAANEN, B.B. 1991. 'Itinerant gold mines: Prostitution in the Cross River Basin of Nigeria, 1930–1950'. *African Studies Review* (Emery University, Georgia), Vol. 34, No. 2, p. 71.

NIEBOR. 1910. *Slavery as an Industrial System: Ethnological Researchers*. 2nd ed. The Hague, Nijhoff.

PERROT, C. 1982. *Les Ani-Ndenye et le pouvoir aux XVIIIe et XIXe siècles en Côte d'Ivoire*. Paris, Sorbonne Publications.

SMITH, M. (ed.). 1969. *Baba de Karo*. Paris, Plon (Collection 'Terres humaines').

TERRAY, E. 1969. 'L'organisation sociale des Dida de Côte d'Ivoire'. *Annales de l'Université* (Abidjan), series F, Vol. I, No. 2.

THOMAS-EMEAGWILI, G. 1985. 'Class formation in precolonial Nigeria'. In Toyin, F., and Ihonvbere, I. (eds.). *Class, State and Society in Nigeria*.

WRIGHT, M. 1975. 'Women in peril: a commentary on the life stories of captives in 19th century East-Central Africa'. *African Social Research* (Lusaka), No. 20, pp. 800–819, University of Zambia.

———. 1983. 'Technology, marriage and women's work in the history of maize-growers in Mazabuka, Zambia: A reconnaissance'. *Journal of Southern African Studies* (Oxford), Vol. 10, No. 1, pp. 55–69, Oxford University Press.

———. 1988. 'Autobiographies, histoires de vie et biographies de femmes africaines: des textes militants'. *Cahiers d'études africaines* (Paris), Vol. 28, No. 109, pp. 45–58, Editions de l'Ecole de Hautes Etudes en Sciences Sociales.

———. 1993. *Strategies of Slaves and Women: Life-Stories from East Central Africa*. New York, Lilian Barber Press.

Chapter 2

The Travel and Transport of Slaves

Mame-Kouna Tondut-Sène

... [Bayangumay] composed a poem in her head and attuned it to the
rhythm and melody of the dirge for the absent ...

> Oh, give me a message to take to the ancestors
> For my name is Bayangumay
> And tomorrow I will go away
> Yes, tomorrow I will cease to be an animal.[1]

AFRICA EXPERIENCED THE SLAVE TRADE in two forms: the internal trade affecting
African societies themselves and the external trade towards the Mediterranean,
the Arab countries and the Americas. The external Mediterranean trade goes
back to ancient times, while the Atlantic trade began in the fifteenth century
and continued to grow from the sixteenth century until its abolition in the nineteenth century. The two trades reflected a single brutality. Within the continent,
slaves were used to underpin the power of local rulers. As regards the external
trade, the use to which this all-purpose labour force was put depended on
whether it went to the Arab world or to the Americas. In the Spanish colonies
in America, African slaves were initially intended to replace the Indians, who
were less able to stand up to work in the mines. This 'traded immigration' of
Africans became a lucrative business, structured and organised through European companies set up to conduct it, a commerce which made a decisive contribution to changing the economy of the Western world. The slave trade was
thus the motor of the triangular trade that linked the three continents: Africa,
America and Europe. In Africa, it led to one of the greatest forced movements
of population that the world has ever seen and constituted a sort of unsuspected
and, very often, deliberately concealed genocide. The transport of slaves by
land, in columns in caravans, or by sea on slave ships meant nothing but physical and moral suffering, in an attempt at the depersonalisation that is the prelude to every form of enslavement. Human beings, subjugated by sheer force of
arms, would then, as Aimé Césaire said of colonisation, become mere 'things'.

The Movement of Captives by Land

Wars, acts of brutality, raids and seizures were the chief means of supplying 'black ivory' (as the slavers called black slaves). After being brutally seized by force, the first move in their delivery to markets for captives began with the formation of lines of men and women. Chained together – yoked to one another at the neck by wooden shackles – they began their long walk surrounded by local brokers or Arab traders, as contemporary documents show.

The caravans made up of men and women chained together followed the traditional routes of the trade in gold, ivory, salt or kola, depending on where the slaves had been captured. Ibrahima B. Kaké distinguishes four main routes for delivering captives to the Arab world: from west to east, from the Maghrib to the Sudan, from Tripolitania to central Sudan and from Egypt (the Upper Nile and Ouadai-Darfur) to the Middle East. The regions of the Atlantic trade were Senegambia, the Gulf of Guinea, the Gold Coast, and the countries of the Bight of Benin and Angola, where forts, trading posts and slave pens awaited consignments of slaves. Exhausted by long forced marches in the torrid regions through which they had passed, the slaves would be stored in baracoons. And there they would wait, still chained, for the dealing to be done, while each of the partners, brokers or slavers, attempted to make the most profit. This forced rest allowed the captives to rebuild their strength a little before resuming their route, halting only in the evening. Water and food rationing, the loads carried, made up of bundles that the brokers transported for their trade, and the lash of the whip made any attempt at flight pointless. Death offered the only way out. In the precarious calm of these waiting areas of the forts and slave pens on the coast, a quite different, quite irreversible adventure was awaiting the slaves: separation from their known world. The great distances covered in caravans would be followed by promiscuity and crowding in huge ships that would take them even farther away. Thus, some would leave the east coast, crowded in the holds of an *aloua* headed for the countries of the Gulf, while others, having reached the west coast, would enter the darkness of ships leaving for the Americas. There another, even more inhuman fate awaited them.

The Transport of Slaves by Sea

In the Atlantic trade, the movement of slave vessels was governed by a financial organisation that had already been well prepared in Europe. Licences – such as the notorious *asiento* or thing agreed – contracts, state monopolies, etc. regulated the movement of slaves, and a Casa de Contratación had been set up in Seville for this purpose. British, Danes, French, Germans, Italians, Portuguese, Spaniards and others freighted ships laden with barter goods that reached the coast of Africa and exchanged their cargo for a human shipment which would be the source of the economic wealth of the plantations of the sugar islands of the Americas. There should be no need to stress that the exchange was intrinsically unequal. Once rid of its cargo destined for barter (brandy, guns, cloth, glassware, iron bars, etc.), the ship would undergo some reorganisation in order to take on its human cargo. The carpenter would have to divide the midships area and put in a ledge, called a platform, halfway up. The space between the upper and lower deck being at most only 1.80 m, the slaves thus had only 90 cm to manage in. They would thus of necessity enter what was to be their home for the long months of the crossing with their backs bent. In the case of the flying trade, the slaves might be on board several months.

The earliest slave ships were large carriers of up to 350 tons deadweight, with several tons of foodstuffs and barrels of water on board. For reasons of handling and speed, these enormous ships were replaced in the nineteenth century by British brigs that were better equipped to cross the bar so common on some parts of the West African coast, especially given the heavy dependence of sailing vessels on the winds and atmospheric conditions along that coast. Torrential rain or equatorial calm would further worsen the conditions in which the slaves were held. In *La France au temps des négriers*, Deveau quotes the case of the *Mars* bound for the island of Príncipe: 'With constantly changing winds and currents, inadequate maps, perhaps, too, inadequate men, she [the *Mars*] wandered around for two months before making landfall there. After a short stop, she set off for a four-month crossing to Cayenne. In all, the first slaves taken on board would have been nine months on the ship.' It will be noted that the names given to various slaving vessels – the *Ange*, the *Jésus*, the *Notre-Dame-de-la-Pitié*, the *Afriquain*, the *Contrat social*, etc. suggest a subconscious desire for protection, which is paradoxical given the nature of the trade being engaged in, which had little place for compassion, although a 1740 Liverpool pamphlet did claim that by moving them 'under the gentle influence of the law and the Gospel, they [the blacks] advance several steps in happiness, albeit not in complete freedom'.

Embarkation and Accommodation of the Slaves on Board

After the anatomical examination that they were subjected to and after the 'formalities' of embarkation, the slaves would get to know their floating home. The surgeon-doctor on board would look closely for the slightest sign of malformation, since only those in perfect health, Negroes in their prime – what the French called *pièces d'Inde* – with no physical or mental defects and no obvious illnesses were saleable. The last operation before the crossing was the branding on the chest or back with the initials of the purchaser. Chained together, in twos or fours or sixes, the slaves were embarked, the men packed tightly in the hold, separated from the women and children, who were not chained and could move about freely on deck. In order to be able to breathe, and, given their large numbers, the men would stretch out for the night arranged in a quincunx, especially as ventilation was provided by only two openings, on each side of the vessel, crudely covered by two criss-crossed planks. However carefully the captives made their sleeping arrangements, it sometimes happened that the openings were too tightly closed, and some would be stifled to death. That is what happened in 1824 on the ship the *Louis*, where 50 slaves perished. The following day, the captain returned to the coast at Calabar to buy a new cargo of slaves.

In his *Histoire de la traite des Noirs*, Deschamps gives a detailed description of life on board these ships. A day could be summarised as follows. When the weather was fine, at 8 a.m., the slaves came up on deck, where they were washed and hosed with sea water. Teams emptied the night-soil buckets and washed the deck and the hold. Then, at 9 a.m., they took their first meal, made of dried vegetables together with fresh vegetables purchased on the coast, so long as they could be kept. Fresh water was filtered to remove impurities and any insects that had fallen into it. The afternoon was taken up with a variety of odd jobs and, to restore circulation in stiff limbs and drive out melancholy, a dance would be organised. On some ships, a member of the crew was expressly responsible for making the slaves dance, using the whip if need be. A second meal, consisting of a mess of groats, was served at 4 p.m. Then, the slaves went back down into the hold to sleep at 5 p.m. During these long nights, the slaves were chained and every movement would hurt their flesh. In such conditions of promiscuity and enclosed space, sickness was not uncommon.

Sickness, Mortality and Revolts

Despite the vigilance of the ship's doctor, who was anxious to get the slaves in good condition to the American points of sale, a variety of sicknesses arising from the poor conditions of transport would strike slaves and crew members alike. The tight packing of so many human beings into the tiny space of a ship and inadequate food weakened immune defences. The most widespread shipboard infections were malaria, scurvy – for lack of vitamin C – dysentery, yellow fever, smallpox, ophthalmia and yaws. Deschamps cites two terrible cases. In 1819, on the ship *Le Rôdeur*, every man lost his life except one sailor who was able to steer the ship to Guadeloupe. Similarly, in 1772, the *Nicolas Theodorus* suffered an epidemic of smallpox, yaws and dysentery, had to change captains four times and lost 148 slaves out of 200. To deal with these infections, the treatment available was derisory: vomitives and vegetable-based liquid food. Given the impurity of the water, contagious illnesses spread rapidly.

In addition to sickness, bad weather, such as cyclones, as well as revolts and mutinies – even if they had little chance of success, since they were invariably bloodily put down – led to many deaths. And if the mutineers succeeded in taking control of a ship, their inability to navigate the sea inevitably led to their deaths. In the eighteenth century there were numerous mutinies on board slave ships: the *Afriquain* in 1714, the *Samuel Marie* in 1750, the *Nécessaire* in 1771.

Furthermore, at the time of embarkation or in the prison-like world of the ships, attempts at suicide were common, despite the rituals designed to combat despair by making the victims forget their identity. In Benin, the 'tree of forgetting', which the slaves had to walk around a number of times in order to forget their pre-captivity identity, can still be seen. Enslavement bound only the body, so it was also appropriate to make three turns around the 'tree of return' to ensure that the soul of the captive would return to the land of his or her ancestors. These various psychological preparations, however, were not always enough to drive out melancholy, and some preferred death to another life far from their village, their traditions, their community, the spirits of their ancestors and the protection of their totemic animal from the forces of the universe: '*Tungan ma lambe lon*' (Elsewhere does not know your patronymic), says a Mandinka song. In 1774, the captain of the ship the *Soleil* reported that on 9 November 'fourteen women threw themselves all together from the top of the poop into the sea'.

What They Took with Them

What did the survivors, the ones who arrived on the other side, those who reached Elsewhere, carry with them? What lesson would they give to the world? Naked and in chains, these men, women and children left their homes with no hope of returning. Travellers without luggage, all they had left was their muscle power, their spirit and their soul. Of these three, only their soul would be theirs alone, and again and again, over there beyond the sea, their beliefs and cultural practices would come back to life. One cannot speak of Haiti without mentioning the voodoo of the Bight of Benin, Cuba without the *santería* or the United States without the fundamental contribution of its blacks. The Africans, still generous despite all that had happened to them, would give their new homelands the best of themselves, their key contribution being spiritual. For they are

> those who know the humblest corners of the land of suffering …
> Those who give themselves up to the essence of all things
> Ignorant of surfaces but struck by the movement of all things
> Free of the desire to tame but familiar with the play of the world
> Truly the eldest sons of the world….

For the fact is that each of them carried with him or her three forms of expression, three languages. The first was *myth*: a primary essential language that founds and organises the world. It expresses the relation to the visible, to the initiation into the invisible; it makes the world explicable, though one single event may shatter it and only a few splinters remain. The Africans also carried with them a 'pregnant' language of condensed wisdom, the means of every exchange, the preface to all knowledge and all thinking: the *proverb*. These two senior languages drew in their wake the language of relaxation, the daughter of the evening: the *tale*, which was written into every muscle of the body, rhythm and syncopation, borne by a long musical river with many tributaries, feeding the sensitivity of the world.

What can we say by way of conclusion about this human adventure in the guise of a commercial transaction? What is known as the 'slave trade' or the 'triangle of trade' brought together in an unprecedented combination peoples who would take time to appreciate one another. Africa, America and Europe would leave the world of mythical knowledge and come into sudden contact with one another. To try to understand the iniquity of the conditions in which the slaves were transported, must we always refer to the image that Europeans and Arabs had of the black? Both long regarded the Negro as a devil – witness some patristic church writings. The attitude of eighteenth-century philosophers at the time of the Enlightenment was hardly more enlightened; it retained the residue of received ideas that we wrongly believe today to be dead and buried. It must be said that the *Code noir*, drawn up at the end of the seventeenth century, added something to the 'reification' of blacks by baptising them. In his *Spirit of Law*, Montesquieu found it possible to set out some of the reasons that justified the enslavement of blacks! As for Voltaire, the scourge of injustice, he has the one-armed, one-legged Negro of Suriname say to Candide's astonishment: 'That is the price of your eating sugar in Europe.' Yet this same Voltaire was the owner of bills of exchange of the Compagnie des Indes, one of the companies engaged in the triangular trade.

What emerges from our analysis is that the study of slavery and its many ramifications is essential for an understanding of humankind and history, particularly in its relation to the notion of human rights. The evolution of this notion, said to be the daughter of the 1789 revolution, treated side by side with the means of enslavement, from the most everyday to the most sophisticated, provides ample food for thought that deserves to be offered to all, and especially to children and adolescents who have the task of building the future. There can be no dreams of peaceful tomorrows without a reactivation of mutual knowledge. Let us remember the Wolof proverb: 'Before we gained knowledge, ignorance almost killed us.'

Note

1. A. Schwarz-Bart, 1972.

Bibliography

CÉSAIRE, A. 1981. *Toussaint Louverture.* Paris, Présence africaine.

_____. 1983. *Cahier d'un retour au pays natal.* Paris, Présence africaine [Eng. tr. J. Berger and A. Bostock. *Return to My Native Land.* Harmondsworth, Penguin, 1969].

_____. 1989. *Discours sur le colonialisme.* Paris, Présence africaine [Eng. tr. J. Pinkham. *Discourse on Colonialism.* New York, Monthly Review Press, 1972].

De la traite à l'esclavage du Ve au XVIIIe siècle. Actes du Colloque international sur la traite des Noirs. Nantes, 1985.

DESCHAMPS, H. 1971. *Histoire de la traite des Noirs de l'Antiquité à nos jours.* Paris, Fayard.

DEVEAU, J.-M. 1994. *La France au temps des négriers.* Paris, France Empire.

KI-ZERBO, J. 1978. *Histoire de l'Afrique.* Paris, Hatier.

MEYER, J. 1986. *Esclaves et négriers.* Paris, Gallimard (Coll. Découvertes).

SCHWARZ-BART, A. 1972. *La mulâtresse Solitude.* Paris, Le Seuil [Eng. tr. R. Manheim. *A Woman Named Solitude.* London, Secker & Warburg, 1973].

UNESCO. 1979. *La traite négrière du XVe au XIXe siècle.* Paris, UNESCO (Coll. Histoire générale de l'Afrique. Etudes et documents).

Chapter 3

The Transition from the Slave Trade to 'Legitimate' Commerce

Robin Law

THE LEGAL ABOLITION OF THE SLAVE TRADE by the European and American nations that were involved in it occurred over a period of more than thirty years, from the banning of the trade by Denmark, effective in 1803, to the eventual acceptance of abolition by Portugal in 1836 – the critical step being the outlawing of the trade by Britain, the principal slave-trading nation, in 1807. Legal abolition was, of course, by no means the same as effective suppression, and the trade continued illegally well into the nineteenth century, while there remained a market for slaves in the Americas (principally in Brazil and Cuba). The transatlantic slave trade did not come to a total end, therefore, until the 1860s.

While the slave trade was in decline, other forms of trade between western Africa and Europe were developing. Although various alternative commodities were exported, the new trade was principally in agricultural produce, especially palm-oil and groundnuts, both used in Europe mainly as a raw material in the manufacture of soap, and later in the nineteenth century also palm kernels, used in the manufacture of margarine. The new trade thus reflected shifting patterns of demand in Europe, arising from the Industrial Revolution. The modern economic relationship between western Africa and Europe, based on the exchange of African raw materials for European manufactured goods, thus had its origins in the era of the abolition of the slave trade in the first half of the nineteenth century.

In the nineteenth century, the slave trade being now illegal, trade in any other commodities, including palm-oil and other agricultural produce, became known by contrast as 'legitimate (or lawful) commerce'. For modern historians, the use of this term is clearly open to objection, especially to those studying these processes from the perspective of Africa rather than of Europe, because it is evidently Eurocentric – since the slave trade initially remained 'legitimate' for the African societies involved in it, although it was now illegal for Europeans. Its use also tends to obscure the fact that trade in commodities other than slaves, including agricultural produce such as palm-oil, existed even before the legal abolition of the slave trade. It remains, however, so firmly embedded in the historical literature that it is difficult to avoid, and is adopted in this essay on grounds of its familiarity.

The transition from the slave trade to 'legitimate' commerce has been a topic of major interest in the historiography of western Africa. The very first substantial academic monograph – based on detailed original research – on any aspect of African history, the late K.O. Dike's study of the Niger Delta in the nineteenth century dealt centrally with this commercial transition, and more especially with its implications for the indigenous African societies involved in the Atlantic trade (Dike, 1956). Subsequently, the subject has continued to attract considerable attention from historians, with not only the accumulation of detailed case-studies, but also significant attempts at general synthesis. The best known and most influential among the latter has certainly been that by Hopkins (1973) in his pioneering survey of the economic history of West Africa, but other substantial contributions have been made by Austen (1970) and Manning (1986). It would be out of place in this context to offer a detailed survey of the development of the historical debate on the commercial transition, in part because I have done so elsewhere.[1] However, some of the general issues and controversies that have emerged in the course of the historical debate will be identified and briefly discussed in order to provide an orientation for future research in the field.

Preliminaries

There are a number of difficulties in coming to terms with the historiography of the transition from the slave trade to 'legitimate' commerce. One is that any judgement on the significance of this commercial transition must necessarily also imply a parallel judgement of the significance of the impact of the slave trade, which is itself an enormous and hotly contested issue. Some historians have argued that the Atlantic trade was simply not great enough in volume or value to have had a major effect on the development of West African societies, with the implication that the transformation of the nature of this trade in the nineteenth century can likewise have had only marginal significance for them: this case has been most systematically argued, in recent times, by Eltis (1987), while the counter-case for attributing a major impact to the Atlantic slave trade has been restated by Lovejoy.[2]

In part, the resolution to this controversy may lie through disaggregation. The experience of all regions of western Africa was evidently not the same. First, the Atlantic trade (and therefore, presumably, the nineteenth-century transformation of its nature) was not equally important for all West African societies. It was clearly of critical importance for coastal communities which lived, essentially, by trading, such as Bonny and other Niger Delta communities; of less but still considerable importance for societies immediately behind the coast, such as Asante and Dahomey; presumably of diminishing importance for societies situated farther inland; and perhaps of no importance at all for some very remote or isolated societies, which may have been wholly unaffected by the Atlantic trade.

The need for disaggregation extends further than this, since the experience of the nineteenth century was also significantly different from area to area within western Africa. The precise chronology of the decline of the slave trade varied considerably. On the Gold Coast, owing to the existence of a substantial European military presence, abolition was relatively easy to police and the export of slaves declined quickly after 1807, whereas elsewhere attempts to enforce the abolition of the slave trade took much longer to become effective. In Dahomey, for example, the critical decade in the decline of the slave trade was as late as the 1850s. Equally, there were local variations in the chronology of the development of 'legitimate' trade: the palm-oil trade, for example, developed first in the Niger Delta, from the late eighteenth century onwards, but took off from the Gold Coast only in the 1830s and from Dahomey only in the 1840s.

Even beyond this, the process of commercial change in the nineteenth century was rather more complex than is implied by the concept of a 'transition' from the slave trade to 'legitimate' commerce. The areas which supplied agricultural produce for the Atlantic trade were not always the same as those which had supplied slaves. In particular, whereas slaves had been taken from almost the whole area of West Africa, produce such as palm-oil and groundnuts was supplied from a relatively restricted area near the coast. The reason for this contrast was the high cost of transport in precolonial West African conditions. Slaves presented relatively few problems of transport because they were self-transporting: they could walk, and were often made to walk, hundreds of miles to their points of sale on the coast. Produce, on the other hand, required transportation, either by water or, if suitable navigable waterways were unavailable, by human porterage, carried on people's heads. The quantities of produce that needed to be moved in the new trade, moreover, were very considerable: in the mid-nineteenth century, the coastal price of a single slave was roughly equivalent to that of a ton of palm-oil, which would require about 60 porters to carry. In these circumstances, it was simply not profitable to produce palm-oil or groundnuts for export unless the producing area was close to the coast, or at least to a navigable river affording relatively cheap transport to the coast. Societies in the interior, therefore, were simply unable to participate directly in the new trade in agricultural produce. For them, there was not so much a 'transition' from the slave trade to 'legitimate' trade as a decline in their involvement in overseas commerce.

The Incidence of Enslavement

One critical area of interest – and controversy – in relation to the commercial transition of the nineteenth century is the question of its effects on the incidence of warfare (and of violence and disorder more generally) in West Africa.

In the most general terms, it seems clear that there was a critical link between the slave trade and violence/warfare, since most of the slaves exported were originally enslaved through violence, mainly by capture in warfare, but also in smaller-scale and less licit kidnappings. But the nature of the link can be contested. Was the slave trade a cause of warfare in West Africa, as European and American abolitionists in the eighteenth century argued?[3] Or did African wars have an independent, autonomous (and cultural/political rather than economic) origin, so that the slave trade fed off wars rather than causing them, as was argued by anti-abolitionists including Dalzel in his pioneering historical study of Dahomey?[4] In short, was African involvement in the Atlantic slave trade supply-driven or demand-driven? This issue is a matter of controversy, not only in general, but also in relation to specific historical episodes. The collapse of Yorubaland (south-western Nigeria) into internecine warfare in the early nineteenth century, for example, certainly generated many captives who were sold into the Atlantic trade. But it is debated whether the origins of these wars should be understood in purely political terms (e.g. Ajayi and Smith[5]) or whether the pressure of demand for captives for the Atlantic trade may have played at least a contributory role in stimulating local warfare (cf. Law[6]).

An assessment of the implications of the ending of transatlantic slave exports will, evidently, depend to some degree upon the view taken on this prior question. The issue is further complicated by the fact that slaves were also exported from West Africa across the Sahara to the Muslim world, and indeed extensively used within West Africa itself. The quantitative importance of the transatlantic market, relative to the trans-Saharan and internal West African markets, would evidently materially affect the significance of the closing of the former, but can be a matter of no more than (more or less) informed speculation. Moreover, the growth of 'legitimate' trade increased the demand for slaves within West Africa, since export commodities such as palm-oil were often produced and transported by slave labour, to some degree offsetting the decline of overseas demand.[7]

The common assumption has been that transatlantic demand was sufficiently significant for the ending of the Atlantic slave trade to have caused a glut of slaves in West Africa (though this effect would presumably have been felt in different areas at different times) and a fall in the price they commanded in local markets. Analysis of the price of slaves (and indeed, of any other commodities) in West Africa during the nineteenth century, however, presents very considerable methodological, as well as empirical, problems. Slave prices are normally cited in European or American currencies, but this may be misleading, since the prices in Europe of many of the goods imported into Africa (such as textiles) were falling in the early decades of the century, in consequence of the cost-reducing innovations associated with the Industrial Revolution (in other words, the terms of trade at this period were moving in favour of African suppliers); a fall in nominal price may therefore mask a rise in the real price, in terms of quantities of imported manufactured goods. The obvious alternative which suggests itself, of citing prices in African currencies, such as cowry shells, may be equally misleading, since these were subject to massive inflation during the nineteenth century[8] (this quite apart from the difficulties caused by price differentials from one part of the coast to another, and between the interior and the coast). The evidence on slave prices is therefore ambiguous, and the question is one which urgently requires further detailed research.

Assuming that there was indeed a fall in the price of slaves (even if only temporarily and to a limited degree), the implications of this for the incidence of warfare and enslavement may be considered. If it is held that war was conducted for solely non-economic reasons, presumably there would be no effect: the level of warfare would remain the same, generating the same number of captives, though fewer of the latter could be sold (leading perhaps to a higher proportion being killed, or perhaps ransomed back to their home communities). If, on the other hand, expectations of profit from the sale of slaves are assumed to have played some role in the origins of wars, what would have been the consequences? From a commonsense view, lower slave prices, by making war less profitable, would have diminished the incidence of war. This is indeed argued, in the case of Asante, by Wilks (1975), who suggests that the diminishing economic attractiveness of war strengthened the 'peace party' against the 'war party' in the national councils of that state. Against this, however, for Sudanic West Africa, Meillassoux (1991) has suggested quite the reverse, i.e. that falling slave prices stimulated increased warfare, as military leaders sought to compensate by increased output of slaves. In Meillassoux's view, this commercial factor played a role in causing the Western Sudanic *jihads* of the nineteenth century. It may be that these alternative hypotheses are not, strictly, contradictory, but may each be applicable to different cases, depending upon the degree to which viable alternatives to slaving were available. Withdrawal from the slave trade would have been a rational option for those who could transfer their energies into other forms of exports, while an increase in output to compensate for falling prices would have made sense for those for whom no such alternative was on offer.

Compatibility

A second general issue relating to the decline of the slave trade and the rise of 'legitimate' trade is that of the nature of the relationship between these two processes. British abolitionists in the nineteenth century tended to believe that the slave trade and 'legitimate' trade were mutually contradictory and incompatible with each other – that the persistence of the slave trade would prevent alternative forms of trade from developing and that, conversely, the growth of legitimate trade would effectively drive out the slave trade. The growth of 'legitimate' trade might thus be either a cause or a consequence of the decline of the slave trade, but on either hypothesis the two processes were presumed to be closely interlinked. Recent research, in contrast, has stressed the compatibility of the two trades. A study of the Bight of Biafra by Northrup

(1976), for example, showed that far from 'legitimate' trade expanding at the expense of the slave trade, both trades in this region expanded simultaneously up to the 1830s.

One possible implication of this 'compatibility' of the slave and palm-oil trades (espoused by Northrup himself) might be that they were, at least in the main, produced and marketed by distinct groups and by different trading networks, prior to delivery to the coastal ports. From the perspective of the coast itself, however, it seems clear that the compatibility of the slave and palm-oil trades reflected the fact that they were not so much distinct as complementary. To some degree, coastal merchants who were engaged in the slave trade took up the palm-oil trade as a hedge against fluctuations in the former. But in some cases, at least, it was rather a question of multilateral patterns of exchange, in which the slave and palm-oil trades reinforced each other. By the 1840s, for example, locally resident Brazilian slave traders in the Bight of Benin began selling palm-oil, not as a substitute for the slave trade but as a support for it: they sold palm-oil for European goods, which were in turn exchanged for slaves. An example is Domingo Martinez, who 'frequently stated that he considered the two trades complementary'.[9] This phenomenon was, indeed, a major problem for European abolitionists, who recognised that 'legitimate' trade conducted with slave traders amounted, in effect, to indirect participation in the slave trade, but were unable to find a clear legal basis for prohibiting it.[10]

If we extend the concept of the slave trade to include the supply of slaves for the internal as well as the export market, of course, the growth of 'legitimate' trade depended upon continued slaving, since (as was noted earlier) considerable use was made of slave labour in the production of agricultural produce for export. At another level (and, perhaps, in the longer run), however, it may be that fundamental contradictions can nevertheless be discerned. In the case of Dahomey, for example, both ideological and material contradictions have been suggested. One of the problems faced by the king and chiefs of Dahomey in moving into the production of palm-oil in the mid-nineteenth century was that the Dahomian ruling élite was essentially a warrior class, whose martial values involved a disdain for agriculture. The shift to commercial agriculture was seen as incompatible with this traditional warrior ethos, and threatened to undermine the legitimacy and authority of the Dahomian State. It has been suggested that these tensions were reflected in debates within Dahomey over the reduction or abolition of 'human sacrifice' (which in Dahomey was closely bound up with the state's military values and mainly involved the killing of war captives in celebration of military victories) under King Gezo in the 1850s.[11] Once Dahomey had committed itself to large-scale participation in the palm-oil trade, moreover, a further contradiction became evident: mobilisation of the population for warfare (in Dahomey, on an annual seasonal basis) withdrew labour from the agricultural sector. This tension became critical when Gezo's successor Glele attempted to revive Dahomian militarism and the slave trade after 1858, consequently undermining the production of palm-oil for export.[12]

The 'Crisis of Adaptation' for African Rulers

A long-established tradition has held that the transition from the slave trade to 'legitimate' trade had destabilising effects on African political and social structures, undermining the position of existing rulers and creating political disorder. The idea was already propounded by Dike in his pioneering study of 1956, which argued that in Bonny and other states of the Niger Delta the fortunes of existing rulers declined with the slave trade, while the rise of trade in palm-oil enabled men of slave origin to acquire wealth and bid for political power, creating tensions which were reflected in recurrent civil wars between the free and slave classes – a process personified above all by the famous ex-slave chief Jaja, who eventually seceded from Bonny to establish his own kingdom at Opobo.[13]

The idea of a 'crisis of adaptation' was subsequently applied by Hopkins to the case of Yorubaland, explaining the endemic warfare in that area in the late nineteenth century as reflecting the undermining of the incomes of local warrior élites by the decline of the slave trade, and their inability to make a comparable revenue from trade in palm produce, which led them to bolster their incomes by increasing the scale of their exaction of tribute and plunder.[14] A similar analysis was applied by Klein (1972) to the case of Senegambia, where the shift to 'legitimate' trade (here in groundnuts rather than palm-oil) was held to have contributed to the overthrow of the existing warrior élite by the Islamic *jihads* of the 1860s.

More clearly than Dike, both Hopkins and Klein explained that the military chiefs who had dominated the slave trade were less able to control the new trade in agricultural produce, because the latter was readily open to participation by small-scale farmers and traders. A memorable epigram of Klein states: '[W]hereas the slave trade strengthened the élite, the peanut trade put money, and thus guns, in the hands of peasants.' Hopkins also stressed the significance of the collapse of West African produce prices in the 'Great Depression' of 1873–96 (when, in contrast to the initial period of 'legitimate' commerce, the terms of trade moved against African suppliers), which compounded the problems facing local rulers by further reducing their incomes from exports.

The classic formulation of the hypothesis of a 'crisis of adaptation' was given by Hopkins in his *Economic History of West Africa*,[15] which generalised the argument to the whole of West Africa. Hopkins here identified various ways in which West African rulers might respond to the commercial transition (singly or in combination). They might, of course, seek to enter the new trade, employing slave labour on large estates to produce agricultural commodities for export, but this was unlikely to yield revenues comparable to those from the slave trade, first, because the new trade was less profitable than the old (production and transport costs being higher, relative to selling prices at the coast), and second (critically) because in any case, rulers no longer had a natural monopoly of supply, as they had in the slave trade, but faced competition from the mass of ordinary farmers who could produce for export on a small scale. They might also try to bolster their incomes by taxing the activities of the independent small-scale producers and traders, or (as in Yorubaland) simply use their military power to appropriate wealth through increased raiding and plunder. But the former was difficult to make effective, and the latter was in the long run counter-productive, since the resulting disorder disrupted the export trade, threatening to provoke European intervention.

This view has not, of course, commanded universal support among historians. An alternative view, propounded perhaps most influentially by Austen, holds that, in fact, existing ruling élites were able to dominate the new trade, as they had the old, so that West African economic and political structures remained substantially intact until they were destroyed by the European colonial conquest at the end of the nineteenth century.[16] Manning, in his general survey of 1986, takes an intermediate view, though one closer to Hopkins than to Austen. Although supporting Hopkins's idea that the new 'legitimate' trade favoured the entry of small producers and traders, he stresses also the need to periodise the development of the trade: the early nineteenth century, when the slave trade was in decline and the palm-oil trade, although expanding, remained limited, 'favoured powerful monarchs and wealthy slave merchants'; the middle decades, when the volume and price of palm-oil exports soared, was marked by 'free-swinging competition and unusual upward social mobility'; but the later nineteenth century, when trade was stagnant due to the collapse of oil prices, was again marked by 'consolidation of political and economic power'.[17]

Although many points remain contested, a degree of consensus may be said to have been reached with regard to certain key questions. First, it is generally agreed (and acknowledged by Hopkins in his *Economic History*) that a distinction needs to be made between conditions in coastal middleman states (such as Bonny) and hinterland producing states (such as Yorubaland). Even if Hopkins is correct in holding that palm-oil was originally made by small-scale producers, it was normally bulked up by the coastal traders before being transported to the coast where large-scale enterprise remained dominant. Historiographically, the critical contribution in this area was John Latham's study of Old Calabar, which showed that the ruling élite there retained their dominance of the new trade in palm-oil and that the role of petty traders remained marginal. Although some ex-slaves in Old Calabar (as in Bonny) were able to become substantial merchants, they rose through the patronage of their masters rather than in competition with them – effectively from *within* the existing commercial and political structure rather than through its overthrow.[18] Other research has shown that this was basically true of the rise of ex-slaves such as Jaja in Bonny itself.[19] Dike's argument linking the rise of such ex-slaves, and political disorder in the coastal states more generally, to the shift from slaves to palm-oil is now generally held to be unsustainable, at least in the form in which he expounded it.

Second, although there were certainly many cases in the hinterland producing states in which existing rulers appear to have had difficulty in maintaining the degree of control over 'legitimate' trade that they had in the slave trade, the process was rather more complex than Hopkins's original formulation allowed. While Hopkins had stressed only the entry of small-scale farmers and traders, analyses of several case-studies suggest that the principal threat to the chiefs' control of 'legitimate' trade came less from small-scale enterprise than from wealthy merchants operating on a large scale. This was argued, for example, for Asante by Wilks (1975) and for Dahomey by Law.[20] Whereas the slave trade depended on warfare, and therefore favoured the domination of the chiefs who controlled the military forces, the new trade in agricultural produce offered no special advantages to warrior élites, and enabled private individuals of wealth to strengthen their position by moving into large-scale production for export.

Third, the destabilising potential of the commercial transition might not in practice be realised because existing rulers could use their political power to enforce monopolies of trade. Latham's study (1973) of Old Calabar, for example, showed that the established merchant chiefs, through the ruling Ekpe society, legislated against petty trade, acting in 1862 to prohibit trading in quantities smaller than the puncheon (240 gallons, or two-thirds of a ton). The king of Dahomey also proclaimed a temporary monopoly of palm-oil exports in 1852.[21] The possibility of such administrative intervention in the market was not, of course, denied by Hopkins, though he was sceptical about its effectiveness in the long run. Given the more dispersed nature of the palm-oil trade (involving a multiplicity of small producers), it must have been more difficult to monitor and control than the slave trade. Moreover, attempts to enforce monopolies of trade, or to increase the level of taxation on the private sector, were likely to provoke resistance and create political problems of their own – as Wilks, in fact, argued in the case of Asante, where the grievances of wealthy merchant entrepreneurs against state regulation and taxation of trade allegedly played a role in the civil wars that occurred there in 1883–88.[22]

It also seems clear by now that the outcome of these tensions and difficulties varied from case to case, with ruling groups in different societies more or less successful in defending the political status quo in the face of economic change. Such differing outcomes presumably reflected, in part, the differing character of the societies involved, with stronger and more centralised states (such as Dahomey and Asante) likely to be better able to contain the strains of the transition than those which were weaker or more decentralised. The precise outcome was presumably also affected by other factors (such as Islam in Senegambia, or European imperialist intervention in many coastal societies), which interacted with and modified the impact of the commercial transition. Future research might perhaps elucidate the reasons for these differing responses to and experiences of the transition, a project here again of disaggregation, rather than seeking to construct further general syntheses which may obscure these particularities.

Gender

A further aspect of the impact of the commercial transition on participating African societies should be noted here, though as an area generally neglected rather than seriously addressed in historical research hitherto: namely, its implications for gender relations. The starting point for this issue is that whereas the capture and trading of slaves were always overwhelmingly male activities, the manufacture and trading of palm-oil were (at least in many coastal societies) traditionally done predominantly by women. The shift from slaves to palm-oil as the principal export must be presumed, therefore, to have had significant implications for relations between the sexes. The only published account which deals centrally with this issue (though with primary reference to the twentieth century rather than the precolonial period) is an article by Susan Martin (1984) on the palm-produce trade in the Ngwa area of Iboland (south-eastern Nigeria). Martin argues that with the rise of an export trade in palm-oil, men moved into oil production in order to appropriate the proceeds for themselves, thus largely depriving women of potential benefit (though the trade in palm kernels, which developed later, remained in female hands, and gave women some opportunities for independent accumulation). It is possible, however, hypothetically at least, to envisage alternative outcomes in other cases. If women had been able to retain control of the palm-oil trade, its growth would presumably have tended to enrich and empower them, and to increase their effective autonomy *vis-à-vis* their menfolk. The whole topic should be a major priority for future research on the nineteenth-century commercial transition.

Abolition and Imperialism: Towards the Partition of Africa

A further and final area of interest in relation to the commercial transition of the nineteenth century is its relationship to the growth of European imperialism and the ultimate partition of Africa among the European colonial powers at the end of the century. This relationship can be conceived as having three distinct aspects, which also roughly represent three successive chronological phases.

First, as was stressed in a neglected article by Austen and Smith,[23] the debate about the abolition of the slave trade dealt, among other things, with the nature of African societies and its relationship to the impact of the slave trade. Abolitionists and anti-abolitionists normally agreed in a negative valuation that regarded Africa as savage and brutal. But whereas anti-abolitionists tended to regard African societies as essentially backward, explaining their supposed barbarism as reflecting the low stage of their social evolution (and inferring that those Africans who were taken as slaves were being rescued from even worse conditions within their own societies), abolitionists tended to regard them as the victims of distorted or corrupted development, their alleged brutalisation being not a pristine state but the consequence of the impact of the slave trade. The logical consequence of the abolitionist view was that Europeans were, in the final analysis, responsible for the current state of Africa, and thus had the moral responsibility to take action to remedy it. The abolition of the slave trade was therefore a means of transforming Africa, as well as a means of ameliorating the conditions suffered by African slaves in the Americas.

One aspect of this abolitionist ideology was its implicit assumption that it was the right, as well as the obligation, of Europeans to determine the future course of African development – an 'imperialism' of intent, if not of execution. The idea is nicely captured by Hopkins in his recent study (with Cain) of British imperialism, in which the campaign against the slave trade in the early nineteenth century is described as 'Britain's first development plan for Africa'.[24]

A second aspect of the abolition issue was that, in practice, the campaign against the slave trade drew European governments, especially the British, into interference in the affairs of African societies on a scale unparalleled during the history of the slave trade itself. The initial assumption was that the slave trade could be suppressed with action on the demand side by negotiating treaties for the legal abolition of the trade with European and American states whose citizens were engaged in the trade, and by maintaining naval patrols in the Atlantic to police this legal abolition and to intercept ships involved in illicit slaving voyages. The evident failure of this policy in bringing the trade to an end, however, led from the late 1830s to a shift towards a supply-side approach, which sought to cut off the supply of slaves from within Africa itself. The best-known symbol of this new policy was the disastrous British expedition up the River Niger to establish a model farm to promote export agriculture in 1841–42, recently restudied by Temperley.[25] More generally, the British government sought to negotiate treaties banning the slave trade with African societies, as with Bonny (beginning in 1839). Although this policy was initially conceived as one of merely diplomatic intervention, it quickly led on to more. Where African rulers proved reluctant to accept anti-slave trade treaties, there was the temptation to apply pressure upon them to do so by the threat, or if necessary the actuality, of military intervention. The classic (but by no means the only) instance was the intervention at Lagos in 1851 to depose the existing ruler, who refused to accept an abolition treaty, in favour of a rival claimant to the throne, who was willing to co-operate with British policy.[26] This was even more obviously a policy of 'imperialism', although not in the sense that it necessarily involved annexation of African territory. The policy still assumed that, in general, the desired transformation could be achieved within a framework of continuing African sovereignty. Although in particular cases an ultimate consequence might be intervention, it was not as a result of a policy of colonial expansion. The policy was 'imperialist' in the looser sense of the use of state power to promote overseas commercial interests – what it has become conventional among historians to term 'informal imperialism'.

A third aspect of the abolition question relates to the shift from this sort of 'informal imperialism' to formal imperialism, i.e. the partition of Africa among rival colonial powers in the late nineteenth century. Although the reasons for the partition of Africa have been a matter of great historical controversy, it may safely be asserted that, at the very least, a significant role was played by European commercial interests, which sought annexation as a solution to what were perceived as problems of Africa's commercial development. The nature of these perceived problems, it may be suggested, is usefully illustrated by the two great international congresses of this period, which discussed and (to some extent) regulated aspects of the process – at Berlin in 1884–85 and at Brussels in 1890. Of these, the first congress, at Berlin, was mainly concerned with intra-European commercial rivalries. But the second, at Brussels in 1890, was mainly concerned with the reconstruction of African societies and, more specifically, with the suppression of the slave trade.[27] By the late nineteenth century, it was clear that the attack on the slave trade from outside Africa had been only partially successful. While the export trade in slaves had been largely suppressed (though less effectively in the east than in the west), slave trading and trading within Africa persisted. More decisive intervention was therefore needed, in the interior as well as on the coast of Africa.

Although this concern for the suppression of the slave trade has often been seen as an excuse or a rationalisation rather than a real motive for European intervention in Africa, it might more illuminatingly be thought of as a symbol. The issue of slavery and its suppression symbolised Europe 's desire (and, in its own eyes, obligation) to effect the 'modernisation' of African societies, and more specifically the diffusion to them of the capitalist mode of production. The move to formal annexation reflected a growing conviction that the more limited forms of intervention adopted earlier were inadequate to effect the desired transformation of African socio-economic structures.

In this context, attention should also be addressed to the argument of Hopkins[28] that the strains of the original transition from the slave trade to 'legitimate' commerce earlier in the nineteenth century themselves contributed to this European pressure for annexation of African territory. In some cases, as Hopkins argued in that of Yorubaland, the problem was that the commercial transition had undermined and weakened the position of African ruling élites, leading to warfare and disorder which Europeans condemned as injurious to trade. But even in those cases in which African rulers had succeeded in maintaining effective control, the policies that they adopted to manage the commercial transition were regularly condemned by Europeans as inimical to free trade, and to modern economic development more generally. Insofar as African ruling élites had coped with the transition to 'legitimate' trade by asserting monopolies of trade, by increasing taxes, and by the more extensive and intensive use of slave labour for export production, they were reinforcing the very practices whose abolition, in the longer run, European capitalism would demand. Even if successful in the short run, the ways in which African rulers responded to the 'crisis of adaptation', therefore, brought down upon them in the end the greater crisis of colonial conquest.

Notes

1. R. Law, 1993, 1995.
2. P. Lovejoy, 1989.
3. For example A. Benezet, 1788.
4. A. Dalzel, 1793.
5. J.F.A. Ajayi, 1964, and R.S. Smith, 1978.
6. R. Law, 1977a.
7. P. Lovejoy, 1983.
8. J.S. Hogendorn and M. Johnson, 1986.
9. D. Ross, 1965.
10. See, for example, L.C. Jennings, 1976.
11. R. Law, 1985.
12. J. Reid, 1986.
13. K.O. Dike, 1956.
14. A.G. Hopkins, 1968.
15. A.G. Hopkins, 1973.
16. R. Austen, 1970.
17. P. Manning, 1986.
18. A.J. Latham, 1973.
19. S.M. Hargreaves, 1987.
20. R. Law, 1977b.
21. Ibid.
22. I. Wilks, 1975.
23. R.A. Austen and W.S. Smith, 1969.
24. P. Cain and A.G. Hopkins, 1993.
25. H. Temperley, 1991.
26. R.S. Smith, 1978.
27. S. Miers, 1975.
28. A.G. Hopkins, 1973.

Bibliography

AJAYI, J.F.A., and SMITH, R.S. 1964. *Yoruba Warfare in the Nineteenth Century*. Cambridge, Cambridge University Press.

AUSTEN, R.A. 1970. 'The abolition of the overseas slave trade: A distorted theme in West African history'. *Journal of the Historical Society of Nigeria,* Vol. 5, No. 2, pp. 257–274.

AUSTEN, R.A., and SMITH, W.S. 1969. 'Images of Africa and British Slave-Trade Abolition: The transition to an imperialist ideology, 1787–1807'. *African Historical Studies,* Vol. 2, No. 1, pp. 69–83.

BENEZET, A. 1788. *Some Historical Account of Guinea*. 2nd ed. London, Frank Cass (1968).

CAIN, P.J., and HOPKINS, A.G. 1993. *British Imperialism: Innovation and Expansion 1688–1914*. London, Longman.

DALZEL, A. 1793. *The History of Dahomy*. London, Frank Cass (1967).

DIKE, K.O. 1956. *Trade and Politics in the Niger Delta 1830–1885*. Oxford, Clarendon Press.

ELTIS, D. 1987. *Economic Growth and the Ending of the Transatlantic Slave Trade*. New York, Oxford University Press.

HARGREAVES, S.M. 1987. The Political Economy of Nineteenth-Century Bonny (University of Birmingham, Ph.D. thesis).

HOGENDORN, J.S., and JOHNSON, M. 1986. *The Shell Money of the Slave Trade*. Cambridge, Cambridge University Press.

HOPKINS, A.G. 1968. 'Economic imperialism in West Africa: Lagos, 1880–92'. *Economic History Review*, Vol. 21, No. 3, pp. 580–600.

————. 1973. *An Economic History of West Africa*. London, Longman.

JENNINGS, L.C. 1976. 'French policy towards trading with African and Brazilian slave merchants, 1840–1853'. *Journal of African History*, Vol. 17, No. 4, pp. 515–528.

KLEIN, M.A. 1972. 'Social and economic factors in the Muslim Revolution in Senegambia'. *Journal of African History* (Cambridge), Vol. 13, No. 2, pp. 419–441.

LATHAM, A.J.H. 1973. *Old Calabar 1600–1891*. Oxford, Clarendon Press.

LAW, R. 1977a. *The Oyo Empire c.1600–c.1836*. Oxford, Clarendon Press.

————. 1977b. 'Royal monopoly and private enterprise in the Atlantic trade: The case of Dahomey'. *Journal of African History*, Vol. 18, No. 4, pp. 555–577.

————. 1985. 'Human sacrifice in pre-colonial West Africa. *African Affairs*, Vol. 84, pp. 53–87.

————. 1993. 'The historiography of the commercial transition in nineteenth-century West Africa'. In Toyin Falola (ed.). *African Historiography: Essays in Honour of Jacob Ade Ajayi*. Longman, London. Pp. 91–115.

————, (ed.). 1995. *From Slave Trade to 'Legitimate' Commerce: The Commercial Transition in Nineteenth-Century West Africa*. Cambridge, Cambridge University Press.

LOVEJOY, P.E. 1983. *Transformations in Slavery: A History of Slavery in Africa*. Cambridge, Cambridge University Press.

————. 1989. 'The impact of the Atlantic slave trade on Africa: A review of the literature. *Journal of African History*, Vol. 30, No. 3, pp. 365–394.

MANNING, P. 1986. 'Slave trade, "legitimate" trade and imperialism revisited: The control of wealth in the Bights of Benin and Biafra'. In Paul Lovejoy (ed.). *Africans in Bondage: Studies in Slavery and the Slave Trade in Honour of Philip D. Curtin*. Madison, University of Wisconsin Press. Pp. 203–233.

MEILLASSOUX, C. 1991. *The Anthropology of Slavery*. Chicago, University of Chicago Press.

MIERS, S. 1975. *Britain and the Ending of the Slave Trade*. London, Longman.

NORTHRUP, D. 1976. 'The compatibility of the slave and palm-oil trades in the Bight of Biafra'. *Journal of African History* (Cambridge), Vol. 17, No. 3, pp. 353–364.

REID, J. 1986. Warrior Aristocrats in Crisis: The Political Effects of the Transition from the Slave Trade to Palm-Oil Commerce in the Nineteenth-Century Kingdom of Dahomey (University of Stirling, Ph.D. thesis).

ROSS, D.A. 1965. 'The career of Domingo Martinez in the Bight of Benin 1833–64'. *Journal of African History* (Cambridge), Vol. 6, No. 1, pp. 79–90.

SMITH, R.S. 1978. *The Lagos Consulate, 1851–1861*. London, MacMillan.

TEMPERLEY, H. 1991. *White Dreams, Black Africa: The Antislavery Expedition to the Niger 1841–1842*. New Haven, Yale University Press.

WILKS, I. 1975. *Asante in the Nineteenth Century*. Cambridge, Cambridge University Press.

Chapter 4

Submarine Archaeology and the History of the Slave Trade

Max Guérout

ARCHIVE DOCUMENTS have enabled us to write the history of the slave trade and to understand how it operated. They underlie all historical studies on the subject. In comparison with the copious manuscript or printed sources, however, very scant material testimony of that dramatic time has come down to us. As a result, museum showcases are often surprisingly bare. An exceptional effort is needed to put together a significant collection, as was done in Nantes in 1992–94 for the exhibition entitled 'The Chains of Memory'.

All that now bears witness to the trading of millions of human beings is a mere handful of objects. But, come to think of it, could things really have been otherwise? The people involved were utterly destitute, and their living conditions as labourers in the new world were most elementary. When slavery was eventually abolished, we can imagine how eager those freed were to destroy anything reminiscent of their past lives, and also how eager their former masters were to do away with all such compromising evidence.

The idea of looking for the wrecks of slave ships arose in part from this awareness, for anyone following the progress of underwater archaeology realises that the seabed holds a very valuable heritage. It must nevertheless be emphasised that the wreck of a slave ship is not just a collection of objects: it is above all a site where all the remains form part of a single coherent whole, where everything is organised around the ship and re-creates for us the reality of a closed world in which captives and crew were united, not for better but for worse. Unlike most objects that have come down to us in a disorganised manner, those found in a shipwreck all belong to the same context and bear witness to one and the same moment in time. It is this simultaneity that makes an underwater site so valuable and so unusual. What we have is a veritable cross-section of time, so that each object carries an incomparable evocative force and emotional impact.

Being able to observe a slave ship at first hand means being able to study it from three angles: as a machine illustrating a particular state of the art in shipbuilding, as an instrument suited to a particular function or need, and as living quarters and workplace. From a study of its cargo the ship can be situated in the organisation and history of the triangular trade, its home base identified and an operating circuit determined. Close analysis of the sediment gives us a clearer idea of living conditions on board, including health and food.

Many of these aspects are admittedly known to us from archive material, but what makes a wreck so valuable is the amount and consistency of the data it provides, together with the fact that much of the data did not find its way into the ledgers of the shipowners, the ships' logbooks or the accounts of the companies. The reason could be that the objects are too lowly or familiar to have been worth mentioning, or that they are connected with non-official or even fraudulent practices that were never recorded, such as the transport of unlawful goods or parallel trading. As for ships wrecked during the period when slave trading was illegal, no mention would have been made of the operation in any written sources.

It is thus clear that the information that may be obtained from a well-preserved wreck can be far more valuable than that obtainable from a more haphazard collection of objects representative of the slave trade.

One may wonder how many slave ships were lost and where, and in what state one can expect to find them. Several recent historical studies, including the doctoral thesis of Ducoin (1993), have assessed the percentage of ships lost by shipowners engaged in slave trading. Ducoin's study is of course limited in both time and space, since it concerns ships fitted out in the port of Nantes between 1700 and 1792. The proportion of ships lost on the triangular voyages, termed *circuitous*, was 4 to 9 per cent, averaging close to 5.4 per cent and representing the loss of 82 ships. This figure, arrived at by rigorous calculation, may serve as a basis for an overall assessment.

Let us take a figure of ten million for the number of slaves transported (not to make a statement as to the extent of the slave trade, but to choose a convenient figure for purposes of calculation). If we reckon, regardless of the period, that 250 slaves on average were to be transported on each ship, this gives a total of 40,000 voyages. If we then apply the percentage of ships lost (for Nantes over the space of a century), we would have a figure of 2,160 ships lost. This is of course only a rough calculation not reflecting reality but giving an approximation, and very probably a conservative estimate. We can therefore be certain that several hundreds or indeed thousands of ships engaged in the triangular slave trade were lost. Incidentally, this figure does not concern ships plying a direct route to America to bring back to Europe the proceeds of the sale of slaves; for that, it has to be remembered, two or three ships were needed for a single slave ship.

Jacques Ducoin's examination of the causes of the shipwrecks shows that navigational error, damage to vessels and bad weather accounted for the loss of 30 to 60 per cent of the ships that went down off the coast. The rest were lost on the high seas as a result of mutiny, major damage or capture, some going down without trace. It can thus be stated with certainty that 1,000 to 1,300 ships were lost on the coasts of the countries bordering on the Atlantic Ocean.

Where and how should these wrecks be sought in the first place? Two methods, not mutually exclusive, may be used. The first consists in proceeding from archival research to identify a shipwreck whose position can be ascertained with some accuracy and which is likely to be of some interest due to the circumstances, the nature of the location and the significance of the cargo. If these conditions are met, a special search can be considered. Our team has on several occasions succeeded in locating a particular wreck very quickly. For instance, the wreck of the trading vessel *Patriote*, sunk on 3 July 1798 off Alexandria, was found in one day; the wreck of the brig *Le Cygne* of the French imperial fleet, sunk off Martinique on 31 December 1808, was found in the course of the first dive; the wreck of the armour-plated frigate *Magenta*, sunk at Toulon on 30 October 1875, was also found in less than a day. On the other hand, the first attempt to locate the slave ship *Marie-Anne*, sunk in 1734 at the mouth of the Loire, was unsuccessful.

The second method of locating sunken vessels consists in running systematic searches in dangerous zones where shipwrecks are likely to occur, usually in the vicinity of the major ports of departure or stopover, or in dangerous waters along the most frequently used routes. The method used depends on the surroundings and ranges from the simplest techniques, such as diving without an aqualung, to more sophisticated procedures involving such devices as the lateral sonar or the magnetometer.

What archaeologists call the mechanics of shipwrecks is another factor to be taken into account before launching any search. What is meant is the manner in which a ship has sunk, thus transforming the craft into an archaeological site. In many cases the vessel will have been completely destroyed and only a few scattered objects at best will be found at the site. This applies to ships that ran aground on rocky or coral shoals during a storm whose violence scatters ship, cargo and equipment more or less without trace. The slave ships were among the most vulnerable in such conditions, for we know that the craft engaged in the triangular slave trade were generally quite modest vessels, displacing less than 200 tonnes on average. Their meagre scantling made for the rapid destruction of the ship. But this was not always the case, particularly if there was enough sand or mud on the seabed to deaden the action of the swell. In such conditions the archaeologist can hope to find sites that deserve a full excavation. Our experience in Senegal and Martinique has demonstrated the soundness of these prospecting methods, resulting in the discovery of some twenty wrecks, of which only one was connected with the slave trade.

For those not familiar with submarine archaeology, it needs pointing out that the immediate environment is all-important for the preservation of the remains. When the ship lies fully exposed in the water, micro-organisms, marine fauna and the mechanical effect of sea and current make short work of its structure, equipment and cargo. The parts best preserved are those buried in the sediment. Shut off from the light and in a medium poor in oxygen, organic matter may be preserved. Metals are more or less sensitive to the complex chemistry that comes into play, but the noblest among them – gold, bronze and copper, as well as lead – keep well. Pottery and glass are also remarkably well preserved and constitute the basic material enabling a site to be both dated and identified.

Materials that have been preserved in a marine environment usually deteriorate irreversibly when brought into contact with the ambient air if nothing is done to halt the process. After a period in protective sediment, wood maintains its shape and external aspect but cannot be preserved in the open air without a long period of expensive treatment. The same goes for nearly all organic matter and ferrous metals. Several conservation laboratories have started specialising in the treatment of items from underwater excavations. Their work is moreover not confined to stabilising the objects entrusted to them; the additional analyses they conduct complete the documentation and work of the archaeologist. Some techniques – such as industrial radiography of the calcareous concretions that usually cover metals – yield remarkably precise information. It is therefore essential to establish a special organisation for the conservation of items, to secure the services of such a laboratory and to arrange the necessary funding before embarking on underwater excavation. The storage and transport of items from the site to the chosen laboratory are also demanding and costly operations that need careful planning.

Very few wrecks of slave ships have so far been found. There are two main reasons for this. The first is that in view of the low monetary value of their cargoes, they have never been systematically tracked down by treasure-seekers in the Caribbean region. The second, as we have seen, is the relative fragility of the structure of the slave ships, whose hulls are bound to disappear more rapidly than others. A site we discovered in 1991 off Martinique, on the cays of the Atlantic coast near the small island of Loup Garou, illustrates this very well. An elephant tusk, found encysted in the coral, most probably marked the site of a ship connected with the slave trade. Yet all that remained of the ship itself were an anchor and a short length of chain, together with a rudder hinge. Around the ivory tusk, a few hundred bricks were all there was to be seen of the cargo. The ship had completely broken up. With the disappearance of the hull, which forms a receptacle in which anything left of the equipment and cargo is usually found, individual objects had been smashed and swept away by the Atlantic breakers that usually pound that outer reef.

Close on a hundred elephant tusks were found by Loïc Letiec[1] in 1987 at another mysterious site, Saint-Quay-Portrieux in Brittany. There again, no trace of a ship's hull was found. All that remains of the cargo are a few beads, a copper bracelet and the familiar manilla that was employed as a form of currency along the African coast. Modest though they be, these traces nevertheless bear witness to the triangular slave trade in those parts.

However, the wreck that best illustrates the usefulness of the archaeological excavation of slave ships is that of the *Henrietta Maria*, an English ship sunk early in the eighteenth century. The wreck was discovered in 1972 by a team of treasure-hunters in the Marquesa Keys off Florida. Passed on eleven years later to another team of treasure-hunters, it was studied by David D. Moore, a student at East Carolina University (North Carolina) who made it the subject of his Master of Art thesis. However much the site was disturbed by previous operations, and despite the difficulties by which its scientific study was beset, interesting results were none the less obtained.

The ship was identified and dated by the discovery of its bell bearing the date 1699. Some parts of the ship's structure have been conserved and some items of equipment studied, but the main interest of the site lies in the remains of the cargo. The three branches of the slave trade are evoked by different items: the Europe-Africa branch by a whole consignment of English pewter-ware intended for trading with the Africans, together with a collection of small mirrors and thousands of yellow and green beads. The latter puzzled archae-ologists, who eventually found an explanation in a report written in 1699 by a certain James Barbot, who was the supercargo of the slave ship *Albion Frigate*. He reported that the demand for yellow and green beads was very low on the Guinea coast and that such colours should no longer be carried. The Africa-America branch of the voyage is represented by sinister iron shackles, of which 75 pairs were found, and also by a whole consignment of elephant tusks. The third branch – from America to Europe – is illustrated by trunks of Campeche wood (the precious wood used in Europe for dyeing) from the city of the same name in the Mexican province of Yucatan.

Another wreck, although not that of a slave ship, provides additional fas-cinating information. The *San Antonio*, a Spanish vessel sunk in 1621 in the Bermudas, was explored by Teddy Tucker,[2] an American treasure-hunter, in the 1950s. In addition to some colonial products in the cargo, several thou-sand cowries (*Cypraea moneta*) were discovered. Like the copper bracelets already referred to, they were used as money on the African coast. A few dozen pounds of them bought an adult slave. Their presence on the Spanish ship illustrates the strange circuit followed by these little white shells gathered in the Maldives and taken across the Pacific to Mexico by the famous Manila galleons before being carried overland to *La Veira Cruz* to be loaded on the Spanish vessels.

The wreck of the former slave ship *James Matthews*, which went down in 1841 off Freemantle in Australia, has also been found.[3] Seized in 1837 off Dominica by a ship of the Royal Navy when engaged in the unlawful trade, it was refitted as a merchant vessel. Only the relatively well-preserved structure of the craft tells us a little more about the slave ships. Of three other wrecks of slave ships found off England, Florida and Panama, little or nothing is known.

The results achieved are thus meagre indeed when set against the poten-tial mentioned earlier as being beneath the oceans. To put this great potential to good use, a systematic research and study programme is essential. The task is immense and, if no effort is to be wasted, care should be taken to choose the most favourable locations and the most appropriate means of research.

It is necessary, initially, to collect existing information on wrecks of slave ships from researchers studying the slave trade, to undertake research on the theme and to gather this information together in a computer file constituting a common base that can be made available to archaeologists and historians. A register should be compiled of all known slave-trading centres and the avail-able historical documentation on each of them gathered. At the same time, a closer study should be made of the environment of the routes used by the slave ships in order to decide on the best areas for prospecting: around the major departure and arrival ports in Europe (Bristol, Liverpool and London for England, Bordeaux, Le Havre, La Rochelle and Nantes for France, etc.); in the main slave-trading zones along the African coast from Mauritania to Angola, namely, Argun, Senegambia, the Grain Coast (from Sierra Leone to Cape Palmas), the Côte d'Ivoire, the Gold Coast (which comprises the former trading post of El Mina and the old kingdoms of Ardres and Juda), the Gulf of Benin and the zone stretching from Cape Lopez to Angola; in the places used as ports of call before the Atlantic crossing (the islands of Príncipe, São Tomé, Cape Verde, etc.); around the main ports of arrival (in Brazil, Venezuela, Guyana, Colombia, the Lesser Antilles, the Greater Antilles and North America). Nor should we forget the slave trade to the Ile Bourbon and the Ile de France (now Reunion and Mauritius) from Mozambique and Madagascar.

To the historical documentation concerning the slave-trading centres in all these zones should be added geographical, geological, hydrographic and meteorological data. By correlating all this information we should be able to determine the best places for systematic investigation or preliminary searches. We shall of course also need to take account of work already done or under way and consider the symbolic significance of particular places. Any systematic – by nature, slow – approach should be accompanied by more high-profile operations aimed at capturing the public imagination and maintaining interest in the project as a whole. It is important, in particular, following the model of the programme set up by the French Underwater Archaeology Group (GRAN),[4] that the initial research should be conducted on all three continents and that other initiatives should gradually cluster around these first poles selected.

For this clearly interregional type of project, the flow and exchange of information are all-important. It is therefore necessary to decide on common working methods, to train multidisciplinary teams (archaeologists, divers and technicians) and to ensure that teams exchange information and experience so as to pool ideas and methods. For it seems essential that a subject that has caused so much controversy in the past should today provide an opportunity for joint reflection and work. The participation in marine operations of researchers from different backgrounds is the best way of establishing practical scientific and technological co-operation.

It is furthermore to be hoped that the 'output' of this programme – publications, conferences, symposia, exhibitions and even artefacts themselves – will be circulated among the different centres and thus encourage active cultural co-operation.

Notes

1. D. Brisou, 1987, p. 40.
2. R.C. Smith, 1988, p. 90.
3. K. Muckleroy, 1978, p. 116.
4. The GRAN programme, 'The Sunken Memory of the Slave Trade Triangle', is being carried out simultaneously in Martinique, Senegal and the approaches to Nantes. It has received the label of UNESCO's World Decade for Cultural Development (1988–97).

Bibliography

BRISOU, D. 1987. 'L'épave de Saint-Quay-Portrieux'. *Chronique d'histoire maritime*, No. 16, 2ᵉ semestre, Paris, CFHM.

DUCOIN, J. 1993. *Naufrages, condition de navigation et assurances dans la marine de commerce du XVIII e siècle. Le cas de Nantes et de son commerce colonial avec les îles d'Amérique*. Paris, Librairie de l'Inde.

MOORE, D.D. 1989. Anatomy of a Seventeenth-Century Ship: Historical and Archaeological Investigations of the Henrietta Marie, 1699 (East Carolina University, M.A. thesis).

MUCKLEROY, K. 1978. *Maritime Archaeology*. Cambridge, Cambridge University Press.

SMITH, R.C. 1988. 'Treasure ships in the Spanish Main: The Iberian-American maritime empires'. *Ships and Shipwrecks of the Americas*. London, Thames & Hudson.

Chapter 5

Origins of the Slaves in the Lima Region in Peru (Sixteenth and Seventeenth Centuries)

Jean-Pierre Tardieu

THE PERUVIAN HISTORIAN FERNANDO ROMERO affirmed in 1977: 'I have identi-fied the existence ... of slaves belonging to 80 different ethnic groups (and hope to find more), but have not as yet been able to determine the number of individuals in each group.'[1] A few years later, in *El negro en el Perú y su tran-sculturación lingüística*,[2] he admitted that the provenance of these slaves had not yet been elucidated and that one should be wary of information gathered in the past, according to which there were 10 principal castes in Peru, i.e. Terra-novos, Lucumís, Mandingas, Cambundas, Carabelíes, Cangoes, Chalas, Huaro-chiríes, Congos and Misangos. These names had in fact been taken from slave-trade contracts drawn up in the eighteenth century.

At that same time, the American historian F. Bowser, in a chapter of his book *El esclavo africano en el Perú colonial*, presents two extremely interesting tables, based on data culled from the notarial registers of the Peruvian histor-ical archives in Lima.[3] The first table examines the origin of Afro-Peruvians (1560–1650), and the second, the provenance of Peruvian *bozales* (blacks from Africa) over the same period. The figures presented in the latter have enabled us to establish the classification presented in Table 5.1.

According to F. Bowser, three major areas can be distinguished for slave supply: Senegambia and Guinea Bissau with 1,281 individuals (blacks), cen-tral and southern Africa with 716, and the part of western Africa located between these two regions with only 248. He assures us that for most of the sixteenth century the Spaniards preferred Africans from the north-western coastal regions for their industrious and happy nature and for their ability to adapt easily. In the late 1580s Spanish America began to receive an increas-ingly large percentage of Africans from Angola.[4]

The Data

Notarial registers are by no means the only source of such information. Parish records also provide documentation of considerable importance. In this study,

Table 5.1 Origins of Peruvian *Bozales*, 1560–1650

Angola	719	Balanta	27
Bran	394	Jolufo	26
Biafra	189	Cazanga	16
Bañon	168	Guinea (unspecified)	13
Folupo	150	Soso	13
Mandinga	125	Terranova	11
Bioho	100	Berbesí	7
Arará/Ardá	71	Anchico	8
Zape	64	Lucumí	5
Caravalí	58	Malamba	4
Nalú	52	Mina	3
Cocolí	36	Mozambique	2
Congo	33	Fula	1
		Total	**2,295**

I shall be using a series of data taken from the collection of the archiepiscopal archives of Lima, specifically:

(a) the *Libro I de bautismos de indios, mulatos, negros (1570–1628)* of the parish of San Marcelo de Lima (Libros parroquiales);

(b) the list of parishioners confirmed in January 1632 by the pastoral visitor of the archdiocese of Lima, Lic. Hierónimo Santa Cruz y Padilla, in his visitation to the parishes of Heruay, Chincha, Pisco, Caucato and Cóndor *(Visitas 1601–1774*, bundle 1);

(c) the *Libro I de matrimonios de negros y mulatos (1640–93)* of the parish of San Marcelo de Lima (Libros parroquiales);

(d) the section *Causas de negros (1630–1702)*.

Documents (a) and (c) deal with urban blacks, while document (b) deals with rural slaves belonging to the haciendas in the rich valleys to the south of Lima. *Causas de negros* (d) includes blacks for the entire archdiocese of Lima, or rather for the capital of the viceroyalty and its environs.

In these documents, the priests use names of ethnic groups as surnames, which makes it possible to determine the origins of the slaves' relatives, if not of the slaves themselves.[5] It must be acknowledged, however, that these names are not always an accurate reflection of the actual provenance of the slaves but are often those of the ports of embarkation scattered along the entire length of the African coast. To these names we have added those of relatives or witnesses whenever their 'caste' or 'nation' is indicated.

Ethnic Origins

Table 5.2 Origins of Blacks of the Parish of San Marcelo de Lima, 1583–89
(*Libro de Bautismos*)

Castes	Number	%
Bran	98	34.02
Biafra	39	13.53
Bañón	38	13.19
Cazanga	24	8.32
Mandinga	19	6.59
Congo	15	5.20
Angola	11	3.81
Jolufo	11	3.81
Biafara	10	3.47
Zape	9	3.12
Bioho	4	1.38
Nalú	4	1.38
Mosanga	3	1.04
Terranovo	2	0.69
Caboverde	1	0.34
Total	**288**	

Table 5.3 Origins of Blacks of Hernay, Chincha, Pisco, Caucato and Cóndor, 1632
(list of parishioners confirmed)

Castes	Number	%
Angola	105	34.20
Bran	39	12.67
Mandinga	22	7.15
Folupo	20	6.50
Bañón	17	5.53
Carabalí	16	5.20
Congo	16	5.20
Terranovo	15	4.85
Biafra	9	2.92
Nalú	7	2.27
Arará	6	1.95
Bioho	6	1.95
Zape	5	1.62
Cazanga	4	1.30
Jolufo	4	1.30
Balanta	3	0.97
Caboverde	3	0.97
Cocolí	2	0.65
Mozambique	2	0.65
Anchico	1	0.32
Biafara	1	0.32

(*cont.*)

Table 5.3 Origins of Blacks of Hernay, Chincha, Pisco, Caucato and Cóndor (*cont.*)

Castes	Number	%
Cacheo	1	0.32
Matamba	1	0.32
Mina	1	0.32
Santomé	1	0.32
Total	307	

Table 5.4 Origins of Blacks of the Parish of San Marcelo de Lima, 1640–80
(*Libros de matrimonios*)

Castes	Male	Number Female	Total	%
Angola	70	92	162	17.68
Congo	57	50	107	11.68
Malamba	53	46	99	10.79
Terranovo	49	39	88	9.59
Bran	46	35	81	8.82
Angú	29	24	53	5.77
Mina	31	16	47	5.12
Popó	18	19	37	4.03
Folupo	18	18	36	3.92
Bañón (or Baño)	12	16	28	2.99
Bioho	14	7	21	2.28
Biafara	9	11	20	2.18
Nalú	10	10	20	2.18
Matamba	11	7	18	1.96
Bamba	8	8	16	1.74
Caravalí	6	6	12	1.30
Arará	4	7	11	1.19
Luanda	5	4	9	0.98
Zape	5	4	9	0.98
Mandinga	5	3	8	0.87
Goja	4	3	7	0.76
Jolufo	3	4	7	0.76
Lucumí	4	3	7	0.76
Biafra	2	3	5	0.54
Mosanga	3	2	5	0.54
Anchico	3	1	4	0.43
Balanta	0	4	4	0.43
Caboverde	2	2	4	0.43
Cocolí	3	1	4	0.43
Cazanga	1	1	2	0.21
Malanta (Balanta?)	1	1	2	0.21
Santomé	1	1	2	0.21
Mozambique	1	0	1	0.10
Total	488	448	936	

Table 5.5 Origins of Blacks in Lima, 1630–1702 (*Causas de Negros*)

Castes	Male	Number Female	Total	%
Congo	32	37	69	16.56
Angola	35	28	63	15.12
Terranovo	30	16	46	11.04
Bran	22	11	33	7.92
Folupo	6	15	21	5.04
Biafara	10	8	18	4.32
Malamba	10	7	17	4.08
Arará	7	9	16	3.84
Mandinga	13	2	15	3.60
Mina	10	4	14	3.36
Bañón (or Baño)	6	6	12	2.88
Lucumí	7	5	12	2.88
Popó	6	4	10	2.40
Zape (or Cape)	4	5	9	2.18
Bioho	5	3	8	1.92
Carabalí	3	5	8	1.92
Nalú	3	3	6	1.44
Caboverde	4	1	5	1.20
Cocolí	3	2	5	1.20
Biafra	1	3	4	0.96
Anchico	2	1	3	0.72
Jolufo	1	2	3	0.72
Mosanga	3	0	3	0.72
Soso	2	0	2	0.48
Agí	0	1	1	0.24
Andosu	1	0	1	0.24
Angú	1	0	1	0.24
Bamba	0	1	1	0.24
Cazanga	1	0	1	0.24
Cacheo	1	0	1	0.24
Masa	1	0	1	0.24
Mozambique	0	1	1	0.24
Santomé	1	0	1	0.24
Total	231	180	411	

Geographic Location

The different ethnic groups presented in Tables 5.2 to 5.5 come from three large areas.

The 'Guinean Rivers'

In slave-trade contracts, the expressions 'Cape Verde islands' (Islas de Caboverde) and 'Guinean rivers' (ríos de Guinea) correspond to the area comprising Senegambia, Guinea-Bissau and Sierra Leone.

The Jolufos, also called Gelofes in other documents of the same period, are today's Senegalese Wolofs. The Cazangas come from the region of the Casamance river along the left bank of which were found the Bañones or Baños. Their true ethnic designation is Bagnoun. The Balantas or Balantes lived along the right bank. The Folupos or Folupes came from this same region.

The Biohos controlled the archipelago of Bijagos (Guinea-Bissau). To the north of these islands, on the continent, the port of Cacheu played a key role in the slave trade, giving rise to the toponym Cacheo. Across from these islands were located the Biafaras, and further south the territory of the Nalús was to be found. What is today Sierra Leone was home to the Sosos, the Zapes or Capes, and the Cocolís, a subgroup of the Zape family.

Between these groups and the Niger were found the Mandingas, inhabitants of the former empire of Mali, who were Muslims much given to proselytising and whose name came to be synonymous with 'demon' in Latin America.[6] We must concede that this name related more to the victims of the Mandingo hegemony than to the ruling élite.[7]

The 'Castes' of São Tomé

Following the coast, we reach the Gulf of Guinea and the infamous 'Slave Coast' which stretches from present-day Togo to present-day Nigeria. Before reaching the shores of these countries, one has to travel along the Costa de Malagueta, which corresponds roughly to the coastline of Côte d'Ivoire, whence came the Branes, otherwise known as the Abrons, who are now settled in the province of Bondoukou, and the Gojas or Gandjas of the Akan group.

The term 'Mina' was used to designate the slaves supplied by the slave-traders of the Gold Coast, now Ghana. This group owes its name to the area's renowned gold 'mines', which were quick to attract the Portuguese; there they founded the São Jorge da Mina fort which served as the headquarters for the slave trade throughout the entire region.

Popó is obviously derived from the Slave Coast port of Grand-Popó, the port of embarkation of slaves probably from the neighbouring kingdom of Ardá, or Alladá, a toponymic designation that gave rise to the term Arará, which is familiar throughout all of Spanish America and the Caribbean. Terranavos was perhaps the name given to the slaves supplied by the Gouns of the kingdom of Porto-Novo.

The masters of the south-west of present-day Nigeria, the famous Yorubas, known at the time by the name Lucumee, supplied the Lucumí slaves.[8] Further east, on the deep Calabar Bay, lived the Caravalís.

Many slaves were concentrated on the island of São Tomé, having been bought following the razzias that were carried out all along these coasts, and were subsequently shipped across the Atlantic under the name Santomés.[9]

The Bantu Zone

The Biafras, according to travellers' accounts, occupied the territories bordering on the Cameroon river. Formerly known as Bafan, they now live in Gabon and are known by the name of Fan.

The Congo river region was for a time under the direct colonisation of the Portuguese, who imposed their Christian beliefs. Their faith did nothing to prevent the development of the slave trade, which spread inland as far as the territory of the Batékés, the latter being imported into Peru under the name Anchicos. The Mosangas belonged to another branch of the same family. The Angus ruled the dukedom of Mpangu, at the confluence of the Kasai and Zaire rivers. The province of Bamba was also a part of the renowned kingdom of the Congo.

A great number of slave ships left Angola laden with slaves from this kingdom, or those from Matamba, to the north, and Malemba, to the south. In the name Luanda one can easily recognise the name of the capital and the principal port of the Portuguese colony (San Pablo de Loanda).

Finally, we must not neglect to mention the existence in seventeenth-century Peru of a group of slaves known as Mozambique, which points up the complexity of the slave trade.[10]

Now that the regions where the *bozales* slaves of Peru originated have been identified, we should ask how the selection process may have evolved. One look at the tables presented above reveals a gradual diversification of the sources of supply.

Changes in the Selection Process

It would of course be rash to base overly categorical conclusions regarding the provenance of slaves on the documents examined in this chapter. As I pointed out, the names assigned to slaves were frequently those of their ports of embarkation. Moreover, it is not at all easy to delimit the geographical area corresponding to the various ethnic groups mentioned, given the inaccuracy of data, the mobility of certain groups over the centuries, the vagueness of the terms 'ethnic groups' and 'ethnic subgroups', and finally the repercussions of colonial policies on the original populations. Therefore, the separation between the three major regions defined in this study cannot be clear-cut as far as the border regions are concerned.

The percentages presented in Table 5.6 thus cannot be said to be scientifically precise: they represent a trend derived from Tables 5.2, 5.3, 5.4 and 5.5, and correspond to the areas previously defined.

Table 5.6 Percentages of Ethnic Origins for Each Period

	Area 1	Area 2	Area 3
T.2 1583–89	41.66	34.72	23.61
T.3 1632	30.94	25.40	43.64
T.4 1640–80	17.62	31.19	51.17
T.5 1630–1702	25.79	34.54	39.65

Based on the figures given for the period 1583–89, there is a clear predominance of area 1 over area 2, while slaves from area 3 represent a minority (barely a quarter of the total). Comparing these percentages with those determined by researchers for other regions of the 'Indies', one can observe that the Bantus were still far from holding the predominant position they already held in Havana.[11] On the other hand, the Branes and the Biafras were in the same position (i.e. second and third, respectively). However, on examining the situation in Córdoba de Tucumán, one senses that these proportions were soon to change. The data gathered by Carlos Sempat Assadourian for the period 1588 to 1610 reveal a percentage of 52.4 in favour of the Angolas, while the Guineos did not exceed 24.85 per cent.

Fifty years later, the results of a trend in favour of the Bantu area in the haciendas of southern Lima were evident. Even in the capital itself, this trend continued well into the second half of the seventeenth century.

It would appear that the area of São Tomé 'castes' put up a fairly effective resistance to Bantu competition, particularly in Lima itself. This trend therefore occurred at the expense of the Senegambia, Guinea-Bissau and Sierra Leone area, a fact corroborated by the figures in Table 5.5, which covers a broader time frame.

Within the areas themselves, the change is just as obvious – a significant example being that of the Branes and the Angolas, as shown in Table 5.7.

Table 5.7 Changing Percentages for the Branes and the Angolas

	1583–89	1632	1640–80	1630–1702
Branes	34.02	12.67	8.82	7.92
Angolas	5.20	34.20	17.68	15.33

The changing levels of these two groups in the slave workforce of Peru admittedly do not exactly balance one another: the continuous decline in the number of Branes listed in our documents is *not* matched by a linear increase in the number of Angolas. The latter appear to have reached their peak in the early decades of the seventeenth century and to have undergone a gradual tapering-off that lasted until the end of the century. Apart from these two groups, the decline in the numbers of Jolufos is also evident: 3.81 per cent (Table 5.2), 1.30 per cent (Table 5.3), 0.76 per cent (Table 5.4) and 0.72 per cent (Table 5.5).

Conclusions

The trends pointed out above may be explained by historical and economic factors. With regard to historical factors, the figures in Tables 5.2, 5.3, 5.4 and 5.5 justify Bowser's emphasis on the increase in the numbers of Angolas at the end of the 1580s, although it appears to have begun before that time. The Portuguese did not begin to 'actively colonize' Angola until 1570.[12] The region was capable of supplying 'inexhaustible quantities' of slaves. After a century of relentless slave-trading, the slave-traders needed to exploit a new, virgin territory – if for no other reason than to lower the unit cost of slaves and thus increase their profit. The decrease in the supply of slaves from Angola in the period 1640 to 1702 finds its natural explanation in Portugal's secession from Spain. Be that as it may, the Bantu area continued to supply a large proportion of slaves (see Table 5.5).

In America, the behaviour of the slaves led to a change in the selection process. The royal schedules banning the passage of Gelofes to the West Indies indicate that these slaves were more rebellious than the others, undoubtedly because they were already Islamised. On 11 May 1526, the Holy Roman Emperor, Charles V, proclaimed: 'Great care should be taken at the *Casa de Contratación* not to transfer to the Indies any so-called Gelofe slaves, nor those from the Levant, nor any brought from (the Indies), nor any others brought up with Moors, even if they are related to the blacks of Guinea without our express permission.'[13]

The central government was forced to return innumerable times to this subject. The schedule of 1532 reveals the reasons underlying this concern:

I have been informed [by the queen] that all the destruction caused on San Juan island and the other islands by the revolt of the blacks and the killings of Christians there were done by the Gelofes living there who by all accounts are arrogant, uncooperative, troublesome and incorrigible. Few receive any punishment and it is invariably they who attempt to rebel and commit every sort of crime, during this revolt and at other times. Those who conduct themselves peacefully, who come from other regions and behave well, they mislead into evil ways, which is displeasing to God, our Lord, and prejudicial to our revenues. This matter having been examined by the members of our Indies Council, and considering the importance for the proper peopling and pacification of these islands that no Gelofe should be moved there, I hereby command you for the future to ensure that no one, absolutely no one, transfers to India, islands and terra firma of the ocean any slave from the Island of Gelofe without our express permission to that end; any failure in this regard will result in confiscation.[14]

The Crown regarded any contact between blacks and Islam to be a threat to peace in the 'Indies': '... and in a new land where our Holy Catholic Faith is now taking root, it is not appropriate to transfer people of the kind because of the negative consequences this could have.'[15]

Such considerations, despite their serious nature, did not entirely convince the slave-traders, who were obliged to follow the dictates of the market. This being said, the intervention of the Crown undoubtedly contributed to the decline noted above. Were the Spanish being more cautious than the Portuguese? The slave uprisings in northern Brazil during the early decades of the nineteenth century were in fact organised by Muslim blacks.[16]

On the other hand, the Indies Council seemed less suspicious of the Mandingas, although they came from a people who had been Islamised since the eleventh century.[17] It is true that their numbers became relatively less significant in the seventeenth century, owing to a massive influx of Congos and Angolas, who were theoretically Christianised. Moreover, the Church assumed responsibility for controlling these blacks.[18]

So much for the historical factors. The economic factors are equally illuminating. In the 'Indies', slave owners were in need of a flexible, industrious workforce that specialised in farm work or possessed craft skills, according to their needs. The slave trade quickly became specialised as a result. The Jésuit Alonso de Sandoval, in *De Instauranda Aethiopum Salute* (1627), relied on the opinions of the slave-traders regarding the different ethnic groups mentioned in this study. The Guineos (from Senegambia, Guinea-Bissau and Sierra Leone) were the most highly prized by the Spaniards for their services.[19] They took readily to instruction in the Christian faith, distinguished themselves by their capacity to reason and their loyalty, and, as an added bonus, had a robust physical constitution, which predisposed them to hard labour: 'They are infinitely more loyal than any of the others, use their heads and are skilful besides being more comely and of finer build; healthy, hard-working blacks; they are accordingly known to be worth more and are more highly appreciated than any other people in the world.'[20]

Although the blacks from São Tomé were less prized than those from Guinea, they were none the less healthier and more fit for work than the Angolas and the Congos. Moreover, they were braver and less likely to run away: 'They are less highly appreciated than those from the Rios de Guinea and worth less; yet they are worth more and cost more than the Angolas and Congos and are very hard-working; they are less vulnerable to sickness; they are not as timid nor as liable to run away.'[21]

The slave-traders did not have a very favourable opinion of the third group, whose members were susceptible to illness and died easily. They were therefore the least useful: 'Blacks of these castes are less valuable and less useful; they are less capable than any other people, the most subject to disease and the most faint-hearted and those who give in to death most easily.'[22]

It was the low cost and poor trade skills of the Angolas that explain their large numbers on the haciendas of southern Lima (Table 5.3). Thus, Peruvian buyers took these criteria into account, despite the fact that the laws of the market, conditioned by monopolistic contracts and historical factors, limited their freedom of choice.

The conclusions reached in the course of this modest study on the provenance of the slaves in the region of Lima logically correspond to other analyses of the slave trade in the 'Indies'. The religious sources used make it possible to shed light on certain aspects that are not revealed by conventional sources (notarial registers, customs records such as the *almojarifazgo,* municipal tax records, etc.). They provide as accurate a picture of the origin of slaves as possible for a given area as far from the African shores as the Pacific coast, which is something that traditional documentation is not always able to establish, owing to the geographic mobility intrinsic to slavery.

Notes

1. F. Romero, 1977, p. 160.
2. F. Romero, 1987, p. 84.
3. F. Bowser, 1977, pp. 66–71.
4. Ibid., pp. 62–65.
5. On onomastic structures applicable to slaves, see G. de Granda, 1971.
6. J.-P. Tardieu, 1985, pp. 99–123.
7. W. Rodney, 1969, pp. 335–336.
8. For the origin of the term *Lucumí,* made famous by Nicolás Guillén but already known in Peru in the seventeenth century, see O.B. Yai, 1976, p. 42.
9. This name was already well known in Spanish literature of the sixteenth and seventeenth centuries. See Tardieu, 1977, p. 26.
10. For further information about the localities of these ethnic groups, see Beltrán, 1972.
11. M.-J. Rojas, 1956, pp. 1278–1279.
12. F.P. Bowser, 1977, pp. 64–65.
13. M.B. De Quirós, 1864–84, Vol. 1, p. 313.
14. *Idem,* Vol. 52, pp. 141–142.
15. A. García Gallo, 1945–46, Vol. 52, pp. 141–142.
16. R. Reichert, 1964, pp. 621–625.
17. In the government of Popayán (present-day Colombia), there was also a large number of slaves originating in the Islamised areas; see G. de Granda, 1972, pp. 89–103.
18. J.-P. Tardieu, 1993, pp. 287–716.
19. A. de Sandoval, 1987, pp. 110–111.
20. Ibid., p. 136.
21. Ibid., p. 139.
22. Ibid., p. 141.

Bibliography

AGUIRRE BELTRÁN, G. 1972. *La población negra de México*. Mexico City, FCE.

BOWSER, F.P. 1977. *El esclavo africano en el Perú colonial*. Mexico City, Siglo Veintiuno Editores.

DE GRANDA, G. 1971. 'Onomástica y procedencia africana de esclavos negros en las minas de la gobernación de Popayan (siglo XVIII)'. *Revista Española de Antropología Americana*. (Madrid), No. 6.

———. 1972. 'Datos antroponómicos sobre negros esclavos musulmanes en Nueva Granada'. *Thesaurus* (Bogota), No. 27.

DE QUIRÓS, M.B. 1864–84. *Colección de documentos inéditos relativos al descubrimiento, conquista y colonización de las antiguas posesiones Españolas de América y Oceanía, sacadas en su mayor parte del Real Archivo de Indias*. Madrid.

———. 1943. *Recopilación de leyes de los Reynos de las Indias, ed. facsímil de la impresa en Madrid en 1791*. Madrid, Consejo de la Hispanidad.

GARCÍA GALLO, A. 1945–46. Cedulario indiano recopilado por Diego de Encinas, reproducción facsímil de la edición de 1596, con estudio e índices de Alfonso García Gallo. Madrid.

REICHERT, R. 1964. 'El ocaso del islam entre los negros brasileños'. Actas del XXXVI Congreso Internacional de Americanistas. Sevilla, Vol. 3, pp. 621–625.

RODNEY, W. 1969. 'Upper Guinea and the Significance of the Origins of the Africans Enslaved in the New World'. *The Journal of Negro History* LIV (4), October.

ROJAS, M.-T. 1956. 'Algunos datos sobre los negros esclavos y horros en la Habana del siglo XVI'. *Miscelánea de estudios dedicados a Fernando Ortiz*. Vol. 2.

ROMERO, F. 1977. 'El habla costeña del Perú y los lenguajes afronegros'. *Boletin de la Academia Peruana de la Lengua* (Lima), No. 12.

———. 1987. *El Negro en el Perú y su transculturación lingüística*. Lima. Ed. Milla Batres.

SANDOVAL, S.J.A., DE. 1987. *De Instauranda Aethiopum Salute*. Ed. Enriqueta Vila Vilar, 1627 *(Un tratado sobre la esclavitud)*. Madrid, Alianza Editorial.

SEMPAT ASSADOURIAN, C. 1969. 'El tráfico de esclavos en Córdoba, 1588–1650'. *Cuadernos de Historia*, No. XXXD, Universidad Nacional de Córdoba, Facultad de Filosofía y Humanidades.

TARDIEU, Jean.-P. 1977. Le Noir dans la Littérature Espagnole des XVI° et XVII° siècles (Doctoral thesis, University of Bordeaux).

———. 1985. 'Ambivalence du personnage du "Mandingue" en Amérique Latine au XX° siècle. Tradition populaire et élaboration littéraire'. *Historiografía y Bibliografía Americanistas* (Sevilla), Vol. XXIX, No. 2.

———. 1993. *L'Eglise et les Noirs au Pérou (XVI° et XVII° siècles)*. Paris, L'Harmattan.

YAI, O.B. 1976. 'Influence yoruba dans la poésie cubaine: Nicolás Guillén et la tradition poétique Yoruba'. Actes du XLII Congrès International des Américanistes, Paris.

Chapter 6

Returning Afro-Brazilians

Bellarmin C. Codo

THE PRESENT CHAPTER examines two events that are significant for Benin. The first event occurred on 3 March 1835, when Francisco de Souza Martins, president of Bahia province, declared that it was necessary 'to send out of Brazilian territory all liberated Africans who constitute a danger to our tranquillity. Such individuals, not having been born in Brazil, possessing a different language, religion and customs, and having shown themselves to be enemies of our tranquillity during recent events, should not benefit from the constitutional guarantees set down only for Brazilian citizens'.[1] This declaration gave the signal that led to the departure for the coast of Africa of the black slaves of Brazil. That is how an Afro-Brazilian society, which made a deep impression on the development of that part of the 'Slave Coast' between Porto Seguro and Lagos, came into being. The second event occurred in 1988 when the Afro-Brazilian-style chapel built by the Christian community of Agoué in the last century, having become too small for the town's Catholic community, was pulled down. These two events mark, on the one hand, the arrival on the coast of Guinea of African slaves from Brazil and, on the other, the disappearance of one of their achievements.

Since the increasing speed of change within African societies is threatening to obliterate a whole cultural heritage from the past – of which the church at Agoué is but one example – it is important that research be carried out on the Afro-Brazilian communities of the old Slave Coast. The political, economic and social achievements of the Afro-Brazilian communities are generally little known and are currently tending to disappear from the collective memory, helped by the fact that we are witnessing the rewriting of some family histories with the aim of idealising their origins.

This chapter will survey the Afro-Brazilian presence on the Slave Coast, particularly in the Republic of Benin, in order to throw light on its origins, to assess its influence and to indicate new paths of research.

Origins

As is well known, the transatlantic slave trade was born of the desire of Europeans to obtain a servile labour force to replace the indigenous Indians, who were decimated by disease, in order to exploit the plantations, the new lands discovered in the Americas and the mines. The resulting drain of men, women and children in which, in one way or another, the political authorities of the Gulf of Guinea participated and which continued from the fifteenth century to the nineteenth century is what gives the sad name of supplier of slaves (Slave Coast) to the portion of the coast from Porto Seguro, in the west, to Lagos, in the east.

The organisation of this vast deportation led to the emergence of communities of European slave-traders in various urban centres which grew rich on this trade. On the Slave Coast, there came into being in Anecho, Badagry, Grand Popo, Lagos, Ouidah, Porto-Novo and, later, Agoué, white communities – more or less mixed depending on the degree of integration into the local African societies – made up of Europeans and Brazilians engaged for the most part in the slave trade. Brazilians and Portuguese were in a majority, particularly at Ouidah, which, by the beginning of the nineteenth century, was the main slave-trading port. The Portuguese language came to be used in political and commercial relations with the African authorities. The Brazilians in particular who came from the Bahia region – such as Francisco Felix de Souza, called Chacha, in Ouidah, or Domingo Martinez in Lagos and later in Porto-Novo[2] – established close economic relations with the Slave Coast, particularly with the centres at Lagos, Ouidah and Porto-Novo. It was these white or mixed communities that would take in the former slaves returning from Brazil to the African continent at the beginning of the nineteenth century.

At that time Brazil was experiencing a whole series of events that had repercussions on slavery. From 1807 onwards, a succession of slave revolts occurred, in particular in the Bahia region, whose principal leaders were liberated Yoruba or Hausa Muslim Africans and which left a deep mark on Brazil. In 1835, the Malè revolt further heightened the fear of seeing Brazil dominated by blacks, whose emancipation, it was feared, would lead to their participation in political decision-making. Thus, added to the desire to reduce the number of blacks by sending out of Brazil the slaves brought in illegally was the desire to send back to Africa liberated former slaves.[3]

It was therefore to satisfy white public opinion, which was demanding that not only captured rebels but also liberated Africans be expelled, that Francisco de Souza Martins, president of the province of Bahia, was authorised to send suspect persons out of the province 'without the formalities of legal proof of guilt'.

It was once again by force that former slaves were returned to the coast of Benin, along with those returning willingly as freed slaves. Although the latter had become Brazilian citizens, they were weary of the hostility of the whites and nostalgic for Africa. All returned to the old Slave Coast and the mixed communities of white slavers and traders whose language – Portuguese – they shared, along with some customs copied from those of whites ('like whites', as people used to say at the time).

How were these migrants received, both by the indigenous African community and by mixed-race Europeans? In Ouidah, Francisco Felix de Souza himself welcomed them, arranging their settlement in the Brésil and Zomaï quarters of the town. In Lagos, the British went so far as to make provision from Brazil itself to receive them. Generally speaking, the Afro-Brazilians arriving on the Slave Coast were rapidly integrated.

The massive arrival of these population groups during the first half of the nineteenth century radically transformed the communities of European slavers and traders who had settled on the African coast since the beginning of the triangle of trade. Most of the former slaves from Bahia had been captured in the wars in which the political authorities of the region engaged in the hinterland: the Fon, Fulani and Hausa prisoners from Oyo were embarked at Lagos and Sèmè (Porto-Novo); the Yoruba and Mahi, prisoners of the kingdom of Danxomè, were embarked at Ouidah, the kingdom's gateway to the ocean. Former slaves who had intended to return to their home country in the hinterland ended up settling on the coast for fear of being captured again, since the wars were still continuing.

In addition, as Gilberto Freyre explains, in the Americas they had assimilated new cultural influences which could only develop in the small, mixed-European communities with whom they shared a language, a religion – Catholic, for the most part – and various customs. In short, they had become 'Brazilianised'.[4] The fact that their reception had often been well organised made their integration that much easier.

Other former slaves, from Cuba (the Abul, the Ahmaral and the Carena) or from São Tomé (the Aguidisso) also settled on the Slave Coast. But those who peopled the towns along the coast were, for the most part, Portuguese-speaking Afro-Brazilians – called *aguda*. Moreover, many bore the same surname despite having different ethnic origins. We shall take the surname d'Almeida as an example. The first, Manuel Joaquim d'Almeida, was a white Brazilian captain of a slave vessel, master of the next two d'Almeidas. The second d'Almeida, also named Joaquim, also known as Zoki Azata, is said to be from the Azima family in Mahi country, to the north of the kingdom of Danxomè. Freed from slavery by his master, captain Joaquim d'Almeida, he returned to Ouidah and finally settled at Agoué. It seems that it was he who had the first chapel at Agoué built. The third, Antonio Olufade d'Almeida, son of Olukokun of Iseyin, not far from Oyo (in what is now Nigeria) was of Yoruba origin. He, too, is said to have been the slave of the slaving captain Manuel Joaquim d'Almeida. Other sources claim that his father, who was of noble birth, entrusted his son to a white man, who, when he returned to Portugal and then Brazil, 'presented' him to Manuel Joaquim d'Almeida. On his return to Africa, Antonio Olufade d'Almeida settled in Ouidah, where he prospered. The fourth, Pedro Felix d'Almeida, whose real name was Ahyi Manko, is said to have been from Elmina, in what is now Ghana. Brought up in the household of Francisco Felix de Souza, he is said to have excelled in his command of the Portuguese language and to have been adopted by the captain of a Portuguese vessel, Felix d'Almeida, who named him Pedro Felix d'Almeida. It would thus seem that he never crossed the Atlantic: he is said to have lived in Ouidah, where his business prospered, before settling in

Anecho, in what is now Togo. Thus we have four d'Almeida lineages, which spread all through the urban centres of Anecho, Agoué, Grand Popo, Ouidah and Porto-Novo.

The Influence of the Afro-Brazilians in Africa

As stated earlier, the slaves who returned to the Slave Coast – Fon, Mahi and Yoruba[5] – were people who had originally come from the area. They had forgotten neither its language nor its religion, to which they added new cultural practices learned during their enforced stay in Brazil.

Trade was the preferred activity of the Afro-Brazilians who settled on the Slave Coast. Some, like the former slave Joaquim d'Almeida, originally from the Mahi country, at Agoué, even engaged in the slave trade. Usually, they acted as middlemen between the Portuguese or Brazilian traders and the big European trading companies specialising in the triangular trade, before going on to engage in legitimate trade.

Political Influence of the Afro-Brazilians

The Afro-Brazilians returning to Africa did not all serve the same political interests, which indeed were sometimes in conflict. It was with the kings of the kingdom of Xogbonu – the object of bitter rivalry between the French and the British – that their political influence was greatest. Under the pretext of abolishing the slave trade, the British attempted to lay hands on that part of the Slave Coast lying between Lagos and Cape Coast and, in particular, on Porto-Novo, which was still involved in the slave trade and resisted such a move. The king of Xogbonu, Dè Sodji, allied himself with the French on the advice of his Afro-Brazilian friends, Joachim Manuel de Carvalho, Joachim José Santa-Anna and Manuel Ferreira, who were anxious to continue their trade. Faced with the refusal of the established authorities in Porto-Novo, the British bombarded the capital in March and April 1861, which led to the signing of the first protectorate treaty with France in February 1863.

In September 1864, Dè Mikpon, who succeeded Dè Sodji on the latter's death, expelled Joachim Manuel de Carvalho. In December 1864, Dè Mikpon terminated the treaty with France, which didn't recover its influence in the kingdom until twenty years later.

On the advice of the Afro-Brazilians and as his father had done before him, King Toffa, who had been placed on the throne of Xogbonu with the help of the king of Danxomè, appealed to France, with which he signed the second protectorate treaty in July 1883. By this treaty, the Afro-Brazilians, led by Georges Pinto, Pedro d'Almeida and Edouardo de Souza, hoped to develop further their business as middlemen between the Africans and the Europeans. They also expected it would afford them protection against local rulers, abolition of taxes and duties due to the king of Porto-Novo, and acknowledgement of their special status as collaborators with the new French power.

The hopes of most of the Afro-Brazilians were disappointed, although some succeeded in profiting from the alliance with France by becoming spokesmen for the community. Ignacio Paraïso, for example, the indispensable intermediary between the royal palace and the French rulers, converted to Islam and became the unofficial leader of the Muslims of Porto-Novo and their spokesman to the colonial power. He went on to become the first African member of the Council of Administration of the new colony of Dahomey in 1894.

Political life in the small kingdom of Agoué revolved around the rivalry between two Afro-Brazilians, Joachim d'Almeida and Pedro Landjekpo da Silveira. But it was above all in the kingdom of Danxomè that the interplay of alliances involving the powerful Afro-Brazilian community, settled by Chacha Francisco de Souza, the friend of King Ghezo, in Ouidah, was the most eventful. Until his death in 1849, Chacha Francisco de Souza nudged the external policy of Danxomè in a direction favourable to the Europeans.

In the second half of the nineteenth century, the European desire to have control of the African coast became more pressing. The rivalry among the imperialist powers enhanced the role of the Afro-Brazilians; the French and the Portuguese in particular sought to win them over to their side.

Development of the European Presence on the Slave Coast

The Blockade of Ouidah (1876–77). An Afro-Brazilian trader, Jacintho Costa Santos, was the unintentional instrument of the advancement of British designs on Danxomè and the rivalries between France and Britain. Summoned by the Yovogan of Ouidah, three charges were laid against him: intercepting a British ship to buy products and failing to respect the royal right of priority in the matter of purchase; refusing to sell to the king some of his products with the prescribed large reductions; non-payment by Santos's father – who had been dead five years – for the purchase of 40 slaves, although the king had already collected his share of the inheritance, naturally the bulk of it.

On 5 January 1876, Jacintho Costa Santos was ordered to pay a heavy fine and his goods were seized immediately. At once, the representatives of the European trading house in Ouidah protested to the king of Danxomè and threatened to leave the town and the kingdom and settle elsewhere if justice was not done. King Glele was unimpressed and ordered the whites, who had previously been more respectful of local customs, to leave the country.

Turnbull, the agent of Swanzy's, a British company, was set upon by the Yovogan's guards at an audience with the representatives of the European houses, and then thrown into prison. Freed a few hours later, he made a complaint to the commander of the British squadron charged with combating the clandestine slave trade. Meanwhile Flandrin, the representative of the French company Régis, left Ouidah for France.

Britain seized this opportunity to issue an ultimatum to the king of Danxomè: by 22 June 1876, King Glele was to provide 80,000 gallons of oil or pay a fine of 160,000 F; otherwise, Ouidah would be blockaded. When the king refused, the blockade was instituted on 1 July and went on for ten months.

Danxomè did not yield. It was a setback for the British, who did not send a punitive expedition, and French traders paid the fine for the king.[6]

Juliano de Souza and Portugal's Claims on Danxomè. Under cover of a commercial agreement, a treaty of protectorate was signed on 5 August 1885 between Portugal and Danxomè. The fraud was made possible by the complicity of the viceroy of Ouidah, Chacha Juliano de Souza, the official intermediary between King Glele and the whites. When a Portuguese mission arrived to inquire about the reasons why he was opposing implementation of the treaty of protectorate, King Glele realised that he had been tricked. He summoned Chacha Juliano de Souza to Abomey, dismissed him and had the Portuguese establishments at Godomey destroyed: 'I give my lands to no one, not even a spoonful, but I want my friends to trade there.... It is better that each nation govern its own lands, the whites in theirs with their kings, and I, King of Dahomey, with mine' (letter from King Glele to King Luiz I of Portugal, 16 July 1887).[7]

On 16 December 1887, Portugal officially renounced its claims over Danxomè but retained the fort at Ouidah.

The Division of the Afro-Brazilians in the Face of the Conquest of Danxomè. After the Conference of Berlin, French penetration of the Slave Coast was stepped up. The Afro-Brazilians, the indispensable intermediaries between whites and blacks who enjoyed privileged status, had to choose sides: France or the kingdom of Danxomè.

As the nineteenth century drew to a close, the Afro-Brazilians who had gone over to the French side thought that their alliance with France would allow them to develop their businesses further and would enhance their political influence. But quite the reverse happened: the supporters of Behanzin, the new king of Danxomè, wanted at all costs to preserve the independence of African states and to be their spokesmen to the outside world.

The Establishment of French Rule. French, the new language of communication, led to the end of the predominance of the Portuguese language. According to a decree of 1892, the term 'Monsieur' described a European, 'Sieur' an Afro-Brazilian and 'le nommé' (the person named) a Dahomeyan subject. Thus France, at least at the level of vocabulary, was acknowledging the special status of the Afro-Brazilians. But the latter's hopes were soon disappointed, and, inexorably, the indigenous economy based on the slave trade went into decline. Many Afro-Brazilians then entered the new French colonial administration as assistants, teachers, interpreters and so forth.

Cultural Influence of the Afro-Brazilians. For the Africans, the Afro-Brazilian community symbolised cultural mimicry. It was proof that European culture could be copied and imitated. Many indeed would entrust their children to the community so that they could be educated 'like white people' (in the sense of 'learning good manners'). As cultural models and referents, the Afro-Brazilians set the tone for the cultural and social life of the region. Their influence was enormous, and even today it is visible everywhere, if only at the level of language,[8] with the contribution of words of Portuguese origin (*adja*, *mina*, etc.), or of cookery, with the introduction of Portuguese or Brazilian dishes. Thus in the nineteenth century the Afro-Brazilians exposed Africans to a new way of life.

It is obvious that the African origin of the Afro-Brazilians gave them a degree of legitimacy among the people of the area. They also influenced the outlook and social behaviour of both Africans and Europeans living in the urban centres along the Slave Coast. As an example of the irresistible character of this prestige, Nicolas Olivier de Montaguère, a great friend of Francisco Felix de Souza and a man of French descent, 'Brazilianised' his surname to Nicolas d'Oliveira. As another example, the dark or black colour previously banned in mourning clothes was, as a result of contact with the Afro-Brazilians, permanently adopted – *lutu*, or dark clothing, is today the distinctive sign of mourning.

Some Directions for Research

Given the wealth of the Afro-Brazilian contribution to the African continent, there is a great need for further study. A number of lines of approach could be followed. One might consist of collecting written archives and oral accounts relating to families of Afro-Brazilian origin, including the litanies or praise-songs that refer to their origins, which, as we know, are extremely varied within the Afro-Brazilian community. For example, in Benin there are descendants of whites who came from Europe either directly or by way of Brazil (some already mixed) to trade on the African coast; descendants of the natural children of passing European traders or captains of slave ships; descendants of slaves deported to Brazil who returned in the nineteenth century; descendants of the children of blacks who had been 'entrusted' to some Portuguese or Brazilian associate to teach them 'how to live like whites'; descendants of Europeans who assimilated themselves into Brazilian society, for example by 'Brazilianising' their surnames; and descendants of slaves of Brazilian masters who had never left the coast and who had been given Portuguese-sounding names.

Today we are seeing changes in the opposite direction, for example, the d'Oliveiras have reverted to being the Olivier de Montaguères. What is the meaning of this development, which is tending to eradicate from the collective memory the symbol of the Afro-Brazilian influence that led a full-blooded Frenchman to 'Brazilianise' his surname? Do people today prefer to be descendants of a European, whether a trader and/or a slave dealer, rather than of a slave?

In this way, many family histories are being rewritten. More and more people are attributing to themselves an ancestor who, they claim, was sent to Brazil to learn a trade and 'how to live like a white person'. There will soon be few left who acknowledge themselves to be the descendants of freed slaves who returned to the African coast. That is why the history of these Africans should be reconstructed through collection and analysis of data, and this must be done before all the data are falsified.

How can such research be organised? It goes without saying that it should be the object of effective co-operation between national governments and international organisations. In concrete terms, we need to establish a documentation centre where written and oral archives on the subject would be centralised. In 1983, following a meeting in Cotonou on 'The Cultural Contributions to Africa of Blacks from the Diaspora', UNESCO envisaged the establishment in Ouidah of such a cultural centre or international research centre on the diaspora and its relations with Africa (CIERDA). The purpose of this centre would be as follows: to list the archives relating to the black diaspora in the various host countries (Brazil, Portugal, etc.); to put these archives on microfilm and microfiche so as to make them available to as many researchers as possible; to collect oral accounts passed down within the communities of those who had returned to their country of origin; to train African researchers in the Portuguese language to enable them to make good use of the sources in Portuguese; to facilitate exchanges and meetings between researchers and cultural organisations of Africa and the black diaspora, both in the field of historical research and in the framework of contemporary relations.

And within the framework of the Slave Route project, the following research programmes might be considered:

- Analysis of the influence of Afro-Brazilians on the dominant political authority and the evolution of their attitudes towards colonial imperialism. In the 1880s, it has been said, some (in Porto-Novo, in particular) wanted to make a treaty of protectorate with France, while in Ouidah, in the kingdom of Danxomè, a treaty with Portugal was preferred in the belief that it would promote trade. What was at stake in the alliances with Europe? What role did Afro-Brazilians play in the imperialist rivalries when dealing with Europe in the late nineteenth century? No thorough study has yet been made of this.
- Analysis of the social and economic impact of the Afro-Brazilians within African societies and of the evolution of their political and social situation in the colonial and post-colonial periods. It is possible to distinguish several phases in the influence of the Afro-Brazilians. Expanding on their return in the nineteenth century, their influence diminished between 1900 and 1920 because of the establishment of French colonial rule. Then, from 1920 to 1940, the Afro-Brazilian community collaborated effectively in the general movement of the struggle against colonialism before gradually losing its influence, so that today it can hardly be distinguished from other groups that have largely assimilated its cultural contributions.
- Analysis of the history and development of secular and religious festivals among the Afro-Brazilians, which would involve a systematic overall study of festivals, songs, dances, musical instruments and various accoutrements of the returning former slaves.
- Study and conservation of the architectural heritage of Afro-Brazilian origin.

Notes

1. P. Verger, 1976 [Eng. trans.], p. 314.
2. D.A. Ross, 1965, pp. 79–90.
3. P. Verger, 1976 [Eng. trans.], p. 314.
4. P. Verger, 1966, pp. 5–28.
5. See, in particular, P. Verger, 1966.
6. C. Coquery, 1962, pp. 373–419.
7. ANSOM, Afrique VI, 67, b, Ministry of Foreign Affairs to Ministry of the Marine and Colonies, Paris, 12 June 1888.
8. T.Y. Tchitchi, 1983, pp. 293–305.

Bibliography

BOUCHE, abbé P. 1885. *Sept ans en Afrique occidentale: la côte des Esclaves*. Paris, Plon.

BURTON, R. 1864. *A Mission to Glele, King of Dahome*. Vol. I. London, Tinsley Brothers.

COQUERY, C. 1962. 'Le blocus de Whydah (1876–1877) et la rivalité franco-anglaise au Dahomey'. *Cahiers d'études africaines* (Paris, Mouton), Vol. II, No. 7.

COQUERY-VIDROVITCH, C. 1971. 'De la traite des esclaves à l'exportation de l'huile de palme et des palmistes au Dahomey au XIXe siècle'. In C. Meillassoux (ed.). *The Development of Indigenous Trade and Markets in West Africa*. London, Oxford University Press for the International African Institute.

DUNCAN, J. 1847. *Travels in Western Africa*. London, Richard Bensley.

GAYIBOR, T. 1972. *Evolution politique et sociale des Mina des origines à 1885*. Paris, Université de Paris I.

KAKE, I.B. *Les Noirs de la diaspora*. Libreville, Léon.

MEDEIROS, F. DE. 1984. *Peuples du golfe du Bénin*. Paris, Karthala.

REIS, J.J. 1993. *Slave Rebellion in Brazil: The Muslim Uprising of 1835 in Bahia*. Baltimore/London, Johns Hopkins University Press.

ROSS, D.A. 1965. 'The career of Domingo Martínez in the Bight of Benin (1833–1864)'. *Journal of African History* (Cambridge), Vol. 6, No. 1.

SANVI, A.M.C. 1977. *Les métis et les Brésiliens dans la colonie du Dahomey, 1890–1920*. Cotonou, UNB (M.A. thesis).

TCHITCHI, T.Y. 1983. 'Le port du deuil, *lutu*, et ses implications culturelles'. *Cultures africaines*. Cotonou, UNESCO.

TURNER, J. M. 1982. *Les Brésiliens. The Impact of Former Brazilian Slaves upon Dahomey*. Ann Arbor, Mich., University Microfilms International.

UNESCO. 1983. *Cultures africaines*. Documents for the meeting of experts on 'Les apports culturels des Noirs de la diaspora à l'Afrique'. Cotonou, UNESCO.

VERGER, P. 1953. 'Influences du Brésil au golfe du Bénin'. *Les Afro-Américains*. Mémoires de l'IFAN (Dakar), No. 27.

———. 1966. 'Retour des 'Brésiliens' au golfe du Bénin au XIXe siècle'. *Etudes dahoméennes*, new series, No. 8.

———. 1968. *Flux et reflux de la traite des nègres entre le golfe du Bénin et Bahia de Todos os Santos du XVIIe au XIXe siècle*. Paris/The Hague, Mouton. [Eng. tr.

E. Crawford. 1976. *Trade Relations between the Bight of Benin and Bahia from the 17th to the 19th Century*. Ibadan, Ibadan University Press.]

VIDEGLA, M. 1993. 'Une approche du rôle économique et politique des Africains émancipés de retour dans les sociétés de la côte des Esclaves, 1830–1900'. *Actes du colloque de la dispersion négrière vers les Amériques aux retrouvailles à Ouidah*. Cotonou (duplicated typescript).

Chapter 7

The Slave Trade to Russia

Dieudonné Gnammankou

THE SLAVE TRADE TO RUSSIA is as yet a little-studied subject. In Volume 5 of the *General History of Africa* published by UNESCO, this issue is examined by Professor Harris.[1] He urges that 'serious research is particularly needed in Turkey and its neighbours on the major entrepôts for slaves from Tripoli and Benghazi', particularly the trade in African children in the late seventeenth century between Turkey and Russia. One of these victims of the traffic in African children (Ibrahim or Abraham Hanibal) became the great-grandfather of the greatest Russian writer, Alexander Pushkin. Why was there such a trade? How extensive was it and what impact did it have? What route did the slave-traders take from Constantinople to Moscow?

Being intrigued by the fate of Abraham Hanibal, a very well-known figure in Russian military history and the most famous African in Russia, we undertook research on the African presence in Russia at the beginning of the eighteenth century.

It can be said that, from the eighteenth century to the twentieth, Abraham Hanibal was the source of the Russian public's interest in Africa. Of course, Pushkin also contributed to the popularity of the man whom Russians still today call 'Peter the Great's Negro', as the great Russian writer was pleased to call him in an unfinished novel written in 1827.

What were the circumstances of this forced exile that took black children from Turkey to Russia? There exist but a few archive documents on this subject.

Africans in the Ottoman Empire

The Ottoman customs authorities recorded slaves entering the empire in registers. These documents, which are still in existence, are in the Ottoman archives in Istanbul. Little use has been made of them, since there are few experts, even in Turkey, who are familiar with the old Ottoman language. Systematic study of these registers should make it possible to have an exact idea of the number of Africans who were victims of this trade.

The black slaves from Africa who were taken to the Ottoman Empire suffered the same fate as the white ones from the European territories (Albania, Bosnia, Bulgaria, Greece, Macedonia, etc.) under Ottoman rule. For the most part, they were girls and boys aged between eight and fifteen. As in the Arab countries, the prettiest girls were sent to the harems of the sultan and powerful men at court, and the rest became servants in the wealthy families of the empire. The boys were employed as pages, soldiers, eunuchs, etc., or formed a servile labour force engaged in various occupations in the Ottoman provinces.

Thus, the Ottoman army at one point included in its ranks thousands of African soldiers. A document dating from 1717 and published in France records the presence of African troops in the Ottoman armies raised in that year to 'serve against H. I. M. in Hungary and against the Venetians, consisting of cavalry and infantry, from the east, the west, the south and the north'.[2] The multiethnic make-up – Africans (Egyptians, Ethiopians, etc.), Armenians, Assyrians, Brazilians, Macedonians, Persians, Wallachs – of the Ottoman army speaks volumes.

In the first Ottoman army sent to Hungary in 1717, there were:

- in the cavalry, out of a total of 105,000 men, '10,000 "Affricains"'[3] (the document that we are citing mentions, apart from 'Affricains': '4,000 "Étyopiens", 10,000 Egyptians, 4,000 Brazilians', or 24,000 men whose origins lay in Africa). (NB. The national origin of the Brazilians not being supplied, they are not included in this total and those below);
- in the infantry, out of a total of 251,000 men, '20,000 "Affricains", 16,000 "Étyopiens", 4,000 Egyptians and 15,000 Brazilians', or 40,000 sons of Africa.

In the second Ottoman army, deployed the same year against the Venetians, there were:

- in the cavalry, out of a total of 62,000 men, '6,000 "Affricains", 5,000 "Étyopiens", 7,000 Egyptians and 6,000 Brazilians', or 18,000 Africans;
- in the infantry, out of 116,100 men, '1,000 "Affricains", 2,000 "Étyopiens", 18,000 Egyptians and 1,000 Brazilians', or a total of 21,000 Africans.

Furthermore, there is ample evidence indicating a Negro-African presence in various institutions of the Ottoman state, particularly between the sixteenth and eighteenth centuries. The Ottoman sultans caused eunuchs and children intended to be employed at various levels of the Ottoman administration to be brought from Africa, especially from Ethiopia and the Lake Chad region.

The first black eunuchs living in the Ottoman sultan's palace can be traced back to the fifteenth century, from 1485. In 1587 one of them even became the grand eunuch or head of the black and white eunuchs (*Kizlar Agasi*). 'The most feared man in the whole of the Ottoman Empire', he had great authority: he had the rank of pasha, commanded the palace halberdiers (*baltadji*) as well as many senior Ottoman officials, including the superintendent of the treasury.

As intendant of the imperial mosques and pious foundations in Mecca and Medina, he also enjoyed great religious authority. He alone could speak to the sultan at any hour of the day and night. And when, as an old man, he left his office, he enjoyed a gilded existence in Egypt.[4]

On the trade in European child slaves, we have the remarkable book by the eminent Serb historian Radovan Samardzic, who sets out the political role played in the sixteenth century by a 'little shepherd from Bosnia', a victim of the *devshirme*,[5] who subsequently became grand vizier of the Ottoman Empire under the name of Mehmed Pasha. As regards children from Africa, so far as I know there has as yet been no study of the impact of influential Africans in the Ottoman administration.

The emotional bond between these African 'exiles' and their mother country was never broken. It is enough to visit in Istanbul, for example, in the palace of the Ottoman sultans, the former black eunuchs' apartments (the palace housed 600 of them) to see that the walls of some rooms were decorated with African landscapes.[6]

There were slave markets in several towns in the Ottoman Empire, for this was a highly prosperous trade. This gave rise to a traffic between Constantinople and other European countries, including Russia, where African children ended up who had been bought in Ottoman markets by Russian merchants.

The research that we have done on this subject covers only the period of the late seventeenth and early eighteenth centuries, in the reign of Peter the Great.

The Traffic in Black Children to Moscow around 1700

The first point to note is that this traffic – which involved above all children intended as pages at the Russian imperial court – was, when all is said and done, rather limited. According to Russian writers, the tsars were simply imitating other European courts where black pages were fashionable.[7] In all likelihood, the arrival of the first African children at the Russian court dates back to the late seventeenth century.

From what parts of Africa did they come? Judging by two archive documents – correspondence dating from 1698 between General Lefort, who was employed at the Russian court, and Tsar Peter I, then on a journey to London, and the report by Admiral Apraxin, dating from 1699, in which mention is made of a black child coming from England – it seems plausible that the first black children employed at the Russian court before 1700 came from Africa by way of London. Evidence for this consists of two letters sent from that city to the tsar by General Lefort: 'Poujalest nie zabouvat coupit arabi'[8] [Don't forget to buy the Negroes] and, a month later, his request: 'Scholo biou, milos twoia, schto ti iswolis arapof dosetats'[9] [I make this request to your good grace, please be so good as to buy the Negroes].

Grunwald, in his *Peter the Great*, also reports that on his journey to Western Europe, the tsar had bought 'two little Negroes'.[10] Admiral Apraxin's 1699 report confirms 'the dispatch of a black child named Kaptiner from England'.[11]

Three other Africans, adults, had been not bought but rather recruited in Amsterdam by the same General Lefort on that journey. The first, Ian Tushekurin, was a painter of ships under construction. The second, Thomas Izes, was a shipbuilder (between 1703 and 1705 he had taken part in the building of the *Etoile* and the *Loukas*). The third, Petro Seichi, was employed for a few years in the fleet before being taken on as a naval officer.[12] The Russian archives also mention a black in the house of boyar Matveev.[13]

At the end of the seventeenth century there were Africans in Russia – few in number, it is true – who were living at the court or in some of the highest noble families.

The Presence of Africans from 1700 to 1725

From the eighteenth century to the first half of the nineteenth century the number of blacks in Russia increased quite significantly, although it is impossible to be precise about the figures, as the subject has been insufficiently studied. Nevertheless, it is not particularly difficult to find traces of them during this period. Some writings about what was happening at the Russian imperial court show clearly that the household of Russian tsars sometimes included between 10 and 25 black pages. Russian iconography of the time testifies to this. When they arrived, these children from Africa would be taught Russian in monasteries.[14] When they grew up, some of these pages became soldiers, particularly regimental drummers, like Alexis Petrov, who arrived in Russia as a child in 1699 and became an oboist in a Moscow regiment.[15]

During the first quarter of the eighteenth century, several archive documents – the best known concern the arrival of three African children in Moscow in November 1704 – reveal that some Africans were reaching Russia by way of the Ottoman Empire. Various letters and official reports throw some light on the traffic in black children in Constantinople and make it possible to map the route taken by African slaves from Turkey to Russia. For example, there is the letter from the merchant Savva Raguzhinsky in Constantinople to Count Golvin, the head of the Chancery in Moscow, dated 21 July 1704:

> This letter will be handed to Your Excellency by my servant Andrew Georgiev whom I shall send with three young Negroes. Two of these are intended for Your Excellency and the third for your Ambassador. I had a great deal of trouble purchasing them ... I pray God that they arrive safe and sound. I hope that they will suit you as they are very black and beautiful; they are not Turks, they are not circumcised ...[16]

and the letter from Ambassador Peter Tolstoy (from Constantinople, 22 July 1704), also to Count Golovin:

> Mr Savva Vladislavich told me that you ordered him to purchase two blacks. He has bought them as you ordered and I have authorized one of Savva's servants to leave with them by way of Wallachia. I have given them a laissez-passer and ordered that they be given carriages from Kiev to Moscow. I have written to the

lords of Wallachia and Moldavia for them to ensure their safe passage as far as Kiev. And I hope that, by the grace of God, they will reach you, my dear sir, safe and sound. As for Mr Savva, he has taken ship for Azov....[17]

The Slave Route to Russia

The safest route at the time for the traffic in slaves was as follows: Ottoman Empire – Wallachia – Moldavia – Little Russia – Moscow. In the case mentioned above, the children were bought in Constantinople illicitly, doubtless because it was very dangerous to buy slaves at that time (in 1704, Ahmed III came to power following political disturbances), so the traders concealed the children when they were passing through Ottoman-ruled territories. The route from Constantinople to Jassy, on the border between Wallachia and Moldavia, was full of danger for the traders in black children. The slaves were conveyed in greater safety after Wallachia, the lord of the place being an ally of the tsar. In addition, the merchants had safe-conducts issued by the Russian ambassador in Constantinople.[18]

One of the three children described in the letter from the merchant Savva Raguzhinsky as 'very black and beautiful' was baptised during the journey and received the name of Abraham. Everything suggests that it is he who, a few decades later, became the famous black general of the Russian imperial army – Abraham Hanibal, Alexander Pushkin's great-grandfather.

Blacks in Russia in the Eighteenth Century

In ancient times, the Russian term used to describe blacks was borrowed from the Greek Ethiopian. In the seventeenth and eighteenth centuries, it was replaced by a word of Turkish origin, *Arap*, the equivalent of *More* or *Mohr*, used at the same time in French and German.[19] We must be careful, therefore, not to confuse the words *Arap* and Arab, a mistake made by several translators from Russian into French which caused serious misunderstandings, in particular by distorting the origin of Negro-African individuals. (An example is a French version of Tolstoy's historical novel *Peter I*, in which the translator, in two separate paragraphs, translates the word *Arap* once as Arab, and once as Negro; in the first case it involved a child who was good at his studies, in the second, a servant!)

As long ago as the late seventeenth century, some dwarfs at the Russian imperial court were of Negro-African origin. One of them was employed by Tsar Peter I as a translator of Greek and Latin documents into Russian. Thus, in the reign of Peter I there were in Russia pages who were either of African origin (victims of the slave trade by way of the Ottoman Empire) or of European origin, together with soldiers and sailors of African origin residing in other European countries who had been engaged on contract in the Russian army or navy. One of them, Petro Seichi, mentioned above, had been registered under the Russified name of Piter Elaïev – which does not make identifying him any easier. The Europeanisation of African names complicates research, although Africans were not the only ones to whom this happened;

other European foreigners, from Sweden or Greece, Russified their names to facilitate integration into Russian society. This means that even a close examination of the archives of the Russian navy at the beginning of the eighteenth century did not reveal the presence of blacks, including Piter Elaïev, alias Petro Seichi. It was only when studying the imperial *ukases* that the researcher N. Teletova discovered quite by chance that the word *Arapy* [Negroes] appeared in front of the names of Elaïev, Tushekurin and Izes. Petro Seichi or Peter Elaïev was a captain in the Russian navy in 1704. He lived at Petersburg, was appointed head of the galleys and in 1712 commanded a fleet of 26 supply ships at Vyborg. He left Russia on 11 October 1715 at the end of his contract.[20]

In the Russian archives of the time can be found a number of pieces of information about Africans present at the Russian imperial court. Thus we learn that one black child was taking Russian language classes in a monastery, that 10 roubles were spent on the purchase of a caftan for another black child, and that on one of the outings of the Empress Catherine, wife of Peter the Great, four black pages in her entourage were dressed in Indian style.[21] At this time, one young African was known to everyone at court: Abraham Petrov, adopted son of Peter I, who took a personal interest in his education.

It is this young *Arap* (black) who practically single-handedly – given the small number of Africans in Russia – made such a deep impression on Russia, such was his popularity. He was in fact one of those few Africans in eighteenth-century Europe who was able to develop his potential in complete freedom and dignity. By becoming one of the most highly educated people of his time, he gave proof that genius knew no racial boundaries. Abraham Hanibal was a general in the Russian imperial army, head of the corps of engineers, mathematics teacher to the future Emperor Peter II and, in 1725–26, author of a treatise on geometry and fortification. In addition, as we have already stated, he was the great-grandfather of one of the greatest literary geniuses of the nineteenth century – Alexander Pushkin, the poet 'with black blood in white veins'.[22]

Thus African genius, in the form of Abraham Hanibal and his descendants (two of his sons were army generals, and Pushkin's mother, known in the salons of Saint Petersburg as the 'beautiful Creole', was his granddaughter), participated in the military, technological and literary development of Russia in the eighteenth and nineteenth centuries.

The Black Presence in Russia in the Nineteenth Century

In the nineteenth century, the African presence in Russia can be seen from the banks of the Neva to Saint Petersburg and the Caucasus Mountains.

Africans in the Caucasus

According to Golden-Hanga, there were Abkhazians of African origin living near the town of Sukhumi, capital of Abkhazia: 'Before the First World War, the Russian press began to publish reports on Africans who had settled in the

Caucasus. The Tbilisi newspaper *Kavkaz* even devoted a special space to them entitled "On the Blacks of Batumi."'

According to documents of the time, 500 individuals of African origin were living in the Caucasus region, chiefly in Abkhazia,[23] in Sukhumi district.

American Blacks

Two blacks, Nelson and Claude Gabriel, who were in the service of the first American ambassador to Russia from 1809 to 1814, John Quincy Adams – president of the United States from 1825 to 1829 – left him during his stay in Saint Petersburg. They were subsequently taken on at the Russian imperial court, where they were made responsible for guarding the tsar.[24]

A black American woman, Nancy Prens, whose husband was in the service of the Russian emperor Alexander I (1801–25), records her life in the Russian capital in her memoirs, *The Narrative of Nancy Prens*. There we learn that at that time there were twenty blacks in the tsar's service and that several others were serving in the wealthy homes of the capital. Nancy Prens further asserts that she endeavoured to spread Protestantism in Saint Petersburg.[25]

Ira Aldridge, the black tragedian, born in New York on 24 June 1807, was invited to Russia in 1858 and was a great success there. The following year, disappointed by the reception he had received in England from producers and public alike, he responded to an invitation from theatre people in Russia and returned there at the beginning of 1861, the year serfdom was abolished, where he made a long triumphal tour – so much so that the French writer Théophile Gauthier, who was in Russia at the time, nicknamed him 'The lion of Saint Petersburg'.[26]

Aldridge, whose father was Fulani and whose mother was Afro-American, acted in Shakespeare's plays – including *Othello*, in which he gave a masterly performance – and was highly praised by the Russian press. In its March 1856 issue, the journal *Golos* (The Voice) wrote:

> Kazan. The performances of the famous Shakespearean actor, the tragedian Ira Aldridge, have caused a storm in the town. The theatre, which had practically never been more than half full, was now too small for the audience. People who had saved a few pennies were spending them on going to the theatre. People who had thought it beneath them to go to the theatre were going every day.

It was the same in Jitomir, Kiev, Nizhni-Novgorod, Odessa, Penza, Rybinsk, Samara, Tambov, Yaroslavl and elsewhere.

People at the time, including the historian Pogodin – who had little sympathy for blacks – recognised that blacks were human beings just like whites.

> General opinion places Negroes as the very lowest link between human species; many forced them to give way to the superiority, mental and moral, of their white relations, apparently of a more noble breed.… Under the dark skin, the same flaming blood is excited, the poor heart beats with the same common human feeling,

from the strained breast bursts the same heavy sigh as ours, a black body quivers from pain the same as white.... Circumstances, history whose laws are as yet unknown to us, have placed them in a position which is presently base and unhappy.... These are the thoughts that were awakened in me by the acting of the African Negro, Ira Aldridge....[27]

Thus, from the late seventeenth to the nineteenth centuries there was a black presence in Russia – small, it is true, but continuous and not insignificant, a consequence of the slave trade to the Ottoman Empire and, to some extent, the slave trade to the New World and the Old World. This traffic, of whatever proportions, deserves our attention, even if only to clarify further the African origin of the Russian poet Pushkin. Contrary to a widely held opinion that the African presence in Russia dates from the era of decolonisation in Africa – from the twentieth century – there were older contacts between these two widely separated areas of the world, as detailed in this chapter.

Notes

1. UNESCO, 1992, p. 129.
2. *Mercure de France*, 1717, p. 95.
3. The spelling here is as in the original document.
4. *Archeologia*, 1970.
5. Professor Samardzic gives the following definition of the *devshirme*: 'It is the raising of Christian children intended to enter the sultan's administration or one of the Porte's regiments. A blood levy.'
6. *Archeologia*, 1970.
7. M. Vegner, 1937.
8. Archives du Cabinet impérial, II, B, No. 2.
9. Ibid.
10. C. de Grunwald, 1953, p. 153.
11. Archives du Cabinet impérial, ibid.
12. Archives de la Marine, Saint Petersburg, 1885, Part I, p. 334.
13. M. Vegner, 1937.
14. D. Anuchin, 1899, p. 7.
15. N.I. Granovskaia, 1989, p. 7.
16. *Historical Archives* (Moscow), No. 1, 1992, pp. 182–188. Report of the interrogation of the Serb employee of the trader Raguzhinsky on his return to Constantinople with three Negro children in November 1704 (copy of the original text). Letter from Savva Raguzhinsky to Golovin, head of the *prikaz* (ministerial department) of ambassadors, July 1704.
17. Ibid.
18. Ibid.
19. D. Blagoy, 1937, p. 175.
20. N. Teletova, 1981, p. 133.
21. *Mémoires du règne de Catherine*, 1728, pp. 512–517.

22. M. Tsvetaeva, 1987.
23. L. Golden-Hanga, 1966; C.L. Holte, 1993, pp. 274–275.
24. A.B. Davidson, 1975.
25. Ibid.
26. Ibid.
27. N.P. Barsukov, 1902 (in part as quoted in M. Marshall and M. Stock, *Ira Aldridge the Negro Tragedian*, Washington, Howard University Press, 1993, p. 233).

Bibliography

ANUCHIN, D. 1899. *A.S. Pushkin. Antropologicheskii eskis.* Moscow, Moskovskie Vedomosti.

Archeologia (Dijon, Editions Faton), No. 35, July–August 1970.

BASURKOV, N.P. 1902. *Zhizn'i trudy M.P. Pogodina* [Life and works of M.P. Pogodin]. Saint Petersburg, Kn. 16.

BLAGOY, D. 1937. 'Abraham Petrovich Hanibal – Arap Petra Velikogo'. *Molodaïa Gvardia* (Moscow), No. 3.

CURTIS, M. 1968. 'Some American Negroes in Russia in the nineteenth century'. *The Massachusetts Review* (Spring).

DAVIDSON, A.B. 1975. 'Makrushin.' *Oblik dalekoy strany* [Profile of a far-away country]. Moscow, Vostochnaia Literatura.

GOLDEN-HANGA, L. 1966. *Africans in Russia.* Moscow, Novosti.

GRANOVSKAIA, N.I. 1989. *Esli ekhat vam sluchitsa.* Leningrad, Leninzdat.

GRUNWALD, C. DE. 1953. *La Russie de Pierre le Grand.* Paris, Hachette. [Eng. tr. V. Garvin. *Peter the Great.* London, MacGibbon & Kay, 1956.]

HOLTE, C.L. 1993. 'The Black in pre-revolutionary Russia.' In I. van Sertima (ed.). *African Presence in Early Europe.* 6th ed. Oxford (New Brunswick), Transaction Books.

Mémoires du règne de Catherine, impératrice et souveraine de toute la Russie. The Hague, 1728.

ORHONLU, C. 1974. *Habes Eyaleti* [The Abyssinian Province]. Istanbul, Edebiyat Fakultesi, Matbaasi.

SAMARDZIC, R. 1994. *Mehmed Sokolovitch: le destin d'un grand vizir.* Lausanne, L'âge d'homme.

TELETOVA, N. 1981. *Zabytye rodstvennye sviazi A.S. Pushkina* [The forgotten branches of Pushkin's genealogy]. Leningrad, Nauka.

TSVETAEVA, M. 1987. *Mon Pouchkine.* Paris, Clémence.

UNESCO. 1992. *General History of Africa.* Paris, Heinemann/UNESCO.

———. 1999. *Histoire générale de l'Afrique.* Vol. V. Paris, UNESCO (English version, Paris, Heinemann/UNESCO, 1992).

UZUNCARSILI, I. 1988. *Kapukulu Ocaklari* [Military history of the Ottoman Empire.] Vols. I and II. Basimevi-Ankara, Türk Tarih Kurumu.

VEGNER, M. 1937. *Predki Pushkina* [Pushkin's ancestors]. Moscow, Sovietski Pissatiel.

WILSON, E.T. 1974. *Russia and Black Africa before World War II.* New York/London, Holmes & Meier Publishers.

Part II

Demographic Impact and Economic and Social Dimensions of the Slave Trade

Chapter 8

From the Slave Trade to Underdevelopment

Yves Bénot

OBVIOUSLY, MANY THINGS HAVE CHANGED in Africa since the days of the European slave trade, which lasted for some four centuries. However, there is at least one word bequeathed by those dark times which is still significant today. This is the word *comprador* (literally, buyer), which designated the African middlemen whom the slave-traders needed for their traffic: in short, dealers in human cargo without any productive function. This term is now commonly applied to a section of the African middle class which is chiefly, but not exclusively, engaged in the import-export business and acts as a bridge between the major industrialised powers from what has come to be known as the 'countries of the Centre' – which continue to be the main focal points of economic and financial decision-making – and the rest of the African world.

It is true that at the time of the slave trade, neither the slave-traders nor their European backers saw anything pejorative in the word *comprador*, whereas the French term *bourgeoisie compradore* has become negative everywhere. The persistent use of the term is none the less indicative of the continued existence of a phenomenon whose forms have varied to a considerable extent but whose general principle remains the same: the foreign powers which burst upon the life of all the African continent south of the Sahara in the mid-fifteenth century needed constantly to create and support a particular local social category which, although not very large in terms of numbers, acted as an intermediary and a channel for their activities. Like any human group, the *compradores* always had their own interests to defend.

However, regardless of the clashes or conflicts which might arise from time to time, the main decisive fact is that the history and development, or rather non-development, of Africa were not the result of independent action by the African people, but were caused by external factors and by enforced insertion into the world economic system that was created following the European invasion of both Africa and the Americas. From that time onwards, the continent was always to suffer – as it still does today – from the repercussions of developments in the capitalist system which existed outside Africa, a system in which Africa was always to be in a subordinate position. This is reflected in the European vocabulary, which also came from outside the continent. Another example, specific to French imperialism but nevertheless significant, is the word *traite* (transport) which, after having been applied to the traffic in slaves, was used in the period of direct colonisation to designate the exploitation of African producers by large trading companies. Both by forcing Africa to become mainly a producer of human commodities in the form of slaves, and by obliging it to devote itself to producing crops or minerals which the developed countries of Europe wanted to acquire cheaply, the countries of the Centre subordinated the continent and dragged it down the path of underdevelopment.

Naturally, when this tragic story began with the arrival of the Portuguese on the coasts of Africa, the concepts of development and underdevelopment did not exist; the words would have been meaningless at that time. In the fifteenth-century world, there were different developments, sometimes in contact with one another, at other times unaware of one another. However, there was not yet any ranking order among them. In particular, even in military terms, there was no huge gap between Africans and Portuguese in the fifteenth and sixteenth centuries. Thus, two attempts at direct penetration into the interior of Africa, in the Congo and Ethiopia, resulted in military defeats which convinced the Portuguese and the other European powers that followed them – the Dutch, English and French – that they should confine themselves to occupying a few trading stations or establishments on the coast (plus the islands of Cape Verde and São Tomé and Príncipe). This did not restrict the influence they exercised on the interior, but it highlighted the importance of the *compradores*. In the context of the slave trade, direct political control was not necessary.

Initially, however, the Portuguese were not driven by the search for slaves, although they did acquire a limited number compared with what was to follow. Rather, they were looking for gold, of which they obtained a certain amount from the area of present-day Ghana, although admittedly not as much as they would have liked. In any event, even if the search for gold had been as lucrative as they had expected, it is unlikely that Africa's destiny would have been very different from what it was following the slave trade.

In its initial stages, the slave trade shed light on the situation in certain European states such as Portugal, Spain and Venice. These states, in spite of professing their Christian faith, and doing so quite aggressively in the case of the first two, were by no means averse to employing slaves as servants, farm labourers and even gondoliers.

Moreover, in the early years of the Spanish invasion of the Caribbean, indigenous Indians were also shipped to Spain as slaves, but they soon succumbed. This first instance of slave-trading, no matter how regrettable, could certainly never have been as serious as the type of trade that followed. However, its effect was that the second wave of the slave trade started with the deportation of African slaves to Haiti and Cuba, not from Africa itself but from Spain, where they had been working in the fields.

A change in scale occurred when, following the annihilation of the Indians of Haiti, the Spanish possessions needed labour for the mines. This was a key factor in changing relations between the Europeans soldiers and traders, entrenched in their forts and trading stations, and the African heads of state or chiefdoms. In appearance, these relations had not been openly colonial; the slave-trading powers established themselves as a result of concessions granted by local potentates and on certain conditions, rather after the manner of a rental arrangement, in the same way as the right to trade in slaves was granted to them in exchange for what were called the 'customs', a kind of tax which varied from place to place and at different periods. However, this trade was already inequitable – indeed, highly so. The products with which the 'customs' were paid, such as glass beads, cloth, iron bars, alcohol and rifles, were prized by the Africans for the use they could make of them. However, when their exchange value was calculated, as was already the practice in Europe, their value was derisory in itself and even more so by comparison with the exchange value of the slaves, not to speak of the value of slave labour production. In this exchange, the Africans were in fact duped under the apparent guise of a contract concluded by mutual agreement.

Yet that was not the most serious factor. The slave-traders' demands, which increased constantly, especially when labour began to be needed for sugar and other plantations and no longer for mines, brought about a far-reaching breakdown of political, economic and social systems over the greater part of the continent, because the hunt for slaves, who had become raw materials for European capitalism, had increasingly profound repercussions in the interior of the continent. More and more wars were waged in a bid to ensure the delivery of slaves, and the slave-trading stations were not averse to encouraging the conflicts by supplying arms and stirring up political intrigues. Some states disintegrated, while others founded their power and their (relative) wealth on control of the slave trade. The social fabric of the latter group was affected by the presence of the small stratum of middlemen who became increasingly important in their states' way of life and very existence. It should be noted that this applies to peoples who had already developed some form of state structure. The slave-traders knew full well that there were stateless African peoples, such as the Balante of Guinea Bissau, but they were not interested in them because they needed some authority with which to negotiate – in other words, which they could influence.

In order to examine the consequences of the slave trade, it is necessary to start out from one firm and obvious fact. Previously, West Africa's trade had always been directed towards the north and north-east, across the Sahara, and the African empires had been situated in the heart of the continent. With the slave trade, the situation was reversed: the direction became the Atlantic instead of the Indian Ocean, and the major states of the interior collapsed. Europe was interested only in the seaboard (in addition to the British colonies in North America, later to become the United States) and only in connection with its own development. It was not until the final years of the slave-trade period that alarm at the depopulation of Africa was suddenly voiced in some quarters – for highly selfish reasons – and that Europe, which had just embarked on the Industrial Revolution, began to be interested in exploring the interior of the continent. This turn seawards, which was a result of European needs and demands, is an early illustration of the phenomenon of dependence which subjected Africa to foreign interests.

Researchers have tended to concentrate on the demographic consequences, and the population drain was certainly enormous. Attempts have been made to calculate, with varying degrees of approximation, the number of African men and women – perhaps slightly more women than men – all of them young, who were deported to the Americas. It is generally agreed that the figure ranges from 12 to 15 million people over a period of four centuries. However, Africa's losses were much more substantial, firstly because this drain of men and women of child-bearing age – the slave-traders were not interested in older members of the population – naturally cut back normal population growth to a degree which can probably never be exactly ascertained. Added to this are all those who died while being marched from the interior to the coast, not to mention the human cost of wars and raids aimed at capturing slaves. It would clearly be pointless to try to put a figure to the considerable population deficit which the slave trade inflicted on Africa and which left the continent mortally weakened when the former slave-trading powers undertook to conquer it and carve it up. The slave trade, which had become largely illegal, continued until the second third of the nineteenth century and even slightly later: slavery in the Americas was only finally abolished by Brazil in 1888. By that time, the process of conquest was already under way, and was in turn accompanied both by slaughter during wars in which different African peoples were enlisted to fight against one another and also, perhaps to an even greater extent, by the decimation of Africans who were forced to act as porters for columns of colonial troops. There were also those who died collecting rubber in the Congo under the harsh rule of Leopold II of Belgium, those who died building the Congo-Ocean railway in the 1930s, and the 'maroons' hunted down and killed by forced labour in the forestry camps of Côte d'Ivoire. The inhuman conditions of the forestry camps were denounced in 1927 by the journalist Albert Londres in his report *Terre d'ébène*. This list is not exhaustive and only mentions the most striking examples. In short, the depopulation of Africa, which began with the slave trade, went on under the horrors of the conquest and the establishment of the colonial system, and lasted until quite recent times.

When the new states gained their independence, they were underpopulated. Because population growth has recovered in the past 30 or 40 years in most of these countries, there has been a tendency to cite excessive population growth as the reason or justification for the low standards of living of their peoples. Yet, when nineteenth-century Europe embarked on the Industrial Revolution in the wake of Great Britain, it, too, was going through a phase of high population growth (except in France), but it did not lapse into underdevelopment. The sources of African poverty and underemployment therefore lie elsewhere.

The effect of the collapse of political and social structures has proved to be more lasting than the population drain, however terrible that may have been. It has lasted longer because, in both present and past, the collapse of these structures stems from the same principle and the same method which, in economic terms, works both ways.

During the slave trade period, during direct colonialism, and even in the years that followed, African production has always been geared to exporting the products demanded and needed by the leading capitalist countries. During the centuries of the slave trade, no account was taken of the fact that the massive export of human commodities was responsible for uprooting part of the labour force needed to produce subsistence crops for Africa itself, while another part of that labour force had to produce crops to maintain the camps where the slaves were assembled before they were shipped away. Matters were not very different in the subsequent period, much vaunted by the conquerors as that of 'free labour', when, for example, African peasants were required to produce the quantity of groundnuts demanded by the European oil mills, to the detriment of their own subsistence production and actual land, and to produce less or nothing at all when the Centre no longer needed the groundnuts or could obtain supplies elsewhere at lower cost. Matters are no different today when it comes to applying the notorious structural adjustment plans imposed by the International Monetary Fund (IMF). In the final analysis, these entail exporting enough to cover debt servicing, which provides the Centre with fresh capital. The principle has remained the same from the time of the Portuguese to that of the IMF: Africa's productive economy has been geared to the outside world – not to the needs of Africans, but rather to those of the capitalist nations which were developing countries in the sixteenth century and then became developed countries.

In addition, the corollary, as far as reverse flows from Europe to Africa are concerned, is that Africa had to open up its markets to products which Europeans saw fit to introduce; in other words, the system of needs in Africa had to be changed, or to some extent adapted, to whatever suited European traders. This was not, however, true of society as a whole: the slave-traders supplied their shoddy goods to the sovereigns and local aristocracy, and then to the local *compradores*. Over and above the slave trade, the aim of opening up the continent to the new industrial products from fast-developing nineteenth-century Europe – and hence of creating new and more 'civilised' needs in Africa – was one of the driving forces behind the penetration of the continent by explorers, missionaries and, eventually, colonial armies. For a long time, the Africans in the social category capable of absorbing a given quantity of manufactured products from the colonial powers were fairly limited in number, as were the *compradores* of the earlier period. The broadening of markets which followed, particularly from the time of independence, was much more a broadening of modern-style needs than of the possibility of satisfying them.

Be that as it may, the method remains the same, and the IMF now ensures that the door remains open and that the African countries abandon the idea, which some of them had in the 1960s, that they should protect their products in the same way as the developed countries of Europe and the Americas had protected theirs when they were becoming industrialised. This twofold action, which made the entire African economy an exogenous economy governed by the outside world, which requires in the present as it did in the past a social category to act as a go-between for external agents – in return, naturally, for certain advantages – reflects the overall pattern which was established with the slave trade and which, in a slightly different form, was to remain the pattern of colonialism and neo-colonialism, a pattern which ensures the creation and reproduction of underdevelopment. It is the continued existence of this pattern which appears to be the most pernicious, and at the same time the most lasting, outcome of the slave trade or of the period and system which the slave trade ushered in. The horrors briefly mentioned above, the population drain itself – all these crimes, however monstrous, could have been mitigated to some extent in the long run and the continent could, little by little, have recovered its spent force. However, the social and economic process which was set in motion and constantly maintained was irremediable and has remained so.

The social category of people acting as intermediaries was naturally transformed, in the same way as the types of production demanded of Africa also changed. At the outset, one of the constituents of this social category were people of mixed origin, since the European men who arrived on the African coasts without their womenfolk were by no means self-denying and soon struck up relationships with African women. We are all familiar with the role played by the mulattos of Saint Louis, in Senegal, where there were never more than 200 Frenchmen at the time of the slave trade; we also know about the role of certain Anglo-African mulatto slavers in Sierra Leone towards the end of the eighteenth century. However, the *comprador* category extended far beyond this necessarily limited circle and, although it remained a minority, grew to form a larger percentage of the population in the colonial period and, above all, after independence.

Naturally, resistance occurred during all of these periods. In the first place, there was resistance to the slave trade, which was obviously never accepted by the mass of the population. It is likely that there were individual instances of resistance. We have more information – although not enough – about resistance at the points of embarkation, sometimes by slaves who escaped and formed liberated enclaves, and often taking the form of revolts on board the slave ships before they weighed anchor, which did not always end in failure. Other developments can also be linked to the efforts which people made to escape deportation. One example was the spread of Islam (a grassroots Islam as opposed to an aristocratic Islam) in West Africa, inasmuch as the Islamised states protected their Muslim subjects from the slave trade, but not their other subjects or the peoples of neighbouring countries. Even so, as a result of wars and slave raids, some African Muslims were deported, but they represented only a small proportion of the total number.

African kings, too, had ways of resisting European demands, such as raising their prices or by prohibiting slave-trading with particular European countries for a given length of time. However, although they could sometimes take advantage of the rivalry between the European powers on the coast, this outcome did not call into question the system itself; at most, in the final analysis, it worked to the advantage of the middleman category. In fact, in this game, the African states often ended up in competition with one another and thereby ensured the recurrence of wars that were useful for the production of slaves as a commodity. Another method to win over these chiefs was occasionally to invite their sons to spend some time in Europe, on the pretext of acquiring a modern education, as a result of which the young men generally also acquired new tastes and needs. It is true that instances can be found here and there of chiefs who were resolutely opposed to the slave trade – at the mouth of the Sierra Leone river, for example – although they were few in number.

The influence of the *compradores* and of the material and political interests that were created during those centuries made it difficult for real resistance to be successful. Even so, this factor should not be neglected because the slave uprisings in the Americas (in particular in Jamaica and Suriname), the simultaneous revolts at the time of shipment in Africa and the ensuing destruction of a number of slave ships, especially towards the end of the eighteenth century, gave the European opponents of slavery and the slave trade food for thought and powerful arguments. The movement that was organised in the English-speaking world of America and Europe from about 1770 onwards was to result in the principle of the slave trade being outlawed much earlier (in 1815) than the abolition of slavery itself, which didn't come about until between 1833 and 1888.

What might appear paradoxical, but is basically not so, is the fact that it was at the heart of the European and American anti-slavery movement at the end of the eighteenth century that an outline substitute plan was clearly formulated – a plan which was to be put into practice by the colonial conquest of virtually the whole of the African continent at the end of the following century. In other words, even before those working for the end of the first form of dependence had achieved their aims, the subsequent pattern of dependence – from which Africa has yet to emerge – was being designed. Some European anti-slavery circles thought in terms of arranging for the colonial commodities produced by slaves in the Americas to be cultivated by free African workers in Africa itself. This was to come about for coffee, cocoa and cotton and also, with more difficulty and at a later date, for sugar. In more general terms, it was agreed that, in exchange, Africans should be able to benefit from European material progress and should acquire new needs – in short, should modernise their way of life. The philanthropists, who put forward these ideas concurrently with economists and technical experts, did not see – and this can be said in their defence – that they were once again proposing an unfair exchange and a state of dependence. Yet this was clearly the turn history took when lasting underdevelopment came to be established on the continent. Naturally, these philanthropists did not foresee or wish for the violence of the colonial conquest, and they would certainly have been horrified by it. This applies especially in England, to Grenville-Sharp and Thornton, the promotors of the most democratic 'free settlement' project and the only one to have been put in practice for some years, that of Sierra Leone at the present-day location of Freetown. Yet that was the thinking behind the historical process to which they contributed, even though they did not realise it. As it turned out, the free settlement of Sierra Leone became the first British crown colony on the continent, in 1808.

From the point of view not of the philanthropists but of the growth of capitalism, which had spread all over the world, the abolition of the Atlantic slave trade and the exploitation of Africans on their own continent repre-sented a change in practice which could be profitable only if African workers cost less than their slave predecessors and even represented a comparative advantage. The conquest succeeded in bringing this about, and consequently exploitation by the Centre spread everywhere, even in areas that had been rel-atively unaffected by the slave trade. Naturally, whether colonialism was direct or indirect (as it has become), it was still just as important to maintain and reproduce the social category of middlemen, bound by their interests more closely to those of the Centre than to those of their own people. Furthermore, we must take account of the situation that has recently arisen with the new stage of globalisation: whole areas which no longer offer profitable prospects or no longer cater for the needs of the world economy are abandoned or, more precisely, are plunged into chaos, famine, insecurity and death.

If this infernal logic of the relations between underdeveloped Africa and the developed Centre is to be overcome, a radical break has to be made with the 'laws' of the worldwide capitalist market, which have assigned a depend-ent function to Africa. However, these so-called 'laws' are not an absolute necessity in the face of human struggles, any more than slavery was an absolute necessity. It is admittedly difficult to make the break, but what was undertaken in Burkina Faso under Thomas Sankara in 1983 clearly represents 'a hope for Africa', this being the title of the book by one of the protagonists involved in the project.

Bibliography

AMIN S. 1972. *Accumulation on a World Scale: A Critique of the Theory of Under-development*. Vols. 1 and 2, trans. B. Pearce. New York and London, Monthly Revew Press.

———. 1985. *La déconnexion*. Paris, La Découverte.

———. 1988. *L'Eurocentrisme*. Paris, Anthropos.

ANSTEY, R. 1975. *The Atlantic Slave Trade and British Abolition, 1760–1810*. Atlantic Highlands, N.J., Humanities Press.

BALANDIER, G. (ed.). 1956. *Le tiers-monde, sous-développement et développement*. Paris, Presses Universitaires de France.

———. 1992. *La vie quotidienne au royaume du Congo du XVI° au XVIII*. Paris, Hachette.

BOUBACAR, B. 1985. *Le royaume du Waalo, 1659–1859*. Paris, Karthala.

BRION DAVIS, D. 1966. *The Problem of Slavery in the Western World*. Ithaca, Cornell University Press.

———. 1975. *Slavery in the Age of Revolution: 1770–1820*. Ithaca, Cornell University Press.

COQUERY-VIDROVITCH, C. 1985. *Afrique noire, permanences et ruptures*. Paris, Payot. 2nd ed. Paris, L'Harmattan (1992).

CURTIN, P.D. 1969. *The Atlantic Slave Trade: A Census*. Madison, University of Wisconsin Press.

———. 1975. *Economic Change in Precolonial Africa*. Madison, University of Wisconsin Press.

DAGET, S. 1975. 'Le trafic négrier illégal français de 1814 à 1860: historiographie et sources'. In *Annales de l'Université d'Abidjan*, No. 3 (series 1, History).

———, (ed.). 1988. *De la traite à l'esclavage, du XV° au XIX° siècle. Colloque international sur la traite des Noirs* (1985). 2 vols. Nantes/Paris, Centre de recherche d'histoire vivante and Socété française d'histoire d'outremer.

DESCHAMPS, H. 1971. *Histoire de la traite des Noirs de l'Antiquité à nos jours*. Paris, Fayard.

DRESCHER, S. 1977. *Econocide: British Slavery in the Age of Abolition*. Pittsburgh, Pittsburgh Press.

GEMERY, H.A., and HOGENDORN, J.S. (eds.). 1979. *The Uncommon Market*. New York, Johns Hopkins University Press.

GUISSOU, B. 1995. *Burkina Faso, un espoir pour l'Afrique*. Paris, L'Harmattan.

HAILEY, L. 1957. *An African Survey*. 2nd ed. Oxford/London, Oxford University Press.

INIKORI, J.E. (ed.). 1982. *Forced Migration: The Impact of the Export Slave Trade on African Societies*. London.

JALEE, P. 1965. *Le pillage du tiers-monde: sous-développement et développement*. Paris, Maspero.

LOVEJOY, P.E. 1983. *Transformations in Slavery: A History of Slavery in Africa*. Cambridge/London, Cambridge University Press.

M'BOKOLO, E. 1985. *L'Afrique au XX° siècle*. 2nd ed. Paris, Le Seuil.

MEILLASSOUX, C. (ed.). 1975. *L'esclavage en Afrique précoloniale*. Paris, Maspero.

METTAS, C., and DAGET, S. 1978, 1984. *Répertoire des expéditions négrières françaises au XVIII° siècle*. 2 vols. Nantes/Paris, Bibliothèque d'outremer.

NYONGO, P.A. (ed.). 1988. *Afrique, la longue marche vers la démocratie*. Paris, Publisud.

RAWLEY, J.A. 1986. *The Transatlantic Slave Trade*. New York, Norton.

RODNEY, W. 1972, 1981. *How Europe Underdeveloped Africa*. Dar es Salaam, Tanzania Publishing House; Washington D.C., Howard University Press.

UNESCO. 1979. *The African Slave Trade from the Fifteenth to the Nineteenth Century* (The General History of Africa, Studies and Documents). Paris, UNESCO.

WILLIAMS, E. 1944. *Capitalism and Slavery*. Raleigh, University of North Carolina Press.

Chapter 9

The Unmeasured Hazards of the Atlantic Slave Trade: Sources, Causes and Historiographical Implications

Joseph E. Inikori

EVEN BY THE STANDARDS of the pre-industrial world, in which international trade was conducted under the constant menace of pirates, the Atlantic slave trade was seen by contemporary observers as unusually hazardous for the traders' capital and for the lives of both the seamen employed and the human beings traded and transported as commodities. The private correspondence and public statements of the traders make it abundantly clear that this was not a business for the frail-hearted. In his description, James Jones, by far the largest slave-trader in late eighteenth-century Bristol, stated tersely: 'It is [a] very uncertain and precarious trade, and if there is not a probable prospect of considerable profit, no man of property who hath any knowledge of it would embark or continue in it.'[1] Robert Norris, a Liverpool counterpart of James Jones, expressed the same view: 'If I could have £5 per cent [profit], at home, I think I should not risk it [his capital] to Africa under £10 [10 per cent].'[2] A Liverpool entrepreneur of the period, who was not directly involved in the slave trade and, therefore, supported its abolition, described the trade similarly as 'a commerce of Enterprise and Risk', for which reason, 'the profits have occasionally been very great'.[3]

But why was the trade that risky for all those involved in it? What are the specifics of the hazards, and what factors explain them? How do we measure their magnitude and frequency, and what are the implications of such measurements for various aspects of the historiography of the Atlantic slave trade?

Historians have always been aware that the slave trade was a risky business. But emphasis was always exclusively on the undeniable suffering of the slaves during the Atlantic crossing, euphemistically referred to as the middle passage.[4] Bored by the repeated horror stories of slaves suffering during the Atlantic crossing, historians turned their back on the hazards of the trade. This is not simply because these hazards cannot be studied analytically and statistically, as was argued recently (Walvin, 1994, pp. 57–58). It is partly because the whole range of the risks, the factors behind them and the complex issues that they raise were hitherto not seriously considered. This chapter attempts to narrow this gap by focusing on the incidence of wartime privateering, wrecks at sea, and losses of ships and cargoes arising from slave insurrections and conflicts with coastal Africans. The qualitative and quantitative evidence, and its analysis, raise a host of issues: issues about the reaction of the coastal African communities (particularly the non-trading ordinary citizens) to the trade in human beings conducted daily before their eyes; issues relating to the implication of the measured evidence for the volume of slave exports estimated by historians, and for the overall mortality rate among the slaves purchased by the European traders; and issues of what the evidence implies about the pattern of profits for the European traders. In what follows, we discuss the sources and examine these issues. For some of the issues, while the evidence provides enough justification for some speculative reasoning, it is too thin to sustain definitive statements. But, even so, the speculations in these cases are worthwhile if only to call attention to the need to focus research on the questions raised.

The Sources

The main source for this study is the *Lloyd's List* kept in the library of the National Maritime Museum in Greenwich, London. The history of the collection, numbering many volumes, is bound up with that of Lloyd's of London. It dates back to the establishment of Lloyd's Coffee House by Edward Lloyd near the Tower of London in about 1689 (Wright and Fayle, 1928, pp. 11–13). As became the custom in seventeenth-century London and later, the coffee houses operated as business centres and places of refreshment for London's merchants.[5]

The regular publication of *Lloyd's List* provided much-needed information for the community of merchants, shipowners and marine insurance brokers in London. While showing information on several important aspects of domestic and international business, such as the course of the stock exchange, it was the ship news that made *Lloyd's List* an invaluable publication for the merchants of London. Published weekly at the beginning and bi-weekly (Tuesdays and Thursdays) from 1737, the ship news provided information on British ships trading overseas. The reports tended to concentrate on losses of ships and cargo arising from various causes, especially wartime captures by enemy privateers. Until recently, the publication of *Lloyd's List* was believed to have begun in 1734 (Wright and Fayle, 1928, p. 72). Evidence produced by John McCusker (1991, pp. 427–431) now shows that before the series which began in 1734 or 1735, there was an earlier one, first issued in January 1692, and another which started in September 1699.

Information for the ship news published in *Lloyd's List* was gathered by correspondents in different ports and transmitted through the Postmasters-General (Wright and Fayle, 1928, pp. 74–75). The degree of reliability for the published information is indicated by the report of a special subcommittee of Lloyd's, appointed in 1837 to consider improvements in the method of publication. Dated 21 June 1837, the report states that 'Lloyd's List has existed 103 years, and during the whole of that long period it has been considered the most correct, authentic, and official document of the kind' (cited by Wright and Fayle, 1928, p. 72).

The early issues have not survived. For the series dating to January 1692, only two issues have been discovered; for that dating from 1699, there exist only the issues for May 1702 to March 1704 (McCusker, 1991, p. 429); while for the third series (1734/1735), the earliest extant issue is that of Friday 2 January 1741,[6] numbered 560. Apart from the early ones, some other issues of the third series are also missing or damaged. A note in the first volume of the collection in the National Maritime Museum states specifically: 'The collection does not include any issues for 1742, 1743, 1745, 1746, 1754, 1756, 1759 or 1778; while various issues are lacking from certain volumes.... Each volume of the reproduction includes as appropriate a list of missing and damaged issues....'[7]

The serial numbering of each issue makes it possible to indicate the extent of the collection. As mentioned previously, the earliest extant issue of the third series (1734/1735) is numbered 560. The last issue inspected for this study, with reports on African ships, is numbered 3832 and dated 11 December 1772. For the *New Lloyd's List*, which began early in the 1770s, the last issue inspected is numbered 4215, being that of Tuesday, 29 December 1807. Descriptions of the routes – 'Liverpool to Africa', 'from Africa to the West Indies', etc. – or locations on the African coast make it possible to identify the reports on African ships in the ship news covering all British vessels trading overseas. Reports on African ships homeward from the Americas are difficult to identify because these are shown frequently as on route from American territories to England, without mentioning Africa. It is likely, therefore, that a significant number of ships on this route, reported on in the ship news, have not been included here. However, as will be shown later, this has no adverse effects on the main arguments of the study.[8]

For the early years of the period covered, additional information is provided by the records of the African companies among the Treasury papers, and the Board of Trade papers among the Colonial Office records, all of which are in the Public Record Office, London. *The Parliamentary Papers, Accounts and Papers*, in the British Library, London, containing data transmitted to House of Commons committees by the Custom House in London, make it possible to reconstruct the movement of each vessel from the point of outward clearance from a port in England. Since the mid-1970s, there have been repeated comments on the relative reliability of the Parliamentary papers (Anstey, 1975a; Inikori, 1976; Richardson, 1989; Inikori, 1992). I have taken advantage of the adequate data available for the years 1796–1805, a particularly important period for the study, to compare the shipping data provided by the *Parliamentary Papers* and *Lloyd's List*.

Some readers may be interested in comparing the list of ships compiled from these sources and presented in this chapter with that produced for the eighteenth-century French slave ships by Jean Mettas (1978 and 1984) some fifteen years ago. The latter has been the basis of several recent estimates of the volume of the French slave trade (Becker, 1986, pp. 633–679; Eltis, 1990, pp. 485–492). It should be noted, however, that there is a fundamental difference. While Mettas attempted to compile a catalogue of all French slave ships during a specified time period, what is presented in this chapter is only a list of British slave ships that were lost as a result of various causes.

The Hazards: Nature and Frequency

For the whole period of the study, 1689–1807, I have information covering 1,053 vessels lost as a result of various causes. Of this number, 679 vessels, or 64.5 per cent of the total, were taken by the enemy in wartime; 188, or 17.9 per cent, were wrecked at sea off the African coast; and 186, or 17.7 per cent, were lost as a result of slave insurrection, conflict with coastal Africans or shipwreck on the African coast.

Thus, war was by far the greatest hazard faced by the traders. This was particularly so because the struggle to control overseas trade was a major factor in these wars (Wilson, 1957; Israel, 1989; Kaiser, 1990). In fact, competition in international trade in Western Europe of the seventeenth and eighteenth centuries was, for all practical purposes, hardly distinguishable from war. When wars actually broke out, governments did not hesitate in granting licences (letters-of-marque) to private individuals to prey on enemy merchant ships. This became a lucrative business for those with adequate resources to properly arm private ships for privateering. Many of the larger British slave-traders, especially those in Liverpool, combined slave-trading and privateering in wartime (Williams, 1897). Because the Atlantic slave trade was conducted triangularly across the entire Atlantic – North and South, East and West – and required relatively long permanent stationing of ship and cargo in Africa and the Americas, it was unusually vulnerable to privateer attacks.

Between 1688 and 1807, England was involved in seven major wars that affected the slave trade (Dowell, 1965, p. 534).[9] Earlier in the seventeenth century, there were the Anglo-Dutch Wars.[10] But of all these wars, the French Revolutionary and Napoleonic Wars, 1793–1815, had by far the greatest impact. Over one-third of the 679 vessels mentioned earlier (248 in all) were taken between 1793 and 1807. These wartime captures constituted a major headache for the traders and for the marine insurance underwriters who provided cover for the trade. It will be argued later that they affected the distribution of profits between the larger and smaller slave-traders. But, in terms of the lives of the seamen employed and of the people traded and transported as commodities (the slaves), the adverse effect was relatively less.

Privateering was a profit-oriented business. The privateers had to preserve their captured property in order to make a profit from the sale. Of course, some lives and property were destroyed in the fighting that preceded capture.

And on occasion some privateers behaved irrationally, as was reported in the *Lloyd's List* of 23 June 1747: 'The *Ogden*, Tristram, of Leverpool [sic], from Africa for Jamaica, with 370 Negroes, was taken off the East-End of that Island by a Spanish Privateer. The Spaniards were so Irritated at their gallant Defence, that, on boarding, they killed Whites and Blacks without Distinction: Soon after the *Ogden* sunk, and only 1 Man, 5 Boys, and 3 Negroes were saved.'[11] A somewhat similar incident was reported in February 1760: 'A store ship from Cape Coast, with about 130 slaves, whose crew consisted of 23 men, fell in with two or three French Privateers, whom he fought for two Days, but was at last taken; and in Return for such a bold Defence, the crew were cut and wounded in a most barbarous manner.'[12] In general, however, irrational behaviour by the privateers was rare. The cost of fitting out a ship for privateering was quite high. To recover the cost and make a profit, the privateers had to properly manage their captured property.

Though they occurred relatively less frequently, the most destructive events affecting the ships and the lives of seamen and slaves were wrecks at sea, slave insurrections and conflicts with coastal Africans. Conflicts with coastal Africans and the insurrection of the slaves before the ships departed the African coast raise some interesting questions that deserve relatively detailed treatment in the section that follows. To conclude this section, let us examine briefly the problem of wrecks at sea.

These wrecks were an important part of the unmeasured risks of the Atlantic slave trade. The perils of the vast ocean separating Africa from the Americas and the annual hurricanes of the Caribbean took their toll. In Africa, the ship captains had to contend with sandbars, limited natural harbours and tropical thunderstorms. As Crosby[13] observes with some exaggeration: 'The worst large expanse of ocean in the world for thunderstorms lies off the coast of Africa from the Senegal River to the Congo River.' For the wooden vessels to spend several months anchored in open waters, with few natural harbours, during the period of trade in Africa, then several weeks of Atlantic crossing, and several weeks more in New World ports (with the possibility of being caught by the annual hurricanes), before spending yet more weeks returning from the Americas to England, several wrecks would have to have been expected annually.

The extant issues of *Lloyd's List* for 1741–1807 show a total of 188 vessels that were wrecked at sea off Africa. The rather imprecise phrase, 'Lost on the coast of Africa', makes it difficult to say how many wrecks in Africa were reported by the same issues. In some cases, additional information makes it clear that the reference is to a loss by wreck. But there are 61 instances in which it is unclear as to whether the loss occurred by wreck or some other cause. If we assume that all 61 cases were wrecks (which may not be altogether correct), then there were 107 wrecks in Africa reported by the extant issues for the period. This makes a total of 295 wrecks reported by the available issues for the period, as compared with 451 losses due to wartime enemy action during the same period. Of the 188 wrecks outside Africa, 72 occurred between England and Africa, 88 during the Atlantic crossing and in New

World ports, and 28 on the way back to England from the Americas. In all likelihood, many wrecks on the last route have not been picked up because of the difficulty of distinguishing between the slave ships and other vessels reported wrecked on this route by *Lloyd's List*.

The reports indicate that sandbars and limited natural harbours on the African coast may have been mainly responsible for the wrecks in Africa. Thunderstorms are rarely mentioned, contrary to what Crosby's description would lead one to expect.

Reaction of Coastal Africans and the Enslaved

Of the 186 vessels lost, 79 were related primarily to slave insurrection and conflict with coastal Africans. Of those connected with slave insurrection, only three occurred during the Atlantic crossing. All others took place on the African coast, very often just before or at the point of departure of the ships from the African shores.

The evidence indicates that insurrection among the export slaves occurred more frequently on the African coast than during the Atlantic crossing. The sight of the African shores may have given the slaves the assurance that they could escape to freedom if they succeeded in overpowering the crew. In fact one such incident in 1773 involved the *Industry*, a London slave ship. Four days after leaving Gambia for Carolina the slaves succeeded in killing all the crew but two and took the ship back to Sierra Leone where they ran her ashore and made their escape. There is also some indication that during such uprisings on the coast, the slaves may have received some assistance from ordinary free Africans in the coastal societies. This is suggested by an extract from *Lloyd's List* relating to the *Nancy*, helmed by Captain Williams, out of Liverpool, in 1769. The gunshots fired by the crew while the insurrection was in progress on the shores of New Calabar attracted the attention of the town's people. They went to the ship in their canoes, boarded and took off the slaves. The ship was set adrift after ivory and other goods were removed.

It is not clear whether the latter incident was simply an act of robbery that took advantage of the uprising or a show of solidarity with unfortunate fellow human beings. Whatever the case, this incident does bring to mind the attitude of ordinary free Africans in the coastal societies to the trade in human beings conducted regularly on such a vast scale before their very eyes. I am referring here to free Africans who were neither traders, nor soldiers, nor government functionaries of any sort, and who could not afford to own slaves in any form. It is not unreasonable to expect such people to dislike the trade and the maltreatment of the export captives they daily observed. Whenever they calculated that the risk to their own lives was not very great, some of these people may have assisted the slaves in their insurrections on the African coast. This is highly speculative. The attitude of this segment of the coastal populations to the Atlantic slave trade is a neglected subject which deserves some attention. However, the possibility of such assistance, real or imagined, may have been a factor in the greater frequency of insurrections on the coast than in the middle passage.

More generally, the extracts from *Lloyd's List* suggest a degree of hostility felt by coastal Africans towards European slave-traders that is much greater than is usually acknowledged in the literature.

I infer from the evidence that when the term 'Negroes' is used, reference is being made to the export slaves, while the term 'Natives' refers to free coastal Africans. We may thus distinguish between incidents involving the export captives primarily and those initiated by the coastal Africans. The latter show a considerable degree of hostility. Even when the vessels were involved in normal wrecks on the coast, the surviving crew were, more often than not, humiliated and brutally treated. A case in point is the *Matthew*, a tender to the *Sawrey*, which was wrecked on the Gold Coast in 1766. All the crew survived, but they were 'stripped naked by the inhabitants'. In another incident involving the *Ann*, helmed by Captain Irving of Liverpool, in 1789, the ship's cargo was plundered and the 'crew made slaves'.

Such incidents may not represent the dominant attitude of the coastal populations to the European slave-traders. All the same, they do indicate a level of hostility not adequately reflected in the literature. Part of the explanation may be the attitude of the ordinary coastal Africans mentioned earlier. Quite often, however, the hostility was ingrained by the intemperate behaviour and sharp business practices of the European traders on the African coast that the following cases illustrate.

In the early nineteenth century, there was a disagreement between a British trader and an African merchant prince in Cape Coast town on the Gold Coast (now Ghana) over the quality of gold that the trader had bought. The African merchant agreed to take the gold back and return the goods he had received in payment. But this did not satisfy the British trader. The African trader was seized and locked up, with no regard to the fact that he was a chief in the area. This provoked a crisis in the town, to which the British company's officials on the coast responded by burning the entire town. In its report of this incident in October 1803, the Gold Coast governor and councillor of the British company wrote:

> We are extremely sorry that the licentious conduct of the Cape Coast people should be such as to compel us to commence Hostilities against them, but their great insolence was not to be borne longer, and required a curb, in consequence of which, we have destroyed their Town by fire.... The loss of the natives is not known; but from what we can learn, many must have been killed and wounded.[14]

The matter was subsequently investigated by Captain W. Brown of His Majesty's Ship *Rodney*. In his report dated 2 January 1804 he condemned the action of the British company's officials in no uncertain terms, and held them totally responsible for the disruption of peace on the Gold Coast.[15]

Earlier in the late eighteenth century, Duke Ephraim of Old Calabar wrote several times to the Bristol slave-trading firm of James Rogers and Co., complaining that one of the firm's slave ships, *Jupiter*, carried off his free citizens to the Americas.[16] The extent of the conflict provoked by this and similar incidents in the area was referred to indirectly by a Mr J. P. Degravers, M.P., in a communication to Rogers and Co.:

> I have now finished the History of the Kingdom of Haifock, Commonly called Old Calabar... I have not mentioned the transactions of your ship masters, nor those of others, leading to the ideas which a copy of my journal have naturally raised within you; the barbarians would most undoubtedly have been productive of another argument to abolish the slave trade, which obviously is clearly demonstrated humane in the actual state of that part of Africa.[17]

Similar incidents were reported by *Lloyd's List*. For example, the issue of 23 April 1773 carried a report from Cape Coast Castle, dated 12 December 1772:

> A sloop about 60 tons, and which by all accounts must be a Pirate, has considerably hurt the Trade for Gold at Assinee and Basam, having carried off several of the free Blacks from those places and killed several others, so that no English Boats can go to those places, which is a great hurt to the Trade at Annamaboe.[18]

Lloyd's List also contains an extract relating to the *Ave Maria*, helmed by Captain DuBlays, in 1770 involving an incident 'occasioned by some of the crew endeavouring to defraud the natives'. Again, it can be argued that these and similar incidents were not typical of the relationship between coastal Africans and European traders at the time. Nevertheless, they must have contributed to the deep-rooted hostility of the coastal African populations towards the European slave-traders, which flared up from time to time along different parts of the coast during the period.

Historiographical Implications

The evidence displayed on the loss of ships and cargo has important implications for various aspects of the historiography of the Atlantic slave trade. The rest of this chapter is devoted to an examination of three of these: (1) the volume of British slave exports derived from British custom records, (2) the mortality rate among slaves purchased by the European traders calculated from the records of ships that actually arrived at their American destinations and (3) the pattern of profits in the British slave trade.

As stated above, the evidence presented shows that 1,053 vessels were lost by their owners to privateers, wrecks at sea and other causes. For the period 1698–1807, the number comes down to 976. The latter figure is 8.8 per cent of the 11,106 ships indicated for the period by the most recent estimate of the volume of slaves transported from Africa by British traders.[19] It should be noted that the evidence does not cover all the years of the period, as shown above. While there are indications of double counting in the report of losses, it may be reasonable to add about 200 vessels to the figure to make up for miss-ing reports. This brings the total for the period to 1,176, or 10.6 per cent of the number of ships produced for the period by the estimate mentioned earlier.

Now, how does this relate to the estimated volume of British slave exports from Africa for the period in question? In the first place, it should be noted that the reports in *Lloyd's List* do not regularly distinguish between slave and non-slave ships, although this is done occasionally. The losses reported include slave ships and non-slave ships, as well as vessels trading from the Americas, and even a few from continental Europe. On this account, the above calculations exaggerate the proportion of slave ships cleared out from England that were lost during the period. More important, however, is the extent to which the vessels lost had loaded their cargo of slaves before they were cap-tured or lost.

The latter problem would have been easy to resolve had the sources regu-larly stated the content of every vessel at the time of capture or loss. *Lloyd's List*, our main source, shows this for a few ships only. For most ships, this vital infor-mation is not given. Even ships in the Atlantic crossing are frequently reported as captured or lost on their way from Africa to the Americas, without stating specifically that they had slaves on board or providing their number. Based on the available evidence, I have attempted to solve the problem in two stages.

It is clear enough that vessels captured or lost outward, that is, between England and Africa, had not yet bought any slaves before the incident. It is equally clear that ships captured or lost during the Atlantic crossing[20] or homeward (that is, from the Americas to England) were carrying or had car-ried a full cargo of slaves before the incident. The only area of uncertainty involves the captures or losses that occurred on the African coast. The evi-dence relating to the point of capture or loss, in terms of these four geographic locations, is very good and permits the grouping of the 1,053 vessels men-tioned above accordingly.[21]

Between 1698 and 1807, 170 of the English vessels listed were captured or lost en route for Africa, 355 on the African coast, 293 on their way to the Americas and 100 homeward. Thus, of the 918 ships of the period, whose geographical points of capture or loss are known, we know for certain that 393 had their full cargo of slaves before the incident occurred, while 170 had no slaves at all on board at the time. The problem now is to determine the proportion of their full cargo of slaves already purchased by the remaining 355 vessels before being captured or lost on the coast of Africa. However, this cannot be computed directly from the reports. But it can be done if we know the average length of time the vessels had spent on the African coast before their capture or loss, and also the average length of time it took to purchase a full cargo of slaves during the period. The detailed information we have for the 10 years from 1796 to 1805, a critical period for the study (as stated above), permits the computation of these lengths of time. Using the date of clearance from England for each ship and the date the loss was reported, we are able to determine the average time interval between clearance and when capture or loss was reported. *Lloyd's List* does not state the actual dates the vessels were captured or lost in all cases. This is done for only 12 of the 48 vessels reported. These 12 cases have been used to determine the average time interval between the actual date of loss and the date the loss was reported by *Lloyd's List*. I have taken four months as the average. From all the evidence, the average time interval between clearance and loss for the 48 vessels comes to 4 months and 18.5 days.

A table of extracts made from the logbooks of British slave ships that cleared ports in England to Africa in 1797 makes it possible to compute the average length of time it took to sail from ports in England to the main place of trade on the African coast, and the average length of time it took to purchase a full cargo of slaves for the ships.[22] From this evidence, the average sailing time from England comes to 2 months and 11 days,[23] and the average length of time it took to purchase a full cargo of slaves was 3 months or 90 days.

Relating the average sailing time from England to the average length of time between clearance and loss for the 48 above-mentioned vessels shows that on average those vessels had spent 2 months and 7.5 days (67.5 days) trading on the African coast before they were captured or lost. Since the evidence also shows that it took 90 days on average to purchase a full cargo of slaves during the period, this means that, again, on the average, the vessels were 75 per cent fully slaved before being captured or lost.

The bulk of the losses reported between 1689 and 1807 occurred in wartime conditions. Hence, the result for the years 1796–1805, a major war period, can reasonably be applied to the whole period of the study. In fact, of the 355 ships captured or lost on the African coast during the period, 166 (46.8 per cent) occurred in the wartime period 1793–1807. What is more, available qualitative and quantitative evidence for the wartime period 1776–1783 – the War of American Independence – basically agrees with our estimates for the years 1796–1805. In particular, the evidence shows, as would be expected, that there were usually more slaves on the African coast in wartime, awaiting sale to the European traders, than there were European ships available to take them away. Thus a British trader wrote in November 1776 to a European trader resident on the African coast: 'Sorry to hear the times are so bad, depend on it that you will have slaves in greater plenty ere you've more ships, for the payments in the West Indies are so very long and uncertain, that untill [sic] times mend there few or no ships will be fitted out; there has not been one fitted out of this place since the *Africa* in July last, indeed all the Guineamen belonging to this port are in Government service as Transports.'[24]

The information we have relating to seven vessels, which arrived and departed the African coast in 1778 and 1779, is consistent with this statement:[25]

- the *Lord Germaine*, Chalmers, Commander, belonging to London, arrived the Gold Coast on 19 January 1778, and left for Jamaica on 17 March 1778, with 556 slaves, 3 tons of ivory and 300 ounces of gold;
- the *Nancy*, Hammond, Commander, of Liverpool, arrived the Gold Coast on 8 January 1779, and departed for Jamaica on 19 March 1779, with 420 slaves;

- the *Nancy*, Nelson, Commander, of Liverpool, arrived the Gold Coast on 8 February 1779, and left for Jamaica on 16 April 1779, with 420 slaves and 1 ton of ivory;
- the *Adventure*, Muir, Commander, of London, arrived the Gold Coast on 17 July 1779, and left for Tobago on 25 September 1779, with 404 slaves, 2 tons of ivory and 550 ounces of gold;
- the *Lord Germaine*, Thoburn, Commander, of London, arrived the Gold Coast on 22 July 1779, and left for Jamaica on 23 October 1779, with 506 slaves and 550 ounces of gold;
- the *Will*, Charles, Commander, of Liverpool, arrived the Gold Coast on 26 July 1779, and left for Jamaica on 25 September 1779, with 310 slaves;
- the *Nancy*, Paisley, Commander, of Liverpool, arrived the Gold Coast on 16 September 1779, and left for Granada on 9 December 1779, with 370 slaves and 100 ounces of gold.

It is significant that only one of the seven ships, the *Lord Germaine*, Thoburn, Commander (22 July–23 October 1779), spent up to three months on the African coast before departing with a full cargo of slaves. Every one of the remaining six spent substantially less than three months, in spite of the fact that they all loaded very large numbers of slaves each, together with ivory and gold. This is a clear indication of the abundance of slaves on the African coast in wartime, relative to the number of European ships trading there, which helped to shorten considerably the length of time the ships took to collect full cargoes of slaves at such times.

We can, therefore, be reasonably sure that we will not err seriously, either way, by applying the result produced earlier for the years 1796–1805 to the 355 vessels captured or lost on the African coast during the whole period. As computed above, this means that in terms of slaving capacity lost, 25 per cent of the 355 vessels should be regarded as having purchased no slaves at all before their destruction, and the remaining 75 per cent as having already had their full cargo of slaves before the incident. This gives 89 and 266 vessels, respectively. Thus, of the 918 vessels stated above, the equivalent of 659 ships completed slave purchases, while 259 made no purchases at all. If these ratios are applied to the 58 vessels, whose geographical point of loss is not stated, and the 200 vessels added for missing reports, we have the equivalent of 332 vessels in slaving capacity wiped out by captures and other losses in the whole period from 1698 to 1807. This is approximately 3 per cent of the total figure of 11,106 vessels for the period, as stated above. As pointed out earlier, if allowance is made for non-slave ships, and the vessels belonging to ports in the Americas and continental Europe included in the Lloyd's reports, the proportion may go down to about 2 per cent. Small as it appears, it is still important in volume estimates to recognise this depressant factor.

Incidentally, a comparison of the shipping data in the *Parliamentary Papers* with the *Lloyd's List* confirms the limitations of the former that have been stressed in the literature (Anstey, 1975a; Inikori, 1976; Inikori, 1992). Of the total number of 245 ships reported captured or lost between 1796 and

1805, no fewer than 80, that is, 33 per cent, could not be found on the rather detailed clearance lists for the period among the *Parliamentary Papers*. The implication of this finding is similar to that of the seizure of Dutch cargo in 1803, discovered by the late Roger Anstey (1975b, pp. 11–12, n. 31).[26]

Non-slave ships, together with vessels belonging to ports in the Americas and continental Europe, may account for about one-half of the vessels. This rather generous allowance still leaves about 16 per cent of the vessels reported captured or lost between 1796 and 1805 unaccounted for in the Parliamentary clearance lists. It is reasonable to conclude that these lists understate the magnitude of British slave ships at least in the same proportion (over 16 per cent) that they underrepresent the ships reported captured or lost by *Lloyd's List* between 1796 and 1805. Hence, even after allowance has been made for lost slaving capacity due to wartime captures and other causes, the fact still remains that existing estimates of the volume of slaves transported from Africa by British traders are minimum estimates with a significant room for upward adjustment, although the exact proportion may be difficult to determine.[27]

As to the implication of the evidence presented for the rate of mortality among the slaves purchased by the European traders in Africa, no exact measurement can be made. It is clear from the evidence that privateering accounted for a large proportion of the losses reported. While these were clear losses to the traders who owned the ships and slaves captured by privateers, as far as slave imports into the Americas were concerned, there was no loss of imports, except to the extent that a few slaves may have been killed in the process. All that happened was a change of destination in the Americas. And quite often this was counterbalanced by captures on the other side. *Lloyd's List* reports for 1744, and for some other years, show prizes taken by British privateers, their slaves being sold in the British Caribbean. In fact, the account of Gomer Williams (1897) indicates that British privateers may have captured more ships than British traders lost to the enemy.

The evidence shows clearly that many slaves died in the wrecks at sea and in various incidents on the African coast, yet these deaths are not captured by existing measurements of slave mortality. These existing measurements are derived exclusively from ships that actually arrived in the Americas.[28] Hence, no account is taken of mortality relating to those ships that never arrived at all. Unfortunately, the reports in *Lloyd's List* do not provide adequate evidence for exact measurements. Quite often the number of slaves killed in these incidents is not stated. However, given that these cases constituted a rather small proportion of the shipping employed, as shown above, they may have added altogether no more than 1 or 2 percentage points to the overall mortality rate. So, again, taking account of the probable magnitude of the understatement of the volume of the trade by the extant records, existing import estimates still leave significant room for upward adjustment, although to a relatively lower degree than the export estimates.

We now come to the implication of the evidence presented for the pattern of profits in the British slave trade. Certainly, the wartime captures posed serious problems for all the traders and for the marine insurance underwriters. As one of the traders wrote in a private letter to a friend in September 1777:

> I take this opportunity by Capt. Chalmers to acquaint you of my misfortune in losing the *St. George* & the *Gascoyne*, both having been taken by the Americans ~ carried into the French Islands. The loss I have sustained by this stroke of ill luck is very considerable, not only as I was short insured upon the property, but many of the underwriters have failed, from the frequent captures since these American troubles, so that I am a sufferer of at least four or five thousand pounds.[29]

Given the magnitude of the losses documented in the letter, readers may wonder whether it was ever possible for the traders to make long-run profits. The archival research of the last two decades makes it clear that the traders did in fact make long-run profits in the trade, although the authorities differ in their estimate of the overall magnitude and pattern of the profits (Anstey, 1975a, 1975b; Richardson, 1975; Inikori, 1981). Significantly, the evidence presented by the researchers shows unmistakably that the wartime conditions of 1776–83 produced one of the abnormally large short-run profits in the trade (Inikori, 1981, pp. 758–761). Among the reasons accounting for this apparent paradox is the fact that most European traders left the trade temporarily in wartime, thus reducing considerably the level of competition on the African coast. This substantially reduced the coastal price of slaves and the time it took to purchase a full cargo of slaves for the ships. In addition, ship captains not only regularly filled up their shipping space, but also crowded their ships beyond the general practice in normal times

The increased security provided by the spreading of the risks through marine insurance also contributed positively to maintaining profits, even when some of the underwriters failed in wartime. What is more, the fact that most of the losses occurred as a result of wartime captures by enemy privateers would mean that traders with adequate resources to properly arm their ships for both protection and privateering suffered fewer losses and were also able to recoup such losses with the proceeds of prizes taken by their well-armed ships. In fact, the evidence indicates, as mentioned above, that they may have made additional net gains from privateering in wartime (Williams, 1897). Again, all this further supports the argument in the literature that the larger traders with more resources made larger profits than the smaller ones, because it was the former that had the resources to heavily arm their ships for protection and for privateering.[30]

Conclusion

The evidence presented and analysed in this chapter confirms the view of the slave-traders that theirs was an unusually hazardous business. The single most important contributing factor was war: seven major wars were fought during the period studied. A second factor, distant to war in quantitative importance, was the occurrence of normal wrecks at sea. Also important, although occurring relatively less frequently, were slave insurrections and conflicts with coastal African populations. The evidence reveals a level of hostility felt by coastal Africans towards the European slave-traders that has hitherto not been adequately reflected in the literature. Although the evidence is thin and sometimes ambiguous, it does lend itself to the speculation that the ordinary folks in the coastal societies – people who were not in government, who were not soldiers or traders, and who held no slaves – were appalled by the trade in fellow human beings conducted daily on a vast scale before their very eyes. Some of these may have assisted the export slaves in their insurrections. They may also have expressed their disapproval by attacking the European traders whenever this could be done with very little risk to themselves. All this would help to explain why far more insurrections by the export slaves occurred on the African shores than in the Atlantic crossing. This speculation suggested by the evidence presented deserves further research to confirm or invalidate. On current evidence, however, we have to conclude that much of the hostility of the coastal Africans was provoked by the intemperate behaviour and sharp business practices of the European traders.

The frequent loss of ship and cargo suffered by the traders has important implications for the historiography of the Atlantic slave trade. Some of the ships were lost before slaves were taken on board; others perished with their full cargo of slaves; and yet others were captured and diverted to other American destinations with their slaves. The evidence analysed in this chapter shows that the loss in slave shipping capacity due to these causes may be as high as 2 per cent of the total volume of slave exports produced by recent estimates. In addition, slaves killed in these incidents may be as much as 1 or 2 per cent of the import estimates. On the other side of the coin, the sources employed confirm the limitations of the extant records employed by historians in the volume estimates. At least 16 per cent of the slave ships reported lost by *Lloyd's List* could not be found on the lists of slave ships cleared from English ports to the African coast. Thus, even after taking account of the aforesaid lost slave shipping capacity and the additional slave mortality, existing export and import estimates still leave significant room for upward adjustment, the former more so than the latter. Recent attempts to explain low estimates of the volume of the black slave trade in terms of these losses are not supported by the evidence.

Notes

1. British Library, London, Additional Manuscripts, Add. MSS. 38.416, fols. 154–156, James Jones to Lord Hawkesbury, Bristol, 26 July 1788.
2. British Library, Parliamentary Papers, Accounts and Papers, 1789, vol. 82, no. 633, evidence of Robert Norris, 2 June 1788, p. 8.
3. J.E. Inikori, 1981, p. 761.

4. H.S. Klein, 1978; J.A. Rawley, 1981, pp. 283–306; J. Walvin, 1994, pp. 38–58. An attempt made a few years ago to relate the risks to the profitability of the trade was limited to middle passage mortality in slave ships that arrived at their American destinations (Richardson, 1987, pp. 178–196).

5. Wright and Fayle (1928, p. 8) state that the first coffee house in London was established in 1652, and that the number grew rapidly after the Restoration (1660).

6. The year shown in the issue is 1740. This is because of the Julian calendar in use at the time, in which the year began on 25 March. The two issues of the 1692 series and those of May 1702 to March 1704 have not been consulted. These years are relatively well covered by the evidence of the Royal African Company for the years 1689–1708.

7. Of the over 100 issues published each year, the missing and damaged issues listed in the volumes up to 1807 include: 1741: 20 issues; 1747: 9; 1748: 5; 1749: 8; 1750: 7; 1751: 7; 1752: 5; 1753: 2.

8. To say that compiling and organising the data from the thousands of reports was tedious and time-consuming is certainly an understatement.

9. These were the war in Ireland and against France, 1688–97; War of Spanish Succession, 1702–13; War with Spain, 1718–21; War with Spain (Right of Search) and of Austrian Succession, 1739–48; Seven Years' War, 1756–63; War of American Independence, 1776–83; French Revolutionary and Napoleonic Wars, 1793–1815.

10. C. Wilson, 1957.

11. *Lloyd's List*, report of Tuesday, 23 June 1747, No. 1208.

12. *Lloyd's List*, report of Friday, 29 February 1760.

13. A. Crosby, 1986, pp. 114–115.

14. PRO, T70/1580, Governor and Council on the Gold Coast to the African Company Committee in London, Cape Coast Castle, 31 October 1803.

15. PRO, T70/1581, Report of Captain W. Brown of His Majesty's Ship Rodney, 2 January 1804.

16. PRO, Chancery Masters Exhibits, Master Senior, C.107/12, Duke Ephraim to James Rogers and L. Roach, Old Calabar, 16 October 1789, and 17 November 1789.

17. PRO, Chancery Masters Exhibits, Master Senior, C.107/7 Part I, J.P. Degravers, M.P., to James Rogers and Co., Bath, 7 October 1791. I have searched in vain for the book on Old Calabar referred to in the letter.

18. *Lloyd's List*, report of Friday, 23 April 1773, No. 426.

19. J. Inikori, 1992, p. 651.

20. This route is described as going from Africa to the Americas. It includes vessels captured or lost after their arrival in the Americas, but before their departure for England.

21. Of the 1,053 vessels, only 58 ships lost by the private traders between 1708 and 1711 cannot be grouped according to the points of capture or loss.

22. See PRO, T70/1576, pp. 338–346: A Table of Extracts made from all the Log Books of African Slave Ships, deposited in the Custom Houses of London, Liverpool and Bristol, for the years 1791 and 1797; and presented at the Bar of the House of Lords by the Commissioners of His Majesty's Customs. See pp. 343–346 for the 1797 vessels, 30 in all. Only the vessels of 1797 are employed in the calculations because they are the ones relevant to the period, 1796–1805, being specifically examined.

23. In all the calculations, the average length of each month is put at 30 days to avoid awkward fractions.

24. PRO, T.70/1534, John Cockburn to a trader on the African Coast, Bristol, 30 November 1776.

25. PRO, T.70/1535, Packet B No. 7, Export of Slaves 1778 [from Annamabo and Cape Coast]; T.70/537, Ships, Arrivals and Departures from the Gold Coast, 1779.

26. See also Inikori, 1992, pp. 659–660, n. 20.

27. It is clear from the evidence in this chapter that the rather low figures recently estimated for the British slave trade before 1714 by David Eltis (1993) cannot be explained in terms of uncompleted voyages due to wartime captures and other losses as Eltis proposes. It is particularly important to note that the losses by the Royal African Company during the period studied by Eltis occurred largely between England and the Americas, after the slaves were landed in the Americas. Those low estimates can only be explained by the limitations of the rather poor import data upon which they are primarily based. Historians using these import data must be reminded of their description by Thomas Irving, the meticulous inspector-general of British imports and exports in the eighteenth century (Inikori, 1992, pp. 670–671).

28. In his discussion of this subject, Stephen Behrendt (1993) accuses Joseph Inikori (1976) of misrepresenting the evidence in Parliamentary Papers. Accounts and Papers, 1792, Vol. 93, No. 766. Contrary to Inikori's statement that this source shows only 35 slaves lost in the middle passage by all the British vessels that landed slaves in the British Caribbean in 1790, Behrendt says, 'this document gives no indication that only thirty-five slaves died on the Middle Passage' (Behrendt, 1993, p. 88, n. 42). But an examination of this source shows that of all the ships that imported slaves into the British Caribbean in 1790, only those that landed slaves in Dominica recorded a middle passage mortality of 35 out of a total of 2,142 landed in that island. All the vessels that landed slaves in the other islands in this year showed no middle passage mortality. In fact, the heading for this document specifically states, 'An Account of the Number of Vessels, their Tonnage, and Number of Men, that have arrived from Africa in the British West India Islands, between the 5th Day of January 1789 and the 5th day of January 1792; with the Number of slaves imported therein… Together with the Number of *Negroes* that died from the Time of being taken on Board until their arrival in the West Indies …' (emphasis added). For 1789, the total number landed by the vessels measuring 16,157 tons is 21,425 slaves, while 1,225 died in the middle passage; for 1791, the respective figures are 24,041 tons for all ships landing slaves, 30,763 slaves landed, and 1,427 slaves died in the middle passage. It is thus clear that Stephen Behrendt did not read this document carefully. See British Library, House of Commons Sessional Papers of the 18th Century. Reports and Papers, Vol. 82, 1791 and 1792, pp. 297–323, for another copy of this document. They both contain identical information.

29. PRO, T70/1534, Geo. Burton to Richard Miles, London, 19 September 1777.

30. The impact of middle passage mortality on profits, analysed by David Richardson (1987), can also be shown as favouring the larger traders, although Richardson does not seem to be aware of this. Adequate resources to properly equip their ships would mean less frequent wrecks at sea.

Bibliography

ANSTEY, R. 1975a. 'The volume and profitability of the British slave trade, 1761–1807'. In S.L. Engerman and E.D. Genovese (eds.). *Race and Slavery in the Western Hemisphere: Quantitative Studies.* Princeton, N.J., Princeton University Press. Pp. 3–31.

―――. 1975b. *The Atlantic Slave Trade and British Abolition 1760–1810*. London, Macmillan.

BECKER, C. 1986. 'Note sur les chiffres de la traite atlantique francaise au XVIIIe siècle'. *Cahiers d' Études africaines*, 104, XXVI (4), pp. 633–679.

BEHRENDT, S.D. 1993. The British Slave Trade, 1785–1807: Volume, Profitability, and Mortality (Ph.D. diss., University of Wisconsin, Madison).

CROSBY, A.W. 1986. *Ecological Imperialism: The Biological Expansion of Europe, 900–1900*. Cambridge, Cambridge University Press.

DOWELL, S. 1965. *A History of Taxation and Taxes in England from the Earliest Times to the Present Day*. 2 Vols., Vol. 2. London, Frank Cass; first published by Longmans Green (1884).

ELTIS, D. 1990. 'The volume, age/sex ratios, and African impact of the slave trade: Some refinements of Paul Lovejoy's review of the Literature'. *Journal of African History*, Vol. 31, pp. 485–492.

―――. 1993. The Transatlantic Slave Trade to the British Americas before 1714: Annual Estimates of Volume and Direction. Unpublished paper.

INIKORI, J.E. 1976. 'Measuring the Atlantic slave trade: An assessment of Curtin and Nasty'. *Journal of African History*, XVII (2), pp. 197–223.

―――. 1981. 'Market structure and the profits of the British African trade in the late eighteenth century'. *Journal of Economic History*, Vol. 41, No. 4, pp. 745–776.

―――. 1992. 'The volume of the British slave trade, 1655–1807'. *Cahiers d' études africaines*, 128, XXXII (4), pp. 643–688.

ISRAEL, J.I. 1989. *Dutch Primacy in World Trade, 1585–1740*. Oxford, Clarendon Press.

KAISER, D. 1990. *Politics and War: European Conflict from Philip II to Hitler*. Cambridge, Mass., Harvard University Press.

KLEIN, H.S. 1978. *The Middle Passage: Comparative Studies in the Atlantic Slave Trade*. Princeton, N.J., Princeton University Press.

McCUSKER, J.J. 1991. 'The early history of "Lloyd's List"'. *Historical Research: The Bulletin of The Institute of Historical Research*, Vol. 64, No. 155, pp. 427–431.

METTAS, J., and DAGET, S. 1978, 1984. *Répertoire des expéditions négrières francaises au XVlIIe siècle*. Nantes/Paris, Bibliothèque d'outre-mer.

RAWLEY, J.A. 1981. *The Transatlantic Slave Trade: A History*. New York and London, W. W. Norton.

RICHARDSON, D. 1975. 'Profitability in the Bristol-Liverpool slave trade'. *Revue française d'histoire d'outre-mer*, 62, nos. 226–227, pp. 301–308.

―――. 1987. 'The costs of survival: The transport of slaves in the middle passage and the profitability of the eighteenth-century British slave trade'. *Explorations in Economic History*, Vol. 24, No. 2, pp. 178–196.

―――. 1989. 'The eighteenth-century British slave trade: Estimates of its volume and coastal distribution in Africa'. *Research in Economic History*, Vol. 12, pp. 151–195.

WALVIN, J. 1994. *Black Ivory: A History of British Slavery*. Washington, D.C., Howard University Press.

WILLIAMS, G. 1897. *History of the Liverpool Privateers and Letters of Marque with an account of the Liverpool Slave Trade*. London.

WILSON, C. 1957. *Profit and Power: A Study of England and the Dutch Wars*. London and New York, Longmans Green.

WRIGHT, C., and FAYLE, C.E. 1928. *A History of Lloyd's from the Founding of Lloyd's Coffee House to the Present Day*. London, Macmillan.

Chapter 10

The Slave Trade and the Demographic Evolution of Africa

Patrick Manning

INTERPRETATIONS OF THE DEMOGRAPHIC EVOLUTION OF AFRICA in the era of the slave trade continue to range widely. The past generation's research, however, has brought to light a great deal of detail on Africa's population history, and has provided an outline of main patterns in African demography. The growing empirical record, when combined with established demographic principles, enables us to make with some confidence a distinction between patterns of population that are likely to have happened in Africa's past and patterns that are unlikely to have happened.

As the demographic past is currently understood, the African population varied substantially in size and structure from region to region over the past several centuries. The slave trade and slavery had significantly negative effects on African population from the sixteenth to the twentieth century, though these effects too varied considerably. The interaction of enslavement with other demographic factors sharply restricted African population growth and increased African displacement, especially during the eighteenth and nineteenth centuries, the very period when the population of most other world regions underwent steady growth.

This essay identifies the major topics in African demographic history as they relate to slavery, addresses the main areas of debate, summarises current interpretations and notes important areas for further research.

Intrinsic Patterns of African Population

For the period before the twentieth century, we have unfortunately little information on African rates of birth and death, or on African patterns of family structure and marriage. Most of the reliable data refers to the migratory process of the Atlantic slave trade. Observations on African populations at home are extremely rare, and they have been linked with guesswork to construct estimates of birth and death rates.

John Thornton has been especially adept at locating early demographic data. For instance, he found a set of seventeenth-century baptismal records from Angola. He tallied these records, and from them estimated an age structure for the Angolan population: average age at death, 27.5 years.[1] This estimate became the basis for other work by himself and others. For instance, in my simulations of African population under the impact of slavery, I accepted this age structure, and went on to assume an intrinsic birth rate sufficient to yield population growth of 0.5 per cent per year.[2]

The weight of so much analysis, however, was more than a single set of baptismal records could bear. The first weakness is that these figures, even if correct as averages, could not have applied to the whole African population. Second, both these assumptions, and particularly that of average age at death, seem on further study to have been too optimistic. The baptismal records Thornton studied are consistent with a much lower age at death, almost as low as 20 years.[3] With that higher death rate, the same number of births would yield a lower rate of population growth.

The best set of demographic records on precolonial Africa applies to a very special case – the immigrant population of Americo-Liberians during the nineteenth century. The illnesses and deaths in Liberia of this American-born black population were recorded by physicians in great detail, and these records have now benefited from an excellent analysis by McDaniel (1994). His calculations show the Americo-Liberians to have undergone the highest rate of mortality ever reliably recorded: malaria was the single greatest cause of death, but pulmonary and other diseases were also significant. These results cannot simply be extended to the surrounding African-born population, though they do suggest that mortality in that population may have been high.

While the search for new data on precolonial birth and death rates must go on, we are left with two other strategies for estimating these rates. One of these is estimating African demographic rates from what is known of human populations in general. Several scholars have utilised this strategy; the problem is that it is difficult to resolve differences among them.[4]

The other strategy is to project twentieth-century patterns backwards in time. In this approach, nineteenth-century populations are estimated by starting with a twentieth-century population and assuming a certain growth rate from the earlier population – where the assumed growth rate is made up of an assumed birth rate less death rate less emigration rate.[5] One main problem with this approach is that twentieth-century population statistics for Africa are not very reliable. For instance, there is no clear answer as to whether polygamy yields a higher or a lower birth rate than monogamy.[6] A second problem is that recent rates of birth, death and migration may not be applicable to earlier periods. African birth rates seem to have been rather consistently high – based on early marriage of women – and these may not have varied much. Death rates, however, are likely to have varied sharply over the last century. The long-term trend has been a great reduction in death rates, but fluctuations may have been severe, as African regions underwent war and colonial conquest, famine and epidemics, in addition to the slave trade.[7]

This is perhaps a gloomy and sceptical report on the evidence touching precolonial African demographic rates. The other side of this report is the implication that any new empirical data will magnify our understanding significantly. We need therefore to continue research on the basic demographic variables for precolonial Africa.

Fluctuations in African Population

In contrast to the limited information on the size, structure and basic rates of African populations, we have rather more evidence and debate on the fluctuations in African population, especially for zones where drought and famine were common: the savannah areas of West Africa and south Central Africa. Following the early work of Lovejoy and Baier on the mid-eighteenth-century drought in the Central Sudan, other scholars have documented cycles of drought and famine in Senegambia, the Cape Verde Islands and Angola.[8] Famine brought the sale of many children into slavery. Noting this and other evidence, Miller has gone so far as to argue that the impact of periodic famine on African population was greater than that of the slave trade.[9]

Warfare, when it became severe, brought redistribution and decline in African population. Studies of West and Central Africa have documented the effects of warfare ranging from the dispersal of towns to regional population decline.[10] As with famine, warfare is difficult to separate from enslavement.

On the other hand, some scholars have argued that the arrival of new crops enabled African rates of population growth to increase, so that the loss of slaves was offset by new births. This reasoning, sometimes accompanied by reference to an offhand remark by Curtin that American maize might have spurred African population growth, has never been developed in a sustained argument.[11] Maize and manioc had spread widely through West and Central Africa by the end of the nineteenth century, but we have no detailed knowledge of the timing or the routes by which these crops spread, nor of the intensity of their utilisation. If the new crops had an advantage over the pre-existing yams, it may have been not so much their calorie content as their greater ease of storage – they were better food for the era of the slave trade.[12]

Other factors may have caused fluctuations in precolonial African population. Marriage practices, for instance, might have been influential. For instance, Vansina (1992) argues that the peoples of the equatorial forest had a deeply rooted preference for low population density that kept population from soaring, presumably by restricting marriage. We have only to consider the colonial era to see ways in which changes in religion, education and occupation, and exposure to disease brought sharp changes in birth and death rates. Similar fluctuations must not be excluded for the precolonial era.

Slavery-Related Influences on African Population

The main focus of this essay is the influences of slavery and the slave trade on the African population. To be clear, we must distinguish several dimensions – eight, as I count them – of the relationship between slavery and African population. These eight dimensions of that relationship are logically distinct, though they overlap significantly in practice. The sections that follow address each of these dimensions.

The export slave trade has received more attention than any other factor, but even it consists of at least two issues. The first dimension is the number of African captives successfully transported in the transatlantic slave trade, and in the trade to the Mediterranean, Southwest Asia and the Indian Ocean. The second dimension is mortality during transportation: the losses during the middle passage of the Atlantic trade and other trade, to which we may add the mortality just before embarkation and just after the voyage.

Three more dimensions of the relationship between slavery and African population stem from the slave trade within Africa. The third dimension is the mortality within Africa of captives taken to be sent overseas. The fourth and fifth dimensions are the number of African captives successfully transported to slave status within Africa, and the additional number of captives who died before becoming slaves in Africa.

Further, while the trade in slaves was the most violent and severe in its influence on population, the institution of slavery itself also led to significant demographic impact in two ways. The sixth dimension, though indirect, was the conditions of slavery on other continents that affected the demand for more African slaves. That is, the high death rates of slaves in the American tropics ensured a continuing demand for more African captives, and thus helped replicate the violence of the whole system. The seventh was the impact on African population of the condition of the large numbers of persons held as slaves within Africa.

The eighth and final dimension of this relationship was the African population itself – its size and structure, in all its regional and temporal variability, as influenced by the other seven dimensions.

The Export Slave Trade

The debate over the export slave trade was launched by Philip Curtin's census of the Atlantic slave trade, with its broad sweep and its detailed estimates. This debate encompasses the first three dimensions of the impact of slavery on African population: export trade, export mortality and mortality in Africa. The debate over the size of the export trade and export mortality is well known and has been summarised elsewhere.[13] The debate on African implications of the export slave trade began quietly in 1969, when Fage, noting the strength of and continuity in West African societies, responded to Curtin's estimates by proposing calculations suggesting that it had virtually no influence on the size or structure of African population (Fage, 1969).

In sharp contrast, Marie Diop-Maes, impressed by the work of Cook, Borah and others in estimating the dramatic population decline in the Americas brought about primarily by disease contact with the Old World, developed analogous estimates for Africa.[14] She concluded that the human agency of the slave trade, added to natural problems of disease, brought an equally terrible decline in African population.

Rodney, surely one of the strongest critics of the European impact upon Africa, argued that the export slave trade brought the expansion of African slaveholding (thus, an influence of the first on the sixth dimension above), but he never went so far as to argue that Africa suffered severe demographic decline under the slave trade.[15] Inikori, however, has made just such an argument in several fashions: first arguing that the volume of the Atlantic slave trade was greater than the 1969 estimate of Curtin, then arguing that the total continental export was sufficient to bring population decline, and finally arguing that the slave trade within Africa, when added to export slave trades, brought population decline for Africa.[16] While the specifics of his arguments have been debated by other scholars, his work has the strength of having touched on all the dimensions of the relationship between slavery and African population.

Many other scholars have argued for a minimal African demographic impact of the slave trade. A number of scholars, following Fage, did so by utilising a simple additive model of the effects of migration: they took the annual number of slave exports, subtracted it from an estimated annual excess of births over deaths (or net population increase), and concluded that African population increased, on average, during the era of slave exports. Northrup (1975) and Anstey (1975) followed Fage in making such estimates. Independent work published by Thornton and the present author in 1981 showed the need to take the age and sex composition of the population into account in such calculations. That is, the slave trade not only removed some people, but caused the number of births to decrease and the number of deaths to increase.

Thornton's 1981 case-study of two Angolan censuses of the 1770s suggested the significant distortion in the age and sex structure of African populations brought by the export slave trade: adult males were roughly half the number of adult females.[17] My study, a more general review, also noted the importance of the age-sex composition of slave exports.[18] Additive calculations were insufficient.

While agreeing on demographic principle, Thornton and I parted ways in estimating demographic impact. I estimated that African population was likely to have declined as a result of slave exports. Thornton, noting the heavily female population of Angola, concluded that it could have produced enough children to grow despite the export of slaves. His conclusion, however, relied on two faulty estimates, one empirical and one theoretical. Empirically, he assumed (from his earlier work on baptismal records, as noted above) that the average age at death of an Angolan population was 27.5 years. A review of his data suggests that they give more support to an average age at death of about 21 years – meaning, in short, that the children born to the women of Angola would not survive to adulthood (Manning, in progress). Theoretically, he neglected the loss of fertility brought by the export of adult women. Even if they were lost in smaller numbers than men, the loss of their fertility meant that the losses to African population included not only current individuals but future births.

Miller, in his 1988 study of Angola, repeated the additive estimates of his predecessors, with its consequent underestimate of African losses, but he added a new empirical twist, which may be labelled as the 'ring of fire'.[19] He argued that the most serious declines in population occurred in frontier regions which, once incorporated under the control of slave-trading states, tended then to return to population growth. Miller's emphasis on regional differentiation in demographic impact is important, but it underestimates overall regional population decline. The simple additive approach continued to exercise its influence: even Vansina (1992), in a study of the equatorial forest notable for its methodological brilliance, neglected the debates of the 1980s and followed the simple additive approach, concluding that population decline was avoided for the forest region during most of the era of slave exports.

My mixture of computer simulation and empirical analysis has shown how a modest stream of surviving slave exports can lead to the halt and reversal of the natural growth rate in an African population. The result may run counter to elementary intuition, but it can be shown to be a consistent pattern of the slave-trade era. An African population with a natural growth rate of five per thousand per year would have its growth halted and reversed by a modest stream of slave exports, averaging some two per thousand of the population annually (and with only one-third of that population being female). The combination of the deaths in enslavement and transport with the loss of fertility would result, given African rates of birth and death, in a decline in the overall population.

The logic of this result has been asserted in several publications.[20] While some reviewers have expressed scepticism, no effort to refute it has yet appeared. One reason is that others have not been able to comment on the details of my simulations. To address this issue, first, I will complete the more detailed study (Manning, in progress). Second, the simulation itself will soon be available in a form enabling other scholars to utilise it and revise it without having to learn details of programming languages.

One advantage of the simulation model is that it permits experimentation by varying all of the data. In an extended sensitivity test, varying all input data and observing the resulting predictions on African population, I was able to identify the variables which are most crucial in influencing the overall impact of enslavement on African population, and on which it is therefore most important to collect new data. Four factors stand out clearly in this analysis: the intrinsic African rates of birth and death, the sex ratio among captives, and the proportion of captives sent abroad.[21]

The results of my estimates of the demographic impact of the export slave trade, including an attempt to account for the work of other scholars, may be summarised as follows. For the western coast of Africa as a whole – the region from Senegal to Angola, up to 600 kilometres from the coast – population declined in the period from about 1730 to 1850. For the eastern coast of Africa, from Mozambique to Kenya, population declined in the middle and late years of the nineteenth century. For the lands of the savannah extending from Senegal to the Nile Valley, and including Ethiopia and the Horn of Africa, the export slave trade was sufficient to slow population growth, but not to halt it, even during the peak of slave exports in the late eighteenth and nineteenth centuries. Details of these estimates are given elsewhere.[22] Overall, I believe these are a lower bound for estimates of the severity of the impact of slavery: they were made with optimistic estimates of African life expectancy and birth rate, and they account for only a portion of the mortality brought by the slave trade within Africa.

Additional patterns, besides the decline in African populations, mark the impact of the export slave trade. First, since more men were transported across the Atlantic than women, significant shortages of adult males developed in African populations in rough proportion to the intensity of the slave trade. Thus, for the Bight of Benin, where the slave trade was the most intense in the early eighteenth century, the population is likely to have had an unusually high disparity in the sex ratio at that time.

A second pattern distinguished littoral areas (within 100 to 200 kilometres of the coast) from interior areas. Slave exports from interior areas were overwhelmingly adult males; exports from coastal areas included adult females, and male and female children.[23] Hence, Bambara, Hausa and Lunda slaves in the Americas were virtually all adult males, while Wolof and Igbo slaves in the Americas included numerous women and children. I have hypothesised that the main cause for this pattern was the differential in slave prices on the African continent. In inland areas far from European buyers, there was little demand for adult male slaves, and the value of a female captive was much higher than that of a male captive. So female captives were retained in slavery, and male captives were taken to the coast to be sent to the Americas.[24]

A third pattern led to a distinction separating the Atlantic slave trade of the nineteenth century from that of earlier centuries. Transatlantic slave cargoes of the nineteenth century included a larger proportion of children, both male and female, than in earlier times.[25] My hypothesis is that the main reason for this difference can also be expressed in terms of prices. In the Americas, the value of child slaves increased as the threat of abolishing the slave trade rose: purchasers gave increased value to the long-term prospect of holding slaves in comparison to the short-term benefits of exploiting adult slaves. At the same time, the rapid expansion of slavery in Africa caused the relative prices of children to fall. African slave owners preferred to buy adult slaves who could be exploited immediately. Later on, when the slave trade was restricted in Africa by colonial powers, the prices of child slaves rose sharply as they had earlier in the Americas.[26]

A fourth set of patterns is the movement of slaves from the various regions of the African continent. We are well acquainted with the powerful images of slaves being embarked on ships from castles along the Gold Coast, or from factories on Goree. In contrast to these images, it appears that the great majority of those who made the middle passage across the Atlantic started their crossing from other points along the coast. The greatest numbers came, in order, from Angola, the Bight of Benin, Loango (Central Africa north of the Congo River), and the Bight of Biafra.

Each of these regions underwent at least a century of decline in population. And, since most of the slaves transported were male, each of these regions experienced a severe shortage of adult males during that time. The decline in population for the Bight of Benin has been debated in some detail, and is becoming increasingly well established.[27] The population declines for Angola and the Bight of Biafra remain in dispute.[28]

The loss of population in Loango is the most difficult to estimate, but it may have been the most severe. That is, if the slaves exported from this region included only a small proportion who originated south of the river, and if birth rates in that era were as low as in the early twentieth century, then a severe decline in population, and an equally severe disparity in the adult sex ratio, must be projected for the eighteenth and nineteenth centuries.[29]

For the eastern coast of Africa, the nineteenth century brought a severe expansion of the export slave trade which lasted until late in the century, and which brought significant decline in population to areas of Mozambique and Tanzania, and perhaps to Madagascar as well.[30]

For remaining areas of the continent – the savannah lands from Senegambia to the Nile Valley, plus the Horn of Africa – the number of slaves exported increased at the end of the nineteenth century, as a result of new demand in the Mediterranean and Southwest Asia. Most of the slaves exported were women. At present, however, it appears that the loss of these persons, by itself, was sufficient to slow but not to reverse the growth of population in the home areas.[31] The South African case stands out, in that the slave trade there did more to bring population into the region than to reduce it: the slaves came mainly from Mozambique, Madagascar and Southeast Asia.

The social impact of these demographic fluctuations and transformations is mostly a matter of speculation, but the shortage of direct evidence does not make this social history any less important. Whether the enslavement of Africans was by warfare, by kidnapping or through the courts, it must have been disruptive to society. The loss of young adults, even at the rate of 1 per cent or so each year, must have weakened African productive capacities. The significant shortages of adult males in many regions must have affected the sexual division of labour: women must have taken on men's work.

Further, the overseas slave trade must have had important implications for African patterns of marriage and family. As Thornton has argued for the case of Angola in the 1770s, the women who remained in relatively large numbers in Africa had a normal number of children.[32] This may mean that the number or proportion of polygamous marriages increased – itself a social change of note. On the other hand, we cannot be sure that the women were married: we do not know whether these relatively numerous women had their children as wives in established marital patterns, as concubines or as women with no man to support them. In general, it seems possible that a series of alternatives to earlier patterns of marriage developed as a result of the export slave trade. To put it crudely, slave concubinage grew at the expense of marriage contracted between families.

The Continental Slave Trade

Here we address the fourth and fifth dimensions of the linkage between slavery and African population: the number of African captives successfully transported to slave status within Africa, and the additional number of captives who died before becoming slaves in Africa.

It is difficult to estimate the number of persons enslaved and held within Africa in any century. The export slave trade led systematically to the development of domestic enslavement as a by-product of its depredations, and some estimates have been constructed of the number of persons enslaved in this way. But for some times and places, it is clear that the number of persons enslaved in Africa went far beyond any amount that could be treated as a by-product of slave exports. The large number of slaves held within the sixteenth-century Songhai empire provides an important early example.[33] Inikori has recently argued that this continental enslavement in the eighteenth and nineteenth centuries caused sufficient mortality to have become a major impediment to African population growth.

There is need therefore to determine the significance of this slave trade and the level of its mortality. The writings of some European travellers suggest that the mortality rates in capture may have been extremely high.[34] It will take judicious research to determine whether such observations are representative of a general pattern, or whether they are exaggerated instances selected because they reaffirmed the developing imperialist ideology of Europeans.

The demographic implications of the slave trade to African destinations, especially during the nineteenth century, must have been severe, though they remain difficult to estimate. If its mortality was at all severe, then – adding the effects of the continental and export slave trade – one may project that the regions of the savannah and the Horn of Africa, in common with the rest of the continent, underwent population decline in the early nineteenth century, and that this decline went on until near the end of the century.

Slavery Abroad and in Africa

Let us turn now to the sixth and seventh dimensions of the relationship between slavery and African population. Here we focus not on the trade in captives, but on the lives of people held in slavery and on the implications of their life patterns for African population.

The millions of captives sent to the Americas created large African-descended populations, born mainly into slavery. In most instances, these populations suffered high rates of mortality and low rates of fertility (the latter reinforced by the shortage of women), and were unable to reproduce themselves under conditions of slavery. As a result, and especially for sugar-producing areas of the Caribbean and Brazil, there was a steady demand for new slaves both to replenish and to expand the slave populations of the Americas.

In addition, as noted above, the nineteenth-century demand for slaves, mainly for Cuba and Brazil, centred increasingly on children of both sexes. The Central African regions from which most of these captives came may therefore have retained less of their children than in earlier times.

Meanwhile, during most of the nineteenth century, growing populations of enslaved Africans developed in Southwest Asia, the Indian Ocean, North Africa and the Sahara. The descendants of these populations are less easily visible than the African population of the Americas, in that African women in the Middle East bore most of their children in unions with their masters rather than with male African slaves. For instance, a substantial demand on the Arabian peninsula brought a stream of Somali and other women of the Horn.[35] These captives became workers as well as concubines: Mozambican and Malagasy captives were purchased as contract labourers by French planters of Reunion into the twentieth century, and many other captives were sent to the Sahara to work as miners and agricultural labourers.[36]

For Africa, numerous studies attest to the large holdings of slaves in many parts of the continent in the late nineteenth century, in such areas as Nupe, Yoruba country, the Western Sudan, the Upper Nile, the Swahili coast and the Congo basin.[37] Areas of the Horn may also have had large slave populations at that time. Paul Lovejoy has offered some rough estimates of numbers of persons held in slavery in Africa in the nineteenth century, which suggest that the slave population of Africa had grown nearly equal to the slave population of the Americas.

Just as the demographic effects of large-scale slavery are obviously significant yet difficult to specify, so also are the social effects. The end of the export slave trade meant that the sex ratio in Africa ought to have returned to near equality. Where there were large slave populations, they ought to have included nearly equal numbers of males and females. These slaves would then have formed their own families, so that slave women would have their children more often by slave men than by masters. In a number of instances, this pattern seems to be supported by the evidence.[38] But Meillassoux and especially Klein, reporting on the Western Sudan in the last half of the nineteenth century, note exceptionally large proportions of females among slaves, suggesting the possibility that large numbers of males were captured and then killed.[39] This issue must remain unsettled for now, but it indicates the limits of the possibilities for both demographic and social implications of continental African slavery.

Two recent works are outstanding in showing the continuing importance of slavery in twentieth-century Africa. Miers and Roberts (1991), in an edited collection, provide examples of colonial slavery drawn from all over the continent. Lovejoy and Hogendorn (1993), in a monographic study of the largest single slave society of the twentieth century, that of Northern Nigeria, provide an analysis whose detail is equivalent to that of the best studies of slavery in the Americas. The additional information available in these studies of slavery in recent times will help us to make sense of both the human and demographic costs of slavery in earlier times.

The African Demographic Regime

The eighth dimension of the relationship between slavery and African population is the African population itself, or, as we may term it, the African demographic regime. The notion of the demographic regime, as developed by Gregory and his associates, refers to the ensemble of the social and demographic conditions in which a population makes its life.[40] For African populations in the era of the slave trade, this meant, above all, the continuation of high death rates. High death rates were reproduced through warfare, dispersal of population to poor lands, and disease spread by migration. Second, African marriage patterns seem to have allowed no real way for birth rates to rise as the slave trade expanded. Women's age at marriage was already young, so it could not be lowered. Women could perhaps have continued having children to a later age, but this effect would have been small because of lower fertility at higher age, and because some women were removed as captives.

We have in addition the question of what happened to the birth rates of women held in slavery in Africa. Meillassoux and Harms have argued that slave status sharply reduced fertility; Meillassoux notes that children belonged to masters, not to the parents.[41] Such an effect, though smaller than Meillassoux and Harms suggest, has been noted for slave women in the Americas, and may have constituted another negative element of the African demographic regime.

These influences of slavery and the slave trade on rates of birth, death and migration brought changes to the structure of African populations. The slave trade brought uneven sex ratios to much of Africa: a shortage of males along the western coast of Africa, and a shortage of females in savannah and eastern coastal areas. Of perhaps similar importance was the shortage of young adults resulting from continuing enslavement.

A further issue of significance, which remains unresolved, is the overall pattern of mortality and migration of children in the slave trade. It is known that the proportion of children arriving as captives in the Americas was small, though it tended to grow with time. Does this mean that few children were enslaved in Africa? Or does it mean that large numbers of children were enslaved, but failed to survive? The rates of mortality for young children in transport are likely to have been high, so the latter possibility cannot automatically be excluded. If children were captured in large numbers, the demographic effects of enslavement must be seen as yet more negative.

African Population in a Global Context

The arguments and evidence presented above reveal that much is in doubt when it comes to assessing the details of African population in the era of the slave trade. Despite this uncertainty of detail, a contrast of great clarity emerges when the outlines of African population are compared with equivalent outlines for other continents.

From the early sixteenth century to the end of the seventeenth century, the population of the Americas declined drastically, from a peak of perhaps fifty million (or, as some have argued, twice that amount) to a low of little more than five million. African and European immigrant populations grew from a low level during this time. In the eighteenth century the total population of the Americas began to grow rapidly as the Native American population began to recover and as immigration from Africa and Europe accelerated.

Europe, after a period of stasis in its population from the fifteenth to the seventeenth centuries, returned to growth in the eighteenth century as well, in part because of younger age at marriage and rising birth rates. European growth accelerated in the nineteenth century as death rates declined.

The populous regions of Asia – Southwest, South, Southeast and East Asia – all seem to have undergone modest population growth in the eighteenth century, while China, India and Japan experienced rapid growth in the nineteenth century.

Africa, in contrast, experienced population stagnation and decline. There may have been modest population growth from the fifteenth to seventeenth centuries. But in the eighteenth century, Africa seems to have experienced no increase in birth rate and no decline in death rate, so that the migration and mortality of the slave trade cancelled population growth in many areas of the continent. In the nineteenth century the death rate was kept high directly and indirectly by the slave trade, so that the migration and mortality due to the slave trade again restricted population growth.

The result, unmistakably, was that the African population declined significantly as a proportion of the world population between 1700 and 1900, a decline that can be attributed in large part to the effects of slavery and the slave trade. Even accounting for African migrants to other continents as part of the total, the proportionate population of African descent declined during these centuries.

Quite aside from limiting the size of the total population, it seems clear that the experience of slavery had other bad effects on Africans. Poor health conditions, racial discrimination, class and ethnic division and conflict, and gender hierarchy were all reinforced by slavery.

The end of slave raiding can only have been beneficial for African populations. The arrival of European colonial rule, in contrast, had mixed effects. In areas of coastal West Africa, the result seems to have been a rapid rebound of population beginning in the late nineteenth century and continuing to the present. In contrast, in many parts of Central Africa – under Belgian, French and Portuguese rule – population seems to have declined in the late nineteenth and early twentieth centuries.[42]

Towards Future Research

The research agenda on the slave route in Africa remains lengthy and significant. For all the study that has been conducted on slavery and its impact on African demography and society, there is need for more. At the level of the monograph, we need thorough and imaginative research to learn about rates of birth and death, enslavement and liberation, as they varied over time and space. At the level of broad interpretation, we need to study the background to the severe problems of inequality separating Africa from other world areas, and the equally severe problems of inequality within Africa. We need to learn more about the extent of slavery in Africa in precolonial and colonial eras, and the relationship of slavery in Africa to the overseas demand for slaves.

Notes

1. J. Thornton, 1977; A.J. Coale; P. Demeny, 1966.
2. P. Manning, 1988.
3. P. Manning (in progress); J.C. Caldwell, 1982.
4. P. Manning, 1981; J.C. Caldwell, 1982; J.E. Inikori, 1982; J. Thornton, 1981b.
5. P. Manning; W.S. Griffiths, 1988.
6. J.C. Caldwell, 1982.
7. B. Fetter, 1990.
8. P.E. Lovejoy; S. Baier, 1975; P.D. Curtin, 1975; J.R. Dias, 1981; J.C. Miller, 1982; C. Becker, 1985; K.D. Patterson, 1988.
9. J.C. Miller, 1982.
10. J.F.A. Ajayi; R. Smith, 1964; R.A. Kea, 1982; J. Thornton, 1988; R. Law, 1991.
11. P.D. Curtin, 1969.
12. P. Manning, 1990; J.C. Miller, 1988.
13. P.D. Curtin, 1969; J.E. Inikori, 1976; P.E. Lovejoy, 1982.
14. L.-M. Diop-Maes, 1985; S.F. Cook; W.W. Borah, 1971–79.
15. W. Rodney, 1966 and 1972.
16. J.E. Inikori, 1982, 1987 and 1988.
17. J. Thornton, 1981a.
18. P. Manning, 1981.
19. J.C. Miller, 1988.
20. P. Manning, 1981, 1988 and 1990; P. Manning; W.S. Griffiths, 1988.
21. P. Manning, 1988.
22. P. Manning, 1990.
23. D. Geggus, 1989.
24. P. Manning, 1990.
25. D. Eltis; S.L. Engerman, 1992.
26. S. Miers; R. Roberts, 1988.
27. P. Manning, 1990; J.E. Inikori, 1988; R. Law, 1991.
28. P. Manning, 1990; J.C. Miller, 1988; J.E. Inikori, 1988.
29. R. Harms, 1981; J.C. Miller, 1988; P. Manning, 1990; J. Vansina, 1992.
30. P. Manning, 1990.
31. Ibid.
32. J. Thornton, 1981a.
33. J.-P. Olivier de Sardan, 1975.
34. D. Livingstone, 1874; G. Nachtigal, 1971.
35. C.M. Doughty, 1979.

36. D.D. Cordell (in progress).
37. M. Mason, 1973; M.A. Klein, 1987; C. Meillassoux, 1986; J.F. Searing, 1993; J. Ewald, 1990; D.D. Cordell, 1985; F. Cooper, 1977; A. Sheriff, 1987; F. Renault, 1989
38. M. Mason, 1973; P.E. Lovejoy; J.S. Hogendorn, 1993; F. Renault, 1989.
39. C. Meillassoux, 1983; M. A. Klein, 1987.
40. D.D. Cordell and J.W. Gregory, 1987.
41. C. Meillassoux, 1983; R. Harms, 1981.
42. C. Coquery-Vidrovitch, 1982.

Bibliography

AJAYI, J.F.A., and SMITH, R. 1964. *Yoruba Warfare in the Nineteenth Century*. Cambridge, Cambridge University Press.

ANSTEY, R. 1975. *The Atlantic Slave Trade and British Abolition, 1760–1810*. Atlantic Highlands, N.J., Humanities Press.

BECKER, C. 1985. 'Notes sur les conditions écologiques en Sénégambie aux 17e et 18e siècles'. *African Economic History*, 14, pp. 167–216.

CALDWELL, J.C. 1982. 'Comment on Manning'. *Canadian Journal of African Studies*, No. 16, pp. 127–130.

COALE, A. J., and DEMENY, P. 1966. *Regional Model Life Tables and Stable Populations*. Princeton, Princeton University Press.

COOK, S.F., and BORAH, W.W. 1971–79. *Essays in Population History: Mexico and the Caribbean*. 3 vols. Berkeley, University of California Press.

COOPER, F. 1977. *Plantation Slavery on the East Coast of Africa*. New Haven, Yale University Press.

COQUERY-VIDROVITCH, C. 1982. *Histoire africaine: permanences, ruptures*. Paris, Payot.

CORDELL, D.D. 1985. *Dar al-Kuti and the Last Years of the Trans-Saharan Slave Trade*. Madison, University of Wisconsin Press.

———. 'The Saharan Slave Trade'. (in progress).

CORDELL, D.D., and GREGORY, J.W. 1987. *African Population and Capitalism: Historical Studies*. Boulder.

CURTIN, P.D. 1969. *The Atlantic Slave Trade: A Census*. Madison, University of Wisconsin Press.

———. 1975. *Economic Change in Precolonial Africa: Senecambia in the Era of the Slave Trade*. 2 vols. Madison, University of Wisconsin Press.

DIAS, J.R. 1981. 'Famine and disease in the history of Angola, c. 1850–1930'. *Journal of African History* (Cambridge), Vol. 22, pp. 349–378.

DIOP-MAES, L.-M. 1985. 'Essai d'évaluation de la population de l'Afrique noire aux XVe et XVIe siècles'. *Population*, 40, pp. 855–894.

DOUGHTY, C.M. 1979. *Travels in Arabia Deserts*. 2 vols. New York, Dover.

ELTIS, D., and ENGERMAN, S.L. 1992. 'Was the slave trade dominated by men?' *Journal of Interdisciplinary History* (Cambridge), 23, pp. 237–257.

EWALD, J. 1990. *Soldiers, Traders and Slaves: State Formation and Economic Transformation in the Greater Nile Valley, 1700–1885*. Madison, University of Wisconsin Press.

FAGE, J.D. 1969. 'Slavery and the slave trade in the context of West African history'. *Journal of African History*, 10, pp. 393–404.

FETTER, B. (ed.). 1990. *Demography from Scanty Evidence: Central Africa in the Colonial Era*. Boulder and London, Lynne Reinner Publishers.

GEGGUS, D. 1989. 'Sex and age ratios in the Atlantic slave trade: Evidence from French plantations in the eighteenth century'. *Journal of African History* (Cambridge), No. 30.

HARMS, R. 1981. *River of Wealth, River of Sorrow: The Central Zaire Basin in the Era of the Slave Trade and the Ivory Trade 1500–1891*. New Haven, Yale University Press.

INIKORI, J. 1976. 'Measuring the Atlantic slave trade: Assessment of Curtin and Anstey'. *Journal of African History* (Cambridge), 17, pp. 197–233.

———. 1982. 'Introduction'. In Inikori, J.E. (ed.). *Forced Migration*. London.

———. 1987. 'Slavery and the development of industrial capitalism in England'. *Journal of Interdisciplinary History* (Cambridge), 17, pp. 771–793.

———. 1988. 'The sources of supply for the Atlantic slave exports from the Bight of Benin and the Bight of Bonny (Biafra)'. In Daget, S. (ed.). *De la traite à l'esclavage*. Nantes, Vol. 2. Pp. 25–43.

KEA, R.A. 1982. *Settlements Trade and Politics on the Seventeenth-Century Gold Coast*. Johns Hopkins Studies in Atlantic History and Culture. Baltimore, BKs Demand.

KLEIN, M.A. 1987. 'The demography of slavery in Western Soudan: The late nineteenth century'. In Dennis, D., Cordell, D.D. and Gregory, J.W. (eds.). *African Population and Capitalism: Historical Studies*. Boulder, Westview Press. Pp. 50–61.

LAW, R. 1991. 'The slave coast of West Africa, 1550–1750: The impact of the Atlantic slave trade on an African society'. *Studies in African Affairs*. Oxford, Clarendon Press.

LIVINGSTONE, D. 1874. *The Last Journals of David Livingstone in Central Africa*. 2 vols. London, Horace Waller.

LOVEJOY, P.E. 1982. 'The volume of the Atlantic slave trade: A Synthesis'. *Journal of African History* (Cambridge), 23, pp. 473–501.

LOVEJOY, P.E., and BAIER, S. 1975. 'The desert-side economy of the Central Sudan'. *International Journal of African Historical Studies*, No. 7, pp. 551–581.

LOVEJOY, P.E., and HOGENDORN, J.S. 1993. *Slow Death for Slavery: The Course of Abolition in Northern Nigeria, 1897–1936*. Cambridge, Cambridge University Press.

MANNING, P. 1981. 'The enslavement of Africans: A demographic model'. *Canadian Journal of African Studies*, 15, pp. 499–526.

———. 1988. 'The impact of slave trade exports on the population of the Western Coast of Africa, 1700–1850'. In Daget, S. (ed.). *De la traite à l'esclavage*. 2 vols. Pp. 111–134.

———. 1990. *Slavery and African Life: Occidental, Oriental. and African Slave Trades*. Cambridge, Cambridge University Press.

———. *African Population in the Slave Trade Era*. (in progress).

MANNING, P., and GRIFFITHS, W.S. 1988. 'Divining the unprovable: Simulating the demography of the Atlantic slave trade'. *Journal of Interdisciplinary History* (Cambridge), 19, pp. 177–201.

MASON, M. 1973. 'Captive and client labour and the economy of the Bida Emirate, 1857–1901'. *Journal of African History* (Cambridge), 14, pp. 453–471.

MCDANIEL, A. 1994. *Swing Low, Sweet Chariot*. Chicago, University of Chicago Press.

MEILLASSOUX, C. 1983. *Women and Slavery in Africa*. Madison, Robertson and Klein.

———. 1986. *Anthropologie de l'esclavage: le ventre de fer et d'argent*. Paris, Presses Universitaires de France.

MIERS, S., and ROBERTS, R. (eds.). 1988. *The End of Slavery in Africa*. Madison, University of Wisconsin Press.

MILLER, J.C. 1982. 'The significance of drought, disease and famine in the agriculturally marginal zone of West-Central Africa'. *Journal of African History* (Cambridge), 22, pp. 17–61.

———. 1988. *Way of Death: Merchant Capitalism and the Angolan Slave Trade, 1730–1830*. Madison, University of Wisconsin Press.

NACHTIGAL, G. 1971. *Sahara and Sudan*. 4 vols. London, Humanities Press International.

NORTHRUP, D. 1978. *Trade without Rulers: Pre-Colonial Economic Development in South-Eastern Nigeria*. Oxford, Clarendon Press.

OLIVIER DE SARDAN, J.-P. 1975. 'Captifs ruraux et esclaves impériaux du Songhay'. In Meillassoux, C. (ed.). *L'Esclavage en Afrique précoloniale*. Paris, Maspero. Pp. 99–134.

PATTERSON, K.D. 1988. 'Epidemics, famines, and population in the Cape Verde Islands, 1580–1900'. *International Journal of African Historical Studies*, 21, pp. 291–313.

RENAULT, F. 1989. 'The structures of the slave trade in Central Africa in the nineteenth century'. In Clarence-Smith, W.G. (ed.). *The Economics of the Indian Ocean Slave Trade in the Nineteenth Century*. London, Frank Cass. Pp. 146–165.

ROBERTSON, C., and KLEIN, M. (eds.). 1983. *Women and Slavery in Africa*. Madison, University of Wisconsin Press.

RODNEY, W. 1966. 'African slavery and other forms of social oppression on the Upper Guinea Coast in the context of the Atlantic slave trade'. *Journal of African History*, 7, pp. 431–443.

———. 1972. *How Europe Underdeveloped Africa*. Kent, Howard University Press.

SEARING, J.F. 1993. *West African Slavery and Atlantic Commerce: The Senegal River Valley 1700–1860*. Cambridge, Cambridge University Press.

SHERIFF, A. 1987. *Slaves, Spices and Ivory in Zanzibar: Integration of an East African Commercial Empire into the World Economy 1770–1873*. London, James Currey.

THORNTON, J. 1977. 'An eighteenth-century baptismal register and the demographic history of Manguenzo'. In Fyfe, C., and McMaster, D. (eds.). *African Historical Demography*. Edinburgh, University of Edinburgh Press. Vol. 1. Pp. 405–415.

———. 1981a. 'The slave trade in eighteenth-century Angola: Effects of demographic structures'. *Canadian Journal of African Studies*, 14, pp. 417–427.

———. 1981b. 'The demographic effects of the slave trade on Western Africa, 1500–1800'. In Fyfe, C., and McMaster, D. (eds.). *African Historical Demography*. Edinburgh, University of Edinburgh Press. Vol. 2.

———. 1988. 'The art of war in Angola, 1575–1680'. *Comparative Studies in Society and History*, 30, pp. 360–378.

VANSINA, J. 1992. *Paths in the Rainforests*. Madison, University of Wisconsin Press.

Chapter 11

The Mental Route of the Slave: A Few Thoughts Inspired by the Present-Day Situation of the Black Peoples

Joseph Ki-Zerbo

THE SLAVE TRADE should not be a tragic, closely circumscribed episode like a file that has been archived; nor should it be a situation that is regularly cited or recalled with a perverse relish verging on masochism. But is this possible?

One thing is certain: when Africans are today encouraged, or indeed forced, to close the parentheses formed by the past and take their place in the world economy – the fundamental (or fundamentalist?) basis for salvation – bad memories are bound to come flooding back.

What sort of integration? For whose benefit? These are not metaphysical questions. For centuries, Africa's induced or forced integration into the world economy took place against a background of exploitation and domination. It could be described as the integration of the 'horse with the rider', although even horses had a higher status than the slaves integrated into the plantation economy.

The emigration from Europe was celebrated in lyrical or epic language, especially by poets like Luis de Camoens (1525–80) and José María de Heredia (1842–1905):

> Like a flight of falcons from their native charnel house,
> Tired of bearing their haughty distress.

These were the 'conquerors'. This type of emigration had nothing in common with the slave route. The emigration of Europeans making a break with the past led to immigration as a structural phenomenon, with the creation on another continent – whether Africa, America or Asia – of fellow nation-states built on the ruins of formerly independent entities. No connection can be made between such migration and the centuries-long draining from Africa of 'tools' for the West, of its people considered as 'ebony' or 'black ore',[1] as timber or firewood for the 'triangular trade'.

Black African history is unique because of the gaps in its itinerary. In spite of the tremendous efforts made by UNESCO to reconstruct this longest evolution in the world, the history of Africa[2] is little known or is misunderstood, through the fault of the African leaders themselves. Above all, we should make no mistakes about objectives or adversaries. The history of Africa should not be a Wailing Wall but should fuel the collective consciousness which leads peoples to self-fulfilment.

Although the slave trade is a phenomenon whose dates and places are known, it is difficult to situate it strictly in a limited time or space. It was planet-wide in scale, if only because of the host of diasporas it created and the economies it strengthened or ruined. Its long-lasting effects constitute a problem that cannot be considered in terms of the ecological, demographic, economic and other results which, like stigmata, still affect the landscapes, the shape of the population pyramid and the unbalanced structure of misdirected development.

Even today, the slave trade still tolls like a funereal bell in the innermost recesses of the conscious and subconscious minds of peoples. Back in the nineteenth century, its abolition was celebrated with great pomp, following the generous campaigns led by various philanthropists, who deserve tribute. People had applauded the end of a continent-wide genocidal exodus and had decided that the answer lay in the integration of Africa with the rest of the world through legitimate trade.

However, from the fifteenth century onwards and for four hundred years, under the impetus of medieval trading across the Sahara and of the prevailing mercantile system, the Europeans had been satisfied to harvest rare and precious commodities on the basis of their ratio of value to weight. In this respect, 'black ore' topped the list, as we know.

At a second stage, with the emergence of industrial capitalism, the time came to exploit Africa on a different basis by 'abolishing' slavery and developing the mining industry – which accounted for 50 per cent of all African exports in 1913 – and the cash crops needed to supply European factories, and by using the Africans' ability to buy and consume, as well as their productive capacity. Territories were conquered and occupied, and the best land was expropriated in order to guarantee sources of supply. It was no mere chance that the United Kingdom, the leading industrial power at that time, was, through its actions and its ideological approach, in the forefront of this movement, which sought the abolition of slavery as a 'legitimate trade'. On the basis of the dual mandate which the 'powers' arrogated to themselves at the Berlin conference (1884–86), the Europeans formulated their concept of a duty to provide Africans with the benefits of material and moral civilisation, while exploiting Africa's wealth. This was the basis on which Lord Lugard proposed the system of indirect rule, designed to ensure that the mandate to exploit the continent did not overshadow the civilising mission.

Similarly, it was not by chance that South Africa, which was the country best fitted for that type of exploitation, was not only the first where the mining industry took off, but also the first to demonstrate that the mandate for exploitation was incompatible with the civilising mission.

With the coming of colonisation, it was no longer the Africans themselves who were bought and sold but the sweat of their labour, through a kind of refining of the 'black ore'. Thus, by spreading over almost the entire continent, colonisation may have extorted as many working hours from Africans in more or less a single century as the slave trade had done over four centuries. In the Belgian Congo of King Leopold II, for example, the whole population was forced to collect rubber in appalling conditions. In fact, the harvesting of commodities lasted for as long as cost calculations made it preferable to any new technical input, and it went on right into the twentieth century – from spices at the time of the sailing ships to shea nuts in the atomic era. For centuries, investment in Africa amounted to less than the cost of maintaining the African labour force. In order to put this force to work, a whole array of legal, administrative, financial and policing measures was deployed, including forced labour, 'compulsory work', poll taxes, the development of new needs, monetisation, unequal terms of trade, and structural adjustment.

Nowadays, financial capitalism has given rise to an economy that is mainly speculative and electronically driven, and is completely dissociated from the production of goods. It does not leave much 'market share' to Africa in terms of quantity (only 1.5 per cent of the world market). Above all, however, in qualitative and structural terms, the role and function of almost all the African countries have not changed significantly. The structure of the balance of trade or of payments has not varied.

As in the past, our exports consist almost exclusively of raw materials. There are very few exceptions to this rule, and the liberalisation of trade does not leave much choice for national production units other than to be swept away or to be integrated into foreign or transnational parent companies.

African workers who are addicted to gambling on horse-racing in France and who know more about the pedigree of the horses running at the Longchamp or Chantilly racecourses than about the realities of their own countries or even their families, African plutocrats who transfer their countries' inheritance to banks in the developed world, and African parliamentarians who sell off their peoples' assets in privatisations imposed by the international financial institutions – all take part in the 'mining' economy which has not fundamentally changed since the fifteenth century. In terms of structural history, the overall pattern of Africa's relations with the 'powers' has not been transformed for the past five hundred years. It is true that the presentation and packaging of its 'black ore' has changed but, as the Secretary-General of the Organisation of African Unity (OAU) has said, the net capital flows from Africa to Europe demonstrate that the drain is still continuing. The 'slave traders' are also still there in the person of arms sellers or traffickers as in the eighteenth century, and of financial experts laden with files, advanced technologies and 'conditionalities'. There are often also petty African monarchs who are privileged partners, or middlemen who cannot be bypassed.

Unfair terms of trade often lead to a stage of 'non-trade', which is still more serious for Africa's national micro-economies because it means that there is no work for a high proportion of young Africans, whether they are qualified or not. Subsidised milk and meat from Europe reduce to naught the labour and the skills of workers in the Sahelian countries.

The end of the slave route does not lie in the dead-end of the Wailing Wall or in a radical breaking away, which is in fact physically impossible because satellites and cable television do not recognise non-alignment. What is needed is more a radical mutation, in the first place in people's minds – a Copernican revolution in people's consciences, an ethical and cultural about-face founded on a number of structural and infrastructural conditions. However, if we are to change routes, we have to know where we are going. As Seneca said: 'There is no such thing as a favourable wind for those who do not know where they are going.'

Knowing ourselves and knowing where we are going are the two most urgent conditions for leaving the slave route.

From the standpoint of methodology, a distinction has to be made between history as a 'science' and history as 'consciousness'. History as a science involves factual research and the interpretation of history by a reading of the facts. History as consciousness entails going beyond science (but not abolishing it) through an investment of bygone times in a future in which both past and present act as a fertilising agent.

If that is true, the slave route must end outside the world of servitude, of unhappy and vanquished consciousness, far from what Aimé Césaire has called 'the fugitive night of bitter salt; the night of the snuffed-out Negro and the dog'. This is why freeing minds, as the founders of UNESCO understood rightly and intuitively, is the first stage in the exodus to salvation which must follow the violent and bloody exodus imposed on tens of millions of Africans.

Nowadays, history as consciousness is vital to the citizens of the world. How can we pull the human caravan out of the slave route, out of the beaten track of acquisition, knowledge and, ultimately, power? One of the main ways out of this predicament is endogenous development, which starts by changing peoples' minds and directing them towards everyday democracy and African integration. All the rest only amounts to the shedding of crocodile tears in the muddy river of human violence, whether naked or 'legal'. There is no point in weeping. An African saying puts this in a nutshell: 'What point is there in weeping when it is raining? Nobody will notice!' What we say is that there has to be 'endogenous development'.

What we have to understand is that the slave's route cannot be the same as that of its master. Trying to make up for lost time by forcing the pace or by aping others will not help Africans to draw level with those who are ahead of us. Nobody has ever seen railway carriages catch up with the engine. It is for Africans to become the engine in our turn, if only in our own sphere, by taking the short cut of our own personality.

The slave trade meant that one of the varieties of humankind's unique and common species was turned into an object. We need no greater proof than the notorious contract concluded by the Compagnie de Cacheu et du Cap-Vert in 1690, which stipulated that 10,000 tons of black slaves corresponding to a given amount of 'pieces of India' (the units of accounting for the trade in human merchandise) should be collected.

Africa's inhabitants were valued in currency of accounting, with fractions and multiples of the slave standard ('the piece of India'), which was worth, for example, one woman and two adolescents. This accounting value is therefore totally divorced from the legal and ethical value of each human individual. For special purposes, slaves' body parts that were considered a hindrance would be cut off, such as genitals to create eunuchs, tongues to produce mute domestic servants, and arms and legs to prevent escape. The slave trade went on for so long that Negroes were by definition identified as slaves. In the *Dictionnaire Universel Français* published in 1709, the term 'Negro' meant 'a slave taken from the coast of Africa'.

It can therefore be readily understood why, at the insistence of Moshud Abiola, who chaired the 'Group of Eminent Persons', the OAU demanded reparations for the damage suffered by the African continent. The economic and material damage pales in comparison with the ethical crimes committed, not only against the black variety of *Homo sapiens* but against the human species as a whole. The slave's struggle was a combat for humankind. Pope John Paul II clearly understood this when, in Gorée, he publicly asked Africa for forgiveness.

As long as there is no official recognition of this historic and fundamental crime against the species, as has been the case for other systematic genocides, slaves routes will continue to spread all over the world.

All in all, however, in the final analysis everything is in the hands of the slaves themselves: both their future and that of their masters. In the circumstances, one's self-image and one's image of others are the greatest tyrants, but also the first liberators. The image of oneself and for oneself and awareness of oneself and for oneself are the most precious capital assets. Economic parameters alone show only a limited part of African reality. However, on the African continent, the collective image of the self and of others remains blurred or misleading. This image has been exploded, in social terms, by inequalities that are constantly growing but (unlike inequalities elsewhere) are completely sterile, because they do not generate a dynamic process. They create wealth without accumulation.

Furthermore, from the ethnic standpoint, this image has been shattered by national borders. Old identities are lost, while new ones – those of the nation-state – remain embryonic or are trapped between grass-roots communities and geo-cultural areas or economic giants operating on a worldwide scale.

Real development, which entails starting out from the self to move towards the self at a higher level through exchanges with others, has been blocked in Africa. How can we 'develop ourselves' if we do not know ourselves? However, knowing ourselves means perceiving ourselves and coming to terms with ourselves as the embodiment of memory and of designs for the future.

In the outside world, the image of Africa for which we are responsible is often negative. Disqualifying Africans as being congenitally incapable of development – virtually forcing them to turn their backs on themselves in order to attain development – gives rise to many and sometimes monstrous contradictions whereby aid is seen as the take-over of a continent regarded as innately handicapped and accordingly 'excused' from making the necessary efforts to develop itself. The way Africans are looked at by others gives many of them crippling complexes, and this lack of self-assurance starts off the vicious circle of stagnation.

Indeed, self-confidence is the first step towards real development.

Whenever young Africans, crushed under the weight of vague and unhappy consciousness, ask themselves 'Are we cursed?' it means that they are still following the slave route.

Whenever an African leader chooses to enlist the services of an 'expatriate', whom he automatically regards as being more credible, and mistrusts those of his own compatriots who are among the leading experts, he drives his people into a kind of prison from which there is no escape.

Whenever African intellectuals prefer to quote or recite the paradigms with which the master peoples have filled their brains instead of taking the difficult short cut of independent thought and inventiveness, of the harsh journey of initiation, they still have a long way to travel on the slave route.

There are still countless Africans who, willingly or reluctantly, take the well-worn paths of slavery imposed by native or foreign tyrants. The petty African kings who are the same colour as their subjects are, in some respects, even more of a threat. Yet, just as in the past, it sometimes happens that they, too, come to be included among the mass of people they have sold.

Too many black people travel this route. They laugh out loud in self-exculpation or smile cynically or irresponsibly; they do not have to account for their actions to anybody since there are no courts to judge memory, no collective purpose. There are likewise no courts to judge the consciences of people who are deaf, dumb and blind.

The mass of the people are too downtrodden to react with a burst of energy. The leaders are often too cunning or too drunk with success to allow civil society greater freedom of action.

What can be done? We have to change our route and take the nearest turning off, if possible through the force of reason and if necessary through the force of arms – the peaceful arms of the people.

Notes

1. The expression is taken from the Haitian poet René Depestre.
2. *The General History of Africa* is published by UNESCO in eight volumes. The English version is complete, and the last two volumes of the French version (5 and 8) have gone to press.

Chapter 12

Conditions of Slaves in the Americas

Paul E. Lovejoy

The Importance of the African Dimension

As a specialist on slavery in Africa and the slave trade, I am pleased to make suggestions on the directions and themes that might profitably be explored in future research in elaborating on the conditions of slaves in the Americas. Such a broad theme might be approached in a variety of ways, including an examination of the material living standards of enslaved Africans in the Americas, their working conditions, their medical problems and general state of health, or numerous other aspects of their existence as human beings in a situation of chattel slavery. While there is already extensive research on many aspects of these questions, it is very likely that future research will add much to our collective knowledge of the slave experience. Certainly an Africanist perspective on these topics can provide a comparative dimension that would assist in understanding the backgrounds of enslaved Africans.

Instead, I would like to suggest that the methodologies and research results of the past several decades of Africanist history can be used much more effectively in the examination of the conditions of slaves in the Americas than has been the case until now. Specifically, it is now possible to say much more about the identities of the enslaved people who were brought to the Americas from Africa; that is to say, the enslaved black population in the Americas can be viewed as Africans, not just as people who were forcibly transported from Africa. In so doing, I am suggesting that there be a fuller appreciation that Africans in the Americas were active agents in reformulating their own cultural and social identities, despite the oppressive settings to which they were subjugated. By emphasising the individuals who comprised the enslaved population, I am constituting an 'Afrocentric' historical view of the evolution of the African diaspora.

The issue of agency is important in unravelling the history of Africans outside of Africa. Of course, scholars have frequently taken the conscious actions of slaves into consideration in studying slave resistance, and there have been important contributions in our understanding of religion, cultural expression (including music, cuisine, naming patterns, etc.) and social relationships (kinship, ethnicity and shipboard friendships). Once upon a time these cultural artefacts were perceived as 'survivals' of a pristine African civilisation that was both unchanging and timeless.[1] Only recently have scholars generally accepted these features of slave culture as the conscious and not-so-conscious decisions made by the people themselves, selecting from their collective experiences those cultural and historical attributes that helped make sense of their experience of slavery in the Americas. Although the slave regime brutalised individuals to the extent that some died without entering into meaningful and sustainable forms of social and cultural interaction with their compatriots, most slaves more or less successfully re-established communities, reformulated their sense of identity and reinterpreted ethnicity in the context of slavery or freedom in the Americas. More than simply the foundation for individual and collective acts of resistance, these expressions of agency involved the transfer and adaptation of the contemporary world of Africa to the Americas and were not mere 'survivals' of some diluted and lipid African past. Despite the 'social death' of which Patterson speaks,[2] slaves created a new social world that drew on the known African experience. Certainly the horrors of enslavement, the rough march to coastal ports and the trauma of the middle passage affected the psychological and medical health of the enslaved population, but not to the extent imagined by Elkins, at least not in most cases.[3] After their arrival in the Americas, Africans entered upon a new social life, one which drew on the past but adapted to the present. While their resurrection from Patterson's 'social death' was distorted by chattel slavery, many enslaved Africans were none the less healthy enough to participate in the '200 Years' War' of which Patterson also writes.[4]

From the perspective of Africa, therefore, it would be fruitful to examine the condition of slaves in the Americas on the basis that they were still Africans, even if they did not perceive of themselves in the pan-African terms of recent times; the evolution of such solidarity has to be examined historically for different times and different places. Rather, I am arguing that many slaves in the Americas, perhaps the great majority, interpreted their lived experiences in terms of their personal histories, and in that sense the African side of the Atlantic continued to have meaning. Often slaves, former slaves and their descendants still considered themselves Africans, no matter whether they reinterpreted that identity in reformulated ethnic terms (Nago, Coramantee, Mandingo, Pawpaw, etc.), in religious terms (Male/Muslim, Kongo Christian, animist) or in some other manner. Efforts to return to Africa by boat or by joining the world of the ancestors through suicide have special meaning in this sense.

This emphasis on the African context of slave identity affects how we understand the process of creolisation under slavery. The influential approach of Sidney Mintz and Richard Price emphasises the blending of cultures in the formation of a new Creole identity.[5] In my opinion, their approach underestimates the importance of the contemporary African experiences of those enslaved individuals who were deported to the Americas. Consequently, the Mintz/Price emphasis on the creolisation process has tended to minimise the continuities between Africa and the Americas. Once the importance of the African dimension is recognised, the creolisation of the slave and free populations of the Americas becomes a dynamic merger of cultures — European and African. The Africa that entered the Creole mentality was neither static nor ossified as if caught in an anthropological past. Rather, the Africa that was taken to the Americas was the product of the specific historical contexts that had shaped individual slaves.

Problems of Methodology

Because enslaved Africans sometimes interpreted their American experience in terms of the contemporary world of Africa, efforts to understand the conditions of slaves in the Americas have to take full cognizance of the political, economic and social conditions prevailing in those parts of Africa from which the individual slaves had actually come. The intellectual and cultural lens through which they viewed their new lives in the Americas had been fashioned in Africa. Hence, there was a tendency for many enslaved Africans to make sense of their oppression through reference to religious and social norms brought from Africa. The conditions of slavery were set on board ships, at the auction block, in the mines and on plantations. But how enslaved Africans responded to these conditions depended as much on their roots in Africa as on the labour regime of the Americas. How to get at this carry-over of experience presents difficulties for historians and other scholars, but there is no reason to doubt that there was a transfer of experience, whether voluntary or involuntary, as was the case with other immigrants.

As a first approximation, it is essential to unravel the complicated and often incompletely known movement of individuals from point of enslavement to coastal port and from there to the different parts of the Americas. This exercise includes a study of the demography of the trade, an effort which has made considerable advances in the past 25 years, since the pioneering study by Curtin.[6] Despite ongoing critique and revision, the regional origins of slaves by specific time period and according to age and sex are now known with reasonable certainty. The correlation of these quantifiable data with local political events and economic factors, at least in broad outline, is now possible as well.[7] No matter how they are viewed, large or small numbers cannot adequately express the terrible suffering of the people who were caught up in the trade. In order to compensate for this weakness, biographical accounts of individuals and a sociological analysis of such accounts can usefully supplement statistical data to help in understanding not only where individual slaves came from but also how they were enslaved, and thereby assist in analysing the process by which individuals formed new communities and new identities under slavery. What demographic analysis can do, however, is contribute to our knowledge of the regional and ethnic origins of the exported slave population and thus guide scholars along fruitful lines of enquiry. Statistical data are therefore useful in identifying patterns in why, when and how individuals were enslaved and indirectly may assist in revealing what aspects of personal experience were important to slaves in the Americas. Although not all contemporary events in Africa continued to have meaning for people once they arrived in the Americas, the reasons for enslavement and deportation almost certainly did. Subsequent ethnic and religious identification in the Americas was often based on common experiences at the time of enslavement, transfer to the coast and transatlantic passage. Hence, greater knowledge of the experiences of slaves from the time of enslavement until the point of export is essential in unravelling the Africanness of slave identify. The underlying factors contributing to this African identity were intertwined with the history of specific regions, states and places, which requires an understanding of local history in as much detail as possible. The task of reconstructing this local history clearly is not limited to the study of slavery and the slave trade, although surely the relative importance of transatlantic slavery is a major issue in the study of the African past. This agenda of historical reconstruction is now being pursued both in national universities within Africa and among scholars worldwide to an extent that is daunting to specialists and non-specialists alike. For scholars of slavery in the Americas who seldom venture across the Atlantic to the African homeland, the rapid and voluminous changes in documentation and analysis are a special problem. It is hard enough to stay abreast of advances in any area of specialisation, and crossing the Atlantic to look closely at African history is a big task. But difficulties duly considered, it is fully as important to keep abreast of advances in African history as to do so in European history. The proper study of slavery in the Americas requires the study of two diasporas and their interrelationships with their home cultures and societies, both African and European, and with each other. Unfortunately, though perhaps to be expected, if no longer acceptable, the African dimension has suffered from an ongoing status of inferiority and neglect while the European dimension has not.

The methodology that is required to uncover the active linkages between Africa and the Americas must begin with a comprehensive knowledge of African history and the application of standard historical techniques in reconstructing the past of Africans who were forcibly moved to the Americas. It is a sad comment on the state of slave studies in the Americas that this common sense is often ignored. Some of the best scholarship makes assumptions about the African past that ignore the application of standard historical methodology, including the central importance of chronology, the examination of change over time, the critique of all available source materials, the insistence that later events and phenomena not be read back into the distant past, and other aspects of the discipline that are or should be taught in virtually every introductory history course. In defiance of these fundamental principles of historical scholarship, slave studies are too often imbued with historical generalisations about the nature of the African past. The treatment of religion and ethnicity, to mention two of the most glaring applications of historicism, can be cited as examples. Twentieth-century anthropological data on African religious thought and practices cannot be used with much effect to explain slave religion any more than late twentieth-century Christianity in all its complexity can tell us about Christianity under slavery. Similarly, twentieth-century ethnic labels cannot willy-nilly be applied to the seventeenth and eighteenth centuries. Indeed, terms such as Yoruba and Igbo, to cite two of the most important examples, had no currency in Africa in the days of the transatlantic slave trade. The terms appear to have arisen in the context of the slave trade itself.

The complexities of African religious history are blurred for a variety of reasons, most especially because there has been little research done on this important topic, except with respect to Islam. Instead of a full examination of how religion is interpreted differently in different times and places and how religion is related to ideology and political structure, 'traditional African religion' is presented as static and all-embracing in vast parts of the continent. Observations from widely different times and places are merged to fabricate a common tradition that may or may not have legitimacy, untested and generalised as the concept is.[8]

As a result, the religious history of Africans from the Bight of Benin, the Bight of Biafra, Kongo and the interior of Angola is reduced to the meaningless concept of being 'traditional'. By contrast, Christianity in the Americas receives full treatment in its complexity, while until recently the African contribution to the spread of Christianity among slaves in the Americas has received little attention.[9] The same standards of historical reconstruction should apply to the study of the African religious tradition as to the examination of the impact of missions and evangelicalism in the Americas. Twentieth-century anthropological analysis of religion cannot be read back into the eighteenth century without considerable risk and certainly not without confirmation from contemporary documents. Unfortunately, specialists of slavery in the Americas generally have not sought such confirmation.[10] The result is bad anthropology and even worse history. A critical examination of the condition of slaves must begin in Africa, and that examination must use the same rigorous historical methodology that characterises other areas of history.

One area of analysis that is particularly fraught with historical generalisation concerns issues relating to ethnicity.[11] With few exceptions, the study of slavery in the Americas has tended to treat ethnicity as a static feature of the culture of slaves. Twentieth-century ethnic categories in Africa are often read backwards to the days of slavery, thereby removing ethnic identity from its proper contemporary context – both political and social. Mullin, for example, is certainly correct in noting that 'tribal' is no longer 'good form', though not for the reasons that he supposes, and certainly 'ethnicity' is not 'a euphemism for tribal', as he claims.[12] The concept of ethnicity is a particularly valuable tool for unravelling the past because it is a complex phenomenon tied into very specific historical situations. What should one make of the fact that 'Akan' or 'Coramantee' were the backbone of maroon communities in Jamaica[13] or that 'Yoruba' or 'Nago' were often behind slave unrest in Bahia?[14]

Since specific ethnic identifications had meaning only in relation to other ethnic categories, their importance has to be examined with reference to the boundaries that separated different ethnic categories from each other, including the political, religious and economic dimensions of these differences and how these changed over time. Certainly, historical associations with Africa were also essential features of these definitions of community, and rather than being static, the links with Africa were seldom disconnected from events across the Atlantic.

Before the abolition of the transatlantic trade in enslaved Africans, new slaves were constantly arriving and thereby infusing slave communities in the Americas with new information and ideas which had to be assimilated in ways that we do not fully understand at present. The movements of former slaves, both before abolition and especially afterwards, continued these contacts. Being 'Nago' in Bahia in the early nineteenth century was not the same as being 'Yoruba' in West Africa. Uncovering why this was so and what was meant by these labels at the time is a major task whose undertaking will inform any analysis of the slave condition.

Personal Profiles of Slaves

The analysis of ethnicity, religion and culture can benefit from the collection of biographical information on individual slaves. The importance of this material in examining the condition of the enslaved population once it reached the Americas is widely recognised, but such materials are also important in understanding the African background of slave culture and identity. Instances of princes and prosperous merchants who found themselves in the Americas after being kidnapped, 'panyarred' or otherwise 'wrongly' seized dot the historical record. Some of these cases have been well-documented,[15] but I would suggest that their full significance in the formulation of identities and communities among slaves in the Americas has yet to be explored, and that the main task of collecting such information has scarcely begun. Plantation records, newspaper advertisements and other materials that are now standard sources of information should be re-examined for their African content because crucial information that makes sense to specialists in African history is unrecognisable to non-specialists.

Sometimes the circumstances surrounding enslavement and export surface clearly and sometimes they are obscured, but it should not be doubted that there is considerable documentation that awaits analysis. Even the well-known biographies that have struck us as oddities deserve to be reread more carefully, whether those of literate Muslims who dumbfounded their less educated masters or those relating chance encounters between European merchants and African merchants and princes who had once done business with each other, especially those of precocious youths who gained the favour of masters or mistresses who themselves were atypical, and similar unusual circumstances. Most of these instances pertain to males, and given the extent to which white masters and overseers controlled the fate of African women, it is astonishing that less is known about the personal histories of women.

Once European abolitionists began to patronise freed slaves and relatively visible domestic servants, these biographies became more numerous. Unfortunately for our task in unravelling the African dimension, many of these later cases tend to involve individuals born in the Americas, and the efforts to publicise the tragic stories of these individuals for abolitionist purposes usually suppressed memories of the African past, other than to emphasise the 'enlightenment' arising from conversion to Christianity. None the less, these stories, whether published or not, have the potential for revealing much additional information on the extent of the linkages between the lived experiences of slaves in the Americas with the remembered past of Africa.

What is required are new techniques to analyse these biographical materials, especially when they are derived from testimonies of individuals born in the Americas and not in Africa. Linguistic data, African names, social customs associated with birth, marriage and death, and other materials may be suggestive of the African connection, but their significance has to be examined carefully. In any event, such methodologies must be rooted in a thorough understanding of the contemporary African setting.[16] In many cases, it is essential to examine the process whereby the African experience was reduced to tradition in the Americas. Personal names, religious practices and other features of the African past — the very items referred to by previous generations of scholars as 'survivals' — can provide keys that open unexpected doors back to Africa. A chance Muslim name, for example, may well reveal a tradition of Islam that might otherwise pass unnoticed.[17] As cultural features entered into tradition their significance changed, and hence it is essential to distinguish among a variety of possible meanings in analysing (1) specific attributes and what they reveal about the past and the association with Africa, (2) how an attribute has become a device for the transmission of tradition and hence has become divorced from historical reality and entered the realm of myth, and (3) how European recording and interpretation of information has distorted, simplified or otherwise changed the material being analysed.

Resistance to Slavery and the Abolition Movement

The African dimension stands out in some notable examples of resistance to slavery in the Americas, which can be re-examined in the light of additional research conducted in Africa and after renewed consideration of methodological issues arising from their interpretation. As Genovese has observed, there was a fundamental shift in the patterns of resistance by slaves, which he correlated with the French Revolution and the destruction of slavery in Santo Domingo.[18] Before the 1790s, slave resistance tended to draw inspiration from the African past; afterwards, the creolisation of slave society brought slave thinking more into line with the revolutionary movement emanating from Europe. The difficulties with this interpretation are twofold. First, Genovese and other scholars who have followed this line of argument have not been well-versed in African history; hence, their image of the African contribution to resistance remains cloudy. Secondly, influences from Africa remained a strong force in the struggle against slavery well after the 1790s, especially in Brazil and Cuba. Despite these reservations, Genovese has drawn attention to an important trend: the complex blending of African and European experiences through the process of creolisation. Undoubtedly, motivations and inspirations for resistance to slavery changed over time.

Rebellion and running away (*marronnage*) were fundamentally political acts, but except for a vague notion that the African backgrounds of slaves influenced the decisions of slaves to conspire, there has been very little attempt to correlate slave resistance in the Americas with events in Africa. None the less, there are clear examples of such overt links, as in the case of the Male uprising in Brazil in 1835. Muslim slaves from the Central Sudan, many seized in the *jihad* associated with the foundation and expansion of the Sokoto caliphate, were responsible for staging this revolt, which came after almost thirty years of intensive and active discontent among the slave and former slave populations of Bahia, particularly those identified as Nago and/or Muslim.[19] As I have argued elsewhere, the uprising of Muslim slaves in Ilorin in 1817 and again in the early 1820s, which was an extension of the *jihad*, was a much more likely source of inspiration for Muslim Yoruba in Bahia than the slave revolt in Santo Domingo. Furthermore, the fact that a very large proportion of the Muslim population in Bahia appears to have been political prisoners who were deliberately deported to the Americas from the Sokoto caliphate highlights the role of agency to an extent that fleshes out our earlier attempts to equate some forms of slave resistance to the African experience.[20] It should be noted that these particular acts of resistance occurred well after the French Revolution and are much better understood within the tradition of *jihad* in West Africa than with revolutionary events in Europe.

As this example demonstrates, readily available information can be used to elaborate on the slave condition and the response of slaves to their tragic predicament. Although the Male revolt was one of the most serious instances of resistance to slavery, my purpose here is not to emphasise once again the extent of resistance to the violence of slavery, important as that was. Instead, my purpose is to draw attention to the kinds of information that can be used in deciphering the African component to the slave condition. The testimony that often surrounded the repressive measures following rebellions and the efforts to suppress *marronnage* allows not only an analysis of the resistance itself, but also a deeper penetration into the cultural identities and expressions of community solidarity that underlay much of the slave experience.

The association between the abolition movement and African resistance to slavery is a controversial point. Abolitionism is usually associated with European thought, especially as expressed by Enlightenment thinkers in Britain and in northern North America. Davis and other scholars have provided useful, even insightful, analysis of this phenomenon, but the premise of much of this analysis overlooks the slaves themselves.[21] Even specialists of

Africa have inadvertently overlooked the importance of black abolitionist thought and action. Thus Klein writes:

> There is no evidence … that slavery was seriously attacked in any part of the world before the eighteenth century. The abolition movement had its origins in a change in European consciousness.[22]

Klein attributes this change to the Enlightenment, thereby ignoring changes in thinking that were taking place among slaves and former slaves in the Americas.

However, as Beckles has argued, there was an 'indigenous antislavery movement' among Africans in the Americas. That is, abolitionism was as much a black response to slavery as a European phenomenon, and hence the concentration on the abolition movement in the standard literature as a white, European movement is only part of the story.[23] It remains to be seen how Africans who were subjected to slavery in the Americas transformed their ideas about slavery, particularly about an institution of servitude that was acceptable in Africa and to which many Africans had been exposed even before their own enslavement, but which was no longer acceptable in the Americas. The conditions of slavery in the Americas were such that the ideological framework that countenanced slavery was transformed into abolitionism.

The transition in the patterns of resistance which eventually merged African and European historical experiences ultimately resulted in a movement to abolish slavery itself. The reasons for this fundamental development arose directly out of the condition of slaves in the Americas as well as the European Enlightenment. Whereas in Africa slavery had been common, opposition to slavery as an institution appears to have been confined essentially to Islamic prohibitions (which were frequently not observed) to the enslavement of Muslims and to the individual actions of disgruntled slaves.[24] Certainly, many slaves who remained in Africa also objected to their bondage, and it is apparent that some of those who were exported to the Americas had proved difficult to their masters and hence were sold as a consequence. As in the Americas, flight from slavery and other acts of resistance were common in Africa, and there were efforts to restrain excessive abuse, to redeem family members and to ransom prisoners from bondage. Despite this tradition of resistance that can be traced back to Africa, the experiences of the enslaved men, women and children before they reached the Americas had not otherwise led to the formulation of abolitionist ideas.

The renewed deracination accompanying the ocean voyage and the humiliation of racial stereotyping that followed in the Americas fundamentally altered the perception of slavery as an institution for many slaves. Individuals who had previously not been noted as opponents of slavery as such now had to struggle against their bonds in the Americas to the point that many became firm opponents of the institution. In the Americas, there were added dimensions to this resistance, especially reactions to the racial characteristics of chattel slavery. This fundamental difference from the condition of slaves in Africa emerged gradually, although the roots of racial categories were established early. Acts of resistance that combined the efforts of indentured Irish workers, African slaves and Amerindian prisoners did occur, although in the end these alliances disintegrated.[25] Furthermore, slaves did not consolidate ethnic identifications on the basis of colour, but it was widely understood that most blacks were slaves and no slaves were white. Although there were black, mulatto and American-born slave owners in some colonies in the Americas, and although many whites did not own slaves, chattel slavery in the Americas was fundamentally different because of the racial dimension.

Conclusion

In setting out to examine the condition of African slaves in the Americas, I have chosen to concentrate on a neglected theme in the consideration of the slave condition: the African identify of the slaves themselves as perceived in the historical context of the period in which individual slaves lived. As a focal point for reflection, I want to emphasise the central place of Africa in the slave experience. By bringing Africa to the fore, my intention is to highlight the importance of agency. While it is often claimed that slaves were active participants in shaping the societies of the Americas, and studies of slave resistance often come close to demonstrating that active role, I am suggesting that Africans cannot be fully appreciated as agents in their own fate, no matter how constrained by chattel slavery that was, until there is greater appreciation of the lived experiences of slaves in Africa itself. Rather than maintaining a few cultural 'survivals' that were quaint and symbolic, Africans brought with them real issues and live interpretations of their predicament. How these were subsequently interpreted in the Americas lies at the basis of the African contribution to the process of creolisation and of resistance to and accommodation with the slave experience.

As a guideline for future research, I am suggesting that information that has often been passed over for want of significance to researchers needs to be re-examined. Specifically, biographical data need to be gathered, collated, compared and analysed with the assistance of specialists who know the history of the period and area in Africa from which individual slaves came. These biographical data are far too extensive for individual scholars to collect, although they are scattered and may not appear to be numerous enough to be significant in the context of other research. Only through a massive, international collaborative effort will it be possible to harvest this abundant resource. Equally important, the details of cultural 'survivals' – names, attributes of culture, kinship relationships, religious observances, etc. – must be collected *in situ*; that is, the exact wording of references with full supporting context has to be recorded so that specialists of African history can have the opportunity to debate the possible meanings of the data.

Oral source material is also essential. Much data of this type has already been collected scientifically by scholars over the past several decades, and there is much additional data, ultimately oral in origin, that has been gathered haphazardly by contemporary observers and transmitted through families to the descendants of slaves. Moreover, additional data are still being collected. Because of the diverse types of oral data and the many and diffused collections of such data, there is urgent need to collate information on oral data holdings and then provide for the dissemination of such data to appropriate depositories. Moreover, the complexity of the methodology required to examine these materials lends itself to a collaborative effort involving Africanist specialists as well as researchers in the Americas. Additional research should concentrate on the descendants of former slaves who returned to Africa and other identifiable groups of slaves who have been careful to preserve their family histories.

Sites and monuments that require urgent inspection, together with the collection of available oral and written documentation that explain their significance, must also be a focus of research. Such sites include the locations of returned freed slaves in Africa and cemeteries and religious shrines in the Americas. The linkages to the historical record that may be revealed in such locations will vary considerably. Cultural activities, including carnivals and the Yoruba symposia that are now being held in Cuba, also offer possibilities for identifying and isolating the ongoing historical connections among Africans in the Americas and in Africa. This focus of research is intended to be suggestive, and nothing more. The purpose is clear: to uncover the rich linkages between Africa and the Americas during the days of slavery and the period following abolition so as to correct the historical balance, which has hitherto emphasised and elaborated the linkages between Europe and the Americas out of context and with only marginal reference to Africa. It cannot be repeated too often: the conditions of slaves in the Americas depended as much on the reinterpretation of African issues and institutions as on European oppression and economics. Slaves were active agents in the establishment of new identities under slavery in the Americas, despite their forced migration and subjugation. In formulating new communities or joining established ones on existing plantations, these enslaved Africans inevitably brought Africa to the Americas. One priority of the research agenda of the Slave Route project must be the recovery of these African voices which have much to say about African history as living and suffering under slavery.

Notes

1. The search for 'survivals' or 'Africanisms' was initially associated with the anthropological research of M.J. Herskovits, 1941, and R. Bastide, 1971. For a recent addition to this approach, see J.E. Holloway, 1990.
2. O. Patterson, 1982.
3. S. Elkins, 1964.
4. O. Patterson, 1970, pp. 289–325.
5. S. Mintz and R. Price, 1992.

6. P. Curtin's study (1969) has been regularly revised, extended and amplified. The standardisation of the various statistical studies being done at the W.E.B. Dubois Center, Harvard University, is an outgrowth of this scholarship. For a recent assessment, see P.E. Lovejoy, 1989, pp. 365–394.

7. Among the preliminary attempts to correlate the export trade with developments within Africa, see P.E. Lovejoy, 1983, and P. Manning, 1990.

8. Until recently, this failure to examine contemporary religious expression and experience *within* Africa during the period of slave exports was due to the want of historical study by African historians, but this is no longer the case. See, for example, the excellent research of R. Law, 1991.

9. See J. Thornton, 1992, although at times Thornton may have overstated the case with respect to the extent to which Africans from the interior of West Central Africa were already Christian before reaching the Americas.

10. Even such classic studies as E.D. Genovese (1974) fall into this trap. Consequently, the juxtaposition of the African religious tradition and Christian conversion is an inadequate mechanism for examining the development of slave culture. At its worst, this approach fails to grasp the major developments in the historical reconstruction of the role of religion in Africa in the specific context of the slave trade.

11. Many studies consider ethnicity, although rarely in detail and without an attempt to explore the meaning of different ethnic identities in Africa and the Americas at the time. See, for example, D.C. Littlefield (1981) and P.H. Wood (1975). Demographic data, including ethnic identification on slaves in the British Caribbean, have been tabulated by B. Higman (1984), but the meaning of the different ethnic labels in historical context has yet to be studied. Similarly, Geggus (1989) has explored French shipping and plantation records to identify ethnic patterns but without analysing the historical origins in Africa in detail. Karasch (1987) has studied ethnicity in Rio de Janeiro, but again her discussion is largely static. Similarly, Hall has identified the backgrounds of many slaves in eighteenth-century Louisiana and has attempted to relate the evolution of Bambara identity in Louisiana with the history of the western Sudan in the same period. Her approach has great potential and should be contrasted with the numerous errors and superficial treatment of ethnicity in Mullin (1992).

12. M. Mullin, 1992, p. 14.

13. Cf. M. Schuler, 1970, p. 831. See also M.C. Campbell, 1990.

14. See the excellent study by J.J. Reis, 1993.

15. For an excellent collection, see P.D. Curtin, 1967. Also see the much neglected study by A.D. Austin, 1984.

16. For a preliminary study of a sample of 108 slaves exported to the Americas from the Central Sudan in the first half of the nineteenth century, see my 'Background to rebellion: The origins of Muslim slaves in Bahia', in P.E. Lovejoy and N. Rogers, 1994.

17. See A. Austin, 1993, and M.A. Gomez, 1994.

18. E.D. Genovese, 1974.

19. Reis, 1993.

20. It should be noted that my interpretation of the African component in the Male revolt is more in line with the earlier interpretation of Rodrigues and Verger than with that of Reis. See P.E. Lovejoy and N. Rogers, 1994, R.N. Rodrigues, 1932, P. Verger, 1968 and J.J. Reis, 1993.

21. D. B. Davis, 1966.

22. M.A. Klein, 'Slavery, the international labour market and the emancipation of slaves in the nineteenth century', in P.E. Lovejoy and N. Rogers, 1994.
23. Contrast H.McD. Beckles, 1990, with D.B. Davis, 1966, and R. Blackburn, 1988. Similarly, S. Drescher, 1987, frames his historical questions about abolition in terms that ignore the African contribution to the anti-slavery movement.
24. There has been little study of resistance to slavery in Africa before the late nineteenth century, but see my 'Fugitive slaves: Resistance to slavery in the Sokoto Caliphate', in G.Y. Okihiro, 1986, and 'Problems in slave control in the Sokoto Caliphate', in P.E. Lovejoy, 1986.
25. Cf. H.McD. Beckles, 1994.

Bibliography

AUSTIN, A.D. 1984. *African Muslims in Antebellum America: A Sourcebook*. New York, Garland.
———. 1993. 'Islamic identities in Africans in North America in the days of slavery (1731–1865)'. *Islam et société au sud du Sahara*, No. 7.
BASTIDE, R. 1971. *African Civilizations in the New World*. New York, Harper and Row.
BECKLES, H.McD. 1990. 'Caribbean anti-slavery: The self-liberation ethos of enslaved blacks'. *Journal of Caribbean History* (Bridgetown, Barbade), Vol. 22, No. 1/2.
———. 1994. 'The colours of property: Brown, white and black chattels and their responses to the colonial frontier'. *Slavery and Abolition* (London), Vol. 15, No. 2.
BLACKBURN, R. 1988. *The Overthrow of Colonial Slavery, 1776–1848*. London, Verso.
CAMPBELL, M.C. 1990. *The Maroons of Jamaica, 1655–1796*. Trenton, Africa World Press.
CURTIN, P.D. 1967. *Africa Remembered: Narratives by West Africans from the Era of the Slave Trade*. Madison, University of Wisconsin Press.
———. 1969. *The Atlantic Slave Trade: A Census*. Madison, University of Wisconsin Press.
DAVIS, D.B. 1966. *The Problem of Slavery in Western Culture*. Ithaca, Cornell University Press.
DRESCHER, S. 1987. *Capitalism and Antislavery: British Mobilisation in Comparative Perspective*. Oxford, Oxford University Press.
ELKINS, S. 1964. *Slavery: A Problem in American Institutional and Intellectual Life*. Chicago, University of Chicago Press.
GEGGUS, D. 1989. 'Sex ratios, age and ethnicity in the Atlantic slave trade: Data from French shipping and plantation records'. *Journal of African Study*, No. 30.
GENOVESE, E.D. 1974. *Roll Jordan Roll: The World the Slaves Made*. New York, Vintage Books.
HERSKOVITS, M.J. 1941. *The Myth of the Negro Past*. New York, Harper and Bros.
HIGMAN, B.W. 1984. *Slave Populations of the British Caribbean, 1807–1834*. Baltimore, Johns Hopkins University Press.
HOLLOWAY, J.E. (ed.). 1990. *Africanisms in American Culture*. Bloomington, University of Indiana Press.
KARASCH, M. 1987. *Slave Life in Rio de Janeiro, 1808–1850*. Princeton, Princeton University Press.

LAW, R. 1991. *The Slave Coast of West Africa, 1550–1759*. Oxford, Oxford University Press.

LITTLEFIELD, D.C. 1981. *Rice and Slaves: Ethnicity and the Slave Trade in Colonial South Carolina*. Baton Rouge, Louisiana State University Press.

LOVEJOY, P.E. 1983. *Transformations in Slavery: A History of Slavery in Africa*. Cambridge, Cambridge University Press.

———. 1989. 'The impact of the Atlantic slave trade on Africa: A review of the literature'. *Journal of African History* (Cambridge), Vol. 30, No. 3.

LOVEJOY, P.E., and ROGERS, N. 1994. 'Background to rebellion: The origins of Muslim slaves in Bahia'. In *Unfree Labour in the Development of the Atlantic World*. London, Frank Cass.

LOVEJOY, P.E. (ed.). 1986. *Africans in Bondage: Studies in Slavery and the Slave Trade*. Madison, University of Wisconsin Press.

MANNING, P. 1990. *Slavery and African Life*. Cambridge, Cambridge University Press.

MINTZ, S., and PRICE, R. 1992. *The Birth of African-American Culture: An Anthropological Perspective*. Boston, Beacon Press. [Published in 1976 in Philadelphia under the title *An Anthropological Approach to the Afro-American Past.*]

MULLIN, M. 1992. *Africa in America: Slave Acculturation and Resistance in the American South and the British Caribbean, 1736–1831*. Urbana and Chicago, University of Illinois Press.

OKIHIRO, G.Y. (ed.). 1986. *In Resistance: Studies in African Caribbean and Afro-American History*. Amherst, University of Massachusetts Press.

PATTERSON, O. 1970. 'Slavery and slave revolts: A socio-historical analysis of the first maroon war, Jamaica, 1655–1740'. *Social and Economics Studies*, Vol. 19, No. 3.

———. 1982. *Slavery and Social Death*. Cambridge, Mass., Harvard University Press.

REIS, J.J. 1993. *Slave Rebellion in Brazil: The Muslim Uprising of 1835 in Bahia*. Baltimore, Johns Hopkins University Press.

RODRIGUIES, R.N. 1932. *Os Africanos no Brasil*. Sao Paulo, Editora Nacional.

SCHULER, M. 1970. 'Akan slave rebellions in the British Caribbean'. *Savacou*, No. 1, pp. 8–31.

THORNTON, J. 1992. *Africa and Africans in the Making of the Atlantic World, 1400–1680*. Cambridge, Cambridge University Press.

VERGER, P. 1968. *Flux et Reflux de la Traite des Nègres entre le Golfe du Bénin et Bahia de Todos os Santos des XVII° et XVIII° siècles*. La Haye, Mouton.

WOOD, P.H. 1975. *Black Majority: Negroes in Colonial South Carolina from 1670 Through the Stone Rebellion*. New York, Knopf.

Chapter 13

Slavery and Society in the Caribbean (1900–1930)

Francisco López Segrera

IN THIS STUDY[1] we shall offer some pointers to an understanding of the social structure of the islands of the Caribbean. We shall first identify the similarities and differences between the former Spanish and French colonies (Cuba and Haiti), which won independence quite early, and the countries that became independent at a later date, such as Jamaica. We shall then go on to complete this comparative approach with brief case-studies of the Caribbean societies in the first decades of the twentieth century, with their particular class structures, by referring back to their forerunners in the nineteenth century.

A number of points can be singled out from among the common features which conferred a specific image on the social structure of the Caribbean. Irrespective of the dates when slavery was abolished (1791–1804 in Haiti, 1834–38 in the British colonies, 1848 in the French colonies, 1863 in the Dutch colonies, 1873–76 in Puerto Rico and 1882–86 in Cuba), social structures were deeply marked by the region's integration into the international capitalist system as a peripheral agent exporting primary commodities produced by a slave-labour based plantation economy.

The extroverted nature of economies geared to the outside world, on which they depended for inputs and markets, was reflected in the social structure, with a governing class that was both dominant and dominated. Leaders and representatives of foreign capital, associated with the white Creoles, stood at the apex of the social pyramid. Anti-nationalist oligarchies accordingly came into being, drawing their income from the services they rendered to the metropolitan colonial or neo-colonial structure of domination.

As a rule, the black majority were debarred from exercising any control over large-scale industry, trade and finance. The blacks were doubly victims of a class-based, discriminatory social structure. This was an accurate reflection of their contribution to the economy, which was essentially that of an unskilled labour force.

The economic structure of the islands of the Caribbean created the social conditions for a migratory movement to the United States, which had the effect of reducing the average cost of poorly skilled labour in the host country: unemployment in Haiti, Jamaica, Puerto Rico and Santo Domingo gave rise to migratory flows which benefited North American employers.

In order to understand the social structure of the Caribbean, it is important to supplement any study of the population of African origin by also studying the specific relations which grew up in the different types of plantations existing in those islands.

In the plantation economy of the Caribbean, the social structures had the following features in common: (1) the large-scale monopolisation of agricultural land by Europeans or white Creoles gave rise to a land-owning aristocracy exporting a small number of primary products; (2) extremely rigid social barriers – slightly less rigid in the Spanish-speaking Caribbean – were erected between the planters and their free or slave-labour force; (3) social divisions were exacerbated by racial divisions which had grown up under slavery and were to continue after its abolition.

Among the differences, it should be noted that, firstly, except in the atypical case of Haiti and that of Puerto Rico which had a specific colonial character, the fact that the non-Spanish-speaking countries became independent relatively late was both the consequence and the cause of their less acute awareness of national identity. This was due to owner absenteeism – which was typical of these colonies – and to the obstacles inherent in the system which prevented the emancipation of slaves. The result was a much greater curb on the integration of the black population into economic and social life in those colonies than in the Spanish-speaking Caribbean. Secondly, again unlike the situation in the Spanish-speaking Caribbean, their late accession to independence after a transitional process that was generally non-violent made it possible for those countries to assimilate the parent country's political model. Thirdly, each colonial power, whether Britain, France, the Netherlands or Spain, left its mark on the economic, political, cultural and social structures of its former colonies, regardless of what these had in common. This is why there were significant differences in the social structures of Cuba, Jamaica and Haiti during the period from 1900 to 1930.

In this connection, let us see what two classic sociological analyses of the countries of the Caribbean have to say about the social and ethnic composition of the region. According to Pierre-Charles:

> the social configuration was marked to varying degrees by the racial factor. Since the whites formed the slave-owning class and the blacks the mass of the slaves, class contradictions commonly led to racial conflict. The domination of the whites over people's lives was linked to their power to regulate the existence of the blacks. As a result of this inequality, there was a deep-rooted identification of the fundamental master-slave conflict with racial antagonism, accompanied by many prejudices on both sides which found expression in legal, religious and ethnic norms. The ideological rationalisation of these norms transformed the racial factor into a factor defining social status, thereby transposing the antagonism

between oppressor and oppressed into a conflict between social strata differentiated by skin colour. This effect of the social factor took on a life of its own as an element of social contradiction, which caused all class conflicts to display some degree of racial antagonism.[2]

Mintz, in his turn, wrote:

The 'racial' composition of the countries of the Caribbean is extremely diversified. In the first place, the variety of phenotypes is unusual, owing to the circumstances of immigration and to the length of the colonial period, both of which differed from one society to another. Secondly, the codes of social relations characterizing these societies take account of the variety of phenotypes, but each society uses its code with its own distinctive style. This is why, even though the concept of 'race' is important everywhere in the Caribbean, its significance and its specific applications in terms of social classification vary from one society to another. The 'maps' of these societies in terms of 'race' indicate different races, but ethnicity covers what many theoreticians consider to be the most obvious and fundamental basis of classification, namely, the class structure.[3]

Historical Background: Comparison between the Cuban Plantations and the Plantations of Haiti, the Southern United States and the Sugar-Producing Islands

The history of the plantation economy countries shows the extent to which their underdevelopment stems chiefly from their exploitation by the home country. For the European mercantilists, the wealth of a country lay in its ability to sell its factories' and colonies' goods abroad. That was why they set up a system of exploitation based on supplying slave labour and high-priced manufactured products to the colonies in exchange for raw materials to feed their budding industries. The sugar cane, cotton and indigo plantations which existed in the Caribbean in the seventeenth century supplied the burgeoning capitalist factories with cheap raw materials. These inputs, coupled with the slave trade, played a decisive role in accumulating the capital needed to finance the Industrial Revolution.[4]

The triangular trade offered British industry a threefold advantage. The blacks were bought with British manufactured products. They were transported to the plantations where they produced sugar, cotton, indigo, molasses and other tropical commodities whose processing created new industries in Great Britain; at the same time, the planters and their slaves provided an additional market for British industry, the agriculture of New England and the fisheries of Newfoundland. By about 1750, it would have been difficult to find a trading or manufacturing city in England that was not in some way involved in triangular or direct trade with the colonies. The profits generated were one of the main sources of capital whose accumulation served to finance the industrial revolution in Great Britain.[5]

That being said, if we really want to understand the factors responsible for the originality of the plantation system in Cuba over and above the sociological features which it shared to some extent with the plantations of Haiti, the sugar-producing islands and the southern United States, we must ask a number of questions. Why did the plantation economy develop in Cuba in spite of metropole – as Humboldt and Moreno Fraginals claim – and not at its instigation, as was the case in Virginia and Barbados? Why did this economy not put an end to the process of diversification but, on the contrary, find itself able to cope with some – admittedly a smaller and subordinate – measure of diversification? How can it be explained that in Haiti, Virginia and Barbados, virtually all of the slave labour was employed in the plantations, compared with less than 50 per cent in Cuba? Why was there not the same degree of awareness of national identity in the British and French West Indies (with the exception of Haiti) as there was in Cuba?

While the energetic economic policy of mercantile Great Britain enabled it to adapt its colonial empire to its capitalist economic development from as early as the seventeenth century, the economic short-sightedness of Spanish governments, coupled with the crisis which Spain was undergoing in the same century, prevented that country from organising its colonial empire in such a way as to develop its factories and achieve the initial accumulation of capital that would have made it possible to finance its industrial revolution. In Cuba, the process of autonomous development which took off in the seventeenth century generated economic interests linked to the economic development of the island. Although those interests were not major, they prevented the plantation economy from monopolising all the land.

> Thus, the development of large sugar plantations in the rest of the West Indies led, after a short period of rapid growth, to the white population monopolizing the land and replacing the small independent farmers by slaves, thereby bringing about the irremediable decline of the islands. In Cuba, on the other hand, the *cabildos* (municipal councils) took over plots of land and distributed them among neighbours, giving rise to a large class of indigenous or creole smallholders with very strong, deep rural roots.[6]

By contrast, the emergence of the plantation system in Barbados and the other sugar-producing islands reproduced a disastrous cyclical pattern in which 'the land was monopolized by the more affluent planters – who were mainly absentee landlords – while ownership of small and medium-sized plots was eliminated, white peasant farmers emigrated, and slaves were imported on a large scale'.[7]

A variety of factors account for the qualitative difference between Cuban society and the societies that grew up in the British colonies. Land in Cuba was never monopolised on the same scale as in Barbados, since the large-scale cattle breeders of Oriente and Camagüey provinces, even though dependent on the plantations in the western part of the island which they supplied with meat, did not allow themselves to be dispossessed of their land until after the Ten Years' War. Small and medium landowners did not disappear in either the eastern or the western parts of the island because the tobacco planters driven out of the area around Havana by the large sugar estates did not emigrate like those in Barbados, but went off to settle the province of Pinar del Río, where the plantation economy had not yet been established. Thus, the quantitative differences in the degree of development of the large estate-owning structures, as well as the qualitative differences – Creole owners living on their own land, the powerful economic interests of the ranchers and a large rural middle class – prevented Cuba from adopting the plantation system as thoroughly as Barbados, Virginia or Haiti. In addition, since the sugar-cane plantations, and hence the sugar trade, were in the hands of Cubans right from the outset, the interests linked with Spanish mercantilism focused not so much on the plantation system as a whole as on the labour and instruments of production to which the Creoles did not have access. Thus, the slave merchants, who at the same time lent capital for the sugar mills, grew fabulously wealthy and, with the end of the favourable economic situation (1790–1840), were responsible for the impoverishment of the Creole oligarchy. However, the export sector, which was predominantly Spanish, was unable to take control of the sugar trade until after 1860. This led to the emergence – among the ranchers and sugar-cane farmers in the eastern region and the rural and urban middle class in the over-exploited sectors of the economy linked with autonomous development – of a revolutionary ideology which brought that sector of the population closer to the slaves ('The blacks must have felt the emotion and awareness of being Cuban', wrote Fernando Ortiz, 'not with more intensity but earlier than the whites') and the burgeoning proletariat, so that political and military expression was given to the libertarian aspirations of the over-exploited masses. This prompted the oligarchy of the eastern region to take the lead in the Ten Years' War (1868–78), in the heat of which differences of colour and class faded and gave rise to the separatist ideology. In other words, in 1860, when the capital-lending Spanish traders succeeded in virtually monopolising the sugar trade and dispossessing the Cubans, the factors which were to work in favour of the integration of the Cuban nation for 30 years (from 1868 to 1898) were already present to an extremely high degree.[8] Without this dissension between the two oligarchic sectors of Cuban society (the Spanish traders lending capital to the sugar industry and the sugar plantation owners of the western region), without the contradiction and antagonism between the privileged corporatist block of Havana (Creole landowners and traders from Spain, who were advocates of the status quo and opposed the revolutionary sector of the middle class in the eastern region which aspired to independence through armed struggle) and, finally, without the other factors mentioned above, Cuba would have suffered the same fate as Barbados.

In short, the autonomous development achieved by Cuba in the seventeenth century, then the support given to the expansion of the sugar industry by colonial officials between 1790 and 1820 – under the governorships of Las Casas, Someruelos and General Cienfuegos the sugar plantation owners in the western part of the island obtained virtually everything that Arango y Parreño demanded – and finally the absolute power exercised by Governor Tacón (1834), all concurred to prevent the hegemony of a single oligarchic group which would have brought about the disappearance of the middle classes and the weakest sectors of the bourgeoisie and imposed a plantation economy system all over the island. This had a particular influence on the use of slave labour: production designed to meet domestic demand – the middle classes and the new rural and urban proletariat had to be fed and clothed – was entrusted to slaves because of the highly profitable nature of these activities, the scarcity of labour and the refusal of whites to do manual work, a prejudice that was to result in their idleness becoming a cause for concern.[9]

Some figures on the economic role of the slaves make it possible to understand more clearly how, in contrast to the situation in the British and French West Indies and the southern United States, the blacks were progressively integrated into Cuban society, in spite of the delaying and disintegrating influence of the plantation economy compared with the patriarchal slavery practised at an earlier date. These figures make it easier to grasp the decisive role played by the blacks in the emergence of Cuban nationalist sentiment during the nineteenth-century wars of independence.

In other words, in Cuba, sugar never mobilised slave labour to the same extent as in the British and French West Indies and the slave-owning south of the United States. Even in the mid-nineteenth century, when Cuba had a large number of slaves, the island's sugar industry absorbed less than 50 per cent of the slave-labour force.

We know from Humboldt that out of the 140,000 slaves engaged in the export-crop sector in 1825, only 66,000 were employed on sugar-cane plantations, and also that out of a total population of some 260,000 slaves, 28 per cent, or more than 73,000, lived in towns, where they were employed in the non-agricultural sector. According to this author, 'emancipation, encouraged by the wisdom of the legislators, was so effective that, to speak only of the present time, it created more than 300,000 emancipated blacks'.[10]

When Francis Robert Jameson visited Cuba in 1820, the island had 204 churches, 42,268 houses, 625 sugar mills, 229 coffee plantations, 1,197 horse-breeding studs, 830 ranches, 11,583 farms and workshops, and 1,691 tobacco plantations for 627,238 inhabitants, 40 per cent of whom were slaves and 15 per cent coloured freemen. The coloured population therefore represented 55 per cent of the total population.[11] Jameson concurred with Humboldt in stressing the relatively humane character of slavery in Cuba compared with the other plantation economies. For example, he wrote, 'There are many coloured people who have obtained their freedom through the additional gains authorized by the law' and who went on to work as public criers in markets, small tobacco retailers and so on; and 'Those who live in the countryside are no different from the poorest whites, with whom they have a perfectly friendly relationship'.[12] Moreover, he writes that under Spanish colonial law:

> ... they have the right to emancipation and their masters cannot refuse. In addition, they can gradually buy their freedom in the long run, depending on their means; these slaves, who are known as *coartados*, can thus work wherever and for whomever they wish by paying their masters one *real* per day for each of the hundreds of *pesos* outstanding on the loan they have contracted. Many others, although not *coartados*, are likewise authorized by their masters to work wherever

they wish on the same terms, so that an industrious slave can earn the price of his emancipation in a few years.[13]

According to the 1827 census, Cuba had 286,942 slaves. Half of these not only did not work on the sugar-cane plantations but lived in towns and engaged in non-agricultural work. Between 1830 and 1860, the manufacturing boom put an end to this predominance of urban slavery, but the sugar industry never absorbed the bulk of the slaves.[14]

According to de la Sagra, the value and distribution of rural activities in Cuba in 1830 were as follows:[15]

Type of Agriculture	Number of Slaves	Value of Slaves (in US dollars)
Sugarcane plantations	50,000	15,000,000
Coffee plantations	50,000	15,000,000
Small farms and ranches	31,065	9,319,500
Tobacco plantations	7,927	2,378,100
Total	138, 992	41,697,600

According to Pezuela,[16] in 1860, when the number of slaves employed in the sugar industry was at its peak, there were 150,000 slaves in the sugar-cane plantations, representing only 38 per cent of the total slave population and 24 per cent of the coloured population.

The figures given by de Arboleya[17] in 1855 show that at the peak of the demand for slave labour in the sugar industry, 20,000 slaves lived in towns (42 per cent of the urban adult labour force employed in manufacturing) and that the total number of wage-earning workers, blacks and whites combined, was not greater than 32,500. According to the same author, in Havana alone 400 slaves worked in the footwear industry, and out of the 14,000 workers recorded in the tobacco industry, there were 4,000 slaves who worked for themselves or were hired out by their masters.

Ramón de la Sagra provides additional evidence of the fact that the Cuban plantation economy did not succeed in completely destroying the diversification of the economy as in Virginia, Haiti or Barbados. In 1830, only between one-fourth and one-half of the rural slave population worked and lived on small tobacco plantations or on large ranches. At that time, the economic importance of ranching was such that it represented the same volume of wealth as the whole of sugar production.[18]

However, in spite of the relative integration of blacks in the Cuban plantation economy compared, for example, with the situation in Haiti, Barbados or Virginia, racial discrimination was still very marked in Cuba in the nineteenth century. This discrimination, along with the harsher slave-labour conditions implicit in the plantation economy (as opposed to the patriarchal-type slavery associated with medium-sized landowners), was to become even more marked following the criminal slaughter of blacks in the episode known to history as the Staircase Conspiracy (1884).[19]

In what way did the plantation economy in Cuba differ from those in Haiti or Virginia? The main feature of the economy of Haiti, like that of the sugar-producing islands, was the removal of the white settlers associated with the development of the national economy. These were replaced by a white oligarchy of generally absentee landlords – who employed managers and foremen to run their estates abroad – and an enormous number of slaves. There was nothing similar in Cuba, where it had not proved possible to eliminate the powerful national interests linked with the development of the island. In addition, at the outset, the sugar trade was in the hands of the Creole élite. Comparison of a few figures clearly shows up the distinctive features of the plantation economies of Cuba and Haiti and the differences between them, and the reason why the revolutionary mass movement of the Haitian slaves was able to triumph over the white French élite. In 1790, Haiti had 31,000 whites, 24,000 emancipated blacks and almost 500,000 slaves of African origin. By contrast, in Cuba in 1791, there were only 138,700 blacks out of a total population of 272,200 inhabitants, with 133,500 whites. Haiti's economic downfall had two important consequences for Cuba: it pushed up the prices of sugar and coffee, which became scarcer on the world market as a result of the collapse of Haitian production, and it was instrumental in driving French emigrants out of Haiti who proceeded to invest a large amount of capital in coffee-growing by setting up plantations in the eastern region of Cuba.

A comparison of the plantation economy in Cuba with that in the southern United States – in Virginia, for example – will help us to pinpoint the originality of the Cuban model even more closely.[20] When a Cuban landowner had one of his slaves taught a trade, it was no doubt profitable to him, but it was also profitable to the slave, whose training, in many cases, helped him to buy his freedom. In Virginia, on the other hand, the mass of the slaves were not skilled and worked only in the plantations among the whites, since competition among small craftsworkers was such that blacks were automatically debarred from that sector. As a result of their training, the blacks in Cuba, unlike those in Virginia, occupied a crucial and indispensable position in the country's economy – a position that was clearly instrumental in advancing their social integration. Whereas Cuba was characterised by a fairly diversified economy and a very active urban life, in Virginia the dependence on a single crop, tobacco, led to urban development being relegated to second place. In 1790, 72 per cent of the slaves in Virginia worked on the plantations (73 per cent in 1860), as against 17 per cent in Cuba in 1830. In 1846, the latter figure had risen to 18 per cent, and in 1860, when the curve peaked, no more than 38 per cent of the slaves were employed in the sugar-cane fields, while only some 40 to 45 per cent of the total work force was employed on plantations producing export crops such as sugar cane and coffee.

In short, a diversified economy, a sizeable domestic market, the development of towns and cities, and the white population's reluctance to engage in manual labour enabled the Cuban blacks to acquire skills which fostered their social integration and the emergence of a national consciousness. On the other hand, the blacks in Barbados, Jamaica, Haiti and Virginia did not have access to such skills. The only prospect for them was unskilled work on the plantations.

The Case of Haiti

In the nineteenth century, a land-owning, commercial and political oligarchy based on coffee-growing grew up in Haiti. This governing elite was composed firstly of mulattos, the children of settlers (usually slave-owning landowners before the revolution of 1791–1804), who had inherited their parents' land, and secondly of blacks who had obtained land through having been in the army during the war of independence or having served as senior officials or generals. This process, which began with the liberator Dessalines (1804–1806), continued under the reign of Henri Christophe (1806–20), whose life is vividly portrayed by the Cuban writer Alejo Carpentier in his novel *El reino de este mundo* (The Kingdom of This World). The black bureaucracy obtained grants of land mainly in the northern parts of the country, since the southern and western parts were controlled by Alexandre Pétion (1806–18) and the mulatto oligarchy. The latter was represented in its trading activities by agents – some of them whites but most of them mulattos – who acted as a bridge between the international capitalist system and the powers that were the embodiment of that system at the time.

This agro-commercial oligarchy of blacks and mulattos appropriated the profits from the labour of the mass of slaves which it exploited, and was therefore quite as parasitic as the former settlers. It wielded its hegemony over the economy and society, and monopolised the machinery of government without allowing the mass of the population to take part in the political life of the country.

The history of Haiti between 1804 and the country's occupation by the United States in 1915 was one of conflict between two oligarchies. The mulatto oligarchy specialised in the export of foodstuffs and became increasingly urbanised, whereas the black oligarchy mainly continued to be large landowners. In fact, the mulattos eventually came to form the dominant economic and political group, even though the blacks benefited from their predominance in the army and from their number, which gave them a broad and legitimate base among the population. This was the political framework and particular class structure, with economic legitimacy depending on skin colour, with which the United States occupants had to contend in 1915. Apart from a few nationalist voices as exceptional as that of Rosalvo Bobo, the oligarchy did not oppose American intervention and tried to take advantage of it. The United States decided to back the mulattos, the most powerful economic and political group. Indeed, the four successive mulatto governments, between 1915 and 1946, continued to rely on the machinery of government to strengthen their social and economic power to the detriment of the black majority.

In economic terms, the remodelling of the oligarchic alliance, which became an 'American-mulatto bloc' from 1915 onwards, and the inflow of international capital, particularly under the United States' influence, turned the agricultural economy into a capitalist economy, although without quite succeeding either in restoring the plantation system or in modernising the traditional agricultural sector. It is true that the large-scale estate system was scarcely conducive to this new process which, though it did not prevail, helped to enrich the American capitalists and the dominant mulatto classes. In addition, expropriations were instrumental in releasing a considerable labour force which worked for American capital, and in triggering off mass emigration abroad. Thus, United States imperial expansion in the Caribbean shaped the regional labour market to suit the interests and needs of American capital.

The waves of emigrant workers from Haiti, but also from Jamaica and the Virgin Islands, supplied uncontrolled cheap labour to the plantations in Cuba, Panama, Costa Rica, Honduras and the Dominican Republic. This had the twofold effect of cutting the cost of local labour and of denationalising the political movements in the agricultural sector by breaking down their unity when workers with different languages and cultures began to be mixed in with the mass of local workers. In the short run, this delayed national integration and jeopardised the unity of the working class.

After some 15 years of American intervention and of puppet heads of government – Sudre Dartiguenave (1915–22), Louis Borno (1922–30), Eugène Roy and Stenio Vincente (1930) – a powerful nationalist current re-emerged in 1928 and showed its strength in the elections in 1929. The outgoing president, Louis Borno, sought re-election despite the opposition of nationalist leaders such as Georges Sylvain, Georges Petit and Jacques Roumain, who struggled for the restoration of Haiti's sovereignty and for free elections. This gave rise to mass agitation, which was put down increasingly harshly by the United States Marines. However, even before the 1929 crisis, the American dominant class and the political class that was its mouthpiece set out to alter the neo-colonial scheme of things with a view to absorbing the mass protests so as to preserve the status quo. In a bid to modernise the system of domination, President Hoover encouraged the holding of elections, as a result of which a section of the dominant Haitian oligarchy, personified by Stenio Vincente and marked by a purportedly nationalist message, came to power in November 1930. In reality, his government's task (like that of Batista in Cuba in 1934) was to preserve the structure of dominance and dependence which already existed in the economic, political, administrative, financial and ideological fields, and to perpetuate its reproduction with the support of the anti-national oligarchic bloc benefiting from it. Thus, on 1 August 1934 (the year in which the Platt amendment was repealed in Cuba), the Marines were able to withdraw from Haiti. Henceforward, the Haitian neo-colony functioned under the authority of a local oligarchy benefiting from the American plan for hegemony which had been set up in those same years in the Caribbean and Central America by forcing political, economic and social structures that differed in their affinities into the relatively uniform mould of dependence on American imperialism.

The Case of Jamaica

In spite of its area of only 11,000 square kilometres, Jamaica was the main sugar-producing island in the Caribbean from the time it became a British colony in the eighteenth century. Under British domination, the island acquired a sugar-plantation economy based on the labour of slaves brought by force from West Africa. Unlike the case of Cuba, in which the eastern part of the island had been spared the plantation system, or that of the plantation economies which had come to maturity (Barbados, Martinique and Antigua) and where the plantation system had very quickly occupied all the available land, Jamaica represented a model midway between these two extremes – that of the Cuban and Barbadian plantations – which could be described as a mixed-plantation economy. Even though Jamaica was much closer to the Barbadian model than to that of Cuba, a small-farmer sector managed to emerge, leading to some diversification of production, which acted as a counterweight to the power of the planters and partly accounts for political and social developments on the island during the first decades of the twentieth century.

This in no sense means that Jamaica stopped displaying the main features of a plantation economy, such as the monopolisation of the land by the richest planters (most of whom seldom lived on their estates), the elimination of small and medium-sized landowners (to a greater extent than in Cuba but less than in Haiti), the emigration of small white settlers and the mass import of slaves. Production was exclusively geared to exporting for the home country's markets, while virtually all foodstuffs and manufactured products were imported. As a result, the social structure was extremely inegalitarian and fundamentally racist, to the detriment of the black mass of the population.

When it comes to analysing the class structure in Jamaica in the first three decades of the twentieth century, the report which Marcus Garvey sent to the black American leader Major R. Mutun, on the occasion of his visit to Jamaica in 1916, is still an invaluable source of information. At that time, the population breakdown in Jamaica was as follows: 15,605 whites, 163,201 mulattos, 630,181 blacks, 17,380 East Indians, 2,111 Chinese and 2,905 persons of undefined origin.[21] Marcus Garvey noted in his report that in spite of the fact that Jamaica's blacks accounted for the overwhelming majority of the population (the proportion was 6 to 1) and in spite of their economic importance as the working class, they had not, unlike the blacks of the United States, produced racial ideals or leaders.

Apart from a very small minority, the blacks of Jamaica were debarred from trade and from employment in the public sector. The only profession open to them was teaching. In rural areas, the master of the plantation was white, the officials and office employees (as well as some landowners) were mulattos, and blacks of both sexes formed the bulk of the labour force. At the time, 90 per cent of the black population were labourers or domestic servants, while the remaining 10 per cent were engaged in various occupations, including trading or small-scale farming.

From 1930 onwards, the class structure in Jamaica crystallised in the pattern described by Michael Manley in his analysis of the 1940s:

> The last characteristic we have to stress stems from the distribution of wealth. Owing to its economic structure and its education system, in 1945 Jamaica had three almost completely isolated social systems. First, there were the traders and the planters, the former with considerable capital and high earnings, the latter with considerable capital but uncertain earnings. Then came the skilled trades with earnings but no capital and, lastly, the workers and peasants, the former with no income and virtually no capital and the latter with very little capital and virtually no earnings. The distance separating the first two groups from the third represented a real challenge to social justice.[22]

Needless to say, most of the blacks were to be found in the third group of workers and peasants.

The Case of Cuba

The first thing to be noted is the weakness of the dependent middle class compared with the importance which that class eventually came to have in most of the countries of Latin America.[23] That weakness was due to historical circumstances. The long, cruel and belated struggle for freedom from Spain did not come to an end in 1825, as in South and Central America, but in 1898. In fact, the most powerful sector of the Creole oligarchy established in Occidente province was not in favour of independence, since it did not want to lose the capital invested in slaves and dreaded an uprising on the lines of the one in Haiti. The liberation struggle brought about the ruin of a large part of the Cuban middle class – indeed, of the whole of that class in the eastern region, which was devastated by the fighting – since the wars of independence and the competition from sugar beet set off a process of industrial concentration with which only the most affluent could contend. In addition, it prompted the oligarchic interests of the surviving sector of the Cuban middle class to form an anti-nationalist coalition with powerful, mainly North American, sugar interests, which offered them better profit-making opportunities than the Spanish market. These interests were favoured in the first instance by the American intervention at the end of the war in 1895 – an intervention encouraged by the most privileged sections of the population – and then by the government of the first president, Tomás Estrada Palma. The Cuban economy became integrated into the American market and received a rapid, massive inflow of American capital. The utter weakness of the Cuban dependent middle class in 1930, and especially of its industrial sector, coupled with the rise in American capital investment, which determined Cuba's role as a producer of sugar and a consumer of manufactured products from the United

States, led to the collapse of the government that had emerged from the revolution of 1930 – a government inspired by an industrial and nationalist ideology similar to that of the circles which came to power in many Latin American countries during the same period.

The social structure of Cuba at that time (1900–30) can be readily explained in terms of land distribution. While it is true that non-sugar-producing estates occupied more or less the same area (250,000 *caballerías* or 3,357,500 hectares) as the sugar monoculture, the crops they produced were by no means of the same economic importance as sugar cane, which dominated the Cuban economy in qualitative terms. According to the 1929 census, sugar cane accounted for 67.81 per cent of the country's agricultural output as compared with 10.5 per cent for foodstuffs, 10.3 per cent for meat and 4.2 per cent for tobacco. In 1924, sugar accounted for 84 per cent of all exports and in 1933, when production fell to its lowest level, it still accounted for 70 per cent.

In 1933, out of a total population of some 4 million, there were 682,000 agricultural workers, 211,000 industrial workers, 123,000 employees in the commercial sector, 50,000 civil servants and 32,000 people in a variety of self-employed occupations. The working class was therefore chiefly employed in agriculture, half of it in the sugar monoculture. Some 230,000 people from the rural proletariat worked in the sugar-cane industry, and 58,000 people from the industrial proletariat worked in urban centres.[24]

An eyewitness report dating from the 1930s noted:

> Cubans really have little they can call their own on their island, with the exception of the government. Wall Street owns the sugar mills or controls them through loans. English and American capital owns the railways; the Electric Bond and Share has a monopoly of electric power in the island; International Telephone & Telegraph has a telephone monopoly. The bulk of city property and much farm land is owned by Spaniards. The majority of commercial firms are owned by Spaniards or Jews. Cubans have one ambition – to be professional men, preferably doctors or lawyers, and to become connected with the government.[25]

In 1916, in the best analysis of Cuba's social structure produced at the time, J.A. Ramos claimed that '31,657 of the 931,341 Cuban men in the 18- to 64-year age-group recorded in the last census, to which their families have to be added, draw all or part of their livelihood from government service'. If 7,000 day labourers, 1,000 lottery agents and 5,000 temporary employees are added to this figure, 'there are an estimated 45,000 government employees'. In addition, Ramos emphasised the fact that the 'middle class' included 'a large core of coloured families whose patriotic fervour sets an example which white Cubans would do well to emulate'.[26]

Moreover, the denationalisation of the nascent Cuban working class between 1900 and 1930 was due, among other factors, to the gradual arrival during this period of one million immigrants (mainly from Haiti and Jamaica), who made it difficult for the members of this class to unite and express their political opinions.

Conclusion

From the sociological standpoint, the plantation economy and the American interventions (in Haiti and Cuba) in the early twentieth century can be said to have given rise to similar patterns in Cuba, Haiti and Jamaica, at least until 1959, when the Cuban revolution broke out. That being said, if the historical evolution of these countries is studied individually, it can be seen that there are significant differences in the social processes involved.

On the one hand, in Jamaica and above all in Haiti, the plantation economy absorbed virtually all of the slave labour, whereas in Cuba it was easier for slaves to win their emancipation, which fostered their integration into Cuban society. In addition, whites represented a distinctly higher proportion of the Cuban population than in Haiti or Jamaica.

On the other hand, independence (which came early in Haiti and later in Cuba) gave rise to the formation of oligarchic blocs allying international capital to domestic capital, thus creating a particular social class which dominated the people but was subordinated to a higher power. In Jamaica, belated independence and the island's status as a British colony fostered 'assimilation' with the structures and 'values' of the metropole, whereas Haiti and Cuba were subjected to the influence of American neo-colonialism.

Thirdly, the main social – and ethnic – inequalities which existed in Jamaica and Haiti inhibited the growth of any national consciousness, whereas in Cuba, from 1930 onwards, a powerful class somewhere between the middle class and the mass of the population was formed and came to protest against oligarchic and imperialist domination. In Jamaica and Haiti, the dominant classes were subordinated to the home country, and the nationalist movements barely succeeded in destabilising the anti-nationalist oligarchic bloc. This could explain, at least partially, the triumph of the Cuban revolution in 1959 and the belated and reversible emergence of nationalism in Haiti and Jamaica.

This is why I feel that it would be useful to engage in research, firstly on the impact of the world capitalist system in the Caribbean on the basis of the theoretical model developed by I. Wallerstein, and on the practical applications of the theory of dependence. Secondly, research could be conducted on the plantation economies, with due regard for the following factors, among others: the different forms taken by colonisation and the mechanisms of transculturation and deculturation; the tools of deculturation (the diversity of ethnic origin, age, sex and culture of the African slaves); plantation work as a factor in deculturation; cultural integration in relation to the presence of slaves in urban areas, in particular in the Spanish-speaking Caribbean; the impact of the different forms of colonisation and plantation economy on the independence process and on the subsequent economic, political, social and cultural evolution of plantation societies. Lastly, a study should be made of the new forms of culture arising out of the encounter between African slaves, Europeans and Asians in particular, and of the special features of the various emancipation processes and their subsequent evolution in the plantation economies. This should not be confined to an economic and social analysis, and a clear distinction should be drawn between historical singularity and sociological typology.

Notes

1. This is a summary of a chapter that will be published in one of the volumes of the *History of the Caribbean* being prepared by UNESCO.
2. G. Pierre-Charles, 1981, p. 5.
3. S.W. Mintz, 1974, p. 52.
4. F. López Segrera, 1972, p. 125.
5. E. Williams, 1964, p. 52.
6. R. Guerra y Sánchez, 1970, pp. 37–38.
7. Ibid., p. 23.
8. J. Ibarra, 1967.
9. J. A. Saco, 1963, Vol. I, p. 177.
10. A. Humboldt, 1959, p. 284.
11. J. Pérez de la Riva, 1966, p. 4.
12. F.R. Jameson, 1966, p. 26.
13. Ibid., p. 27.
14. R. de la Sagra, 1831, p. 7.
15. Ibid., p. 123
16. Pezuela, 1863, Vol. 1, p. 61
17. G. de Arboleya, 1855, pp. 176, 180, 183.
18. R. de la Sagra, 1831, p. 125.
19. V. Martínez Alier, 1968.
20. H.S. Klein, 1967, pp. 163–192. See also the comparative studies of social structures in the Caribbean by S. Mintz, H.S. Klein and S. Engerman, in M. Moreno Fraginals, F. Moya Pons and S. Engerman (eds.), 1985. See also J. James, 1989.
21. M. Garvey, 1973.
22. M. Manley, 1974, p. 94.
23. F. López Segrera, 1972, 1980, 1985.
24. Foreign Policy Association, 1935, pp. 20, 308 and 313.
25. R. Hart Phillips, 1959, p. 72.
26. José Antonio Ramos, 1916, pp. 42, 197, 199 and 200–209.

Bibliography

ARBOLEYA, G.DE. 1855. *Manual de la isla de Cuba. Compendio de su historia, geografía, estadistica y administración.*

BAGU, S. 1973. 'Las clases sociales del subdesarrollo'. In Bagu, S., Dos Santos, Theotonio, et al. *Problemas del subdesarrollo latinoamericano.* Mexico City, Editorial Nuestro Tiempo.

BECKFORD, F., and WITTER, M. 1982. *Small Garden ... Bitter Weed: The Political Economy of Struggle and Change in Jamaica*. Morant Bay, Jamaica, Maroon Publishing House.

BECKFORD, L. 1980. 'Cambio socioeconómico y continuidad política en el Caribe Anglófono'. In Pierre-Charles, G. *Relaciones internacionales y estructuras sociopolíticas en el Caribe*. Mexico City, Universidad autónoma de México, Instituto de investigaciones sociales.

BELL, W. 1980. 'Equality and social justice: Foundations of nationalism in the Caribbean'. *Caribbean Studies* (Amsterdam), No. 2.

BENOIST, J. 1977. 'The social organization of the West Indies'. In Fraginals, M. Moreno. *Africa in Latin America*. Paris, UNESCO.

BOSCH, J. 1977. *De Cristóbal Colón a Fidel Castro: el Caribe frontera imperial*. Madrid, Alfaguara.

———. 1983. *De Cristóbal Colón a Fidel Castro*. Havana, Instituto del libro.

BRAITHWAITE, E. 1971. *The Development of Creole Society in Jamaica, 1770–1820*. Oxford, Clarendon Press.

BRAITHWAITE, L. 1973. *Social Stratification in Trinidad: A Preliminary Analysis*. Kingston, UWI/ISER.

CARPENTIER, A. 1967. *The Kingdom of This World*, London, Noonday Press.

CARRION, M. 1921. 'El desenvolvimiento social en Cuba en los últimos veinte años'. *Revista Cuba Contemporánea* (Havana), Vol. 27, No. 105.

CARY, H., and MARION, L. 1981. 'La burgesía haitiana: una clase en vía de transformación'. *Lecturas* (Havana), No. 9, Centro de Estudios sobre América.

CASIMIR, J. 1977. 'The problems of slavery and colonization in Haiti: A case-study'. In Fraginals, M. Moreno. *Africa in Latin America*. Paris, UNESCO.

CASTOR, S. 1971. *La ocupación norteamericana de Haití y sus consecuencias, 1915–1934*. Mexico City, Siglo Veintiuno Editores.

CLARKE, E. 1974. *My Mother Who Fathered Me*. London, Allen and Unwin.

COMITAS, L. 1977. *The Complete Caribbean (1900–1975): A Bibliographical Guide to the Scholarly Literature*. New York, Millwood KTO Press.

COMITAS, L., and LOWENTHAL, D. 1973. Vol. I: *Slaves, Freemen, Citizens*. Vol. II: *Consequences of Class and Color: West Indian Perspectives*. New York, Greenwood Press.

CRAIG, S. 1981. *Contemporary Caribbean: A Sociological Reader.* Vol. I. Maracas, Susan Craig.

FOREIGN POLICY ASSOCIATION. 1935. *Problemas de la nueva Cuba*. New York, Foreign Policy Association Incorporated.

FRUCHT, R. 1971. *Black Society in the New World*. New York, Random House.

GARVEY, M. 1973. 'The race question in Jamaica (1916)'. InComitas, L., and Lowenthal, D. *Consequences of Class and Color: West Indian Perspectives*. Vol. 2. New York, Greenwood Press.

GIRVAN, N. 1971. *Foreign Capital and Economic Underdevelopment in Jamaica*. Kingston, ISER.

———. 1980. 'Aspectos de la economía política de raza en el Caribe y las Américas'. In Pierre-Charles, G. *Relaciones internacionales y estructuras sociopolíticas en el Caribe*. Mexico City, Universidad autónoma de México, Instituto de investigaciones sociales.

GIRVAN, N., BERNAL, R., and HUGHES, W. 1970. *The International Monetary Fund and the Third World: The Case of Jamaica*. Kingston.

GIRVAN, N., and OWEN, J. 1971. *Readings in the Political Economy of the Caribbean.* Trinidad, New World Press.

GOVEIA, E. 1965. *Slave Society in the British Leeward Islands at the End of the Nineteenth Century.* New Haven, Yale University Press.

————. 1984. *Estudios de la historiografía de las Antillas inglesas hasta finales del siglo XIX.* Havana, Casa de las Américas.

GUERRA Y SÁNCHEZ, R. 1970. *Azúcar y población en las Antillas.* Havana, Instituto Cubano del Libro.

HUMBOLDT, A. 1959. *Ensayo político sobre la isla de Cuba.* Havana, Oficina del historiador de la ciudad de la Habana.

IBARRA, J. 1967. *Ideología mambisa.* Havana.

JAGAN, C. 1974. *Race and Politics in Guyana.* Georgetown.

JAMES, C.L.R. 1963. *The Black Jacobins.* New York, Vintage Books.

JAMES, J. 1989. 'Sociedad y nación en el Caribe'. *Del Caribe* (Santiago, Chile), No. 14 (1st ed., 1938).

JAMESON, F.R. 1966. *Cartas habaneras.* Havana, Instituto Cubano del Libro.

KLEIN, H.S. 1967. *Slavery in the Americas: A Comparative Study of Virginia and Cuba.* Chicago, Elephant Paperbacks.

KNIGHT, F.W. 1985. 'Jamaican migrants and the Cuban sugar industry (1900–1934)'. In Moreno Fraginals, M., Moya Pons, F., and Engerman, S. *Between Slavery and Free Labor.* Baltimore, Johns Hopkins University Press.

LEPKOWSKI, T. 1968. *Haiti.* Havana, Casa de la Américas.

LEWIS, G.K. 1969. *The Growth of the Modern West Indies.* 2nd ed. New York, Modern Reader Paperbacks.

LÓPEZ SEGRERA, F. 1972. *Cuba: capitalismo dependiente y subdesarrollo (1510–1959).* Havana, Casa de las Américas.

————. 1980. *Raíces históricas de la revolución cubana (1868–1958).* Havana, Unión de escritores y artistas de Cuba.

————. 1985. 'Cuba: Dependence, plantation economy and social classes'. In Moreno Fraginals, M., Moya Pons, F., and Engerman, S. *Between Slavery and Free Labor.* Baltimore, Johns Hopkins University Press.

LOWENTHAL, D. 1972. *West Indian Societies.* London, Greenwood Press.

LUC, J. 1976. *Structures économiques et lutte nationale en Haiti.* Nouvelle optique.

MAINGOT, A., PARRY, J.H., and SHERLOCK, P. 1991. *A Short History of the West Indies.* New York, Westview Press.

MANLEY, M. 1975. *The Politics of Change.* Cambridge, Mass., Harvard University Press.

MARTÍNEZ ALIER, V. 1968. 'Color, clase y matrimonio en Cuba en el siglo XIX'. *Revista de la Biblioteca Nacional José Martí* (Havana) No. 2.

MAU, J.A. 1968. *Social Change and Images of the Future in Jamaica.* Cambridge, Russell Press.

MINTZ, S.W. 1974. 'The Caribbean region'. *Daedalus* (Spring).

MINTZ, S.W., and PRICE, S. 1985. *Caribbean Contours.* Baltimore, Johns Hopkins Press.

MORENO FRAGINALS, M. 1977. *Africa in Latin America.* Paris, UNESCO.

MORENO FRAGINALS, M., MOYA PONS, F., and ENGERMAN, S. 1985. *Between Slavery and Free Labor.* Baltimore, Johns Hopkins University Press.

NETTLEFORD, R. 1970. *Identity, Race and Protest in Jamaica.* Kingston, W. Collins and Sangster.

————. 1979. *Caribbean Cultural Identity (the Case of Jamaica).* Los Angeles, UCLA.

PÉREZ DE LA RIVA, J. 1966. *La isla de Cuba en el siglo XIX vista por los extranjeros.* Havana, Biblioteca Nacional José Martí.

PEZUELA. 1863. *Diccionario geográfico, histórico, estadístico.*

PHILLIPS, R.H. 1959. *Cuba, Island of Paradox.* New York, Obolensky.

PIERRE-CHARLES, G. 1973. 'Para una sociología de la opresión: el caso de Haití'. Santiago, Chile, Ed. Quimantur.

———. 1980. *Relaciones internacionales y estructuras sociopolíticas en el Caribe.* Mexico City, Universidad autónoma de México, Instituto de investigaciones sociales.

———. 1981. 'Haití: la crisis ininterrumpida (1930–1975)'. In Gonzalez Casanova, P. (ed.). *América latina: historia de medio siglo.* Vol. 2. Mexico City, Siglo Veintiuno Editores.

PRICE, R. 1979. *Maroon Societies: Rebel Slave Communities in the Americas.* Baltimore, Johns Hopkins University Press.

RAMOS, J.A. 1916. *Manual del perfecto fulanista.* Havana, J. Montero.

RODNEY, W. 1972. *How Europe Underdeveloped Africa.* London, Howard University Press.

RUBIN, V. 1962. *Culture, Politics and Race Relations: Social and Economic Studies.* Vol. 11, No. 4. New York, Chicago Press.

RYAN, S. 1974. *Race and Nationalism in Trinidad and Tobago: A Study of Decolonization in a Multisocial Society.* Kingston, UWI/ISER.

SACO, J.A. 1963. *Papeles sobre Cuba.* Havana, Dirección general de la cultura, Ministerio de educación.

SAGRA, R.DE LA. 1831. *Historia económico-política y estadística de la isla de Cuba.* Havana, Impresa de las viudas de Arazoza y Saler.

SERBIN, A. *Etnicidad, clase y nación en la cultura política del Caribe de habla inglesa.* Caracas, Academia Historia (Coll. Estudios, monografías y ensayos, 93).

SMITH, M.G. 1965. *The Plural Society in the British West Indies.* Berkeley, University of California Press.

———. 1973. 'The plural framework of Jamaican society'. In Comitas, L., and Lowenthal, D. (eds.). *Slaves, Free Men, Citizens.* Vol. 1. New York, Anchor Press.

STONE, C. 1973. *Class, Race and Political Behaviour in Urban Jamaica.* Kingston, UWI/ISER.

———. 1986. *Class, State and Democracy in Jamaica.* New York, Praeger Publishers.

THOMAS, C.Y. 1982. *From Colony to State Capitalism: Alternative Paths of Development in the Caribbean.* Paramaribo.

VILAS, C.M. 1983. 'Movimientos internacionales de población y valoración del capital en el Caribe'. *Anales del Caribe* (Havana), No. 3.

WATSON, H.A. 1980. 'Imperialism and Caribbean dependence: Resistance and adaptation'. *Carabisch Forum*, Vol. 1, No. 3.

———. 1986. 'Economic dependency and geopolitics: Recurring ideological themes in Caribbean intellectual culture'. *New West Indies Guide*, Vol. 60, Nos. 3 and 4.

WILLIAMS, E. 1964. *Capitalism and Slavery.* London, A. Deutsch.

———. 1984. *From Columbus to Castro: The History of the Caribbean, 1492–1969.* London, Random House.

Part III

Abolition of the Slave Trade and Slavery, and Changing Mentalities

Chapter 14

The Abolition of the Slave Trade and Slavery: Historical Foundations

Joseph C. Miller

NEARLY EVERYWHERE AROUND THE WORLD, enslavement was, before the modern era, a near ubiquitous misfortune. Victors captured and then enslaved the vanquished – when they did not slaughter them on the spot – and stole their women. The household economies of prosperous families rested on the services of outsiders taken in as slave domestics, and wealthy and powerful men assembled harems of slave women. Rulers built their power on the skills of imported slave retainers, skilled because they could be controlled and trained, and loyal because they were so dependent. In bureaucratic states they filled sensitive offices, and some of them rose to ministerial status, so important were they to the administrative structures of control. Military rulers armed others as palace guards dedicated to preserving the masters to whom they owed their lives. The wealthy and honourable, or merely the prestige hungry, expressed their superiority by surrounding themselves with conspicuously superfluous, lavishly costumed retinues of slaves. Merchants sent slaves out in caravans and canoes as commercial agents and stationed them in trading factories to facilitate flows of goods – and sometimes slaves as well – between sellers and buyers in distant markets, because they could trust dependants who had no other sponsors. Cities consigned to slaves the labour of building municipal works, provisioning town populations and cleaning their refuse. And, occasionally, massive inflows of captives allowed owners of agricultural estates, operators of mines and industrial processors to employ them, as slaves, to develop significant, even dominating, new productive economic sectors.

The most familiar occasion of this last sort, and one that vastly exceeded all previous such instances in scale and significance, became the starting point for the historic ending of what had previously been pervasive in world history.[1] Europeans in the seventeenth and eighteenth centuries built huge American mining and plantation enterprises on the enslavement of Africans and created a massive pan-Atlantic commercial network of slave transport to keep up the numbers of the millions of Africans on whom they had come to depend.[2] The gradual abolition of slavery around the world in the nineteenth century, and of the various trades in slaves serving it, is therefore well worthy of the attention it has received in the historical literature, not only as an anomaly in the many centuries of world history but also as a key feature of the road to modernity, with all of its discontents, as well as the present worldwide concern for recognition of universal human rights.

The unprecedented character of Atlantic abolition in the nineteenth century stands out all the more prominently on a world scale. Although the enslaved had never accepted the utter subordination of their condition and, arguably, had invented the very idea of 'freedom', the valuing of individual autonomy, against the ethos of 'belonging' that characterised societies everywhere in the world prior to the eighteenth-century European Enlightenment, always before they had found self-respect and had created communities of their own within the framework of their masters' formal, nominal control.[3] Nor had any previous élite's impulse to abolish the trade actually terminated slaving or slavery anywhere else in world history.[4] Normally, trading of modest proportions continued unhindered, if only as an activity secondary to other primary forms of commerce. Even in the earlier economies most reliant on slavery, such as that of Italy under Roman imperial rule, where the transport and sale of slaves had been consequences of military conquest and plunder, slavery had declined with the waning of imperial wars of expansion without formal rejection of the principle in philosophical discourse or government policy. The descendants of Roman slaves in Italy and elsewhere in Europe had gradually become indistinguishable from dependent labourers of other sorts, locally born, gradually endowed with limited rights, and not replaced with other enslaved newcomers.[5] In contrast, although American slaves also resisted their masters, sometimes violently and collectively,[6] nineteenth-century abolition also became a matter of public initiative, of government policy, in Britain and in a few other Western European and American nations. Clearly, something had changed, specifically in the countries where the movement arose from mass popular initiative. Elsewhere, British measures developed to enforce abolition were systematically evaded, by the slavers in the colonies and by political authorities in other European nations. Slave-trading did not decline because of its own inefficiencies or immorality but rather had to be suppressed, thus creating the unprecedented phenomenon of persistent organised intellectual, political, diplomatic and – in extreme cases – military assaults against it.

In Asia and Africa, the end of the slave trade in the Atlantic contrasted also with simultaneous expansions in the exodus of slaves from Africa north across the Sahara Desert, from the upper Nile Valley northeast across the Red Sea, and from nearly the entire Indian Ocean coast of eastern Africa to Arabia, the Persian Gulf and the Mascareignes Islands.[7] Also at the same time, slavery spread more widely than ever before throughout Africa.[8] Slave-raiding and slavery in parts of Asia grew as well.[9] A deep sense of paradox therefore arises in attempting to understand the historical roots of global abolition in the nineteenth century, just as more people than ever before were becoming slaves in many parts of the world, and at a time when the institution remained economically viable around the Atlantic basin itself.[10]

The modern sense of paradox as to how and why slavery and the slave trade ended was lost on reforming abolitionists in England and the United States, filled with the moral righteousness of their cause, who explained their success either as the fulfilment of God-given commandments or as part of the ascent of the human race towards European-led progress and modernity. Disillusionment with such optimistic and progressive visions spread in the wake of the First World War and world economic collapse during the 1930s; the nineteenth-century sense of unproblematic inevitability gave way to efforts to understand what had happened in historical terms. Abolition was no longer seen as destiny but rather as a human achievement, a triumph of principled altruism against considerable odds of economic self-interest. Historians' first interpretations of the movement itself thus brought the earlier spirit of confident optimism in the realm of professional history, against the harsh realities of the Depression. They took the reformers, especially in Britain, on their own terms and elevated their inspiration to the level of sufficient historical cause.[11] By this interpretation, religious dissenters in England – Evangelicals, Methodists, Quakers – combined Enlightenment faith in the possibility of worldly progress with religious fervour to spark broad-based popular opposition to the slave trade, and to slavery, and eventually, in 1807, a Parliamentary prohibition of further dealing in slaves by British subjects, to take effect in 1808. In the United States, an act of the new federal congress had earlier, in 1794, forbidden North American traders to bring slaves from the West Indies but had failed to hinder United States imports of slaves significantly; a second statute, of 1807, took effect in the same year as its British counterpart.[12] By these laws, the greatest naval power in Europe and the American nation destined to dominate the Western hemisphere had declared international trafficking in human beings morally unacceptable.[13] Though the United States government failed notoriously to prevent its citizens from further involvement in Atlantic slaving, Britain gradually established a naval presence along the sea lanes of the slave route[14] that, combined with persistent diplomatic pressure, ended the continuing slaving of the other nations – the French,[15] Portuguese and Brazilians,[16] the United States itself,[17] and the Spaniards[18] – by the 1860s.

The challenge to the triumphant accent in this tale of abolition came almost at once from the West Indian scholar Eric Williams.[19] For him, the rectitude of the reformers contained elements of self-congratulatory rationalisation for a self-interested national adjustment to economic circumstances profoundly changed since the creation of the British slave-worked sugar plantations in the West Indies, and the trade to support them, more than a century earlier. According to Williams's materialist analysis, the great profitability of slave-grown sugar had brought the accumulation of capital in Britain to levels capable of sustaining the Industrial Revolution. But by the end of the eighteenth century, and particularly following the loss of the North American colonies after 1783, profits from the plantations were declining. At home, British consumer markets, agriculture and new industries had begun to grow beyond mercantilist protectionism and its reliance on favourable balances of trade with closed colonial possessions, particularly the sugar colonies. Britain was therefore turning to free trade, seeking new markets in the colonial economies of other nations, importing sugar from plantations in the Indian Ocean and drawing its capital from by-then-viable industrial sectors at home. West Indian sugar, having given birth to capitalism, had become superfluous as it matured and could be cast loose to fend for itself. The slave trade supplying it with labour, under fire from reformers in England, was inefficient and lethal to British sailors on the ships, and could be done away with. With industrial capitalism generating the profits, the reformers' humanitarian rhetoric was thus shown to have hidden an underlying, entirely rational self-interest, as Britain first ended the Atlantic trade in slaves in 1807, and then slavery itself in 1833, a tone that prevails in the succeeding historiography still today.[20]

W.E.B. Du Bois had long since established a second approach to the process of abolishing the maritime trade that was equally critical of the righteous rhetoric of humanitarian reform. He had demonstrated the ineffectuality of US legislation nominally prohibiting national shipping from participation in the trade after 1807, and indeed the collusion of public authorities in subverting its nominal intent.[21] The collaboration of British merchants and captains in the mercantile, if not the slave-carrying, phases of the full trading cycle out to Africa and back through from the Americas to Europe had been noted by Williams in 1942,[22] and its full dimensions became clearer with detailed study of the continuing Portuguese-Brazilian and Spanish trades.[23] At the same time, recognition grew of increased slaving and slavery within Africa and of the thriving nineteenth-century trans-Saharan, Red Sea and Indian Ocean trades.[24] A sense of paradox has deepened, at least in economic terms, as the certainties of Europe-centred moral rectitude or West Indian economic decline, determinisms ideological and material, gave way to global perspectives on the realities of political pragmatism, opportunistic contingency and contradiction behind the orderly rhetoric of the process.

In this new vision, the trades in slaves have been seen more clearly in their full global context, as aspects of the historical creation of the modern world economy. Abolition, in these terms, was a long-running process that coalesced intellectually in Britain in the middle of the eighteenth century and spread outward politically through the Atlantic in the first half, or two-thirds, of the nineteenth century,[25] then moved into the Indian Ocean and the Ottoman domains after 1870, and later, in the early twentieth century, into Africa and parts of Asia with the imposition of European colonial authority there.[26] It exhibited certain characteristics specific to the global scale of the nineteenth-century trade in slaves itself. Unlike many earlier, and some contemporary, slaving networks, the nineteenth-century trade was entirely maritime and moved in international waters by then covered by layers of intra-European diplomatic conventions. It was thus potentially subject to treaty agreements with other powers and accessible to the British navy, then by far the most powerful maritime force in the world. Because slaves were – almost by definition[27] – 'deracinated',[28] taken and resettled far from their homes, abolition became a transnational phenomenon distinctively subject to control only on an international scale. Further, on the assumption – largely true[29] – that political authorities at the destinations of the slaves by definition depended on and gained from maintaining slave populations through continued importation and would not themselves harm the goose that laid their golden eggs, abolition was an inherently intrusive process. Abolition thus took place in terms of specific local contexts that produced highly variable manifestations of the long-running, single broad trend.

Economic and Political Factors in Great Britian

Britain's prominence as an advocate of abolition has kept historians' attention focused on the circumstances in late-eighteenth-century England – intellectual and political – that converted the reformist ideals of a relatively small number of zealots on the fringes of power into public policy, the expenditure of government funds and intrusion into affairs that other nations regarded as their own domestic matters. Although the abolitionists' humanitarian idealism encompassed many other social injustices, the slave trade remained a principal focus of their efforts in part because it stood as an effective moral – or more precisely, immoral – proxy for slavery itself, the most brutal, and lethal, phase of the long path that slaves followed from their homes to resettlement and bondage elsewhere. Conditions in Africa were seldom clearly visible to European reformers in the eighteenth century,[30] and slaves' lives on New World plantations contained elements that could be represented as relatively benign. However, the cramped and pestilential conditions beneath the decks of ships that slaves endured during transport at sea, and from which many died, lent themselves to direct observation and to graphic descriptions that aroused strong feelings back at home. The widely circulated diagram of dark figures arrayed like so many clothespins aboard the slave ship *Brookes* became perhaps the most notorious symbol of these abuses.[31]

The abolitionists directed their initial efforts at slave-carrying also because continued supplies of slaves were in fact critical to the survival of slavery itself in most parts of the world. Suppression of the trade would, it was rightly assumed, inflict a lethal wound on the entire slave system in the long run.[32] At the level of the most basic, economic pressures, at least up to the end of the eighteenth century, slavers could deliver raw Africans to planters at costs lower than those of maintaining self-reproducing populations of captive workers.[33] Mortality among slave populations nearly everywhere in the New World, though lower than the deaths suffered during the middle passage across the Atlantic itself, carried away more individuals than the relatively few females in the captive population could replace through reproduction, particularly during the first years of residence.[34] That largely inescapable demographic fact – given limited understanding of nutrition,[35] rudimentary medical techniques, endemic epidemiological hazards and planters' complacency, or resignation, about the fragility of their African workers' lives – meant that tropical

American slavery faced debilitation within a few years of ceasing to replenish the numbers of the enslaved population through continuous importation. In addition, an annoying, though seldom large, erosion in the numbers of slaves continued through escapes of 'maroons' to independent settlements located in the inaccessible forests and mountains near the plantations.

These basic demographic limitations of New World slavery were accentuated also by the higher costs inherent in attempting to manage populations of settled slaves, particularly those born and raised in Africa. The profitability of slavery in most areas depended heavily on the sheer vulnerability of these new arrivals.[36] Though not always highly productive, since they were sometimes inexperienced at the more technologically complicated tasks at hand, particularly on sugar plantations, they were often weakened by the physical stress and psychological shock of the middle passage, socially isolated and helpless, and therefore subject to being driven to greater degrees than planters could impose on more experienced individuals.[37] After months or years, slaves who survived the initial stages of their captivity learned how to exploit the interstices of the network of controls that surrounded them; earned support within the community of slaves among whom they lived; acquired friends, spouses and other protectors; and cultivated the patronage of their masters. Slaves tended to move from initial assignments to rough labour in remote fields, mines or forests towards the towns and the plantation houses as they became 'seasoned', from exile with other recent arrivals to close association with their bosses. As they lived out this process of social and cultural, if not legal, assimilation, they also became more difficult, and more costly, to control than were newcomers just off the boats. In the Iberian parts of the Americas, the life cycles of surviving slaves often led to semi-autonomy in the towns, in which slaves earned the costs of their modest successes themselves. With a frequency distinctive in the Americas, they even purchased formal manumission and, particularly in Brazil, bought the freedom of loved ones.

Management of people born into slavery and raised in the New World – far from the now rejected stereotype of broken spirits, accepting of their servitude – was even more expensive from the perspective of the system as a whole. They grew up as members of family networks, spoke their masters' language, or a dialect of it, as their mother tongue, could sometimes exercise considerable informal influence from skilled and sensitive positions in households or at key points in plantation production cycles, and had other resources available only to the native-born. They were consequently more productive than newcomers, but the number of positions in which their abilities could be utilised profitably was limited, particularly in colonies with competing populations of artisans and managers of European origin. Too many such assimilated and able slaves became liabilities, costly to contain and control.[38] Without the Atlantic trade to provide poorer, more exploitable replacements in the early stages of integration, slavery lost some of its economic advantage over other methods of coercing labour. Suppression of the trade thus threatened the long-term viability of economies based on the labour of slaves, and the reformers initiated their broader strategies of eventual full emancipation by concentrating on the trade.[39] Abolition of slave-trading thus provided access to a key artery carrying the lifeblood of the American – and later other – slave systems themselves.

The New World exceptions underscore the sensitivity of slavery to continuing imports. By the end of the eighteenth century, prices of slaves from Africa had risen high enough to lead slave owners in the Americas to contemplate natalist policies that would replace imports with native-born populations of slave workers.[40] Denmark terminated slave deliveries to its small sugar islands in the West Indies in 1792, effective 1803, and thus became the first slave-holding nation in Europe to abolish the trade.[41] This was accomplished due to largely economic considerations and by means of a royal edict unencumbered by the increasingly popular political processes upon which abolition had to be based in Britain, the United States and France. Prominent among the Danes' calculations was the prospect of developing a self-reproducing slave population that would continue to support Danish sugar, without continued imports of new labour.[42] The ten-year delay in implementation of the abolition edict was intended to allow time to import enough women of child-bearing age and to improve social conditions in the islands to allow slaves there to replace themselves.

The prospect of such amelioration of the slaves' lives conditioned calculations, and also debates, in Britain and its slave-holding possessions in the West Indies.[43] The extreme hardships of early eighteenth-century slavery in the British Caribbean had begun to lessen by the middle 1700s, and even prominent abolitionists in Britain soothed slave-holding opponents of their campaign against the trade with toleration for continued slavery, under more humane circumstances for the slaves. With gradual abolition of the trade and a period of selective importation of females, the planters of the West Indies contemplated the prospect of rearing a self-reproducing, Creole slave population on the islands. They would provide family living arrangements and offer incentives – tax abatements, exemptions from labour obligations and other concessions – to slave women able to bear and raise four or five children. In the interim they would have to bear the additional costs of doing so, in the form of lost working days of the mothers, and some generous estimates placed these prohibitively high.

Finally, in the United States, behind the intricate and intense partisan and sectional politics of the congressional vote to abolish its trade in 1807 lay fundamental economic considerations. Alone among the slaves of the New World, the African-Americans of the Chesapeake and the Carolina coasts had managed, perhaps as early as the 1740s, to achieve natural population growth without continued replenishments from Africa.[44] Imports of slaves to North America had declined before the American Revolution, and the war had disrupted further deliveries. Arrivals at Charleston, South Carolina, surged after peace returned in 1783, but American slavers themselves were already in the 1790s shifting their attention towards more remunerative markets in Cuba. In the Chesapeake, where the largest populations of slaves lived, tobacco was in decline and planters there had extra hands whom they hoped to sell in the domestic market. In this context, crucial slave-owning interests did not oppose abolition of further imports that might compete with their own prospects of selling surplus labour, and the necessary bill passed the United States Congress in 1807.[45] Only with more slaves than needed and prospects for further population growth could a slave-holding regime terminate imports of slaves on its own. That imports actually ceased to the considerable extent that they did had everything to do with withdrawal from the trade by the principal participants as smugglers, the British and the French.

Revision of the original humanitarian thesis of the origins of abolitionism in Britain, often in explicit refutation of the overtones in Williams's thesis critical of British political motives, came into clear focus with Anstey's addition of parliamentary politics to the array of factors seen as influential in producing the Act of 1807. Starting from a refutation of Williams's implied, or sometimes rhetorically asserted, claim that the trade itself had generated unusually, and critically, large profits for the merchants who conducted it,[46] Anstey took the abolitionists' moral commitment very seriously as the basis for explaining the ability of sectarians otherwise theologically divided to ally in united political campaigns against the trade and thus to form a single, politically efficacious 'anti-slavery lobby' or a 'national abolition lobby'. Emphasising the novelty of such a combination in British politics at that time, he then examined closely the strategies and tactics of the campaign itself: '[A]n intellectual climate favourable to abolition, though important, was in no way sufficient to secure it.'[47] Anstey went on to trace the shifting political coalitions in the Parliament in the 1790s and early 1800s to a moment in 1807 when the abolitionists found it possible to portray their cause as serving the national interest in time of war against France. The abolitionists were thus rehabilitated as men of principle but also shown as politicians endowed 'with consummate tactical skill'. Domestic politics had been added to the historical roots of abolitionism in Britain.

National self-interest, rather than humanitarian sentiments and philosophical premises, also became a theme, since similar considerations in France blocked the rise of popular pressures to abolish the slave trade there. A small, élite abolitionist society, the *Société des Amis des Noirs*, had been founded in 1788 on the eve of the French Revolution, but it never developed, or attempted to develop, the mass political involvement, whether effective or not, that swirled around the ending of the trade in Britain. The lack of popular participation in abolition movements in France compared to the highly populist course of abolition in Britain appears all the more striking, at least superficially, in view of the massive surge of popular participation in French national politics in 1789 and after.[48] The French trade had become significantly less important after the revolt in 1791 by the slaves in the largest French sugar colony in the West Indies, St-Domingue, and it all but disappeared during the wars of the period after 1793. Abolitionists in the first French Republican governments thus found it possible to pass a measure declaring the illegality of the trade in 1794 at low political cost. Slaving was opportunistically restored in 1802 and 1814, though again terminated as a concession made in the peace agreements with Britain of 1815. Thereafter, the abolitionist cause in defeated, and increasingly nationalistic, France bore the stigmata of a foreign ideology imposed against French national interests.[49] Economic recovery policies, in the wake of the wars and the continental blockade that the British had imposed on French shipping, gave priority to the prosperity of Nantes, Bordeaux and the other ports serving the colonial trade, which the Assembly seemed to have little discomfort in interpreting as including slaving. The fortunes of the remaining French colonies in the Antilles also seemed at stake. Though French abolitionism bore a philosophical family resemblance to its British cousin in its humanitarian Enlightenment rhetoric, its political character was entirely different in its utter lack of mass participation. However, its political fortunes in the French National Assembly paralleled those of the British Parliament in depending finally on perceived rational, national self-interest.

Politics, once added to the brew in Britain, proved even more influential when considered in terms of the profound social transformation proceeding at home simultaneously with the pursuit of reform abroad. The other side of Anstey's emphasis on the professional abolitionists' political skill in Parliament was their ability out on the hustings to mobilise hundreds of thousands of lay supporters of the cause in a mass political movement so agitated that it penetrated even the remote and lofty halls of Westminster at the time. Starting with the evangelical churches, the most democratic and participatory institutions in British society at the time, and moving to organisation at the level of whole communities through the formation of local abolition societies, and then on to national campaigns, abolitionists convinced people who had never before exercised any role in national affairs that they could influence the votes, in Parliament, of their political betters. They generated a massive outpouring of abolitionist and anti-slavery petitions that presented the parliamentarians with concrete, countable evidence of the strong popular convictions in their boroughs among people who did not have the vote and of their expectations of responsiveness. The abolitionist campaign in the towns and country parishes thus formed the cutting edge of a profound shift towards expanded participation in electoral politics in Britain, one that would lead within a generation to formal broadening of the British franchise in the parliamentary reform bills of 1831 and 1832 and the consolidation of mass politics.[50] Abolitionism thus also emerged from and focused deep-flowing currents towards maturation of the modern British body politic and towards social issues paramount in the minds of the unrepresented masses of the nation.[51] Abolitionist opposition to the slave trade may also have refracted and displaced less easily resolvable domestic social and economic tensions animating reform campaigns directed at perceived evils within the British Isles. As the Industrial Revolution gathered momentum, country people were moving to new and rapidly growing towns and cities, places very inadequately equipped for their arrival. Visibly unsanitary conditions, seemingly intemperate behaviour, poverty and crime, all became matters of concern to authorities, as well as to social reformers, as issues of controlling potentially dangerous lower classes. The employed and unemployed in the cities were creating new urban cultures out of the social displacement and suffering of the times, and these emerging masses of labourers and the unemployed appeared threatening not only to older, landed gentry but also to members of the respectable middle classes. On the one hand, awareness of, and faith in the ability of reform measures to solve, growing tensions at home sustained the comprehensive humanitarian and ameliorative impulses that fuelled abolitionism. On the other hand, to the extent that reformers lived in the midst of these dislocations, they could see the intractability of the problems in England and experienced the opposition of the conservatives to reform. However, the West Indies were far away, and 'slavery' and the slave trade were available for them to idealise as manageable and eradicable causes of social injustice. Furthermore, since slavery was a legal status and slaving a regulable trade, both were susceptible to 'solutions' by parliamentary vote. Much more difficult measures would be necessary to feed, employ, educate or control the teeming human crowds of London. Reformers could therefore find apparently effective vents there for their generalised sense of malaise and their determination to remedy it in the distant Caribbean. Reformers saw abolition as a laboratory for experiments in social change that might be applied later at home.[52] Conservative interests in Britain, those who wished to control the problems at home rather than to reduce them, tolerated this displacement of the 'problems' of industrialisation to remote colonies across the ocean and onto the backs of idealised enslaved Africans. It seemed far less costly to achieve a measure of social justice, or to deflect the inconvenient, seemingly naive pressures of the reformers, by tolerating an end to slaving than by investing in adequate housing, constructing urban sanitation systems or facing the growing reality of profound working class discontent in Britain. In a strong version of this argument, abolitionism had the effect of 'strengthen[ing] the invisible chains being forged at home'.[53]

Sustained historical research into Williams's principal economic hypothesis – that declining prosperity and profitability in the West Indies in the late eighteenth century brought recognition that the sugar colonies of the West Indies had outlived their economic utility to Britain – has greatly clarified the precise contribution of the American plantations to British economic development at the time. Seymour Drescher argued that the economy of the British West Indies had not gone into decline after the loss of the North American colonies, as Williams had asserted, but rather had continued to expand after 1783 and had continued to benefit Britain until well after termination of the trade in 1807.[54] The economic paradox of a metropolis that appeared to destroy, by deliberated legislative enactment, a valuable colonial system of slavery and the trades supporting it by ending slaving then left Drescher to seek the political and other non-economic factors at work.

While the inattention to economic rationality that Drescher asserted diverted attention to the complexities of British political and ideological trends at the time, the economic paradox was deepened by growing appreciation of the indirect ways in which the West Indies and African slaving had, in fact, made critical contributions to British economic growth. On the issue of the wealth that the profits of slavery and slaving had brought to Britain, the first formal economic analyses of Williams's broad, rather circumstantially argued claims for their importance had concentrated narrowly on demonstrable gains to the shipping firms engaged in the trade.[55] These, even generously calculated, proved miniscule in relation to the size of the British economy of the time.[56] Nor could formal models of export-led economic growth show the aggregate volume of trade to the West Indies to have accounted for a proportion of total British foreign and colonial commerce adequate to explain the far-reaching changes under way.[57] But a more detailed consideration of the many specific and often indirect ways in which components of the British economy had gained momentum from 'the impact of foreign trade' showed that 'the export slave trade from Africa and New World slavery were crucial to the capitalist transformation of England in the seventeenth and eighteenth centuries'.[58] Arguments of considerable ingenuity and economic refinement revealed critical linkages between internal sources of economic growth and the external linkages specific to the West Indian trade, replacing Williams's much simpler attribution of a direct influence of the latter. The size of the available market was critical to the development of mass production, and hence to the creation of a high-volume industrial plant in the modern sense. In this model, the slave trade and slavery had the effect of transporting millions of captives out of largely self-sufficient African economies, then still relatively inaccessible to British manufacturers, to islands where they had no choice but to consume British exports.[59] Recent contributions of similarly broad scope have added such other economic variables on a global scale as opportunities for investment (in labour, where land was cheap) and flexibility in moving labour to new production sites to conclude that slavery and colonial possessions in the New World gave Britain a critical edge in the eighteenth century over competitors confined to domestic markets and local sources of raw materials.[60]

Finally, close attention to the initial phases of specific British manufacturing sectors critical to what became the Industrial Revolution demonstrated how captive West Indian markets for the relatively unsophisticated product of infant industries allowed British manufacturing interests to survive and gain momentum which they could not have achieved in a more competitive environment.[61] This demonstration of the precise economic utility of the colonies and the slave trade supporting them *before* the rise of abolitionism, combined with the probability that the slavery and slaving remained important to Britain *during and after* the mass popular campaigns, deepens the paradox of abolitionism in terms of economic self-interest. The multiple value of the slave colonies would have been apparent to political economists of the eighteenth century, at least in theoretical terms, and thus could hardly support Williams's implication that abolition had proceeded from a conscious calculation of the sugar colonies' economic disutility.

If the political and economic roots of metropolitan abolition have been identified in refining, and revising, Williams's challenge to his predecessors' faith in the power of ideas,[62] separate lines of inquiry have returned to intellectual history and the interplay of thought and behaviour, combining it with social history to wonder how it was that 'ideas, antislavery in this instance, became social facts, cultural attitudes, and motives and means for collective action'.[63] The effect has been to refine greatly the implicit, consciously self-interested psychology by which Williams linked 'capitalism' and the ending of the slave trade. The contributors to these debates all accept some sort of connection between capitalism, as ideology, and anti-slavery, but they reject Williams's cynicism and disagree as to the nature of the link. Davis's association of conservative class interests in late-eighteenth-century England with the deflection of popular attention to social injustice towards slaves in remote colonies resembles Antonio Gramsci's neo-Marxist notion of a 'hegemonic ideology', a construction of reality through which classes disadvantaged or exploited by accumulating capitalist interests are led to accept and even unknowingly support their own exploitation. Haskell seeks similarly to connect abolitionism with capitalism, but his idealist Weberian view has 'capitalism', through the notion of an abstract, universal 'market', bringing a consciousness of shared interests and even identity with strangers one has never seen. Such awareness, coupled with the similarly novel notion of social efficacy, the feeling of being able to make a difference in the fortunes of oneself and of one's fellows, drove the abolitionists and their supporters to end abuses that, once recognised, they could no longer morally tolerate. It is, however, avoiding all but one level of this intensely subtle and accomplished debate to emphasise that the issues involve how one might reconcile the obviously sincere altruism of the reformers and others with effective self-interest, however unconscious, and whether, or how and to what extent, one must invoke class antagonism and exploitation to do so.

The early abolition movement thus released and channelled deep, unresolved intellectual and ideological tensions and broad social and political changes arising from late-eighteenth-century British industrialisation, but not its economics. The moral and philosophical humanitarianism of the reformers was undoubtedly altruistic and ameliorative in intent, and it was inspiring, because of its nobility, to large numbers of people worried about their own futures in times of rapid and bewildering change. Animated also by the growing eagerness of those excluded from formal British politics to influence national affairs, the movement elicited broad popular participation. Although the clearly demonstrated restiveness of the working classes and others of the 'popular orders' might have alarmed conservative, propertied or industrialist interests still well positioned to block their objectives, the cause of the slaves in the far-away Caribbean seemed less threatening and might deflect attention away from much touchier potential reforms at home. In the environment of a compelling cause thus serving multiple interests, not all of them consciously held, it became just barely possible for skilled parliamentarians to seize a momentary identification of abolition with the national interest in 1807 and thus to enact the legislation that ended the trade, even against immediate economic self-interest. The slave trade and West Indian slavery had contributed in critically significant ways to accelerating British economic growth in the second half of the eighteenth century, and they remained dynamic and viable for their participants after abolition in 1807, even as Britain's domestic economy and European and Asian trades grew. It was thus the social and political consequences of the Industrial Revolution, not economic ones, that both promoted and permitted the abolition of slaving; economic decline in the West Indies came later and was more a consequence of the trade's termination than a cause.

The slaves' own sense of self-respect and their struggles to preserve their identities under a system premised upon utter subjugation of their wills to those of their masters provided the essential predisposing condition of success underlying the efforts of abolitionists in Europe, far from the fields, plantations, mines and cities of the New World. Slaves had, however, previously directed their efforts to defend and define themselves largely at finding viable places within hierarchical orders of the sort they had known in Africa, or accepting the premises of human inequality underlying the American plantation regimes – including slavery: in refugee settlements (maroons in English colonies, *cimarones* and *palenques* in Spanish-speaking areas, *quilombos* and *mocambos* in Brazil),[64] by creating and maintaining communities of their own in the cities[65] and plantations[66] on which they laboured, and occasionally – though always without threatening or even questioning slavery itself – in violent assaults against particular masters, in protest against specific abuses, or in unpoliticised outbreaks in the wake of subsistence or other crises of survival.[67] A recurrent objective of these revolts – though not a surprising one from 'outsiders' defined by social exclusion at the most profound level from the rights of human beings – had been to be included by the standards of the times in which they lived. However, neither retreat to the margins of society in maroon settlements nor the solace of the slave community, embedded within alien frameworks belonging to others and created out of self-defense against them, could adequately meet the slaves' deep longing to participate.

Self-Deliverance in the New World

The Enlightenment, and the North American and French revolutionary ideologies of individual human rights deriving from it, proclaimed a new and absolute standard of belonging that slaves appropriated – first, and definitively, in the French island of St. Domingue.[68] There, slaves won political independence from France and defeated the armies of three major imperial powers in the Caribbean after an uprising that began in 1791. Their victories both terrified masters throughout the hemisphere and inspired their slaves. Threats of slave violence in the United States – Gabriel Prosser's in Virginia in 1800[69] and the conspiracy led by Denmark Vesey in Charleston in 1822[70] – reflected slave incorporation of libertarian revolutionary ideals, triggering reactions among their masters and later inspiring abolitionist forces in the northern states in degrees that far exceeded their immediate failures. Throughout the Western hemisphere from the 1770s onward, conflicts among the imperial powers or between metropolitan armies and patriotic American forces had forced both sides to enlist slaves in causes that increasingly involved the quest for, or defense of, 'freedom'. In the United States, freedmen and -women and escaped ex-slaves – Sojourner Truth, Frederick Douglass, Solomon Northrup, Maria Stewart, Martin Delaney and many others – used their personal experience and intimate knowledge of slavery's denial of fundamental human dignity to give the American abolitionist cause much of the mass appeal that led eventually to political confrontation, civil war and emancipation.[71] The confederacy of the southern states lost its coherence in the crucible of war and went down to defeat along a road paved with unmanageable slaves' abandonment of their masters gone to the front and of the women left to try to keep the economy running at home.[72]

The slaves' dignity and independence, even when it did not intensify to the level of active or visible restiveness, worked through innumerable indirect channels to encourage abolitionists in Europe. The slaves' resistance forced American slave-holders to take defensive, authoritarian and expensive steps that slowly, but surely, discredited them in the increasingly egalitarian and participatory political atmosphere of the nineteenth century. Growing slave numbers in themselves provoked masters' fears of a 'black majority'[73] and brought forth local calls for the ending of further imports. Open revolts by slaves provoked reprisals of the most extreme cruelty, not rendered acceptable by the *pro forma* legalities that frightened masters employed to attempt to justify them. Alarm at the possible inspiration offered American slaves by the Haitian revolution contributed to pressure to close the trade to South Carolina in the 1790s and to the final, national prohibition of imports in 1807. In North America, Chesapeake slaves, who had been reproducing themselves since the 1730s and 1740s, became English-speaking, increasingly Christian Americans, well aware of the liberal ideals circulating among their masters by the 1770s and 1780s. The end of slave importing to the British West Indies accelerated the Americanisation of slave populations there during the 1810s and 1820s, while flat sugar prices simultaneously increased pressures on them to work. The slaves' initiatives and their resistance to hard driving and other deprivations of the years after abolition of the trade became more and more difficult and expensive to contain. The growing impasse contributed to both the willingness of the British government to abandon its commitment to slave labour and to the acquiescence of the planter regimes in the islands to ameliorating and, ultimately, emancipating pressures from the metropole.[74]

With Britain's own slaving eliminated and its ideological and political dilemmas moving into domestic channels of reform, abolitionism did not decline but rather gained new force abroad.[75] London established the West Africa Squadron of the Royal Navy to patrol Atlantic slaving routes. For more than 30 years, it interfered with the transport of slaves by the ships of the continental powers. The Foreign Office simultaneously began to apply diplomatic pressure on the continental governments that allowed their citizens and subjects to remain active in the trade, in particular France and Spain. After 1823 a new wave of British social humanitarians raised their ambitions to move directly to eliminate slavery itself in the West Indies and at the Cape of Good Hope, in southern Africa, as well.[76] Nineteenth-century abolitionist opposition to the slave trade, that is, after 1807, became a vehicle for the promotion of British naval hegemony and, in the long run, for imperialist expansion and nationalistic confrontation with Britain's European rivals. Beyond displacing domestic tensions,[77] it became an instrument of British imperialist expansion around the world, useful because it wrapped the most aggressive intrusions in others' affairs in a cloak of moral justice. Slavers seemed to deserve any punishment that the British could give them.

Britain and British Imperialism

Britain channelled its reforming energies, blended with imperialist impulses, against the slaving of defeated nations in Europe as it and its allies triumphed in the Napoleonic wars. The Dutch, recently liberated from French control in the Napoleonic wars, found themselves compelled by British fiat to abandon their slaving enterprises, in spite of their clear perception of continued economic advantage for themselves in the trade.[78] The defeated French were led, reluctantly, to accept a prohibition against slaving by the terms of the 1815 Treaty of Vienna, but twice restored the trade before finally conceding its demise in 1845.[79] Having boarded a British fleet in 1807 to escape Napoleon's advance into peninsular Portugal, the Portuguese king and court were vulnerable – due to their huge Brazilian possessions in America – to subsequent abolitionist pressures from London. Agricultural Portugal and Brazil were, however, more economically dependent on continued slaving than were the industrialising nations of northern Europe. The 'Declaration on the Slave Trade' that Lisbon signed at the Congress of Vienna in 1815 committed Portugal to eventual termination of slaving but had only very limited effect for more than three decades, since both Portugal and Brazil were determined to avoid implementing its terms. Having declared its independence from Portugal in 1821, Brazil then in 1826 had to declare further imports of slaves illegal within three years as one cost of obtaining British diplomatic recognition. Brazilian slaving then thrived illegally until 1851 in the southern Atlantic and expanded into the Indian Ocean as well.[80]

Spain, with virtually no domestic abolitionist pressures, was primarily concerned to sustain the rapid nineteenth-century growth of its profitable sugar plantations in Cuba. It was also fearful that interference with the slave-based prosperity of Cuban planters would open them to overtures from the expansive slave-holding United States just to the north. Spain therefore managed to resist British diplomatic pressures to abolish its trade, with minor exceptions, until the 1860s. United States slavers, particularly from the 1830s onwards, became important suppliers of slaves to Cuba. Lingering US concerns to avoid domination by its former colonial ruler, the sensitivity of any issue involving slavery in the domestic political conflicts between northern and southern states, and US expansionist designs on Cuba made the United States generally hostile to British pressure to terminate its citizens' slaving. Formal agreement to end the trade, and effective suppression of it, came only in 1862, after the rupture between the Confederacy and the Union and the need for British support during the trials of the US Civil War.

Slave-trading in the Atlantic thus continued into the 1860s in spite of Britain's naval patrols and its persistent engagement of the issue in negotiations with the slaving nations over other matters. At times, the continuing trade included significant – and in some sectors even dominant – participation by ships of the two English-speaking powers that had first declared its end. Clearly, the merchants understood the continued economic viability of slaving and of slavery itself.[81] Although popular indifference abroad and tolerance, if not sympathetic support, among most politicians in Europe, combined with active hostility among planters and their suppliers in the New World and continued eagerness to provide slaves among African suppliers, delayed the ending of the trade, by the 1870s it had dwindled to insignificance nearly everywhere in the Atlantic.[82] Thereafter, legally and – for the moment at least – morally acceptable 'indentured' labourers from India, China, Japan and other parts of Asia, peasants from the rural regions of the Americas, and free immigrants from Europe supplemented enslaved Africans as low-paid workers in the commercial agriculture of the tropical Americas.[83]

Abolitionist energies in Britain then advanced into Asia and the Indian Ocean, still at the leading edge of Britain's expanding imperial power all around the globe. As the East India Company claimed increasing authority in South Asia during the first half of the nineteenth century, abolitionists at home brought increasing pressure to ameliorate the conditions of labour in its vast Asian domains.[84] Abolitionism remained a strong current of British reformism throughout the nineteenth century, repeatedly deriving renewed strength as it merged with other contemporary social and humanitarian causes. Perceived conflicts between needs for reform at home and conditions found, or created, abroad – like the connections that had flickered just below the surface of the original campaigns to end slaving in the Atlantic – became a more and more explicit theme. Prominent among them was the idea that the increasing government funds and energies being expended in military expansion abroad deprived Britons at home of badly needed social benefits. In addition, the justice of the dominion increasingly being claimed over independent peoples in other parts of the globe was profoundly dubious in these circles. The cause of imperial expansion could then be defended only in similarly moralising terms, including the opportunity that colonial rule offered to eradicate, around the globe, practices contrary to what Europeans came to understand as universal standards of progress and 'civilisation'.[85] Racialist beliefs rationalised the ability, and responsibility, of the Europeans to undertake this 'civilising mission'. Slavery became a primary symbol of the evils to be eradicated.

The limited effectiveness of early efforts at colonial rule severely compromised these reform impulses and delayed the ending of slavery in colonial possessions all around the world until after the First World War. As is well known, European nations competed for control in Asia and Africa through the nineteenth century. To defend against claims by rivals to areas of even potential interest there, colonial powers tended to declare spheres of influence, or to 'protect' local authorities, for the range of their ability to exercise more than nominal control. This pattern emerged first in India. In the period of Britain's direct conflict with Napoleonic France, the Company Raj in South Asia had thus asserted its authority over, and hence implicitly assumed responsibility for, territories that it barely knew, much less could control. It in fact could 'rule' only through elaborate understandings with the Indian regimes, often quite independent in spirit and capability, of the era. Since most of these rulers relied heavily on bonded labour of many sorts, including slaves, the British East India Company found itself vulnerable to its domestic opponents on the profound contradiction of its being able to maintain its presence in South Asia only by supporting coercive systems contrary to British principles of free labour and in clear violation of the mission to 'civilise' backward lands.

In India, with its many gradations of servility, slavery was only the most extreme of the coercive labour arrangements in effect and not often the critical factor in the economic control of Britain's Indian partners in rule. The 1838 Parliamentary act abolishing slavery in British possessions had extended to the American colonies and to South Africa but had none the less specifically excluded India and Ceylon. The Company regarded it as impossible to interfere too strongly in domestic arrangements on which it was entirely dependent, and so authorities turned to the relatively marginal trade in people legally termed 'slaves' as a conveniently visible target that would give an impression at home of action against slavery without arousing undue and uncontrollable local opposition in India. Dealing in slaves was prohibited in 1843, and British courts were forbidden to acknowledge slavery itself within the confined areas in which they exercised direct jurisdiction, according to a doctrine known as 'legal status abolition'.[86] It was argued that this formula, which temporarily mollified the abolitionists but did not directly threaten the local authorities in power, also protected slaves from eviction and destitution. It also planted seeds that in time would mature into effective termination of slavery, as the reach of British legal jurisdiction expanded, as interference with slaving limited the number of new captives and as the slaves already in residence followed the usual paths into other subordinated, but not legally enslaved, statuses. This policy extended the logic that had linked abolition of the trade in slaves to deferred emancipation in the New World at the end of the eighteenth century. And it maintained efforts to suppress trading in slaves at the cutting edge of much broader programmes of social reform emanating from Britain and, after the 1830s, extending to more and more areas of the world. The simultaneous growth of 'indentured' labour exports from India and other British possessions in Asia received notably less attention.

The anti-slaving initiative in India thus arose at the initial phases of Britain's developing strategies of modern colonial rule and was internal to British domains and therefore directly responsive to domestic policy formulation. In the international sphere, abolitionist attention shifted from European rivals to the trade supplying captives to the vast Ottoman domains, which extended from northwestern Africa to the Persian Gulf. Growing Ottoman commercial prosperity in the nineteenth century had stimulated demand for

Africans (and also Circassians and other central Asians) to work as urban domestics, in municipal services and in other dangerous and disdained occupations.[87] Exports of captive people from Sudanic Africa, from Senegal east to the Nile, from the fringes of the Ethiopian plateau and from eastern and south-eastern Africa had grown significantly during the middle third of the century.[88] At the same time, consolidation of political authority and economic integration on Madagascar under the Merina kingdom had made that island a further centre of slave-trading by the 1850s.[89] Britain thus became significantly more involved not only in inhibiting Ottoman slaving, but also by concluding in 1873 a treaty with the Sultan of Zanzibar, who was responsible for a key centre of Indian Ocean slaving that permitted British naval patrols to substantially reduce the movement of Africans by sea in the Indian Ocean by the 1880s.[90] The directness with which Britain was able to interfere in the slaving of the Indian Ocean grew in direct proportion to its vastly superior military and economic power and to the absence of the dense network of interests and diplomatic conventions that had precluded overt intrusions into the domains of its European rivals in the Atlantic. The racialist sense of a civilising mission justified measures in Asia and in Africa that would have been unacceptable among Europeans. Abolition had become the leading edge of Britain's assertion of powers that would culminate in formal colonial rule.

Bilateral Anglo-Ottoman anti-slaving conventions, to which the Ottoman Porte agreed but did not enforce, also began to take effect during the 1880s. A formal agreement was signed in 1880, conceding to Britain the right to search vessels suspected of carrying slaves to Ottoman territories and subjecting those found guilty to seizure. After Britain's occupation of Egypt in 1882 cut off, or diverted, the major source of captive Africans at that time, the disrupted regions of the Upper Nile valley, access to further supplies declined. The trade dwindled to a covert flow, particularly across the Red Sea to Arabia, that continued into the 1920s at least.[91]

Abolition in Africa

These successes in bilateral relations with weaker Asian powers coincided with a major effort to internationalise the late nineteenth-century abolitionist effort among the European powers. Once the campaign shifted to non-Western slaving, otherwise divided Europeans could find common cause, at least superficially, in suppressing it. The British Government was goaded at home by a very active British and Foreign Anti-Slavery Society which had emerged as the principal pressure group organised around the issue of slaving. It therefore kept up international pressures throughout the years following diminution of the issue – if not also the flow of coerced labour – in the Atlantic. Attention had turned to Africa itself with the signing of the Berlin Act of 1885, the multilateral European treaty that defined standards of international recognition of European nations' competing colonial claims in Africa. The Berlin Act contained limited condemnation of slavery in Africa, in tacit recognition of the lesson learned from attempting to confront strong local authorities dependent on unaccept-able forms of coerced labour in India. In Africa the horns of the dilemma were all the more sharply pointed. Europeans, particularly the British, were acutely sensitive to the ubiquity, and inequities, of slavery there.[92] David Livingstone's widely popular descriptions of his celebrated travels in central, southern and eastern Africa during the 1850s and 1860s had effectively dramatised the trade to the coast, particularly the routes feeding the Indian Ocean trade. Mission-ary societies had at once dispatched personnel to Christianise and 'civilise', and combat the trade. Later European travellers through the interior had enhanced sales of their published journals by appealing to the antipathy of the reading public to the slavery and slaving they observed.

The obviously widespread slaving within Africa during the 1870s and 1880s meant that the Berlin Act of 1885 awarded nominal political authority to European nations that would have to implement it, in the initial years, through the collaboration of African authorities more than marginally depend-ent on slavery. Early colonial estimates of the proportion of enslaved people in the populations they ruled produced numbers above 50 per cent and in local areas higher percentages still. In Africa, unlike in India, slavery was the prin-cipal means by which landowners and rulers in many parts of the continent, particularly in western Africa, controlled dependants beyond their immediate circle of relatives.[93] Even where colonial conquest eliminated the major mili-tary powers engaged in the most violent and systematic seizures of large num-bers of people – Samory in Upper Guinea, Rabeh in the Chadian and Nilotic Sudan, the Sokoto caliphate west of Lake Chad, Tippu Tib and his Swahili 'Arab' allies on the upper Zaire – the nascent colonial governments found themselves heavily dependent on Africans who could not maintain themselves without their slave dependants. Humanitarians in Africa, too, as in India, could worry about the fates of former captives suddenly turned out, far from home and with no means of supporting themselves, by masters prevented from exercising their rights as owners.[94] The solution would be the same: an initial prohibition of further dealing in slaves, along with refusal by colonial courts to recognise the status of slavery under African or Muslim law, and quiet collaboration with slave-holding African authorities while both sides waited for the growth of colonial power, the spread of the cash economy and diminished supplies of new captives to erode the institution and replace it with new forms of control over workers and women.[95]

The formal discussions in Europe, far from the realities of attempting to exercise effective authority from very weak positions on the ground in Africa, took the form of an international convention adopted at Brussels in 1889–90, piously opposed to all of the evils then perceived as besetting Africans. In addition to the continuing liberal concerns of British abolitionists, impetus from France came from Catholic religious sources. Cardinal Lavigerie and the Pères du Saint-Esprit, or White Fathers,[96] publicised the horror felt throughout Europe at the slaving still thriving in Central Africa and added to the momentum building up for a second international conference to deal specifically with issues of the slave trade. The Brussels Conference pledged the participating nations – including all of those active in colonial subjugation in Africa – to a range of reforms, including prohibition of the trades in arms and liquor to African possessions, the continued suppression of international slaving and the ending of slavery in Africa itself.[97]

The colonial powers proceeded cautiously against slaving within their colonial possessions in Africa, focusing first on ending continued trading.[98] Some treaties confirming conquest obligated defeated African powers to terminate raiding as part of the price of submission. Imposition of terms like these suppressing slave-trading on a defeated rival continued policies first established at the Congress of Vienna in 1815. But many other treaties signed in the last decades of the nineteenth century discreetly failed to mention the issue. When European rule became more firmly established during the first decade of the twentieth century, colonial authorities issued bans against slave-trading, nearly two decades after formally assuming authority. The French formally moved first, in 1903.[99] However, people whom they could not control, such as the Berbers of the Saharan regions in French Mauritania, escaped suppression into the 1930s. The Portuguese in Angola tacitly collaborated with some of the people they ruled in Angola to supply labourers for Portuguese enterprises until well into the colonial period. And none of the powers was exempt from tolerating slaving that they could not prevent. Only with the advent of much more dense institutions of police control, the spread of cash economies and rural impoverishment – particularly with colonial needs to mobilise labour and resources during the First World War – did slaving diminish along the course foreseen. It continued longer in Ethiopia, which was not subject to colonial strictures and was adjacent to small surviving markets for captive Africans across the Red Sea. Slavery, or its residual effects on the descendants of those who came to their present homes in captivity, lasted longer still.

Conclusion

Abolition thus originated at the cutting edge of social reform in Britain, gained force in the New World, with the efforts of the slaves themselves, and later advanced as an entering wedge for British consolidation of power around the Atlantic, in India, through the western Indian Ocean, on the fringes of the Ottoman empire and in Africa. It was transformed from a movement primarily domestic in its dynamic to an aspect of intrusion into the American colonies of Portugal and Spain and the independent Latin American nations that emerged from the dissolution of their New World empires. It then justified imperial and colonial rule with extension of the campaign to suppress maritime slaving into the Indian Ocean and the shores of the Ottoman Mediterranean in the 1860s and 1870s, more than incidentally coinciding with the opening of the Suez Canal in 1869. Suppression of slaving became an issue in the delicate politics of the early, weak years of colonial rule in India in the 1840s and then, later in the 1890s, in Africa. Throughout, it marked increased public intervention in local affairs and state interference in relationships between masters and slaves that had historically been matters of intense, if also often hostile, privacy – including preserves of masters' honour and resistance to government intrusion.

Abolition thus followed in the wake of integration of each of these world regions into Europe's growing economic sphere, injecting government power into the lives of masters and slaves alike. Throughout the years from the 1770s until the First World War, when Europe's reforming impulses returned closer to home, abolition remained a convenient vehicle for presenting control by the powerful as commitment to the cause of social justice, in the midst of insoluble social problems at home. In the Americas, slaving was seldom ended by direct suppression, because abolition, by its inherently transformative nature, continually focused attention just beyond the effective reach of European – usually British – power. In Asia and Africa, the pattern remained the same. Abolition thus remained dynamic for a century and a half, continually renewed because it could never fully attain the ends it proclaimed. But the beginnings of local economic decline around the world – as industrialisation and agricultural mechanisation sent people from impoverished rural areas into the cities and abroad to the industrialising nations where the abolitionist impulse had arisen through movements of 'free' indentured contract labourers and 'voluntary' emigrants – eventually imparted more than nominal effect to the principles proclaimed. Coercion has not yet, of course, ended, and substandard and sub-subsistence conditions are still imposed on 'undocumented aliens', *Gastarbeitern*, oscillating labour migrants and other modern successors to the Africans transported as slaves in the eighteenth and nineteenth centuries. The abolitionist impulse has, accordingly, broadened and been further internationalised through the activities of the League of Nations in the 1920s and, since 1949, those of the United Nations into contemporary programmes defending universal human rights.

The essence of abolitionism, viewed over the full century and a half of its expansion around the globe, thus appears as its conversion of the quintessentially intimate relationship between master and slave into a public travesty, a cause enabling generations of politicians to hide self-interest, conservation of the privileges of the rich and powerful, and national aggression behind the cause of humane justice. The movement's ideologues, from French *philosophes*, Scottish liberals and English evangelicals in the late eighteenth century to socialist-leaning reformers in the twentieth century, have been moved by sincere dedication to improvement of the human fate. But their ideals alone had little effect. American slaves – to a vastly greater degree than those enslaved in Africa or Asia – contributed to their own emancipation by creating and maintaining cultures of their own and by resisting, openly and violently as well as insidiously and subtly. Elsewhere abolition served as an entering wedge for the consolidation of European governmental power over economic links spreading outwards through the nineteenth century towards the most remote corners of the globe. A similar case may be made for the extension of northern industrial influence through the rural states of the Old

South that followed abolitionism in the United States. If abolition was an aspect of an essentially political process of expansion and consolidation of governmental power, domestically and around the world, it should not be a matter of surprise that it often defied the economic interests of those who gained, even indirectly, from transporting, provisioning, owning or working the slaves and their products.

Notes

1. Against a background of narrow scholarly focus on slavery in the nineteenth-century United States and elsewhere in the Americas, recognition of the ubiquity of slavery had been growing slowly through two decades of research, when the publication of Orlando Patterson's *Slavery and Social Death* (1982) made the point emphatically and with elegant theoretical sophistication. Moses I. Finley had earlier stressed the importance of slavery to the societies of the ancient Mediterranean and the blindness to it in European scholarship, culminating in his *Ancient Slavery and Modern Ideology* (1980). Slavery in Africa had been similarly obscured by scholarly preoccupations until the work of Claude Meillassoux, most significantly *L'esclavage en Afrique précoloniale* (1975), and then the collection edited by Suzanne Miers and Igor Kopytoff, *Slavery in Africa: Historical and Anthropological Perspectives* (1977). European stereotypes of Muslims as 'master slavers' yielded to more analytical studies of the persistence and varying forms of enslavement under Islam; see J.O. Hunwick, 'Black Africans in the Mediterranean world: Introduction to a neglected aspect of the African diaspora', in E. Savage, 1992, pp. 5–38, and M. Gordon, 1989. Numerous studies then followed revealing the significance of the institution in other parts of the world, including Russia (R. Hellie, 1982), Southeast Asia (A. Reid, 1983), medieval and Renaissance Europe (W.D. Phillips, 1985), and in general, J.D. Watson, 1980, and L.J. Archer, 1988.
2. More than a million of them passed through Whydah (Ouidah), the very spot where the international conference on 'The Slave Route' assembled in September 1994. I am grateful to UNESCO for the opportunity to be present on that occasion and to conference participants for comments that I have found vital in preparing the present revised text.
3. O. Patterson, 1991. The literature on slavery has not developed 'subaltern' theories of cultural domination parallel to those characteristic of much recent work on the colonised parts of the modern world, in particular South Asia. I attribute the emphatic recognition of slave integrity and initiative to the intensity of the effort necessary to break free of 'slavish', or 'Sambo', stereotypes of the docile, acquiescing slave personality; W.E. Evans, 1980, pp. 15–43 (and reprinted in The Black Diaspora Committee of Howard University, 1986, pp. 80–112). For other work on subordinated non-industrial cultures, see J.C. Scott, 1976, 1985 and 1990. For further references in the context of peasants in Africa, see A F. Isaacman, 1990, pp. 1–120. The connections between this literature and that on working classes in industrial societies are intimate, complex and beyond the scope of the present note. A useful recent discussion is found in J. Glassman, 1991, pp. 277–312.
4. D.B. Davis, 1966, for the ancient Mediterranean and Christian Europe. More generally, O. Patterson, 1982.

5. P. Dockès, 1979 (translated [by Arthur Goldhammer] as *Medieval Slavery and Liberation* [Chicago, 1982]), gives late Roman and early medieval slaves a determining role in the broad transformation of European institutions leading to the consolidation of feudalism by the twelfth century. In a very complex Marxist model, Dockès's rural slaves' resistance forced masters into accommodations that eventuated in rights to land and other concessions that finally left European slavery an exclusively urban institution by the fifteenth and sixteenth centuries. In sharp contrast to the leading role of government in nineteenth-century abolitionism, for Dockès the state was then the primary guarantor of slavery, as guarantor of the masters' superiority over their resisting bondsmen and -women.

6. Most of the extensive historiography of slave resistance in the New World has been limited to descriptive studies demonstrating that it existed. The relationship of slave resistance to abolition receives forceful and systematic treatment primarily in E.D. Genovese, 1979, and in the elaborate analysis of R. Blackburn, 1988. For the full general bibliography, see J.C. Miller, 1993, especially index entries 'Resistance' (108 refs.) and 'Revolts' (190 refs.).

7. As specialists in the history of Africa have emphasised: P.E. Lovejoy, 1983; P. Manning, 1990; W.G. Clarence-Smith, 1988; Savage, 1992. From the perspective of international efforts to end these trades around the fringes of the Ottoman empire, E. Toledano, 1982.

8. Since P.E. Lovejoy, 1983: J.E. Inikori et al., 1986; G.R. Campbell, 1981, pp. 203–227, and idem, 1989, pp. 1–27; E.A. Eldredge and F. Morton, 1994.

9. J.E. Harris, 1971; U. Patnaik and M. Dingwaney, 1985; J.F. Warren, 1981; R. Needham, 1983.

10. D. Eltis, 1987.

11. The paradigmatic study is R. Coupland, 1933. Coupland was himself concerned primarily to trace the history of the reform movement in Great Britain, and only secondarily – since he took it for granted – with how the campaign there might have *caused* the end of slavery in the broader senses in which subsequent historians have understood the process. Economic historians, considering the movement in the context of British industrial and commercial development, contemplated additional levels of significance.

12. J. Coughtry, 1981.

13. Though not internal trading. For the US, M. Tadman, 1989.

14. In addition to Eltis, 1987, see C. Lloyd, 1968; W.E.F. Ward, 1969; R.C. Howell, 1987.

15. The definitive work on the ending of the French trade was rather later than its counterparts: S. Daget, 1990. For a preview, see S. Daget, 1975, pp. 23–54, or idem, 1981, pp. 193–217.

16. L. Bethell, 1970; R.E. Conrad, 1985, translated as R.E. Conrad, 1986.

17. W.S. Howard, 1963; P. Duignan and C. Clendenen, 1963.

18. D.R. Murray, 1980. Of course, Eltis, 1987, has synthesised and superseded the first generation of specialised studies.

19. Although his critical response, *Capitalism and Slavery* (1944), did not reach print for several years. C.L.R. James, 1938, according to Darity, picked up French historians' more cynical assessments of Britain's reasons for abolishing its slave trade; also see W. Darity, Jr., 1988, pp. 29–41, for previous British economic historians' development of arguments that Williams drew together into his master synthesis.

20. Though one that was slow to develop and was largely critical; Centre of African Studies, 1965. Recent, rehabilitative, studies are in B.L. Solow and S.L. Engerman, 1987.

21. W.E.B. Du Bois, 1896 (new ed., with foreword by John Hope Franklin, 1969).

22. E. Williams, 1942, pp. 175–191.
23. L. Bethell, 1970; D.R. Murray, 1980. Also D.M. Williams, 1973, pp. 103–115.
24. Most approachable through two recent collections of papers. For the trans-Saharan trade, see E. Savage, 1992, and for the Indian Ocean and Red Sea trades, W.G. Clarence-Smith, 1988.
25. As developed by D.B. Davis in his sequel, 1975.
26. See the substantial collection of papers edited by S. Miers and R. Roberts, 1988, and more broadly, M.A. Klein, 1993.
27. See Moses Finley's seminal definition in the *Encyclopedia of the Social Sciences* (1968), Vol. 14, pp. 307–313. Claimed exceptions are celebrated, and doubtful: e.g. R. Hellie, 1989, p. 24. He also lists 'sub-continental Indians ... and perhaps Koreans'.
28. Patterson's term, in *Slavery and Social Death*, for the same emphasis.
29. Exceptions – Denmark and the US – noted below.
30. Although depictions of the horrors of 'the path' in Africa became standard fare in the travel accounts of the first Europeans to send back eyewitness reports of conditions there; e.g. Mungo Park.
31. Ubiquitously reproduced; or a recent version, Conrad, 1983, illus. 1 (p. 21); J. Walvin, 1994, pp. 46–48, emphasises the propaganda impact of the diagram; also see the similar diagram reproduced facing p. 174. A 1789 broadsheet utilising the *Brookes* is reproduced on the jacket cover of H.S. Klein, 1978. Men who, as slaves, had survived the Atlantic crossing contributed to the campaign as well with gripping accounts of their experience; notably, *The Interesting Narrative of the Life of Olauda Equiano* (1789), subsequently republished many times, and recently a subject of critical literary analysis; E. Abanime, 1979, pp. 80–84; P. Edwards, 1990, pp. 216–226. Also see G. I. Jones, 1967, pp. 60–98.
32. It was also true that the existence of slavery kept the traders in business and that emancipation of the slaves would put an end to slaving. In practice, emancipation was a domestic issue, not an international campaign like abolitionism, and in the Americas normally followed the suppression of slave imports by about a generation.
33. A point developed with elegant theoretical force, though in different terms, by C. Meillassoux, 1986, and translated (by Alide Dasnois) as *The Anthropology of Slavery: The Womb of Iron and Gold* (1991).
34. A point first established in demographic terms and emphasised in P.D. Curtin, 1969, and subsequently studied in great detail in many specific regions, perhaps most comprehensively in B.W. Higman, 1984.
35. K.F. Kiple, 1985.
36. The psychological disorientation and passivity – and, as is now suspected, nutritional deprivation – of slaves just off the ships could be extreme, as the high death rates among recent arrivals emphasise. But slaves regained more than sufficient resiliency and initiative after recovering from the traumas of the middle passage to survive, to resist their captivity and to build communities and worlds of their own. Key landmarks in the development of this theme, one of the most pervasive in scholarship on slavery anywhere in the world during the last thirty years, include S.M. Elkins, 1959, and subsequent editions, which overstated the slaves' disability and attributed it primarily to life under slavery rather than to the process of enslavement; J. Blassingame, 1972, revised 1979; and E.D. Genovese, 1974.
37. Circumstances emphasised most systematically in S. Mintz and R. Price, 1976. The slaves' inability to arrive with personal initiative intact, and even social and cultural group coherence, is currently subject to careful re-evaluation; J.K. Thornton, 1992, and a lengthening series of case-studies: 'African dimensions of the

Stono Rebellion', *American Historical Review*, Vol. 96, No. 5 (1991), pp. 1101–1113; 'African soldiers in the Haitian revolution', *Journal of Caribbean History*, Vol. 25, Nos. 1–2 (1991), pp. 58–80; '"I am the subject of the King of Congo": African political ideology and the Haitian revolution', *Journal of World History*, Vol. 4, No. 2 (1993), pp. 181–214; 'Central African names and African-American naming patterns', *William and Mary Quarterly*, Vol. 40, No. 4 (1993), pp. 727–742; 'The role of Africans in the Atlantic economy: Modern Africanist historiography and the world systems paradigm', *Colonial Latin American Historical Review*, Vol. 3 (1994), pp. 125–140.

38. Veteran slaves' acquired skills clearly earned their keep, but the costs of containing them in bondage clearly exceeded the differential between slavery and freedom, as the frequency of manumission and the encouragement of self-purchase demonstrated everywhere outside the US.

39. Although, in the throes of political campaigns to end the trade, they usually tolerated claims that self-reproducing slave populations were possible and even viable in the long run, the futility of this strategy soon became apparent and was used to support further efforts to emancipate.

40. P. Manning, 1990, pp. 18–19.

41. S.E. Green-Pedersen, 1979, pp. 399–418.

42. Other factors included the prospect of abolition in the British islands, which Danish traders supplied with slaves, and the high costs and low profits of attempting to maintain a small African commerce in a market dominated by giant competitors.

43. J.R. Ward, 1988.

44. A point emphasised first in P.D. Curtin, 1969, and still not fully explained in spite of sustained scholarly investigation.

45. D. Eltis, 1987, p. 207, citing D.L. Robinson, 1971, pp. 232–233, 295–346.

46. A relatively simplified version of Williams's entire case, although Williams at certain points indulged in rather strong statements of aspects of this particular point: 'It was the capital accumulation of Liverpool which called the population of Lancashire into existence and stimulated the manufactures of Manchester. That capital accumulation came from the slave trade, whose importance was appreciated more by contemporaries than by later historians.' However, earlier in the same paragraph he had qualified the point, even contradicting himself, by writing that Thomas Clarkson, certainly a contemporary and leading abolitionist, had acknowledged 'that the rise of Liverpool is due to a variety of causes'. See Williams, *Capitalism and Slavery* (New York: Capricorn Books edition, 1966), p. 63.

47. R.T. Anstey, 1975, pp. 406–407.

48. Differing national attitudes towards Africans, as blacks, were also influential. While the English might respond to abolitionists' images of slaves as redeemable 'noble savages', as 'men and brothers' brutalised only by the corruption of slavery, the French saw Africans, enslaved or not, as irredeemably brutish. See S. Daget, 1981, pp. 193–217; S. Drescher, 1992, pp. 361–396.

49. And French politicians, and later historians, cast a jaundiced eye on British humanitarianism as a cynical distraction from the real underlying economic and aggressively imperialist impulses that abolition served, particularly as Britain developed it as an international cause after 1815. Eric Williams (see note 15), had he referred to the French strain in the historiography, would have found ample support for his version of the case against humanitarian complacency.

50. And to the abolition of slavery itself almost at once, in 1833 (to take effect in 1834). J. Walvin, 1981, pp. 63–79; idem, 1986; S. Drescher, 1987a.

51. In this context, the élitism of the French abolitionists seems explicable. If the populist aspects of abolitionism in England amounted to an assault on the exclusivism of British politics as practised in the late eighteenth century, they relieved anti-government pressures of the sort that led to the fall of the Bastille in 1789 in Paris. Conversely, in France the fundamental impulses of the masses towards political participation were drawn into republican governments in the early 1790s, then diverted into war and finally, after 1815, channelled again into politics. The release of political energies in French domestic institutions meant that abolitionism did not assume the burden of expressing social tensions at home in the same way that it did across the Channel.

52. D.B. Davis, 1966. Davis restates and amplifies this argument in Davis, 1987, pp. 209–227. H. Temperley, 1981, pp. 21–35, inverted the ideological thrust to argue that it was faith in the ideal of 'free labor' as it was emerging in industrialising Britain that animated popular efforts to extend the same privilege to slaves elsewhere.

53. S. Drescher, 1987b, pp. 191–208 (citing p. 195).

54. S. Drescher, 1977. There has also been a restatement of the Williams 'decline' thesis by S.H.H. Carrington, in three essays; the first version to appear was 'Econocide': Myth or Reality? The Question of West Indian Decline, 1783–1806', 1986, pp. 13–38 (with response by Drescher and 'postscriptum' by Carrington). This is not the place to enter into the technicalities of the subtle discussions among economic historians in this debate; but for recent positions and a summary, see Solow and Engerman, 1987.

55. E.g. R.T. Anstey, 1975, chap. 2, in an analysis appearing first in 1968.

56. J.E. Inikori, 1981, pp. 745–776.

57. This was the key variable in Williams's implicit model, and the ground on which Drescher demonstrated its factual weakness.

58. J.E. Inikori, 1987, pp. 103–133, pp. 79–101 (quote from p. 92), caps Inikori's lengthy series of detailed, highly creative and intensely debated empirical arguments in presenting a formal model of the process. The previous quoted phrase is from the subtitle of Inikori's doctoral dissertation (University of Ibadan, 1973).

59. Or, stating the point in terms of productive efficiency, the effect was to transport workers from African environments in which their productivity was low to more productive, capital-intensive plantations. Alternatively, it was extremely expensive to transport, by land, bulk products produced by free labourers in Africa, but it was much less costly from islands accessible to early modern European maritime shipping.

60. B.L. Solow, 1987, pp. 51–77,

61. D. Richardson, 1987, pp. 103–133.

62. R.T. Anstey, 1975, is an exception in combining in emphasis on the efficacy of ideas with political applications.

63. A three-way debate initiated by Thomas Haskell in reaction to D.B. Davis, 1966, and joined by John Ashworth. The principal statements are collected and introduced in T. Bender, 1992; for the quote, see p. 3.

64. See J.C. Miller, 1993, for the full bibliography. The index entry for 'maroons' shows 178 works focused on these communities; the standard starting-point remains R. Price, 1973; second edition with a new afterword (Baltimore, 1979); translated as *Sociedades cimarronas: comunidades esclavas rebeldes en las Américas* (Mexico, 1981).

65. A paradigmatic study for Brazil is J.J. Reis, 1986, revised and expanded in an edition translated in 1993 by Arthur Brakel as *Slave Rebellion in Brazil: The Muslim Uprising of 1835 in Bahia*. Also see J.J. Reis, 1988.

66. J.W. Blassingame, 1972; revised edition, 1979; and discussion in A.-T. Gilmore, 1978. The most theoretically developed Marxist case for the slave community is, of course, E.D. Genovese, 1974. As Genovese phrased the issue in 1979, p. xviii: '... the rich and contradictory process whereby the slaves fashioned their own history within the contours of the dominant modes of production.'

67. R. Dirks, 1987; idem, 1978, pp. 122–180; idem, 1988, pp. 167–194.

68. C.L.R. James, 1963.

69. G.W. Mullin, 1972; M. Mullin, 1978, pp. 235–267.

70. William W. Freehling, 1986, pp. 25–47, for the most recent, and penetrating, statement.

71. W.E.B. Du Bois first drew attention to US slaves' awareness of, and dedication to, the libertarian ideals of the ambivalent founders of the North American republic; Herbert Aptheker, 1943, and many other writings, including idem, 1987, pp. 68–71. For a retrospective and appreciation, see G.Y. Okihiro, 1986.

72. D.G. Faust, 1996.

73. P.H. Wood, 1974. The point had been made earlier by Du Bois.

74. E.D. Genovese, 1979, and R. Blackburn, 1988, both provide sweeping recent interpretations of abolition and emancipation that emphasise the slaves' contributions to their own liberation in the midst of the imperial struggles of the era, and the shifting balances in the conflict between conservative regimes in Europe and the growing populist challenges that they faced.

75. D.B. Davis, 1987, makes clear that displacement of immediate domestic tensions outward also left a domestic residue of reformism that continued to thrive.

76. This latter domestic emancipation campaign developed a dynamic of its own and will not be pursued here, where attention remains fixed on abolition of slave-trading in the international environment. For South Africa, R.L. Watson, 1990; J.E. Mason, 1996; M.I. Rayner, 1986.

77. Unless one emphasises Lenin's explanation of imperialism and nationalism as a means of lessening class conflict in the capitalist metropole.

78. P.C. Emmer, 1981, pp. 177–192.

79. S. Daget, 1990.

80. L. Bethell, 1970; R.E. Conrad, 1986.

81. D. Eltis, 1987, provides a masterful and comprehensive study of the trade, including numerous insights on the ironies and contradictions of abolitionism after 1807.

82. The French continued to transport 'indentured' Africans (*engagés*) into the 1860s and 1870s, and the Portuguese supplied labour on various pretexts to Cuba, preserving a local export in *libertos* (freedmen) to São Tomé into the twentieth century. For the Portuguese, W.G. Clarence-Smith, 1993, pp. 150–170; idem, 1984, pp. 25–33; J. Duffy, 1967.

83. Although not a subject that can receive more than passing acknowledgement in a survey of slaving and its abolition, for emphasis on the continuity, see Eric Wolf, 1982, chap. 12, and other modern global histories. Stanley L. Engerman has written extensively on the economics of the transition from 'coerced' to 'free' labour in the nineteenth century; e.g. S.L. Engerman, 1986, pp. 263–294. Also, for late-nineteenth-century Atlantic emigration in the context of slaving, see Emmer, 1990, pp. 11–24; idem, 1992, pp. 1–12; M. Twaddle, 1993 – also as special issue, *Slavery and Abolition*, Vol. 14, No. 1 (1993).

84. H. Temperley, 1972.
85. It is, of course, impossible to enter seriously into the scholarship on these vast changes in Europe and around the world in this era; for a recent survey, see M. Adas, 1989.
86. D. Khumar, 1993, pp. 112–130, and G. Prakash, 1993, pp. 131–149. Also U. Patnaik and M. Dingwaney, 1985.
87. W.G. Clarence-Smith, 1988; F. Savage, 1992; E. Toledano, 1982.
88. For a survey of the events in Africa contributing to these exports, see P.E. Lovejoy, 1983.
89. Among the numerous studies of G.R. Campbell, 1988, pp. 166–193.
90. A. Sheriff, 1987.
91. E. Toledano, 1982, esp. chap. 7.
92. They were much less aware of the extent to which the 'legitimate' nineteenth-century trades in palm oil, groundnuts, ivory and other products – which the abolitionists had championed as substitutes for slaves in promoting European trade with Africa – had also stimulated slaving and slavery; P.E. Lovejoy, 1983.
93. C. Meillassoux, 1986. Also Claire C. and M.A. Klein and C.C. Robertson, 1983. For central Africa, R. Harms, 1981; and for other dependent statuses, J. Vansina, 1990. One alternative, close to but distinct from slavery, was pawnship; see T. Falola and P.E. Lovejoy, 1993.
94. A further ironic subtheme in the process of abolition in Africa therefore became the dilemma faced by missionaries committed to ending slavery, who redeemed captives, sometimes by direct purchase, and thus in more than a technical sense themselves became involved in slaving.
95. M. Wright, 1993.
96. F. Renault, 1971.
97. S. Miers, 1975.
98. S. Miers and R. Roberts, 1988. See also the thorough monograph by P.E. Lovejoy and J.S. Hogendorn, 1993; C.N. Ubah, 1991, pp. 447–470; F. Cooper, 1980.
99. Forthcoming work by Martin A. Klein will provide similarly comprehensive and probing coverage of the end of slavery in French West Africa; for a preview, see M.A. Klein, 1988–89, pp. 188–211.

Bibliography

ABANIME, E. 1979. 'Equiano, précurseur de la littérature nigériane anglophone'. *Éthiopiques* (Dakar), No. 19.
ABZUG, R.H., and MAIZLISH, S.E. (eds.) 1986. *New Perspectives on Slavery in America: Essays in Honor of Kenneth M. Stampp.* Lexington, University Press of Kentucky.
ADAS, M. 1989. *Machines as the Measure of Men: Science, Technology and Ideologies of Western Dominance.* London, Ithaca/Cornell University Press.
ANSTEY, R.T. 1975. *The Atlantic Slave Trade and British Abolition, 1760–1810.* Atlantic Highlands, Macmillan.
APTHEKER, H. 1943. *American Negro Slave Revolts.* New York, Columbia University Press.

————. 1987. 'American Negro slave revolts: Fifty years gone'. *Science and Society* (New York), Vol. 51, No. 1.

ARCHER, L.J. 1988. *Slavery and Other Forms of Unfree Labour.* London, Routledge.

BENDER, T. (ed.). 1992. *The Anti-Slavery Debate: Capitalism and Abolitionism as a Problem in Historical Interpretation.* Berkeley/Los Angeles, University of California Press.

BETHELL, L. 1970. *The Abolition of the Brazilian Slave Trade: Britain, Brazil and the Slave Trade Question, 1807–1869.* Cambridge, Cambridge University Press.

BLACK DIASPORA COMMITTEE OF HOWARD UNIVERSITY (ed.). 1986. *The African Diaspora: Africans and Their Descendants in the Wider World to 1800.* Lexington. Mass., Ginn Press.

BLACKBURN, R. 1988. *The Overthrow of Colonial Slavery, 1776–1848.* London, Verso.

BLASSINGAME, J.W. 1972 (revised 1979). *The Slave Community: Plantation Life in the Antebellum South.* New York, Oxford University Press.

CAMPBELL, G.R. 1981. 'Madagascar and the slave trade, 1810–1895'. *Journal of African History* (Cambridge), Vol. 22, No. 2.

————. 1988. 'Madagascar and Mozambique in the Slave Trade of the Western Indian Ocean, 1800–1861'. *Slavery and Abolition* (London),Vol. 9, No. 3.

————. 1989. 'The East African slave trade, 1876–1895: The Southern complex'. *International Journal of African Historical Studies* (Boston), Vol. 22, No. 1.

CARRINGTON, S.H.H. 1986. 'Econocide': Myth or reality? The question of West Indian decline, 1783–1806'. *Boletín de estudios latinoamericanos y del Caribe*, Vol. 36.

CENTRE OF AFRICAN STUDIES. 1965. *The Transatlantic Slave Trade from West Africa.* Edinburg, University of Edinburg.

CLARENCE-SMITH, W.G. 1984. 'The Portuguese contribution to the Cuban slave and coolie trades in the nineteenth century'. *Slavery and Abolition* (London), Vol. 8, No. 1.

————. 1988. 'The economics of the Indian Ocean slave trade in the nineteenth century'. *Slavery and Abolition* (London), Vol. 9, No. 3.

————. 1993. 'Cocoa plantations and coerced labor in the Gulf of Guinea, 1870–1914'. In Klein, M.A. (ed.) *Breaking the Chains: Slavery, Bondage and Emancipation in Modern Africa and Asia.* Madison, University of Wisconsin Press.

CONRAD, R.E. 1983. *Children of God's Fire.* Princeton, Princeton University Press.

————. 1985. *Tumbeiros: o tráfico de escravospara o Brasil.* São Paulo, Brazil, Cunha Press.

————. 1986. *World of Sorrow: The African Slave Trade to Brazil.* Baton Rouge, Louisiana State University Press.

COOPER, F. 1980. *From Slaves to Squatters: Plantation Labour and Agriculture in Zanzibar and Coastal Kenya, 1890–1925.* New Haven, Yale University Press.

COUGHTRY, J. 1981. *The Notorious Triangle: Rhode Island and the African Slave Trade, 1700–1807.* Philadelphia, Temple University Press.

COUPLAND, R. 1933. *The British Anti-Slavery Movement.* London, Oxford University Press.

CROW, J.J., and TISE, L.E. (eds.). 1978. *The Southern Experience in the American Revolution.* Chapel Hill, University of North Carolina Press.

CURTIN, P.D. 1969. *The Atlantic Slave Trade: A Census.* Madison, University of Wisconsin Press.

———— (ed.). 1967. *Africa Remembered: Narratives by West Africans from the Era of the Slave Trade.* Madison, University of Wisconsin Press.

DAGET, S. 1975. 'Le trafic négrier illégal français de 1814 à 1860: historiographie et sources'. *Annales de l'Université d'Abidjan.* No. 3. (Série 1, Histoire.)

———. 1981. 'France, suppression of the illegal trade, and England, 1817–1850'. In Walvin, J. and Eltis, D. (eds.). *The Abolition of the Atlantic Slave Trade: Origins and Effects in Europe, Africa and the Americas.* Madison, University of Wisconsin Press.

———. 1990. *La traite des Noirs: bastilles négrières et velléités abolitionnistes.* Paris, Ouest-France Université.

DARITY, W. JR. 1988. 'The Williams thesis before Williams'. *Slavery and Abolition* (London), Vol. 9, No. 1.

DAVIS, D.B. 1966. *The Problem of Slavery in Western Culture.* New York, Cornell University Press/Ithaca.

———. 1975. *The Problem of Slavery in the Age of Revolution, 1770–1823.* New York, Cornell University Press/Ithaca.

———. 1987. 'Capitalism, abolitionism, and hegemony'. In Solow, B.L., and Engerman, S.L. *British Capitalism and Caribbean Slavery: The Legacy of Eric Williams.* New York, Cambridge University Press.

DIRKS, R. 1987. *The Black Saturnalia: Conflict and Its Ritual Expression on British West Indian Slave Plantations.* Gainesville, University Presses of Florida.

———. 1978. 'Resource fluctuations and competitive transformation in West Indian slave societies'. In Laughlin, C.D. Jr, and Brady, I.A. (eds.). *Extinction and Survival in Human Populations.* New York, Columbia University Press.

———. 1988. 'The black saturnalia and relief-induced agonism'. In KIPLE, K.F. (ed.). *The African Exchange: Toward a Biological History of the Black People.* Durham, N.C., Duke University Press.

DOCKÈS, P. 1979. *La libération médiévale.* Paris, Flammarion.

DRESCHER, S. 1977. *Econocide: British Slavery in the Era of Abolition.* Pittsburgh, University of Pittsburgh Press.

———. 1987a. *Capitalism and Antislavery: British Mobilization in Comparative Perspective.* London, Oxford University Press.

———. 1987b. 'Paradigms tossed: Capitalism and the political sources of abolition'. In Solow, B.L., and Engerman, S.L. *British Capitalism and Caribbean Slavery: The Legacy of Eric Williams.* New York, Cambridge University Press.

———. 1992. 'The ending of the slave trade and the evolution of European scientific realism'. In Inikori, J.E., and Engerman, S. (eds.). *The Atlantic Slave Trade Effects on Economies, Societies and Peoples in Africa, the Americas and Europe.* Durham, Duke University Press.

DU BOIS, W.E.B. 1896. *The Suppression of the African Slave Trade, 1638–1870.* New York, Longmans Green. (New edition, Baton Rouge, J. H. Franklin, 1969.)

DUFFY, J. 1967. *A Question of Slavery.* Cambridge, Mass., Harvard University Press.

DUIGNAN, P., and CLENDENEN, C. 1963. *The United States and the African Slave Trade, 1619–1862.* Stanford, Stanford University Press.

EDWARDS, P. 1990. 'Master and father in Equiano's interesting narrative'. *Slavery and Abolition* (London), Vol. 11, No. 2.

ELDREDGE, E.A., and MORTON, F. 1994. *Slavery in South Africa: Captive Labour on the Dutch Frontier.* San Francisco/Oxford, Boulder/Westview Press.

ELKINS, S.M. 1959. *Slavery: A Problem in American Institutional and Intellectual Life.* Chicago, University of Chicago Press.

ELTIS, D. 1987. *Economic Growth and the Ending of the Transatlantic Slave Trade.* New York, Oxford University Press.

EMMER, P.C. (ed.) 1986. *Colonialism and Migration: Indentured Labour before and after Slavery.* Dordrecht, M. Nijhoff.

EMMER, P.C. 1981. 'Abolition of the abolished: The illegal Dutch slave trade and the mixed courts'. In Walvin, J., and Eltis, D. (eds.). *The Abolition of the Atlantic Slave Trade*. Madison, University of Wisconsin Press.

———. 1990. 'European expansion and migration: The European colonial past and intercontinental migration – an overview'. *Itinerario* (Leiden), Vol. 14, No. 1.

———. 1992. 'European expansion and migration: The European colonial past and intercontinental migration: An overview'. In Emmer, P.C., and Mörner, M. (eds.). 1992. *European Expansion and Migration: Essays on the Intercontinental Migration from Africa, Asia and Europe*. New York, Berg.

EMMER, P.C. (ed.) 1986. *Colonialism and Migration: Indentured Labour before and after Slavery*. Dordrecht, M. Nijhoff.

EMMER. P.C., and MÖRNER, M. (eds.). 1992. *European Expansion and Migration: Essays on the Intercontinental Migration from Africa, Asia and Europe*. New York, Berg.

ENGERMAN, S.L. 1986. 'Servants to slaves to servants: Contract labor and European expansion'. In EMMER, P.C. (ed.). *Colonialism and Migration: Indentured Labour before and after Slavery*. Dordrecht, M. Nijhoff.

EQUIANO, O. 1789. 'The interesting narrative of the life of Olauda Equiano'. 2 vols. London. Printed and sold by the author (also by Mr Johnson, St Paul's Churchyard).

EVANS, W.M. 1980. 'From the land of Canaan to the land of Guinea: The strange odyssey of the "Sons of Ham"'. *American Historical Review* (Washington D.C.), Vol. 85, No. 1. Reproduced in Black Diaspora Committee of Howard University (ed.). *The African Diaspora: Africans and Their Descendants in the Wider World to 1800*. Lexington. Mass., Ginn Press, 1986.

FALOLA, T., and LOVEJOY, P.E. (eds.) 1993. *Pawnship in Africa: Perspectives on Debt Bondage*. San Francisco/Oxford, Boulder/Westview Press.

FAUST, D.G. 1996. *Mothers of Invention: Women of the Slave South in the American Civil War*. Chapel Hill, University of North Carolina Press.

FINLEY, M.I. 1968. In Sills, D.L. (ed.). *Encyclopedia of the Social Sciences*. New York, Macmillan and the Free Press.

———. 1980. *Ancient Slavery and Modern Ideology*. New York, Viking Press.

FREEHLING, W.W. 1986. 'Denmark Vesey's peculiar reality'. In Abzug, R.H., and Maizlish, S.E. (eds.). *New Perspectives on Slavery in America: Essays in Honor of Kenneth M. Stampp*. Lexington, University Press of Kentucky.

GEMERY, H.A., and HOGENDORN, J.S. (eds.). 1979. *The Uncommon Market: Studies in the Economic History of the Atlantic Slave Trade*. New York, Academic Press.

GENOVESE, E.D. 1974. *Roll Jordan Roll: The World the Slaves Made*. New York, Pantheon.

———. 1979. *From Rebellion to Revolution*. Baton Rouge, Louisiana State University Press.

GILMORE, AL-TONY (ed.). 1978. *Revisiting Blassingame's* The Slave Community: *The Scholars Respond*. Westport, Conn., Greenwood Press.

GLASSMAN, J. 1991. 'The bondsman's new clothes: The contradictory consciousness of slave resistance on the Swahili coast'. *Journal of African History* (Cambridge), Vol. 33, No. 2.

GORDON, M. 1989. *Slavery in the Arab World*. New York, New Amsterdam.

GREEN-PEDERSEN, S.E. 1979. 'The economic considerations behind the Danish abolition of the Negro slave trade'. In Gemery, H.A. and Hogendorn, J.S. (eds.). *The Uncommon Market: Studies in the Economic History of the Atlantic Slave Trade*. New York, Academic Press.

HARMS, R. 1981. *River of Wealth, River of Sorrow: The Central Zaïre Basin in the Era of the Slave and Ivory Trade, 1500–1891.* New Haven, Yale University Press.

HARRIS, J.B. 1971. *The African Presence in Asia: Consequences of the East African Slave Trade.* Evanston, Ill., Northwestern University Press.

HELLIE, R. 1982. *Slavery in Russia, 1450–1725.* Chicago, University of Chicago Press.

———. 1989. 'The manumission of Russian slaves'. *Slavery and Abolition* (London), Vol. 10, No. 3.

HIGMAN, B.W. 1984. *Slave Populations of the British Caribbean, 1807–1834.* Baltimore, Johns Hopkins University Press.

HOWARD, W.S. 1963. *American Slavers and the Federal Law, 1837–1862.* Berkeley/Los Angeles, University of California Press.

HOWELL, R.C. 1987. *The Royal Navy and the Slave Trade.* London, Groom/Helm.

HUNWICK, J.O. 1992. 'Black Africans in the Mediterranean world: Introduction to a neglected aspect of the African diaspora'. In Savage, E. (ed.). *The Human Commodity: Perspectives on the Trans-Saharan Slave Trade.* London, Frank Cass.

INIKORI, J.E. 1981. 'Market structure and the profits of the British African trade in the late eighteenth century'. *Journal of Economic History* (Raleigh), Vol. 41, No. 4.

———. 1987. 'Slavery and the development of industrial capitalism in England'. In Solow, B.L., and Engerman, S.L. (eds.). *British Capitalism and Caribbean Slavery: The Legacy of Eric Williams.* New York, Cambridge University Press.

INIKORI, J.E., and ENGERMAN, S. (eds.). 1992. *The Atlantic Slave Trade Effects on Economies, Societies and Peoples in Africa, the Americas and Europe.* Durham, N.C., Duke University Press.

INIKORI, J.E., OHADIKE, D.C., and UNOMAH, A.C. 1986. *The Chaining of a Continent: Export Demand for Captives and the History of Africa South of the Sahara, 1450–1870.* Paris, UNESCO.

ISAACMAN, A.F. 1990. 'Peasants and rural social protest in Africa'. *African Studies Review* (Atlanta), Vol. 33, No. 2.

JAMES, C.L.R. 1938 (2nd rev. ed. 1963). *The Black Jacobins: Toussaint Louverture and the San Domingo Revolution.* New York, Vintage Books.

JONES, G.I. 1967. 'Olaudah Equiano of the Niger Ibo'. In Curtin, P.D. (ed.). *Africa Remembered: Narratives by West Africans from the Era of the Slave Trade.* Madison, University of Wisconsin Press.

KHUMAR, D. 1993. 'Colonialism, bondage, and caste in British India'. In Klein, M.A. (ed.). *Breaking the Chains: Slavery, Bondage and Emancipation in Modern Africa and Asia.* Madison, University of Wisconsin Press.

KIPLE, K.F. 1985. *The Caribbean Slave: A Biological History.* Cambridge, Cambridge University Press.

———. (ed.). 1988. *The African Exchange: Toward a Biological History of the Black People.* Durham, N.C., Duke University Press.

KLEIN, H.S. 1978. *The Middle Passage: Comparative Studies in the Atlantic Slave Trade.* Princeton, Princeton University Press.

KLEIN, M.A. 1988–89. 'Slavery and emancipation in French West Africa'. *Indian Historical Review* (New Delhi), Vol. 15, Nos. 1–2.

———. (ed.) 1993. *Breaking the Chains: Slavery, Bondage and Emancipation in Modern Africa and Asia.* Madison, University of Wisconsin Press.

KLEIN, M.A., and ROBERTSON, C.C. 1983. *Women and Slavery in Africa.* Madison, University of Wisconsin Press.

LAUGHLIN, C.D. Jr, and BRADY, I.A. (eds.). 1978. *Extinction and Survival in Human Populations.* New York, Columbia University Press.

LLOYD, C. 1968. *The Navy and the Slave Trade: The Suppression of the African Trade in the Nineteenth Century.* London, Cass.

LOVEJOY, P.E. 1983. *Transformations in Slavery: A History of Slavery in Africa.* New York, Cambridge University Press.

LOVEJOY, P.E., and HOGENDORN, J.S. 1993. *Slow Death for Slavery: The Course of Abolition in Northern Nigeria, 1837–1936.* New York, Cambridge University Press.

MANNING, P. 1990. *Slavery in African Life: Occidental, Oriental and African Slave Trades.* New York, Cambridge University Press.

MASON, J.E. 1996. *Social Death and Resurrection.* Charlottesville, University Press of Virginia.

MEILLASSOUX, C. (ed.). 1975. *L'esclavage en Afrique précoloniale.* Paris, Maspero.

———. 1986. *Anthropologie de l'esclavage. Le ventre de fer et d'argent.* Paris, Maspero.

MIERS, S. 1975. *Britain and the Ending of the Slave Trade.* New York, Africana.

MIERS, S., and KOPYTOFF, I. 1977. *Slavery in Africa: Historical and Anthropological Perspectives.* Madison, University of Wisconsin Press.

MIERS, S., and ROBERTS, R. (eds.). 1988. *The End of Slavery in Africa.* Madison, University of Wisconsin Press.

MILLER, J.C. 1993. *Slavery and Slaving in World History: A Bibliography, 1900–1991.* Millwood, N.Y., Kraus.

MINTZ, S., and PRICE, R. 1976. *An Anthropological Approach to the Afro-American Past: A Caribbean Perspective.* Philadelphia, Ishi.

MULLIN, G.W. 1972. *Flight and Rebellion: Slave Resistance in Eighteenth-Century Virginia.* New York, Oxford University Press.

MULLIN, M. 'British Caribbean and North American slaves in an era of war and revolution, 1775–1807'. In CROW, J.J., and TISE, L.E. (eds.). *The Southern Experience in the American Revolution.* Chapel Hill, University of North Carolina Press.

MURRAY, D.R. 1980. *Odious Commerce: Britain, Spain and the Abolition of the Cuban Slave Trade.* New York, Cambridge University Press.

NEEDHAM, R. 1983. *Sumba and the Slave Trade.* Melbourne, Monash University Centre of Southeast Asian Studies.

OKIHIRO, G.Y. 1986. *The Resistance: Studies in African, Caribbean and Afro-American History.* Amherst, University of Massachusetts Press.

PATNAIK, U., and DINGWANEY, M. (eds.). 1985. *Chains of Servitude: Bondage and Slavery in India.* Madras, Sangham Books.

PATTERSON, O. 1982. *Slavery and Social Death.* Cambridge, Harvard University Press.

———. 1991. *Freedom in the Making of Western Culture.* New York, Basic Books.

PHILLIPS, W.D. 1985. *Slavery from Ancient Times to the Early Transatlantic Trade.* Minneapolis, University of Minnesota Press.

PRAKASH, G. 1993. 'Terms of servitude: The colonial discourse on slavery and bondage in India'. In Klein, M.S. (ed.). *Breaking the Chains: Slavery, Bondage and Emancipation in Modern Africa and Asia.* Madison, University of Wisconsin Press.

PRICE, R. 1973. *Maroon Societies: Rebel Slave Communities in the Americas.* New York, Anchor Press.

RAYNER, M.I. 1986. Wine and Slaves: The Failure of an Export Economy and the Ending of Slavery in the Cape Colony, South Africa, 1806–1834 (Duke University, Ph.D. thesis).

REID, A. (ed.). 1983. *Slavery, Bondage and Dependency in Southeast Asia.* Sainte-Lucie, University of Queensland Press.

REIS, J.J. 1986 (revised 1993). *Rebelião escrava no Brasil: a história do levante dos Malés, 1835.* São Paulo, Brazil, Brasiliense.

————. (ed.). 1988. *Escravidão e invenção da liberdade: estudos sobre o negro no Brasil.* São Paulo, Brazil, Brasiliense.

RENAULT, F. 1971. *Lavigerie, l'esclave africain et l'Europe.* 2 vols. Paris, De Boccard.

RICHARDSON, D. 1987. 'The slave trade, sugar, and British economic growth, 1748–1776'. In Solow, B.L., and Engerman, S.L. *British Capitalism and Caribbean Slavery: The Legacy of Eric Williams.* New York, Cambridge University Press.

ROBINSON, D.L. 1971. *Slavery in the Structure of American Politics, 1765–1820.* New York, Harcourt Brace Jovanovich.

SAVAGE, E. (ed.). 1992. *The Human Commodity: Perspectives on the Trans-Saharan Slave Trade.* London, Frank Cass.

SCOTT, J.C. 1976. *The Moral Economy of the Peasant: Rebellion and Subsistence in Southeast Asia.* New Haven, Yale University Press.

————. 1985. *Weapons of the Weak: Everyday Forms of Peasant Resistance.* New Haven, Yale University Press.

————. 1990. *Domination and the Arts of Resistance: Hidden Transcripts.* New Haven, Yale University Press.

SHERIFF, A. 1987. *Slaves, Spices and Ivory in Zanzibar: Integration of an East African Commercial Empire into the World Economy 1770–1873.* London, James Currey.

SOLOW, B.L. 1987. 'Capitalism and slavery in the exceedingly long run'. In Solow, B.L., and Engerman, S.L. *British Capitalism and Caribbean Slavery: The Legacy of Eric Williams.* New York, Cambridge University Press.

SOLOW, B.L., and ENGERMAN, S.L. 1987. *British Capitalism and Caribbean Slavery: The Legacy of Eric Williams.* New York, Cambridge University Press.

TADMAN, M. 1989. *Speculators and Slaves: Masters, Traders and Slaves in the Old South.* Madison, University of Wisconsin Press.

TEMPERLEY, H. 1972. *British Antislavery, 1833–1870.* London, Longman.

————. 1981. 'The ideology of antislavery'. In Walvin, J., and Eltis, D. (eds.). *The Abolition of the Atlantic Slave Trade.* Madison, University of Wisconsin Press.

THORNTON, J.K. 1992. *Africa and Africans in the Making of the Atlantic World, 1400–1680.* New York, Cambridge University Press.

TOLEDANO, E. 1982. *The Ottoman Slave Trade and Its Suppression, 1840–1890.* Princeton, Princeton University Press.

TWADDLE, M. (ed.). 1993. *The Wages of Slavery: From Chattel Slavery to Wage Labour in Africa, the Caribbean and England.* London, Cass.

UBAH, C.N. 1991. 'Suppression of the slave trade in the Nigerian emirates'. *Journal of African History* (Cambridge), Vol. 32, No. 3.

VANSINA, J. 1990. *Paths in the Rainforests: Towards a History of Political Tradition in Equatorial Africa.* Madison, University of Wisconsin Press.

WALVIN, J. 1981. 'The public campaign in England against slavery, 1787–1834'. In Walvin, J., and Eltis, D. (eds.). *The Abolition of the Atlantic Slave Trade.* Madison, University of Wisconsin Press.

————. 1986. *England, Slaves and Freedom,* London, Macmillan.

————. 1994. *Black Ivory: A History of British Slavery.* Washington, Harvard University Press.

WALVIN, J., and ELTIS, D. (eds.). 1981. *The Abolition of the Atlantic Slave Trade.* Madison, University of Wisconsin Press.

WARD, J.R. 1988. *British West Indian Slavery, 1750–1834: The Process of Amelioration.* New York, Oxford University Press.

WARD, W.E.F. 1969. *The Royal Navy and the Slaves: The Suppression of the Atlantic Slave Trade*. New York, Pantheon.

WARREN, J.F. 1981. *The Sulu Zone: The Dynamics of External Trade Slavery and Ethnicity in the Transformation of a Southeast Asian Maritime State*. Singapore, Singapore University Press.

WATSON, J.D. 1980. *Asian and African Systems of Slavery*. Berkeley/Los Angeles, University of California Press.

WATSON, R.L. 1990. *The Slave Question: Liberty and Property in South Africa*. Middletown, Wesleyan University Press.

WILLIAMS, D.M. 1973. 'Abolition and the re-deployment of the slave fleet, 1807–1811'. *Journal of Transport History* (Leicester), Vol. 2, No. 2.

WILLIAMS, E. 1942. 'The British West Indian slave trade after its abolition in 1807'. *Journal of Negro History* (Washington D. C.), Vol. 27, No. 2.

WOLF, E. 1982. *Europe and the People without History*. Berkeley/Los Angeles, University of California Press.

WOOD, P.H. 1974. *Black Majority: Negroes in Colonial South Carolina from 1670 through the Stone Rebellion*. New York, Knopf.

WRIGHT, M. 1993. *Strategies of Slaves and Women: Life-Stories from East Central Africa*. New York, Lilian Barber Press.

Chapter 15

The Liberated Slaves and the Question of the Return to Africa: Interaction along the Upper Guinea Coast

Florence Omolara Mahoney

THE UPPER GUINEA COAST of West Africa from Cape Verde to Cape Mount was a region well watered by numerous rivers flowing in a westerly direction: the Senegal, the Gambia, the Casamance, the Rio Grande, the Pongo, the Sierra Leone and others. Over many centuries African peoples had established settlements along the banks of these rivers, some building centralised states and others decentralised. Communities of fisherfolk and peasant-farmers, salters, weavers and dyers, potters, blacksmiths and goldsmiths, ironsmelters, and even long-distance traders into the hinterland of the Western Sudan made this region 'a congenial place for the mixing and mingling of peoples'.

The arrival of Europeans in ships gave a new significance to the coast, with the rivers determining the pattern of European settlement in the region. In the fifteenth and sixteenth centuries, a succession of European traders and adventurers had followed in the wake of Portuguese explorers: Alvise da Cadamosto, Diego Gomes, Valentin Fernandes, Pacheco Pereira and others. Attracted by prospects of trade in African commodities – gum, wax, ivory, hides, camwood, civet cats, gold and slaves – which could be exchanged for horses, cloth, iron, brass pans, beads, silver coins, firearms and alcohol, these Europeans sought protection from African rulers in whose states they resided. Many of them married local women according to local law and custom, although they did not give up their national dress, language or religion, which was Christian.

It was from these liaisons that the Portuguese mulatto community[1] emerged with its own cultural identity – distinct from yet adopting some European and African features. It was this community that produced many 'middlemen' (and there were women agents, too) for the slave trade. By the eighteenth century, some of them had amassed enough capital to trade on their own account and were formidable rivals to well-established European trading companies. Their participation in the socio-economic life of the region improved the skills of their African apprentices in boat-building, seamanship, carpentry and the building trade generally.

Private European traders also found it an advantage to live in close proximity to trading forts. The Royal African Company founded in 1672 had obtained permission from the 'king' of Barra to rebuild James Fort in the lower River Gambia, and British factors established villages, like Pisania in the ruler of Niani's domains, where they lived with Mandingo wives and servants in the same way as the Portuguese had done before them. These villages became centres of trade and 'crucial points for the diffusion of European culture' in Upper Guinea.[2]

None the less, relations between Africans and Europeans in this region deteriorated once the trade in slaves, firearms and alcohol became the dominant factors in that relationship. What had been 'a congenial place for the mixing and mingling of peoples' became a turbulent place where the political independence of African rulers was compromised and African society was damaged socially and economically. The violent removal of millions of Africans from their homeland was catastrophic for the whole continent of Africa. Mutual respect between peoples was lost, and the course of development impeded.

Slaves in Strange Lands

In the fifteenth century, free Africans had been kidnapped by European adventurers along the Upper Guinea Coast, transported to Lisbon and Andalusia, and sold. However, special manumission laws opened avenues to freedom, and many slaves were absorbed into Portuguese or Spanish societies, their ethnic identity becoming lost with the passing years.

Slavery in the New World, on the other hand, took on different and varied forms. Generally the experience was harsh and cruel – only a handful returned unscathed. The growing demand for labour on sugar and tobacco plantations in the Caribbean Islands and in North and South America gave fresh impetus to slaving on the Upper Guinea Coast. Merchants of London and other cities in Europe sent out ships laden with specialised goods for the purchase of slaves in Upper Guinea for their agents in the New World, and for African commodities for European markets. By the eighteenth century this highly developed triangular trade had uprooted and displaced millions of able-bodied persons from West Africa, for only the best and healthiest were saleable.

Slave Narrative of the Eighteenth Century: Ayuba ibn Suleiman ibn Ibrahima Diallo (alias Job Ben Solomon)

In 1731, Ayuba ibn Suleiman ibn Ibrahima Diallo – 31 years old, the son of a prominent Muslim cleric in the Fulbe state of Bondou (beyond the upper reaches of the River Gambia) – was kidnapped and sold while passing through the Mandigo state of Jarra on the south bank of the Gambia, some two hundred miles from home. Captain Pike, the American who bought him, agreed to delay his departure so that Ayuba's father could send slaves to redeem his son. Unfortunately, the fortnight's journey to Bondou and back was too long for Pike to wait, and his ship the *Arabella* set sail, calling at James Fort on its way out of the river, according to the account given by Francis Moore, factor of the Royal African Company, stationed there at the time. Sailing into Chesapeake Bay on the coast of Maryland, Captain Pike delivered his consignment of slaves (Ayuba among them) to Vachell Denton, agent of a London merchant, William Hunt. It was this agent who sold Ayuba to a Mr Tolsey, owner of a tobacco plantation on Kent Island in the Bay.[3]

Ayuba's experience of plantation slavery was so disagreeable that he tried to escape to look for less arduous work. Indeed, it was a common practice for slaves with initiative and courage to use every opportunity that came their way to break the shackles of slavery. Sometimes the environment of the plantation was not entirely unfavourable; for there existed manumission laws and persons with humanitarian sentiments to implement them. Besides, hope was an essential element for survival.

His distinctive physical Fula features and his faithful observance of the five daily prayers of Islam made Ayuba quite conspicuous. Captain Thomas Bluett, who knew Ayuba, described his countenance as 'exceeding pleasant, yet grave and composed, his hair long, black and curled, being very different from that of the Negro commonly brought from Africa'.[4] Indeed, his ability to write Arabic became his passport to freedom, for a letter he had written to his father relating the misfortune that had befallen him and pleading with him to find some means of redeeming him from slavery was seen by General James Oglethorpe, a well-known philanthropist and a director of the Royal African Company. He responded generously to Ayuba's cry for freedom, offering to buy Ayuba from his owner for the price that the owner had paid for him. This done, Ayuba was invited to England, and thus began the quest for the return to his homeland of Africa.

THE QUESTION OF THE RETURN TO AFRICA. Ayuba Suleiman, the freed slave from the tobacco plantation (he had been made a herdsman when he could not cope with the gruelling work in the fields), became a celebrity in England. He was presented at court, and met many members of the royal family, the nobility and members of learned societies interested in exploring the interior of Africa, including Sir Hans Sloane, President of the Royal Society, First Physician to King George II, and an Arabic scholar. The Duke of Montague, a courtier and philanthropist, invited Ayuba to his estate in the country for the purpose of demonstrating to him the use of agricultural and other implements and tools which might be introduced to his people on his return home to Bondou. Many of these implements were then packed in chests to be put on board one of the Royal African Company's ships bound for the River Gambia. Meanwhile, General James Oglethorpe accommodated him in Africa House, the Company's headquarters in London, until he could return to the Gambia. So it was that, in July 1734, this Fula, laden with 'rich presents – worth upwards of

500 pounds; besides – well furnished with money – embarked on board one of the African Company's ships, bound for Gambia …'.[5]

The Royal African Company, and indeed merchants of London, hoped that their friendship with Ayuba Suleiman and the numerous implements he was carrying back to Africa would promote agriculture and commerce in Bondou and neighbouring states. There was growing interest in the lucrative gum and gold trade of Bambuk to the east of Bondou, quite apart from the trade in slaves, and exploration of the interior might facilitate access to the Ferlo gum forest. Ayuba, for his part, was dreaming of his homeland where he would be reunited with his father, his two wives and his children, especially the youngest who was his favourite. He was proud of the rich gold watch that Her Majesty Queen Caroline had been pleased to give him, and the sumptuous dinners in the homes of the English nobility must have been exhilarating, if somewhat daunting. Yet real freedom could only be fully enjoyed with his own kith and kin in Africa.

HOMECOMING. On 8 August 1734, Ayuba Suleiman disembarked from the *Dolphin Snow* at James Fort in the River Gambia and was welcomed by Francis Moore, the same factor who had waved him goodbye as he sailed into slavery across the seas three years before. He had left as a miserable slave in shackles, convinced that white men were cannibals, since no one had ever returned from slavery. He was going home, the only black man on a slave vessel of the Royal African Company, whose directors had ordered their agents in the River Gambia to show him the greatest respect. The chest of tools, costly gifts and personal effects were stored in the Company's warehouse until they could be transported to Bondou. Meanwhile messengers were sent to Ayuba's father to announce his safe arrival. What irony that Ayuba's return dispelled the horror his people felt for slavery among the English; for he spoke kindly of them. What must the James Fort slaves have made of such a phenomenon?

Ayuba, for all his glowing account of his life across the seas, was incensed one evening when a group of Mandingo men appeared in Doomasensa in Jarra, and was restrained only with difficulty from drawing his broadsword and pistols.[6] The men were those who had robbed him and sold him into slavery three years before: the loss of freedom especially by violent means is quite intolerable.

BONDOU-BRITISH FRIENDSHIP. This friendship was built on the goodwill of a single individual, Ayuba, and his family and members of his ethnic group who saw evidence of the kindness shown by white folk in strange countries they could not imagine. Even though all the chests laden with gifts were lost en route to Bondou, the lost son had been found, and he had brought reams of writing paper[7] with him for his Islamic community. Ayuba travelled between Bondou and James Fort, acting as guide and adviser to any mission into the interior. In 1744, for example, he took with him to Bondou one Melchior De Jaspas, an Armenian (who knew Arabic) employed by the Royal African Company, from where he travelled overland to Cacheo south of the Casamance River. Ayuba himself kept up a personal correspondence with friends in Britain. He even requested to be given another opportunity to visit England, but the directors of the Royal African Company did not think this would be wise. By the 1750s, however, the declining fortunes of the Royal African Company made it impossible to pursue its trade in the interior.

Ayuba Suleiman had not lost his cultural identity, having been away from his homeland for only three years. He seems to have had few problems of adjustment on his return to Africa, and enjoyed good health until his death in the 1770s. His experiences in the New World and later in England had made him a 'man of two worlds' and an agent of Western civilisation in the interior of West Africa. While remaining a devout Muslim and reverting to life in a polygamous society, his interaction with Europeans had broadened his perspective of the world, and he wanted to remain a part of that world.

Other Narratives of Liberated Slaves in the Eighteenth Century

The Story of Johnson – Language Skills and African Exploration

There were others, too, who were enslaved and shipped across the Atlantic Ocean, and who were fortunate to return home to the River Gambia. It is from the the late-eighteenth-century *Travels in the Interior Districts of Africa* of the young Scottish doctor, Mungo Park, that we read of his faithful and knowledgeable guide 'Johnson'. His brief account fails to provide us with Johnson's family background, except that he belonged to the Mandingo people along the River Gambia, and that he was sold as a young man and transported to the West Indian island of Jamaica. According to Park's record, Johnson 'had been made free, and taken to England by his master, where he had resided many years; and at length found his way back to his native country'.[8] Following Lord Chief Justice Manfield's judgement of 1772,[9] which outlawed slavery in England, hundreds of African slaves obtained their freedom. After the American War of Independence in 1783, the black community in London (which came to be known as 'the black poor') increased with huge numbers of demobilised black soldiers and sailors.

It was among these paupers in London that Johnson must have lived for seven years before he found his way back to the Gambia, where he and his Mandingo wife set up house at the British factory of Pisania. Johnson's knowledge of English, first acquired under slavery in Jamaica and improved upon as a liberated slave in London, enabled him to find satisfactory employment as an interpreter for private European traders. It was one of these, Dr John Laidley of England, who had started business on the banks of the River Gambia in 1771 and knew Johnson well, who recommended him as a reliable interpreter and companion to Mungo Park. Park was commissioned in 1795 by the African Association in England to explore the interior of Africa by way of the river. Johnson was to be paid ten bars of iron monthly, and his wife five bars monthly during his absence. During the slave trade, the iron bar was the most common item of currency in Sene-Gambia. If a bar could buy one ounce of silver, two pounds of gun powder or two pints of brandy (according to Francis Moore's calculation), then these salaries were certainly not insignificant.

Liberated slaves like Ayuba and Johnson had intimate knowledge of their own people, were fluent in their vernacular, and practised their religion and traditional customs. Park was amused that after seven years in England, Johnson 'still retained the prejudices and notions he had imbibed in his youth' such as offering a white chicken as a sacrifice to the spirits of the woods through which their caravan of 30 persons and six loaded asses was to pass, so that the journey might be successful.[10] Superstitious beliefs aside, these returned Africans who straddled two worlds were endowed with the kind of wisdom, insight and ingenuity required for survival. Indeed, it was Johnson's ingenuity that saved Park from being captured by the Moors of Ludamar and engineered his escape.

Though he well understood that Park's mission of exploration in the interior might open up new channels of commerce from which he himself could derive personal benefit, Johnson was not prepared to press onwards to the banks of the Niger once the hazards of the journey seemed overwhelming. Preferring to forfeit his wages rather than continue, he accepted custody of Mungo Park's journal (Park keeping the duplicate), bade him farewell in Jarra in Kaarta, and set off on the return journey to Pisania. On Park's return from the banks of the Niger, 18 months after his departure, he was distressed to learn that Johnson, his trustworthy and faithful companion, had never returned.

Liberty for the returned blacks, as indeed for most people in Upper Guinea, was fragile during the turbulent period of the slave trade. Indigenous rulers, especially the Moors, objected to the penetration of their interior states by Europeans, and Africans who acted as guides spearheading such missions of exploration were themselves looked upon as spies and enemies. In spite of the risk to their lives, and the suspicion and undisguised disapproval of their society, returned Africans were ever ready to leave the relative security of the Guinea coast and accompany explorers, traders and missionaries into the interior. The tragedy of Johnson did not deter others from following in his footsteps, and in 1805 Park was able to engage another guide, one Isaaco, described as 'a Mandingo who spoke English ... of exceptional intelligence, fortitude, and devotion'.[11] Happily, he survived the hazards of the journey, for Park – who had entrusted his papers to him before setting sail down the River Niger – never returned.

Thomas Joiner: Freed Slaves Return – Rehabilitation through Assimilation

A young Mandingo musician, who played the *kora* and belonged to the *jaliba* caste, recounted his misfortune along the banks of the Gambia at the height of the slave trade. He too had been captured in a raid and sold with others to a mulatto slave merchant, named Robert Aynsley, who traded at the British factory of Pisania. With an American vessel then in the river, Aynsley had no difficulty in disposing of his consignment of slaves. On landing in America (slaves from the Gambia were often delivered to agents in Maryland or Virginia), the Mandingo musician was sold to a master who found him hardworking, intelligent and honest, and was given a post of responsibility. After several years of faithful service, Thomas Joiner, as he was then called, had saved enough money to purchase his freedom from his master. With a few dollars in his pocket, he found employment on a British man-of-war as captain's steward, intending to make his way back to Africa.[12] This experience on board ship was to serve him in good stead.

Thomas Joiner returned to the Upper Guinea Coast and set up a small business in Goree after it was recaptured by the British in 1800 during the Napoleonic Wars. From that base he traded to the River Gambia, his homeland, sending canoes as far as Fattatenda in the Upper River. Once the slave trade was abolished in 1807, and the British had established a military base on St Mary's Island in the estuary of the River in 1816, British merchants and their dependents were encouraged to transfer their businesses from the River Senegal. Thomas Joiner moved with them. He returned to find his old roots and to sink new ones in an environment that could have been hostile, for the man who had sold him into slavery, Robert Aynsley, was now his neighbour in the commercial centre of Bathurst on St Mary's Island. Their children attended the Wesleyan school. Joiner had become a Christian.

The early years of repatriation were difficult for returned slaves, for the Upper Guinea Coast was still destabilised by the slave trade and its aftermath. It was by dint of hard work and perseverance, with a sense of purpose and sometimes luck, that some were able to plant cautious feet on African soil and survive the vicissitudes of life. Joiner was among those who had survived the trauma of the New World and returned home with some awareness of commercial opportunities for Africa, apart from the abominable trade in slaves. His participation in the new economic life of the British settlement of Bathurst caused him to withdraw from his people who lived on the banks of the Gambia and become a part of the multicultural society of the coast. Having saved capital, he bought a good house in Bathurst, 'furnished it genteelly, and lived as a first-rate gentleman',[13] reported Reverend William Moister, a Methodist missionary from England who knew him. From there Joiner established a broad-based business, carrying on an extensive trade with his Mandingo people in the River Gambia and dispatching his trading vessels as far as Cape Verde, the Bissagos Isles, Sierra Leone, other settlements on the Upper Guinea Coast and beyond as far as the West Indies. As an ambitious entrepreneur, Joiner's interests were now closer to those of the European and mulatto merchants than to Mandingo producers and traders in the interior. His signature was appended to many memorials and petitions from the mercantile community of Bathurst demanding government protection of trade in the River Gambia.

Communities of Freed Slaves and Their Return to Africa

During the American War of Independence (1776–83), thousands of black slaves on the American plantations escaped to freedom by rallying under the British flag. They came to be known as 'Black Loyalists', and included some 'free persons of colour' dissatisfied with the limitations put on their freedom in America. In 1775, Lord Dunmore, Governor of Virginia, declared that freedom would be granted to any slave who bore arms and joined His Majesty's troops against the American rebels.[14] It was reckoned that nearly 100,000 slaves (one-fifth of the black population of America) joined the British troops. Many came with specialised skills and training – blacksmiths, carpenters, tailors, coopers, cooks, bakers, orderlies, etc., or acted as guides and intelligence agents for the invading British armies. Some served as soldiers with their own non-commissioned officers in black regiments, and others as sailors in the Royal Navy or as pilots on coastal vessels. When Britain lost the war, it was committed to freeing these loyalists who had fought on its side. They were settled in London, Jamaica, Nova Scotia and elsewhere.

Solidarity and Identity

In 1783, 30,000 Black Loyalists (3,000 of whom were free blacks) were located in Nova Scotia, Canada.[15] They found the climate unfavourable and their freedom sadly restricted, but, above all, the promised land grants seemed indefinitely delayed. Their newly gained freedom was meaningless without land, and their proximity to America put them at risk of being seized by former masters there. Thus, the road to freedom was not yet found. The 'promised land'[16] might be distant, but preparation for the journey was ongoing. Their hope of survival generated enthusiasm for new initiatives, resulting in a written petition to the British government's Secretary of State for the Colonies, William Grenville, which stated that some of them were 'ready and willing to go wherever the wisdom of Government may think proper to provide for them as free Subjects of the British Empire'.[17]

Thomas Peters,[18] former sergeant of one of the black regiments, was given power of attorney by over 200 families to go personally to London in December 1790 to deliver the petition. Arriving in London, he made his mission known first to the community of the 'black poor', some of whom had accepted the challenge to venture to Africa to form a settlement on the Upper Guinea Coast which they had named Granville Town (after their patron and benefactor, Granville Sharpe, the philanthropist). Could this be the road to real freedom? Could Africa provide the freedom and land they longed for? Thomas Peters hastily returned to Canada with an invitation for the petitioners to join the exodus to Africa which might indeed prove to be that 'promised land'.

Liberated Slaves Found West African Nationalism

The first generation of liberated Africans had to accept a dependent status in society. Their positive response to relief programmes organised by government, missionary and mercantile agencies, as well as other benefactors like the freed blacks from the New World, contributed to their rehabilitation and equipped them to rise from servitude. Professor Arthur Porter identified 'Education …

[as] a crucial instrument providing … the knowledge and skills necessary for movement into new and more highly valued roles than those occupied by their parents'.[19] By the 1860s, these displaced black refugees from diverse ethnic origins had been moulded into a homogeneous community – a people, that now spoke a common language, *krio*, practised a common religion, Christianity, and accepted a common leadership for the attainment of new goals. A.B.C. Sibthorpe, writing in Freetown in 1868, observed that they had been 'compelled by fortune and nature to become one people, or nation'. Writing in the same year, James Africanus Horton acknowledged too that 'The inhabitants of the colony [Sierra Leone] have been gradually blending into one race, and a national spirit is being developed'. He described them as 'an industrious, exploring race, determined to advance their position in life', that could be found 'in every part of the [West] coast'.[20] The impact of this community on Gambian society was as important as it was elsewhere on the coast. As trading agents for European merchants, and later as merchants in the groundnut trade of the river, liberated Africans contributed substantially to the colonial revenue. Their women (dressed in the traditional *kaba-sloht*)[21] joined in commercial activity, primarily in cola nuts, as soon as shipping along the West Coast improved in the late 1850s.[22]

Indeed, it was in recognition of their importance to the economic life of the colony that the first liberated African, J.D. Richards, was nominated to the legislative council of the Gambia in 1883.[23] Three years later, another liberated African, S.J. Forster, joined him in council.[24] In the latter part of the nineteenth century, members of this community were represented in all grades of the civil service. Their loyalty to the British Crown and British institutions was so passionate that they organised opposition to the proposed transfer of the Gambia to France in the 1870s.[25]

There were ugly manifestations of European imperialism in Africa in the late nineteenth century through conquests of indigenous states and peoples, and increasing antipathy between British officials, and even missionaries, and the liberated African élite. Those who had been their benefactors and their allies in the promotion of Christianity and Western civilisation into the interior of Africa now ridiculed their hybrid *krio* culture, and declared openly that senior posts in church and state were to be reserved for Europeans. Such open hostility distressed the liberated African élite at the time of its greatest achievement and forced its leaders to look to the future with foreboding. It was out of this desperate situation that they founded the National Congress of British West Africa in 1920, for the purpose of bringing self-government to British West Africa.

Notes

1. W. Rodney, 1970, chap. 8.
2. A.W. Lawrence, 1963, p. 29.
3. 'The capture and travels of Ayuba Suleiman Ibrahima', relation of Thomas Bluett, in P.D. Curtin, 1967, chap. 1. See also F. Moore, 1738, pp. 202–203, 205–209, 223–224.
4. P.D. Curtin, 1967, p. 51.
5. Ibid., pp. 46–47.
6. F. Moore, 1738.
7. Ibid.
8. M. Park, 1799, pp. 42–43.
9. G.M. Trevelyan, 1993.
10. M. Park, 1799, pp. 105–106.
11. Ibid.
12. W. Moister, 1850, p. 175.
13. Ibid., p. 176.
14. J. St G. Walker, 1976, p. 1.
15. Ibid., pp. 12, 18.
16. Ibid., p. 87.
17. 'Memorial and petition of Thomas Peters a free negro'. In J. St G. Walker, 1976, p. 95.
18. C. Fyfe, 1953.
19. A. Porter, 1963.
20. J.A. Horton, 1868, p. 83, and H. Wilson, 1969, p. 164.
21. B. Wass and S.M. Broderick, 1979.
22. F. Mahoney, 1974, unpublished.
23. Ibid.
24. Ibid.
25. J.D. Hargreaves, 1963, chap. 4.

Bibliography

ASIEGBU, J. 1969. *Slavery and the Politics of Liberation, 1787–1861*. London, Longmans.

CASSIDY, F. 1961. *Jamaica Talk*. London, Macmillan.

CURTIN, P.D. 1967. *Africa Remembered: Narratives by West Africans from the Era of Slave Trade*. Madison, University of Wisconsin Press.

DAVIDSON, B. 1961. *Black Mother*. Victor Gollancz.

FOX, W., Rev. 1851. *A Brief History of the Wesleyan Mission on the Western Coast of Africa*. London.

FYFE, C. 1953. 'Thomas Peters: History and legend'. *Sierra Leone Studies*, No. 1.

———. 1962. *History of the Gambia*. Cambridge, Cambridge University Press.

HARGREAVES, J.D. 1958. *A Life of Sir Samuel Lewis*. London.

———. 1963. *Prelude to the Partition of West Africa*. London, Macmillan.

HORTON, J.A. 1868. *West African Countries and Peoples*. London, W.J. Johnson.

HUNTER, Y.L. 1982. *Road to Freedom*. African University Press.

JULY, R. 1968. *The Origins of Modern African Thought*. London, Faber and Faber.

KOPYTOFF HERSKOVITS, J. 1965. *The Sierra Leoneans in Yorubaland 1830–1890*. Madison, University of Wisconsin Press.

KUCZYNSKI, R.R. 1948. *Demographic Survey of the British Colonial Empire, West Africa*. Vol. 1. London, Oxford University Press.

LAWRENCE, A.W. 1963. *Trade Castles and Forts of West Africa*. London, Jonathan Cape.

MAHONEY, F. 1963. *Government and Opinion in the Gambia, 1816–1901*. London.

———. 1974. Liberated Africans in the Gambia in the Nineteenth Century. (Unpublished.)

MARTIN, E.C. 1927. *The British West African Settlements, 1750–1821*. London, Negro University Press.

MOISTER, W., Rev. 1850. *Memorials of Missionary Labours in West Africa*. London, John Mason.

MOORE, F. 1738. *Travels into the Inland Parts of Africa*. London, E. Cave.

PARK, M. 1799. *Travels in the Interior Districts of Africa in the Years 1795, 1796 and 1797*. London, Bulmer and Co.

PORTER, A. 1963. *Creoledom*. Cambridge, Cambridge University Press.

RODNEY, W. 1970. *A History of the Upper Guinea Coast, 1545–1800*. Oxford, Clarendon Press.

ST G. WALKER, J. 1976. *The Black Loyalists*. London, Longman and Dalhousie University Press.

TANNENBAUM, F. 1947. *Slave and Citizen*. New York, Alfred Knopf.

TREVELYAN, G.M. 1993. *Histoire sociale de l'Angleterre*. Paris, Laffont. (Coll. Bouquins.)

WASS, B., and BRODERICK, S.M. 1979. 'The kaba-sloht'. *African Arts* (UCLA, Los Angeles), Vol. 12.

WILSON, H. 1969. *Origins of West African Nationalism*. London, Macmillan.

WYSE, A. 1989. *The Krio of Sierra Leone*. London, International African Institute.

Chapter 16

Former African and Malagasy Freed Slaves: Comprehensive Listing and Conclusions

Norbert Benoît

HISTORIANS SAY that the Arabs discovered Mauritius, although some dispute this. The island was not colonised until the eighteenth century. Holland was the first colonial power, with Dutch rule lasting more or less continuously from 1638 to 1710. When the Dutch finally abandoned the island, which they had named Mauritius, a number of slaves fled into the forests in the interior of the island. Five years later, on 20 September 1715, the French arrived, but effective French settlement began only in 1721 when the first settlers landed. After much hesitation, the French decided to stay on the island, turning it into a major colony, especially as the Ile de France, as they named it, was strategically well situated on the route to India. In 1810, unwilling to tolerate any longer the harassment of the pirates operating out of the Ile de France and attacking their ships, the British captured the island. The settlers were granted generous surrender terms, which guaranteed respect for their laws, customs and religion. The British remained on the island until 1968, when Mauritius became an independent state within the Commonwealth of Nations. It has been a republic since 1992. All of the colonisers, Dutch, French and British, resorted to slaves to develop the country. However, the British, from the very beginning, were against retaining slavery. Proclamations by the first British governor, Robert Townsend Farquhar, demonstrate the sincere desire on the part of the new masters of the country to get rid of this system. On 1 February 1835, the theoretical abolition of slavery was proclaimed; it became finalised five years later. The settlers received compensation and found in India the workers who were destined to replace slave labour.

The Quest for an Identity

Most of the slaves owned by the British were Africans. It is with these that we are concerned in this chapter, with one very clear aim in mind. In the history of Mauritius, there have been numerous studies of the Indian immigrants who came to replace the slaves to work the land, but very little is so far known about the descendants of African slaves.

It would not be far from the truth to say that, as regards the descendants of these slaves, we are, generally speaking, more or less totally in the dark. We know virtually nothing about how they have lived their lives from the time their ancestors were liberated down to the present day. It is also important to remember that the slaves were not prepared for their new status of freedmen. For example, what useful purpose could it serve to put up posters aimed at the apprentices if they could not read? We shall quote an extract from one of the country's newspapers published a year after abolition:

> Laws have been made on vagrancy, and the new apprentices are being asked to obey those laws. That is all very fine, since vagrancy is a plague that is already eating into the social fabric and that could, if care is not taken, become incurable. But there has not been sufficient appreciation of the fact that the governor's best laws, or the police's wisest advice regarding the newly freed slaves might just as well not exist for all these unfortunate people. 'Can you read?' ' No.' 'Read, then' – and so later the police turn an uneducated person into an offender. You could cover the walls of the city with notifications, decrees and proclamations aimed at these freed slaves, and it would all be pointless.[1]

Other evidence could be cited to show that, in the years following the abolition of slavery, the former slaves were always regarded as second-class persons.

It has been observed for some time now that more and more Mauritians are claiming their descent from African and Malagasy slaves and attesting their identity as Africans and Malagasies. They describe themselves as Creoles of African and Malagasy descent and want to trace their roots. In other words, they are embracing something that earlier generations were ashamed of. They cling to everything that might bring them closer to Africa and Madagascar but, unfortunately, the loss of cultural identity has been going on for too long, and the route to be retraced seems very difficult. The descendants of African and Malagasy slaves are more than ever feeling enclosed in a ghetto from which they simply have to escape. Consciousness-raising groups have been formed and Mauritians – not necessarily all of Afro-Malagasy origin – have joined them. The Catholic Church is not insensitive to what is happening and is lending its support to this movement to reclaim an identity.

We have placed our study in the framework of this quest for identity by this target group, mainly using original documents available in the National Archives of Mauritius at Coromandel.[2] We have consulted registers of correspondence of the time and have looked in particular at documents in which former freed slaves were writing to administrators. We have built up a *répertoire,* a comprehensive listing – rather as is being done with ships, in the library of the port of Lorient, in Brittany, where we did some research – which presents the bulk of the information collected about former African and Malagasy slaves, in particular in 1869 and from 1871 to 1874.

Findings

What have we been able to discover from the fifty-odd cases that we have examined? What are our conclusions? In most cases, the former freed slaves were social outcasts, living on nothing but the food and clothing rations allocated by the government. But for that they had to apply to the state and supply proof that, at some time or other, they had indeed been slaves of the state. Only if they could furnish proof would they receive assistance. To enjoy that assistance they thus had to make a written request to the government, accompanied by supporting documents. After these had been examined, the request would be rejected or approved if the police felt that the applicant merited it. Most of the time, the former freed slaves lived in the direst poverty and were often ill (there were many who were suffering from fever or who were blind or paralysed).

These former freed slaves were known as Mozambiques. This pejorative term has long been used to describe all descendants of Africans or any individual with frizzy hair. Some engaged in petty trades, such as carpenters or cooks for the governor, but were not very welcome in the neighbourhood. Land that had belonged to them for generations would sometimes be seized, so the British government would grant them a plot of land in exchange for a small rent that they were often unable to pay, being too old to work. Often married when they were far from young, they had young children whom they could only with difficulty manage to feed. Most were living in the capital, Port-Louis, or on the outskirts. Others were settled together near Moka, in the centre of the country, in a village popularly known as the Malagasy village, since the Mauritians often regarded the Malagasy as Africans. In spite of everything, some Mozambiques managed to become landowners – but that was rather the exception. Others left for the Seychelles to work and peopled the islands.

Many of the former freed slaves continued to bear their African names: Onomacoah, Arokanga, Aramrookoo, Matoomba. Onomacoah was also called Jolicoeur, as many Mauritian families are today. The other African names no longer exist. Often the former freed slaves were blessed with nicknames: Mars, Fou, Lindor, Apollon, La Providence, some of which still exist. Thomy Apollon is one such example. His mother was a Friquin, but he was called Apollon, a name he liked and wanted to pass on to his children. A fisherman on the south-south-west coast, he was literate and soon became a notable, leaving many descendants. He is the exception that proves the rule.

Our study has also revealed a number of aspects of the history of these freed slaves.

- Despite the prohibition of slavery, the clandestine trade continued to flourish. A child of eight, who was given the name Jim Hunt, was captured on board a slave ship by one of His Majesty's ships, the *Sidoa*, as late as 1861.
- To make up for the shortage of labour in agriculture, an attempt was made to use freed Africans who had come from Aden but who had actually signed their contract of employment in Mauritius itself.

- Some freed slaves continued to be slaves. Voltaire Dorothée, for instance, lived eight years in slavery after steps had been set in motion for his freedom and compensation had been paid. What is most surprising is that he was not freed until 1838, long after 1 February 1835.
- Raids for slaves in Madagascar between 1820 and 1830 were organised with the complicity of some tribes.
- Finally, and above all, some slaves were freed long after the abolition of slavery, since there are freedom certificates dating from 1843 and 1847.

Why did Mauritians who acknowledge themselves to be descendants of African and Malagasy slaves come to find themselves in this ghetto from which they wanted to escape? First, because for generations the descendants of slaves were regarded by others – and by themselves – as belonging to the so-called lower classes. They learned to be content with the bare minimum amid general indifference. To be an African at that time was a stigma. Of their own free will, the descendants of African and Malagasy slaves rejected everything that could link them to their origins. Second, because of the loss of culture consequent upon conversion to Catholicism. Once baptised, Africans, even if they were only second-class Christians, would forget the gods of their origins. Today, the descendants of former African and Malagasy slaves no longer know anything about animism or voodoo. What binds them to the past, we might say, is the *sega*, a dance long condemned, and the Creole language. Mauritius boasts a varied and cosmopolitan cuisine, but has retained almost no African dishes.

Thus, it seems to me that we need to make a comprehensive listing of all the documents concerning the ancestors of Mauritians descended from slaves, who have been so long ignored. Rooted in a rediscovered identity, these Mauritians would be able to look to the future with greater serenity, and no longer be satisfied with *sega* and Creole alone. Moreover, we now know that it is sometimes possible to reconstruct the pedigree of families of descendants of slaves. All these measures would help to reconstruct a lost heritage.

Notes

1. *Le Mauricien* (Port-Louis, Mauritius), 20 February 1836.
2. National Archives of Mauritius, Coromandel, Mauritius. Registers: RA 2135, RA 2136, RA 2137, RA 2138, RA 2139, RA 2140, RA 2141, RA 2142, RA 2173, RA 2176, RA 2178, RA 2179, RA 2180, RA 2182, RA 2183, RA 2214.

Chapter 17

Slavery in Law Codes

Lluís Sala-Molins

HAVE WE EVER SEEN a drive for expansion, invasion and subjection achieve its purpose without being inspired by a solid, well-worked-out theory that can always be reduced to some such slogan as 'It's God's will'? Too simple? Then put anything you like in place of God. There's plenty to choose from: the people, the king, the nation, the empire, class, etc. Of course, whoever it is you are occupying, invading or subjugating does not immediately have the same feeling. They take a long time to be convinced. That doesn't matter. When you subjugate, you always indoctrinate, and you can count on the sheer impact of power for the subjugated to come round to an understanding that subjugation fits them like a glove, that they have been unbelievably lucky to have been chosen by the supreme will of *these* particular masters – good, powerful, civilised believers – and not some other masters.

Such is the case with that perfect form of subjugation known as slavery. Go back to the earliest evidence of history accessible to us, and come forward to slavery as practised today, in the twenty-first century. You will never find naked slavery, because it is never self-evident, anywhere, that one human being can become the thing of another. Yet he or she does become so. When people are cast out of humanity, expelled from among human beings and consigned to the world of animals, tools, things, this is all justified and described by 'ideologists', partly to assuage any possible bad conscience on the part of those who purchase, inherit or sell, but much more in order to ensure that the subjection of the slave to the master is a matter of a properly drawn-up contract (varying according to the latitude, the season and the climate).

Ejected from the category of human being and reduced to the status of animal or thing, the slave comes within the purview of the law, a matter of interpersonal relations, at the very point at which the law declares that the slave is *not* a human being. It would be paradoxical, were this not a logic against which there is no appeal. The law, according to the time-honoured formula, is about 'giving to each his due'. If the law deals with relations between persons as owners – whether of three grains of millet or of a fortune, it is all the same – then slaves appear under the heading of property: they are the three grains of millet, they are the fortune. The law will tell the owner of the three grains how to keep them, the owner of the fortune how to keep it, transfer it or squander it.

Because it has always inevitably been so since slavery began and will always be the same so long as it continues to be there (and it is still there), it is both useful and highly instructive to follow down through the ages the intertwining of 'ideologies' and 'laws' in the matter of slavery. How, in each period and in each country, does the law go about translating what the ideology says about slaves as property and their relationship to their owners?

Although the slave trade went on everywhere under very similar legal rules and over very long periods, we shall look at these things in two broad geographical areas and two specific periods: the medieval Mediterranean and the modern and contemporary Atlantic. We must not lose sight of the fact that when the Christian European powers wished to legitimise their centuries-long acts of banditry in Africa and codify the enslavement of millions of slaves in the Americas, they went to look for their justifications not only in the codes of ancient Greece and Rome but also in the legal provisions produced by Mediterranean Christianity. What this means is that we can see in the legal language an unbroken continuity between the classical Greek bestialisation of the slave (the well-known classical Greek and Roman justifications for their position will not be addressed in these pages) and the modern European bestialisation of the slave, by way of the medieval Christian bestialisation. The contextual texture and images of the ideology change, but the concern to make a clear distinction between the humanity of the free and the sub-humanity or non-humanity of the slave remains.

Christianity did not know quite what line to take. On the one hand, it posited each individual in an economy of salvation (every soul can be saved or condemned in the future life). On the other, it extended tacitly – without building it into a theory but accepting its practice – the Graeco-Roman pattern of the reification of the slave, accepting implicitly the effective description of situations of economy, war, kidnapping and birth resulting in reduction to slavery and hence the shift of someone from the legal status of 'person' to that of 'property'.

The followers of the three religions of the Book would demonstrate unflagging zeal for stealing, raiding, buying and selling (it was not yet called 'slave-trading'), and, along the way, castrating for the needs of Muslims in particular. As for those who prayed to 'God the Father', people trafficked notably on the fringes of Christendom (theoretically, a Christian did not reduce a Christian to slavery, as the Jew did not a Jew, but the exceptions were so many that the rule itself went by the board) among the Slavs, also called Sclavs, whose frequent appearance on the market produced, among other effects, the creation of the common noun 'slave'. Among those worshipping Allah, people penetrated deeper and deeper beyond the borders of the Islamic world, raided or negotiated hard in East Africa, and did plenty of castrating as they went. Muslims and Christians, as they now and again came to blows in the Iberian peninsula, happily threw themselves into capturing one another – so much so that some aspects of economic life came to depend on the presence of a 'captive' labour force on both sides. It only took peace to break out and alliances to follow punch-ups, and 'captive' labour became scarce; once that state became endemic, it was replaced by slave labour. As for the followers of Jehovah, they did a little enslaving for themselves and a lot for others, that is, for business. Thus we had trans-European and trans-Mediterranean networks of slaves convoyed by Jews to markets, where Christians and Muslims, depending on the place, would brand with the cross or the crescent the same places on the body where, later, the modern and even contemporary slavers would brand the fleur-de -lys or the initials of the slaver.

The three religions of the Book, each with its own peculiarities, were everywhere on these routes and in these markets. If we look into this ideological-religious morass, it is marvellous to behold the contortions of priests, imams and rabbis to claim that a person is both man and beast, seeming to save the man in the very gesture whereby the beast was forever enslaved. We have only to consult the municipal laws in some Italian cities, such as Genoa, Florence or Venice, or Catalan ones such as Tortosa, to find particularly clear traces of this continuity of slavery, whose death knell – or so everyone is asked to believe – was sounded with the establishment of Christianity as a power in Europe.

There is no need to look farther than the cupboards of notaries or lawyers in the Mediterranean-Christian countries: they are packed with deeds for the purchase and sale of slaves. Any unbiased person who consults the trail that slave-traders left from the Slav countries to the Adriatic, and as far as Catalonia and Al-Andalus, will observe that the slave trade was being carried on under the aegis of royal grants and properly signed and sealed safe-conducts, with the full approval of the Christian authority that supplied the law.

Shall we describe the sting of the hot iron, the nights in the dry tanks with the entrance padlocked? Shall we linger over the tearing of children from parents, of wives from husbands, over the wounds and the blows? Shall we elaborate on the constant flights (there were 'maroons', runaways, in Europe, too)? Or the police regulations designed to keep slaves away from the coast? Or the steps taken to ensure that the masters of runaway slaves were compensated? Or stress the countless cases with which (slave-owning) Barcelona harassed Toulouse (which did not have slavery) because slaves of the Catalans took refuge in lands ruled by Toulouse?

The law covers all that. The codes cover all that. Under the heading of property, naturally. In this Mediterranean practice of slavery, the slave, invisible to the law as a person, is made into a non-person, removed completely from view. As if Roman law had set the tune. Slaves make no appearance in the treatises, or in the summa, or in the collections of sermons or in the *exempla* with which priests edified the masses. It was as if, invisible to the law, they had become invisible *per se*. Yet they were there, and their name was legion The serf was a person; the law knew it and said so. The captive was a person; the law said so and insisted on it, since captives could be exchanged for money that would return them to where they belonged. The slave was not legally a person. Those who decided such things lent them souls to be saved, which they enclosed in bodies to be mastered, the bodies of beasts about which they were not in the least concerned. The law and the codes proclaimed all that. They did so more bluntly in Iberia than elsewhere because of the centuries-old clash between Islam and Christianity fought on its soil.

All through the late Middles Ages and beyond, the Iberian peninsula had Slav and Albanian slaves, Moorish and Greek slaves, Finnish slaves and black slaves. There is no need to do more than look at the map and follow the routes of the Euro-African and Afro-European slave trade. Iberia is there, looming very large. And it made laws, vast quantities of laws. Then, when the story of the enslavement of Africans shifted westward as the West Indies and the American continents were discovered, then – contrary to what has been foolishly written to reinforce the lie that slavery had been effectively eliminated there by the adoption of Christianity – Spain and Portugal did not have to reinvent this type of subjection. They simply intensified a system of exploitation that was an integral part of their history and restricted themselves, if I dare put it thus, to providing the extension with the 'seriousness' necessary for an 'industrial' exploitation of a system of enslavement and legal bestialisation of which they had hitherto made only 'non-industrial' use.

But the quantitative increase in the scale of a phenomenon may lead to a qualitative alteration. That is undeniably the case if we compare the earliest trans-Mediterranean slave systems with the scale of transatlantic or Afro-American slavery. The law records this qualitative, if not substantial, shift. Portugal piled document on document, enactment on enactment, provision on provision in an amazing disorder but with formidable effectiveness to 'domesticate' its slaves and depopulate Angola for the benefit of Brazil. It was not drawing on a void but on what it had already developed to give its African voyages and southern settlements ideological backing. Spain drew on the *Siete partidas* of King Alfonso X the Wise to give the slave owner a tighter grip on the whip handle. Long after ravaging the Canaries, it wore out the indigenous peoples of the Caribbean, laid waste the coast of Venezuela and then settled its slaves over there – black Africans who had first tasted in the peninsula the exquisite pleasure of having a white master – in the mines of the land of the setting sun. We know what followed. The *Siete partidas* begat measures, decrees, provisions to make it all conform with the interests of the moment, whose ideology made the logic unassailable. Before long, all the white-Biblical nations with a coastline, all the nations of Christendom off-loaded into the Americas their 'excess' population, as Victor Hugo would later say to encourage these to work in Africa, and all made laws. Each of them erected strong, quite unambiguous legal frameworks to 'domesticate' slaves and keep them outside the law. And there would be a Dutch, a Portuguese, and an English *Code noir* (Black Code) that would have to be reconstructed by comparing the haphazard mass of convergent, divergent, complementary or contradictory decrees with one another.

What do these codes tell us that the archives do not? They tell us of the normality of slavery because they set out the will of sovereigns, how they intend to control the many ways of enforcing a single law, the law of owner-ship that their subjects, whether Dutch, Portuguese, etc., will apply to their own slaves. The pattern is simple: the sovereign codifies the law of subjects as owners of slaves. We keep finding the same model: between the sovereign and the slave-property there is the subject owner. And what is it that the sovereign wants? Whatever he may want – the code knows how to state it starkly – he wants it according to the harmony between his strategy and the ideology that prevails in his state and in his time. What the sovereign wants is a slave whose capture, purchase and enslavement can be exalted, whose sufferings can be made commonplace and whose degradation to the status of beast can be legit-imised by the dominant ideology – the very site where his sovereignty is legit-imised. The sovereign signs the letter of a code whose spirit and intention are the spirit and intention of the king himself insofar as they are assimilable and comprehensible in the ideological framework that legitimises a multitude of manifestations of the link between sovereign and subject. The circle is com-plete. But a circle can be interpreted.

Only the ideology is better at playing tricks than the code. It encloses absurdities in reasons, approximations in certainties, prophecies in predic-tions, myths in histories. It shakes everything up a little and persuades, and it's over. The codes operate a selection. No useless fantasies, no silly consider-ations or long-winded procrastinations: it is the law in all its stark dryness and priestly rigour.

After so much trial and error – if we are prepared to read in the conver-gence and historical linearity the codification of Afro-American slavery – the day came when France produced the juridical monster which states slavery and law in the same line. The *Code noir* (the word is French, the 'perfect' com-pletion of the thing is French) has the perfection of a total subjugation – the branding of the body and soul – of the black slave in the Caribbean, Louisiana, the Ile Bourbon, everywhere that France had colonised.

Is it possible to read the history of the slave trade without constantly dig-ging in the *Code noir*? Of course it is. Is it possible to grasp clearly and easily its interconnection with the ideology of the white-Biblical nations without constantly digging into it? Surely not. Should we talk of planned genocide when we begin to compare the code with what the archives of the slave trade show? Of that there can be no doubt. Should we seek an explanation from the European ideology (*Aufklärung, Ilustración, Lumières,* Enlightenment) that was contemporary with the widespread development of slavery, the 'excesses' of which it did bring itself now and then to criticise in measured tones, with fine gestures, without demolishing the principle of it? We must.

The *Code noir* was a judicial monstrosity which, from the time of its promulgation under Louis XIV in 1685 to its abrogation by Arago in 1848, deprived the slave of all legal reality and admitted only that he or she had a soul to be saved. The code was almost a century old when official Spain dis-covered its virtues and, for its own slaves, drew up a new version of it known as the *Código negro carolino* (*carolino* as a tribute to Charles III of Bourbon, the *ilustrado* king, that is, a supporter of the Enlightenment) – a century, in the time-scale of the history of ideas, between formulating a programme for slavery in French Saint-Domingue that had as much to do with genocide as with profit and the project of 'industrialising' slavery for the benefit of Spanish Santo Domingo.

The two codes need to be compared. While the *Código negro carolino* is a bastard child of the French *Code noir*, the drafters of the latter had conscientiously scoured the old Spanish-Dominican provisions to formulate it. The result was that while the Caroline code borrowed from the French *Code noir* in its time, it was also drawing indirectly on old Spanish documents that had come down to it through a bit of French technique. But times had changed and Catholicism weighed more heavily on Spain in the eighteenth century than it had on France in the seventeenth and eighteenth centuries. Whereas the French *Code noir* made a clear distinction between freedom and slavery, its Spanish bastard went to great lengths to treat free blacks and black slaves alike, removing both outside Spanish 'common law'. The *Code noir* laid down once and for all the rejection of the slave outside the legal category of 'person'. The *Código negro* explicitly regretted having to impose the crushing burden of a yoke on brothers so poorly equipped by natural law, whose freedom is mentioned in one paragraph only for their unfreedom to be stressed in the next. It regrets, but it crushes. Suddenly, it takes for granted that slavery exists only for a time and hence leads eventually to emancipation – and then an article simply removes all doubt about its permanence. It dilates on the coming end of a calamity which is solely due to the economic and political imperatives of the colony, but it contrives to hedge about that legal outcome with moral obstacles. In short, Spanish legal drafters are repugnant in their half-measures, sighs and lamentations about the terrible absurdity of something whose management they are exhausting themselves trying to organise and whose profitability they are exhausting themselves trying to build, as were the French 'poets' of moratoria wearing themselves out suggesting how to manage the worst possible abuse, the worst possible injustice without placing undue strain on justice.

Cold reason in France? The French *Code noir* is coldly rational. Reasonable whining on the part of Spain? The Spanish *Código negro* whines. Each throne has its own strategy, each nation its ideology, each one the slaves it wants to see. Like the others elsewhere, these two want slaves prostrate, humiliated, bestialised and well-behaved, 'domesticated'.

The codes say all that.

Humboldt, the great Humboldt, went to see the lands of slavery. When he returned, he recorded and stressed the four consolations which lightened the lot of the black male slave in Spanish lands and of which he was deprived in the other colonies: the slave could choose his master; he could choose his wife as his heart dictated; he could purchase his freedom through work or obtain it as a reward for his good service; and finally he could purchase the freedom of his wife and children.

Touching, but false. If you read at night, by the light of a pathetic candle, the *Código negro carolino* and the documents that preceded it and the one that abridged it and followed it in historical reality (the *Código negro carolino*, ratified by the Spanish crown, was still-born), and if you skip pages, you might think that paradise was being programmed for black slaves. For blacks, it described hell. But since when has anyone sipping coffee with the masters read it with the eyes of the slaves?

The genealogy of all the European slave codes – not only the two discussed at length here – is being reconstructed, but it is work that will take a long time. In this area, bringing out clearly the will of sovereigns will only confirm the murderous constancy of what was a single, undivided project.

Bibliography

LUCENA SALMORAL, M. 1996. *Los códigos negros de la América española*. Alcalá de Henares/Paris, University of Alcalá/UNESCO Publishing.

SALA-MOLINS, L. 1986. *Le Code noir ou le calvaire de Canaan*. Paris, Presses Universitaires de France.

———. 1992a. *L'Afrique aux Amériques. Le Code noir espagnol*. Paris, Presses Universitaires de France.

———. 1992b. *Les misères des lumières*. Paris, Laffont.

VERLINDEN, C. 1955 and 1977. *L'esclavage dans l'Europe médiévale*. 2 vols. Brugge/Ghent, Rijksuniversiteit te Gent.

Chapter 18

The Incomplete Past of Slavery: The African Heritage in the Social Reality, Subconsciousness and Imagination of Guadeloupe

Dany Bébel-Gisler

> *Lè ou konnèt la ou sôti,*
> *Chimen douvan-ou ka vin pli klè.*

> When you know where you come from,
> The road you have left to run, your future, becomes clearer.

> *Pa konnèt mové.*
> *Rasin a-y anmè. Rasin a-y pwazon.*

> Ignorance is bad.
> Its roots are bitter. Its roots
> Are poison.

The Incomplete Past of Slavery

Sété léstravay

> It was the time of slavery.
> White men then were so cruel. The things they did to black folks!
> Grab the men from their homes, throw them in chains, carry them across the ocean, bring them here, to work.
> To work without any clue, without saying things should be done this way or that …
> Isn't that real cruelty?
> And if a black man didn't do well … A stake planted in the ground, the man attached. And then the whip …
> That's how whites treated blacks then.
> …

Some people, having seen these atrocities, cried out:
'Oh, oh! They carried us away from our homeland.
They threw us in chains.
They dragged us here.
They forced us to work.
They don't tell us how to do things.
They kill us with their lashes.
They sting us, they burn us.'
The sorcerer replied:
'They will see. Get ready, we are leaving, the time has come.'
'How will we manage?'
'I am telling you, get yourselves ready.'
'We can never return to Africa.
We came by boat.
We cannot walk across the sea on our feet made for the mud.'
'Get ready. I will return soon.'
The black man entered the white man's hen-house.
He opened the hen-house. He took two eggs.
'I am telling you, let us be off.'
Some followed him and others remained.
They went to Moko Bridge, at La Boucan, where the boats leave for
    La Pointe.
'We cannot walk across the sea on our feet.'
But the African knew how.
They went under the bridge. He used his magic to break the two eggs.
A large ship appeared.
They left and returned to Africa.

This story of the imaginary return to Africa shows how imagination and symbolism help people to survive. It is an imaginary resistance associated with other forms of struggle waged by slaves against the attempt to deprive them totally of their identity, the absolute physical, cultural and symbolic violence used against them.

As regards Guadeloupe, the return to Africa, long awaited and long hoped for by our ancestors the slaves, never happened, except in the imagination as described to me in 1980 by Anmann, a ninety-eight-year-old Guadeloupian woman married to an 'African' whose parents had arrived in Guadeloupe as part of the clandestine trade shortly after the abolition of slavery, in 1848.[1] And today, a group of Rastas, the 'Sainte famille Jah', claiming to have been much moved by this story, is advocating a return to Africa by ship in order to put its resources and technology, as well as its spirituality, at the disposal of its brothers.[2]

In Guadeloupe, revolts, insurrections and *marronnage* – that is, running away from the plantations to escape slavery and demonstrate opposition to the slave system – did not, as they did in Haiti, end in independence. In the 1980s, the image of *marronnage*, the moment when a special language is reconstructed and an attempt made to build up a force of opposition, underwent a reassessment, with the rise of nationalist ideas. The activists of the Action Révolutionnaire Caraïbe (ARC) declared themselves '*Nègres marrons modernes*' and turned against the state, rejecting the negative labels (bandits, savages, criminals, etc.) that the state had used against their ancestors. Thus a 1983 communiqué was headed: 'General statement. Appeal to the Guadeloupian people for armed struggle against the *French bandits*.' Some advocates of independence even went so far as to argue that to escape from the crisis and throw off the colonial yoke, it was necessary to practise what the '*Nègres marrons*' had done, in particular, to practise economic development based on self-reliance – to take up the resistance agriculture practised by the slaves, diversifying crops to put an end to sugar-cane monoculture.

Sugar-cane growing left its mark on the formation and structure of Caribbean societies (agrarian landscape, housing, class/race hierarchies) and led, after the establishment of slavery, to the extermination of the natives of the Caribbean and the destruction of the ecological landscape and a civilisation based on sugar cane. The life of the poor people of Guadeloupe, which once moved at the pace of the sugar harvest, even recently was conditioned by the sugar factories. All work depended on it. Today, only three factories remain, and soon there will be only one left. On the land formerly planted with cane, concrete is king. The cane workers have had to suffer not only unemployment but also loss of their homes and exclusion from the environment to which they were accustomed. And there can be no retraining for them, since no other industry is about to replace the doomed sugar industry.

Guadeloupe and Martinique are areas deeply scarred by the slave trade, since in the history of the slave system are to be found the roots of the still unresolved social and economic conflicts affecting Caribbean societies and contaminating and confusing discourse and practice. It is an area that has today by fiat been opened up to the European single market, the bridgehead of the European Union on the American continent.

The slave system remains a close and present reality in the collective memory of the Caribbean. And it is against this background of the incomplete past of slavery, of the growing impoverishment of sugar-cane workers and a serious economic crisis linked with the world economic crisis, that the social structures and political problems – in particular those of economic development, cultural and national identity, and the African cultural heritage – unfold and become embroiled. Are the art of speech, the relation to the Other in popular culture and Guadeloupian society, and the conception of the body-person (to mention just a few of the topics that I shall look at in this chapter) practices and a philosophy inherited from Africa?

Leaving aside music and a number of magical and religious phenomena for which there is evidence in the Creole language, it is difficult to locate the survivals of African civilisations in the societies of the Caribbean and understand the strategies put into effect to conserve them. It is difficult because there are so many factors that complicate the analogies, similarities and divergences to be observed. In some cases, how can we know whether something derives from this or that cultural tradition, from commodity relations that are deeply implanted in the region or from the constraints of adaptation? In addition, many things held to be peculiarly African are to be found in other peasant societies.

In general, traditions may last as long as the relations of law and duty that support them. When those relations become frayed, the principles disappear. Yet in Guadeloupe, for example in the stories created by the children of Bwadoubout,[3] we find the same bitter and ambiguous vision of the boy as in the traditional folktale: deprived of his childhood, usually an orphan and poor, he wins the status of a person only by deception and revolt. At the end of the story he is an adult, rich and respected, far removed from both poverty and childhood. Hunger, poverty, revolt, deception to escape from an oppressive situation, these constants of the traditional folktale are taken up, transformed of course, by the children of the Guadeloupian countryside today.

How, then, are we to interpret and analyse this strategy of indirectness and avoidance, widely present in Guadeloupe in the behaviour of both young and old, rich and poor? The principle of indirectness 'must be looked on as immediately descended from the African scene ... and the implications of this fact in giving form to Negro behaviour ... if a true picture of Negro life is to be had, cannot be overlooked', argued Herskovits[4] almost half a century ago.

In theory, we could go on forever glossing on whether or not it is necessary to go back to the African past to explain the strategy of deception, since it is a feature of all dominated, disinherited classes, who use it as a method of protection. There should be no need to recall that the slave who refused to deceive died. What is this strategy of survival through deception? Could it be that the economic situation of the peasants has scarcely changed since slavery, considering that the ideology of folktales continues to exist? That slavery weighs heavily on all the structures of Guadeloupian society? That there is a Guadeloupian popular culture that is very much alive and distinct from French culture?

My questioning is rather about the role that these behavioural traits may play and the use that can be made of this African heritage. Why, when the material underpinnings and the symbols disappear, do the practices survive? Is it because these practices are the product of the individual *habitus*, the *ethos* of a society and the economic, political, ideological and symbolic interests of an individual or a group? Then, in that case, should we not be identifying what underlies the interests at stake in retaining this or that trait, this or that mode of production of one civilisation rather than another?

Beyond these theoretical considerations and scientific caution, popular wisdom says to me: 'When you know where you come from, your future becomes clearer.' How, then, can knowledge of the past of the slaves in the Americas, knowledge of all that they have bequeathed us as a legacy – thought, spirituality, knowledge, know-how, etc. – serve the movement to win back control of ourselves and help us to construct a future different from the one that has been imposed? How is the African sociocultural heritage represented in the Caribbean, and in Guadeloupe and Martinique in particular?

Who are the men and women who have decided to make this heritage bear fruit and why? What is the state of knowledge of that past and what might be its contribution and political function?

- To reconstruct the collective memory, to alter the relationship of Caribbeans to Africa, an Africa that is present in us but denied and repressed, and that is beginning to be taken on board;
- To save from oblivion, indifference and contempt the memory of those African men and women deported to the Americas and the Caribbean to whom we are so much indebted;
- To mobilise collective knowledge about the slave route and its conditions of life and death, about the slave community's genius for adaptation and creativity of which, for us, the most original were jazz and the Creole languages;
- To invite Caribbeans to dare to plunge themselves into oral tradition to track down and dispel, in the depths where it is hidden, 'ignorance, bitter root, poison' – ignorance of ourselves, our history and our past.

First Training for Research

Before setting out a few aspects of African civilisation and culture present in the sugar-cane civilisation and Caribbean popular culture that are the primary components of the African sociocultural heritage in Guadeloupe, I want briefly to show where I am coming from. Following shocks that precipitated a crisis in the system of certainties that had been inculcated into me in the colonial school, I came to question my relationship to Africa, have become aware of the African roots present in Guadeloupian words and cultural practices, and call into question theses about the loss of the African cultural heritage.

Very powerful experiences in my family environment and a hands-on practice of literacy teaching with African workers who had migrated to the Paris region were, for me, the causes of my research training. I learned that science is passionate interrogation, openness, ongoing dialogue throughout the research with data and facts, an intimate combination of objectivity and subjectivity, and of political and partisan commitment – all are essential to approach topics including the future of Guadeloupian language and culture, the responses to be given to social demands, and the need to develop new links with our cousins in the Americas and the Caribbean and our grandparents in Africa.

My family environment was the first place where I got my training in research. Why were my educated, French-speaking relatives on my father's side described as 'good people' and those on my mother's side – small farmers unable to read or write, speaking only Creole – as idiots, people without culture, blacks good enough for sugar cane, the banana and the hoe, when the stories that they used to tell me by moonlight enchanted me.

My father was the son of an important landowner, my mother, a mulatto, a farm worker on my grandfather's plantation. If, by clinging to the paternal side of the family, I was able to prolong my studies, it was always with the maternal side that I felt at ease. Today, I know why. My mother's family nurtured my imagination and sensitised me to the buried story of Guadeloupe, never studied, that thrilled me and gave me a taste for observing, for questioning the most common, everyday language and for exploring our roots and our words.

As a child, I experienced the relations between masters and slaves, and later between masters and workers on the coffee, banana and sugar plantations through my mother's family. The overseer of the plantation where they worked and lived forbade us to pass in front of the master's house. We had to make a detour of several kilometres to fetch water from the spring. When I passed my secondary school final exams, all of my mother's side of the family, on whom this honour reflected, were granted the right to pass by. In other words, for the master of the plantation, my promotion made my kinsmen and -women achieve the rank of human beings! The shock that gave me awakened in me the desire to understand what a language is and the role of the colonial school in society and in the construction of identity.

Much later, I understood that the behaviour of this big landowner was simply reproducing the prejudices induced by the slave system: the master was simply recognising the validity of his racist criteria of humanity, while the black had to prove that he was a human being, in short that he existed – and was capable of being absorbed into the dominant French model.

Forty years ago, when I left Guadeloupe to study in France, I carried with me in my luggage a certain knowledge of the white people's country, society and cultural practices, those peculiar to poor Guadeloupian peasants. I had the desire to understand scientifically the foundations of our subjectivity, to bring out the repressed history, to recover that subconscious in the sense in which Durkheim said 'To recover the subconscious is to recover history', to give voice to the nearest descendants of former slaves, the workers in or around the sugar industry, in order to attempt to reconstruct with them the memory of this shameful past – slavery. And to do that meant tracking down the 'unspoken', the African repressed, the hidden face of social and cultural life in Guadeloupe, grasping the 'obscure', that basic anthropological category, in order to bring all these out and analyse them.

Encounter with Soninke and Bambara Workers at Ivry-sur-Seine (France)

In the Creole language, people say: *Lè ou fè-ou kontré fondal natal, dabôpouy-onn, i ka dékostonbré-ou. Aprédavwa i travay vou konsa, si ou asèpté woté is an zyé a-ou, woté kras an tèt a-ou, ou pé woufè kô a-ou* (When you make an important encounter, it at first throws you off balance. Then it reconstructs you, on condition you consent to lift the veil from your eyes and clean out your brain. In short, with your certainties upset, you can then pull yourself together for a new departure),

That is how it was with my encounter with the Soninke and Bambara workers of Ivry. I arrived as a colonised, intellectual woman with an overall plan for literacy teaching and consciousness-raising, puffed up with theoretical knowledge. I quickly found myself thrown back on my own resources. My political commitment was endlessly called into question: the African workers did not ask me what I knew of Marx, Lenin or Mao, but *who* I was. Concretely, I was faced with the question of my identity: was I African, French, Caribbean? How could I, a black woman like them, sometimes have behaviour similar to that of the French people in their group? Might I be a 'coconut'? The African comrades helped me to understand myself as objectively formed and deformed by the phenomenon of assimilation and subjectively deprived of Caribbean reality.

The second place where I acquired training was thus, for six years, the 'African village at Ivry', in the suburbs of Paris. Those who trained me were these African brothers – more especially, one old man who taught me so much about myself and about Africa.[5]

It was at this time that I began to practise action research, that is, research that attempts to combine action and science and involve the population in the process of research itself. This approach makes it possible to modify a situation and, by transforming it, to lay bare the mental mechanisms impossible to grasp using the traditional methods that turn subjects of research into passive objects. As I listened to the different types of knowledge of the Soninke, my knowledge of Africa, my image of Africans and, in particular, my representation of the Soninke and the Bambara, were modified, relativised and even corrected.

From a Fractured and Mutilated Heritage to the Reconstruction of Memory and the Appreciation of African Roots

The Question of the African Sociocultural Heritage in Guadeloupe

I have been engaged in investigating Caribbean reality, elucidating and understanding Guadeloupian sociocultural reality and the distinctiveness of Caribbean culture for the past 25 years, and from my very earliest research work I was faced with the problem of features of African civilisation in Caribbean societies. Were they something that ran deep, or were they mere relics?

As I devoted myself to deciphering the collective memory and the Guadeloupian world of the imagination, I could not fail to encounter Africa. It was an Africa that was at first denied, the black contributions to the world unknown and/or not appreciated. The story of the imaginary return to Africa and study of the conception of the human person (*ko/kadav*) and of the art of speech still alive in popular culture, together with original data collected on modes of physical and imaginary resistance on the part of both slaves and present-day peasants, gave irrefutable confirmation of the continuity of features of African civilisation in Caribbean societies and the strength of the African heritage, whether rejected or accepted, in particular in Guadeloupe.

For some researchers, it is impossible to speak of a cultural heritage left by slaves: '[F]rom the moment the slaves set foot on the slave ship, the African culture in which until then they had been integrated vanished, since they would never recover the socio-economic bases on which it rested.... Once in the West Indies, the African culture carried by the slaves was thus annihilated.'[6] For some researchers, both the Creole language and the Creole culture developed and produced by the slaves are simply by-products of European cultures.

Because of colonial policy, the black contribution to Caribbean societies was not recognised and acknowledged as a fundamental feature, any more than was the imprint of Africa in the identity of the Americas. As for Guadeloupe and Martinique, not so long ago they were regarded as the least 'black' countries of the Caribbean, and as having lost all African roots, thus being the most 'civilised'. It should be noted that they have the 'extreme and original' characteristic of offering an example of a situation in which French colonialism, because of the origin of the social pattern and the length of its centuries-long domination (360 years), was able to follow through to its extreme consequences the effects of its own logic.

What strategies were used by the population that had come from Africa to resist hegemony, to keep alive some of the basic features of African civilisation and not allow themselves to be totally dispossessed of the cultural and symbolic achievements handed down by their ancestors?

Taking Guadeloupian popular culture to be a culture of deception and prevarication, I began to answer these questions in part. In my view, Africa is present in a good many Guadeloupians, of course as the 'splinter in the wound', but in a way that is very much alive – by actualising itself in everyday practices, in the thousand and one ways that Guadeloupians of all social classes have of using the capacities for resistance and withdrawal developed by the slaves and enriched by their descendants.

Even with the repression and absolute oppression introduced by the slave system, the powers that be failed to deprive the Africans held in slavery and their descendants of their cultural values, nor were they successful in imprisoning their imagination. How could we explain that they were able to survive in the concentration and labour camps of the sugar and cotton plantations, that they were able to resist the vilest of all debasements – slavery – and the rejection beyond the pale of humanity if, in the holds of the slave ships, there had not been songs?

How can we explain their survival without the remembrance of those folktales and myths in which African man is described as proud and strong. If, after the master's whip, fourteen hours of back-breaking toil, food barely sufficient for the body, there had not been the reinvigorating sound of the drum, music locked into the noises of the body-person to whom it communicated strength and energy to mark the soothing steps of the dance. If there had not been, anchored in them, the deep roots of African tradition, transformed, enriched and adapted to the new world. If they had not made imagination part of their community life. If they had not, while accommodating themselves to legality in order to survive, clung to African cultural and symbolic benchmarks. If, finally, they and their descendants, from 1635 to 1848, from 1848 to 1946, had not practised the ways of 'cunning intelligence'[7] and 'indirectness' to create, keep alive and enrich a culture condemned to clandestinity from its very creation and then fiercely repressed.

What was the universe of this culture? From the very beginning, a specific manner of approaching and understanding situations and events, and of acting on them, succumbing to them or resisting them. Ways of being and doing, like every culture. A culture in warlike coexistence and unequal exchange by virtue of its social status in relation to French culture.

What I mean by 'Caribbean popular culture in its Guadeloupian particularity' is neither the faithful and exact reproduction of African cultures, nor a by-product of French culture. For we are neither Africans nor French but Guadeloupians – men and women of African, Indian or European origin who, like the Creole language (*kaz a kô a yo*: the house of their being) that unites them, are made of tensions that are always present, contradictions that are unresolved and wounds that have not healed over.

Survival through Resistance in the Imagination

In addition to the revolts and insurrections that terrorised the colonisers, everyday actions on the plantation, passivity, suicide and *marronnage*, the slave could 'withdraw his body', flee, resist through the imagination. The slave in revolt was creating for himself another imaginary and symbolic space where he was endeavouring to represent himself differently, to 'live his body', to live for himself, that is to say, to push aside the bars of the cage in which people were trying to hold him completely enclosed, allowing the master to exploit only his physical strength.

Imagination and symbolism were part of community life, and cultural *marronnage* was woven into the Creole language, in which there was a distinction between the body and the corpse. Even today one can still hear: *Misyé la ka konprann i sé mèt a kô an mwen. Awa, sé kadav la tousèl i ka komandé poutoutbo'* (The gentleman [boss, employer] thinks himself master of my body. But he isn't. He really only commands my corpse. He does not possess me entirely. He thinks he has me, but it's only my corpse that I let him have). The lexeme *kô*, in Creole, corresponding to *corps* (body) in French, reflects a philosophy close to the Yomba theory of personality, of the vital principle of *lémi* that makes a distinction between the living body and the corpse.[8]

For the mass of Guadeloupians, man is not made up of a soul and a body. His perceived body, named sometimes 'body', sometimes 'corpse', is inhabited and traversed by spiritual forces which make a person a real and living body and not a corpse. When these forces let go of you, you begin to decline because it is they that 'keep' the body alive.

The expression *kenbé kô* (keep your body) signifies controlling your psychological life so that the good and bad spirits that rule it live in equilibrium, ensuring that your 'great big good angel', the essential principle of psychological life, is not taken away from you. To inquire after someone's health is to ask how his body is doing – if the body is leading him or if he is leading the body. Use of the word *kadav* sometimes indicates to another what you think of him or her and introduces nuances into the ongoing relationship. When you say *kô*, you are by the same token referring to all the relations that bind the individual to his family, both the living and the dead, in a symbolic chain which embraces relations with illness, life, death, the ancestors, the spirits and nature.

Another fundamental element of this heritage is the relation between human beings and nature. In Guadeloupe, a certain type of this relation still survives which is not one of domination and exploitation but one of alliance. Nature is not an inert space to which *Homo sapiens* alone give life by exploiting it with technology, but rather is an inhabited place, full of living forces centred around the body-person. This way of seeing things, inherited from Africa, is still very strongly present in Guadeloupe. It is unfortunately often treated as superstition – thinking that has more to do with magic than with reason.

Such an approach differs totally from Western thought, one of the first effects of whose colonisation of the New World was the destruction of the ecological and human environment and the introduction of a relationship of domination and profit.

But the world cannot be saved by ratiocination alone. Saving the Amazon, for example, the greatest gene bank in the world, involves the local populations 'who have protected this region for all the years of their existence, thanks to their very special ancestral wisdom'.

An Art of Speech Still Very Much Alive

In tracing the sources of oral tradition and, in particular, ways of naming and expressing reality, I have listed more than 40 ways of characterising speech. A world of words in which *pawôl a bouch a manjé an nou* (words proffered by the mouth with which you eat, true, sure words) is certainly not comparable to *pawôl yo kraché an bouch an nou* (words that were spat into our mouth, reported, booby-trapped words).

Laying bare the thousand and one ways of characterising speech in Creole – a speech given exclusively and sovereignly to the masters and denied to the slaves – offers a particularly effective way of entering intimately into the everyday universe of slaves, and feeling the tension from which they were forever escaping through repeated inventiveness. Whence these *pawôl anba dousou* (clandestine words), *pawôl kokomakak* (bludgeon words that strike like a blow with a stick), *pawôl vant* (words coming from the belly, essential words), *pawôl masyé* (masked, allusive words), *pawôl a Nég Kongo* (words of Congo blacks, the last to arrive, scorned and despised).

Words distorted by the iron muzzle that was put on slaves. Forbidden, smothered words that in order to express things were obliged to resort to paths that were *kosyé*, roundabout. Words drawn from the deepest depths of nature, attentive to day, to night, to the rustling of leaves, the bark of trees. Animist words to celebrate the fusion, the marriage of humanity with the cosmic universe. Like this magnificent ox-driver's song:

Désawa é	Disarray eh
Désawa o	Disarray oh
An tout bwa pa ni vwa	In every wood no voice
Lalin tèt anba	The moon hangs its head ...
Latè o sé frè mwen	The earth, oh, is my brother
Dlo sé sésé mwen	The water is my little sister ...
Manman-ou sé manman mwen	Your mother is my mother
Papa-ou sé papa mwen	Your father is my father
Latè o sé frè mwen	The earth is my brother
Woulé, Yèy, woulé!	Move, ye-up, move!

Words of indirectness, too, to hide and conceal one's own thought, not to attack the adversary head on. Oral tradition and Caribbean peasant culture are a mine of maxims and advice on how to deceive, overcome through ridicule, protect oneself, etc.

If, one hundred and sixty years after the abolition of slavery, children tell folktales and proverbs which, like *griots*, they embellish with events and people from their own everyday life or the everyday life of the country, it is because African oral tradition has been kept alive and passed from generation to generation. Its words have remained living words: *Davwa bwa ka pouri, pawôl pa ka pouri* (Wood rots, words don't).

I could explain many other attitudes manifesting this continuity of the African presence, such as the principles that govern relations between adults and children, the respect due to the elders, the custom of saying 'hallo' to everyone, known or unknown, whom you meet on your way – which is a way of recognising him or her as another self – and all the unwritten rules that make up tradition. Or the way of appropriating land, work relations, the continuing importance even today of joint ownership, and so on.

I could also describe the cult of the ancestors by the descendants of the Congo blacks who arrived in Guadeloupe after the abolition of slavery in 1848, or the *grap a kongo* (cult of the ancestors on All Saints' Day) practised by Massongo families in Capesterre-Belle-Eau or Pointe-Noire. Or show how, down to the present day, musical instruments (trombones, siyaks) continue to be made at Marie-Galante that are identical to those of the Bantu homeland.

For centuries the Creole language and Guadeloupian culture have been continually changing, and the African heritage has been constantly redefined. The former will not save us, but they constitute that 'critical mirror' that can send us back our past and present image and teach us what we are, and ensure that concepts such as national language, science, technology, revolution, socialism, integrated development, freedom and peace cease to be mere symbols and are given concrete form in programmes.

Conclusion

In a paper at a symposium on sugar and literature, I suggested that the slave, like the cane for which he or she was deported, was an essential component of our personality, representing flexibility, apparent submission and fragility, but also, in our innermost being, resistance – assured as we are of the power of our life-force and the strength of our roots.

Unfortunately, not all the peoples of the Caribbean are clearly conscious either of the original African roots present in their own cultural characteristics or of the devastating effects of the slave trade. Perhaps this is because, as the late Miles Davies suggested, unlike the Jews, the blacks have been unable to assert their tragic heritage in the face of the world, the crimes against humanity of deportation and enslavement, or to tell their children about our holocaust in order to perpetuate slavery in the collective memory and produce enough documents, literary and artistic works, films, etc., for their children and grandchildren never to be able to forget.

In 1986, a Guadeloupian, Paul Louis, convinced of the necessity of having 'a symbol to bring us together and serve as a focus for us as others do before their statues and their museums', conceived the project 'of erecting a black memorial of the deportation and slavery' and launched an appeal for it. In Guadeloupe, this appeal met with only indifference or rejection. In the light of the low impact that this project had, Lluís Sala-Molins wrote in the journal *Afrique-Asie* (No. 397): 'Has the white work of burying the centuries-long black African and Afro-American disasters succeeded, then, in dragging the black memory to the depths where whiteness has buried the memory of its crimes?... If the peoples do not need heroes, they must draw from their history, and also from the monumental reminders of their disasters, the determination to survive and the will to rebel.'

However, over the last ten years or so, a number of men and women from Guadeloupe have been recognising themselves as *Guadeloupian blacks*, originating from Africa. And they are doing this irrespective of whether they are mulattos, *gwo Nèg*, 'black Negroes', as we say here, *bata blan, bata nèg* or *bata zendyen*. They want to know their slave past in order to rescue slavery from oblivion and indifference, give the African contribution to the American continents in particular its due, and encourage Guadeloupians to be reconciled with Africa and thus with themselves.

Various associations are working to this end, including:

- the Cercle d'Étude Cheikh Anta Diop, which was set up in 1987 and whose aim is 'to study, disseminate and promote the work of Cheikh Anta Diop and its consequences and influences';
- the Comité International des Peuples Noirs de Guadeloupe, which looks into the political, human, socio-economic and cultural realities of blacks in the world in terms of economics, alternative development and reparations: 'Is the black world a reality or a myth? Why, at the dawn of the twenty-first century, do we have all the ills, all the weaknesses, all

the contradictions and all the handicaps? What can we do, if there is still time, to develop and make a reality of this reintegration in which what is at stake is the survival or disappearance of a whole swathe of humankind? Does the West owe reparations to the black world and how might such reparations serve to support economic development?';

- the Association Nkelo Wa Kongo, set up in June 1992 around the Masenbo family living in the commune of Capesterre-Belle-Eau in Guadeloupe and practising *grap a kongo*, and whose objective is 'to collect, present and promote Congo traditions and cultures in Guadeloupe and, more generally, African culture';

- the Association Sa ki ta-ou sé ta-ou (what is yours is yours) has the aim of 'promoting Guadeloupian culture and studying the African contributions to that culture, notably music';

- the Comité 94, set up to commemorate the two-hundredth anniversary of the abolition of slavery in 1794, an abolition unknown to most Guadeloupians and which the Comité 94 is seeking to impress on people's memory through concrete symbols: a monument bearing in three languages – French, Creole and English – the text of the decree of 16 Pluviôse Year II;

- a monument to the memory of the 'Unknown black maroon';

- a 'Torch of Freedom'.

In February 1994, in the commune of Lamentin, the Maison de l'Esclavage et des Droits de l'Homme (House of slavery and human rights) was established in order to 'safeguard, defend and enhance knowledge, through collective memory, of the slave past as one of the essential elements of the Guadeloupian cultural heritage, promote better knowledge of our history, in particular that of slavery, through undertaking and disseminating research and making it widely available, and create a new pedagogy to deal with issues associated with slavery and human rights'. This building, a witness to the past, will house all the remains, documents, objects and writings from the slave period and the results of our contemporary research in order to explain to present and future generations where they come from, who they are, and what made them, and to make them *vin byen èvè sa ki ta yo*, reconciling themselves with this past erased from consciousness with the complicity of official history.

It is high time to save from oblivion and indifference these millions of men and women murdered by the slave trade and to rehabilitate slaves in all their humanity. Of course, by bringing us together to pursue this issue further, we compare and contrast our ideas, but everything must be done to ensure that our proposals for research and action bear fruit.

Notes

1. This narrative about the imaginary return to Africa is taken from D. Bébel-Gisler, 1985. Anmann, the Guadeloupian peasant woman, repeated to me again and again: 'Those who had done three turns were able to return to Africa. Those who had not were unable to leave and remained in Guadeloupe.' *Lantou a ki biten Anmann?* (Around what, Anmann?) I got no details or clarifications. But I got the reply in Ouidah. I discovered the 'tree of return'. It was quite emotional to learn that as they left the Zonaï, the African prisoners had to walk round this tree three times. It was a ceremony that would enable the spirits of the slaves to return to their country after their death. Three centuries later, this story of a mystical journey testifies to the strength of symbolism and the imaginary and how they make it possible to grasp the social logic and reality.
2. The 'Sainte famille Jah', embracing a small community of about twenty individuals, is leading an autarchic existence in the district of Capesterre-Belle-Eau. It has endeavoured, so far without success, to collect the money needed to hire a sailing ship to return to Africa.
3. A dwelling place established in 1979 for young people with educational, family or social problems. All the teaching there is in Creole.
4. M.J. Herskovits, 1941.
5. See D. Bébel-Gisler, 1970 and 1975.
6. J.-L. Bonniol, 1980, p. 268.
7. M. Detienne and J.-P. Marcel-Vernant, 1978. 'Cunning intelligence' is here defined as 'a type of intelligence and of thought, a way of knowing; it implies a complex but very coherent body of mental attitudes and intellectual behaviour which combine flair, wisdom, forethought, subtlety of mind, deception, resourcefulness, vigilance, opportunism, various skills, and experience acquired over the years'.
8. I should stress that I did not start from the Yomba to verify if this view of things existed in Guadeloupe. After the publication in 1980 of my article 'Corps, langage, politique, une expérience d'alphabétisation en Guadeloupe', African researchers commented on it to me. The same thing happened after the publication in 1985 of *Léonora, l'histoire enfouie de la Guadeloupe*, a story of the life of a peasant woman who had lived forty years on a sugar plantation. Everything that Léonora said about rituals of birth, death and relations with others is very close to what happens in Africa, I was assured by several African readers.

Bibliography

BÉBEL-GISLER, D. 1970. Migration et organisation communautaire: le cas des travailleurs immigrés soninké de la région parisienne. Paris, Sorbonne. (Master's thesis in ethnology.)

———. 1975. *Quelques principes pour écrire le créole.* Paris, L'Harmattan.

———. 1980. 'Corps, langage, politique. Une expérience d'alphabétisation en Guadeloupe'. *Actes de la recherche en sciences sociales.*

———. 1985. *Léonora, l'histoire enfouie de la Guadeloupe.* Paris, Seghers. (Mémoires vives.) [Eng. tr. Leskes, A. 1994. *Leonora. The Buried Story of Guadeloupe.* Charlottesville, University Press of Virginia.]

BONNIOL, J.-L. 'Les contradictions culturelles antillaises'. *Historial antillais*. Vol. 1. Société Dajani.

DETIENNE, M., and MARCEL-VERNANT, J.-P. 1977. *Les ruses de l'intelligence, la métis des Grecs*. Paris, Flammarion. [Eng. tr. Lloyd, J. 1978. *Cunning Intelligence in Greek Culture and Society*. Chicago and London, University of Chicago Press.]

HERSKOVITS, M.J. 1958. *L'héritage du noir*. Paris, Présence africaine. [Orig. Am. ed. 1941. *Myth of the Negro Past*. New York, Harper and Brothers.]

Chapter 19

From the Slave Trade to the 'Screening' of Immigrants

Hagen Kordes

A 'German' Approach to the Dialectic between Integration and Rejection[1]

It was in the course of some years spent in what used to be Dahomey in the late 1960s that I first heard of someone called Carolof,[2] a Brandenburger who had set up a trading post in 1682 on the coast of Ouidah and organised the slave trade for the French Compagnie des Indes Occidentales. In 1892, King Behanzin clandestinely traded slaves for weapons that were delivered to him by the big German companies established at Ouidah. This last piece of slave-dealing gave rise, in Cameroon, to a tribe called the Fon tribe.

The Germans, as is well known, made only a minor contribution to the slave trade.[3] Much more significant, on the other hand, was the barbarity of a number of governors during Germany's brief colonial period. The massive atrocities under the command of Carl Peters in South-West Africa seemed to foreshadow the Holocaust. Indeed, many officials of this old-fashioned colonial empire would later help Hitler take power at the head of the Reich and reduce millions of Jews, Gypsies (Rom and Sinti) and disabled people to slavery.

Although I am not particularly given to mentioning my German identity, I cannot avoid this burden that weighs on the shared history of Germans and Jews or Germans and Africans. I cannot but accept the atrocities committed by my compatriots of another age, in all the horror that they inspire in me. My ambivalent relations with my status as a German make me run a risk similar to the one – as Frantz Fanon explains – hovering over black Caribbeans in their relations with their origins: '... after the great white terror, the [Caribbean black] is now living in the great black mirage.'

Fleeing both mirage and utopia, I shall try here to analyse the development of human oppression from the slave trade to the present day, the age of the screening of immigrants, through the intermediate stages – colonialism and Nazism – and their transmission belt of racist fantasies and discourse, always masked or moulded to suit the trends of the time.

The Nuremberg Judgement Is No Longer Binding

Europeans and North Americans Attempt to Absolve Modern Times
of a Past Based on Slavery, Genocide and the Holocaust

Fifty years ago, the leaders of Nazi Germany who ordered the deportation and extermination of the Jews were tried, found guilty and executed. Their misdeeds were declared to be 'crimes against humanity'. Today, after the fall of the Berlin Wall, the collapse of the socialist bloc and the reunification of the two Germanys, the Nuremberg trial seems to be no longer binding.[4] This loss of authority is apparent not only in public opinion but also in the German legal institutions that succeeded the Nuremberg tribunal. Recently, the lower court of Mannheim granted a far-right politician that the fact of 'denying Auschwitz' – and thereby the industrial murder of millions of Jews in the gas chambers – was not an offence serious enough to constitute incitement to discrimination. The dignity of those killed might – 'possibly' – suffer from such denials, but not that of survivors. The judges gave credit to the accused for the fact that he condemned the persecution of the Jews while protesting, 'with a legitimate interest', against the fact that 50 years after the end of the Second World War, Germany was still in the dock, whereas crimes against humanity committed by others were passed over.[5]

The Nuremberg judgement seems to have been in force only for as long as Germany was defeated and the victors could impose their own ideas of law and justice. In other words, had the Germans emerged victorious from the war, they would doubtless have celebrated their deeds as exploits that were part of the story of human emancipation. Perhaps, too, they might have called the Allies to account for their crimes against humanity, such as the gulag and the genocide of the American Indians (which some German historians have indeed recently started to do).

Since the fall of the Berlin Wall, the end of the Cold War and reunification, Germany has ceased to be the great loser, not only in the images people have of it but also in the political, moral and judicial institutions of Germany itself. This change of focus heralds a new ideological era that will see a radically new set of assumptions as well as a complete reversal of historical memory. Even the re-emergence since 1991 of the issue of the slave trade (like that of the Soviet gulag) could be interpreted as an indicator of this trend towards putting the victors in the dock.

Although monstrously intolerable, the persecution, enslavement and extermination of the Jews, the Rom and the Sinti by Nazi Germany cannot be isolated from the global history of the subjugation of human beings by human beings. They alone no longer monopolise historical memory and the moral accomplishment of the past. But the Mannheim judgement is not designed to keep the memory alive. On the contrary, that judgement reflects an opinion predominant in Germany, which is that this country ought to enjoy the same acquittal of its crimes as have other nations, in other circumstances, that also enslaved peoples. In the name of justice between dominant nations, where there is no longer either victor or vanquished, the modern age as a whole – responsible for both slavery and genocide – must be absolved. Condemnation of the slave trade, colonial exploitation, extermination of the Jews and the hell of the gulag are seen as having more to do with the vexation aroused by defeat than with any commitment to international law. How else can we explain why memory of the barbarities of yesterday offers no guarantee against the bestialities of today: ethnic cleansing in Yugoslavia, tribal extermination in Rwanda, racial civil war in the United States of America, the violence suffered by immigrants and asylum-seekers in Germany and all over Western Europe?

From Repressive Tolerance to Open Violence against Foreigners

The behaviour of gangs of skinheads continues to express this collective subconscious attitude that comprises not only the Nazis' desire to exterminate but also the cruelty of colonisers and slavers. Since the reunification of Germany, not a week has passed without immigrant workers (mainly Turks) or refugees (especially Africans and Vietnamese) being physically attacked and their houses burnt down. Those committing these acts of vandalism are largely young people in gangs of skinheads who flaunt Nazi symbols simply to be provocative. When they were interrogated by the police, some of them justified their misconduct as follows: 'These foreigners are the pits. They are invading us and taking our money, our women and our houses. They are like vermin, layabouts who need to be given a good hiding, beaten up and wiped out. They overturn rubbish bins, pour motor oil in children's sandpits and eat our dogs and cats. [I, a skinhead] am doing openly what others – the politicians and the bourgeois – want deep down. In other words, I am doing other people's dirty work.'

In my opinion, the violence of skinheads against immigrant minorities is an echo of a collective memory made up of the Nazi desire to exterminate, the drive for colonial exploitation and the slave mania of the 'slavers'.[6] Nazi inspiration and mimicry are evident in the actions and language of young people belonging to the third generation after the Holocaust, fascinated by Hitlerite esotericism. More deeply, their symbolic gestures reveal a desire for extermination (they want to 'wipe out the vermin', they say) which now extends beyond its traditional object (the Semite) to attack new groups that are 'objectified', regarded as inferior and subordinated: foreign and immigrant minorities like the Turks, who have only a limited-period residence permit, or refugees from Africa and Asia whose asylum is precarious. The skinheads want to annihilate them because, in their view, they are decadent and inferior beings. In other words, discrimination is no longer aimed at simply humiliating the other symbolically but at liquidating him or her physically.

Like the Nazis and the skinheads, the colonialists felt contempt for those they viewed as underdeveloped and 'uncivilised'. They paternalistically advocated ambiguous attitudes: either assimilation ('they [foreigners] ought to reach our level of development'), or marginalisation ('so long as they provide cheap labour, they can stay, but don't let them ask for anything!').

The xenophobes thus behave like slavers, perceiving foreigners only as cattle: 'They are savages, creatures of instinct, vermin. All these blacks, browns and yellows come from the depths of darkness or the jungle. No one – either in the population or in the media – knows their face, still less their name.'[7] In order to explain the racist violence of East German skinheads, it must be remembered that it was only very recently that, in the former GDR, a socialist government presided over a peaceful, decent life: 'We were doing all right in the [then Communist] German Democratic Republic. We didn't have any Turks. And the blacks didn't dare give us any trouble. The *Stasi* [security service] would have stepped in immediately.'

It is not only the Nuremberg verdict that is no longer binding: the historical condemnations of slavery have also lost their hold on much of public opinion. Segregation, the forerunner of extradition, is spreading to all the dominant nations in Europe and North America.

Ambiguous Attitudes

The strategies of integration and segregation are complementary. That segregation is simply another form of apartheid is something shown, *inter alia*, by an experiment that I conducted with students at the University of Münster[8] where, in front of the university restaurant, we set up two separate entrances, one for Germans, the other for 'foreigners'. Using leaflets, a committee of German students justified the operation by pointing to the growing number of foreign students, the rise in the price of meal tickets and the many disadvantages suffered by German students. This experiment showed that 95 per cent of students followed the instructions spontaneously: Germans to the left, 'foreigners' to the right. Thus, people who were otherwise charming, intelligent, sensitive and open grouped themselves into one mass without asking themselves any questions about the segregationist character of the instructions. This inability to ask questions does not simply demonstrate the weakness of the whole and the herd instinct of individuals, it also shows that each individual has his or her own personal strategy, in which integrationist ('anthropophagic', i.e. absorbing people into society) attitudes and segregationist ('anthropemic', i.e. ejecting people from society) attitudes are combined.[9]

I shall take up here some comments by an economics student: 'At last, our prerogatives are being taken seriously.... I want it to be easier to find an empty seat.... Well, they [foreigners] should be obliged to adapt: to our language, of course, in order to be able to study, but also to the food here. The university kitchen can't pander to every religious and cultural taboo.' This student's remarks indicate a segregationist attitude, since he thinks that nationals have prerogatives over foreigners. The indigenous person – allegedly superior – is thus prepared to tolerate the foreigner only if the latter acknowledges, on the one hand, that he/she (the native) is entitled to privileges, and that he/she (the foreigner) must not claim rights to which he/she does not yet have access. In other words, the foreigner must accept whatever margin of tolerance people care to grant. That is called marginalisation. Beneath this attitude – a very common one in the experiences of 'foreignness' (*Verfremdung*) – lurks the desire to exclude foreigners in accordance with the well-known slogan: 'Foreigners or migrants whose way of life is not compatible with ours may, possibly, work (or study) here but they should live in their own homes or areas and, above all, ask for nothing.'

This marginalising restriction masks a latent, unacknowledged racism, since foreigners are tolerated solely because of their discretion and reserve – in other words, their ability not to annoy nationals. To the desire for segregation the student quoted above adds the desire to assimilate foreigners: those who live and work in Germany should behave like genuine German citizens and adapt to both the laws and the customs of the country. In other words, 'foreigners may live in our society on condition that they become like us, that they adopt our language and our culture and forget their original language and culture'. If the reverse happens, they will be seen as 'foreign bodies' that are unassimilable and therefore responsible for their own marginalisation. Thus, assimilation refers to marginalisation and vice versa. Assimilation itself harbours a latent racism to the extent that it takes foreigners away from their culture of origin and considers them unable to contribute to the growth of the host society. What is important is only integration, or adaptation, or isolation in national culture.

- Female student: What you are doing is not right.
- Teacher: Why?
- Student: Aren't you afraid that it will harm the university's reputation?
- Teacher: How?
- Student: But it's misanthropic!
- Teacher: Come on, what's at stake here is not people, it's money!
- Student: The running costs that you are talking about cannot pose such a problem. You're ignoring human rights.
- Teacher: No, I'm not. All that we are trying to do in these times of recession, unemployment and large-scale immigration is to control running costs. Furthermore, as far as human rights are concerned, especially equality between men and women, there are people in the south who do not resp ...
- Student: That's definitely true, the Koran-Turks with their two-faced morality should be thrown out!

When we analyse this exchange, we observe that the student feels that the human rights situation is intolerable since she contrasts the discriminatory method of our experiment with the principle of a type of integration in which 'foreigners would be invited to contribute their differences to our country, the task of a liberal society being to help manage diversity'. However, that same generosity reveals an implicit penchant for segregation, or even rejection. In the interview quoted above, the student ends up letting drop what she is really talking about: 'Even a multicultural society has borders: anyone who violates human rights and does not behave properly should be excluded from the legal, social and moral order of that society.' In other words, the notion thus deduced from human rights is assumed to be universally valid: others – Africans, Asians, Muslims or Hindus – are left with no possibility of not accepting this approach, even if the Western social reality – pornography and capitalism – that this order and this law regulate seems to them immoral or unjust. What representations others have of humanity and its civil order is of no account. Thus the student feels that the other's culture is of no importance for the majority culture, whatever may be the culture of his or her society or that of the world. Of course, even if it is subconscious, what we have here is another latent form of racism under cover of multiculturalism. Worse, by reducing Muslim Turks ('Koran-Turks') to stereotypes, she is demonstrating what I shall call an attitude of fixation. By attributing to those she lumps together as 'Koran-Turks' collectively and to all appearances permanently a double morality and a macho 'pasha' attitude, she sees in them only their ethnic and religious identity, which assigns them indefinitely to their collective origin. This fixation expresses the desire to put down benchmarks and send foreigners back over the border: 'Foreigners whose culture is not compatible with ours can stay only temporarily in our country as tourists or guests: we thus have every right to send them back to their own country.' Such an attitude is racist because the other is perceived solely and permanently in terms of his or her collective origin and because, at the same time, the other's culture is asserted to be incompatible with that of nationals.

The ambiguity does not stop there. There are those who see in our experiment the translation of atavistic remorse and tormented 'Germanness', a self-critical attitude which is not without (auto)-racist and discriminatory overtones. Like those blacks who, according to Frantz Fanon, fall from a great white error into a black mirage, many Germans have developed self-hatred. Some state they are 'sick of' Germans, whom they see as short-sighted petty bourgeois full of racist resentment, while others spend all their lives endeavouring to 'de-Germanise' themselves.

The international and interracial imagination emerges from the asynchronicity of the simultaneous and manifests itself in the ambiguous strategy which never experiences an integrative attitude without an attitude of rejection. The racism complex – the socio-psychological and politico-economic burden that weighs on relations between master and slave, coloniser and colonised, national majority and immigrant minority – is continually exacerbated by these two antagonistic forces (see Tables 19.1 and 19.2 at the end of the chapter): on the one hand, by the force from 'above', an integrative force, which tends to produce, preserve and co-ordinate cultural differences in order to work on 'strange' and alienating situations between individuals and between peoples; on the other, by the force from 'below' which tends – at least within a single country – to level out these differences and head off and repress experiences of 'strangeness'. This ambiguity reminds me of a Janus head. Table 19.1 is an attempt to represent this two-faced head. (The god Janus had to satisfy the need of Roman aristocrats to secure divine protection at the doors to their house. The illustrious two-faced guard thus watched both sides of the house: the entrance – integration – and the exit – rejection.) Racism is thus not a monolithic bloc always underpinning the same constructs and articulating the same discourses. On the contrary, its complexity combines, often in a single individual or a single community,[10] these two tendencies that are at first sight antagonistic.

Slavery, Colonisation, Extermination and Discrimination

These various forms of subordination in modern times are linked to one another through the 'medium' of a racism that is forever taking on new disguises and associating, as the situation dictates, with dominant contemporary movements.

The current ambiguity appears in the worst possible circumstances, at a time when nation-states are being rocked by a profound crisis. Of course, the history of these nation-states is closely tied up with slavery, colonialism and National Socialism. But it is precisely just when they are beginning to open their constitutions to egalitarian and integrationist norms that these states are giving up or abdicating. Two forces then emerge: on the one hand, that of a *trans*national media communication capitalism with but a single goal – to put an end to state intervention in the market and promote the privatisation of the state; and, on the other, that of a *sub*national tribalism (or ethnicity) which attempts to cater for the social needs of individuals by seeking aims for their collective identity. The weakened nation-states are faced with two impossible tasks: on the one hand, the original strategy of transnational or multicultural integration, or even incorporation, which is increasingly being perverted by popular ideologies of exclusion or rejection; on the other, the construction of collective identities whose artificial and historically based character now stand starkly revealed.

The upshot is no longer slavery, or colonisation, or extermination. Postmodernism produces scattered omnipresent and abundant sorting processes. Extradition, expulsion, persecution and every other form of rejection are no longer the monopoly of the state, which is increasingly being replaced by a wide range of local initiatives. That is equally true of the anti-racist struggle within civil society (*Bürgerinitiativen*).

How are we to explain the failure of the concepts of a melting-pot and a multicultural society? The nations that were the mother countries of colonialism (above all the United States of America, the United Kingdom, France and the Netherlands) from the very outset practised forms of exploitation, subjection, discrimination and deprivation of rights towards their immigrants. The industrial societies without a continuous colonial past (in particular Germany) have always transformed the ethnic identity of workers recruited abroad into a *sub*legal status that restricted their political rights and social demands, denying them dual citizenship and limiting the length of their stay, thus legalising a de facto discrimination. Faced with a majority society perceived as hostile, a growing number of immigrants are withdrawing, either internally, by joining ethnic and religious groups, or externally, by going 'home'. But neither of these withdrawals is easy. Many immigrants are treated unequally both in the host society and in their society of origin. Majorities and minorities confront one another in a conflict between modernity and tradition, fundamentalism and universalism and so forth. The weakened states of Europe and North America then construct regional unions. Simultaneously, the opening-up of the market and frontiers promotes the establishment of fortresses: internally, minorities that are the product of established immigration are fed illusions with promises of ever more assimilation and integration, while at the same time threats are made to deprive them of their rights or even expel them; externally, measures of intimidation and isolation are stepped up, while there are more and more establishments where labour is cheaper and state control less oppressive.

Discrimination against immigrants is not the same as that associated with slavery, colonialism and National Socialism, though there are comparisons: extermination by the Nazis, after a short period of deportation and slavery in the shape of forced labour; exploitation by colonisers drawing strength from their alleged civilising mission ('using a tone that was usually not very civil', as Léopold Sédar Senghor observed); and subjection by slave traders, who were, however, forced to combine the useful (absence of rights) with the necessary (care or help afforded to those to be transported). But these distinctions have little more than an abstract value, since the masters, whoever they may be, live through their times like Janus. Consequently, there is no age which has typical structures of subjection. The slave trade did not affect every member of a tribe, a people, a continent or a 'race'. On the contrary, it was sustained by monarchs who handed over to slavers on the spot the subjects of their kingdom whom they wished to exile – prisoners of war, or victims of raids and razzias. These chiefs, as well as members of their clan, dealt on an equal footing with the white slavers and the European chartered companies that the slavers were representing. As for colonial imperialism, it not only promoted ethnic differentiation and the stabilisation of castes but also genocide and massacres, and did so right up to the appearance of the first concentration camps. Even the Nazis helped Jews or blacks when it suited them – on the occasion of the Olympic games, for example, or in the context of artistic, scientific or industrial productions. 'I will decide who is a Jew!' said Göring, while the attachment of some concentration camp commanders to 'their' Jews or 'their' Gypsies is also well known, though that did not prevent them from carrying out their grim duty.

The main advantage of separating different forms of subjection by period is that it helps us to set out historically their evolution over time. The history of the subjection of human communities is not linear or repetitive but one with many detours, latent phases and peaks. That is why Nazi anti-Semitism, colonial imperialism or even the slave trade should not be regarded as 'models' to be assigned varying degrees of cruelty or atrocity. In the same way, they do not constitute points 'on the slave route' or in the history of racism. They are, rather, living constellations that today help to map the various types of discrimination. These constellations are thus not limited to their own time, but, quite the reverse, are always there, like a volcano that, at times, releases its flow of lava. A dynamic of subjection is that whatever particular stage it first came into being, it can be revived at any moment.

Racism is the ideology that keeps these various forms of subjection alive. From the point when some individuals disputed the divine origin of the division between free men and slaves (and when the immobile slave economy was holding back industrial production based on individual self-interest), those individuals set themselves up as sovereigns of existence. Human beings then became objects for classification and division. This assertion found its rational and scientific justification in biology and later in bio-sociology (social Darwinism), which divided humanity into different races. The myth of (divine) descent that prevailed in the days of slavery was succeeded, during the colonial period, by the myth of the development and progress of civilisation and culture. The colonial powers were thus sustained by a racist discourse which justified the exploitation of peoples deemed inferior because they were allegedly without culture. The discourse of colonialism was directed outwards, that of the Nazis was directed inwards ('Aryans' had to be protected from contamination by the racially inferior foreigner). After Auschwitz, the concept of 'race' lost all legitimacy, as had the concept of 'slave' two centuries earlier. Racism, however, does not involve the death of the other. Dressed up as a sort of, neo-racism – or 'light' or 'soft' racism – contemporary racist discourse highlights concepts such as ethnicity and cultural differences to mark divisions between human groups, a fertile ground for discriminatory practices.

What links the periods to one another and makes them interchangeable is thus a racism comprising fantasies and discourse in which a dominant or majority population creates, for its own use, the signs dividing 'in' groups and 'out' groups, 'superior' and 'inferior', 'one of us' and 'one of them', 'friendly' and 'hostile', 'useful' and 'dangerous'. Those marks that denote inferiority, or assign the quality of outsider, or instrumentalise, or distance, in short, that 'racialise', feed the imagination, in particular that of the dominant groups, and provide them, when the right moment arrives, with justifications for depriving people of their rights and threatening them with expulsion. Racist discourse does not seek to be an analysis or a proper description of relations among human groups, but is itself reproduced by the images that some – the strong, the powerful – project onto others – the weak. In this dialogue, slaves become 'savage', the colonised, 'underdeveloped', the Jews, dangerous and decadent, immigrants and refugees, incompatible, or even irreconcilable, with representatives of European and North American culture.

Racism thus does not operate as a single configuration linking fantasies to discourse in some coherent and stable manner. Indeed, quite the reverse is true. It is flexible, skilled at 'dressing itself up', as Frantz Fanon said, to take a refined form, and to do so at any moment as the opportunity arises.

In order to avoid any misunderstanding, it must be clearly understood that the socio-psychological and politico-economic complex that makes up racism never represents anything but the 'medium' in the chemical sense of the word: in other words, the medium in and through which the correspondences among the various periods are crystallised. Racism thus erupts only if it ties in with the predominant movements of each age. In the post-modern era of discrimination against immigrants, racism takes hold only because of the need for ethnic identification and cultural differentiation and, paradoxically, in a context of transnational communication capitalism. During the colonial period, it was racism of a certain type that enabled the modern nation-states to act in the context of a capitalism of worldwide production. Everything had been prepared by the mercantile capitalism of the age of slavery which produced the 'raw material' for all subsequent periods.

Some might suggest that this analysis is unbalanced, that I am exaggerating the dark side of history, or, worse, that, by linking the slave trade to contemporary history, I am downplaying its tragic aspect. But it is not in the least my intention either to exaggerate or to minimise, but rather, more precisely to explain a hidden tendency which now threatens to undermine world peace, the art of living together and co-operation among peoples. The history of the industrialised world – of Europeans and North Americans – is an odyssey that swings between alienation and emancipation, integration and rejection. This odyssey is not over. It currently finds itself in a situation of turbulence and worldwide disorder and subjection in many different forms. I have suggested a historical analysis starting from an approach that I admit is ethnocentric and German. That is inevitable when one is seeking to elucidate the destructive dialectic of that aspect of history.

If we hope to act, we need a new mode of discourse which overcomes slave, colonialist, anti-Semitic and culturalist projections. We must not be reduced to passive spectators as history unfolds from period to period. We can overcome not only the tendency to forget a past that all too easily becomes part and parcel of the justification of the repressed, but also the rationalisation – or opportunist and post hoc justification – of a future that makes us all slide tacitly towards habits of filtering immigrants and refugees. We are in the process of acquiring bad habits both at the level of everyday life and in institutional life, moving towards greater marginalisation, keeping foreigners in their home countries and discrimination, which are, however, concealed (or indeed 'rationalised') bids for assimilation and integration.

Each of us should therefore face up to his or her own responsibility for solidarity among human beings. We should also call on nation-states and international organisations to account for their contribution to the survival and prosperity of all the peoples on the planet. Is such a proposal realistic? We know Zygmunt Bauman's reply: 'So much the worse for reality!' I am taking the opposite position. My proposal could not be more realistic. So much the worse if we do not succeed in accepting this reality.

Notes

1. See H. Kordes, 1995 .
2. See E. Dunglas, 'Établissements des Européens sur le golfe du Bénin', cited in R. Cornevin, 1962, p. 251.
3. Brandenburg-Preussen an der Westküste von Westafrika, 1681–1721; P.D. Curtin, 1969, pp. 117 and 210.
4. Z. Bauman, 1993, p. 519.
5. *Urteilsbegründung des Landgerichts Mannheim gegen den wegen Volksverhetzung angeklagten Vorsitzenden des rechtsradikalen Partei NPD, Günther Decker*, 11 August 1994. The fact that these judges were subsequently reprimanded and suspended by higher authorities alters nothing. Those measures appear to have been dictated above all by a concern with not harming Germany's international reputation.
6. As Étienne Balibar thinks, although he does not mention slavery. See É. Balibar and I. Wallerstein, 1990.
7. On this point, the German public's perception differs from the French public's. In France, everyone knows the name of Malik Oussekine, the young man killed by the police in a street demonstration. In Germany, no one, or almost no one, knows the names of the Angolan Amadeu Antonio, murdered by skinheads (as the police looked on) or the Turkish Aslan and Genç families, killed when their houses were torched in Mölln and Solingen.
8. H. Kordes and 'Krisenexperiment' working group. (Report on the experiment on segregation between 'Germans' and 'foreigners' at the entrance to Münster university restaurant, 1994.)
9. See Z. Bauman, p. 519, who turns these two distinct strategies, first developed in this way by C. Lévi-Strauss in *Tristes tropiques*, into a single ambiguous strategy.
10. The bourgeois scenario of rumour and manhunt which preceded the attacks by the young skinheads gives a more detailed insight into this dialectic. See H. Kordes (1995).

Bibliography

BALIBAR, É., and WALLERSTEIN, I. 1990. *Race, classe, nation*. Paris, Verso. [Eng. ed. 1991. *Race, Nation, Class, Ambiguous Identities*. London, Verso.]
BAUMAN, Z. 1993. 'Das Urteil von Nürnberg hat keinen Bestand'. *Das argument* (Hamburg), No. 200.
CORNEVIN, R. 1962. *Histoire du Dahomey*. Paris, Berger-Levrault.
CURTIN, P.D. 1969. *The Atlantic Slave Trade: A Census*. Madison, University of Wisconsin Press.
DUNGLAS, E. 1962. 'Établissements des Européens sur le golfe du Bénin'. In Cornevin, R. *Histoire du Dahomey*. Paris, Berger-Levrault.
FANON, F. 1955. *Africains et Antillais*. Paris, L'Harmattan. [Eng. tr. Chevalier, H. 1967. 'West Indians and Africans' in *Toward the African Revolution*. New York and London, Monthly Review Press.]
KORDES, H. 1995. *Einander in der Befremdung begleiten*. Münster, Lit.
LÉVI-STRAUSS, C. 1980. *Tristes tropiques*. Paris, Plon. [Eng. tr. Weightman, J., and Weightman, D. 1973. *Tristes Tropiques*. London, Jonathan Cape.]

Table 19.1 SOS Racism (1) (Graduated scale designed to draw attention to the latent and manifest forms of racism)

Attitude	Discriminate	Settle	Marginalise	Assimilate	Integrate	Syncriticise
Social space	Inequalities	Recognition of difference			Recognition of differences	Equalities
Time-scale Problematic aspect (focus)	Unchangeableness Destruction of the people (genetic potential/race)	Irreconcilability Loss as a result of miscegenation and pluralism (deregulation) Deterioration of culture (customs, nation, ethnic group)	Inadaptability Incompatibility Disorientation in one's own country	Adaptability Heterogeneity of national culture	Integrability Benefit owing to plurality (differentiation) Conflictual character of multicultural society	Variability Ambiguity between identity of majority and minorities
Majority towards minority	Foreigners who, by their origin, are biologically and morally inferior and/ or who behave anti-socially, have no right to be in our country; their quality as human beings is questionable and consequently, they may be expelled, humiliated or even exterminated	Foreigners coming from a culture that is irreconcilable with ours may live in our country temporarily We have the right to send them back to their country of origin which is their home	Foreigners whose way of life is not *compatible* with ours may, if unavoidable, work here but they should live in special places and curtail their demands	Foreigners may live in our country and become like us if they adopt our culture and put theirs aside	Foreigners may bring their differences to our country so long as they respect a civil order based on the rule of law and democracy	In the encounter with the foreigner my humanity and my culture are put to the test; in dealings with foreigners we must together decide where to resist the dissolution of our culture and where we broaden our outlook and that of our own culture
Minority towards majority	We must stand up to the majority that labels minorities, with pride	Faced with a majority trapping us in a provisional	Faced with a majority that marginalises us we	Faced with a majority offering us its own identity, we	With the majority, we observe a civil order so long as the views	We respect the majority for its seniority and we test its capacity for

(Continued)

Table 19.1 SOS Racism (1) (*Continued*)

Attitude	Discriminate	Settle	Marginalise	Assimilate	Integrate	Syncriticise
	in our roots and our race	status, we will have to safeguard our awareness of our culture of origin	will have to revive what gives us honour and dignity: our religion, our language and our culture	ought to set aside our language and culture of origin	and feelings of minorities are taken into account	broadening its outlook and our shared civil order
Overt racism	Bio-cultural	Ethno-cultural and religious	Ethno-economic	National-paternalistic	Advocatory-universalist	Identificatory and antagonistic
	Human beings are strongly determined, hierarchically, by their origin				Ethnic and cultural differences are assessed at their true worth	Account is taken of each individual's ethno-biological circumstances
Action	Discrimination (negative)	Extradition (expulsion)	Marginalisation	Assimilation	Discrimination (positive)	Antagonistic identification
	Extermination Alienation					
Latent racism		Human beings are permanently bound to their collective origin	Individuals are judged by their adaptability	Foreign culture is of no importance to the host culture	Racial and cultural differences are taken into account while Western rights are assumed to be universal	Ethnic origin and personal biography are taken into account while the inevitability of antagonism between individuals and cultures is taken for granted

Table 19.2 SOS Racism (2)

(Future) prospects		
	Syncriticise (Accept antagonism and ambiguity) Make one's way through the *interferences* between the familiar and the foreign In the encounter with the foreigner, my humanity and my culture are put to the test; in dealings with foreigners, we must together decide where to resist the dissolution of our culture and where we broaden our outlook and that of our own culture	Identify (with one's origin)
Relativise	**Integrate** (establish a civil order in pluralism) Work on the impact of the differences between our culture and foreign ones Foreigners may bring their differences to our country so long as they observe a civil order according to the rules of law and democracy	Reflect
Respect	**Assimilate** (adjust the foreigner to one's own culture) Shape *differences* starting from what is familiar to us Foreigners may live in our country and become like us so long as they adopt our culture and set aside their culture of origin	Expose
Total elimination of racist attitudes is not possible	Continuous work on the foreigner's experience	
'Ghettoisation'	**Marginalise** (consign the foreigner to the fringes of society) Foreigners whose way of life is not *compatible* with ours may, possibly, work here but they should live in special places and curtail their demands	'Self-ghettoisation'
Ethnic Cleansing	**Settle** (send foreigners back to their collective origin) Foreigners whose way of life is not reconcilable with ours may live temporarily in our country. We have the right to send them back to their country of origin which is their home	Cultural conservation
Alienate	**Discriminate** (isolate and treat foreigners as inferior beings) Foreigners who are, by their origin, biologically and morally inferior and/or who behave anti-socially have no right to be in our country; their quality as human beings is questionable and, consequently, they may be expelled, humiliated or even exterminated	'Exoticise'

Chapter 20

The Slave's World of the Imagination: Outline of the Foundations of Caribbean Thought

Hugues Liborel-Pochot

Being Torn from the Land of One's Birth

Exile may well begin in the human feeling that one partakes of the duality of mortality and immortality – the 'missed message' of the gods (cf. Tonga myth, or the Asante story of the goat and the sheep). Being torn from the land of one's birth is synonymous with speed, which brings death. Whites are seen as the animals bearing the first message. Torn from their land, thrown into the turmoil of the slave trade, the blacks are seen as taking refuge in the mystical emotion arising from their beliefs. These are the foundations of their spirituality. That is how they will keep up the dialogue between the invisible world and themselves, creating for themselves, first all unknowingly, then more and more unconsciously, the feeling of self-realisation, gradually doing without the help of god. Those who have survived 'will have made for themselves the slowness of the second message'. They will themselves have become that slowness which makes it possible to cling to life. The black person embarking on the journey, gradually becoming one with it, will become the site of an interpenetration between speed and slowness, transition from one to the other, mediator between the heavenly and earthly worlds.

But we are not claiming that in the variety of individuals embarking on the slave ships, coming from different ethnic groups, there was a single black imagination. Did the great propensity among blacks to form for themselves fully formed groups enable those 'torn away' to establish an initial conceptual community based on the new geographical latitude and the new relationship to the everyday world? The diversity of ethnic cultural patterns in Africa, the land from which they came, is such that we shall never be able to identify in the slave a single mode of thought; but we can try to get a better grasp of the language of the imagination used to understand the new environment. Since each element requires different interpretations, anyone seeking to understand must make, as it were, a horizontal crossing through those interpretations.

Is this how the spiritual heritage of the new society of slaves was formed, using its most authentic values in a place where a new fate awaited it? The geometric cosmogony of the Dogon or the myth of the first human being emerging from a reed, among the Tonga, lend support to our remarks here.

Those slaves who arrived in the lands of the Amerindians were the ones who continued to think, to nourish their imagination. They ensured the transition from one meaning to another and linked up the concepts of life, death and time. We feel that essential questions underlay the work of the imagination in the slave. And even then we still need to spell out how and why we moved from the state of being 'uprooted' to that of 'being a slave'. Was the original mysterious forest metamorphosed into this surrounding vastness that was both benign and dangerous, giving a single form to everything, joining or rejoining the organic world and the inorganic world? Each dead man or woman thrown into the ocean became liquid. What are the ones who endured the same ordeals – the same lulls when the wind dropped or the same storms – but yet ill-treat, torture and kill? Who are these new messengers of death?

In the words of Bastide, what we have here, in all likelihood, is the emergence 'of a mysticism without gods and outside all religious life'. Between the 'seeking' subject (the black person, slave) and the object, better and better apprehended (the white person and/or the one ill-treating), this new mysticism eventually eliminated the former in favour of the latter. Would the contemplating subject identify himself or herself fully and completely with the thing so attentively observed, watched and contemplated? Is it in this imitation that Réluse and Longoué are caught, the two blacks who fight on the deck of the ship as it arrives?[1] Did they fight in place of the masters, who have never, so Mathieu thinks, been able to settle their dispute? When this latter says: 'You see, you see yourself…. They haven't done anything, they've imitated, right from the start …', it is as much a revelation for the speaker. In this way he is lifting a veil on the discourse of daddy Longoué. He is laying bare, revealing and showing daddy Longoué something contained in his discourse that he, the one engaging in the discourse, does not see or does not want to say. For the Caribbean, speaking is seeing: speaking of the slavery experienced by his ancestors, seeing in this discourse old and new images.[2]

A Memory That Circulates Like Blood

Essential questions such as 'Why did those who remained behind not prevent this departure? Why did they not keep us with them?' sustained the work of the slave's mental world all through the middle passage. They were questions that combined despair and opposition and from them would arise the individualised body of the male slave. A body primarily of suffering, revealed to itself in its dangerous solitude, 'the space of dreams and wild awakening'; body 'at the end of the small hours', at the end of desolation; in the 'horrible futility of our *raison d'être*'. Aimé Césaire was the first to say it aloud for all the generations of Caribbean blacks to come. Single and multiplied body. Body taken in madness and in ecstasy: space and time of the 'savage sacred'. Instance of pure creation in which the body rises at the same time as everything it sees, body-shred of a memory risen like a river, flat, spread out, which carries along 'an old life's lying smile, its lips opened by disused fear; an old poverty rotting under the sun, silently; an old silence bursting with tepid pustules'.[3] A body upright that cries relentlessly for this squabbling crowd so strangely unaware of its own cry ... its only true cry, the only cry one would have wished to hear because one senses that only this cry alone is *its own*. A standing body, living present, which is simultaneously what it sees, what rises from its red and black swollen flesh of a memory that continues to circulate like blood. 'Like frantic blood over the slow stream of the eye, I would roll words as crazy horses as fresh children as bloodclots as curfew as vestiges of temples as gems deep enough to discourage miners. Whoever would not understand me would not understand the roaring of the tiger either.'[4]

Before being accepted by another 'tense', land, 'drunken land'; in the refuge of these 'hungry West Indies', budding with frail creeks, 'the West Indies pockpitted with smallpox, the West Indies blown up by alcohol, stranded in the mud of this bay ...', before being there, in 'another small hours of Europe', it had been a body which might, at any moment, be seized, beaten up and killed. Then, screaming, it had felt itself becoming this man-bridge, a giant bestriding the reddened seas and oceans, with one foot African and the other Amerindian. In solitude and disaster, a man-land-organ. Land great sex organ rising towards the sun, looking, now gazing fixedly on that elsewhere towards which he was being driven: the Caribbean. Land at the other end of the same fascination with the lost-land-mother, fascination in the midst of which stands the slave.

Man, black, alone, multiplied, divided, separated, borne by the sole part, in him, of the voice of the Africa of the *griots*. The voice that frees itself by wailing in this *Cahier*. 'At last we hear it.... We now make out its share in our voice. We listen to the explanation of the origins, the wanderings of the ancestors, the separation of the elements.'[5]

The voice is with us. It is in us. It has risen from the surroundings. It is the voice that now guides us in *leaving, de-parting* (dividing into parts, parting from someone, departing from a place). Let us listen again to Césaire,[6] who tells us how much it would metamorphose us into all the bodies of men. Just as there is the body of these shamans – hyenas and panthers – so there is the long line of the world's scapegoats, of those who like spittle are always being expelled, cast down and trampled on. The world moves on over their trampled, paved, metalled bodies. Then, in procession, come the pariah-people. There are more and more of them. They always are and always will be in all the exoduses, all the diasporas, all the trades in human beings. E. Williams[7] says that the slave trade is 'the first principle and foundation of all the rest, the mainspring of the machine which sets every wheel in motion'. Later, Marx thought that Africa had been transformed into a preserve (etymologically: place reserved by a lord for hunting and fishing).

How, in our Caribbean heads, did we move from the concept of 'slave' to that of 'racial'? From the state of 'being, man-land-and-bridge' to that of 'becoming, I-we-Caribbean'? We continue the task of digging about in memories, getting used to extracting ourselves from passive irresponsibility, rereading history, our history, finding new readings of this subconscious 'cultural challenge' that the middle passage was. Always saying an old, present, pressing word, like that of Léonora.[8] Acting and singing old sagas like those of Dlan, Silacier and Medellus in *Malemort*. As for myself, the psychoanalysis of which I have become a practitioner enables me, sometimes, to scrutinise the African shadows that still dwell in me and always will. At the end of the slave route, positioned in this present, I continue to ask myself about my belonging to the past, that past of the middle passage. Am I not, necessarily, confronted with an obscurity of my memory beyond which it is virtually impossible to go? How far could I go in exploring this area? For us – blacks, intellectuals, researchers, archaeologists of this common past – what links should always be maintained between our common affectivity, the true terrain and instrument of knowledge, and the intellectual endeavour properly so called? Are we always to be caught in some kind of ambiguity, an ambiguity between the permanent desire to know and the due consideration always charged with emotions of ancient suffering? For us, Caribbeans, that suffering, even when it strikes us powerless, is an integral part of what and who we are.

From the Word 'Slave' to the 'I Caribbean'

'At the end of the small hours', Césaire's *Cahier* set me on fire. Almost half-way through this text (1994, p. 20 [1995, p. 87]), there is a paragraph which creates a rift, a break, between what comes before and what comes after in the text. This paragraph makes us readers shift from the rhythmic, repeated word 'slave', the inheritor in revolt, to the 'I' heralding the birth of the 'other', the Caribbean, the one who will henceforth speak off-stage. His cry has been transformed into a source-word, emerging, difficult, which has found the secret of great communications and great combustions. Speech, storm, river, tornado, leaf, tree, speech that grows. It is soaked by all the rains; all the dews have caused its flesh to rise, calmly, just like that, as new bread rises.

'But who can kill Remorse beautiful as the stupefied face of an English lady finding a Hottentot's skull in her soup-tureen?' It is not our purpose here to present this scene of interrogation – scene of doubt – scene of no and of name. Scene of the mirror first full of a narcissistic image, but one resolutely engaged in denying death. Seeing itself other, it knows that it will not die of it. But will reveal itself beautiful, blinding, obliged to take into account the fundamental resemblance, the structural resemblance that proceeds to split the personality. Here, Césaire's slave, or at least one who felt himself invested with the whole heritage, will recognise himself to be there in the strange double. Because of his new voice, and the different sensations he experiences, he feels himself endowed with a peculiar status. What he henceforth experiences belongs indeed to the past – to the fact of having recognised the true history of his slave ancestors – but that life is now an integral part of the external world. The slave's heir has somehow been made into a subject. Emerging from Remorse. Is this where Césaire could help us to get a better grasp in that history 'the person-of-ourselves', that-of-myself? It did not live but bears the traces of experience. Our proposed reflection on the imagination of the slave would plumb depths and reworkings of received ideas regarding those traces. Should we stop, we too perhaps, this relentless pursuit, always on the lookout to bear what our ancestors bore? Let us get away from endlessly mulling over the morbid entities whose study provides material for the theories of experts like André Green; let us move from a narcissism of death to a narcissism of life: get away from seeing the riven and affected self in order to be in that state of seeing differently. 'See the countries. Hear the countries, behind the little island.... To leave the cry and forge the word is not to renounce the imaginary or the sovereign powers, it is to arm a new time-span anchored in the emergences of peoples', writes Glissant (1981).

Language, Love and Death in Caribbean Discourse

Without lapsing into controversy, let us see what Raphaël Confiant (1993) says in his work entitled *Aimé Césaire, une traversée paradoxale du siècle*: 'It is now clear that Césaire [continues to have] a problematic relationship with the Creole language and with Creole culture in general.' This comment overlooks the fact that, for Césaire, not writing in Creole does not mean that he does not know the language and all the culture it conveys. It is true that he kept quiet when others were taking more overt positions.[9] But what does 'keeping quiet' signify here, for him? We shall examine the silence of the author of the *Cahier d'un retour au pays natal* rather differently from the way Confiant does. Let us, rather, start from what Annie Dick[10] says about the Creole elements in Césaire's writing: 'As for the poet himself, he has little to say by way of explanation about this unless the question is put to him. When he does so, it is in the course of interviews, in response to the questions of those interviewing him. Everything seems to indicate that it is something he does not want to speak about.'

The poet does not want to speak about 'it' ('this within') because it ('that', what he recognises in that 'it') still speaks too much in him. Is the language of the *Cahier*, in speaking for blacks (including those of the post-war generations who lived through the fever of the language demands of the 1970s and 1980s), going first to name the things of the world? To name them, that is to classify them, for blacks, into past, terrifying things seen, into clear things to come that are hard to forge. As in Creole, in its very foundations, by building on the syntax of Creole, that is on what, in that language, essentially involved an ordering of words, giving the phrase a different structure, the language of the

Cahier creates a new field of signs. It is henceforth important for the inheritor of such a painful past to give a name to the things among which he lives.

Césaire makes us think (get away from simple images), and he was the first to do so, using a language not explicitly recognised as such about slaves and their enslavement, about the inheritor and the heritage, about the Caribbean, speaking subject, and the boundless field of sources of concepts opening before him.

With Césaire, we have entered into the dynamic process of conceptualising a new language, spoken and written by a Caribbean. It is a dynamic process in which we remain, particularly those of us who are concerned about language and idiom. The language of Césaire is peculiarly the texture of the language of every Caribbean writer. To quote Hagège (1985), we will say that the language of Césaire, through its new, special signs, 'can in no way be a momentary model of knowledge which we might one day simply get rid of to replace with other, more adequate ones'.

If the language of Césaire seems like an interpretative grid, the figuration of his interpretations is not made up of fixed forms. Césaire also invented the continuous, energetic displacement of that grid. A river-like density of language bearing *Le lézard, Le quatrième siècle, Eau de café, Texaco* and which will bear many more to come.

There might still be a temptation to raise the question of the origin of Creole, our Caribbean Creole, given as Hagège again says, '… that it is not possible to reconstruct experimentally the birth of a language as a manifest faculty of idiom'. Hagège feels that there would be no answer to that question. But by simply asking it again and again, we each time get a better grasp on it: '… Creoles seem to expect that anyone taken with them will integrate them into a consistent linguistic theory.' We may well suppose that Césaire was one of those and the first of us to fall in love with the idea that Creole, our Caribbean Creole, originally the language of slaves, might be present in its original form in the figures of various languages (those of all the peoples making up the population of slaves in the holds and on the decks of the slave ships), figures linked to one another by the same sounds of cries, moans, sufferings and protests.

Let us take the inaugural fantasy of the Caribbean Creole language, Césaire's linguistic dream: is it, and does it still remain, the first attempt to trace the history of the itinerary of the words of slaves, with the suffering bodies of the speakers remaining the first links between those words? Those bodies carried, with them and in them, all the social, ethnological and political assumptions that in Césaire's text are not erased but make us understand, those of us who are not linguists, that 'linguistics cannot be separated from the history of linguistics'.

Does Césaire's language, particularly that of the *Cahier d'un retour au pays natal*, retrace the various successive stages of the ordering of the words of slaves? Whatever the case, it attempts to do so. Is it the reproduction of the unwinding of the sound track that was the first to take bodies and words together?

Caribbean Creole is the site, at once unique and multiple, of the speech of slave-bodies. First figures of the words of suffering. When we decipher them, they enable us to follow all their meanders. Thus, although the Caribbean Creole language began in the upheavals of the embarkation of blacks for a new world in order to sleep, enjoy or die, it has become that 'analogous language', to use René Girard's terms, in which the one speaking first walks.

Far from having problems with Creole, Césaire, in his own – new, invented – language, displaces, transports, transposes, and transforms its tricks and detours. He 'appropriates it', not in the repetition of the same sonorities but in the renewal of magic songs, in a different power of incantation in order to say one is alive. The finest proof that we could give of what we are suggesting here is to say that the most beautiful Creole song would be the translation into Creole of the *Cahier d'un retour au pays natal*.

Aimé Césaire gives us the keys to the Creole language, for its evolution through what each of us may now allow ourselves to bring to it. He has made us understand that the Creole sentence, which is also his, always remains linked to the external world of which it speaks: 'I would come to this land of mine and I would say: "Kiss me without fear.... And if I can only speak, it is for you that I shall speak."' That sentence is to be looked at in its relation to the one expressing it: 'And above all beware, my body and soul too, beware of crossing your arms in the sterile attitude of the spectator, because life is not a spectacle, because a sea of sorrows is not a proscenium, because a man who screams is not a dancing bear....' In the last analysis, it is Césaire who was the first, in a new writing, to give us Caribbean writers the intonative form of the sentence.

In an article entitled 'L'équilibre antillais', which appeared in the April 1962 issue of the journal *Esprit,* Glissant said: 'To recover one's balance, is thus to think Caribbean.' Almost ten years earlier, in February 1955, Frantz Fanon published in the same journal an article entitled 'Antillais et Africains', in which he explained the change in the Caribbean, as early as 1945, in relation to Africa. Quoting Césaire, Fanon said that in Césaire's *Cahier* there is an 'African period':

> 'By dint of thinking of the Congo
> I have become a Congo humming with forests and rivers' ... It thus seems that the West Indian, after the great white error, is now living in the great black mirage.

To link these two Caribbean authors Césaire and Fanon together in this way is to attempt to grasp the quest of the Caribbean intellectual still in search of his 'Caribbeanness'. And Glissant takes up the long litany that seems to underpin this quest for a cultural identity.[11] That quest is a quest, he seems to say, and always will be. Césaire will disprove it.

From the *Cahier d'un retour au pays natal*, which first appeared in August 1939, there has been a split between what, before that date, had been the substance of the writing of the Caribbean intellectual and what came after. Césaire was the first to call a halt to the dead end of imitation-writing by Caribbeans, something explicitly recognised and stated. It is they who, from the outside, look at this new written expression – bodies and written words borne by desire whose object has been rediscovered – land – body – links, desiring, now anchored in a principle of reality – living on the other land – mine – bodies reactualised in the freedom of being, bodies of pleasure, of enjoyment henceforth acting as an alternative to the bodies of suffering where our origins will always lie.

In addition to being a most original and unique artistic and literary creation, Césaire's writing became the response to the aspiration of a whole people. Caribbean unity erupted, burst forth from many sources, not where it was traditionally looked for – that is, in politics or economics – but in that elsewhere of the combat between the oral and the written. Where the spoken language did not succumb to the demands of the written but penetrated this same writing with bursts of assonant rhythms, with new concepts, in individual and/or collective relation to our mother, spoken tongue.

If we want, here, to try and locate the figures of love and death in this same world of the imagination, it is to rediscover the route taken by masculinity and femininity in the conditions of slavery in which they were engaged until their conceptualisation in our Caribbean society.

'Capture and the slave trade set in motion a process through which the captive was rendered extraneous and thus prepared for his or her state as absolute alien in the society into which he or she was delivered.'[12] It is the word 'extraneousness' used by Claude Meillassoux that tells us how much, despite an obvious infrastructural difference between captured black men and women, their processing during the crossing, into human cattle, into living commodities, was the same for all.

The productivity of slave labour, essentially based on agricultural activities, regulated the production capacities of each slave, also controlling the demographic cohesion of the slave population by eliminating useless mouths. Renewal of the generations was not thought of in terms of human reproduction but in terms of the replacement of one producer by another.

It may be thought that the idea of being born and growing old together, of surviving over time, demarcates the community of men (those who work and toil and not those who reproduce). The society of peers is first of all that of men to whom the general phantasmagoria, that of both masters and slaves, will of necessity assimilate women. The social organisation of the domestic community was formed around the constraints associated with agricultural pursuits. Everyday needs, we would say, to ensure passage from one cycle of production to another. But what about co-generation, that is, what is, in the slack season, at night, joint growth, relative to individuals, of men and women, in relation to each other? The regulated access of men to women's bodies, the highlighting of that access, in secret, by the slaves themselves, threw light on the difference between the productive body of the man and the productive body of the woman, replacing the established categories of productive and unproductive.

Not that speculation about the production of the woman maintained in its comparison with the other cyclical, unequivocal, *ogreste* (infernal divinity) production would awaken in the black male slave an archaic feeling of inferiority (we were no longer in the prehistoric times of the discovery of woman's body by man). But it would further reinforce the image of reproducer, stud, that had previously been imposed on him in slave society. In the historical and sociological conditions of existence in the community of slaves, the exploited, domesticated black man, a captive become an outsider, sees his capacities for integration either as genitor or as producer reduced. What can he do against a will, external to him, to employ him as producer? How is one to distinguish the products of which he is the producer? It is probably this ascension to the body of the woman, by night, in mutual agreed desire – an act fantasised as being the only one of freedom, that is leading gradually to the ability to *think oneself* – that will favour the integration of the black male slave first among his peers and later in his relationship to the white man. When Béluse and Longoué fight each other, that fight is also a place where meaning is summarised. They are fighting to prove themselves, to confront their bodies. Giving themselves the possibility of separating (of no longer being the same), of becoming different, of inhabiting henceforth each a body which will be his own. They are also fighting to forget: '… yes. All that forgotten in each day that passed, with each morning the hand held out towards the manners of an other whose gesture or voice it would never be possible to imitate to perfection.'[13] They are fighting because they are alive. It is in this new self-discovery that they are approaching the Amerindian soil: 'That is how it is. They came on the Ocean (they survived), and when they saw the new land, there was no longer any hope; returning was not allowed. Then they understood, it's all over. They fought each other.'[14] A warlike parry to prove that those who set foot on it are arriving on this new battlefield with all their new forces intact. To shed the other's blood on such a new land, to wound him without causing him to die, is also to exorcise the slow dead language, obsessive all through the middle passage, and to emerge from the state of docile, domesticable animal.

Thus masculinity, in the black male slave, was taking shape, emerging from a bedlam made up of the crack of whips, of blood shed, of washing in salt or brine, of bodies thrown into huge lighters, heightened endurance, concentration and materiality of great sufferings above which a new will to live was establishing itself. A will in daddy Longoué to say, to speak and to speak of himself. A will in Mathieu to listen, to understand why there was another history before, to forge his own understanding in relation to what he is hearing.

The wind, between the two men, is a bond; it binds their two figures as if on a stela. The wind, the wind that has always been there – that is still there – bears the voice of daddy Longoué as he turns and shapes Mathieu's body: 'The wind was beginning to blow on the site. Mathieu felt it gentle on his legs, exactly like savannah that was not too high, a low field of lianas.' Masculinity in the black male slave, carried over the oceans, rolled and driven to the new land of the Caribbean, is a metaphor of the wind, 'a wind that drove, this wind, suddenly loosed by its own strength into the gully in front of the trees, it pushed hard: a weed which soon would find support on the chest of the two men.'[15] 'What could still be said, was that the Béluses and the Longoués had as it were come together in a single wind, with a fury arising first from among the Longoués, a force, but which was rooted in the unbelievable patience of the Béluses.'[16] Then death appeared between the Béluses and the Longoués: 'Anne Béluse had killed Liberté Longoué. For love and jealousy.... Stéphanie, née Béluse, had been given to a Longoué.'

Love and death, like two totems that the two slaves carry with them. They keep them in turn, protect them, sacrifice one to leave possibilities of child-bearing to the other. Glissant's images are unhoped-for signifiers. In the new will of the black male slave to be, the dead and the living are not separated. The latter are extensions of the former. They bear them. Doubtless for the living slaves it was a scene of incarnation (a replica perhaps of some primitive scene), when, disembarking from the slave ships, they buried their first dead in the Amerindian soil. Mother earth that had followed them (perhaps driven by the wind) was there awaiting them. It was going to receive the dead, make possible the continuity of a funeral rite, founder of all civilisation. Since they were carrying the dead to land, it was the sign that they had escaped all the madnesses. They could henceforth dismember them.

> the madness that remembers
> the madness that screams
> the madness that sees
> the madness that is unleashed.

By their act of recognising each of them there, present, living people deposed in the reality of another illusion, that of 'the forest that mews', they allow themselves to say: 'Who and what are we?'[17] An admirable rhetorical question which Aimé Césaire turns into a link naming all those of whom henceforth we are made. It is the same symbolism that lets it be understood that between daddy Longoué and Mathieu, whose works are full of historical objects such as iron and rope, there are also crowds of the dead and the living, of whom they are the last of a long line. Admirable indirect question in order to con-solidate an assertion. Intoning a song to express the vision of a new space: wrathful fields, epileptic nations, abyssal sands, nights shot through with musky odours.

In the midst of all these new sensations and visions, the man relieves his own body of its old violence. 'How can I help it?' Do again, do, begin. That is a necessity. 'We have to make a start.' Undertake a new initiation. Enter on another questioning. 'Start what?' This 'End of the world' through which it would be necessary to begin is not so much the destruction of the world of which we, we who survive, we who speak, are the executors, as the consid-eration of the end of the world of the slaves, the end of the voyage, at the end of life, love, death revealed. Stopping in order to depart again. The native of the Caribbean will have to recognise that it was the end of the voyage. That he made the necessary stop. That he had to give up the lost land, perhaps in his fantasy that which had rejected him, in order to adopt another with deceptive appearances.

In truth, you can't understand anything about it.

At the end of a long series of revived images, Césaire outlines the portrait of an age-old mutant, the supreme one, the black woman actualised:

Women are still seen with madras cloth
round their loins rings in their ears
smiles on their mouths babies
at their breast and all the rest of it....

The woman-history, witness to traditions, to changes, to the fact that we belong to the past. She is there, changing and unchangeable, in the depths of time. Aimé Césaire introduces the image of woman into the *Cahier* one step at a time. First as a goddess who 'suddenly calls upon a hypothetical rain and commands it not to fall ... or assumes the sudden grave animality of a peasant woman urinating standing, stiff legs apart.' This woman, this old peasant woman, joins the cohort of goddesses. She is spinner and fate, Hottentot Venus and Ceres-Demeter, inscribed in the order of time long before man discovered her ability to produce his own pleasure.[18] Then she is the figure of the mother, the author's mother, tireless seamstress who defies fatigue, night and day.

Women in our Caribbean heads are the thread along which the generations are told and come to rest. It is in the same belly that they carried us.

What to Say of Our Shortcomings?

Today, when Caribbean people are taking an ever increasing interest in Africans (marriages between the two are common), more and more Africans are choosing to live in Martinique and Guadeloupe. There are more and more *marabouts* there. What other reading(s) can we give to the links that exist between Africa and the Caribbean? Between Africanness and Caribbeanness?

There is a way for the Caribbean to be in the breach, not to be able to opt freely for tradition or for modernity, as if he or she had not altogether renounced the lost land. Who, with us, would help in this work of sublimation? While putting out such an appearance, there is in the Caribbean a dichotomy between his or her conception of the body, individualised, and that of the body of the community to which he or she belongs; how can there be established between them an exchange which, in our view, is fundamental, structural?

Caribbeans as much as Africans are people among whom 'murder of the father' is not committed. What roles are there henceforth for the father?

Notes

1. É. Glissant, 1964.
2. See É. Glissant, 1981. Our discourse on the slave's imaginary is inevitably a work of accumulation at all levels. This is the most suitable technique for unveiling a reality (an image of the real) which is itself scattered.
3. A. Césaire, 1994, p. 8 (1995, p. 73).
4. Ibid., p. 21 (p. 87).
5. É. Glissant, 1981, p. 391.
6. A. Césaire, 1994, p. 20 (1995, p. 85).
7. E. Williams, 1968, p. 73 (Eng. 1944, p. 51).
8. D. Bébel-Gisler, 1985.
9. See, for example, R. Suvelor, 1971.
10. A. Dick, 1990.
11. É. Glissant, 1981, pp. 435–437.
12. C. Meillassoux, 1986, chap. 2.
13. É. Glissant, 1964, p. 31.
14. Ibid., pp. 33–34.
15. Ibid., p. 18.
16. Ibid., p. 20.
17. A. Césaire, 1994, p. 70 (1995, p. 93).
18. Ibid., pp. 9–10 (p. 39).

Bibliography

BASTIDE, R. 1976. *Le sacré sauvage*. Paris, Payot.

BÉBEL-GISLER, D. 1985. *Léonora, l'histoire enfouie de la Guadeloupe*. Paris, Seghers. (Mémoires vives.) [Eng. tr. Leskes, A. 1994. *Leonora: The Buried Story of Guadeloupe*. Charlottesville, University Press of Virginia.]

———. 1989 *Le défi culturel guadeloupéen*. Paris, Éditions caraïbéennes.

CÉSAIRE, A. 1983. *Cadastre*. Paris, Présence africaine.

———. 1994. *Cahier d'un retour au pays natal*. Paris, Présence africaine [Paris, Volontés, 1939]. [Eng. tr. Rosello, M., with Pritchard, A. 1995. *Notebook of a Return to My Native Land*. Newcastle upon Tyne, Bloodaxe Books.]

CONFIANT, R. 1993. *Aimé Césaire, une traversée paradoxale du siècle*. Paris, Stock.

CORNEVIN, R. 1976. *Histoire de l'Afrique. L'Afrique précoloniale*. Paris, Payot.

DICK, A. 1990. 'Le rebelle'. *Cahiers du Centre d'études et de recherches césairien*, No. 2.

FANON, F. 1955. 'Antillais et Africains'. *Esprit* (February).

GISLER, A. 1981. *L'esclavage aux Antilles françaises*. Paris, Karthala.

GLISSANT, É. 1962. 'L'équilibre antillais'. *Esprit* (April).

———. 1964. *Le quatrième siècle*. Paris, Éditions du Seuil.

———. 1981. *Le discours antillais*. Paris, Fayard.

GRIAULE, M. 1966. *Dieu d'eau*. Paris, Fayard. [Eng. tr. Butler, R., rev. by Richards, A., and Hooke, B. 1965. *Conversations with Ogotemmêle. An Introduction to Dogon Religious Ideas*. London, Oxford University Press for the International African Institute.]

GRIAULE, M., and DIETERLEN, G. 1991. *Le renard pâle*. Paris, Institut d'ethnologie. [Eng. tr. of 1st ed. Infantino, S.C. 1986. *The Pale Fox*, China Valley, Arizona, Continuum Foundation.]

HAGÈGE, C. 1985. *L'homme de paroles*. Paris, Fayard.

HOPE FRANKLIN, J. 1984. *De l'esclavage à la liberté. Histoire des Afro-Américains*. Paris, Éditions caraïbéennes. [1st Am. ed. 1948. *From Slavery to Freedom: A History of American Negroes*. New York, Alfred Knopf.]

JAHN, J. *Muntu, l'homme africain et la culture néo-africaine*. Paris, Éditions du Seuil. [Eng. tr. Greene, M. 1961. *Muntu: An Outline of Neo-African Culture*. London, Faber & Faber.]

MEILLASSOUX, C. 1986. *Anthropologie de l'esclavage, le ventre de fer et d'argent*. Paris, Maspero. [Eng. tr. Dasnois, A. 1991. *The Anthropology of Slavery, the Womb of Iron and Gold*. London, Athlone Press.]

ORTIGUES, E. 1977. *Le discours et le symbole*. Paris, Aubier.

UNESCO. 1984. *L'Afrique en Amérique latine*. Paris, UNESCO.

———. 1985. *The African Slave Trade from the Fifteenth to the Nineteenth Century*. (Coll. General History of Africa. Studies and documents.) Paris, UNESCO.

WILLIAMS, E. 1968. *Capitalisme et esclavage*. Paris, Présence africaine. [Orig. Am. ed. 1944. *Capitalism and Slavery*. Chapel Hill, University of North Carolina Press.]

ZAHAN, D. 1978. *Religion, spiritualité et pensée africaines*. Paris, Payot. [Am. tr. Martin, K.E., and Martin, L.M. 1979. *The Religion, Spirituality and Thought of Traditional Africa*. Chicago, University of Chicago Press.]

Chapter 21

Slaves and Slavery in the Study of Fon Proverbs in Benin

Jean-Norbert Vignondé

IF WE ARE TO LOOK AT SLAVERY as a historical topic in oral literatures and traditions, it would certainly be easier to refer to folktales and legends rather than to proverbs which tend to express wisdom handed down through the ages much more than historical facts. And yet, in Benin, there is a specific feature of Fon proverbs that makes such a methodological approach possible.

Fon Proverbs

In many Western cultures, proverbs strictly so called simply express wisdom passed down through generations, and those that refer to slavery put more stress on concepts of an ethical nature than on the historical experience. Leaving aside their 'imagological', metaphorical or analogical specificity, African proverbs also tend to do the same, as Professor Mwamba Cabakulu shows in his *Dictionnaire des proverbes africains* under the entry 'slavery'. 'Slaves have duties', he writes, 'but they also enjoy rights which must be respected. The slavery against which we must fight is that of our passions and our shortcomings.'[1]

    Fon proverbs, on the other hand, and in particular those with a binary structure – also known as proverbs with two statements (or lò)[2] – belong, by their aesthetic qualities, in the narrative genre. They are the summation and therefore the most elliptical form possible of a narrative, which led M. Quenum to say that the Fon proverb is 'a small anecdote [taking the form] of a dialogue. The person using the proverb sets out a story in a few words; his interlocutor's response is the celebrated word of the main character in the story and the proverb strictly so called',[3] a definition which, despite its accuracy, needs to be modified in several respects.[4] Later, Kouaovi took up this same idea, albeit cryptically, speaking of proverbs among the Fon: 'Each proverb conceals an anecdote and each anecdote gives rise to a proverb.'[5]

This fact that the Fon proverb is closely related to the narrative genre justifies its close link with tradition, with the history of the people in general and of individuals in particular – in short, with every aspect of social life. It is also what gives the Fon proverb its eminently living character which explains that it has a beginning and undergoes more or less development depending on the chances of survival given it by those using it and the use they make of it. The whole of the community that speaks the language is involved in the production and use of proverbs, contrary to the idea that, once upon a time, a set of old men made them up and froze them for eternity. For the Fon, the proverbs are nothing short of a poetic activity,[6] at once popular and spontaneous, an ongoing creation which involves all levels of society. This means that the methodological approach which consists in attempting to deduce from its proverbs the conception that a people has of a given matter in order to extract from it, as it were, its 'world-view', is more inappropriate here than elsewhere. Fon proverbs resemble proverbs of the type 'Like father, like son' and 'Miserly father, prodigal son': they cannot be abstracted from the dialectical contradiction which both nourishes and is nourished by them. If it was otherwise, it would amount to posing a priori unanimity as the principle of African societies, as Delafosse did, seeing in the oral nature of our literatures 'a collective production, that reveals the average mentality of which it is the subconscious work', as contrasted with European literatures which are produced by 'individuals whose personal mentalities, such as they are, cannot simply be added together to form the collective mentality of the mass'. At this point we should denounce the myth, also decried by Hountondji, of primitive unanimity 'with its suggestion that in "primitive" societies – that is to say, non-Western societies – everybody always agrees with everybody else … that in such societies there can never be individual beliefs or philosophies but only collective systems of beliefs'.[7]

Before it became part and parcel of popular literature, the Fon proverb, or *lô*, originated in the personal experience of an individual – or a privileged observer – who drew from it a lesson, a moral, a philosophy or a recipe for living. All points of view will thus be expressed in a Fon proverb, which leads Gbégnonvi to speak of the 'reason and unreason' of Fon proverbs and, in particular, of the *lô* with two statements.[8] These proverbs make possible a discussion with opposing points of view in which individual styles appreciated by some and rejected by others are expressed. And that is why the Fon *lô* which deals with slavery is indeed the only proverb in the world to bear witness to its authentic experience with its contradictions and its complementarities.

Some Statistics

Ethnologists will agree that it would not have been wise to scour the villages to build up a corpus of proverbs on slavery, since, despite what would probably have been a good harvest, their authenticity and their historical value would certainly have been highly suspect. That is why we chose to work on the basis of existing collections and, of the three major collections so far published,[9] we have selected that of Gbégnonvi and Vignondé (1983) because not only is it of unimpeachable scientific accuracy but also, owing to the of the number of proverbs that it includes (one thousand), it offers quite a representative sample.

Of the 949 proverbs in this collection built around 65 key words, seven explicitly contain the word 'slave' and four clearly refer to it. That is not many compared to the number of proverbs dealing with death (90) or madness (41), but it is sufficient if one considers the topics that are mentioned in only three, four or five proverbs, at most. Of the 2,739 proverbs in Cabakulu's *Dictionnaire des proverbes africains*, only eight deal with slavery, but not in the sense of the slave trade as in the collection of *lô* but rather in the sense of being slaves to our passions and shortcomings. Examples: 'A female slave is never satisfied; if you give her oil, to her it is a drop of oil; if you give her salt, it is a grain of salt' (Serer proverb from Senegal); 'You will remain a slave of the jackal' (or 'He who takes too much delight in pleasures will remain the slave of his stomach'); 'You cannot ask for the back of the chicken if your mother is not there' (Mossi proverb from Burkina Faso) which the author of the dictionary recommends using 'against the exaggerated pretensions of a slave's child'.

The 11 Fon proverbs (listed below) in the 1983 *lô* collectiondeal not with 'being slaves to our passions and shortcomings' but with the slave trade.

Corpus of *Lô* or Proverbs about the Slave and Slavery

Page	No.	
36	1	Kannumo byó xù:
		A slave claims his share of an inheritance:
		– Hwidésu o, nù mìma à nyi.
		– *You are part of my inheritance that I shall bequeath.*
36	2	Kannumo kplé asi'kwé, bò gàn tón só dù:
		A slave saves money to get married, and his master spends it:
		– Hwi tè we tiín, bò nù towe dè tiin?
		– *How can you claim to possess something when you don't exist yourself?*
36	3	Kannumo kpota bò me e hèn e wá ó dó kpo è:
		A master flogs his slave because he has not been bought by the slave-dealer:
		– Ani we un ka tuun dò masa o me?
		– *But what do I know about the reasons for such a non-sale?*
36	3[1]	E gbo bâ dó xó kannumo dó Aguda ma xo e wú:
		A slave is flogged to punish him because the Portuguese did not buy him.
		– Hwe ce dé wè nyí à?
		– *Is it my fault?*
41	4	Nyadé xwè kú bò Agaja má du n'i:
		As he is about to be sent to the ancestors, a slave is entrusted with a load of powder from King Agaja.
		– Sè we tè magboje mi à?
		– *What? Has God denied me rest forever?*

41	4[1]	Nyadé xwè kú bò Agaja n'e gbadé xúxú d'alò me:

As he is about to be sent to the ancestors, a slave is entrusted with a handful of dried maize from King Agaja:

- Nû è no mo winya d'alixo wè.
- *It's for anything unexpected on the way.*

100	6	Ahwan-kannumo xò Dada-Segbo Cukú:

A slave, originally a prisoner of war, beats His Majesty's dog:

- Gbè-na-no-nu jèn wà à dè à?
- *Do you think you are going to get yourself a long life by doing that?*

100	6[1]	Ahwan-kannumo xò Dada-Segbo Cukú:

A slave, originally a prisoner of war, beats His Majesty's dog:

- È na sí xè, bo na le xefún à?
- *What! Venerate and fear both the bird and its feathers?*

79	7	È wli xesino vi sà:

You capture a fool's son to sell him:

- A na dù 'kwè ne o vo dìn có mì na kpó dò fí.
- *It won't take you long to spend that money which won't make you happy.*

62	13	È xwlè dà nú nyodaxoví bó só sá, b'e kanby'e dò nè é nyí aji:

The head of an old man about to be sold is shaved and he is asked to state his name:

- É dò emi nyí kakanuazandénijè.
- *He says that his name is 'Give me a few more days'.*

36	a	Kannumo ma j'akpa dó negbé.

A slave must not allow himself to be wounded in the back.

A first reading of these eleven proverbs indicates that (1) war provides slaves (6 and 6[1]); (2) slaves have a life of suffering, punishment, ill-treatment, humiliations and arbitrary treatment of all sorts, and that is so because of their lord and master who, in some cases, may be His Majesty the King (proverbs 2, 3, 3[1], 4, 4[1], 6, 6[1], 7); (3) slaves are sold on the slave market (proverbs 3, 3[1], 7, 13); and (4) the slave-trader is the Portuguese (proverb 3[1]).

Origin of Slaves

The collection of *lô* gives very few pointers as to the source of the supply of slaves. Nevertheless, proverbs 6 and 6[1] indicate a distinction between slaves proper and those who were reduced to slavery after being defeated in the wars of conquest that the Fon waged against their Togolese neighbours in Atakpamé to the west or their Bariba neighbours to the north of the kingdom of Danxomé, or the inhabitants of Ketu and Abeokuta to the east. War, it seems, was the chief means of supplying slaves. As Verbeek notes: 'War remained one of the main sources, even the chief source of slavery. Sometimes it involved "conventional" conflicts between kingdoms or tribes divided by deep-seated ancient rivalries, sometimes straightforward territorial conquests.'[10] An example would be the repeated expeditions against the town of Abeokuta in what is now western Nigeria, which Ahanzo-Glèlè starkly describes as 'Agbomé's *Carthago delenda est*'.[11]

Slavery existed among the Fon long before the overseas slave trade. In this very feudal society, some customs required human sacrifice and hence a category of people over whom the master had the right of life or death. In other words, the overseas slave trade – present in proverbs 3, 3[1], 7 and 13 – which only emerged rather late in the history of Agbomé, simply amplified an already old tradition of slavery.

Being a Slave

The slave appears first as a tragically solitary 'being-in-the-world', with no ties and no support. He is wholly dependent only on his own resources, and must at all costs avoid finding himself in a situation in which he would have to ask help of another. Such is the meaning of proverb 'a' with one statement (Gbégnonvi and Vignondé, 1983, p. 36): 'Kannumo ma j'akpa dó negbé '(*A slave must not allow himself to be wounded in the back*), which is not to be translated as 'A slave does not have a wound in his back'. Why this metaphor? Quite simply because, unlike every other part of the body, the care and dressing of a wound in the back requires the kind assistance of another person. But, by his definition, a slave is a person who can count on no one but himself.

To say that the slave is a 'being-in-the-world' is to speak from the standpoint of the slave himself, or of those who sympathise with his lot. It is moreover only from this angle that the slave could allow himself not only to inflict punishment on his master's (His Majesty the King's) dog, as illustrated by the first part of lô 6 and its variant 6[1] (Ahwan-kannumo xò Dada-Segbo Cukú [*A slave, originally a prisoner of war, beats His Majesty's dog*]), but also, thereby, to assert the supremacy of his dignity as a man over a dog, even a royal one (È na sí xè, bo na le xefún à? [*What! Venerate and fear both the bird and its feathers?*]), or again, as a man, nurturing ideas such as saving money – which he will give to his master for safekeeping in lô 2 – with a view to taking a wife and starting a family (Kannumo kplé asi'kwè, bo gàn ton so dù [*A slave saves to get married and his master spends it*]).

Conversely, the gaze that the other focused on the slave was altogether different. This latter was simply one thing among others and the property of his master, as the second part of lô 1 says (Hwidésu o, nù mima à nyí [*You are part of my inheritance that I shall bequeath*]), or a being whose precarious existence could at any moment be ended by his master's decision (second part of lô 6: Gbè-na-no-nu jèn wà à de à? [*Do you think you are going to get yourself a long life by doing that?*]) when this existence was not bluntly denied (second part of lô 2: Hwi tè we tiín, bò nù towe dè tiin? [*How can you claim to possess something when you don't exist yourself?*]).

As we can see, a slave's life was worth less than that of his master's dog, since the fact of punishing the king's dog made him liable to be killed (proverbs 6 and 6[1]).

But the slave did have a value for his master, the value that enabled him to be the king's emissary to the dead ancestors, as can be seen in proverbs 4 and 4[1]: Nyadé xwè kú bò Agaja má du n'i (*As he is about to be sent to the ances-tors, a slave is entrusted with a load of powder from King Agaja*).

In 1927, Father Gabriel Kiti gave the following explanation of this proverb:

> What is being referred to here is a slave destined to be sacrificed to the spirits of the dead king. During his life, he has worked and toiled. His masters, who were tyrants, Agaja in particular,[12] left him no rest on earth. He rejoices at his approach-ing execution: death will finally bring him what he has so long desired. But then King Agaja sends him a packet of powder to deliver to the late kings, his ances-tors, in the other world. The slave is upset and screams: What? After a life of toil like mine, you want to take away from me the rest that every man enjoys in the land of the dead? No! Has God denied me rest forever?[13]

The slave was his master's property exactly like his cattle or his fields, and had no claim to inherit, whence this response made in lô 1, to the unhappy slave who had been saving and asked for his share of the inheritance before the master died: Hwidésu o, nù mima à nyí (*You are also part of this inheritance that I shall bequeath!*).

The slave thus in reality had only a market value. And that is the only rea-son why he would receive any care at all from his master, whose insatiable cupidity, skilfully brought out in proverb 13, led to fraud, deceiving the slaver as to the actual value of the slave-property: È xwlè dà nú nyodaxoví bó só sá … (*The head of an old man about to be sold is shaved …*).

Verbeek provides valuable information about the practice of shaving the head of an elderly slave: 'Once they have reached their destination, they [the slaves] are held in fenced enclosures until the slave ships arrive. The sellers gen-erally put this period to good use to revive the captives, often exhausted by the long distance they have just walked.'[14] The aim was to enhance the value of the slave-commodity awaiting the arrival of purchasers by making him look younger: 'The standard used, if I might put it so, was the *pièce d'Inde*, as the slavers called a well-built adult black man, with all his teeth and no more than 40 years old…. A man who was slightly disabled or aged more than 40 was worth half a *pièce d'Inde*…. The infirm, the sick, the old (as measured by wrinkles, white hair, very acidic sweat) were deemed unsaleable, even at a cut price rate….'[15]

In this proverb, it is thus a matter of removing the old man from the cat-egory of unsaleable slave by making him pass for an adult under 40 years old. The slave was obliged to co-operate with this dishonest dealing on pain of being punished as illustrated by proverbs 3 (Kannumo kpota bò me e hèn e wá o dó kpo è [*A master flogs his slave because he has not been bought by the slave-dealer*]) and 3[1] (E gbo bâ dó xó kannumo dó Aguda ma xo e wú [*A slave is flogged to punish him because the Portuguese did not buy him*]). It will be remembered that, in Prosper Merimée's novel of the same name, Tamango quite simply killed his unsold slaves so as not to have to keep them.

Faced with a tragic fate and no way out, the slave often had only a choice between three attitudes: (1) resignation and fear because of his powerlessness, which are expressed in the candour and innocence combined with naivety contained in the response to proverbs 3 (Ani we un ka tuun dò masa o me?

[*But what do I know about the reasons for such a non-sale?*]) and 3[1] (Hwe ce dé wè nyí à? [*Is it my fault?*]); (2) malicious and sometimes moralising humour (É dò emi nyí kakanuazandénijè [*He says that his name is 'Give me a few more days'*], which means: 'Wait a few days, my hair will grow again and you will see if you are really getting a good deal'); or (3) again, among the boldest, insolence or fearless bravado (A na dù 'kwè ne o vo dìn có mì na kpó dò fí [*It won't take you long to spend that money which won't make you happy*]), as can be seen in proverbs 4 (Sè we tè magboje mi à? [*What? Has God denied me rest forever?*]) and 6[1] (Ahwan-kannumo xò Dada-Segbo Cukú [*A slave, originally a prisoner of war, beats His Majesty's dog*], È na sí xe, bo na le sí xefún à? [*What! Venerate and fear both the bird and its feathers?*]).

The distinction that is made in the collection of proverbs between 'timid slave' and 'rebellious slave' constitutes another historical element which is confirmed by Verbeek: '[There are, among the slaves,] individuals who are recalcitrant or suspected of becoming so' whose 'wrists [were] also shackled' and who 'in addition [wore] a collar whose lock was linked to a rope or a chain, while the fetters on their ankles were joined to rigid irons.'[16]

The Slave-Dealer

Of all the nationalities of slave-dealers, the collection of Fon proverbs has remembered only the Portuguese slave-dealer called *Aguda* in Fon, doubtless because the Portuguese did the most business in this trade. As Ahanzo-Glèlè points out, quoting Berbain: 'The black market [in Dahomey] was held at Xavier (Savi) where the British, the French, the Portuguese and the Dutch had factories. Ships under all flags dropped anchor off Juda (Ouidah) and each year the French took 500–600 blacks, the British 6,000–7,000, the Dutch 1,000–1,500 and the Portuguese 6,000–7,000.'[17] It will also be observed that in Fon proverbs, the European slave-dealer does not play a prominent role in the slave trade.

What can we learn from this brief overview of Fon proverbs about slavery? First, that Fon proverbs, far from simply being a store of ancestral wisdom, are very close to the narrative genre from which they derive and which they serve by becoming a figure of style, and not a literary genre in their own right. They are 'the icing on the cake' or, in the words of Gbégnonvi, 'the extra spirit of discourse'.[18] And it is because their source and strength derive from narrative that they enshrine all that is taken from social life and, thus, from history – national history but also the history of individuals, from the most illustrious to the most obscure – and draw sustenance from it.

There is a further peculiar feature of the Fon proverbs which we have studied, namely, that contrary to the recurrent discourse on slavery and the Atlantic slave trade, the white slave-dealer is not criticised in them. With courage and honesty, the Fon people looks at itself as it is and attempts to understand the role that it played so as to establish its own responsibilities, by showing that blacks, too, participated in the enslavement of other blacks. Fon proverbs thus constitute valuable testimonies of historical reality. For that reason, they should be saved from oblivion and, above all, saved in their integrity.

Notes

1. M. Cabakulu, 1992, pp. 93–94.
2. In our study (1978, pp. 43–53), we drew a distinction between proverbs with a simple structure and proverbs with a binary structure. In his thesis (1985, chaps. 9 and 10), R. Gbégnonvi preferred the distinction 'lô with one statement' and 'lô with two statements'. We accept these names, which we recognise to be more appropriate.
3. M. Quenum, 1938, p. 31.
4. First, highlighting the 'response' alone as being the 'proverb strictly so called' seriously mutilates the lô and drains it of all sociological, ecological, historical, sociological ad cultural references of which it may be the focal point. Next, there are lôs in which what Quenum regards as the 'proverb strictly so called' is found expressed not in the 'response' but in the first statement, the first part of the proverb. Finally, the complexity of the morpho-syntactic structure of Fon proverbs is such that the response may not be 'the celebrated word of the main character in the story'.
5. A.B.M. Kouaovi, 1981.
6. Poetic activity must be understood here in its etymological sense of an activity of artistic creation.
7. P. Hountondji, 1976, p. 62 (1983, p. 60).
8. 'Raison et déraison au royaume d'Abomey ou l'épopée des lô à deux énoncés', in R. Gbégnonvi, 1994, pp. 95–110.
9. G. Guillet, 1971, Les proverbes, pp. 1–57, and Pro manuscripto; A.B.M. Kouaovi, 1981; R. Gbégnonvi and J.-N. Vignondé, 1983.
10. Y. Verbeek, 1978, p. 45.
11. M. Ahanzo-Glèlè, 1974, pp. 34–36 and 162.
12. So far as we know, the tyranny of King Agaja is not well established. But it cannot be ruled out that the young black priest, working under the very colonial Reverend Father Aupais, was the victim of colonial African history textbooks, which, at the time, presented African kings as 'bloody savage barbarians' from whose tyranny the civilising mission of colonisation had come to deliver Africans.
13. In La reconnaissance africaine, No. 39, June 1927, quoted by G. Guillet, 1971.
14. Y. Verbeek, 1978, p. 47.
15. Ibid., p. 51.
16. Ibid., p. 57.
17. M. Ahanzo-Glèlè, 1974, p. 162.
18. Ibid., p. 74.

Bibliography

AHANZO-GLÈLÈ, M. 1974. Le Danxome: du pouvoir aja à la nation fon. Paris, Nubia.
BERBAIN, S. 1942. Étude sur la traite des Noirs au golfe de Guinée: le comptoir français de Juda (Ouidah) au XVIIIᵉ siècle. Paris, Librairie Larose. [Mémoire de l'IFAN.]
CABAKULU, M. 1992. Dictionnaire des proverbes africains. Paris, L'Harmattan/ACIVA.
GBÉGNONVI, R. 1985. Lô ou 'proverbes': structure et fonctions d'un epiphénomène du parler fon des Aja-Fon du Danxome au Sud Bénin (University of Bielefeld/Faculty of Linguistics and Literature, Master's thesis).

————. 1994. 'Raison et déraison au royaume d'Abomey ou l'épopée des lô à deux énoncés'. In *Mélanges Jean Pliya*. Cotonou, Les Éditions du Flamboyant.

GBÉGNONVI, R., and VIGNONDÉ, J.-N. 1983. *Lô*. Paris, Binndi e Jannde.

GUILLET, G. 1971. *Les proverbes* and *Pro manuscripto*. Cotonou, BNF. (Regards sur la littérature dahoméenne.)

HOUNTONDJI, P. 1976. *Sur la 'philosophie africaine'*. Paris, Maspero. [Eng. tr. Evans, H. 1983. *African Philosophy: Myth and Reality*. London, Hutchinson University Library for Africa.]

KOUAOVI, A.B.M. 1981. *Proverbes et dictons du Bénin*. Paris, ACCT.

QUENUM, A. 1993. *Les églises chrétiennes et la traite atlantique du XVe au XIXe siècle*. Paris, Karthala.

QUENUM, M. 1938. *Au pays des Fon. Us et coutumes du Dahomey*. Paris, Éditions Larose.

SAUGERA, E. 1995. *Bordeaux, port négrier*. Paris, Karthala.

VERBEEK, Y. 1978. *Histoire de l'esclavage de l'Antiquité à nos jours*. Geneva, Éditions Ferni. (Le cercle des bibliophiles contemporains.)

VIGNONDÉ, J.-N. 1978. *La littérature orale fon du Bénin. Contribution à la recherche paradémiologique* (Université de Paris III-Sorbonne, Master's thesis).

Chapter 22

Some Remarks on the Christian Churches and the Atlantic Slave Trade from the Fifteenth to the Nineteenth Century

Alphonse Quenum

THERE ARE THOSE who do not like to recall the wounds of a bygone age that affects them, 'in order', as Daget (1960) says, 'to conceal a troubled gaze'. Others avoid remembrance in order not to admit to themselves their own weaknesses. It serves no purpose to shift responsibilities. The presence of the past, whatever that past might be, is the mark and the guarantee of our dignity as human beings – provided that we agree to face it squarely.

Some might be surprised that we have chosen to deal with such a long historical period – ranging from the fifteenth to the nineteenth century – but I wanted to provide an overall view of a phenomenon that people refuse to approach from a religious perspective.

We speak of Christian Churches in the plural because when the slave trade began to be organised on a large scale, there was no longer a monolithic Church in the Christian countries, which were the main actors in the tragedy. The Protestant Reformation had already caused profound rifts in the Catholic West.

As the Holy Scriptures were used to justify slavery and the slave trade – as indeed they were later appealed to in order to fight it – they will be the subject of the first part of this chapter. The second part will look at the tragedy of the Atlantic slave trade with the crises of conscience that it aroused. In the third part, abolitionism will be examined.

The Bible and Slavery

It is impossible to study the slave trade and the position of the Christian Churches on this social phenomenon without exploring the Bible, the key source of Christian thought and ethics. One reason for paying especial attention to the principles set out in the Bible is that one of the major assertions of the theologians of the Reformation concerned the primacy of Scripture, the sole source of faith and ethics.

Those who defended the legitimacy of the slave trade, in particular in countries with a Protestant majority such as England or the United States, regularly referred to the slavery practised in the sacred books. Yet in France, too, a country whose faith was Catholic, some, like the theologian Bellon de Saint-Quentin in his *Dissertation sur la traite et le commerce des nègres*, referred to the Bible to justify slavery.

Slavery in the Old Testament

Slavery is such an integral part of the history of peoples that Israel itself, despite the fact that it had been a victim of this practice, did not escape it (Genesis 24; 37). As a result of the wars that broke out in the reign of King David, numerous slaves were bound to forced labour. The Bible also mentions the slave trade that went on in the Phoenician ports in particular (Amos 1, 6, 9, 10, etc.).

We shall pay particular attention, in the Old Testament, to the myth of the curse of Ham. This recurrent and obscure topic originates in the Book of Genesis (chapters 9 and 10) and is always cited and debated in discussions of the Negro-African odyssey: Noah is said to have cursed one of his three sons who showed him lack of respect, by seeing his nakedness. Ham was condemned, and is said to have become his brothers' slave. The myth of Ham continued to be used tendentiously in many religious circles, down to very recent times. Some Africans even refer to it still.

In the fifteenth and sixteenth centuries and the first half of the seventeenth, the story of Noah was very rarely used against blacks, but in the second half of the seventeenth, the eighteenth and, above all, the nineteenth century, blacks were treated as 'children of Ham' and as an 'accursed race'.

That there may have been misunderstanding, misinterpretation or misreading of the Biblical text may indeed be the case, but the underlying question remains. 'How', said the missionary J. Lecuyer (1988), 'can we evangelise peoples, and how can we make them seek in our old Bible an ideal of life and the strength to follow that ideal, if we begin by giving them to believe that that same Bible, which we tell them contains all truth, includes the story of an alleged curse on them?'

The New Testament and the Slave

The Gospels have little so say about slavery as such (Matthew 24: 24–25; 25: 14; Luke 12: 35, etc.) and do little more than compare slaves to Christians. Nowhere is there an analysis of slavery as a social reality. It is only with the epistles of St Peter and St Paul that we see the beginnings of thinking about the fate of slaves and slavery. But, in both, all is on the spiritual level with its call to look towards celestial happiness and the salvation of the soul. Even the famous epistle that St Paul wrote to Philemon about the slave Onesimus leaves us unsatisfied.

What is certain is that, in both the Old and the New Testaments, slavery constitutes a major social reality. It is sometimes regulated to limit its excesses, as in the Old Testament, or widely accepted, even respected, as in the New Testament. Nowhere is it said that slavery is an evil.

In addition, the prejudice that blacks were the unfortunate children of Ham was so deeply entrenched in attitudes that in the nineteenth century the founders of missionary orders – whose good faith cannot be suspect – referred to it to justify their pastoral commiseration. Naturally, at no point did they wonder about the theological meaning of this curse for the doctrine of universal salvation.

The Christian World and the Atlantic Slave Trade

From the Age of the Apostles to the Fifteenth Century: The Popes and Slavery

Slavery, then, was tolerated and accepted by the Church. Sometimes it was thought to be a lesser evil, sometimes a sin. It was almost never openly regarded as reprehensible. That might explain why, in the days before Europe embarked on colonisation, the Popes did not make a stand against slavery, though it is true that the Church was not indifferent to the fate of the slaves.

Thus, on the issue of slavery, the Church – whether the early Church or the Church of the Middle Ages – was hardly revolutionary. The primitive Church sought rather to justify an institution that was deeply rooted in community life, the acceptance of which was recognised in many sources: the Old Testament, the setting and heritage of Roman law, the ethics of the New Testament according to which the slave was subject to his master, among others.

The Papal Bulls and 'the New Worlds'

The Popes have often been accused of favouring the colonialist and pro-slavery activities of the Christian powers by their stands and moral cover. The bull *Romanus Pontifex* of 1455 was an effective weapon in the hands of Prince Henry. The bulls of Alexander VI, notably *Inter Coetera* of 1493, divided the world to the advantage of Portugal and Spain, in accordance with the doctrine of 'the Pope's universal monarchy', asserting the authority of the Pope over Christian princes and countries.

For the Indians against the Blacks

Like many people of his time faced with the tragedy of the Indians, who were dying in vast numbers, the Spanish missionary Las Casas was hoping that slaves, who were more resistant, like the blacks whom he knew, would take the Indians' place. For a long time, Las Casas did not view the slave trade as an evil; only the fate reserved for the Indians was. Black slaves, of whom it was said that 'the work of one … is worth more than that of four natives', were above all highly regarded for their capacity to work. They should therefore be used as a replacement labour force.

Yet Las Casas soon recognised his error: 'The blood of a black man has the same value as that of an Indian.' Even if he cannot be regarded as the defender of the blacks, as he was of the Indians, he did at least make proper apologies.

The Power of Mercantilism and the Complicity of Silence

In the fifteenth and sixteenth centuries and at the very beginning of the seventeenth century, the trade in blacks was much like slavery as it had been known since the dawn of time. The fate of those sent to the galleys in the same period is sufficient evidence of that.

From the seventeenth century onwards, the Atlantic slave trade emerged from its pre-industrial stage and reached unprecedented proportions, thanks to the well-organised system set up by the large monopoly trading companies. Under the law of supply and demand, slave-trading Europe was matched by the African slave-trading period.

Slave-trading Europe was a mercantilist Europe on the make, whose dominant culture was officially Christian. While Catholic France was not among the first nations to get involved in the triangular trade, it was the first to get out of it. As for the Portuguese and Spanish missionaries, they were always there – in Africa as chaplains in the forts from which the cargoes of slaves that they had baptised set out – and in the Americas at the point where the blacks were sold.

Like Catholics, the vast majority of Protestants were heirs to the dualist tradition which accepted slavery while rejecting violence and injustice. In a world in a state of sin, slavery, it was thought, could save souls. Far then from opposing the slave trade, the Protestants saw in it a means of advancing their work of evangelisation. The proper functioning of trading companies, enriched by the triangular trade, was regarded as proof of divine blessing. To blame the trader for his greed and lack of pity was unthinkable.

Doctrinal Debates and Crisis of Conscience

Despite the collective clear conscience, the slave trade did not proceed without precipitating doctrinal debates, even something of a crisis of conscience. At the beginning of the seventeenth century, the debates that were organised on the subject in Catholic universities, especially the Spanish ones such as Valladolid, were part of a moral and legal debate in which the notion of a just war and the primacy of the right to evangelise were examined.

From the second half of the seventeenth century and all through the eighteenth, things changed with the emergence of Enlightenment humanist philosophy and reason, and the highlighting of the ambiguities of the Holy Scriptures and the use of Christian reason as moral justification. Such was the case with Bellon de Saint-Quentin and de Fromageau at the Paris Sorbonne in France.

The Era of Change: The Abolitionist Movement (Late Eighteenth to Nineteenth Centuries)

The abolitionist movement was the outcome of a new awareness that had several causes.

Protestant Evangelical Radicalism

The anti-slavery campaign emerged from the ranks of Protestants – from the then marginalised Quakers. The evangelical leaders Granville Sharp, Wilberforce, and John Wesley regarded slavery as an evil. Disagreeing with Aristotelian philosophy and ethics, they drew on Gospel theology for the spiritual strength and logic to fight against the slave trade. Nevertheless, their writings are dominated by a philanthropic and humanistic approach in the name of what they saw as 'true Christian ethics'.

Almost all of the sermons and lectures delivered in the framework of this anti-slavery movement made reference to the texts of Holy Scripture and went so far as to accuse the British state, which allowed the slave trade, of being an accomplice in crime.

Catholic Abolitionism

The difficulties that lie in the way of grasping the official position of the Catholic Church in the abolitionist movement arise from the fact that religious analysts or historians favourable to the Church often fail to distinguish between slavery in general and the particular case of the overseas slave trade.

The truth is that the new anti-slavery approach of the Popes began with the Congress of Vienna, in 1814, at which Pius VII addressed clergy and lay people in the following terms: 'And we forbid any clergyman or layman to dare to support as allowed, on whatsoever pretext, this trade in blacks or to preach or teach in public or in private in any way whatsoever anything contrary to this apostolic letter.'[1] This text suggests that at the beginning of the nineteenth century some of the clergy still believed that there was nothing reprehensible in the trade in blacks.

It was Gregory XVI, in his Constitution *In Supremo Apostolatus Fastigio* of December 1839, who first openly condemned – speaking seven times of '*nigritarum commercium*' – the slave trade in blacks. Of course, as was the custom, Gregory XVI placed his action in the tradition of the Church and referred to his predecessors (Clement I, Pius II, Paul II, Urban VIII [1639], Benedict XIV [1741] and Pius VII), but no Pope before him had condemned the slave trade, 'this iniquitous, pernicious, degrading human traffic which must completely disappear among Christians'.

On 16 June 1850, Pius IX beatified the Catalan Jesuit Peter Claver, an admirable monk who in 1622 decided to serve God all his life, in the person of the slaves, and who lambasted the slave traders 'who, in their supreme wickedness, would habitually exchange human lives for gold'.

Finally, in his encyclical letter *In plurimis* (1888), addressed to the bishops of Brazil, Leo XIII criticised the slave trade and slavery which still continued to flourish, even though Christian countries were no longer directly implicated in it.

Conclusion

One after the other, and for a variety of reasons, the European nations of various Christian persuasions put a legal end to the slave trade and slavery, both on their territory and in their American colonies. Thus, by the end of the nineteenth century, the Atlantic slave trade – which had lasted for four hundred years – had officially ended. Yet neither slavery nor the slave trade had completely disappeared from the African continent.

Pride, the humiliating nature of the slave trade, the scale of the Atlantic slave trade and the racist prejudices that accompanied it – at least at a certain level of its development – often impelled African historians to see the cause of the evil only on the European side. But such partiality veils Africa in an innocence that is not always well founded and that does a disservice to Africans, since it prevents them from seeking out the truth and facing it fully.

History has shown us that the Christian Churches were not always successful in living up to the ethical values that they claimed to believe in. But they have nothing to lose by acknowledging that the work of God has often been hindered by human vagaries within the Church itself. That is why they could not or would not develop a systematic doctrine against the slave trade at an early date.

It is unfortunate that history continues to be unfair to black people. There is willingness to acknowledge their tragedy, but its impact is played down. It would surely be in the best interest of Africans to try to understand this tragedy by reflecting on the horrors that their ancestors suffered as much by their own fault and complicity as by the cynical greed and barbarism of others. That is what it will take to escape from fatalism and for the African continent to cease to appear as the laggard of humankind.

Note

1. L. Conti, 1985, p. 274.

Bibliography

BRASIO, A. 1952. *Monumenta missionaria Africana Costa occidental Africana.* Lisbon, Agencia geral do Ultramar.

COLLANGE, J.-F. 1987. *L'épître de saint Paul à Philemon.* Geneva, Labor et Fides.

CONTI, L. 1985. 'L'Église catholique et la traite négrière'. In *La traite négrière du XVe au XIXe siècle.* (Coll: Histoire générale de l'Afrique. Études et documents, No. 2.) Paris, UNESCO. [Eng. ed. 1979. *The African Slave Trade from the Fifteenth to the Nineteenth Century.* (General History of Africa, Studies and Documents, No. 2) Paris, UNESCO.]

DAGET, S. 1960. 'L'abolition de la traite des Noirs en France de 1814 à 1831'. *Cahiers d'études africaines,* Vol. 11, No. 41.

DEBIEN, G. 1967. *La christianisation des Antilles françaises aux XVIIe et XVIIIe siècles.* Montreal.

DUCHET, M. 1965. 'Esclavage et humanisme en 1787'. In *Annales historiques de la révolution française.* Paris, Société des études robespierristes.

FROMAGEAU, G. 1714. *Résolution de plusieurs cas de conscience.* Paris, J.-B. Coignard fils.

———. 1733. *Le dictionnaire des cas de conscience décidées suivant les principes de la morale.* Paris, J.-B. Coignard fils.

LECUYER, J. 1988. 'Le père Liberman et la malédiction de Cham'. In *Liberman 1802–1852. Une pensée et un mystique missionaire.* Paris, Le Cerf.

MAXWELL, J.-F. *Slavery and the Catholic Church: The History of Catholic Teaching Concerning the Moral Legitimacy of the Institution of Slavery.* Chichester/London, Barry Rose Publ. (With a foreword by Lord Wilberforce.)

ROSCOE, M.R. *Slavery and Catholicism.* Durham, N.C., Northsale Publishers.

Chapter 23

The Abolitions of Slavery (1793, 1794, 1848): Overview of a Symposium

Marcel Dorigny

ON 16 PLUVIÔSE YEAR II, the French National Convention voted for the abolition of slavery in all of the French colonies. In the final analysis, it matters little that some publicists here and there declare loudly that the French Revolution was not, chronologically, the first to abolish slavery: we are, of course, fully aware that several of the newly independent states in North America, following the teachings of the Quakers, did so several years before the decree of 16 Pluviôse Year II; we also know that Denmark prohibited the trade on its ships in 1792. However, in those countries, the slave trade and slavery were far from being a key economic component of national prosperity itself, as was the case for the leading colonial powers of the time: Britain, France, Portugal and the Netherlands. For these countries, the colonial economy, almost intrinsically tied in with slavery, was a vital sector of their trade and manufacturing, and it would be foolish to underestimate the weight of special interests, their capacity for resistance and their political influence. Thus, by its gesture of 16 Pluviôse Year II, the Convention was indeed doing something pioneering: for the first time, a country for which the slave-based plantation colonial economy was vital was abandoning slavery.

Yet, once we have re-stated that key fact, we must not ignore the reality of the situation: on 16 Pluviôse Year II, the National Convention ratified a de facto situation that it had not itself created. The fact is that the main French slave colony, Saint-Domingue, had proclaimed universal emancipation on 29 August and 21 September 1793, through unilateral decisions by the civil commissioners Sonthonax and Polverel. However, the Convention extended this abolition to all the other French possessions, that is, essentially, Guadeloupe, Guiana and the Mascarenes. We also know perfectly well that the two commissioners of the republic who proclaimed abolition on the spot, without having been ordered to do so from Paris, acted under the pressure of circumstances, whatever may have been their own personal convictions; the slave uprising was in control of most of the colony and the threat of a British landing was imminent, while Spain was beginning an invasion over the land border.

Thus, the process that led to the abolition of slavery was not as simple and clear-cut as one optimistic republican tradition would for so long have it. It took the Revolution several years, after it had proclaimed the Rights of Man, to apply its own universalist principles to all French possessions, including the colonies, and there is no denying that the uprising by the slaves of Saint-Domingue was a decisive element in the process of abolition.

The symposium organised by the University of Paris VIII on 3, 4 and 5 February 1994, under the auspices of the UNESCO Slave Route programme,[1] was devoted precisely to highlighting, so far as current research allows, the complexity of the path that led to the disappearance of slavery. It was focused particularly on the French colonies, but a comparative approach was also suggested: how can the mechanisms of abolition and its consequences be understood without taking account of the variety of experiences and the ongoing intertwining of the colonies and their commercial networks?

In order to meet the requirements of scholarship, we organised the symposium around six major themes, arranged with the intention of reflecting a novel approach:

- the forms taken by resistance to the slave trade and slavery;
- the Enlightenment and slavery: Was there a demand for abolition?
- uprisings against slavery; the debates in the revolutionary assemblies up to the abolition of 16 Pluviôse;
- the restoration of slavery and the reorganisation of the abolitionist movements;
- the abolitions outside the French colonies;
- the abolition of April 1848: debates and how it was implemented.

Following is an account of all these sessions, grouped around these six themes.

Resistance to slavery and the slave trade constitutes a topic that has been relatively little studied, and, when it has been, it has usually been approached through description of how the slave trade actually operated and the everyday lives of slaves on the plantations. Yet all of our sources indicate that the capture of future slaves and their transfer to the coast, and then the long voyage on the slave ship were never peaceful stages in a perfectly harmoniously organised process. On the contrary, there was fierce resistance: open rebellions, refusal to eat, collective or individual suicide, mutinies on ships and above all escapes, or attempted escapes, by sea to endeavour to return to Africa. Especially, and the symposium papers on the Ile Bourbon and the Windward Islands bring this out in particular, the dominant form of resistance to slavery was *marronnage*, or running away. More than fleeing, to be a maroon, a runaway, was to enter into a clandestine existence and rebuild a new life, trying sometimes to return to where one had been before captivity. All through the period of colonial slavery, the existence of 'communities' of '*Nègres marrons*' (maroons, runaways) was one of the colonisers' great nightmares. The mythical belief in the imminence of a 'general war' launched by thousands of maroons lay permanently at the heart of the collective fears of planters, which always impelled the colonial authorities to be ferocious in applying the punishments provided for in the *Code noir* for captured runaways.

Alongside running away, one of the most common forms of resistance was the refusal to have children, who would be condemned to slavery from birth. This conscious refusal to reproduce sometimes went so far as infanticide, which was harshly condemned by the Church and the planters' justice.

Finally, religious and cultural resistance was of no less importance. Faced with the systematic practice of baptism and conversion to Catholicism, imposed by the *Code noir* as an obligation for the masters, the slaves successfully remained attached to traditional beliefs, which soon became marks of cultural identity, highlighting the refusal to enter into the masters' way of thinking. In Saint-Domingue, voodoo was the most developed form of this cultural resistance on the part of slaves, and the role that it played in the launching of the insurrection of Bois-Caïman in August 1791 is well known. The Catholic Church's relentless struggle against what it regarded as an intolerable survival of fetishism and paganism alone speaks volumes of the significance of cultural resistance on the part of the slaves. To reject the religion of the Europeans was to refuse to be wholly dominated; the labour and even the person of the slave could, by force, be made the property of the white man, but not his spirit, which was subjugated in outward appearance only.

How did eighteenth-century Europe perceive the existence of the slave trade and slavery in the colonies of the most powerful and wealthy nations, which were consequently those most open to the ideals of the Enlightenment, advocating tolerance, justice, individual guarantees and equality among men, at least before the law? The symposium papers on this topic forcefully stressed the message of the Enlightenment, which on one central point was unambiguous: the 'moral' condemnation of slavery gradually imposed itself in the course of the century to become clear and categorical in Montesquieu's *Spirit of Law* in 1748. But in this area, too, it would be dangerously naive to believe in a unilateral commitment in favour of an immediate abolition of a practice that was condemned morally and philosophically: the moral condemnation of slavery did not lead the men of the Enlightenment to a serious political conclusion. There were hesitations and proposals for gradual abolition of the slave trade and slavery, but never, at least before 1770, proposals for the immediate elimination of a system on which the prosperity of the kingdom depended. Among the Enlightenment writers, there was a sort of inner conflict between what justice required and the equally central dogma of the quest for economic efficiency and praise of the enrichment of societies. Before the physiocrats, precisely in the name of economic efficiency, had demonstrated just how perverse slavery was, there was constant hesitation about embarking on an openly abolitionist campaign.

The move from what it is perhaps reductive to describe as 'mere moral condemnation' to a call, even if only rhetorical, for an insurrection by the slaves was a decisive stage in the growth of awareness of the injustice of the foundations of colonial society. Mercier, in 1770, and then Raynal and Diderot set out with moving eloquence the imminence of a revolt by the blacks in the islands, a prelude to a deplorable but just massacre of the whites, paving the way for the independence of the colonies – an independence which would be quite unlike that of the states of North America, where only the whites won their freedom. This rising power of anti-slavery after 1770, marked by legitimation of the still quite hypothetical insurrection of the blacks, had one major consequence: the birth of the first organised abolitionist movement, equipped with a programme, statutes, finance and means of action. With the establishment in February 1788 of the Société des Amis des Noirs, the fight against slavery took on a political dimension that it had previously lacked.

Above all, and it is essential to stress it strongly here, the abolitionist movement had an international base. The American Revolution had put among the foremost values of the young republic the ideas of individual freedom and equality; the Declaration of Independence had enshrined those principles, which became the foundations of the republic with the promulgation of the federal constitution. There is no doubt that abolitionism was invigorated, at least initially, by the very strength of the ideas of 'free Americans', even though, in reality, the birth of the United States was not concomitant with the abolition of slavery, or even of the slave trade, in the southern states, where these were matters of the highest economic importance. In Great Britain, a leading slaving country, a powerful abolitionist lobby was developing at about the same time around Clarkson, Benezet and Wilberforce, which resulted in the foundation in 1787 of the Society for the Abolition of the Slave Trade. At this time there was close co-operation among British, American and French abolitionists: the French Société des Amis des Noirs saw itself as being an offshoot of the British society and as being in permanent relations with the various American abolitionist societies. A sort of 'anti-slavery international' was taking shape, whose role in the late eighteenth century should not be underestimated. It would be ahistorical to see in the anti-slavery members of the Société des Amis des Noirs the last remnants of the literary theorising of the eighteenth century, with its 'narrowly moralising' ideas lacking all boldness. It is true that none of these men was proposing the immediate abolition of slavery, but only plans for gradual abolition, spread out over two or three generations in order to make possible a gradual reconversion of the economies of the metropoles and the colonies. Only the immediate abolition of the slave trade was called for, in order to cut off the system at its source by depriving the settlers of new slaves.

To carry through this reformist programme successfully, the Amis des Noirs were counting on two complementary means of action. First, they launched campaigns aimed at the general public to spread anti-slavery ideas. Second, with regard to the government, they attempted a discreet but continuous tactic of applying pressure and bringing influence to bear on the offices of the Ministry of the Navy, where many Amis des Noirs had contacts and where they were fully aware that enlightened colonial administrators were preparing proposals for a 'reform' of the system which might pave the way for a policy moving in the direction of that sought by the abolitionists. There can thus be no denying that these various anti-slavery 'societies' played a role in the long process that led to the abolitions: they spread anti-slavery ideas among the enlightened public of their time, in particular by publishing translations of British and American works on the slave trade and living conditions in the plantations, thus breaking the silence that prevailed on aspects of colonial society that people were not anxious to see brought out. Even before 1789, the debate on slavery and the colonies pitted the Amis des Noirs against the settlers, a prelude to the great confrontations of the early years of the Revolution.

With the radical transformations of the political system in metropolitan France – brought about suddenly in 1789 by the Revolution – the existence of slavery in the colonies was potentially called into question. For how could the settlers, on the one hand, and the abolitionists, on the other, fail to make an immediate connection between Article I of the Declaration of the Rights of Man (adopted on 26 August 1789) and the practice of slavery in the colonies? The settlers, rightly worried, did not wait for this vote to take political precautions against an abolitionist upsurge in the ranks of the most extreme 'patriots' in the Assembly, among whom the Comte de Mirabeau was then very influential and whose role in the Société des Amis des Noirs was known to every settler.

In order to ward off such 'excesses', the settlers of Saint-Domingue had succeeded in securing separate representation within the National Assembly, bringing with it that of the other colonies. On 20 August 1789, the Club Massiac held its first meeting in Paris: it brought together the leading planters of Saint-Domingue, and could count on close friendships among the deputies who were then most influential – Barnave, the Lameth brothers, Malouet, etc. Thus, by the summer of 1789, a pro-slave 'lobby' was already in existence. The establishment of the Colonial Committee of the Constituent Assembly on 2 March 1790 was the climax of this policy of resistance – almost in anticipation, it might be said – by the settlers to the slightest talk of reforming, however modestly, the colonial status quo. Nine out of ten members of this committee were convinced supporters of the planters' interests. Thus, control of parliamentary debates was assured, and any offensive by the abolitionists could be blocked even before it reached a public hearing. This was the strategy applied all through the session of the Constituent Assembly. There was no debate on slavery itself; on the contrary, the decree of 15 May 1791 constitutionally recognised the existence in the French colonies of 'unfree persons'. The slave trade was also kept in existence, including the payment of bonuses to slave-traders by the government. Only the question of the political rights of 'free people of colour' was raised publicly. The defenders of the claims of these 'free men', a minority in the Assembly, were able on 15 May 1791 to secure a compromise decree granting equality at the second generation only. This modest victory was short-lived: the same assembly revoked its timid decree on the following 24 September, before the end of the session. Finally, to crown this conservative policy of the pro-slavery colonial order, the Constitution of 1791 itself failed to apply its founding principles to the colonies, since its final article specified: 'The French colonies, although part of the French Empire, are not included in this constitution.'

The decisive impulse originated elsewhere. While the Constituent Assembly remained deaf to the proposals, timid though they were, of the Amis des Noirs, insurrections broke out in the colonies without any proven direct links with the revolutionary events in France. A summary of the chronology of these events follows. At the end of August 1789, when the storming of the Bastille was as yet unknown to them, the slaves of Saint-Pierre de la Martinique rebelled; at the beginning of October, an attempted uprising occurred in the south of Saint-Domingue; in November, there was another in Martinique; then, on 4 and 5 December 1789, there was an attempted uprising in Guiana; on 11 and 12 April 1790, it was the turn of Guadeloupe to be affected in the Capesterre-Petit-Bourg area; then again in Martinique in October and November 1790; in Saint Lucia in December of the same year. Finally, on 22 August 1791, came the most important of all the slave uprisings – the only one that was successful – with the start of the revolt in northern Saint-Domingue, which has gone down in history and legend as the insurrection of Bois-Caïman.

While not exhaustive, this list is long enough to convey the widespread nature of the armed struggle in 1789 by slaves in all of the islands. The origins and strategies of these colonial 'revolutions' owed nothing to the one that began in France in the same year, yet it would be unwise to separate the two sets of events. It was in the context of the loss of legitimacy of the power of the absolute monarchy that the colonial edifice was shaken, first by the white challenge to some aspects of metropolitan power over the islands (for example, over the matter of the colonial *exclusif*, even in a 'watered down' form, whereby the colonies could trade only with France, in French vessels), and then by the promulgation in France of a Declaration of the Rights of Man which denied the legitimacy of 'unfreedom' without, however, anticipating all the consequences. Given these new facts, the repressive power was weakened, hesitant and divided. There is no denying that the radicalness of the revolutionary ideas, taken to their extreme consequences between 1792 and 1794, could not but lend support to the desire for freedom which was always latent in the population reduced to slavery. It is through this conjunction – not to say convergence, since nothing proves that the Jacobins in Paris wanted a rapid abolition – that the revolutionary events in France played a positive role in the move towards the first abolition of slavery. A different government in Paris would probably not have endorsed the abolitionist proclamation of the two civil commissioners in Saint-Domingue. The decree of 16 Pluviôse was possible because there existed in France at that time a political balance of power favourable to those among the Jacobins who, some from long before, were convinced of the iniquity of slavery and of the urgency of abolishing it, even if those men had rather 'endured' events in Saint-Domingue than truly sought them. It is surely true that the military circumstances and the strength of the revolt in Saint-Domingue were decisive factors in the final decision-making, but it would be speculative to seek to apportion the share of each of these factors in getting the process under way.

The symposium wished to go beyond this detailed examination of the conditions that resulted in the decision of 16 Pluviôse Year II. The organisers felt that it was necessary to follow through the actual ways in which the abolition decided on in Paris was implemented in the French colonies. The particular, but highly revealing, case of the Indian Ocean islands was treated specifically: it was recalled how, with the connivance of some metropolitan interests, the Ile Bourbon, renamed Réunion, and the Ile de France, together with the small possessions of the Comoros, were able to remain in a state of illegality with complete impunity. These islands simply did not implement the decree of 16 Pluviôse and came through the revolution with their slave system intact. For the settlers of this area, the restoration of May 1802 was not an innovation: they simply returned to being in harmony with a metropole that was rehabilitating the colonial values of the *ancien régime*.

The fights inside the Thermidorian Convention and then the Councils of the Directory to maintain the abolition of slavery were highlighted by several participants: they demonstrated that the heritage of the Enlightenment was not dead, in all its ambiguity. The constitution of Year II had, for the first time, introduced the principle of the 'assimilation' of the colonies to the metropole, with the same laws, the same administration and the same social order. The avowed purpose of this early policy of assimilation was of course to render impossible any restoration of slavery, that 'peculiarity' of the colonies so dear to the settlers under the *ancien régime*. But it had the consequence of denying all autonomy to these distant territories, and thus marked the triumph of the absolute power of the metropole over its colonies, something the old monarchy had dreamed of but had never been able to achieve. If France under the *Directoire* regarded the end of slavery and the slave trade as final, it had no intention of giving up its colonies; nor did it intend to give up conquering new ones. The Treaty of Basel in 1795 exemplified this desire for colonial expansion: France finally took over the whole island of Saint-Domingue, the old dream of the planters in their days of glory. The anti-slavery movement, apparently victorious, was reorganised in a rather different form: the Société des Amis des Noirs et des Colonies. The alteration was significant: colonies without slavery were quite legitimate.

Whatever the symbolic import of the decree of 16 Pluviôse Year II, we know that it was in force for only a short period – from February 1794 to May 1802, little more than eight years. The first abolition, imposed on a metropole engaged in foreign war and revolution, did not survive the circumstances that had made its existence possible. The prospect of approaching peace with Britain in 1802 and, above all, the ending of the republic and its replacement by the personal rule of Bonaparte, following the *coup d'état* of 18 and 19 Brumaire Year VIII, paved the way for the restoration of colonial slavery. The ways and means and consequences of this step backwards were minutely studied: the impact of the planters' lobby in the entourage of the First Consul; the desire for colonial expansion in Africa and Asia, even in Spanish America; the advent of schools of thought that openly denied the central thesis of the Enlightenment on the 'oneness of the human species' in favour of theories seeking to establish a hierarchy of races; the economic importance of the remaining French colonies after the independence of Haiti; but also the slow reorganisation of an abolitionist movement, still timid under the empire, then flowering under the Restoration and even more so under the July Monarchy.

The first half of the nineteenth century, going against what had become French policy since 1802, saw the development of a series of anti-slavery laws in the main European countries that had colonies. Britain abolished the slave trade and then slavery; the Netherlands and Denmark, and even Tunisia shortly after 1840, followed this example.

In the French colonies, both those retained and those recovered after the treaties of 1814 and 1815, the return to slavery was not always painless, chiefly in Guadeloupe, the only colony to have truly experienced the regime of 'general freedom' followed by the full restoration of slavery. There was a return to the 'classic' forms of resistance: running away (*marronnage*), revolts, and refusal to work and to eat. Insurrections, too, once again became widespread, although none took on the scale of the one in Saint-Domingue in 1791. The metropolitan government was vigilant and the repression did not wait for the rebellion to become widespread before coming down with the full force of the restored *Code noir*.

Yet, whatever the settlers may have thought, the restoration of the colonial *ancien régime* could not last forever: the revolutionary upheaval had left a deep imprint on mentalities, and the European colonial powers were moving gradually towards eliminating the slave trade and slavery. France itself could not escape this revival of anti-slavery, despite the return of the Bourbons and their determination – especially under Charles X and his minister Villèle, allied to powerful interests in Réunion – not to touch a system that had ensured the greatness of an *ancien régime* that was then being idealised. The anti-slavery movement slowly reorganised, mainly around philanthropic societies such as the Société de la Morale Chrétienne. Also, especially after 1830, the Liberals moved closer to the positions once defended by Smith, the physiocrats and the Amis des Noirs that the forced labour of the slave was less productive than the free labour of the wage-earner. It is thus highly likely that an abolitionist majority may have existed within the legislative body between 1840 and 1850, all the more so in that the ongoing conquest of Algeria, conceived as the prelude to more extensive settlement in Africa, assumed that France would clearly take an emancipationist line. After all, was it not proposing to bring 'civilisation' to the new colonies? But, whatever the intentions, the historically established fact remains that the regime of the 'citizen king' did not dare take this step of its own authority, perhaps for fear of reminding the then existing French ruling class of the tragic times of Year II, the only time when a French government had dared to vote for the abolition of slavery.

Then came the return of the republic, under the provisional government that emerged from the February days, which linked up with the abolitionist heritage of the First Republic. With the decisive drive of Victor Schoelcher, the decree of 27 April 1848 put a final end to slavery in the French colonies.

The final session of our symposium was wholly devoted to studying the conditions, procedures and implementation of the 1848 legislation, which none of the regimes that followed the Second Republic dared to call into question.

The year 1848 was indeed, for the French colonies, the end of the legal existence of slavery, which does not mean that other forms of unfreedom did not continue to exist, or indeed to be created from scratch by colonisers at the end of the nineteenth or beginning of the twentieth century, as one of the papers at this last session showed for West Africa.

We can thus understand how complex was the process that led to the abolition of slavery. It would be idle, and pointlessly polemical, to claim to be able to say which factor was the single decisive element. The role of slave revolts cannot and must not be minimised. But it is equally certain that the balance of metropolitan political power was another essential component of the process of abolition: how can we fail to observe that the two French abolitions, in Year II and in April 1848, coincided with the coming to power of 'radical republican' political groups? The collapse of the republic in Year VIII paved the way for the return of the colonial *ancien régime*. There was thus indeed a close correlation between the struggles of the slaves for their own freedom and the coming to power in Paris of some of the people who had made the cause of the slaves their chief political battle. On this point, the Jacobins of Year II were just as divided as the republicans of 1848, but in both cases the context made possible the victory of supporters of immediate abolition. We know that in both Year II and 1848 the outcome would certainly have been very different if the events had happened a few months later: it is unlikely that the Thermidorian coalition would have had the temerity to opt for abolition, just as one may doubt the anti-slavery intentions of the conservative republicans who came to power after the bloody repression of June 1848.

Note

1. The proceedings were published in 1995 under the title *Les abolitions de l'esclavage: 1793, 1794, 1848*. Paris, UNESCO/Presses universitaires de Vincennes.

Part IV

Contributions, Continuity and Cultural Dynamics

Chapter 24

The All-Americas/All-American African Diaspora

Sheila S. Walker

IT WAS ONLY WHEN ATTENDING an Afro-Brazilian *candomblé* ceremony more than two decades later that I began to really understand the meaning of something I had experienced as a child at Hopewell Baptist Church in Newark, New Jersey – seeing respectable, well-dressed ladies with hats and purses suddenly 'get happy', 'shout', 'feel the spirit', behave in a way quite different from their everyday secular behaviour.

It was when studying Wolof, the major language of the Senegambia region of West Africa, that I understood the source of terms like 'jive' and 'hip', 'jive cat' and 'hip cat', introduced into American English by African American musicians, and that I learned the origin of the exclamation 'Wow!'.

It was when learning about African naming patterns that I really understood why the last name of a man I met skiing was Coffey and that of a boy I knew in high school was Cuff. It was when learning about places from which enslaved Africans had left the continent that I understood the evocative meaning of the first name, Weda, of a girl from the same high school.

And it was in West Africa that I came to understand why okra and black-eyed peas are part of the diet of white Southerners as well as being important constituents of United States African American soul food nationally.

What I was understanding was that the African American culture to which I belong – even as a northern, urban, middle-class person who grew up in ethnically integrated neighbourhoods, always attended predominantly white schools, and whose father and paternal grandmother were born in New Jersey and New York state respectively – continues to reflect its African ancestry almost two centuries after the official end of the transatlantic slave trade and the importation of Africans to the United States.

I also began to understand that the African cultural presence in the United States and the rest of the Americas is not limited to people whose epidermic melanin visually reflects their African ancestry. It is rather an integral part of the United States 'mainstream' – i.e. presumably white – culture that is allegedly its antithesis, not a recent 'crossover' or 'pop culture' phenomenon. And it is fundamental to the cultural fabric of the nation.

This understanding became the basis for my knowledge concerning the larger issue of both the cultural continuum from Africa to the Americas and the cultural unity of the African diaspora in the Western hemisphere. I also learned that one can not fully understand the societies of the African diaspora in isolation, but only comparatively with respect to both their historical evolution and their contemporary dynamics. Learning more about the unmistakably African elements of other societies of the Americas throws light on certain, less immediately obvious elements of their presence in the United States.

When looked at in the larger African and African diasporan context, 'getting happy', 'shouting' and 'feeling the spirit' in Hopewell Baptist Church take on greater meaning as an aspect, and a symbol, of the African cultural continuum to the Americas and the cultural unity of the African diaspora. This is especially clear when the act of going into a religious trance and doing the holy dance as a manifestation of receiving and being moved by the spirit, in the context of a US African American Protestant ceremony, is seen through the mirror of 'manifesting the *orishas*' in the Afro-Brazilian *candomblé* and having the *loa* 'dance in one's head' in Haitian voodoo. These spiritual expressions are both behaviourally and conceptually analogous although one is 'Christian' and the others are acknowledged to be of African origin and belong to religious institutions that have retained much of their African identity in an American – in the hemispheric sense – context.

In these instances the relationship between the human and the divine is so intimate that the entering of divine beings into the bodies of their human worshippers – who literally *embody* the divine energies when they are 'filled with the spirit' – is the *sine qua non* of religious ceremony. If the spirit does not 'move' anyone to make evident its presence in the human community, if the *orishas* or *loa* do not 'come down' or 'manifest', if no worshippers 'make a joyful noise unto the Lord' by dancing and shouting the divine presence in their bodies, no spiritual communion has taken place. An Afro-Cuban woman, in comparing Euro-Christian worship with the worship of the *orishas* said, 'We understand that your deities are content with just prayers, but our deities like to dance.'

The kind of intimate relationship between human and divine beings which assumes that it is not just a possibility but rather a privilege for divine beings to manifest their presence in the bodies of their worshippers through ecstatic trance and dance is characteristic of some African peoples and their descendants in the Americas. The similarities in behaviour and spiritual explanation thereof reflect their common origins, even for American Afro-Protestants whose Euro-Protestantism has been profoundly modified by underlying African patterns that determine beliefs about how one feels the spirit and manifests its presence – whether the participants know or acknowledge this fact or not. In fact, Sobel, in *The World They Made Together: Black and White Values in Eighteenth-Century Virginia* (1987), even asserts that much of the contemporary ecstatic behaviour of white Christian denominations in the United States was originally learned from their spiritual contact with African Americans.

Elements of African sacred and/or secular culture exist in the societies of the Americas from Argentina to Canada, whether people of African origin are the obvious majority, as in most of the Caribbean, or an almost invisible and often believed extinct minority, as in Argentina, or some more or less significant proportion in between, as in Brazil and the United States – the countries with the second and third largest populations of African origin after Nigeria.

The elements of African culture that exist in the Americas may take the form of religious institutions whose African roots are obvious, such as the *candomblé* in Brazil, *shango* in Trinidad and the *Regla de Ocha* (or *Santeria*) in Cuba, all of Yoruba origin from what are now Nigeria and Benin, and voodoo in Haiti, of predominantly Fon origin, also from Benin. Or they may take the form of behaviour the African origins of which may be less apparent and may even be denied by its practitioners, such as 'getting happy' in traditional African American Protestant churches in the United States.

To the extent that African culture is conceded to exist in some of these American societies, it is usually relegated to the realm of 'folklore'. In reality, however, the African cultural presence is a part of the mainstream national culture, and constitutes some part of the cultural repertoire of the population of non-African as well as of visible African origin throughout the Americas, especially in expressive culture such as music, dance, cuisine and language. Thus, for example, in Argentina, which had a significant Afro-Argentinean population in the nineteenth century, but where the few thousand remaining Afro-Argentineans neither form a community nor share a sense of common identity, both Afro- and Euro-Argentineans have as their national dance the tango, eat *mondongo* (a spicy chitlin' stew) and use expressions such as *Que quilombo* (What a mess), all of which are of Central African Bantu origin.

Elements of specific African societies are represented in different ways in the Americas, the following examples being merely suggestive. As Yoruba and Fon culture are represented in religious institutions, Akan culture from Ghana and Côte d'Ivoire is represented in names and folktales. The Akan people name children according to their day of birth. Some of those names have remained as family rather than personal names in Jamaica, Suriname and the United States, such as 'Coffey' or 'Cuff' from 'Kofi', designating a boy born on Friday. The process of using these day names as family names in conjunction with European first names now also occurs in Africa as a result of the European colonial influence. And stories about Anansi, or Kweku or Kwaku Anansi, the wily spider who, like Brer Rabbit in the United States, outwits bigger, stronger animals, continue to be found in Jamaica and Suriname. In some parts of South Carolina Anansi became Aunt Nancy, an elderly African American woman who outsmarts powerful white men.

Ouidah, or Weda in its English rather than French spelling, a coastal town in the Republic of Benin, was a port from which many enslaved Africans left the continent. Weda remains in the Unites States as an African American female name, in most cases probably without the bearer's knowing its origin.

On the culinary side, okra and black-eyed peas prepared in various ways came to the Americas from Africa. The black-eyed pea fritters that gave birth to bean cakes in North Carolina are known as *acra* or *acara* in much of West Africa and *acaraje* in Brazil. Other dishes also retained their names, such as *calalloo* from Benin, which is found in most of the Caribbean as well as in Brazil with the simple 'l' to 'r' transformation that makes it *caruru*. And Louisiana has its gumbo, whose antecedents are found in the okra stews of much of West and Central Africa.

Traditional African American rhythms and dances of the Western hemisphere tend to have Central African Bantu names, like the Uruguayan *candombe*, the Brazilian samba, the Cuban rumba, the Colombian *cambia* and the Puerto Rican *bamba*. And Wolof, the dominant language of Senegal and the Gambia, has given mainstream United States English as ubiquitous an exclamation as 'wow', which in Wolof means 'yes'. Wolof is also the source of terms such as 'jive cat', 'hip cat' and 'honky'. *Jef* in Wolof means 'not serious', and *khat* refers to someone who does something, such that *jefkhat* is a person who is not serious – a jive cat. *Khipi* in Wolof means to have one's eyes open, to know what's happening, to be a hip cat. And Europeans are described as *khonkhe nopp,* or 'red ears', leading to 'honky' in the United States because of the effect of the sun on skin with only a slight degree of melanin. In American English, it is the neck rather than the ears that is seen as red.

Thus, identifiable elements of specific African cultures have remained in the societies of the Americas, sometimes in obvious ways and sometimes in camouflaged form, either deliberately as a means of preserving prohibited practices, or by historical accident as African cultures evolved in contact with others. European culture was defined as superior by the Europeans and Euro-Americans in power, and was imposed upon and taken on to a considerable degree by people of African origin. What began as a Euro-American veneer most often came to be understood, even by its practitioners, as the substance, obscuring the understanding of underlying African patterns of behaviour and meaning that constitute the real substance.

To return to 'feeling the spirit' at Hopewell Baptist Church, a comparison between the United States and other societies of the Americas makes evident the behavioural and conceptual Africanity of this United States Afro-Protestant phenomenon, even though most of its practitioners would probably deny that they or their religious behaviour had anything to do with Africa, and would insist that what they were doing was purely Christian, meaning European, white and definitely non-African. Such spirit-feeling sisters might even say, 'I ain't left nothin' in no Africa', as many African Americans have been heard to say, consciously distancing themselves from Africa – intellectually denying while simultaneously behaviourally acknowledging their continuing relationship with the continent of origin of their most significant ancestors, those responsible for their social and cultural identity and behaviour as African Americans. African conceptual and behavioural patterns persist all over the Americas, especially in the populations of African origin, whether acknowledged or not, whether denied or not, whether wanted or not.

These church sisters, like most African Americans, have been taught and have learned well that Africa is not the kind of place with which someone aspiring to an All-American (meaning as white as possible under contradicting circumstances) identity with its attendant privileges and benefits should want to identify. And they honestly do not realise how comparatively unsuccessful they have been in ridding themselves of persistent concepts and behaviours that continue to betray their African origins and how their ancestors infiltrated into religious and other cultural institutions of European origin imposed by or acquired from whites.

This denial of African cultural ancestry is superseded by the more generalised denial of – or failure to acknowledge or seek to understand – the African contributions to the national culture of the United States, not just to the culture of the African American community. African Americans have, of course, remained the locus of most culture of African origin because of the historical and contemporary socially and culturally segregated nature of the society. Thus, if northern, urban, middle-class African Americans from integrated environments and institutions continue to have elements of obviously African culture as part of their everyday repertoire – as opposed to those elements they may have deliberately introduced as manifestations of a Pan-African consciousness – it is logical that those African Americans from more culturally dense environments with less ethnically integrated/diluted institutions live a version of African American culture that continues to manifest more clearly and profoundly its African ancestry.

Prior to the 1940s, the general assumption, and the state of the research, was that although elements of African culture may have continued to exist in other societies of the Americas, including ethnically pluralistic ones such as Brazil and Cuba, they had not survived the institution of slavery in the United States because of its more culturally destructive form. Such an assumption satisfied both the Eurocentric perspective that African culture had no value and the position of the majority of African Americans who, in addition to having learned the Eurocentric bias, also believed that an assimilationist stance asserting their 'Americanness' and denying and trying to rid themselves of their 'Africanness' was in their best interests as a way of ending legal segregation and gaining access to the benefits associated with white US citizenship. Hence, the publication in 1941 of anthropologist Melville Herskovits's *The Myth of the Negro Past* – in which he demonstrated on the basis of comparative field research in West Africa and several societies of the African diaspora that, as in other societies of the Americas, aspects of African culture remained in the population of African origin in the United States – was not enthusiastically received by either camp.

The Herskovits-Frazier debate ensued in which Herskovits defended his thesis and African American sociologist E. Franklin Frazier, author of *The Negro in the United States* (1949), countered with the argument that the institution and experience of slavery had destroyed any African culture that had survived the middle passage to the United States. Frazier, as an African American committed to integrating into American society, would not logically have been interested in finding and acknowledging African elements in what was then termed 'Negro' or 'coloured' behaviour, Africa being assumed to be uncivilised at best, and African Americans having distanced themselves from the term 'African American' in the late nineteenth century in favour of assimilation and in reaction to the threat of deportation to the African continent. The idea that there was a legitimate culture that could be characterised as 'African American' by respected scholars, and claimed and affirmed by middle-class African Americans who have made it into one of the major institutions of the larger society, was at that time three decades into the future.

Even then, however, some African American scholars sought to discover the African roots of African American culture. Linguist Lorenzo Dow Turner made a major contribution to this effort with his book *Africanisms in the Gullah Dialect* (1949), in which he discussed the African basis of the speech of the people of the Sea Islands off the coast and in the coastal regions of Georgia and South Carolina. It was not until the 1970s that most linguists began to acknowledge that African American speech constitutes a legitimate system reflecting its African roots, and that African languages have even affected the English spoken by some whites – the Southern drawl, for example, being considered the result of traces left on Euro-American tongues by the tonal languages of some involuntary African immigrants.

A key issue concerning the origins of African American culture in the United States is the nature of the alternative to understanding it as a creolised form blending elements of its diverse African ethnic heritages with elements of the specific European, and sometimes Native American, cultures in the midst of which Africans found themselves in the Americas. This alternative is the outmoded, but not yet eliminated, perspective that African American culture is deficient/defective, that African Americans speak bad English and that the ecstatic spiritual behaviour characteristic of traditional Afro-Protestant churches is at worst pathological and at best an emotional release in response to severe oppression – but certainly not a manifestation of a sophisticated spiritual philosophy that is part of a religious system common to many peoples of Africa and their descendants in the Americas.

As a result of area-specific historical and demographic factors, such as when the importation of Africans ended, the relative proportion of Africans and Europeans, and which specific African and European ethnic groups were in contact, African cultural elements in the different societies of the Americas are more or less obvious, more or less blended both among African cultures and with European and Native American forms, and are more or less limited to the population defined as being of African origin, such definitions varying from society to society. These African cultural elements may be so pervasive that Fidel Castro, for example, could validly characterise multiethnic Cuba as an Afro-Latin society in which the African contribution is an integral and inextricable component of the fabric of the national culture common to all Cubans.

The United States is the only society in the Americas that has created a simplistic binary division into people of African and people of European origin, with any degree of African admixture defining the person as African American – the assumption being that culture can be strictly colour-coded. This binary construction of reality mandates the fiction that African culture can have remained only in the population of African origin and cannot be a part of mainstream United States culture, which is supposedly an exclusively Euro-American preserve. The only problem with this idea, as with the view that African American culture can be seen as insufficiently or ineptly acquired Euro-American culture, is that it is contradicted not only by the nature of culture, but also by the empirical data.

Although culture functions in a much more fluid and dynamic way than that posited by the binary theory, and is no respecter of degree of epidermic melanin, social definitions and barriers in the United States and legal and post-legal segregation have created and reinforced a situation in which African culture remains mainly, but by no means exclusively, concentrated in the African American population. Given the nature of historic and present representations of Africa in the United States, it is logical that those people presumably most marginal to the 'mainstream', who continue to live the most dense elements of African culture, have also learned to be unaware of and to deny the African influences in their behaviour. The wonderful irony, however, is that it is precisely this most African repository of African American culture that unceasingly evolves and creates new cultural forms that continue to infiltrate more and more aggressively and obviously into the United States 'mainstream', even further 'muddying' those already not so limpid waters, the commoditisation and commercialisation of these cultural elements by the 'mainstream' establishment serving to even further embed them therein.

Bibliography

FRAZIER, E.F. 1949. *The Negro in the United States*. New York, Macmillan.
HERSKOVITS, M. 1941. *The Myth of the Negro Past*. Boston, Beacon Press.
SOBEL, M. 1987. *The World They Made Together: Black and White Values in Eighteenth-Century Virginia*. Princeton, Princeton University Press.
TURNER, L.D. 1949. *Africanisms in the Gullah Dialect*. Chicago, University of Chicago Press.

Chapter 25

The Role of Africa and Blacks in the Building of the Americas: Focus on Colombia

Nina S. de Friedemann

> The social sciences have taught us to decipher the various destinations and mul-
> tiple vocations and utilities of commemorations. Often erected into privileged
> moments of withdrawal into oneself, exclusion of the Other and self-exaltation,
> they can also constitute a fruitful opportunity for critical thinking and a clear look
> at oneself, which can generate clear-sightedness, tolerance and openness.[1]

THAT THE CELEBRATION of the fifth centenary of the discovery of America, in
1992, should be regarded as the commemoration of the encounter of not two,
but three or four worlds demonstrates that historiographical knowledge has,
fortunately, lost its innocence. The fact that the historical and contemporary
reality of the participation of Africa and blacks in the building of the Americas
is being debated is evidence of this new perspective, which is in turn paving the
way for a self-reconciliation of the American continents by ending the covering
up of the role played by Africans and their descendants in the New World.

In Colombia, where some new thinking seems to be developing, promoted by the demand for rights to human diversity, there has been a marked
retreat of ideas that were common currency in this Latin American country 25
years ago. At that time, members of the African diaspora were not even
deemed fit subjects for anthropological study, and Africa, the ancestral home
of the black population residing in major pockets in vast areas of the country,
was hardly part of the nation's present. In short, the condition stated by Nobel
Prize winner Wole Soyinka[2] – that, to fulfil its mission, history must be capable of interrogating the present – was far from being met.

At the dawn of the third millennium, we might try to interrogate the present. We might not only ask, as I have been doing for 10 years and more in our
anthropology congresses and those of other disciplines, why there is no teaching of the history of Africa and no anthropology of the African diaspora in
Colombia, but also ask why our universities, our social science faculties, with
their departments and the agencies responsible for education, continue to
avoid this question.

The Senegalese researcher Cheikh Anta Diop has shown that the eradication and destruction of the historical awareness of the past has always been part and parcel of the techniques of colonising, enslaving and bastardising peoples of the African continent.[3] In Africa in the seventeenth century, 'the Ashanti empire, in particular, was built up by conquest. But the *griots* [traditional historians, rather like troubadours, specialists in music, genealogists or ambassadors] of the various basic communities were forbidden to mention the real origin of the basic communities. Any infringement of this rule was punished by death, the *griots* being diligently taught the new official version of national history, in such a way as to eliminate all memory of past confrontations and create consciousness of complete unity and national harmony'.[4] While it is true that the history of the aboriginal peoples of America has also suffered from this kind of technique, the history of Africa and the African diaspora in the Americas has been the most strongly affected.

Contrary to what happened in countries like Colombia, in Africa, since the late 1950s, there has been a growing awareness of the effects of the destruction of knowledge of the past and the urgency of recovering it. African intellectuals are currently using European techniques of investigating the past and endeavouring to develop their own approach in order to bring out, on their continent and in the Western world, the history of Africa as seen from the viewpoint of Africans.[5] Their work has helped to weaken some of the pseudo-scientific racist myths that had disfigured that past, resulting in declarations such as 'Africa has no history'. These myths were based on a sociocultural scale of values closely tied to the degree of skin pigmentation, with blacks at the bottom, among the non-civilised, the *others*. In that context, the history of Africans and their descendants in the New World was a question of no importance or value, and it would have been totally incongruous to mention their contribution to the societies in which they were living.

Thoughts and Actions

The process of decolonisation in Africa brought about a movement of self-assertion among its peoples and nations. The socio-political and economic upheaval of the post-colonial period affected the areas of education and science. The teaching of a decolonised history became a strategic weapon in the battle to eradicate racist prejudices.

In the 20 years that followed 1950, during the process of decolonisation, some five hundred historians with a doctorate or equivalent qualification were trained and became involved in research, and in publishing and teaching their analyses and studies.[6] The Arabic, Chinese, European and Hindu sources written prior to and after the fifteenth century that they have studied[7] reveal encounters between Africa and other worlds long before 1492. Elikia M'Bokolo, one of these historians and currently director of studies at the Ecole des Hautes Études en Sciences Sociales (EHESS) in Paris, has looked at relations between eastern Asia and the African continent. These studies make it possible to grasp the role played by Africa in time, space and historical circumstances, and totally rule out the notion that the year 1492 demarcates an absolute beginning, the inaugural date of the shift from a plural world to a single global space.

On the contrary, M'Bokolo[8] and many African scholars regard what happened in 1492 as part of a series of beginnings from which Africa was never absent. From this angle, the hypothesis – regarded as 'blasphemy' by Western scholarship in particular – of contacts between Africa and America in pre-Columbian times is constantly borne in mind and is encouraging the quest for evidence of all sorts. In the account given by Ibn Fadl Allal Al Omari of a meeting that Kanku Musa, emperor of Mali, had with the governor of Cairo at the time of his pilgrimage to the holy places of Islam in 1324, reference is made to the attempts of Kanku Musa's predecessor, Mansa Abubakar II, to have the Atlantic Ocean explored.[9] Publication of documents such as this reflects the concern to stimulate research on ancient navigation techniques in Africa, one of the most neglected areas of the new historiography of the continent. While the research has not yet been focused on this area, this does not mean that such techniques did not exist. Proof of that is the experiment of Thor Heyerdahl, who left Safi on 25 May 1969 in his reed boat – named *Râ I*, built using the techniques of the Buduma of Chad – and travelled 4,345 kilometres to reach the Caribbean on 18 July.[10]

In Colombia, among the hypotheses regarded as blasphemous is also that of the archaeologist Donald Lathrap,[11] who asserts that certain processes at work in the Old World – in particular, those of plant domestication – derive from a single model of experimentation developed in Africa 40,000 years ago in Early Stone Age times by representatives of the Sangoan and Lupemban cultures.[12] He argues that a group of African fishermen may have landed somewhere on the northern coast of Brazil more than 12,000 years ago. Having set out in search of shoals, they could have been carried by marine currents away from the western coast of Africa to a point between Recife and the mouth of the Amazon. Were they on rafts or in fishing boats? Were they carried along with their nets and with seeds of the bottle gourd (*Lagenaria siceraria*), a plant domesticated in Africa which cannot reproduce without human help? Were these seeds used by the inhabitants of the South American coast?

For a decade, little was made of this hypothesis. But, in recent years, the number and antiquity of settlement sites on the South American continent, such as the site of Pedra Furada, in north-eastern Brazil, which dates back 32,000 years, and other data pointing in the same direction, have restored Lathrap's theories to a place of honour at the centre of the concerns animating the new historiography in Africa. From the viewpoint of the encounter of different worlds, this hypothesis would indicate that contacts occurred at a very early date.[13]

Living Tradition

To return to Africans' thinking about their history and its recovery, we shall mention here studies such as those of A. Hampaté Ba,[14] rooted in oral tradition.

'Living tradition', as he calls it, is synonymous with the 'great history of life', which embraces the history of lands and waters, plants, the veins that run through the depths of the earth, the stars and, of course, the human being, the symbiosis of all the histories, in whom resides something of everything that existed before humankind.

The collection and evaluation of oral tradition with a view to recovering the past are continuing in Africa. Their importance is illustrated by the results of the comparison between traditions collected by the chronicler Cavazzi in the seventeenth century – epics, literary tales and cosmogonic data – and research on local traditions conducted on the ground in 1970. This made it possible to sketch the outline of the dynasties and socio-political changes that had occurred in the region of the upper Kwango in Angola,[15] and to highlight the epic resistance to the slave trade that went on uninterruptedly in this region, as it did in others, from the seventeenth to the end of the nineteenth century.

The Transatlantic Slave Trade: Some Thoughts

Yet the transatlantic slave trade remains a burning topic in the thinking and practice of a new historiography in Africa. For Africans, it is the most visible, lasting and serious consequence of the encounter between Africa, Europe and America. It is also a highly sensitive issue which heightens guilt feelings and arouses a multitude of reactions. While it is true that Europeans did not invent slavery, which was an ancient activity in Africa, practised on a small scale in order to ensure the social reintegration of individuals who had lost their families in wars and other disasters, it remains the case that the arrival of the Europeans changed its nature and turned it into something on an enormous scale[16] – so much so that the effects of the profound upheaval it caused in African society at the time can still be felt today.

African intellectuals also feel that this demographic blood-letting, which deprived the continent of millions of human beings and went on for more than three centuries, was an enterprise of sociocultural elimination directed by alliances made between the ruling strata of the two civilisations, European and African.[17] In the opinion of many researchers, it partly explains the weakness of socio-political resistance to the process of colonisation carried out by Europe in the nineteenth century. Paradoxically, the internal wars and the brutal forced intercontinental migration constituted the stuff of the Afro-American diaspora that has become an integral part of America.

These facts are relatively well known, but those that attest to African resistance to the slave trade in Africa are less so. It is even rarer that they are interpreted as traces of Africanism in the behaviour of the American *cimarrons* (rebel slaves), whose liberation ideology was expressed in the terms used to name them: *palenques*, *kilombos*, *mambises*, *cumbes* or *mocambos*. Works of the new African historiography, such as those of Oruno D. Lara,[18] highlight the evidence of this resistance incarnated, in Guinea, by the Bijagos and, in Kongo, by the Jaga. Between 1568 and 1587, there was a movement of opposition to the slave trade known as the 'long transit of the Jaga, from Africa to the New World'. This involved groups of warriors made up of men and women fighting side by side, equipped with a strong political, religious and military organisation, which operated over vast areas from stockades or *kilombos*, a word which, in Brazil, was to describe runaway black slaves. In the course of their expeditions, they invaded Kongo which they laid waste in order to disorganise the Portuguese slave trade. Their aim, according to Lara, was the conquest and destruction of kingdoms allied to the Europeans for the slave trade.

According to Lara,[19] the writings of Giovanni Antonio Cavazzi provide a description of the African *kilombo* and information on its social and religious organisation. Yet, to date, the historiography of the Afro-Colombian diaspora has been unaware of or, at any event, has made no use of these data on the African past of resistance to the slave trade, despite their importance for the analysis of the phenomenon of the *cimarrons* and, generally, the study of black groups. It is an example which, on the one hand, shows how far the invisibility of African history goes – an invisibility that is manifested in the historiography of black groups as well as in the historiography of Colombia more generally – and, on the other hand, illustrates the urgency of actively organising exchanges between Africanist researchers and Afro-Americanist specialists, not to mention the necessity of encouraging, in our country, the training of teams of scholars from the culture of the diaspora.

The Family: A Different Perspective

In Colombia, particularly in the area of research on the family, the ethnocentric approach adopted by various researchers is a good illustration of the problem of the invisibility of Africa and blacks in the world of academe. By seeking to explain the African situation using concepts such as those of the nuclear monogamous family, research has committed errors and inaccuracies. It would seem that the classical model of the extended family, made up of two nuclear families or more, put forward by Murdock,[20] does not fit the facts, either in Africa or in Afro-America.

The studies by Niara Sudarkasa reveal that in the African extended family, the bond of consanguinity is more important than the conjugal one. As for the conjugal cycle, it comprises two equivalent phases – of monogamy at first and then polygamy. Whether a man has, or has had, one wife and children, two wives and children, or many wives and children, his is only one family. When it comes to defining the monogamous phase of this family, we must obviously go beyond the ideology that underlies the notion of the monogamous nuclear family in Western society, since, in the African extended family, this phase is not institutionally isolated, either in its formation or in its functioning.[21]

It is this aspect that, according to Africanists, is misunderstood and distorted in theoretical discussions of this subject, when it is said that these families are 'multiple families' with a husband-father in common,[22] or when no account is taken of the fact that their stability depends not on the conjugal union, in its monogamous or polygamous phase, but on the exercise of the right of consanguinity within the family group, the foundation of which is generally polygynous.

In Colombia as in other Latin American countries, the nuclear, monogamous Christian family has been made into a paradigm of historical and contemporary analyses of social organisation at the national level, such that no interest is taken in survivals of the African extended family in the lives of the black family. The discovery of polygynous forms has led, on the contrary, to the roles of women and men in the psycho-economic and affective domain being transformed into stereotypes.[23]

To mention, as I have just done, the survivals of 'Africanness' or the chains of iconic associations is to come close to Gregory Bateson's arguments[24] on the language of icons, which may in turn be linked to the concept of 'cognitive orientations' proposed by Mintz and Price[25] for the study of the problems of the development of Afro-American cultures. The Africanist anthropologist Niara Sudarkasa[26] takes the same line: for her, the most important legacy of Africa in the diaspora is that of the extended family, which has re-created ethical principles, modes of behaviour, structural characteristics and cognitive orientations in new codes of kinship which have enabled blacks to survive, both physically and culturally, in the New World.

The Diaspora: A Divergence

I can easily understand that these thoughts might appear to reflect some very particular concerns, even in a work aspiring, as this one does, to disciplinary diversity. Doubtless this would be less the case if our cultural and historiographical training did not exclude groups of African origin. In addition, I have taken the liberty of not exploring the hackneyed topic of the contributions of Africa to the music, dance and religious songs of the Americas. For while they offer valuable material for the study of Afro-American patterns of development, they have provided the basis for the formation of social-scientific imagery that the institutions responsible for administering cultural programmes continue to manipulate, sometimes succeeding in disarming the protests aroused by the denial of historiographical and anthropological knowledge in the self-assertion of the Afro-Colombian diaspora within the nation. There are numerous programmes described as 'folkloric', in which people play the drum and dance the *mapalé*, but there are very few congresses devoted to Afro-Colombian oral tradition, or the development of the black family and black culture in general. That has not prevented the strength of the diaspora from flourishing in such national emblems as the *cumbia*, the carnival, the *vallenato* or the poetic world of Macondo in Gabriel Garcia Márquez's *One Hundred Years of Solitude*. These are all manifestations of the African poetic and narrative heritage and of ancient iconographies, all remodelled by the creativity that made possible the growth of a black America in a new world.[27]

In the context of the reflection prompted by the celebration of the fifth centenary of the discovery of the Americas, it is – as Bonfil Batalla has stressed in Chiapas[28] – the asymmetrical situations of formation and information, like those I have mentioned about Africans and their descendants, that are now in the forefront of concerns, both in the Americas and in Africa. It is they, too, that call urgently for changes.

In Colombia, where blacks lack visibility because, in the national system, they are the Other, it is urgent to begin to explain why their exclusion persists. In an article that he devoted to the new Colombian constitution and the fate meted out in it to the identity and territorial demands of blacks, Jaime Arocha mentions the influence that has continued to be exerted by the binary socio-racial artifice that underlay the constitution of 1886 and from which flowed in 1991 the manifest intention, in particular on the part of politicians and social scientists, to gloss over the history and presence of blacks in the Colombian nation and nationality, and their effort to eliminate them as socio-ethnic subjects.[29]

Thus, I feel it is inappropriate that the new constitution of 1991 should declare that Colombia is a multiethnic nation and, at the same time, make no mention of the presence in the country, for more than two hundred years, of communities of black miners, fishermen and farmers. To do so is to legitimise the territorial exclusion of the Afro-Colombians of the Pacific coast. Provisional article 55 of the constitution provides for the existence of *empty lands* in the rural coastal areas along the Pacific, occupied by black communities. It is not enough to pay lip service to plurality and diversity: they must be respected and legitimised.[30]

The artifice that I have just mentioned consisted in the application of a numerical system in which the number 1 – person – corresponded to the mestizo and the figure 0 – non-person – to the Indian.[31] By adopting ideals of liberty and progress resting on the myth of miscegenation without abandoning the archetype of the white race, post-slavery society adapted itself to new realities.

But this artifice, which gave visibility to the Indian, continued to deny it to the black descendant of Africans and other heirs to the same tradition. This meant the institutionalisation of the norm of socio-biological whitening as a means of social mobility. A single race, a single language and a single religion – this profession of social faith of the new nation was thus turned into a formula for the exclusion of the Other by the One.

In accordance with the hypotheses of Gregory Bateson, this formula has become a conviction that has shaped both perceptions and plans which were originally deliberately pursued. Repetition has incorporated these latter into unconscious forms of behaviour which are expressed in the everyday culture of institutions, disciplines, universities and, of course, individuals whose rules of behaviour and relations with groups and the black population they modify. Bateson[32] adds that in the implementation of plans deliberately pursued by an individual or an institution, all information that does not fit into the theoretical and cultural model previously established is subconsciously eliminated.[33] Any action that does not contribute to the maintenance of a given system, in other words the status quo, constitutes a divergence. Thus, in the process of constructing the Colombian national identity, the goal of introducing into the system knowledge relating to the African diaspora, of which each representative is perceived as the Other, has become a divergence.

That, of course, has not ruled out the pursuit of individual and institutional actions that go against the status quo. The country has a team of eminent researchers who have decided to devote themselves to the study of black groups, although they do not receive at their university the specialist training required. In recent years, in the framework of its *Expedición humana* programme which extends the *América oculta*, the Universidad Javeriana has given a prominent place to *América negra*, an interdisciplinary research project including the publication of studies on Colombian, African and Afro-American black groups, and scholarly exchanges with African researchers and groups. However, Colombia still does not have a proper university course of study that prepares researchers to take up the many challenges that a programme of that scope involves in the specific area of Afro-America. But I am convinced that this gap will be filled soon in the new millennium.

Notes

1. E. M'Bokolo, 1995.
2. W. Soyinka, 1981, p. 157.
3. C.A. Diop, 1981, p. 64.
4. M. Towa, 1986, p. 150.
5. See J.D. Fage, 1980, p. 61 [Eng. ed., p. 40], and P.D. Curtin, 1980, p. 88 [Eng. ed., p. 54].
6. P.D. Curtin, 1980, p. 88 [Eng. ed., p. 64].
7. H. Djait, 1980; I. Hrbek, 1980.
8. E. M'Bokolo, 1995, p. 4.
9. See E. M'Bokolo, 1995; N.S. de Friedemann and J. Arocha, 1986; M.C. Diaw, 1983.
10. E. M'Bokolo, 1995.
11. D. Lathrap, 1977.
12. T. Shaw, 1972.
13. See N.S. de Friedemann, 1995; N.S. de Friedemann and J. Arocha, 1985.
14. A. Hampaté Ba, 1982.
15. J. Vansina, 1983, p. 182.
16. M. Gueye, 1979, p. 1.
17. B.K. Sélassié, 1995.
18. O.D. Lara, 1979, pp. 6 and 7 [Eng. ed., pp. 104–105].
19. Ibid.
20. G.P. Murdock, 1949.
21. N. Sudarkasa, 1980, p. 43.
22. Ibid.
23. N.S. de Friedemann and M. Espinosa Arango, 1994.
24. G. Bateson, 1972.
25. S. Mintz and R. Price, 1976.
26. N. Sudarkasa, 1980.

27. N.S. de Friedemann, in press.
28. G. Bonfil Batalla, 1991, pp. 83–91.
29. J. Arocha, 1992, pp. 39–56.
30. Act 70 of 1993 on the ethnic rights of the black communities was promulgated by the President of the Republic in Quibdo on 27 August 1993.
31. J. Arocha, 1992, p. 39.
32. G. Bateson, 1972.
33. G. Friedemann, 1992.

Bibliography

AROCHA, J. 1992. 'Los negros y la nueva constitución colombiana de 1991'. *América Negro* (Bogota), No. 3. Expedición humana, Pontificia Universidad Javeriana.

BATESON, G. 1972. *Steps to an Ecology of Mind*. New York, Ballantine Books.

BONFIL BATALLA, G. 1991. 'Diversidad y democracia: un futuro necesario'. In *Amerindia hacia el tercer milenio*. International seminar, San Cristóbal de la Casas (Chiapas, Mexico).

CAVAZZI DE MONTECUCCOLO, G.A. 1687. *Istorica descrizione deitre regni, Congo, Matamba e Angola, situati nell' Etiopia inferiore occidentale*. Bologna. [French adaptation published by Father Labat, Paris, 1735, 5 vols.]

CURTIN, P.D. 1980. 'Tendances récentes des recherches historiques africaines'. In Ki-Zerbo, J. (ed.). *Histoire générale de l'Afrique*. Vol. 1. Paris, UNESCO/Stock/Jeune Afrique [Eng. ed., 1981. 'Recent trends in African historiography and their contribution to history in general'. In Ki-Zerbo, J. (ed.). *General History of Africa*. Vol. 1. London, Heinemann Educational Books.]

DIAW, M.C. 1983. *Social and Production Relationships in the Artisanal Fisheries of West Africa: A Comparative Analysis*. Ann Arbor, University of Michigan Press.

DIOP, C.A. 1981. *De l'identité culturelle. L'affirmation de l'identité culturelle et la formation de la conscience nationale dans l'Afrique contemporaine*. Paris, UNESCO.

DJAIT, H. 1980. 'Sources écrites antérieures au XVe siècle'. In Ki-Zerbo, J. (ed.). *Histoire générale de l'Afrique*. Vol. 1. Paris, UNESCO/Stock/Jeune Afrique. [Eng. ed., 1981. 'Written sources before the fifteenth century'. In Ki-Zerbo, J. (ed.). *General History of Africa*. Vol. 1. London. Heinemann Educational Books.]

FAGE, J.D. 1980. 'Évolution de l'historiographie de l'Afrique'. In Ki-Zerbo, J. (ed.). *Histoire générale de l'Afrique*. Vol. 1. Paris, UNESCO/Stock/Jeune Afrique. [Eng. ed., 1981. 'The development of African historiography'. In Ki-Zerbo, J. (ed.). *General History of Africa*, vol. 1. London. Heinemann Educational Books.]

FRIEDEMANN, G. 1992. 'Bateson y el postmodernismo con razón y corazón'. *América Negra* (Bogota), No. 4. Expedición humana, Pontificia Universidad Javeriana.

FRIEDEMANN, N.S. de. 1993. *La saga del negro*. Bogota, Pontificia Universidad Javeriana.

———. 1995. 'Les Amériques africaines, les chemins du retour'. In M'Bokolo, E. (ed.) *L'Afrique entre l'Europe et l'Amérique*. Paris, UNESCO.

———. *Presencia africana en Colombia. Nuestra tercera raíz y proyección histórica y perpectivas de los pueblos afroamericanos*. V Centenario, Mexico, Conaculta (in press).

FRIEDEMANN, N.S. de, and AROCHA, J. 1985. *Herederos del jaguar y la anaconda.* 2nd ed. Bogota, Carlos Valencia Editores.

———. 1986. *De sol a sol. Génesis, transformación y presencia de los negros en Colombia.* Bogota, Planeta.

FRIEDEMANN, N.S. de, and ESPINOSA ARANGO, M. 1994. *La mujer negra en la historia de Colombia. Las mujeres en la historia de Colombia.* Bogota, Norma Editorial/Consejería presidencial para la juventud, la mujer et la familia.

GUEYE, M. 1979. 'La traite négrière à l'intérieur du continent africain'. In *La traite négrière du XVᵉ au XIXᵉ siècle.* Paris, UNESCO. (Working documents). [Eng. ed., 'The slave trade within the African continent'. In *The African Slave Trade from the Fifteenth to the Nineteenth Century.* Paris, UNESCO (Working documents).]

HRBEK, I. 1980. 'Sources écrites à partir du XVᵉ siècle'. In Ki-Zerbo, J. (ed.). *Histoire générale de l'Afrique.* Vol. 1. Paris, UNESCO/Stock/Jeune Afrique. [Eng. ed., 1981. 'Written sources from the fifteenth century onwards'. In Ki-Zerbo, J. (ed.). *General History of Africa.* Vol. 1. London. Heinemann Educational Books.]

LARA, O.D. 1979. 'Résistance et esclavage: de l'Afrique aux Amériques noires, XVᵉ–XIXᵉ'. In *La traite négrière du XVᵉ au XIXᵉ siècle.* Paris, UNESCO. (Working documents). [Eng. ed., 'Negro resistance to slavery and the Atlantic slave trade to black America'. In *The African Slave Trade from the Fifteenth to the Nineteenth Century.* Paris, UNESCO (Working documents).]

LATHRAP, D. 1977. 'Our father the Cayman, our mother the Gourd: Spinden revisited, or a unitary model for the emergence of agriculture in the New World'. In Reed, C.A. (ed.). *Origins of Agriculture.* New York, Mouton.

———. 1983. 'La antigüedad e importancia de las relaciones de intercambio a larga distancia en los trópicos húmedos de Sudamérica precolombina'. *Amazonia Peruana,* Vol. 4, No. 7, pp. 79–97.

M'BOKOLO, E. 1995. 'La rencontre des deux mondes et ses répercussions: la part de l'Afrique (1492–1992)'. In M'Bokolo, E. (ed.). *L'Afrique entre l'Europe et l'Amérique.* Paris, UNESCO.

MINTZ, S., and PRICE, R. 1976. *An Anthropological Approach to the Afro-American Past: A Caribbean Perspective.* Philadelphia, ISHI.

MURDOCK, G.P. 1949. *Social Structure.* New York, MacMillan.

SÉLASSIÉ, B.K. 1995. 'La dimension culturelle des futures relations entre l'Afrique et l'Amérique. L'essentiel et l'accessoire'. In M'Bokolo, E. (ed.). *L'Afrique entre l'Europe et l'Amérique.* Paris, UNESCO.

SHAW, T. 1972. 'The prehistory of West Africa'. In Ade Ajayi, J.F., and Crowder, M. (eds.). *History of West Africa.* Vol 1. New York, Columbia University Press.

SOYINKA, W. 1981. *De la renaissance culturelle africaine. L'affirmation de l'identité culturelle et la formation de la conscience nationale dans l'Afrique contemporaine.* Paris, UNESCO.

SUDARKASA, N. 1980. 'African and Afro-American family structure: a comparison'. *The Black Scholar: A Journal of Black Studies and Research* (Washington), Vol. 11, No. 8, pp. 37–60.

TOWA, M. 1986. *La spécificité et le dynamisme des cultures négro-africaines: une hypothèse de travail.* Paris, UNESCO.

VANSINA, J. 1983. *Oral Tradition as History.* Madison, University of Wisconsin Press.

Chapter 26

The African Presence in Brazil

Kabengele Munanga

Historical and Demographic Data

At the time of the discovery of Brazil, the Portuguese thought they would find gold and silver there as in Mexico and Peru, or spices or other marketable products as they had found in Asia. But they quickly found another source of income with the cultivation of sugar cane, as the Sicilians had done before them in their island. The first plantations came into being in the islands of Madeira, the Azores and São Tomé, which had been occupied by the Portuguese since 1420, and it was from these islands that they introduced sugar cane into the Latin American continent and, with it, the first blacks with some experience of plantation crops.

Sugar was the most important source of profit that Portugal could hope for from its colonies. The development of large sugar-cane plantations was promoted by the import of an abundant servile labour force. At the time, Brazil was inhabited by hundreds of thousands, even millions, of people, since some historians and writers speak of between 2.5 and 5 million Indians, as the Portuguese explorers called them, thinking they had landed in India.

We know that the Portuguese began by using the Indians as free labour. This was a failure: they were rapidly decimated, in particular by alcohol and diseases imported from Europe. So black slaves replaced the Indians in the plantations, all the more easily because the Portuguese had already been engaging in the slave trade with Africa since the fifteenth century.[1] We do not know the precise date at which the first African slaves were introduced into Brazil, but many authors agree that it occurred in the first half of the sixteenth century, probably between 1516 and 1526.[2] The destruction in 1891 of all documents and archives relative to the slave trade and slavery on the orders of the Brazilian government excludes any hope of knowing the precise number of blacks taken by force to Brazil. But on the basis of information gathered from documents found on slave vessels, or from inventories, wills, registers and surveys of captives, or from lists of liberated slaves and population censuses, it is estimated that some 4 million Africans were landed in Brazilian ports between

1551 and 1856,[3] between the legal trade and the smuggling that was intensified after the prohibition of the slave trade in 1850. Others incline to figures between 3 and 18 million for the number of Africans arriving in Brazil between the sixteenth and nineteenth centuries, when anti-slavery laws were promulgated leading to the abolition of slavery in 1888.[4]

We know when and from where the slaves were shipped, how long the crossing lasted and the types of vessel used. We know, too, that 10 per cent of the cargo died during the voyage from ill-treatment or contagious diseases. During the period of 'seasoning', acclimatisation to the country, a further 30 per cent fell ill or died, largely because of the harshness of the work.[5]

The demographic evolution of the Brazilian population shows that, until the 1830s, blacks constituted 63 per cent of the population, whites 16 per cent and mixed-race people 21 per cent (see Table 26.1). After 1850, when the slave trade was abolished, followed by the elimination of the slave system in 1888, the black population began to fall markedly because of bad living conditions and as a result of miscegenation with whites and Amerindians (see Tables 26.2 and 26.3).

Between 1950 and 1980, the criterion of skin colour was excluded from the general census of the Brazilian population, the class in power taking the view that stress should rather be put on the quest for national unity and identity and the reassertion of 'racial democracy'. The black opposition movements saw this retreat as a manoeuvre by the dominant class to conceal racial inequalities and the prejudices from which blacks were suffering. They therefore demanded that skin colour appear in the census of the population of Brazil, which was done in 1980.

As we have shown above, the black population of Brazil began to decline after 1850. By 1980, blacks represented about 6 per cent of the total population, as against 39 per cent for mixed-race, 55 per cent for whites and .6 per cent for Asians. Blacks and mixed-race people thus together made up about 44 per cent of the Brazilian population, as against 55 per cent whites and 1 per cent Asians. These figures must be interpreted with caution, given a racial ideology which, according to Oracy Nogueira, regards as relevant not the race of origin as in the United States of America but rather the apparent type – in other words, skin colour.[6] Thus, in censuses, individuals are classified not only according to their phenotypes but also, and above all, in terms of their position in society, the ideal being white, in skin colour or social position.

Table 26.1 Estimated Population of Brazil

Year	Author	Blacks	Whites	Mixed-Race	Total
1827	Rugendas	72.5%	15.5%	12.0%	100%
		3,758,000	800,000	638,000	5,186,000
1830	Malte-Brun	63.0%	16.0%	21.0%	100%
		5,340,000	1,347,000	1,748,000	8,435,000

Source: F. Mourão, 1977, p. 23.

Table 26.2 Estimated Slave Population of Brazil

Year	Authors	Slaves
1819	Councillor Veloso de Oliveira	1,107,000
1850	Senator C. Baptista de Oliveira	2,500,000
1869	Senator Thomas Pompeu de Souza Brasil	1,690,000
1872	Oliveira Viana	1,510,806

Source: F. Mourão, 1977, p. 23.

Table 26.3 Population by Skin Colour (in thousands)

Colour	1872 Total	1872 %	1890 Total	1890 %	1940 Total	1940 %	1950 Total	1950 %
White	3,854	38.0	6,302	44.0	26,206	63.5	32,028	61.9
Black	1,995	20.0	2,098	14.5	6,044	14.5	5,693	11.0
Mixed-race	4,262	42.0	5,934	41.5	8,760	21.3	13,787	26.5
Yellow					243	0.7	330	0.6
Total	10,112	100.0	14,334	100.0	41,253	100.0	51,838	100.0

Source: F. Mourão, 1977, p. 24.

According to Elza Berquió, the last 40 years have seen a relative decrease in the number of whites and blacks and an increase in the number of mixed-race (see Table 26.4).[7] The white population increased at an average rate of 2.10 per cent per annum between 1940 and 1950, 2.94 per cent between 1950 and 1960 and 2.16 per cent between 1960 and 1980, to reach 64,540,467 in 1980. Blacks fell from 6,035,869 to 5,692,657 between 1940 and 1950, a decrease of 0.58 per cent per annum. During the years that followed, their number rose by about 0.84 per cent and then fell to 0.61 per cent between 1960 and 1980. The number of mixed-race rose by 4.62 per cent between 1940 and 1950. Between 1950 and 1960, that rate fell to 4.09 per cent, and it reached 4.05 per cent between 1960 and 1980.

Today, when some researchers or black opposition movements claim that blacks make up about 45 per cent of the Brazilian population, the term 'black'

Table 26.4 Evolution of the Brazilian Population by Skin Colour (in %)

Year	Whites	Mixed-Race	Blacks
1940	64	21	15
1950	62	27	11
1960	61	30	9
1980	55	39	6

Sources: IBGE population censuses of 1940, 1950, 1960 and 1980.

has an ideological rather than a biological meaning, since it designates not only individuals with a black phenotype but also their mixed-race descendants.

Cultural Resistance

By contributing to the peopling of Brazil and the building of its economy with their unpaid labour, blacks left their mark on this country with the culture they brought from Africa. When they arrived in Brazil in the first half of the sixteenth century, uprooted from their sociocultural environment, the black slaves, who came from various geographical and cultural areas of sub-Saharan Africa, had lost nothing of their collective memory. They were equipped with wide-ranging knowledge not only of medicine, science and technology – in the fields of agriculture, hunting and fishing, and metalworking – but also of artistic creativity – music with its rhythms, dances and songs – and mythical systems of thought related to religions and wisdom. Thus blacks contributed to shaping the current personality of Brazil in every sector of social and cultural life.[8]

How was a culture that had been uprooted from its area of origin, from which it drew its strength, able to hold out against a Western-type dominant culture which asserted its superiority loud and clear? It will be remembered, for example, that aboard the slave ships African slaves were baptised, since the trade in blacks was legitimised – especially in the sixteenth century – by the duty to convert the black pagans. In Brazil, religion was one of the areas in which the resistance of African culture showed itself most tenaciously. Of course, the forces ranged against one another were unequal (how could it have been otherwise under a colonial regime?) since, by law, blacks were not allowed to practise their religion, relegated to the status of superstition, and were converted by force to Catholicism, the sole true faith.

Because abandoning their religious beliefs signified death for them, the slaves from Africa chose to resist – not frontally, but slyly – and they invented a variety of defence strategies, especially symbolic ones.[9] Their response to the dominant religion that was imposed on them by their masters was not immediate. And when, with the permission of their masters, they would meet on Sundays to relax with people from all ethnic groups – for in this way it was hoped to prevent them from forging a class-consciousness – they would take advantage of it to pay their respects to the gods of their traditions. In these practices of dances and rhythmic chanting to the sound of drums and the languages of home, the masters saw nothing more than the amusements of nostalgic Negroes.[10]

Then gradually the blacks became conscious of the lives of the saints and the history of the Catholic religion, with its structural, cultural and sociological features, which they compared to their own beliefs. In this way they came to shape a religious syncretism which enabled them to dissimulate, beneath the veil of a professed Catholicism, beliefs that came from the animist tradition and to protect themselves from any retribution from their masters. In the view of Roger Bastide, the discovery of structural similarities between the two types of religion predated the arrival of blacks in the Americas – their evange-lisation having begun in Africa a couple of centuries before the settlement of Brazil – and certain Dahomeyan and Congolese gods had already been identi-fied with Catholic saints.[11] For example, the Catholic pattern of the saints' intercession for humankind with the Virgin Mary, the Virgin's intercession with Jesus and Jesus' intercession with God the Father is reminiscent of the Yoruba cosmology in which the *orishas* act as mediators between humanity and the god Olorum. Similarly, in the Catholic religion, each saint presides over a human activity or is responsible for healing a certain disease. In the Negro-African religions, the *voduns* and *orishas* also protect certain occupa-tions, such as the hunter, warrior, smith and so forth.[12] The idea of the guardian angel exists in both religious worlds, with the difference that in the Yoruba religious pantheon, each individual can know the nature of his or her guardian angel (head *orisha*), which is not the case in the Catholic religion. Or again, like the saints, the *orishas* lived on the earth with human beings.

In all the traditional Brazilian *candomblés* – in Bahia, Recife, Porto Alegre or Rio de Janeiro in particular – there is always an altar for the Catholic God – a sort of oratory – and several *pegi* sanctuaries for the *orishas*. The Catholic-inspired oratory, which is decorated with photographs of saints, is placed prominently in the dance room, in such a way that every individual who enters this place sees it, whereas the *pegi* sanctuaries, which house the *orishas*, are concealed from the public. The cult objects and religious spaces are not mixed up together and do not impinge on one another: they are simply juxta-posed. That is why the Catholic altar plays no functional role in the cere-monies honouring the *orishas*, and the Catholic altar is not saluted, unlike the *pegi*, whereas the choice of images that decorate the oratory reflects the sym-bolism of correspondences between *orishas* and saints[13] based either on func-tional similarities or on similarities concerning the lives or the temperaments of the saints at the time when they were also human.[14]

These similarities are sometimes fluid or can vary from region to region and from one *candomblé* brotherhood (*terreiros*) to another. Thus, Shango, the god of thunder, violent and virile, is compared in Bahia to Saint Jerome, an old, bald, bearded monk, accompanied by a lion docilely lying at his feet. It is the lion, the symbol of royalty among the Yoruba, that explains why this saint was likened to Shango, who was the third ruler of the Yoruba.[15] Oya-Yansan, Shango's first wife, goddess of lightning and storms, has been compared, in Bahia, to Saint Barbara who, according to legend, was killed on her father's orders because she had converted to Christianity, before being struck by light-ning and reduced to ashes. That is presumably why she is invoked during storms. Yemanja, mother of waterways and many *orishas*, is likened to Our Lady of the Immaculate Conception, since the church of the same name in Bahia was built on All Saints Bay. Also in Bahia, Saint George is likened to Oshossi, the god of hunters, whereas in Rio de Janeiro he is compared to Ogun, the god of war, which is logical since he is represented as a valiant horseman dressed in shining armour mounted on a horse caparisoned with metal, laying low the dragon with his lance. Omolu, the *orisha* protecting humankind from contagious diseases, is assimilated, in Bahia, to Saint Lazarus and Saint Roch, the bodies of these two saints being known to be covered with wounds and sores.[16] Oshala, also known as Obatala, the object of the most popular cult in Salvador, has been assimilated to the Senhor do Bonfim because of the great prestige that both enjoyed. The Senhor do Bonfim is seen as representing God on Earth and Oshala as representing Olorum among men.[17] In the brotherhoods that are particularly open to Catholic influences, Eshu is confounded with the devil, on the one hand, because of his 'immoral' character – as a phallic figure – an irremediably sinning creature in the eyes of Catholic moralists, and, on the other, as master of the offerings, whose presence is required at sacrificial rites and black magic seances.[18] The Catholic missionaries were so shocked by the indecent representations of Eshu that they thought he was a demon. In Brazil, it is because black magic was directed against the lords that it was perceived as diabolical and was associated with Eshu, chiefly in the *umbanda* religion. That is not the case in orthodox (Nago) *candomblés*, where Eshu is not regarded as the incarnation of evil, although he is feared because of his ability to transform himself.[19]

These few examples have shown how the black slaves imported into Brazil were able to bring the two religious worlds together, even if the functional correspondences varied according to time, place and ethnic group. It should also be noted that not all the *orishas* have their equivalent in Catholic hagiography, since there are far more of them than there are saints.[20]

Another rapprochement has been effected between the two religious systems on the temporal level. In Africa, religious ceremonies followed a ritual calendar whose dates were fixed in accordance with the pattern of nature and the community. The export of these ceremonies to another continent was not without difficulties, since the natural and cultural rhythms of the new continent were very different. To make up for them, blacks in some parts of Brazil who had come from Africa aligned the Yoruba religious calendar on the Christian one. Thus, in Recife, the great festivals of the *orishas* are celebrated on the dates set aside for the corresponding Catholic saints: St. George's day, for Ogun; St. John's day for Shango, etc. That does not prevent the two rites from remaining quite distinct, particularly in the area of organisation: for example, people go to mass in the morning and in the evening they dance to the sound of drums until late in the night. These correspondences have been described by Nina Rodrigues as the 'juxtaposition of externalities'[21] – spatially and temporally.

How are we to understand the inner feelings or the images that underlie these correspondences? Let us take the example of the ceremonial cleaning of the church of Bonfim, which takes place in January. This ceremony, typically Portuguese in origin, was introduced by a Paraguayan soldier going off to war in 1888,[22] who promised Jesus that, if he returned unhurt, he would wash the atrium of His church. The blacks adopted this custom, but in doing so they changed its meaning in reference to the Yoruba ceremony in Africa 'of the water of Oshala', whose purpose was to renew the energy of the stones of the gods by washing them with water from the sacred spring. Here, there was probably confusion between two rather similar ceremonies since, in fact, it is not to Christ – who died at the age of 33 on the cross – that the blacks are paying tribute by washing the church with holy water, but to his African counterpart Oshala,[23] nicknamed the 'old one'.

Another example is to be found in the use of a little bell known as the *adja* in summoning the deities. This bell resembles the one rung in Catholic masses at the moment of the consecration. In Recife, the ringing of the *adja* is sometimes interpreted in its Catholic meaning of calling the attention of the congregation to the climax of the ceremony, when homage is in fact being paid to Oshala, the greatest of the *orishas*.

While in some cases we can observe a degree of apparent confusion between Catholic rites and traditional African rites, it seems that in fact, in terms of inner attitudes, the two are kept distinctly separate. This is true of the orthodox *candomblés,* where it is clear that the descendants of black slaves interpret the Catholic rites through the prism of their own original cultural values.

Political Resistance

Brazilian official historiography has long peddled the prejudice that the black was a 'submissive' individual who had accepted enslavement without reacting because slavery was a common practice in Africa. Such an assertion stands refuted by the permanent tensions that prevailed in Brazil during the three centuries that slavery endured: slaves running away, masters being murdered, slaves committing suicide, etc. Escapes in organised bands and the creation of refuges known as *quilombos* or *mocambos* are clear evidence that slave resistance did indeed exist. Over twenty centres of resistance grouped in *quilombos* have been identified all over the country. Because of its sophisticated political and military organisation, the largest one, the *quilombo de Palmares,* was regarded as a sort of republic or state functioning according to African traditions. It lasted for more than half a century – from 1630 to 1697 – and held out against armed attacks by the Dutch, the Portuguese and the Brazilians.[24]

In 1888, the black slaves became theoretically free, but neither economic help nor compulsory assistance was provided for them, nor had any legal steps been taken to enable them to adapt to their new situation. Opportunities for paid employment existed, but only for immigrants, who were mostly white. That is why some writers go so far as to say that with the abolition of slavery, blacks lost their position within the economic system. In other words, the traditional mechanisms of social domination remained intact, and the reorganisation of the society failed to affect in any significant way the pre-established patterns of racial concentration in the areas of income, social prestige and power. As a result, the freedom achieved by blacks bore no economic, social, or cultural dividends.[25]

Just as Brazilian slavery developed in parallel with the process of colonisation, so its abolition coincided with the beginnings of the transformation of the colonial-type rural economy into a capitalist-type industrial economy.

With the revolution of 1930, it was thought that capitalism would triumph and compel the rural aristocracy to share power with the middle classes. Then, the towns would win out over the countryside, a popular-based national culture would emerge and economic development would create jobs, which would promote social mobility, that of blacks in particular, who, as they became equal to whites, would finally lose their inferiority complex born of slavery.[26] It was in this context that the myth of 'racial democracy' *à la Brésilienne* was constructed, which, it is universally agreed, still operates effectively today. Several reasons can be adduced to explain the success of this ideology based on harmonious relations between the races: on the one hand, because it was 'in the nature' of the Portuguese to frequent black women, whence the creation of a whole class of mixed-race people who acted as a buffer,[27] and, on the other hand, because slavery in Brazil was less brutal than it was elsewhere.

This ideology had an enormous impact on the whole Brazilian population, of all colours. Thus, as early as 1924, a 'black press' came into being in São Paulo which, through the pages of newspapers such as *O Clarim da Alvorada* (The Clarion of Dawn), denounced the existing discrimination practised against blacks in employment, education, and leisure activities and facilities. From this emerged in 1931 the Frente Negra (Negro Front), regarded as the first racial movement since the abolition of slavery to put forward demands.[28] It became a political party in 1936 but was banned the following year with the seizure of power by the dictator Gétulio Vargas.[29] In 1945, when the dictatorship was ended, this black movement reappeared under several guises, such as the First National Concentration of the Brazilian Negro or the Negro Experimental Theatre, and continued its action against discrimination.

Between 1945 and 1970, dozens of black movements came and went, all concerned with presenting a new image of the black that was reminiscent of the one propounded by the ideology of 'racial democracy'. This stance gave these groups an integrationist character, as happened within American black movements before Malcolm X. Schooling and education for all were their main objectives: since racism derived from ignorance, it was through education – and tolerance in particular – that it would be ended.[30] A corollary of this was that it was up to blacks, the designated victims of racism, to change in order to get themselves accepted by whites – in other words, to put an end to living in promiscuity, idleness and self-destruction. In short, education, training and assimilation to the white model were the keys to integration. Even the most short-sighted whites would understand that it was in their best interest to open the door to qualified, well-behaved, upstanding blacks.[31] Most of these black movements conducted intensive educational campaigns in Brazil, stressing the good behaviour that was required in society. Cosmetic products designed to straighten hair were advertised, and the drum or anything of African origin regarded as inferior was excluded from the cultural life of blacks. Reference was to the model offered by the dominant – that is, white – society, whence derives the ambiguity of these movements which, while protesting against racial prejudice, nurtured feelings of inferiority with regard to the blacks' African cultural identity.[32]

From 1964 to 1978, Brazil experienced major economic development which culminated in 1968 with what is known as the 'economic miracle'. This period was marked by the military seizure of power and the resulting dictatorship, very rapid economic growth (some 10 per cent in industry), the internationalisation of the economy and the concentration of exports, state control of the economy, wage freeze and control of inflation,[33] and also by the proliferation of private universities whose creation was encouraged by the state in order to ease the crisis in higher education.[34]

Some blacks – few in number – benefited from this economic miracle and were able to get a university education. In accordance with the ideology of 'racial democracy', they thought that the more educated they were, the less they would be rejected. But the opposite happened: once on the labour market, they were the object of discriminatory practices more than any other group. Frustrated in these social ambitions, these young black graduates then understood that capitalist-type growth – as advocated by 'racial democracy' – simply strengthened racial inequality.

New black anti-racist movements came into being in the country, started by young intellectuals from the first black generation to have gone to university, who were later joined by lower-level civilian and military officials, members of the professions with low or average wages, artists, students, self-employed workers on low incomes, etc. In origin, those making up these movements were from the middle class or the élite, drawing not only on the experience of those who had gone before them, but also on external influences, in particular from North America and Africa, such as pan-Africanism and *négritude*. Unlike the movements in the ambit of 'racial democracy', which advocated assimilation to the white society, the new black movements stressed self-acceptance and reconstruction of cultural and racial identity.

Although united by similar ideals – the struggle against racism and the equal participation of blacks in the country's political life, in enjoyment of the social and economic product, and in all sectors of national life – these movements experienced ideological divergences. Some lost sight of the concrete objectives of their struggle and focused on an evasive and vague academic discourse that removed them from the grass roots. Others thought that since racism and capitalism were intrinsically linked, the first would disappear with the taking of power by the proletariat. Others again felt that blacks should organise as a conscious community and take the reins of capitalist power, the only means of having access to social positions hitherto reserved for whites.

Despite their divergences, these new movements initiated common strategies. In a first stage, the black challenge denounced racially discriminatory practices and launched non-violent appeals to the conscience of whites. The aim was to make whites, as well as national and international opinion, aware of the issue and to make the average Brazilian admit that he or she was indeed racist. The weapons used were tears – and sometimes legal action, which was mostly ineffective for lack of white testimony. In a second stage, it was understood that the struggle against racism demanded that the problems of blacks be treated globally, and include history and cultural identity. Knowledge of their historical and cultural past, rediscovery of their identity and a growing awareness of their contribution to the building of the country, in particular economically, would help blacks to rebuild their personality and get rid of any inferiority complex. With the black historian Joel Rufino dos Santos, we would say that it was a 'matter of making Brazilian blacks visible by redeeming their past.... Although that might seem a second-order task, it is the first and indispensable step for raising them to the level of high-level Brazilians'.[35] This stage saw the demand for *négritude*, which implied a symbolic return to Africa and, above all, knowledge of one's history and culture. Its aim was to make blacks proud of being black and of possessing a culture equal to that of other ethnic groups.

After 1980, faced with the new political situation known as the 'democratic opening' by the ruling class, blacks changed tactics. While maintaining the cultural strategy which they continued to use as the platform for joint action, the leaders of these movements sought to mobilise blacks for elections, so as to win seats for their representatives in municipal, provincial and national assemblies and councils, where the major decisions affecting them were taken. But in order to win elections, blacks had to form a united racial group. If, however, ideologically, blacks and mixed-race people were all Negroes because they occupied the lower rungs of the social hierarchy, individually it was quite another matter: the mixed-race refused to be perceived as blacks – one more manifestation of the 'ideology of whitening' which was a corollary of 'racial democracy'. Since to be black was pejorative, they would call themselves *moreno*. There were thus 'dark' *morenos* and 'light' *morenos*, so light that it made them white.

Thus, despite their ideological differences, black militants thought that it was of vital importance to occupy the political space and promote the 'racial vote' in order to fight effectively against racism and discrimination. However, the lack of cohesion sounded the death knell of the black vote in the 1982 elections. Of the 54 black candidates registered in the state of São Paulo, only two – a regional MP and a municipal councillor[36] – were elected, as the programme they were putting forward was of interest to the whole population, not only those of African origin. Moreover, the first candidate defined himself as a convinced socialist, a proletarian and a candidate of the poor. As to the second, a football player, it is likely that he benefited from the votes of both his black and his white supporters.[37]

It should be noted that until 1982, illiterates, half of whom were blacks, did not have the right to vote in Brazil. And yet, despite the vote of illiterates in the 1986 election, the situation changed very little.

Relations between the Races in Brazil Today

Brazil has long presented itself to the world as a country in which a 'racial democracy' prevails, in which all individuals and ethnic groups of whatever origin live in harmony in a climate of festivals and cultural exchanges, and everyone participates equitably in the various aspects of national life.[38] These beliefs permeate all of the social strata and ethnic groups that make up the mosaic of the Brazilian population. Indeed, compared to other multiethnic nations such as the United States of America or South Africa before the ending of apartheid, Brazil is a country in which, apparently, there is no prejudice or discrimination or segregation based on race. If this belief in a genuine 'racial democracy' is so convincing, it is because it rests on a number of realities:

- relations been individuals and ethnic groups are apparently cordial. Thus it would be quite out of place to make fun of somebody because of his or her racial or religious identity;
- the history of Brazil has furnished proof of its great openness to foreign influences by creating a cultural syncretism that is unique;
- the high percentage of mixed-race people and mulattos is clear evidence of the open-mindedness of the population, the white population in particular, in its choice of sexual partners;
- the fame of some individuals of colour in the arts or sport (Pelé, for example)[39] greatly helped to strengthen belief in the reality of a 'racial democracy'.

None the less, sociological studies conducted in the 1950s on social mobility and racial inequalities showed that this belief had no real basis. According to the sociologists, the racial inequalities observed in Brazil were the result of the hierarchical system inherited from the slave past and would disappear with the integration of blacks into the various classes making up society and with the advent of political socialism.[40]

It was only in the early 1970s that the idea of a form of racism resting on the remnants of the slave past began to be displaced. At that time, a number of researchers – while acknowledging that the mechanism of class domination affected all the oppressed, whatever the colour of their skin – demonstrated that 'race' or 'racial descent' constituted in Brazil a variable or a criterion structuring social relations.[41] In other words, in late twentieth-century Brazil, race constitutes a factor of social selection, which would explain the persistence of social and economic inequalities between whites and non-whites (blacks, mixed-race, Indians, Asians)[42]

And yet, at the fourth Afro-Brazilian Congress, which was held in Recife from 17 to 20 April 1994, one of the official speeches asserted that discrimination against blacks in Brazil was more social than racial.[43] This shows that the myth of 'racial democracy' persists, and how difficult it is for Brazilian society to appreciate fully certain realities in the area of unequal opportunities and discrimination.

Paraphrasing the sociologist Carlos Hasenbalg, I would say that Brazilians have forged a gratifying image of social harmony by distancing themselves from avowedly racist 'Jim Crow' and apartheid regimes. But the Jim Crow system no longer exists, and apartheid has recently been legally buried ...[44]

Notes

1. T. de Azevedo, 1975, p. 11.
2. M. Bergmann, 1972, p. 133.
3. T. de Azevedo, 1975, p. 12.
4. J.B. Borges Pereira, 1987, p. 8.
5. M. Bergmann, 1972, p. 25.
6. O. Nogueira, 1954.
7. E. Berquió, 1988.
8. K. Munanga, 1989, p. 100.
9. Ibid., p. 101.
10. P. Verger, 1983, p. 41.
11. R. Bastide, 1971, p. 361 [Eng. tr., p. 262].
12. Ibid.
13. Ibid., p. 377 [Eng. tr., pp. 272–273].
14. W. Valente, 1977, p. 76.
15. P. Verger, 1983, p. 42.
16. Ibid.
17. N. Rodrigues, 1935, p. 177.
18. M. Augras, 1983, p. 102.
19. Ibid., pp. 102–103.
20. R. Bastide, 1971, p. 383 [Eng. tr., p. 274].
21. N. Rodrigues, 1935, p. 168.
22. R. Bastide, 1971, p. 381 [Eng. tr., p. 276].
23. Ibid.
24. D. Freitas, 1973, pp. 10 et seq.
25. R. Bastide and F. Fernandes, 1955, pp. 57 and 59; F. Fernandes, 1978, pp. 457–459 [Eng. tr., pp. 440–442].
26. J.R. dos Santos, 1983, p. 16.
27. On this, see G. de Mello Freyre, 1963 and 1951 [Eng. tr., 1986 and 1956].
28. T. de Azevedo, 1975, p. 30.
29. M. Bergmann, 1972, p. 71.
30. Ibid.
31. S. Body-Gendrot et al., 1984, p. 22.
32. M. Bergmann, 1972, p. 23.
33. J.R. dos Santos, 1983, p. 17.
34. Ibid.
35. Ibid., p. 19.
36. K. Munanga, 1987, pp. 11–12.
37. On this, see A.L. Valente and E. Farat, 1986.
38. J.B. Borges Pereira, 1987, pp. 8–9.
39. Ibid.
40. On this, see O. Ianni, 1962 and 1966.
41. On this, see C.A. Hasenbalg, 1979, and J.B. Borges Pereira, 1967.
42. N. do Valle Silva and C.A. Hasenbalg, 1992, pp. 11–12.
43. *Jornal Diário de Pernambuco*, 1994, p. 89.
44. N. do Valle Silva and C.A. Hasenbalg, 1992, p. 10.

Bibliography

AUGRAS, M. 1983. *O duplo e a metamorfose: a identidade mitica em cumudade nagó.* Petrópolis, Editora Vozes.

AZEVEDO, T.DE. 1975. *Democracia racial.* Petrópolis, Editora Vozes.

BASTIDE, R. 1971. *As religioès africanas no Brasil.* Vol. 2. São Paulo, Livraria Pioneira Editora. [Eng. tr., Sebba, H. 1978. *The African Religions of Brazil: Toward a Sociology of the Interpenetration of Civilizations.* Baltimore, Johns Hopkins University Press.]

BASTIDE, R., and FERNANDES, F. 1955. *Brancos e negros em São Paulo.* 3rd ed. São Paulo, Companhia Editora Nacional.

BERGMANN, M. 1972. *Nasce um povo.* 2nd ed. Petrópolis, Editora Vozes.

BERQUIÓ, E. 1988. 'Demografia da desigualdade. Algunas considerações sobre o negro no Brasil'. Paper presented to the meeting on 'The demography of inequality in contemporary Latin America' (University of Florida, 21–24 February 1988).

BODY-GENDROT, S., et al. 1984. *Les Noirs américains aujourd'hui.* Paris, Armand Colin.

BORGES PEREIRA, J.B. 'La constitution historique de la pluralité ethnique et raciale au Brésil'. Paper presented to the seminar on *Minorités ethniques du Brésil et du Canada*, Québec, Université de Laval, May 1987. (Unpub.)

———. 1967. *Cor, profissão y mobilidade. O Negro e o rádio de São Paulo.* São Paulo, Livraria Pioneira Editora.

FERNANDES, F. 1965 and 1978. *A integração do Negro na sociedade de classes.* 2 vol.s. São Paulo, Editora Atica. [Eng. tr., Skiles, J.D., Brunel, A., and Rothwell, A. 1969. *The Negro in Brazilian Society.* New York, Columbia University Press.]

———. 1972. *O Negro no mundo dos brancos.* São Paulo, Difusão Européia do Livro.

FREITAS, D. 1973. *Palmares, a guerra dos escravos.* Porto Alegre, Editora Movimento.

HASENBALG, C.A. 1979. *Discriminação e desigualdades raciais no Brasil.* Rio de Janeiro, Edições Graal [Eng. orig., Race Relations in Post-abolition Brazil. (University of California, Berkeley, Ph.D. thesis.]

IANNI, O. 1962. *As metamorfoses do escravo: apogen e crise do escravatura no Brasil meridional.* São Paulo, Difusão Européia do Livro.

———. 1966. *Raças e classes sociais no Brasil.* Rio de Janeiro, Civilização brasileira.

Jornal Diário de Pernambuco (city), 18 April 1994.

MELO FREYRE, G.DE. 1951. *Sobrados e mucambos: decadência do patriarcado rural e desenvolvimento urbano.* 2nd ed. Rio de Janeiro, J. Olympio. [Eng. tr., Onís, H. de. 1986. *The Mansion and the Shanties.* Berkeley, University of California Press.]

———. 1963. *Casa grande e senzala.* 13th ed. Brasilia, Editora da Universidade de Brasilia [Eng. tr., Putnam, S. 1964. *The Master and the Slaves.* New York, Knopf].

MOURÃO, F. 1977. 'La présence de la culture africaine et la dynamique du processus social africain'. Paper presented to the Second World Black and African Festival of Arts and Culture, Lagos/Kaduna, Nigeria.

MUNANGA, K. 1987. 'Situation actuelle et avenir des Noirs au Brésil'. Paper presented to the seminar on 'Minorités ethniques du Brésil et du Canada', Québec, Université de Laval, May. (Unpub.).

———. 1989. 'Art africain et syncrétisme religieux au Brésil'. *Revista Dédalo* (São Paulo).

NOGUEIRA, O. 1954. 'Preconceito racial de marca e preconceito racial de Origem'. Paper presented to the Congresso internacional de americanistas, São Paulo.

RODRIGUES, N. 1935. *O animismo fetichista dos negros bahianos.* Rio de Janeiro, Civilização Brasileira.

SANTOS, J.R. DOS. 1983. 'Le Noir brésilien et son histoire'. *Recherche, pédagogie et culture* (Paris), No. 64.

VALENTE, A. L., and FARAT, E. 1986. *Politica e relações raciais: o Negro e as eleições paulistas de 1982*. São Paulo, Faculdad de Filosofia, Letras e Ciencias Humanas, Universidade de São Paulo.

VALENTE, W. 1977. *Sincretismo religioso afro-brasileiro*. 3rd ed. São Paulo, Editora Nacional.

VALLE SILVA, N. DO, and HASENBALG, C.A. 1992. *Relações raciais no Brasil contemporaneo*. Rio de Janeiro, Fundo Editora.

VERGER, P. 1983. 'Syncrétisme'. *Recherche, pédagogie et culture* (Paris), No. 64.

Chapter 27

Influence of African Art on American Art

Joseph C.E. Adande

THE ISSUE OF THE WAYS in which one art has influenced another is not fundamentally new and recent. It is part of every good research methodology in art history and the human sciences. In these disciplines, the questions that are asked always involve the examination of the many facets of a reality whose simplicity, at first sight, is often deceptive: it leaves unseen many other phenomena that need to be brought out, because it is they that give unity to the fact that is being examined. In art history in particular, attention is focused on the single object from which the discourse is elaborated. The object, in its simplicity, has an origin and a destination, such that in the last analysis the before and the after of the object are, for the art historian, part of its present – in other words, part of present-day civilisation. For the fact is that every process of constructing that civilisation proceeds on the basis of cultural contributions from a variety of sources whose more or less harmonious combining and mixing generate a new product, a new civilisation and culture where 'new' people become recognisable. In that sense, the famous American melting-pot is just like so many other human embryonically civilising assemblages that have existed since human beings learned to move and reach out to their fellows – brothers and sisters, enemies or kindred. Human beings borrow from other civilisations what interests them, while adapting it to their own needs, as history bears witness. The same spirit of a return to the 'pagan' sources of civilisation that marked the Renaissance outlook in the sixteenth century is to be found with its own particular features in the Cubist artist endeavouring to escape the heavy hand of academicism in order to rediscover, four centuries later, the naivety of essential forms: it was necessary to discard the accretions to reach the heart.

For many scientists, nature abhors repetition. It invents once and once only and sets its stamp on an archetypal matrix – the 'collective subconscious', for example – from which the original forms of creation can be drawn at any moment.

Long before us, Plato claimed that ideas pre-existed the real world and that it was thus enough to remember – in other words, to bring back to consciousness what was buried in the depths of the self. What is African in American art is thus a matter either of borrowing or of reminiscence. Borrowing, because we may reasonably think that the blacks who landed in the Americas gradually became different from their brothers who had remained in Africa and that they laid the foundations of a new civilisation. Reminiscence, if we stress the African heritage in American art.

Whatever case is taken, the quest for the distinctive character of an influence in a culture or a civilisation is much concerned with identity: it has to answer such questions as 'Who am I?' and 'Where do I come from?' without any beating about the bush. Such a concern is perfectly legitimate, but it must not lead to an artistic narcissism of self-glorification. On the contrary, such a quest should bring out the malleability of the systems producing and receiving influences as well as the high intelligence of the individuals who established them. Cultural traits are, of course, important, but much more important is what people have made of them and what they have become under other skies away from their original home.

In examining the influence of African art in American art, we can thus grasp the civilising flow both before and after the moment when the objects, evidence of and product of encounters, have retold the multifaceted history of human beings. As we shall soon see, there are as many reasons that militate for as against a particular trait's belonging to one culture rather than to another. When art historians have to make a choice, they must, as everywhere in the sciences, adduce evidence that, fortunately, is not always irrefutable.

Before listing and analysing some of the significant traits of the influence of African arts on American art, we shall first make a critical study, by topic and by work. Our aim is to demonstrate that contemporary African art is relevant, as well as offering an appropriate reflection of the reality of human beings.

Much has been published about the influence of Africa on the Americas. That influence is felt above all in the spiritual domain, since many religious rituals from Africa found fertile soil in the New World: Bahia de Todos Os Santos in Brazil and Cuba, in particular, are the chosen homes of voodoo, for example (see works by P. Verger, R. Bastide, A. Métraux, M.J. Herskovits, M. Guérin, R.F. Thompson). Two books are particularly important to this topic: R.F. Thompson's *Flash of the Spirit* (1984), devoted to a synoptic study of African influences and their survival in the Americas, and S. Price and R. Price's work on Afro-American art in Suriname (1980).

In the last 20 years, research, which previously focused essentially on the black contribution to music, dance and entertainment, has been extended to the plastic and graphic arts, architecture and decoration, as well as the useful arts (on this, see the work by E.H. Fine, *The Afro-American Artist: A Search for Identity* [1973], and the catalogue of the Dallas Museum of Art, *Black Art Ancestral Legacy: The African Impulse in African American Art* [1989]).

The influence of Africa on American art thus arouses the curiosity and interest of Americans and more especially of black Americans, in quest of the cornerstones of their own personality in order to reinvent their identity and references to their own civilisation. The Africans have not, it seems to me, invested the same energy in this quest: their equally pressing nationalist demands directed at Europe become blurred in Africa itself, when they do not lapse into ethnic or inter-tribal struggles whose political roots would repay considerable reflection. In Europe, too, researchers at the Ecole Pratique des Hautes Etudes en Sciences Sociales and the Ecole Pratique des Hautes Etudes have embarked on the study of the influence of Africa on the Americas and have organised exchanges of teachers as part of their thinking.

Because it moved millions of human beings from Africa to the Americas, the slave trade made such influences inevitable. The fact that slaves came from particular regions, relative though it may have been, has probably meant that a particular region of the African continent has had more influence on one part of the Americas than another. Thus, voodoo is well established in Haiti and its rites resemble those of the *vodun* of Danhomé (voodoo of Dahomey). In Brazil, there are survivals of cults from Yorubaland – notably from Ketu – to such an extent that these regions, hosts to African traditions, act as a backup source of information to supplement that which researchers go to seek in Africa itself. No study could be complete if it did not focus on both sides of the Atlantic. This cultural kinship is the result of human kinship.

Thus, research conducted in the United States of America using genetic markers has demonstrated the kinship of American blacks with their brothers and sisters on the African continent. Herskovits[1] demonstrated the sub-Saharan provenance of many slaves, and Thompson[2] quotes a Harvard academic attesting the presence of 'Southern Bantu type' blood groups in the ancestry of black North Americans.

The research conducted by the writer Alex Haley, which resulted in the publication of *Roots*, testifies to the reality of slavery in these times of historical revisionism. *Roots* is a credible work; it would have just as much value if it were only a work of romantic fiction. What is called into being through dreaming is just as necessary for the balance of a human being and poignantly recalls each individual's expectations and aspirations. In this way, one provides a solution to the unresolved, and transforms into a lesser evil what, in other circumstances, might have overwhelmed oneself and one's fellows. The memory of a past such as that of slavery might kill if the individual was not capable, not of forgetting, but of transforming reality by dreaming. From this quest for freedom, ill-assuaged or assuaged only with difficulty, many artistic mutations have arisen. It would have been strange if such a presence of Africa in the Americas had not been reflected in religions and their forms of expression, the leading site where one can point to the existence of African artistic influences in American art. Contrary to what is commonly asserted, religion does not create art, but by drawing on a shared root emotion, it enables art to become manifest and to find a setting suitable for multidimensional deployment.

The tenaciousness of religions of African origin in the Americas is to be explained by the fact that those who were forced to make the voyage were unable in the space of a few months to rid themselves of what had hitherto constituted their relationship to the gods of their home country. But they could not, in the particular circumstances of a lack of freedom of which they were victims, retain the full original character of the cults and objects that they were perpetuating. 'In that situation', writes Max Benoît about Haiti, 'under the threat of torture and in fear of "whitening", a punishment in which the colonist had the slaves skinned alive – using a sharp cutlass, the white colour of the sub-epidermal tissue was laid bare – the syncretism of Catholicism and voodoo came into being: the Negroes replied by decking out the images of the Roman Church with the names of African gods.' Historians know that persecution always generates a new religion. They know, too, that human beings have short memories; otherwise, how are we to understand how Christianity, initially the religion of slaves persecuted all around the Mediterranean basin, persecuted other slaves fifteen centuries later in order to uproot their beliefs? The tolerance of African religions doubtless prevented slaves from choosing to reveal their beliefs openly at the risk of losing their lives. On the contrary, they adopted a form of cultural resistance the better to assert their identity: are not 'taking on local colour' and 'adapting' the most eloquent signs of membership of the human race? Of course, this capacity to reinterpret the sign associated with polysemic symbolism runs through all religions, but the *vodun* cultures have been champions at it because of their constant openness to the new. Whether that religious syncretism is called *santería* in Cuba, *macumba* in Brazil or *vodun* in Haiti, it enabled slaves to re-create figures similar to those of their original cultures and religions.

What is commonly described as traditional art is inspired largely by *vodun* cults. This has long been recognised and, while it enshrines the ancient bonds between art and religion, it also expresses the difficulty of studying and knowing art outside its religious environment. That truth prevails on both sides of the Atlantic. We have to turn to Pierre Verger (1968) for evidence, not only of the existence of similar cults, but above all of virtually identical names of gods on both sides of the Atlantic. They are the proof of the conservation of the essential characteristics of each of those cults. The only difference, mentioned by the author, is the constitution of the *orishas* into a pantheon in the New World, whereas in Yorubaland their existence and different groups' knowledge of them are associated with the history of towns. It remains the case that Orisha n'la, Eshu, Ogun, Oshu, Oranyan, Shango, Oya, Oshun, Yemanja, Oshumare and Nana Burucu are names common to *orishas* on both sides of the Atlantic. Some objects of the material and artistic culture of the New World reflect the persistence of artistic links between the two sides of the Atlantic. Thompson[3] reports several that are worth mentioning.

The cult of Ogun is one of the most popular in the Yoruba world. To honour this god, the Yoruba created the *amula*, which is simply a piece of jewellery on which appear most of the emblems of Ogun. Together they make up a chain or collar which dignitaries of the god wear.[4] The same idea in Fon culture probably led to the design of the *asen gubasa* and also the superb Gu crown by Akati,[5] on which are to be found as attributes of that god all the blunt objects known to the culture. In the New World, the *amula Ogun* gave rise in Cuba to the 'cauldron of Ogun'. 'Such objects are full of various expressions of ironwork, such as nails, iron bows and arrows, horseshoes, and fetters, thus fusing token pieces of [Ogun's] medium within the programmatic arrangements of the *amula* with an iron cooking vessel, as if to prepare a mighty broth of iron.'[6] Thompson also informs us that, as a result of Cuban migration to North America, the cauldron is to be found in Miami and New York with fanciful additions such as a pistol. I see nothing fanciful in such an addition – rather, it should be seen as the sign of the modernity and contemporary relevance of Ogun, the god of hunting. The original arrow, although effective, belongs to him just as much as the symbolic gun of the slave trade and one of his last updatings, the pistol. It comes as no surprise to find the same idea in Brazil with the name of *ferramentas de Ogun*. Some Brazilian blacksmiths create sculptures that not only resemble those of the Yoruba world but also conform to the numerology peculiar to Ogun by having seven objects attached to the principal support.

We could go on at length about these resemblances between religious-artistic objects. What we need to note is that most of the cultures of West and Central Africa have left their mark on the black culture of the New World. In the absence of any other sign, the cosmograms would still bear witness to the specificity of African traits outside Africa, the place where they emerged. Apart from the religious-artistic vein, the influence of Africa is still present in folk arts. We shall note a few significant examples in textiles, basket-making and pottery.

In textiles, a kinship with Africa is quite visible. One of the many uses of cloth consists in appliquéing cut-outs on a background that is in principle monochrome. In this way, through a series of more or less connected pictograms, it is possible to tell a story, translate a proverb or, simply, beautify. The art of appliqué is common in Africa, especially in West Africa. By the seventeenth century, this technique was perfectly familiar at the court of the kings of Danhomé, where it was used to transcribe the names of kings, embellish areas set aside for worship or pay homage to the dead. For the court artists of Abomey, this art form was associated with light, since they compared it to a negative made up of a monochrome background cloth which would highlight the pictograms in their varied colours. Recent research[7] has shown that the technique of appliquéd cloth such as is found among the Fante of the Gold Coast in the eighteenth century had been borrowed from Abomey.

The use of a similar technique is to be found in the production of quilts in North America. Thus those made by the ex-slave Harriet Powers, born on 29 October 1837 in Athens, Georgia,[8] with their pictograms inspired by biblical texts and in which each square tells a story, are reminiscent of the appliquéd cloths of Abomey.

The Fon artistic tradition is not the only one present in black American folk art. It also contains evidence of the Gullah tradition, the Gullahs being an Angolan ethnic group whose name has been given to traditional wickerwork makers in South Carolina. The style of so-called Gullah baskets is similar to that of the woven baskets of Senegambia. That they should be given the name of a group from Angola probably reflects the many years of mixing and borrowing between Africans in the New World, where representatives of different ethnic groups could sometimes be found in quite small areas. Many other African cultural traits are to be found in black American folk arts, from circular buildings to walking sticks on which different figures are carved with tools as rudimentary as those used in Africa. And these various forms of art are still very much alive in contemporary America.

The Kongo presence in the United States of America is as substantial as that of other groups.[9] For example, the cosmogram *Tendwa Nza Kongo* – a cross-shaped symbol referring to humanity's relationship to God, and consequently constructed from the top downwards, from the living to the dead – has become the 'singing and drawing points of contact between worlds'.[10] On the island of Cuba, when Kongo ritual leaders wished to make the important *Zarabanda* charm (Ki-Kongo: *nsala-banda*, a charm-making kind of cloth), they began by tracing, in white chalk, a cruciform pattern at the bottom of an iron kettle. This was the signature (*firma*) of the spirit invoked by the charm. It clearly derives from the Kongo sign except that the sun disks were replaced by arrows, standing for the four winds of the universe.

Beyond the cosmograms, the *minkisi* are today part of the black heritage of the Americas. They are to be found in Cuba, where the receptacles to contain them are called *prendas* or pawns[11] and some contemporary artists, such as Renée Stout, draw inspiration from them.[12] The artist is not copying the traditional forms of the *minkisi*, but rather re-creating them by adapting them to current situations, although there is a visual and conceptual continuity between the old and the new. Renée Stout saw a *minkisi* for the first time at the age of 10, in a museum, and was sufficiently marked by the experience to rediscover its formal appearance later. It is easy to understand that for a vision to transform itself so rapidly into creation, it must have brought back to clear consciousness memories and an experience that had probably long been buried away. Is Renée Stout an example of the theory that one learns nothing but remembers everything?

Visual creations in line with the traditions of origin are surely the most informative in our quest for the African influence on American art. Just because they are contemporary, we must not forget the existence of artistic trends that, since the beginning of the century, have been forged in contact with historical reality in the demand for values peculiar to black culture. For black North Americans, these values were part and parcel of their heritage, and to rediscover them was to reconstitute a personality fractured and devalued by the masters of yesteryear. Blacks came to be regarded as authentic creators only very recently, for talented freed slaves or descendants of slaves such as Scipio Morhead, a black painter of the late nineteenth century, often simply drew their inspiration from the rules and models of Western art.

Some North American black artists were involved in the encounter that occurred at the beginning of the century between African art and Western artists, from which Cubism emerged. For example, Meta Warrick Fuller's sculpture *Ethiopia Awakening* (1914) is regarded as the starting-point of the artistic revival of North American blacks drawing their inspiration from their African origin. The numerous struggles waged by North American blacks for their emancipation, along with the actions of such figures as W.E.B. Du Bois and Marcus Garvey, developed this trend, giving rise to various schools of thought, including the Harlem Renaissance. For the first time, North American blacks were making their own assessment, asking themselves questions about their actions and positioning themselves in relation to other currents and traditions with which they rubbed shoulders and from which they drew inspiration, at least in part. Borrowing from, and reference to, Africa increased, whence the increase in the number of contacts between the artists of the two continents in the form of periods of residence or study tours, and even, among some, the desire to return to live in Africa.

Our survey lays no claim to being exhaustive. It has simply sketched African influences on traditional American art or on its more contemporary forms, ranging from sculpture to painting. The contribution of blacks to American music has been deliberately omitted because it is well known.

The African cultural influence was thus able to adapt itself to the reality experienced by slaves in their new adopted home, and religious syncretism has often made it possible to conserve the most interesting features of imported traditions. These influences, as we have said, are still very much alive today in the big American cities, since we find *babalawo*[13] there, along with shrines dedicated to the various gods of the African pantheons. Sometimes African artistic practices are even incorporated into therapies adopted by psychologists or psychoanalysts. African art is thus playing a full part in enabling people in the New World to recover their identity, whatever the colour of their skin.

But much remains to be done on both sides of the Atlantic. These arts, while continuing to develop along their own lines, can be complemented by exchanges of academics, for example, so as to promote the transmission of knowledge about African art and its Afro-American counterpart. We also surely need to encourage Africans to specialise in this area, so as to have a more balanced view of the different contributions of the African and American continents.

In the same way, exhibitions should be organised on the transatlantic slave trade, not only to raise public awareness but also to make more widely known the inventiveness of black people in such tragic situations as slavery, their tremendous physical resistance and their sense of the African homeland that centuries of ill treatment have failed to eradicate. These activities should also lead to the establishment of tourist trails on the slave trade associating the visit of sites with the consumption of traditional dishes, those known to slaves and those not; advantage could be taken of them to get to know those that have been invented since, as they result from the many borrowings from America, including certain plants which successfully adapted to the African tropical climate.

Today, we need to offer Africa new images that transform fears into reasons to go forward and that make our sufferings and the torments that our ancestors endured the springboard for the future. To follow the Slave Route through the arts is to consent, voluntarily, to break the chains of slavery on which we have turned our backs in order to construct, stone by stone, a civilisation that weaves, at the end of an old rope, another one, enriched by all the contributions over time on both sides of that sea, whose name comes from Atlantis. The people of this fabled city, it is said, were great builders of civilisation, and we can decide to be their heirs likewise.

Notes

1. M.J. Herskovits, 1966, p. 58.
2. R.F. Thompson, 1984, p. 35.
3. R.F. Thompson, 1985.
4. Ibid., p 53.
5. S. Blier, 1990, p. 49.
6. R.F. Thompson, 1984, p. 55.
7. M. Chaplain-Riou and C. Bernard, 1980.
8. R.A. Perry, 1989, p. 38.
9. R. A. Perry, 1989, p. 38.
10. R.F. Thompson, 1984 and 1993.
11. R.F. Thompson, 1984, p. 121.
12. M. Harris, 1993, pp. 107–142.
13. *Babalawo*: Yoruba term describing a person responsible for a cult, usually also acting as a soothsayer.

Bibliography

BITON, M. 1994. 'Question de Gu'. *Arts d'Afrique Noire* (Arnouville), pp. 25–34.
BLIER, S.P. 1990. 'King Glele of Danhomè. Part one: Divination portraits of a lion king and man of iron'. *African Art*, Vol. 23, No. 4, pp. 42–53.
CHAPLAIN-RIOU, M., and BERNARD, C. 1980. *Les étoffes en appliqué fon: transformations, diffusion, époque royale et début de la période coloniale.* Paris, Université de Paris I. (Mémoire de maîtrise UER d'arts plastiques et sciences de l'art.)
DALLAS MUSEUM OF ART. 1989. *Black Art Ancestral Legacy: The African Impulse in African-American Art.* New York, Harry Abrams Inc. Publishers.
FINE, E.H. 1973. *The Afro-American Artist: A Search for Identity.* New York, Holt, Rinehart and Winston, Inc.
HARRIS, M. 1993. 'Resonance, transformation, and rhyme: The art of Renée Stout'. In *Astonishment and Power.* New York, National Museum of African Art, pp. 107–154.
HERSKOVITS, M.J. 1966. *L'héritage du Noir, mytbe et réalité.* Paris, Présence africaine. [Orig. Am. ed., 1941. *Myth of the Negro Past.* New York, Harper & Brothers.]

PERRY, R.A. 1989. 'African art and African-American folk art: A stylistic and spiritual kinship'. In Rozelle, Robert V. (ed.). *Black Art Ancestral Legacy*. Dallas, Dallas Museum of Art, pp. 35–52.

PRICE, S., and PRICE, R. 1980. *Afro-American Arts of the Suriname Rain Forest*. Los Angeles, University of California Press.

THOMPSON, R.F. 1984. *Flash of the Spirit: African and Afro-American Art and Philosophy*. New York, Random House.

———. 1985 *L'éclair primordial, présence africaine dans la philosophie et l'art afro-américains*. Paris, Editions caribéennes.

———. 1993. *Face of the Gods: Art and Altars of Africa and the African Americas*. New York, Museum of African Art.

UNESCO. 1985. *Cultures africaines*. Paris. Documents de la réunion d'experts sur 'Les survivances des traditions religieuses africaines dans les Caraïbes et en Amérique latine', San Luis de Maranhao, Brazil, 24–28 June 1985.

VERGER, P. 1968. *Flux et reflux de la traite des nègres entre le golfe du Bénin et Bahia de Todos os Santos du XVIIe au XIXe siècle*. Paris/The Hague, Mouton. [Eng. tr. E. Crawford. 1976. *Trade Relations between the Bight of Benin and Bahia from the 17th to the 19th Century*. Ibadan, Ibadan University Press.]

Chapter 28

Resilience and Transformation in Varieties of African Musical Elements in Latin America

Kazadi wa Mukuna

THE QUEST FOR AFRICANISM in the music of Latin America and the Caribbean has occupied, since the turn of the century, a prominent position on the agendas of individual Latin Americanist scholars and those of research institutions.[1] During this period, researchers have been occupied with the identification of the ethnic origins of musical materials from Africa and the process of their incorporation into the musical expressions of the New World. In some of these studies, applied approaches, which omit consideration of extra-musical phenomena as constituent elements of the context vital to the interpretation and the understanding of processes of retention of these musical elements in the New World, have often led to erroneous results. Recently, with the development of new trends of research focused on the process of the assimilation and rejection of African musical elements in Latin America, scholars have begun to consider the role of both the psychological and the social phenomena in this process. These two levels of consideration are best understood when seen in terms of the resilience of musical elements often strengthened by the renewal of cultural contacts from both sides of the Atlantic. It is in this light that scholars have formulated new theories and have suggested new methodological guidelines to implement them.

More recently, the 'Grupo de Trabajo' of the Interamerican Music Council proposed the following research guideline:

> The identification of African elements in the musical fabric of Latin America should ... take into consideration the historical aspect which includes the impact of all phenomena, social and economic, on the carriers of the cultural material. This sustains the fact that a musical expression is indeed a product of the influence of these phenomena on the conceptual level of its makers. To the latter, music is not conceived as mere organisation of sounds, but rather as integral parts of a total expression, which include languages, dance, movements, games and the particular behaviour patterns of a dynamic society.[2]

Elsewhere I have asserted[3] that the continuity of a cultural element in a new society is a validation of its persistence or its assimilation into that society. In light of the scope of the present discussion, this assertion can be expanded to consider the adaptability of African musical elements in the process of their assimilation, and thus their continuity, into the musical fabric of the New World. Taking into consideration that assimilation is an advanced stage in the process of cultural exchange, it is preceded by other phases at each of which a cultural element may be rejected as being incompatible with the existing needs of the new tradition, or adapted and assimilated in order to fulfil the requirements. Mention may be made of the following phases, *inter alia*: a cultural inventory allows members of different origins in an emerging society to discover, consciously or unconsciously, what they have in common and to define cultural common denominators which might become features of their culture; the common denominators are in turn evaluated according to new sets of norms and values to determine their compatibility in enhancing the lives of their potential new users; those common denominators that have been judged compatible are submitted to reinterpretation when they are transformed and attributed new functions as they gradually reach the point of assimilation. It is at this phase of the process that cultural elements are either retained or rejected. Further examination of this process of cultural extension brings to light four major levels of consideration which operate in concert but not in any particular order: the original cultural manifestation/context of which the musical element is an integral part; the flexibility of the cultural element in the new society which will allow transformation to take place at the physical and/or contextual level, thereby assuring its continuity; the fact that an element which remains inflexible becomes obsolete; the functionality of the cultural element relative to the needs of the ruling class.

African slaves brought to Latin America knowledge of various musical instruments and the concept of organisation of their musical elements. These materials survived in their minds within the framework of the variety of cultural manifestations and the context with which they were associated in the homeland. In the New World, as it became necessary to ensure their own survival,[4] African slaves began to re-create some of what gave meaning to their lives. In some instances this process was made possible by members of the ruling class who encouraged slaves to group into social brotherhoods such as those known in Brazil as *Nations*[5] and in Cuba as *cabildos*.[6] Although the primary intention of the authorities was to control the growing slave population by keeping a firm hand on their leaders who had to answer for the misbehaviour of all members of their brotherhoods, these groups provided opportunities for slaves to re-create and perpetuate their cultural calendar. Mason states: 'These societies provided the foundations for organizing and promoting the observance of fundamentally necessary social and religious festivals and rituals.'[7]

The survival of the Sudanese religion in Latin America within these social groupings is certainly one of the reasons for the survival of a large number of African musical instruments in the New World. Religious syncretism provided the necessary cultural context for the re-creation of an array of musical instruments, ritual songs, rhythmic patterns and dance movements. In this context, these musical elements remained protected within the realm of the ritual whose efficacy is dependent on the proper observance of all its integral parts. The rigidity of this criterion has sometimes led scholars to consider the role fulfilled by music and dance in this context to be secondary to the religious ceremony. 'The dancing is extremely ordered and symbolic', writes Bolaji Idowu. 'Exact timing and placement of foot and hand movements are necessary to the success of the ritual and are therefore religious rather than musical requirements.'[8] Throughout Latin America, the concern for the efficacy of the religious ceremonies has helped maintain the similarity of rituals which includes invocatory song, a hymn to call to worship, a hymn of adoration, a hymn of prayer committing the worshippers to the care of the divinity and a parting hymn, all set at intervals within the order of worship.[9] Musical similarities are apparent in song melodies (differing in their mutilated texts), rhythmic patterns and dance movements identified with particular divinities. These elements are taught to novices who must learn to sing, dance and behave in the manner of the divinity they are prepared to receive.

Numerous membranophones were reconstructed by slaves to serve in this context in Latin America. Although in most of these reconstructions it was not imperative to observe drum shapes identical to their African prototypes, nevertheless, the style of fixing the skin to the drumhead reflected that of the African region of origin of their makers. Perhaps one of the most celebrated of all reconstructed membranophones in the religious context is the *bata*, a set of two-headed, truncated, cone-shaped drums of different sizes. In Cuba, these drums have maintained their morphological structures as well as their Yoruba names and functions within the ritual. The largest of these is called *iya* (mother), the mid-size *itotelee*, and the smallest of the three *konkolo*. Mason expresses the phenomenon in these terms: 'Although the Africans in Cuba were able to reconstruct and invent innumerable musical instruments to represent and assist in cultural reclamation, the sacred set of three Bata drums of the Yoruba can unequivocally be considered the most important musical symbol of this reclamation movement.'[10]

In light of the above discussion, it is safe to reassert that the survival of the Sudanese religion in Latin America was in itself a vital cultural context for the survival of a variety of musical elements. Its acceptance in Latin America guaranteed the continuity of all its integral elements, i.e. music, dance, instruments. ritual, invocations and so on. Outside this sacred context cultural elements were exposed, unprotected from the impact of the myriad phenomena of social structure and dynamic. It is within the secular realm that the aforementioned process of adaptability and transformation of musical elements and the impact of the social structure are detected. In this realm, the survival of a musical element is determined by a combination of several factors, each of which is introduced into the process at different points and levels.

While African religions provided the original cultural context that guaranteed the survival of musical elements in Latin America, most secular manifestations were either innovated or created by slaves or by those of African descent reflecting new social conditions. The principle of innovation implies that musical elements of different origins can be kept intact, modified, transformed or replaced by others independently of each other in order to constitute a new expression. Within the criteria of innovation, the assimilation of a musical element or instrument is dependent on its flexibility to withstand the rigorous test of the reinterpretation which operates in a subtle way and the ability of the instrument to fulfil the musical requirements of the new society, in general, and those of the ruling class, in particular. Several African musical elements survived in the New World under these conditions. In Brazil, as well as in other parts of Latin America, those musical instruments which have been incorporated into the new musical expressions are those which the masters found useful to their own needs. On the other hand, however, certain instruments that were popular among African slaves yet considered obsolete by the dominant class were dropped by the wayside.

Such is the case with the friction drum known in Brazil as *cuica* and in Cuba under its retained Bantu name of *kinfwiti*. The name of these friction drums together with their morphology – a hollow tree trunk with a stretched skin head fixed at one end, at the centre of which is a shaft attached internally – sustain their Congo-Angola origin. Despite the structural differences between the African *kinfwiti* and the Portuguese *sarronca*, which imposes the holding position of the instrument during the execution, their principles of sound production, i.e. transmitting vibration to the drumhead indirectly through frictions on the shaft, are similar. However, while the African used his friction drum primarily for ritual invocations, symbolising the leopard, the lion or the mysterious voice from the dead,[11] the Portuguese friction drums are played preferably at night to accompany songs during Christmas festivities and carnival parades.[12] At the reinterpretation phase of the assimilation process in Brazil, the dominant class adopted the African *kinfwiti* to which they attributed their carnivalesque functions. This instrument is a perfect example of the capacity of African musical instruments to adapt for purposes of survival in the New World. The African slave was compelled to accept the vulgarisation of his instrument from ritual to carnival context.

Two other musical instruments fall into this category of those that were flexible enough to be introduced into an innovated cultural context. The first of these is the musical bow from the Congo-Angola region, known in Brazil as *berimbau*,[13] but reported by Ortiz in Cuba as *burumbumba*,[14] a name that is closely related to its Bantu name *mbulumbumba*. The process of adaptation of this musical instrument in Brazil is a familiar pattern which confirms the influence of the ruling class as in the case of several other musical instruments and cultural elements throughout Latin America. 'White Brazilians', writes Kubik. 'noticed a similarity between the guimbarde of their own cultures and the African bows in that all these instruments created melodies by re-enforcing harmonics.'[15] The second instrument is the basket rattle, which is known as *caxixi* in Brazil and which survived in that country by becoming a sympathetic sound provider to the *berimbau* in a new cultural context of *capoeira*.

Unlike these instruments which survived by becoming functional to the members of the dominant class, three melodic instruments, including the xylophone, were less fortunate. As to why the latter instrument did not take root in Cuba, Ortiz notes:

> The balafon or marimba necessitated the hierarchic social function of a royal ceremony that had no equivalent or valid substitute in the Cuban context. Religious rituals there had specific sacred instruments that made no allowance for the marimba. Without an established religion to sustain it, its melodic function was gradually replaced by the bandola, guitar and other stringed instruments that were more artistic and prestigious, being white people's instruments.[16]

In Brazil, the xylophone is used by a small group on the coast north of São Paulo in the context of a cultural event called *congada*, itself an innovation. However, the gradual disappearance of the *congada* is depriving the xylophone of its sole cultural support so that it is now virtually extinct in Brazil.

Lack of interest on the part of the ruling class also led to the disappearance in Latin America of two other melodic instruments: the *chibumba* bowlute and the *mbira* idiophone. In Brazil, although these instruments were popular among slaves during the eighteenth and nineteenth centuries, as illustrated by Alexandre Rodrigues Ferreira in his *Viagen Filosofica 1783–1792* and by Jean-Baptiste Debret, a French artist who lived in Rio de Janeiro from 1816 to 1832, they did not survive because their limited range prevented them from producing the same variety of notes and harmonies as the chordophones of the ruling class.

Closer examination of most of the cultural manifestations found in Latin America, identified by scholars at one time as originating in Africa, shows that they come under the heading of creations. Unlike the case of innovation, which welcomes earlier instruments as an integral part of a new form of expression in creation, it is the concept of organisation rather than the material factor that prevails in creation. In other words, these manifestations are conceptualised according to the African principles of organisation, which I shall simply refer to as *Africanisms*. They can be seen in many of the cultural manifestations conceived by the descendants of slaves. They provide the groundwork for the structure of the *samba* and the *capoeira* in Brazil, the principle governing satire in Brazilian *Bumba-meu-Boi* music-hall songs, the rhythmic essence of the music of the population of African descent and the outstanding mark of the song and dance of the descendants of slaves throughout Latin America. In his 'Africanism in African-American Music', Maultsby draws this conclusion: 'African retentions in African-American music can be defined as a core of conceptual approaches.... Black people create, interpret and experience music out of an African frame of reference, one that shapes musical sound, interpretation and behaviour and makes black music traditions throughout the world a unified whole.'[17]

In this essay it has been argued that the survival of African musical elements in the Americas was made possible by a combination of factors, principally social, which came into play at different stages of the process of assimilation. One of the most important of these was the 'cultural context', which provided the framework in which the musical elements were attributed new functions. Some survived thanks to the preservation of the cultural manifestations with which they were originally associated. Such is the case of the *bata* drums and the accompanying songs and dances which were essential to religious ritual. Others elements, however, were incorporated into manifestations created by the new society. If it was to succeed in this process of attributing new functions to African musical elements in the New World, such a reinterpretation meant that these elements had to adapt to the new functions and at the same time satisfy the musical needs of the ruling class.

Notes

1. Among individual scholars are Kazadi wa Mukuna, Gherard Kubik, Tiago de Oliveira Pinto, Fernando Ortiz and Fradique Lizardo, to name but a few. The list of organisations include the Consejo Inter-Americano de Musica (CIDEM) of the Organization of American States, and the International Music Council (IMC) of UNESCO.
2. K. wa Mukuna and T. Pinto de Oliveira, 1990–91, p. 47.
3. K. wa Mukuna, 1990, pp. 104–106.
4. Here I am referring to the African philosophy of existence expressed in the concept of belonging.
5. Nago, Gege, Ketu and Congo.
6. LuKumi, Arara, Sango de Dun (Sango arrives with a roar). For further discussion of the *cabildos*, see J. Mason, 1992.
7. Ibid., p. 9.
8. Bolaji Idowu, 1962, pp. 113–115.
9. Ibid.
10. J. Mason, 1992, p. 9. The author also provides a historical account of the survival of the various sets of drums in Cuba and their introduction into the United States.
11. K. wa Mukuna, 1979, p. 144.
12. E. Veiga de Oliveira, 1982, pp. 411–412.
13. For an extended discussion about the *berimbau*, its origin and its reinterpretation in Brazil, see G. Kubik, 1979, pp. 33–36.
14. F. Ortiz, 1952, Vol. 1, p. 21.
15. G. Kubik, 1979, p. 33.
16. F. Ortiz, 1952, p. 298.
17. P. Maultsby, 1990, p. 20. See also K. Nketia, 1981, pp. 82–88, and O. Wilson, 1981, pp. 95–105. A similar concept is implied in the methodological guideline proposed by the 'Grupo de Trabajo'. See K. wa Mukuna and T. Pinto de Oliveira, 1990–91, pp. 47–48.

Bibliography

BOLAJI IDOWU. 1962. *Olodumare: God in Yoruha Belief*. London, Longman Press.

HOLLOWAY, J.E. (ed.). 1990. *Africanisms in American Culture*. Bloomington, Indiana University Press.

KUBIK, G. 1979. *Angolan Cultural Traits in Black Music, Games and Dances of Brazil: A Study of African Cultural Extensions Overseas*. Lisbon, Junta de Investigacoes Cientificas do Ultramar.

————. 1991. *Extensionen Afrikanischer Kulturen in Brasilien*. Kinzel, Alano Verlag/Edition Herodot.

MASON, J. 1992. *Orin Orisa: Songs for Selected Heads*. New York, Yoruba Theological Archministry.

MAULTSBY, P. 1990. 'Africanism in African-American music'. In Holloway, J.E. (ed.). *Africanisms in American Culture*. Bloomington, Indiana University Press.

MUKUNA, K. WA. 1979. *Contriboicao Bantu na Musica Popular Brasileira*. São Paulo, Global Editora.

————. *'Sotaques*: Style and ethnicity in a Brazilian folk drama'. Unpublished paper.

————. 1990. 'The process of assimilation of African musical instruments in Brazil: Theoretical observation'. *The World of Music* (Berlin), No. 3.

————. 'The ox and the slave: *Bumba-rneu-Boi* in Maranhao'. *Progress Report in Ethnomusicology* (in press).

MUKUNA, K. WA, and PINTO DE OLIVEIRA, T. 1990–91. 'The study of African musical contribution to Latin America and the Caribbean: A methodological guideline'. *Bulletin of the International Committee* on *Urgent Anthropological and Ethnological Research* (Paris), No. 32–33.

NKETIA, K. 1981. 'African roots of music in the Americas: An African view'. In Heartz, D., and Wade, B. (ed.). *International Musicology Society: Report of the Twelfth Congress, Berkeley, 1977*. Philadelphia, American Musicological Society.

ORTIZ, F. 1950. *La Africania de la Música folklórica de Cuba*. Havana, Ediciones Cardenas y Cia.

————. 1952. *Los Instrumentos de la Música Afrocubana*. 5 vols. Havana. Dirección de Cultura del Ministerio de Educación.

PINTO DE OLIVEIRA, T. 1991. *Capoeira, Samba, Candomble: Afro-Brasilianische Musik im Reconcavo, Bahia*. Berlin: Museum für Volkerkunde.

VEIGA DE OLIVEIRA, E. 1996. *Instrumentos Musicais Populares Portugueses*. Lisbon, Fundacao Calouste Gulbenkian.

WILSON, O. 1981. 'The association of movement and music as a manifestation of a Black conceptual approach to music'. In Heartz, D., and Wade, B. (ed.). *International Musicology Society: Report of the Twelfth Congress, Berkeley, 1977*. Philadelphia, American Musicological Society.

Chapter 29

African Survivals in the Secular Popular Culture of the Americas

Yolande Behanzin-Joseph-Noël

THE AFRICAN CULTURAL COMPONENTS in the formation of the substratum of American and Caribbean cultures have been identified and widely studied; it is a presence whose depth varies from place to place, depending on history. We shall study this African contribution in a number of regions of the Americas and the Caribbean in the areas of secular popular music and dance – which in fact cannot really be separated – and, to a lesser extent, in a number of other aspects of culture.

It is well known that for slaves dance was a way of both asserting themselves and resisting oppression. According to Bangou, '...for him [the slave], rhythm was an opportunity to be himself, to become aware of his complete spiritual and bodily being, to feel himself its sole master, to have unfettered control of it, to glory in that feeling of being able to do something with oneself and use oneself to exhaustion. Through dance he rediscovered his universe; he became part of a world with which he was familiar: his own; he became one with his "cosmos". He could say: "I dance, therefore I am."'[1]

We have deliberately excluded from our study jazz and its forerunners – ragtime, blues and so on – which have been and are still the subject of numerous and often very detailed studies by experts. Our scope will be limited to a few observations on less well-known aspects of music and dance.

Afro-American reality, that of the American continents and the islands of the Caribbean, becomes explicable only if the historical background of blacks, 'people of colour' and their descendants is kept firmly in mind. In many places in Brazil, Cuba, the Guianas and Haiti, for example, various features of African civilisations have been maintained with great fidelity. Elsewhere, in the United States of America, where Anglo-Saxon culture predominates – except in the islands off the coasts of the Carolinas and Georgia, and above all in Louisiana and New Orleans – that memory is fainter.

Whatever the case, Creole blacks – the largest group – quickly lost much of their ancestral heritage, both in the area of the intangible – tales, proverbs, stories, myths, norms of political and economic thinking – and in that of techniques – goldsmithing, pottery, wood-carving, iron-working, etc. Only some elements of the heritage, whether immaterial or tangible, were preserved, although often reinterpreted and re-created: music, dance, religious beliefs. A careful examination will thus bring out what is purely of African origin and what has been transformed. A song collected by Lafcadio Hearn in the southern United States of America in the late nineteenth century clearly shows this evolution, being expressed in French, Creole and an African language. African languages quite rapidly ceased to be understood by Africans, even where they were perpetuated, for example in voodoo, *santería*, *candomblé* or *macumba* religious rites in the Caribbean, Latin America and Louisiana. Moreover, many secular dances that still exist today are essentially African.

During the slave period, in several northern cities in the thirteen British colonies of North America, masters would grant their slaves several days' respite from work twice a year, at Christmas and Easter, to celebrate their 'jubilees':[2] thus, in 1774, in Maryland, a witness was impressed by 'the musical improvization of Africans on an African music'. In Connecticut and New Hampshire, the custom, which seems to have originated about 1750, of granting a day of rest, 'Lection Day', lasted in some New England towns as late as the 1850s.

'Pinkster Day',[3] was celebrated in Pennsylvania, Maryland and New York. At this time, and for a week after Whit Sunday, the slaves were allowed to dance their 'Congo dances, dancing as they had danced back in Africa'. Eyewitness accounts of the time describe the celebrations in the town of Albany and later ones in Manhattan, at the site now known as City Hall Park. In Philadelphia, like everywhere else, the movements of the dancers – which took place in Potter's Field (now Washington Square) – attracted a host of white spectators. The music for these dances came from drums made from a wooden eel-trap, or a box, or a hollowed-out log. The drum was always covered with a cleanly dressed sheepskin drawn tightly over its wider end. In addition to the drum and 'patting' which predominated, various other instruments were used, like the *banjor* in Virginia,[4] a large hollow instrument with three strings, or a gourd with four strings that was played with the fingers in the same manner.[5]

In her book, Southern deals at length with the dances performed by blacks in Congo Square in New Orleans which were still being performed in 1843. In this Square (now Beauregard Square), from 2,000 to 3,000 people would congregate to see 'Kraels, Minahs, Congos and Mandringas, Gangas, Hiboas, and Fulas' dance.[6] According to the architect Henry B. Latrobe, who attended these dances between 1818 and 1820, 'the music consisted of two drums and a stringed instrument …, [one of which was] a cylindrical drum, about a foot in diameter…. The drum was an open-staved thing held between the knees…. The most curious instrument, however, was a stringed instrument, which no doubt was imported from Africa. On top of the finger board was the rude figure of a man in a sitting posture, and two pegs behind him to which the strings were fastened. The body was a calabash….'[7] Another instrument 'which, from the color of the wood seemed new, consisted of a block cut into something of the form of a cricket bat, with a long and deep mortise running down the center. The thing made a considerable noise, being beaten lustily on the side by a short stick. In the same orchestra was a square drum, looking like a stool, which made an abominably loud noise; also a calabash, with a round hole in it, the hole studded with brass nails, which was beaten by a woman with two short sticks.'[8] The dancers moved in a ring, some using a kind of shuffle step characteristic of West African dancing and which is still used today in some Caribbean dances such as the mazurka in Martinique or the calypso in Trinidad. Much to the dismay of many outraged ministers – even those of African descent – the believers of the black Protestant churches accompanied the singing of the psalms with this step: 'With every word so sung', complained Pastor Watson, 'they have a sinking of one or [the] other leg of the body alternately; producing an audible sound of the feet at every step, and as manifest as the steps of actual Negro dancing in Virginia, etc. If some, in the meantime, sit, they strike the sound alternately on each thigh.'[9]

In 1843, the New Orleans city authorities banned dances on Congo Square. But the dances did not end, continuing in the form of the shuffle step, the music always accompanying the 'ring shout' of the black Protestants. Elsewhere, 'when the fiddler grew tired, the slaves provided a different kind of dance music by "pattin' juba". Basically, this procedure involved foot tapping, hand clapping, and thigh slapping, all in precise rhythm. There seem to have existed, however, a number of ways to accomplish this feat.... [In] Louisiana ... the patting was performed by striking the hands on the knees, then striking the hands together, then striking the right shoulder with one hand, the left with the other – all the while keeping time with the feet, and singing....'[10] This dance is a precise replica of the rhythm to be found in Benin and Togo, throughout the Ewe and Adja culture area (Adja, Fon, Mina, Gun, Watchi, Aïzo) on the occasion of various celebrations. This dance was also to be found in other US states, notably in New York and New Jersey: '[T]he slaves produced a kind of percussion music by beating their hands on their thighs and stomping their heels.'[11] This beating is still very much alive today, for example in the Caribbean, where it marks the rhythm and amplifies it when the dancers enter a trance-like state.

One of the most popular dances of African origin is the *calanda*, which is found in various forms in the Americas. Father Labat, who lived in Martinique and Guadeloupe in the seventeenth century, refers to the *calanda* as one of the most popular dances among the slaves of those islands. He tells us that

> to mark the time, [the slaves] use drums made from two hollowed-out tree trunks of unequal sizes. One end is open, the other is covered with a lamb or goat skin scraped like parchment. The larger of these two drums may be three or four feet long and sixteen inches in diameter. The smaller one, called the baboula, is about as long and is eight or nine inches in diameter. The drummers put them between their legs or sit on them and touch them with the flat of four fingers of each hand. The man who touches the drum beats steadily and calmly, but the one beating the baboula beats as fast as he can ... and as the sound that it makes is much less than

that of the big drum, and very shrill; it simply serves to make a noise, and does not beat out the rhythm or mark the movements of the dancers.[12]

The sound of the instruments composing the orchestra is greatly enriched by the human voice, which, in Africa, has always been one of the foremost means of expression. 'The dancers', adds Father J.-B. Labat, 'form up in two lines, one in front of the other, the men on one side, the women on the other. Those who are tired of dancing and the spectators form a circle around the dancers and the drums. The most skilful one sings a song that he composes as he goes along on any subject he chooses, and the chorus is sung by all the spectators and accompanied by a great deal of clapping.'

Labat also gives a good description of the circle that brings together the essential elements of the group – drummers, singers and dancers – and which is surrounded by the crowd, as well as the art of improvisation, the dialogue between the soloist and the choir, and the clapping of hands that beats out the rhythm. This practice of improvising songs during a festival with the chorus being immediately picked up by the spectators still happens. It is still to be found today in many parts of Africa, in particular on the occasion of events at which collective emotions are running high, as in the funerary ceremonies of the Adja group in Benin. The technique of the antiphon, in which the soloist sings a theme and the choir responds to him, still typifies both Afro-American (the blues, for example) and Caribbean music (*beguine*, *zouk*, calypso, rumba, salsa).

Observing the dancers, Labat further notes that the dancers position their arms a little like

> those who dance while playing the castanets. They leap, pirouette, approach to within two or three feet of each other, withdraw in time until the sound of the drum alerts them to come back together striking their thighs against one another, that is the men against the women. To see them, it looks as if their bellies are bumping together, whereas it is only the thighs that take the blows. They withdraw at once, pirouetting as they go, and then begin the same movement again with gestures that are totally lewd, and as often as the drum gives the signal to do so, which it does several times in succession. From time to time they interlock their arms and do two or three turns while still striking their thighs ...

This *calanda* was danced over a very long period, since Moreau de Saint-Méry reports encountering it in Santo Domingo during the second half of the eighteenth century. His account reveals that the African ingredients that typify it were still visible: the orchestra was made up of two drums identical to those mentioned earlier. The shorter, the *bamboula*, was sometimes made from a single large piece of bamboo. On each drum a drummer would stand astride, hitting it with his wrists and fingers, slowly on one drum in order to give a hollow sound. The sharper sound of small calabashes half filled with pebbles or kernels of corn, which the players shook by striking them on one hand, would harmonise with the drums. Sometimes the orchestra would be made more complete with a *banza*, a sort of violin with four strings which were plucked. It is in fact 'an instrument composed of a little board eight inches long by four or five wide. On it they have a little bit of steel or brass wire, set the long way of the board, under which they pass crosswise the extremely fine tips of marsh reeds or bamboo, of unequal lengths, with an almost equal width throughout, and which hardly exceeds three lines. The negro, holding the little board in his two hands, rests his thumbnail on the very ends of the reeds, which the brass wire forces thus to rise and vibrate'. The *banza* is to be found in many places in Africa but with a variety of names and in varied forms. It also long continued to exist in remote parts of the 'black Americas'.

The instrumental ensemble was accompanied by a female choir, which marked time with the songs by clapping their hands. The audience responded in chorus to one or two solo singers who improvised.

The dancers, always in equal numbers of men and women, came to the middle of a circle, facing each other:

> [This dance] consists of a step wherein each foot is alternately extended and withdrawn, striking the earth hard, first with the toe and then with the heel. It is done somewhat as in the step of the Anglaise. The man turns either around in the same spot or around his partner, who also turns and changes her place, while shaking the two ends of a kerchief which she holds. The woman keeps lowering and raising her arms while holding her elbows close to her body and her fists nearly closed. This dance … is very animated. Its even rhythm adds real grace to it. The dancers perform admirably, vying with each other….[13]

It is again to Moreau de Saint-Méry that we owe precise details of another dance originating in Africa,

> … the Chica, also known as the Calenda in the Leeward Islands, but which is called the Congo in Cayenne, the Fandango in Spain, and so on. This dance has an air especially dedicated to it and the beat is strongly accentuated. The woman shows her quality in the skill with which she makes her hips and the lower part of her back move, while keeping the rest of her body more or less immobile. This does not mean that she stops the movement of her arms, which balance the two extremities with a kerchief or with her short petticoat. A man approaches her, leaps suddenly, and falls, to the beat, almost touching her. He recoils, leaps again, and provokes her to a most seductive struggle. The dance grows wilder and soon she offers a picture in which the facial features are at first voluptuous but soon become lascivious. The true quality of the Chica cannot be described and I limit myself to saying that the impression it makes is so powerful that the African or Creole male of no matter what shade of skin cannot watch it without being stirred – unless he has lost his very final sparks of emotion.

It is this dance, called the *calanda*, that Caribbean folk dance groups still dance today. Until 1902, when Mount Pelée erupted, marking a break in the history of Martinique, it was highly esteemed at the famous carnival of the town of Saint-Pierre. There was more than one *beguine* which told of it, such as the folk version, called *Marka! Marka! Ça ou fè a pa bien*, in which a line in the first verse refers to the mother who *ka dansé kalinda*.

The *calanda*, undeniably of Bantu origin, is the heir to a dance imported into the Americas from Angola. It is reminiscent of the popular 'belly-dance', still danced today in the Cape Verde islands. Eileen Southern tells us that in the second half of the nineteenth century, the *calanda* was danced in Louisiana by slaves and then their descendants. It was 'a kind of quadrille in which two lines of dancers faced each other, advancing and retreating in time to the music. The name of the song and the music were the same'.[14] It was also danced in Peru where, according to Descola, 'Originally a favourite dance of the negro slaves, the *calenda* had penetrated into the best Lima society'.[15] Father Labat wrote of it in the seventeenth century that 'The Spaniards have learnt it from the negroes.... The French ... have forbidden it, because the postures and movements of this dance are most improper.... It is nevertheless popular with the Spanish Creoles of America and is so customary among them that it forms the better part of their amusements and even enters into their devotions. They dance it in their churches and during their processions....' But a stop was eventually put to these excesses, not without difficulty, by the Most Holy Mother the Apostolic and Roman Church.

Bastide[16] reports the presence of the *calanda* in Uruguay and Argentina as late as the nineteenth century, but it had ceased to be danced there by the twentieth century. It bore 'the same name as in Louisiana, and was marked the meeting of navels'. Bastide adds that anther dance of African origin was danced in Peru, the *golpe de frente* or meeting of navels. Such, then, is the common feature of erotic dances originating from Angola which, mixing with the Spanish flamenco, gave birth to the dance that is so popular in Latin America, from Argentina to Bolivia: the *zomba* or *cueca* or *zamacueca* (which represents the amorous pursuit of a woman by a man and ends with the couple locked in a voluptuous embrace). Blacks and whites used to dance it with each group modifying it in the light of its culture and social background. The *zamacueca* or the *mozamala*, was, according to Descola, 'the typical dance of Peru, and especially of Lima.... Depending on the couples who danced it, it could be very pure or lascivious, for it "disturbed both the heart and the senses". Everything depended on the *almea*, the state of soul.... But ... the *zamacueca* was not always innocent'. In Mexico, too, in 1766, the Inquisition mentioned a dance performed by four women and four men also involving *ombligados* (navel against navel). Whatever it was called, the *calanda* enabled the slaves to express their vitality and their sensitivity through the only thing that belonged to them: their own body.

Cuba, too, long retained dances of African origin, such as the *caringa* (*calanda*), or the *mani* dance, a sort of danced fight which has inspired many highly rhythmic modern tunes. One has only to hear the melody or the rhythm to be convinced that the *guarachas*, rumbas and other *habaneras* owe their popularity to their African-derived scansion and their sensuality. Mention must also be made of the many musical instruments, also of African origin, listed and studied by Fernando Ortiz (1952) along with his research on Afro-Cuban music.

The *bomba*, another dance of African origin, performed mainly at Christmas and accompanied by songs in Spanish,[17] is still danced in the valley of the

Rio Chota in northern Ecuador where descendants of former slaves of the Jesuits live.

Brazil (people of all races) is also deeply marked by African culture. Of course, there is the samba which, in Angola, describes the 'meeting of navels' (*umbigada* in Brazilian) and which has become the national dance. In the original samba, the dancers appeared 'either in line, men opposite women, or in a circle with a couple that moves out to dance in its centre, which mimics the choice of sexual partners'.[18]

In Colombia,[19] the African contributions are very much present both in musical instruments and in dances. Thus there is the *curralao*, which expresses the initial amorous approaches of a woman and a man, or the *bambouco*, whose name probably comes from the African *bambouk*, which has today become, 'in sung form, [a] national music'.

The *bamboula*, a very lively dance that is danced in couples, is also of Bantu origin. As Father Labat pointed out, the word *bamboula* doubtless derives from the African bamboo drum which originally accompanied the dance. The *bamboula* was danced on Place Congo in New Orleans on Saturday and Sunday nights with an orchestra consisting of drums, castanets made of two donkey jaws and anklets of little bells worn by the women. Reproduced in Southern's book, a drawing by E.W. Kemble – which illustrated an article by G. Cable, 'The dance in Place Congo' (*Century Magazine*, 31 [1885–86]) – clearly shows the circle of dancers, the couple dancing and the four drummers sitting on the ground. Among the latter, one is astride his instrument and is striking it with two thigh bones, while the other three, with drums placed between their legs, are beating them with their hands. It seems that after it was banned from being performed in public places in 1843, the *bamboula* continued after the abolition of slavery[20] under the name *cabinda*, a new name that confirms its Bantu origin.

Calendas and *bamboulas* continued to brighten the days of the descendants of slaves. As Southern stresses, Afro-American music in the United States today retains traces of at least two *bamboulas* that predate the US Civil War: *Musieu Bainjo*, which 'pokes fun at the city dandy'[21] and *Quand patate la cuite*. It is no surprise that these titles are in Creole, since Louisiana used to be a French colony where Creole was still spoken at the beginning of the twentieth century. Martinique has retained the memory of a dance called the *bamboula*, a joyful affair in which young and old joined with gusto. The term is still used to express a joyous, dancing, relaxed, friendly atmosphere. The *gwoka*, Guadeloupean popular music, comes directly from Africa, as witnessed by the names of the seven rhythms that are indubitably of African origin (*mende* and *kalaja* in particular).

The *danmyé* (draughtboard), a fight danced and mimed by men, is still performed in Martinique. It is a very lively cultural expression which is worth lingering over. It has other names: *laggia*, *laguia*, *ladja* in the northern part of the island, or *kokoyé* or *wonpwen*. The *danmyé* is related to the Haitian *sauvé bâton* or the Brazilian *capoeira*. The rhythm of the dancers' hand-to-hand fight is beaten out by the *tambouyé* (drummer). The drummer bestrides the drum and strikes the tightly stretched flayed sheepskin with his hands. He can also scrape it with his heel to alter the sound. He is accompanied by a second instrumentalist – a singer who pounds rapidly on his drum, which may be an empty barrel struck with two little sticks. Labat had already noted the difference in the rhythm given by the two drums:

> Abruptly, two dancers rise up one in front of the other, the heels strike the ground in step, the arms stiffen forward, every muscle is tensed, their facial muscles are frozen…. The movement speeds up; the drummer of the 'little woods' (*ti boi*) gives the commands and shouts out phrases that make people laugh and are personal…. Other dancers join the dance and the temperature rises. From time to time, a dancer separates himself from the group and, without breaking the rhythm of the group, runs a few jerky steps, making tremendous springs on his hocks.[22]

The AM 4 group[23] has recently established a school of *danmyé* in Martinique, whose aim is to link up with the profound reality of this cultural expression while preserving its martial character, pounded out by the rhythm of the drums which are its life and soul. The fact is that one cannot become a *danmyé* dancer at will. Before meriting that name, a candidate must go through several stages (beginner, senior, *met sava'n*) before reaching the top. For the founders of the AM 4 group, *danmyé* is not simply a fight danced to the beat of drums – it is nothing short of a martial art. The *ladja* or *danmyé* dancer is 'a man who practises a discipline in which esotericism, communion with plants, watercourses and even nutrition are an integral part of a training leading to a special encounter between two *met sava'n*, an evocative term associated with Martiniquan reality, which comes from the observation that in a flock at pasture, the animals are under the charge of a male obliged to defend his patch, *sava'n* (savannah), against intrusion by a male laying claim to leadership'.

The dancer-fighter is in a state of total concentration which enables him to communicate with the music and to fight to the rhythm of the drum. He succeeds in doing so thanks to physical preparation which hardens his body and develops agility and reflexes. Leaf baths, *bains la sous* (bathing in a river at its source), ingestion of certain foods and learning to fight to the sound of the drum are all part of his conditioning. All these exercises are designed to make the dancer-fighter 'at one with the cosmos'. 'The *kha* pose, with hands outstretched to the heavens, which is to be found in Upper Egypt and which prefigures every fight' expresses that he is ready to confront the adversary. Since the rhythm of the drum is fundamental, each fighter has his own *tambouyé* who beats out his dance and, through 'one, two or three time syncopation (defence, attack/defence, continuous attack)', gives him the energy and the strength to destabilise the adversary. But during the fight, a single drummer, chosen beforehand, performs. The challenges having been issued many weeks before the encounter and the drummer having been selected, the dancer now has to train to fight against the chosen drum so as to destabilise the adversary using tricks and to strike him down, thus winning victory. The fighters, according to very detailed rules, use every part of the body. They can hit with the hand closed or open, the elbow, the head, the knee or the foot. They are also allowed to 'grab their adversary, immobilize him or sweep him off his feet'. The blows, delivered with violence, may cause serious injuries, such that people sometimes speak of the *ladja* of death or *danmyé lan mö*. Once the fight is over and before launching into the next one, the fighters undergo a ritual 'preparation' to 'get rid of' the first fight. The seniors (*majo*) and the *met sava'n* have always been the focus of respectful and fearful admiration from both adults and children, doubtless because of their extraordinary power.

Although we do not intend to speak of jazz in depth, we shall nevertheless just mention that this music – which is sometimes separated from dance and is played mostly with instruments unknown to Africa – is fundamentally linked to Africa. Musicians and musicologists are all agreed in recognising that two of the musical peculiarities of jazz derive from Africa: 'the use of scales not usually employed in European art music [the diatonic scale] but derived from West Africa ... or from the combination of African scales with European harmonies ... and another African element, rhythm',[24] to which is added the use of polyphonic, or contrapuntal, rhythmic effects.[25] According to the writer LeRoi Jones, 'the only so-called popular music in this country of any real value is of African derivation'.[26]

The African contribution is not the only one present in American culture. Thus, British, Iberian and French cultures mixed with African cultural traits have each produced original types of music, either Ibero-Anglo-American and Caribbean (Cuba, Puerto Rico, Santo Domingo, Trinidad, Brazil) or Franco-Caribbean and French Guyanese (Guadeloupe, Haiti, Martinique and French Guiana). The French musical tradition combined with that of Africa is also to be found in New Orleans, where the people of colour and the Creoles successfully created a musical style strikingly similar to that of Martinique. In the same way, the satirical and polemical song, the Beninese *han-lo*, for example, has been perpetuated in many songs in the Caribbean which, notably at carnival, criticise, mock and ridicule – sometimes very harshly – unfortunate heroes who would willingly do without such notoriety.

Although it has lost its sacred character, the mask is another example of the survival of African culture in Martinique, such as the *Papa diab* used on Shrove Tuesday.[27] It already existed in the late nineteenth century, since the American Lafcadio Hearn, attending the carnival at Saint-Pierre in Martinique, describes it as a 'hideous blood-colored mask, and a cap, whose four sides are formed by four mirrors, the whole head-dress being surmounted by a red lantern. He has a white wig made of horse-hair and walks about the streets surrounded by children to whom he gives coins and sweets'. At the time, he did not wear horns, but dragged behind him the 'Shrove Tuesday ox'. With Christian influence, the pagan ox became fused with the devil to form a single figure: the *Diab*, dressed all in red, with an ox head bearing mirrors. In 1948, Landry Detho, a docker at Fort-de-France, resumed the tradition of the red devil, a tradition, which, although deeply rooted in the collective subconscious, had disappeared after the eruption of Mount Pelée in 1902. Detho carved a devil mask to which he later added a fork. This *Diab* is the product of Creole syncretism in which African animism is mixed with European Catholicism. The African origin of this mask is verified and recorded in a piece written by Aimé Césaire, which appeared in 1973 in the Martiniquan review *Études littéraires*, in which the poet describes his encounter with the red devil of this island's Shrove Tuesday: 'I was in Senegal, in Casamance, at a big village festival.... Suddenly, I saw my devil appear, the ox of the Martiniquan Shrove Tuesday, with his red covering covered with mirrors, his tail and his ox horns. I rushed up to a villager: I asked him for explanations. He replied that it is the mask of those who have undergone initiation ... that the ox horns were the symbol of temporal wealth and that the mirrors set side by side symbolized spiritual wealth. In short, this mask was a divine mask.' As to Christianity, it manifests itself in the devil's fork and the red of the flames of hell, a remarkable point of contact with the original red. The song that the devil sings also testifies to Christian influence: *Abbi, abbi, abbi, caïman, mi diab'la déwö* (Abbi, abbi, abbi, cayman, the devil has come out, he is outside), *diab'la ka mandé an ti manmaille, an ti manmaille san batinm* (the devil demands an unbaptised child). These two sentences merit a closer look. *Abbi* is a term that is hardly found anywhere else other than in this song and is certainly of African origin. Its precise meaning is not known but we know that it attracts the attention of spectators. Nor are there any caymans in Martinique. This is quite obviously a memory of African fauna. But what the song above all recalls is a ritual that was formerly practised in some parts of Africa, by which bad luck could be exorcised and the village protected by delivering a child or the most beautiful girl in the village each year to the cayman, the master of the watercourse that supplied the village. Many African legends and tales still tell of this ritual, even today.

The pedagogical function of the *Diab* should also be stressed. While dancing, he walks about following a route that is not a matter of chance because he has planned to stop in front of certain houses to sing out his *Abbi*, an air that causes the inhabitants to quake, since it lambastes those who have fallen short of the rules of the community. The *Diab* is in a way the devil-policeman, the *zangbeto* of Adja culture or the *Egun-gun* of the Yoruba. The mask of the *Diab* gives the person wearing it great power: 'Every audacity is allowed him; he cuts into processions, even the *"vidé"* [the processional dance that meanders through the streets], attracts everybody and gives unheard-of strength.' He is the king of carnival. Despite the remoteness in time and space and the changes of meaning it has undergone (for example, the symbolism of the ox has been eliminated), the Martiniquan *Diab* shows that Africa is indeed rooted in the heart of Africans of the diaspora.

Although we have limited our comments to a single area, African survivals are many and are to be found in values (respect for the old, solidarity, a love of children that goes far beyond mere parental affection), behaviour (the sinuous walk of women and the hip-swaying walk of men, the infectious laughter, the interest in games, tales and legends) and language (the structure of Creole has remained very African, as has its sensuality), or in other aspects of culture (religious rituals, pharmacopoeia, cooking, cosmogony and so on).

Fortunately, thanks to the recent growth in awareness of the importance of the common cultural heritage, the path for multidisciplinary studies is open. We shall now be able to study globally the various African civilisations (e.g. Bantu, Yoruba, Sudanic) and the African diaspora, enriched by other historical contributions in the Americas and the Caribbean.

Notes

1. H. Bangou, 1962, Vol. 1, p. 116.
2. E. Southern, 1976, pp. 46–47 (1997, p. 42).
3. Ibid., pp. 47–49 (pp. 53–55).
4. Ibid., p. 128 (p. 172).
5. Ibid., p. 58 (p. 48).
6. Ibid., pp. 111 and 112 (pp. 136–137).
7. Ibid. (pp. 137–138).
8. Ibid.
9. Ibid., p. 84 (p. 88).
10. Ibid., pp. 135–136 (pp. 168–169).
11. Ibid., p. 49 (p. 56).
12. See H. Bangou, 1962, p. 116.
13. M.L.E. Moreau de Saint-Méry, 1958, Vol. 1, pp. 63–64 (Eng. tr., pp. 55–56).
14. E. Southern, p. 148 (1997, p. 171).
15. J. Descola, 1962, pp. 185–186 (Eng. tr., p. 168).
16. R. Bastide, 1967, pp. 178–180.
17. Ibid., pp. 178–179.
18. Ibid., p. 181.
19. Ibid., p. 179.
20. Ibid., p. 178.
21. E. Southern, 1976, p. 149 (1997, p. 171).
22. L. Gabriel-Soime, 1966, p. 215.
23. See *France-Antilles Hebdo*, 13–19 May 1994, p. 36.
24. F. Newton, 1966, pp. 22–23 (1960, p. 26).
25. L. Jones, 1968, p. 38 (1963, p. 25).
26. Ibid., p. 40 (1963, p. 28).
27. See *France-Antilles Hebdo*, 18–24 February 1994, pp. 24–25.

Bibliography

BANGOU, H. 1962. *La Guadeloupe (1492–1848)*. 2 vols. Paris, Éditions du Centre.

BASTIDE, R. 1967. *Les Amériques noires*. Paris, Payot. (Coll. Petite bibliothèque.)

DESCOLA, J. 1962. *La vie quotidienne au Pérou au temps des Espagnols (1710–1820)*. Paris, Hachette. [Eng. tr., Heron, M. 1968. *Daily Life in Colonial Peru 1710–1820*. New York, Macmillan.]

France-Antilles Hebdo, 18–24 February and 13–19 May 1994.

GABRIEL-SOIME, L. 1966. *Ça, c'est la Martinique!* Paris.

JONES, L. 1968. *Le peuple du blues*. Paris, Gallimard. [Orig. Am. ed., 1963. *Blues People: Negro Music in White America*. New York, William Morrow and Company.]

MOREAU DE SAINT-MERY, M.L.E. 1958. *Description de la partie française de l'île Saint-Domingue*. 3 vols. Paris, Société de l'histoire des colonies françaises/Larose. [Abridged and edited Eng. tr., Spencer, I.D. *A Civilization That Perished: The Last Years of White Colonial Rule in Haiti*. Lanham, Md., University Press of America.]

NEWTON, F. 1966. *Une sociologie du jazz*. Paris, Flammarion. [Orig. Am. ed., 1960. *The Jazz Scene*. New York, Monthly Review Press.]

ORTIZ, F. 1952. *Los Instrumentos de la Música Afrocubana*. 5 vols. Havana, Ministry of Education.

SOUTHERN, E. 1976. *Histoire de la musique noire américaine*. Paris, Buchet-Chastel. [3rd Am. ed., 1997. *The Music of Black Americans: A History*. New York, W.W. Norton and Co., 1997 (1st ed., 1971).]

Chapter 30

Survivals and Dynamism of African Cultures in the Americas

Olabiyi B. Yai

> *Traemos nuestro rasgo*
> *al perfil definitivo de América.*
> (We have added our features)
> (to the finished profile of America.)
> Nicolás Guillén

> *Orúko tó wu làá jé léhìn odi.*
> (A person is free to choose a name
> when far from home.)
> Yoruba proverb

LET US DARE TO TALK of the future of humanity: '*La force aussi toujours de regarder demain*' (Strength also [means] always looking to tomorrow). So says Aimé Césaire, that worthy son of Africa, a great observer alert to every breath in the world, who, in his very personal voice, speaks of the destiny of African cultures on the continent and in the diaspora and, with it, that of every culture of the human race.

The echoes of the five hundredth anniversary of 1492, variously celebrated around the world, were barely dying out – and with them the end of apartheid, the most gaping and ugly sore on the slave route – when the pogroms in Rwanda broke out and others in Bosnia, reminding us that peace is never won. All these tragic events constitute so many milestones, or wrong turnings, on the slave route. Regarded individually or together, they should be telling us how urgent it is to seek out together, in solidarity, in our respective cultures, what is needed to give us the 'strength always to look to tomorrow'. Let us not forget that Wells's words, 'Our true nationality is mankind', have never been as true as they are today.

But 'let us take again the useful patient path', as Césaire also invites us. It was in 1492 that Christopher Columbus reached Hispaniola, believing he was landing in India. Instead of semantic disputes over the notion of discovery,[1] we would surely gain by speaking, for the history of the human species, of the Columbus galaxy. For Africa, 1492 marks the beginning of the massive forced exodus of its daughters and sons, victims of the most inhuman traffic in human history. Africa was economically and politically devastated. The world economy, as Immanuel Wallerstein has so well stated it, practically caused it to 'go off the rails'. Its institutions – some of them thousands of years old – and its cultures were devastated. Even today, Africa has not fully recovered from that tragedy. Five centuries later, we must indeed acknowledge, with Basil Davidson,[2] that the Genoese navigator's 'discovery' – 'the curse of Columbus' – had many negative effects on Africa. The Columbus galaxy inaugurated the era of the great empires 'on which the sun never set'. It also gave rise to what, playing on one of Calderón's themes, the great poet Octavio Paz calls '*el gran teatro del immundo*'. It is the continued existence of this 'great theatre of the obscene' that summons us to place the Slave Route project in a new, ecumenical perspective.

The issue is not about promoting some '*visión de los vencidos*'(vision of the vanquished)[3] – a very legitimate and easy temptation, but one which must be resisted. It is illusory and distressing to speak of victors when we are actors participating in the 'great theatre of the obscene'. Of course, Africans were the most numerous victims, but the African cultures that arrived in the Americas with the slaves nevertheless never saw themselves as vanquished. Despite the most sophisticated strategies to destroy cultural identity, despite repeated ethnic cleansing and inhuman working conditions, despite sexual exploitation and the disintegration of their social and economic systems, Africans were able to ensure the survival of the key parts of their original cultures, due to the initiatives that they were able to take or to the negotiating spaces that they were able to extract from – or impose on – their masters. They also assimilated some of the practices of the other cultures with which they came into contact, interpreting and re-creating them as they did so.

Thus, Yoruba culture, for example, sees life as a river[4] of which we are all – individuals and cultural groups – eddies borne along through numerous encounters rolling towards the wide ocean of the great beyond (*Odò layé*). Variants of this concept are to be found in several African cultures. Anyone who tried to separate the eddies from the river would be very unwise indeed! Yet slavery was just such an attempt to do so. And our ancestors were quite aware of that. Thus Afro-Brazilians call Africa not the mother-continent (*Guiné*) or *Africa*, which are borrowed names, but *Ilé Ayé/Ìlú Ayé* (the home of life/the country of life). By using that name, invented overseas in conditions in which life was harsh, the Africans of Brazil were demonstrating that culture is a striving of values towards life – a life *towards* and *for* values. It is this vision of the world that makes it possible to explain four centuries of creativity generated by African cultures imported into the Americas.

But how can we give even a cursory account of *vodun* in Haiti and Louisiana, the art of cooking in Bahia, the Creole vitality of the Caribbean, the blues and jazz, the baroque statues of the Afro-Brazilian sculptor Alejadinho in the eighteenth century, the Rastafarians, the Nossa Senhora de Boa Morte (Our Lady of the Good Death) sorority in Brazil, whose members, worthy heirs of their African ancestors, vow to struggle in dignity against poverty and oppression and for the preservation of African culture. How shall we describe the art of Haiti (naively described as naive), rap and the poetry of Nicolás Guillén, the genius of Zora Neale Hurston and the pictorial art of the Cuban Wilfredo Lam or his contemporary successor Manuel Mendive, the oral art of the poets of the Ecuadorian Esmeralda and the films of Spike Lee?

I shall confine myself first to raising a few methodological and epistemological problems inherent in certain approaches in research on African cultures in the Americas. I shall then examine the survivals and dynamism of African cultures in the Americas, especially in the areas of religions and popular cultures, areas that seem to me to be extensions of African cultures in their relations with other cultures, perhaps even more today than in years gone by.

> The resurgence takes place here
> through wind born in Africa
> ... the resurgence here takes place
> through influx even more than through afflux.

> Aimé Césaire

I shall begin by elucidating a number of terms. The notion of survival, for example, is often criticised and is currently regarded as unfashionable.[5] It has been proposed that it be replaced by the notions of transculturation, adaptation, acculturation or even re-creation. Without our always being aware of it, the issues are not simply semantic. Here, perhaps more than elsewhere, concepts have a sometimes misleading ideological content, always laden with subconscious meaning and unsuspected consequences. We must accept that we shall never be able to pay proper due to what Mintz calls 'the toughness and intelligence of those millions of enslaved people who built their new ways of life under conditions of almost unremitting oppression'.[6] As regards the concept of adaptation, it does not lack relevance, but it is not exhaustive, since it assumes that the initiative was not taken by Africans, who had only to find their niche in an environment created for them by European cultures regarded as being 'already there'. This concept contains an assimilationist assumption, or even a project of implicit integration. Of course Africans did not ask to emigrate to the Americas. But once there, the historical reality that they offer us does not consist only of 'responses'. They must also have questioned other cultures and questioned one another. As Sartre writes, 'the important thing is what people do with what they have been made'. While it does leave room for the creative genius of African cultures in the new host countries, the concept of re-creation still remains silent on the conditions of that creativity. The 'conditions of almost unremitting repression' mentioned above by Mintz have virtually no place in it, since this concept naively assumes a neutral context. It is the same with the concepts of transculturation and acculturation, which say nothing about the conditions of their occurrence. For all these reasons, the concept of survival is still the most appropriate one, since it evokes the tension, the struggle, the selection of individuals, values and cultural traits, all undeniably phenomena in the historical record. It also assumes the clash of two intentions: an intention of cultural genocide on the part of the slave masters, and a firm intention not to die on the part of African cultures, through the women and men in whom they were expressed.

Since the now classic debates between Herskovits and Frazier on the fate of African cultures in the Americas, many researchers have looked at the issues highlighted by those two pioneers, each one in the light of his or her loyalties or theoretical or ideological interest.[7] Herskovits has often been criticised for his predilection for correspondences between African cultural traits in Africa and Afro-American cultural traits. The hunt for 'Africanisms' undoubtedly irritated researchers of succeeding generations,[8] but that is an unreal dispute, as are the criticisms of ahistoricism made against the defenders of a degree of continuity on both sides of the Atlantic. Drawing parallels between the culture of Allada and that of Haiti does not imply that the Fon culture in Africa has not changed 'significantly since the heyday of the slave trade', as Mintz suggests.[9] It simply assumes that the two cultures have changed, sometimes profoundly, while remaining themselves. '*Oko kìí jé ti baba tomo kó máà láàlà*' (There is always room for difference inside the farm that belongs jointly to father and son), says a Yoruba proverb. I also do not see how the approach of R. Price and S. Price, which draws on the Chomskyan model of generative grammar by speaking of 'deep structures and surface manifestations',[10] can do without any reference to an African invariant.

For his part, writing of syncretism in Afro-American religions, Mintz invites us, not unreasonably, to focus more, not on the origins, but on analysis of the specific processes of change: 'What is intrinsically more interesting scientifically (and perhaps aesthetically, as well) than the "blending" of African and European elements in Afro-Cuban belief, for instance, is the system of underlying values and perceptions, and the particular local conditions, according to which that particular "mixture" rather than some other, took on its characteristic form.' And he adds, 'The same may be true of studies of material culture, art, folklore, and all else that is definably Afro-American.'[11] Mintz's approach, assuredly fruitful and apparently radical, seems to us to miss part of its target, for the good reason that it does not pass the test of African historical depth.

It enables us to put our finger on the inadequacy – not methodological but, this time, epistemological – that most studies of Afro-American cultures share, across all schools: namely, their blindness to pre-Atlantic African cultural traditions. In order to account for Afro-Christian religious syncretism in the Americas, for example, the most radical researchers refer us to the same phenomenon in Africa, through missionary contacts in the kingdom of Kongo and on the coast of West Africa and the reaction of both élites and the population to this novelty.[12] We feel that such an approach is still not radical enough, since it encloses African cultural dynamism in an Atlantic strait-jacket. It assumes that innovation requires contact between cultures from Africa and cultures from Europe, whether the encounter occurs in Africa or in the Americas. It suggests that invention always comes from the outside – and that is false. Paradoxically, the Afro-American ideologues who criticise this approach subconsciously agree with it. The two approaches assume, in a worrying blind spot, the exclusion of the African from pre-Atlantic cultural dynamism. The possibility of a continental tradition of Afro-African syncretism is never contemplated. Yet that tradition is a very real one – indeed a massive one – and underlies the cultural dynamisms in the African diaspora. In their enthusiasm to demonstrate the creativeness of enslaved blacks, they simply manage to confine it in its 'reactive' role to a stimulus from elsewhere. In this debate, it is Africans and the African heartland that are the great absentees.

But some questions just cannot be evaded. What is the cultural norm? What is the ideal of cultural behaviour in everyday life of reputedly multiethnic geo-political entities such as ancient Ghana, Kongo, Mali, Allada, etc.? How did the Africans of Walo, Tekrur, Zimbabwe, Oyo or Abomey conceive of culture? How did the peoples of these geo-political entities envisage cultural relations between them and their neighbours? How does one – did one – say 'culture' in Kimbundu, Shona, Efik, Fulfulde, Ciyanja or Wolof? And what can be learned from such concepts? What types of discourse were formulated on culture and cultural relations? (Even if we cannot prove that such discourse always existed everywhere, neither can we prove the contrary, since we are dealing with oral cultures.)

When, in Bahia, the Afro-Brazilian *Aninha*, of Gurunsi origin and knowing herself to be so, was initiated into the Yoruba religion and became *iyalorixa* or saint's mother, that is high priestess – in consequence of which her Gurunsi ancestors became *egúngún* (spirits of the ancestors) venerated in the Yoruba pantheon in Bahia – did she act out of African atavism by creating something new in the framework of an earlier tradition, or did she innovate under the pressure of circumstances and the Brazilian environment? And if there are two determinants, what is the respective weight of African atavism and the response to circumstances, and why and how are they ranked?[13]

It is by asking this sort of question and trying to find a reply that we shall give research on African cultures in the Americas a solid epistemological base and reduce the risk of errors of interpretation. In other words, we need to stress a certain type of research, like the poetics/politics of the African relation so dear to Édouard Glissant. Yoruba wisdom informs us that 'when a child stumbles against an obstacle, he looks in front of him; when an adult does so, he looks behind him' (*Bómodé bá kosè a wowájú, bí àgbà bá kosè a wèhìn*). It is the same thing as regards the understanding of cultural phenomena in the African Americas. Aimé Césaire was not saying anything different: 'The resurgence takes place here through wind born in Africa.'

Another methodological point: an African 'poetics of relation' in the Americas should give ample space to 'implicit survivals'. There has been too much of a tendency to envisage survivals only in terms of explicit evidence. But the cultural memory in a relationship situation is not only what one remembers but also what one has chosen to forget in the other party. Thus, when African cultures refuse to adapt to the values of the European cultures with which they are in contact, the 'black hole' (to play on a term that is one of Césaire's as well as one used in modern science) may be either the presence of an absence or the absence of a presence that is otherwise significant. Let us take the example of the notorious 'lack of success' of Afro-Americans in business, compared to the sometimes amazing 'success' of other newly arrived immigrants. Is this a failing tied to a particular circumstance and one therefore that can be overcome, or is it, on the contrary, a rejection of the economic paradigm on offer, a stubborn refusal not to learn a grammar whose rules are contrary to African ideas of economic and social development? The question remains open.

It is thus to the concept of culture as it is apprehended by different traditions that we must return, as well as to the practices that flow from it. We also need to interrogate, with an open mind but searchingly, the philosophical texts, in particular on wisdom, and not hesitate to debate the issue of slavery,[14] as the 'traditional' intellectuals of precolonial Africa surely did.

I shall be particularly concerned with Yoruba culture, in which the set of characteristics proposed to a community is called *àsà*.[15] This same word may apply also to an individual, in that case describing personality and habits. The word *àsà* derives from the verb *sà*, which means to choose, discern, discriminate, select, sort. When it is applied to a community, it describes a set of collective behaviours normally expected of individuals who have chosen it consciously and responsibly. In other words, in principle, *àsà* cannot be imposed. Since *àsà* brings in the notion of choice, it can be said that Yoruba culture is part of a tradition open to innovation.[16] What has not been the object of a collective choice is not part of tradition. Individuals, professional groups, lineages, ethnic groups, etc., have their own *àsà*, each forming a set that can be pictured as a chain with intersections. In Yoruba culture, as *oríkì* (which means, approximately, mottoes) or oral poetry shows very clearly, the plural character of identities goes without saying.

Faced as they were with the hostility of their New World environment (inhuman work in mines and plantations), making a selection among the flow of cultural traits proposed by tradition took on for the Africans every appearance of a necessity. The African traditionalists of the New World must have learned, probably in a few decades, to choose in their respective traditions which cultural traits and values to retain *in toto* and which traits of other cultures to choose to forge the admirable syncretism that we know today which is, it must be stressed, Afro-American before it is Afro-Christian. As Aimé Césaire reminds us in his poem *Transmission*, 'forces are not exhausted that quickly when one is only their puny trustee'.

Thus, generations of Africans dumped in the plantations, mines and cities of the colonial Americas experienced their common condition as a 'misdeal to negotiate step by step, with it up to them to discover each water hole' (Césaire). Research is needed on this aspect as well, indeed, as on the notion of 'seed', in the sense in which the Soninke of Mali and Senegal speak of the 'seed of the word'.[17] Beyond roots,[18] a useful concept but one which harbours the danger of fixity, it is the seed of African cultures that we ought to be analysing. Césaire made this point in verse when he wrote:

> Let us take up again
> the useful patient path
> lower than roots the path of seed
> the summary miracle shuffles the deck
> but there is no miracle
> only the strength of seeds
> depending on their stubbornness to ripen.
>
> Aimé Césaire

It is above all through their philosophies, religions and attitudes to life and death that African cultures give us the best example of their 'stubbornness to ripen', which is also a stubbornness not to die. The religious aspect, with its multiple sensitivities, is the most representative evidence of that, involving not only religions deriving from the African continent – indigenous or Islamised – but also those in the Americas that are the result of a variety of syncretisms, such as *candomblé* in Bahia in Brazil, or *kumina, umbanda santería, shango, rastafari, obeah, vodun*, shouting, etc. That said, for at least two reasons, it is rather pointless to propose a nomenclature of religions. First, the religious experience in Africa and the Americas did not always deem it useful to give itself a name. Even if it was not always structured, religious belief was no less profound and survived despite the historical pressure of official ideology. Second, in many countries in the Caribbean and the Americas, the presence of African religion is still very much a present-day reality, since 401 gods are venerated – 400 to indicate the necessity, permanence and importance of religion for the population, and the one designating other gods that may be invented (on this, see the works by Fernando Ortiz, Alfred Métraux, Lydia Cabrera, Edison Carneiro, Arthur Ramos, Roger Bastide, William Bascom, Pierre Verger, Melville Herskovits, de Braga, Vivaldo Costa Lima, Santos, Laënnec Hurbon, Montilus Guerin, Isabel Castellanos, Nina de Friedemann, John Mason, Mercedes Sandoval, etc.).

The belief in forces that transcend human beings[19] and the belief in a vital force that animates existence in all its manifestations, divining, invoking or summoning up the supernatural to resolve the problems of everyday life and solidarity, are African cultural traits that survived in the Americas. According to Santayana, 'Every living and healthy religion has a marked idiosyncrasy. Its power consists in its special and surprising message and in the bias which that revelation gives to life.' Co-existing in the Americas with missionary-type ideologies based on conversion,[20] African religions offer individuals not a path to follow, but a variety of possible paths – without the anguish of original sin – in order to achieve harmony with the family, the physical environment, society, the ancestors and other entities of the supernatural world. It is this message of openness and harmony that enabled Africans transplanted by force into a hostile environment to imagine solutions to the most difficult situations and, above all, give meaning to their lives. De Friedemann, for example, informs us that if the Afro-Colombians of Palenque borrowed from Christianity the notion of hell, they made it a provisional place of punishment for those who had not accomplished the mission that God had assigned them on earth, which was to live (*gozar la vida*). Thus, '*la mujer virgen se va pa la candela*' (the virgin woman goes to hell), says the Afro-Colombian Marciano Casiani, while '*el que ha gozado la vida se va pal cielo*' (he who has enjoyed life goes to heaven).[21] This example of creativity in continuity-discontinuity should make us take another look at the concept of 'syncretism', analyse its relevance, identify the issues and explore the potentialities it harbours, in the context of a poetics of relation.

We also need to enlarge the comparative framework of research on African religions in the Americas by including an examination of such phenomena as the rise of the Pentecostal movement in Afro-Latin America (particularly in Brazil) and the Afro-Christian religions of the mother continent itself (Bwiti, Aladura, etc.). In doing so, equal attention should be paid to the theologies and to an analysis of the religious experience in different social settings, the itineraries of individuals and groups, and the institutions that act as a framework for their lives.

I cannot close this brief survey without mentioning the extraordinary dynamism in recent decades of religions such as *santería* or *candomblé* which have carried African cultures far beyond the ethnic settings in which they originated. Thus, in Brazil, more and more Brazilians of Italian, German, Hungarian and Japanese origin – including the petty bourgeoisie, artists or members of the professions – are Africanising themselves by joining Afro-Brazilian religions. In addition, the growing popularity of Brazilian *candomblé* is spreading as far as Argentina, Uruguay and Paraguay, countries which usually have little interest in their African past.

Successive waves of Cuban migration and population movements in the Spanish-speaking Caribbean have virtually transformed the Caribbean Sea into a *mare santeriae*. Even in Cuba, where the official materialist ideology treats it as a superstition, *santería* is winning more and more adherents. But it was chiefly after 1980 that Cuban migrants established *santería* and *palo* in Puerto Rico, Santo Domingo and Mexico. *Santería* is also strongly implanted in Venezuela, where it syncretises the cult, itself a syncretic one, of María Lionza. In Miami, *santería* is increasingly becoming the religion of immigrant workers from the Third World, especially since the Mariel migration. It enables thousands to acquire a shared identity and to experience a sense of belonging to a community threatened by the dominant Anglo-Saxon culture. Beyond Miami, the dynamism of Afro-Cuban religions has penetrated the major American cities: New York, Chicago, Boston, Los Angeles, Atlanta. Moreover, many Americans of African origin, in search of an original ritual purity free of any taint of Catholicism, are being initiated into its practice, either by going to Africa or by bringing Yoruba priests to America.[22] Despite their dynamism and human depth, and the transcendence of their message, these religions do not engage in any proselytism and do not receive any support from governments.

The vitality of Afro-American religions, marked both by the permanence of their messages and by the desire for ecumenism, is making its mark on the

cultures of the various communities, and in particular on the public perform-
ances that are so popular in the Caribbean and the Americas. Similarly, many
classical music composers, such as Amadeo Roldán and Alejandro García
Caturla in Cuba in the 1930s, sought inspiration from the traditional forms of
sacred music of Africa in their work. Nearer to our own time, Leo Brauer and
Hector Angulo continued that tradition of 'bimusicality', to use the expression
of the Nigerian musicologist Akin Euba. It is a fact that bimusicality has
always been a feature of the everyday experience of Africans, in particular in
the prolific arts of orality. It is certainly in the cultural domain that the concept of survival is most relevant. Whereas exile, inhuman working conditions,
racism and marginalisation might have turned the enslaved Africans into simply resentful men and women, they chose, on the contrary, to make the harsh
reality of everyday life poetic – in short, to be joyful.[23]

It is true that orality, dance, music and poetry are universal, but not all
cultures assign them the same place in the everyday life of individuals. It is
well known that Africa was able to make other peoples with whom it came
into contact share its sense of festival and its taste for orality. That is why the
performing arts, for the inhabitants of the Caribbean and the Americas, are an
everyday necessity in the sense in which Ernst Fisher once spoke of the 'necessity of art'. *Cumbia* or samba, jazz or calypso, son or reggae, *pacá* or rap, each
of these dances bears the stamp of Africa, enriched with borrowings from
Europe and the Amerindians.

Carnival, the quintessence of African oral poetry in the Americas,
deserves to be studied in greater depth by scholars, so as to go beyond the
reductive and impoverishing reading that is made of it, in which only its most
visible manifestations are taken into account. But carnival, as an extension
beyond the Atlantic of the festivals and ceremonies organised in villages in
Africa, is above all a poetic activity.

Thanks to the unprecedented advances of technology in the field of communication in recent years, the different artistic genres are criss-crossing one
another, borrowing from and fertilising one another in an innovative syncretism that is giving rise to wholly novel creations,[24] such as world beat and
reggae. This last, derived from *mento*, which combined African rhythms and
melodies and British music, synthesises elements of rhythm and blues, jazz,
calypso, soul and Rastafarian music. Originally the music of the ghettos of
Kingston, it is today Jamaican while already being no longer just that, since its
most illustrious representatives, Bob Marley, Jimmy Cliff and Peter Tosh, are
now part of the cultural heritage of humanity.

Similarly, in Brazil, following the vogue for bossa nova, an offshoot of jazz
and samba, Bahian artists such as Caetano Veloso, and above all Gilberto Gil
after his return from exile, sought to Africanise Brazilian popular music.
Thus *blocos afros* came into being, the best known being Ile Ayé and the
Grupo Cultural Olodum which, resolutely engaged in the quest for musical
material, invented the *afoxe* style and samba-reggae. By whatever name they
style themselves, the musical groups of the African Americas – Eksperyans,
Olodum, Ile Ayé, Sintesis, Irakeré, etc. – are characterised by the same taste

for experimentation – surpassing themselves, returning to the sources – and the search for something that mirrors the religious quest. The important thing about the festivals of performing arts (CARIFESTAS in the Caribbean, FESTAC in Lagos) is that they bring together in one place and for a brief, magical moment, African creative artists from Africa or the diaspora, and thus play a role in synthesising talents.

It is certainly true that African popular cultures in the Americas, as well as the religions that underlie them, carry a universal ethic, transmitting the values of justice, equity and solidarity. What Afro-American music says is that it is absurd to be racist when people are dancing reggae or jazz. It is a lesson that is so necessary in these sad times when '*el sueño de la razón produce monstruos*' (the sleep of reason breeds monsters). Long before Carlos Drummond de Andrade, who called on Brazilians to '*reinventar Nagôs and Latinos*' (reinvent the Nagos and the Latins), Africans had understood this necessity for endless multiple reinvention. Thus, the Slave Route project will offer 'an irreducible memory with the strength always to look to tomorrow'.

Notes

1. That does not mean that the concept of discovery is innocent. I simply mean that for humanity as a whole, the issues go far beyond the puzzle of 'who discovered whom'.
2. B. Davidson, 1994, pp. 334–342.
3. I take this expression from the title of M. León-Portilla's book (1969), an undertaking that is indeed totally legitimate and necessary.
4. A metaphor that is to be found in black America. See L. Hughes, 1940.
5. The meeting organised by UNESCO on the presence of African cultures in the Caribbean and North and South America (Bridgetown, Barbados, 21–25 January 1980) debated these terminological issues at length.
6. S. Mintz, 1984, p. 295.
7. J.E. Philips, 1991.
8. A. Apter, 1991.
9. S. Mintz, 1984, pp. 296–297.
10. R. Price and S. Price, 1972, p. 362.
11. S. Mintz, 1984, pp. 296–297.
12. G. Cossard-Binon, 1976, and J. Thornton, 1992.
13. D. dos Santos, 1988; V. Costa Lima and W. Freitas Oliveira, 1987.
14. In this connection, we do not share the views of Crouch according to whom 'it is important to face the fact that *there was no great African debate over the moral meanings of slavery itself* [his emphasis]. There is no record whatsoever of an African from a tribe that *wasn't* being enslaved arguing against the very practice of capturing and selling other Africans' (Crouch, 1994).
15. A more detailed analysis of culture for the Yoruba will be found in O.B. Yai, 1983 and 1993.

16. Individuals who choose not to submit to the collective choices made by their community are described by the word *asa*, a word whose two middle tones contrast with the two low tones of *àsà*, no doubt in order to stress the difference. Yoruba philosophers often resort to this procedure of tonal counterpoint to give shades of meaning to concepts.

17. See the study by M. Diawara, 1990.

18. See É. Glissant's critique of the concept of root (1997), particularly pp. 17–34.

19. The distinction that most researchers make between monotheism and polytheism and the characterisation of African religions in the Americas as implicit monotheisms or syntheses of monotheism and polytheism (see, for example, J. Castellanos and I. Castellanos, 1992) are beside the point. The Negro-African religions do not ask whether God exists in terms of one or many. Such a theological debate does not arise, and it could even be argued that it could not arise. African polytheism or monotheism exists only as the invention of the revealed religions of the Middle East that claim to be monotheist.

20. Even a liberal modern theologian such as L. Boff is unable to free himself of the language of missionaries. Speaking of the African religions in Brazil, he writes (1977, pp. 582–583): 'When we refer to Christian syncretism, we define it on the basis of the essential core of Christian faith incorporated in the symbolic framework of another culture. That does not happen without conversion. Once the conversion has been made, the process of syncretism gets under way…. The opposite process may also occur: a religion may come into contact with Christianity and, instead of being "converted", it converts Christianity within its own identity (example: Yoruba religion in *candomblé* or *nagô* in Brazil). But even if it has "borrowed" Christic elements into its system, its theological basis has not been affected. From that we may deduce that the Church is in a missionary position vis-à-vis the Yoruba religion.'

21. N. de Friedemann, 1994, pp. 6–8.

22. J. Mason, 1988.

23. See the works of Guillén, René Depestre, Gabriel García Márquez, Aimé Césaire, Jorge Amado, etc.

24. Two interesting analyses of the dynamism of popular cultures of African origin in the New World are M. Roberts, 1992, and O. Patterson, 1994.

Bibliography

APTER, A. 1991. 'Herskovits's heritage: Rethinking syncretism in the African diaspora'. *Diaspora: A Journal of Transnational Studies* (New York), Vol. 1, No. 3, pp. 235–260.

BASCOM, W. 1972. *Shango in the New World*. Austin, University of Texas, African and Afro-American Research Institute.

BOFF, L. 1977. 'Avialação teologicacritica do sincretismo'. *Revista de Cultura Vozes* (Petropolis), Vol. 71, No. 7.

BRAGA, J. 1988. *O Jogo de buzios: un estudo da adivinhacão no candomblé*. São Paulo, Editora Brasilense.

CABRERA, L. 1980. *Yemaga y Ochun: Karocha, Iyalorocha y Olorichas*. New York, Colección de Chicherucu en el Exile.

CANEIRO, E. 1954. *Candombles de Bahia*. Rio de Janeiro, Editorial Audes.

CASTELLANOS, J., and CASTELLANOS, I. 1992. *Cultura afro-cubana 3: las religiones y las lenguas*. Miami, Ediciones Universal.

COSSARD-BINON, G. 1976. 'Origines lointaines du syncrétisme afro-catholique au Brésil et perspectives d'avenir'. *Afro-Asia* (Salvador), No. 12, pp. 161–166. (Publicação do Centro de Estudos Afro-Orientais da Unversidade da Federal da Bahia.)

COSTA LIMA, V., and FREITAS OLIVEIRA, W. 1987. *Cartas de Édison Carneiro a Artur Ramos*. São Paulo, Corrupio.

CROUCH, S. 1994 'Who are we? Where did we come from? Where are we going?' In Early, G. (ed.). *Lure and Loathing: Essays on Race, Identity and the Ambivalence of Assimilation*. London, Allen Lane, The Penguin Press (with an introduction by G. Early).

DAVIDSON, B. 194. *The Search for Africa: History, Culture, Politics*. London, Times Books/Random House.

DIAWARA, M. 1990. *La graine de la parole. Dimension sociale et politique des traditions orales du royaume de Jaara (Mali) du XVe au milieu du XIXe siècle*. Stuttgart, Franz Steiner Verlag.

EARLY, G. (ed.). 1994. *Lure and Loathing: Essays on Race, Identity and the Ambivalence of Assimilation*. London, Allen Lane, The Penguin Press (with an introduction by G. Early).

FRAGINALS, M. MORENO (ed.). 1984. *Africa in Latin America*. New York, Holmes & Meier Publishers Inc.

FRIEDEMANN, N. de. 1994. 'Africanía y religíon en Colombia. Cosmovisiones e imaginarios'. Paper presented to the first International Symposium on Afro-Ibero-American Studies, organised by UNESCO, Alcalá de Henares.

GLISSANT, E. 1990. *Poétique de la relation*. Paris, Gallimard. [Eng. tr., 1997. Wing, B. *Poetics of Relation*. Ann Arbor, University of Michigan Press.]

HERSKOVITS, M.J. 1966. *The New World Negro: Selected papers in Afro-American Studies*. Bloomington, University of Indiana Press.

HOLLOWAY, J.E. (ed.). 1991. *Africanisms in American Culture*. Bloomington, Indiana University Press.

HUGHES, L. 1940. *The Big Sea*. New York, A. Knopf.

HURBON, L. 1993. *Les mystères du vaudou*. Paris, Gallimard. (Coll. Découvertes.) [Eng. tr., 1995. Frankell, L. *Voodoo: Search for the Spirit*. New York, H.N. Abrams.]

LEÓN-PORTILLA, M. 1969. *Visión de los vencidos*. Havana, Casa de las Américas. [Eng. tr., 1992. Kemp, L. *The Broken Spears: The Aztec Account of the Conquest of Mexico*. Boston, Beacon Press.]

MASON, J. 1988. 'Fundamentals'. Paper presented to the Conference on the Yoruba Diaspora in the New World, Gainesville, University of Florida.

MASON, J., and EDWARDS, G. 1985. *Black Gods: Orisa Studies in the New World*. New York, Yoruba Theological Archministry.

MÉTRAUX, A. 1958. *Le vaudou haïtien*. Paris, Gallimard. [Eng. tr., 1974. Carteris, H. *Voodoo*. London, Sphere Books.]

MINTZ, S. 1984. 'Africa in Latin America: An unguarded reflection'. In Fraginals, M. Moreno (ed.). *Africa in Latin America*. New York, Holmes & Meier Publishers Inc.

MONTILUS, G. 1988. *Dieux en diaspora: les loa haïtiens et les vaudou du royaume d'Allada (Bénin)*. Niamey, Celhto.

ORTIZ, F. 1993. *Africanita de la música folklórica cubana*. Havana, Letras Cubanas.

PATTERSON, O. 1994. 'Global culture and the American cosmos'. *World Policy Journal* (New York), Vol. 11, No. 2.

PHILIPS, J.E. 1991. 'The African heritage of white America'. In Holloway, J.E. (ed.). *Africanisms in American Culture*. Bloomington, University of Indiana Press.

PRICE, R., and PRICE, S. 1972. 'Saramaka onomastics: An Afro-American naming system'. *Ethnology* (Pittsburg), Vol. 22, No. 4.

RAMOS, A. 1940 (2nd ed.). *O negro brasileiro*. São Paulo, Companhia Editora Nacional. [Eng. tr. of 1st ed., 1939. Pattee, R. *The Negro in Brazil*. Washington, DC, Associated Publishers.]

ROBERTS, M. 1992. 'World music and global cultural economy'. *Diaspora: A Journal of Transnational Studies* (New York), Vol. 2, No. 2.

SANDOVAL, M. 1975. *La religión afrócubana*. Madrid, Playor.

SANTOS, DEOSCOREDES DOS, M.D. 1988. *História de um terreiro Nagó*. São Paulo, Max Limonad.

THORNTON, J. 1992. *Africa and Africans in the Making of the Atlantic World, 1400–1680*. Cambridge, Cambridge University Press.

VERGER, P. 1968. *Flux et reflux de la traite des nègres entre le golfe du Bénin et Bahia de Todos os Santos, du XVIIᵉ au XIXᵉ siècle*. Paris, Mouton. [Eng. tr., 1976. Crawford, E. *Trade Relations between the Bight of Benin and Bahia from the 17th to the 19th Century*. Ibadan, Ibadan University Press.]

YAI, O.B. 1983. 'Les apports culturels des Noirs de la diaspora à l'Afrique: Bénin, Togo'. *Cultures africaines. Documents d'experts sur les apports culturels des Noirs de la diaspora à l'Afrique, Cotonou (Bénin), 21–25 mars 1983*. Paris, UNESCO.

———. 1993. 'In praise of metonymy: The concepts of "tradition" and "creativity" in the transmission of Yoruba artistry over time and space'. *Research in African Literatures* (Bloomington), Vol. 24, No. 4.

Chapter 31

African Religions in the Americas:
A Structural Analysis

Guérin C. Montilus

IN AN ETHNOLOGICAL APPROACH to the pantheon or ritual of the various African religions in the Americas, it is customary to examine the equivalences of symbolic codes, to identify the correspondences of mythical or ritual figures, or to analyse syntactic resemblances and differences and highlight semantic survivals or changes. Then, borrowings are made from the discoveries of pioneers such as the anthropologists Jean-Price Mars, Melville J. Herskovits, Alfred Métraux, Roger Bastide and Pierre Verger. And finally, on the basis of a few lexemes borrowed from the vast and varied religious pantheon, comparisons are established, some of them surprising.

Our intention is not to draw up a conventional list of the different African religions in the Americas, but rather to present a global comparative study of the range of indigenous cosmological discourse through which the African in Africa – on the west coast above all – and the African in the diaspora organise their universe. We shall therefore analyse the basic concepts of indigenous cosmological discourse on the west coast of Africa with the aim of highlighting the fundamental currents of the religious thought of the African diaspora in the Americas. In the light of this analysis, we shall bring out some implications and conclusions of an anthropological nature.

Preliminary Remarks

The term 'cosmology' refers to the world as an ordered system organised by the word of human beings. It thus belongs to the category of relation. Cosmology analyses the human being as an individual and as a gregarious being. It therefore includes the concepts of life and death, health and illness: in short, fate. But cosmology also deals with the physical, metaphysical, natural, social and individual orders and the relations that these various orders maintain with one another. It is in this context that the concept of cosmology assumes a global meaning, highly significant in the framework of an anthropological study whose discourse extends to the world regarded as a whole.

A discourse that seeks to be global must, however, limit itself to analytical parameters. In the present case, we distinguish three: power, speech and community.

The concept of power is at the heart of all religion. It is thanks to this power which transcends the physical and natural order that humanity triumphs over the contingencies of this world and, in particular, death. It also makes it possible to order and rank beings as humans – powerless in the face of death – and as divine or superhuman beings who, conversely, are omnipotent. The divine beings may either help humans or harm them. That being the case, humans and divine beings are bound by a relation of reciprocity: the superhuman beings may be influenced by the actions of people who, in order to ward off death, beseech them and venerate them with offerings, so as to receive favours from them in return. That is why religion is so profoundly rooted in the life of human beings. And it is from there, too, that the idea of salvation and redemption arises, which covers in fact the idea of submission, subordination, dependence and subjection that results from the fact that we are contingent beings.

The second parameter is that of speech, creator of the myth of the formation of the world which moves from chaos (disorder) to that of cosmos (order). The order of language is cultural. And it is as such, that is, as creator of culture and engine of the process of symbolic representation, that speech is an instrument of civilisation. The symbol is the tool which gives form, which allows me as an individual to appropriate the world for myself but also to define myself within the limits of the indigent and necessitous being that I am. Thus, the symbol gives form to the process of communication through which metaphors and metonyms enable individuals and communities to take on board the cultural process of transcending death.

The third parameter is community. As a sign and system of symbols, religion is also a social matter, which means that it is an instrument of communication. As such, moreover, it develops in a given physical, social, economic and political situation constituting a natural framework which any analysis must take into account. Religion is not abstract; it is contingent and, as such, reflects the varied conditions of its natural framework.

Our study seeks to demonstrate that Afro-American religions constitute thought systems, in other words a cosmology, created by an African speech whose semantics developed within communities that were varied and scattered, in both time and space.

The Cosmology of Afro-American Religions

The world is neither an abstract entity nor a confused mass of elements. It is an object of thought, interpretation and classification. As reality, the world is ordered. Human beings 'arrange' the universe into a coherent whole just as they 'arrange' the community to which they belong into interdependent systems. Here we shall analyse the African cosmos as the place where human beings live their lives, as well as the alterations made to it after the forced departure for the Americas.

The concepts of power, speech and community interlink and overlap to make the universe a coherent whole. In that sense, African thought stresses the equivalences rather than the differences, since it integrates or reconciles in a single unity what other cultures regard as antithesis and opposition. For example: life and death are the two sides of the same coin, or the two lobes of the same bean. That explains why, in African thought, the dead and the living are closely involved with one another so as to form but a single community living in close interdependence.

The dead 'exist' since they are the source of life for their lineage; the living are their offspring, their cosmic extension through time and space. Thus, in African cosmology, the immortality that is sought by all religions has a terrestrial dimension since it is rooted in the world of the departed and its manifestations occur in the world of the living. The immortality of the name or the being is more real than abstract. This tradition has been maintained among Africans in the diaspora carried by force to the Americas: the cult of the dead is in fact one of the most vibrant there, especially in Haiti, where 2 November, the day of the Catholic festival of the dead, All Saints Day, is celebrated with great pomp. Moreover, in addition to the traditional festival of the dead which is celebrated annually, there are the frequent *mangé lé mó* (meals of the dead) that occur throughout the year according to the instructions of the *bòkò* (sorcerer) or the *hungan* (voodoo priest). The link that the living maintain with the dead is a constant feature of African thought in the Americas. The dead communicate with the living in dreams. In fact, it is said that at night the dead come back to see the living to speak to them and pass on messages about the future or the present, for example by punishing the living who stray from essential traditions for commemorating the dead – or by giving winning lottery numbers to those who do follow the rules. Several communities in the African diaspora in the Americas have their own interpreters of dreams. In Haiti, there are publications on the subject and a tradition of dreams being interpreted by the elders. Many Afro-Americans, Afro-Cubans or Afro-Brazilians believe that the dead communicate with the living in their dreams. For Africans, in Africa or the Americas, the world of the dead and the world of the living are in communication.

The living and the dead form a single community. In Detroit, devoted children go so far as to bury their dead in communities in the South where their families come from, just as is done today on the west coast of Africa. In Benin, for example, it is common to organise local funeral ceremonies for the departed. What is more, on the occasion of Mother's Day and Father's Day, sons and daughters travel enormous distances to clean and decorate the graves of their departed and spend the day communicating with their dead. Even Anglo-Saxon Protestant austerity has been unable to eliminate this African spiritual tradition.

African religious thought is concerned with controlling various sectors of the universe as cosmos. The universe needs to be controlled in order to be habitable; it forms a whole divided into various domains. Supernatural beings control the forests, the waterways, the crossroads, the highways, the sky. They form independent entities that all together constitute a sort of 'commonwealth'. The government of the world is not 'monarchical' as in the Judaeo-Christian model, since there are a great many powers, enormously diverse but identical in nature, each in their own domain. They have no inherent *raison d'être* other than to order the universe for humanity's survival. The structure of this type of mythical discourse is not theocentric but anthropocentric, since the essential factor is the human being, who is at the heart of this cosmology. For example, the spirits who control the sky make rain fall which enables plants to grow to feed human beings. Thus, all – divine, mineral, vegetable, animal, human – exist and act for the good of *Homo sapiens*. The world thus finds its unity in the mythological anthropocentricity of a wholly Earth-centred cosmology.

Finally, we would note that the supernatural powers that are, so to speak, 'confederated' are indivisible. Each power administers, legislates, decides, judges, controls and applies its laws and decisions in its own domain, in complete independence. Each mythical power is independent, both in its origins and in its functions. The question of the origin of these powers is regarded as non-vital and is glossed over in favour of the more pragmatic one of living in the everyday world. Thus, African thought is more interested in the real ability of the various powers to control the universe than in their metaphysical meaning.

The Cosmic Order

The cosmic order is global, general and inclusive: it comprises everything. In the centre of the African cosmos is the human being. In every cosmology, of course, questions are raised about the origin of human beings, the meaning of life and death, the presence of people on Earth and the nature of our destiny. The existential questions that human beings ask are central because they give rise to values and the significance that society accords to things. Every society cloaks its thought in more or less elaborate myths, born of the need to define and explain a world wreathed in mysteries. The purpose of developing the mythology is to give birth to a system of values and determinism that makes it possible to give answers to the questions raised. Nevertheless, the myths remain working and thinking hypotheses that present an intuitive vision of reality.

Thus, Judaeo-Christian civilisations are based on the allegedly universal myth of creation, thereby testifying to a pseudo-superiority over other societies. If we look at African religions, we see that the precariousness of the subsistence economy determines the cosmological discourse: the power that commands the world and relieves anxiety is part and parcel of everyday life. The one that controls the contingencies of this world, especially sickness and death, is more important than the one that created the universe. The concept of power over the world is rooted in the experience of ownership or, more precisely, in Africa, according to Pathé Diagne (1967), in the control of land. Whether it be water, hunting, grazing or fishing, who owns the land is always identified and named. Even civilisations that have not conceptualised the notions of kingship or political leader have always conceptualised those of owner or master of the land, simply because these notions are essential to the life of individuals. Diagne adds that appropriation of the land was also deemed to confer control of political power. The foundation of political power is thus possession of the land. Such was, indeed, the case in the ancient kingdoms of Africa in which all land belonged to the king.

Thus, the African cosmic order rests on the action of possessing rather than creating. That does not mean that the system of African thought is inferior: it is simply structurally different. He who possesses is sovereign, not he who creates. If he governs the cosmos, it is because the cosmos belongs to him – the tree (*atin*) and the liana (*kan*), say the Aja Fon. E. Bolaji Idowu (1973) notes that the Yoruba name the supreme ruler *Olodumare*, or owner of spirit or life. Thus it is *Olodumare* who makes the rain fall that waters the earth, who controls the seasons and the course of events, who is the master of the day. His other name is *Olojo oni*, owner of the day. Haitians have remained attached to this tradition: the supreme power, or *Gran-Met-la* (the great Master), is the master of history and the world that he owns. Everything depends on him. He is the father: *Papa Bon Die* – he who owns everything – can avail himself of everything and gives everything to his children. He is omnipotent and his power is universal. He is not a remote God. The cosmic order, which embraces everything except life itself, depends on him. He contains different sectors which are entrusted to immediate powers, whence the urgent and constraining character of relations between these secondary powers (which we call 'spirits') and humans.

The supreme power is thus the ultimate master of history, in other words of space and time. The Aja Fon say '*Kpe Mawu ton*' (if Mawu wills), or '*Ace Mawu ton*' (by the power of Mawu), Mawu being the supreme power. It is thanks to his power that we awaken – '*Mawu ni fon mi*' (May Mawu wake us up) – since sleep is so close to death. Haitians never refer to the morrow without calling the supreme power to witness: '*Demin, si Bon Dié vié*' (Tomorrow, if God wills). We know that for the Yoruba, *Olodumare*, the master of the day, controls time and the course of events. For Afro-Americans, the supreme power is held by the Lord or Almighty God, master of space and time, and, above all, justice, an extremely rich concept among Africans in the American diaspora. This is because the experience of slavery led the latter to conceive mythically (that is, through an effort of language) a sovereign capable of transcending the domination of slave masters. More particularly, Afro-Cubans have developed the African figure of Shango, who takes revenge on human beings by striking them with lightning. This Yoruba *orisha*, like the Haitian Ogu Feray, who came from the Aja of southern Benin, becomes the avenging right arm of the justice-dispensing sovereign.

That is why the Afro-American diaspora, throughout the American continents, makes justice the supreme moral virtue since, in those lands of slavery, racism ruled unquestioned and the fundamental rights of Afro-Americans were – and still are – constantly violated.

To summarise, we can say that the general order of the cosmos – of space and time – belongs to the master of history. Global power is not situated *outside* the world – it is *in* the world. It is inscribed in time, always present and active; it is a function of the experience lived by human beings. It is thus an anthropocentric power which finds its *raison d'être* in humanity. The cosmic order is thus inclusive, yet not absorbing, since the other powers are autonomous and independent.

The Natural Order

Because it produces life, the physical world is particularly important in African mythology. This tradition is still very much alive in the Americas. The land through its fertility, the heavens through their fertilising rains, the rivers and streams through their life-giving power, the trees through their nutritive and medicinal values are not sources of anxiety to the extent that we know that they are under the umbrella of certain powers, conceived of in the sense of ownership or mastery of the land, as we set out above.

Their names may vary, but these powers have the same functions. The Aja of south-eastern Ghana, southern Benin and Togo call them *vodun*, the Yoruba *orisha*, the Akan of Ghana *abosom*, the Ga *wodzi*, the Ibo *alusi ndimmua*. This African semantic diversity crossed the ocean. *Orisha* are to be found in Brazil and in regions where Yoruba traditions are well implanted, as in Cuba. The *vodun* have become *iwa* in Haiti.

The African of the diaspora is not particularly interested in understanding where these powers come from, since the question of origin is, as we have said, not, strictly speaking, an existential question. What matters is to know who has control of the universe, not whence the universe comes. Unlike the one that governs the global cosmic order, the secondary powers do not possess a total power since they are not owners of the cosmos but only its administrators. Their territory is clearly determined and limited to the essential areas of human life: the sky with its clouds that water the earth with its rains, the life-giving waters that make plants germinate and grow, the forests that provide lianas and wood (as the Aja Fon say) for hut-building or the plant-based pharmacopoeia. A *hungan* (voodoo priest) recently told us that the *iwa* – meaning the *vodun* of the Aja – adapt badly to cities. Country life suits them better, since the rural environment is where this religion born of dependence on agriculture belongs. In cities, the rural environment is only a reference point. Myths are somewhat emptied of their meaning in an urban context.

This religion is functional and exists for the good of human beings. This mythical kind of 'arrangement' makes it possible to explain the relationship between humanity and nature which otherwise would be indefinable. The beings that compose it are metaphorical – metonymic, even; their existence is pure language. But these metaphorical beings like Legba, the master of the crossroads in Haiti, Shango, the master of the clouds and thunder in the Caribbean, Agueet Yemanja, the master and mistress of the sea, end up having a genuine ontological reality, as they give meaning to life on earth, the course of events, the world and history. In short, they create a system of values which makes it possible to distinguish between good and evil; they give a concrete existence to realities that otherwise would remain abstract and absurd.

It is well known that in Catholic America these African powers have their correspondences in the catalogue of the saints of Rome. In Cuba, the popular Saint Barbara, with her menacing sword, represents the Yoruba Shango. What matter if the saint is a woman, and a white woman to boot. The essential thing is the sword! Here it is not a matter of metaphor but of metonymy, with the part signifying the whole. This example clearly shows that we are involved here with symbols, that is, images, whose functions, values and meanings are interchangeable. These are synonyms whose equivalences are communicated through various means in different cultures. This is not syncretic confusion. It is a phenomenon of transcultural metonymy and synonymy which is comprehensible once we know that every culture is first and foremost a system of signs whose purpose is to communicate and transmit messages. And signs may well be similar in time and space.

In Protestant America there is no place for such a metaphorical and metonymic reorganisation, simply because there are no saints in the Protestant liturgy. However, metaphorical equivalences can be found in the Old Testament and the Gospels. That is enough to satisfy the old African affinity with nature, which explains why the Afro-American Churches in the United States of America have a particular taste for Old Testament biblical subjects or for the abstract language of the epistles of Saint Paul, which constitute theological reflections that are sometimes more philosophical than real. Biblical figures, like the patriarchs, the prophets, the kings or Jesus himself, all have their equivalents in the African metaphors that control the various sectors of the cosmos. Moses and his serpent bringing salvation to his people are mythical figures to whom individuals may refer. That is why biblical metaphorical figures have such importance in the process of acculturating Africans in the New World. Moses, Noah, Joshua, Jesus and others pacify human spirits and can be converted into African figures because they embody an African semantics. The signifiers may be different but the signified are the same. The resulting spiritual symbiosis is African in nature.

The Social Order

Like animals, human beings are attached to a territory in which they live. They take possession of a space, use it for a specific purpose, mark it out and demand that others respect it. In short, they establish frontiers – visible or invisible – in such a way as to keep others at a distance. They defend their territory against potential usurpers and protect their right of ownership. Moreover, humans, through symbolic acts, use myths and rituals to mark their right of ownership. In this case, the symbols serve as instruments enabling human beings to enlarge their inhabited space.

In the African traditions spread by the Afro-American diaspora, the social order begins with the occupation of the land. The land is inherited from the lineage's founding ancestor. This ancestral heritage is constituted by the soil where one is born, is raised and grows up. It is on that land that our line of descendants is constituted, and, hence, our immortality. More than a mere place of birth, the land where one is born is synonymous with life and accompanies the individual to his or her death. It is the witness of the high points of a life, the initiations peculiar to childhood and adolescence, the periodical rituals of adult life, including the rites of birth, healing and purification in particular.

The land where one is born is thus protected by the founding ancestor and all those who have symbolised that person's power down through the ages. That is where the protective temples built by the ancestors are to be found, the sacred waters, places and trees, the sources of vital powers. This land links all the generations and thereby gives a cosmic dimension to African spirituality. That being so, the role of ancestors becomes central: they represent powers, since they are responsible for the survival of their descendants, whether in life or in death. They are the founders of the ethical code; they are the co-ordinators of the material and spiritual happiness of the family. It is thus on the land of the ancestors that, every year, their descendants celebrate their memory and beseech them with libations, prayers and sacrifices.

On the American continents, some diaspora communities have preserved the concept of 'land of the ancestors'. The Haitians call it the *demambre* or *bitation* (family house, dwelling). It is a special spiritual place where one communicates with the spirit of the ancestors. It has the same characteristics as the Aja Fon *hennu xwe* (home of the extended family) in lower Benin (formerly Dahomey, in Haitian usage). There, the dead watch over the living and protect them. They express themselves through the voice of the elders and in dreams. In Protestant America, the church fulfils this function, the pastor in some sense taking the place of the ancestor as he interprets the word of the Bible. Jesus, meanwhile, is the ancestral figure of the sacred place that is the church, and heaven is the paternal home. To die is to go to the father's home to live with the founding ancestor. In this way, the tradition of the African social order is perpetuated in the spirituality of the Afro-American diaspora. The notion of space as a social framework in which human destiny is concretely realised is very much alive in the African semantic tradition. However, Christian acculturation turns African mythical discourse on its head. Instead of making the earth the place where the living and the dead meet, Christian myth operates a spatial displacement by constructing a celestial and Platonic type of space. Even after conversion to Christianity, the mythical representation continues to express the original African semantics using a Western sign.

The Individual Order

The individual order covers all the domains in which the individual perceives himself or herself as organiser of life and the world. As in the case of the cosmos, nature and society, the concepts of power, control and ownership assume their full meaning here, especially in a methodological approach. The human being is a 'crossroads' of relations with the natural and supernatural powers to ensure that the world is in order. Humanity exists in solidarity with the cosmos. In the individual domain, the concept of power coincides with that of knowledge. This latter serves as a check and makes mastery of every art a possibility. Skill in controlling nature is varied: it may take the form of technology, art, language – anything that overcomes the innate limits of the human being.

We may attempt to establish a typology, which makes no claim to be exhaustive:

- empirical knowledge, such as the pharmacopoeia;
- sociopolitical knowledge – customs, traditions, etc.;
- practical knowledge, such as fishing, hunting and agriculture;
- metaphysical knowledge – myths, rituals, magic, divination;
- arts such as music, song, dance, poetry, literature;
- medical knowledge;
- knowledge of a trade – carpentry, masonry, etc.

All these forms of knowledge confer on the human being a power over nature and a mastery that are respected in society.

African cultures, despite their dispersal on the American continents, continue to give precedence to the community over individuals, for the sake of collective prosperity. The idea of community, which signifies sharing and solidarity and helps individuals to survive, is fundamental in everyday life. It is in this sense that the lineage or the extended family are more important than the nuclear family. It is the lineage that links the individual to the founding ancestor and the community of the departed through the head of the family, who represents the eponymous ancestor. In the head of the family is reproduced the mythical word of life in which the existence of each is rooted.

The purpose of myths is the survival of human beings on Earth. The human being, as we have said, is the measure of all things in these religions with their telluric eschatology, unlike religions with a uranian or trans-telluric eschatology. Unlike the biblical religions, which are theocentric, African religions, we repeat, are anthropocentric. Human beings are not adorers of God. God exists for the good of man, and not man for the glory of God. Furthermore, the individual participates in his or her salvation, and is not passive. That is why magic is so important in religions of African origin, even deep in the Americas. Magic, which is a knowledge (that is a power) of the human being, is integrated into religion, which is submission to the knowledge (that is to the power) of superior beings. That makes it possible to understand why divination is an integral part of religion as the site of the action of the power both of God and of the human being. The individual needs to know the hidden causes and secret reasons that have prevented, and still prevent, triumph over the difficulties of yesterday, today and tomorrow (meaning, over death). It is the urgency of the present that makes the religion real, that is, existential, limited in time and space. African religion is not proselytising; it does not seek to win over other followers nor to convert all nations. It is an institution that is family- and lineage-based, immediate, whose effects are measured on a small scale. It simply seeks the salvation of an individual engaged in the everyday concrete struggle for survival. That explains its success in the time of slavery and after slavery, despite the tireless efforts to convert, in the words of a missionary bishop of Gonaïves, in Haiti, 'these negroes obstinate in their paganism'. It can thus be said that the African religions of the Afro-American diaspora promote integration and combination rather than fragmentation and breakdown. One of the consequences is the interpenetration of the mythical and the cosmic, which explains why the mythical partakes also of the political.

Conclusion

African cosmology, underpinned by the concept of power, speech and community, is the organising element of mythical thought which continues to survive over time and space in the faraway lands of the Americas. Control of time and space, knowledge of the world and its functions – at the centre of which is the human being – contribute to the balance of the world, myths and rituals. It is because the African cosmos closely binds the internal and the external of the various orders that we have described above that the human being lives by myths, beliefs and rituals. The anthropocentric character of this cosmology which gives a concrete dimension to religion is common to all the African religions of the Americas. Only power, speech and community make it possible to disentangle the windings of mythical discourse that are in appearance so varied.

But, in reality, is it not, perhaps, a matter of a universal (anthropological) structure that enables the human being to name what, otherwise, would be anonymous and absurd, or even a discourse that unfolds in a given Durkheimian-type social framework? Religion as a quest for salvation reflects an identical universal preoccupation: victory over death regarded as total destruction. From this viewpoint, religions do not differ from one another, since they are waging a common battle.

Bibliography

AUGÉ, M. 1975. *Théorie des pouvoirs et idéologie*. Paris, Hermann.

BASTIDE, R. 1967. *Les Amériques noires: les civilisations africaines dans le Nouveau Monde*. Paris, Payot. (Coll. Petite bibliothèque.)

DIAGNE, P. 1967. *Pouvoir politique traditionnel en Afrique occidentale*. Paris, Présence africaine.

HALBWACHS, M. 1970. *Morphologie sociale*. Paris, Armand Colin.

HARRIS, J.E. 1982. *Global Dimensions of the African Diaspora*. Washington, DC, Howard University Press.

HURBON, L. 1993. *Les mystères du vaudou*. Paris, Gallimard. (Coll. Découvertes.) [Eng. tr., 1995. Frankell, L. *Voodoo: Search for the Spirit*. New York, H.N. Abrams.]

IDOWU, E.B. 1973. *African Traditional Religion*. London, Longman.

MÉTRAUX, A. 1958. *Le vaudou haïtien*. Paris, Gallimard. [Eng. tr., 1974. Carteris, H. *Voodoo*. London, Sphere Books.]

MITCHELL, H. 1989. *Black Preaching … the Recovery of a Powerful Art*. New York, Schocken Books.

MONTILUS, G. 1988. *Dieux en diaspora*. Niamey, Abington.

———. 1989. *Dompim: The Spirituality of African Peoples*. Nashville, Winston-Derek.

THOMAS, L.-V., and LUNEAU, R. 1975a. *La terre africaine et ses religions*. Paris, L'Harmattan.

———. 1975b. *Traditions et changements*. Paris, L'Harmattan.

THOMPSON, R.F. 1984. *Flash of the Spirit: African and Afro-American Art and Philosophy*. New York, Random House.

UNESCO. 1985. *Le concept de pouvoir en Afrique*. Paris, UNESCO.

VERGER, P. 1957. *Notes sur le culte des orisha et vodun à Bahia, la Baie de tous les Saints, au Brésil et à l'ancienne côte des Esclaves en Afrique*. Dakar, IFAN.

Chapter 32

The Persistence of Clan Identities among Slaves through the *Vodun* and *Orisha* Religious Cults

Jacqueline Roumeguère-Eberhardt

> An individual can no more live without memory than a
> human group can live without knowledge of its past.
>
> Jean Devisse

THEY WERE MERCILESSLY TORN from their native soil, their forests, savannah and rivers glistening with dancing fish, the warmth of their homes, their children and parents, and their totem clans. But there was one thing which could not be taken away from them: *memory*.

They remembered that in their countries, they belonged to Shango, the god of thunder, to the gentle Yemanja, goddess of the sea, to Ogun, the iron smith of martial prowess, to Oxum, she of fresh water, and to so many other *orishas*, the children of Obatala.

> They remembered the rhythms of their drums
> the dances and trances
> with which to beat
> the daily horrors
> of the lives of slaves
> exiles from their land.
> But Africa conquered.
> For the worship of totems
> is that of life itself,
> and stronger than darkness.
> Through worship brothers can be found again
> – even among the Indians, the masters of these new lands
>   and even among the Christians.
> For their saints belong to the waves of the universe,
> and join with the *vodun*, *orisha* and *mutupu* gods
> to dance in the sanctuaries
> and resonate in the different rhythms
> that order the universe
> giving unity
> amid diversity.

African Cultural Identity

Sociology, of whatever kind, implies a historical dimension, and any economic and development action requires an understanding of social structures and cultural identities. The totem concerns, above all, the cultural identity and integration of the individual in the clan, the nation, the state and beyond the borders of the nation-state. *Vodun, orisha* and *mutupu*-totem are our genetic code.

To quote Djim Doumbé:

> The totem is a system which perpetuates tradition, despite the oppressive context of colonisation and neo-colonisation. It has made it possible to resist the homicide of African peoples and nations. Unable to perpetuate a socio-political system, the totem has clothed it in new languages of freedom and cultural assertion.
>
> The totem defends the relationship of individuals with their ancestors and descendants. It is thus concerned with the survival of humanity. It teaches mutual respect in the midst of diversity.
>
> The totemic spirit embraces an essential and fundamental value which lies at the root of all the others, the spiritual religious sense or the sense of the sacredness of life, of honour and of human activities, the true mystic sense. This spirit implies the omnipresence of myth and history, which does not mean that history is absent, but that time is not considered as a linear and inescapable scale of reference.
>
> The totem requires:
>
> * personal and social ethics;
> * the ideology of democratic consensus;
> * community spirit or altruism and a self-subsistent economy;
> * 'from the bottom up' democracy;
> * the fraternity within but, above all, transcending the clan, and a sense of hospitality.
>
> In short, the setting in which the spirit of the totem can be perceived through the great spiritual values. Tradition, the clan, and the special initiation held up by peoples remain strong and ineluctable.
>
> The Map of totems should provide a better understanding and appreciation of totem clans:
>
> * their mechanisms;
> * their processes;
> * their advantages;
> * their consequences.
>
> It is a question of making black people aware of totemism, the basis of their cultural heritage. The project should not only be based on the past, it should illuminate it so that better plans can be made for the future. It is a research project to be conducted throughout the African continent along different lines:
>
> * research;
> * the preservation of what remains of the totem;
> * exchanges of cultural information.

The Map of African Totems

In the nineteenth century, Africa was divided up and given frontiers which were completely arbitrary, but which met the immediate requirements for national borders. Ethnologists began to study 'tribes' (macro-sociological and macro-historical groups), thus increasing the confusion, given that the African tribe is only a very temporary, fluctuating and changing reality, and is essentially arbitrary. One chooses one's tribe, but one is bequeathed one's clan and *mutupu* (totem). The *mutupu* (totemistic clan) is the basic fact underlying the deeply rooted unity which continues to be safeguarded and still operates, linking families beyond different borders.

Thus, it is on the basis of a micro-history of the totem and what I have termed a 'Map of African Totems' that we will be able to gain a new understanding of the totem's macro-history. And far from appearing to be a force that generates conflict, it shows what truly unites the peoples of Africa.

We shall follow the rules of Bantu epistemology – which distinguishes three levels of knowledge – in order to understand the significance of the term *mutupu*, which I have translated as 'totem'. With reference to 'hearing knowledge', the totem is an animal, a bird, an object or a part thereof: it enables people to be divided into totem clans; it forms the basis of clan exogamy and is linked to the prohibition of incest; it leads to the existence of taboos and food prohibitions.

With respect to 'initiatory knowledge', the *mutupu* has a symbolism that the initiates can 'read' and which is used for the immediate hierarchical classification of people in terms of rank, sex and age. Such attributes are rendered explicit by ritual praises (*chidawo*) associated with the *mutupu*-totem.

In the context of what is known as 'real knowledge', the totem is the procreative sister of the same blood. The food prohibition 'not to eat one's totem-*mutupu*' is understood as meaning 'not to have sexual relations with one's sister'; the *mutupu* is thus fundamentally linked to clan exogamy. At the same time, however, it represents the 'ideal' spouse since, in the Second World, twins were destined to marry, and the kings and queens in such societies, as in Pharaonic Egypt, are brother and sister. In our world, the Third World, they continue to personify this 'ideal' union of the Second World.

We thus find that the totem is linked to each social category:

- in sex and age groups, the *mutupu* and its ramifications form the basis of initiatory instruction and hierarchical classification in terms of rank, sex and age;
- in the context of the family, the *mutupu* underlies clan exogamy;
- in regard to territorial divisions, it explains the distribution of land (both mythical and real), the corresponding rites and the choice of officiants (both ceremonial and administrative).

The *mutupu* is also intimately linked to every religious category:

- the totemistic myth provides us with the keys for understanding its role in each of the social categories, more especially with respect to territorial organisation and that of royalty;
- the prohibition against eating the totem primarily symbolises the incest taboo, the prototype taboo, and the establishment of exogamic marriage;
- the rites assume their deep significance when interpreted in relation to the symbolism which pivots on the totem-*mutupu* – which is often actualised during the performance of the rites.

But what story do they have to tell the people to whom this history belongs? That everywhere on the African continent, people with the same totem are *ipso facto* related. That those who live in Zimbabwe, our teachers, can recite the genealogies and the names of the places where they stayed during their migrations. That they can travel right across Africa, in this way, sleeping every evening in a village in the house of people with the same totem, who are therefore related to them.

And we have had the opportunity to verify: that a man from the 'Lion' clan, in the Central African Republic, would not marry a Ndau 'Lion' Venda young lady because, as he said, 'we are brother and sister'; that a 'Monkey' man, in Gabon, would not marry a '*Shoko*' (monkey) woman from Zimbabwe, for the same reason.

This is, without doubt, knowledge which is threatened with extinction if we do not record it because, as its keepers say, 'When our children go to school they forget'. And this is certainly why they have given us this information.

With these lists of totemistic sites in hand, I and my students at the Sorbonne were able to locate the places on maps. We were able to arrive at astonishingly precise results concerning the migration routes of peoples across the African continent. One can see the routes taken by clans travelling together and where they separated. In this way, we can read the Map of totems to reinterpret the entire history of Africa.[1]

Towards a Cultural Renaissance

At the time of independence, the African states had to retain the borders arbitrarily established by the colonising countries, the general assumption being that the forging of national unity required doing away with tribal and clan identities, and even with the cultural traditions of the peoples making up the state. This led to the worst type of repression, and aggravated rivalries and hatreds. But the conclusion which has now been reached is that only the recognition of these specific identities and of their worth and value will enable such peoples to unite of their own accord, with due regard and recognition for other peoples and for the unique and traditionally sanctioned role played by the clans. As was confirmed in Uganda, each clan plays a well-established role when a king is enthroned.

The Totem: The Basis of African Social Structures

'We are making a record of all the totems of the peoples in our kingdom: this is our cultural heritage. We also wish to establish "clan clubs" as each totem clan plays a specific and complementary role in relation to the others.' This statement, made by one of the members of the Committee for the Restoration of the Kingdom of Butwarane ya Toro in May 1993, clearly shows that membership of a totem is recognised as having primordial importance for the functioning of social structures and plays a fully up-to-date role in relation to this cultural renaissance.

In Swaziland, we met T.T. Ginindza, author of a book entitled *Sibongo: Swazi Clan Names and Clan Praises* (1992). *Sibongo* can be translated as 'totem', and the term *sibongo* denotes a vital aspect of all forms of Swazi social behaviour. The frequent use of *sibongo* in social interaction is not only a Swazi behavioural trait; it is found among all the Nguni peoples of southern Africa. In his preface to the above-mentioned work, S.M. Guma declares: 'This book begins a new chapter in the collection and preservation of each clan's most intimate and personal praises; praises which not only link the members of the clan to each other, but also strike a chord in one's innermost being.'

These three relatively recent testimonies to the renewal of interest in the traditional cultural heritage with a view to making it a part of everyday life signal a change in the thinking of the intellectual élite who, during the past few decades, seemed to have rejected such practices.

But the conclusion is clear: the building of the society of tomorrow requires a return to the cultural heritage and, first and foremost, to clan identity, which is based on the totem. As in the past, unity is to be found in this kind of diversity. The message of the cultural renaissance, which has begun to be felt everywhere, is that the way to consolidate the national unity freely chosen by each people, solidly rooted in their traditions, is to accept and mobilise the different cultural heritages in all their diversity.

It is only by acknowledging the importance of the role played by the totem that one can understand the events now taking place in Africa and put them in their proper perspective; they continue to elude our understanding precisely because the totem, which is always the invisible and soundless driving force behind these occurrences, is perceived from the outside. In Africa, membership of a totem clan is inescapable, since one is bequeathed one's totem at birth. Hence, one belongs to a clan which plays a very particular and specific role in relation to the other clans and to society in general. And far from separating people from each other, this awareness unites them.

Even today, the totem is living testimony to the unity of Africa's peoples who did not wait for planes to travel from east to west, from west to east, from north to south and from south to north over their vast continent, which they did by following the sea routes as well as the major routes of land migration, as is shown by our Map of African Totems. These data, which were transmitted to us by the traditional historians of Zimbabwe and by oral tradition, were recently corroborated by archaeological excavations as well as by the persistence, along these routes, of clans belonging to the same totems. Everywhere and in every case, it is the totem which has safeguarded cultural identities.

Moreover, the totem is the guardian of a people's memory. Micro-historic studies of clans lead to a macro-history which reveals the migrations of peoples across Africa and membership of major cultural complexes.

VODUN and ORISHA = TOTEM

The explanation given by Djim Doumbé concerning the *vodun* totem of the cultural area encompassing Benin, Togo and Nigeria is entirely new and of major importance for understanding the significance of voodoo in the Caribbean as well as in Brazil and Haiti. Following his missions to Togo and Benin for the Map of African Totems project, Djim Doumbé reached the very convincing conclusion that *vodun* = totem.

Viewed in this light, we can understand the importance of the *vodun* cults for black people in the Caribbean, Haiti and Brazil. Having been mercilessly torn from their families and clans by slavery and dispersed by the sales which separated brothers, sisters and children to mix them with others who had come from elsewhere, a major concern of these people was the reconstruction of their totem rite, *vodun*. Families had been dispersed, so it was by divination using cowries that the *orisha* (Yoruba name meaning *vodun* or totem) fraternities were put together. The *orisha* families were reconstituted around the *pais de santos* (fathers of saints) in the *candomblé* of Brazil, the voodoo temples of Haiti and the *lukumi* ceremonies of Cuba. The main priority everywhere was the cult of the totem.

The fact that Brazil has *orishas* whereas voodoo is predominant in Haiti could indicate that Nigerian slave ships went to Brazil and to Cuba (the *lukumi* cult has Yoruba drums), and that ships from Benin and Togo went to the Caribbean, more particularly to Haiti.

Djim Doumbé states that there are several categories of *vodun* corresponding to the air, earth and water fraternities. In fact, the *mutupu*-totems of southern Africa are to be found in categories representing the four elements: earth, air, fire and water.

The totem is above all an interrelation between the individual-microcosm and the universe-macrocosm; it is not knowledge frozen in the past but a vital and living source of energy. Its presence is such that it dictates not only the behaviour of individuals in relation to their environment and society, but also, and above all, their interrelationships with others – even their political and economic behaviour. If sociologists, historians and economists do not understand the totem, they will fail to appreciate the real dimension of individual and collective structures in Africa.

According to Bastide (1960):

> Mythology comprises superimposed strata with different ages, or, in other words, a chronology. Religion is not a dead entity, even though it is always conservative. It changes with the social environment, with places and with dynasties, and acquires new rituals in response to the changing needs of the population or the interests of dominant families. When all these transformations, all these changes of regime and palace revolutions subside, they leave behind them, like flood water, layers of myths which are new, but still operate in the context of respect for archaic tradition.[2]

This raises the following question: Are not all religions, inevitably and by definition, the result of syncretism? Yes. The more so as we believe that syncretism (taken to mean 'fusions of several systems') is a constant feature of both social and religious units. Briefly put, it concerns myths, rites and taboos in where religion is concerned, and family structures, sex, age and territorial groupings where social units are concerned.

To quote Leenhardt: 'Myths mark out a reality which reason cannot define, but which is nonetheless a reality. And myths dictate a form of behaviour related to this reality.'[3] This explains how the slaves were able not only to remember their cultural heritage but also, through the syncretic cults, to make it a part of the mythical reality of their everyday lives.

The Persistence of Totemistic Identities in Exile

The fact that *orishas* are associated with the worship of Catholic saints in Brazilian *candomblé* should come as no surprise. It is merely a translation, a dovetailing of two systems which, by definition, have corresponding features for which equivalents can be found, just like the words of two different languages. As taught in initiation schools in Africa,[4] 'certain things go together':

– this stone goes with that grass, or that plant
– goes with this insect
– goes with this animal, this bird, this fish
– belongs to this totem clan.

It is a matter of the same wavelength, the same sound and the same light, the same vibrations and the same rhythm. Thus, each *orisha* has its colour, music, dance step and trance.

When, like the slaves, one has lost the security of one's home, clan and totem priests, the totem – the genetic code which transcends time and space – still remains intact and can be identified by divination. We come from this totem-life when we are born, and return to it when we die. Accordingly, people in the *candomblé* of Brazil who have the same *orisha* form a family and, as in Africa, it is taboo to marry anyone with the same *orisha* as this would amount to incest. Some *candomblé* cults are more specifically devoted to one particular *orisha*, which dwells in certain favourite places.

It is, therefore, no coincidence that the slaves of Yoruba stock had a preference for syncretism with the Catholic saints. In both Christian Catholic rites and Yoruba rites, the priesthood is very hierarchical and worship takes place in a sanctuary with altars made by worshippers. By contrast, the Bantu slaves from Angola were more inclined to practise syncretism with the so-called *caboclo* Indians. Their *catimbo* worship took place in the open in forests, near rivers and in the mountains, and this bore the greatest resemblance to the original cults of these slaves whose totems were explicitly linked to the forces of nature and the four elements: earth, air, fire and water. As among the Indians, the totem is embodied in an animal, a bird, a fish or a tree.

This link with cosmic forces can also be found among the *orishas*, and a systematic inventory could usefully be made. It was no doubt more easily lost in the countries of exile in which the slaves had to face strange natural sur-roundings. This explains why they had to call on the traditional masters of the land: the Indians. But Bastide observes that the Shango procession is accom-panied, in Brazil, by an elephant made of cardboard. And, indeed, in Benin, the elephant is the totem of Shango, as it is of the kingdoms of Lozi and Venda.

To conclude, I should like to invite Benin to join in the Map of African Totems project. It will involve the creation, in each country, of a group of researchers – academics and others – to collect and draw up a list of all the *vodun* and *orishas*, indicating their affinities (animal, vegetable, etc.), taboos (food and/or ritual), favourite food (for example, in Brazil, mutton for Shango), colour, music, rhythm, perfume and ritual praise. The databank thus established could be used to produce a booklet (of the same type as the work on the Swazi)[5] which would be distributed, free of charge or otherwise, at the historic sites during ceremonies, in museums and, above all, in schools. The same type of research could be undertaken in the Americas and the Caribbean, especially in relation to African totems or what remains of them.

As in the case of the Map of African Totems, one would thus be able to determine the geographical dispersion of peoples and the persistence of their clan membership, notwithstanding the contingencies of time and space. As a great sage from Benin once put it: the nation's life-force resides in the *vodun*-totem. It is the major force underlying social, economic, political, cultural and religious integration.[6]

Notes

1. J. Roumeguère-Eberhardt, 1982.
2. R. Bastide, 1960.
3. M. Leenhardt, 1953.
4. I myself received training in the traditional Khomba and Domba schools in the Venda court.
5. T.T. Ginindza, 1992.
6. Statement recorded in Benin in July 1993.

Bibliography

BASTIDE, R. 1960. *Les religions africaines au Brésil: vers une sociologie des interpéné-trations de civilisation.* Paris, Presses Universitaires de France.

GININDZA, T.T. 1992. *Sibongo: Swazi Clan Names and Clan Praises.* Mbabane, Swazi Heritage.

LEENHARDT, M. 1953. *Sociologie religieuse* (Dakar), Vol. 15, No. 2, pp. 768–797.

ROUMEGUÈRE-EBERHARDT, J. 1982. *Le signe du début de Zimbabwe.* Paris. Publisud.

Chapter 33

The Influence of Blacks in the Americas

Luz María Martínez-Montiel

The Economic Dimension of Slavery

The explanation for Spanish expansion in the Americas is to be sought in the accumulation of capital in the form of precious metals derived from mining and the booty of conquest. Until the last decades of the eighteenth century, the economy of the Spanish empire continued to be based on mining for minerals whose importance declined over time. In Brazil, the huge increase in gold mining was made possible only by the introduction of slave labour. The first phase of the economy of the American colonies, known as the gold cycle, corresponds to the arrival of black labour, which was vital to the high production of the metal-producing provinces.

The gold cycle spread from the Caribbean Islands to Mexico in the north and Chile in the south. Employing blacks at this period meant paying high prices, the transatlantic slave trade not yet having reached the sustained rhythm of later years. In some areas where there was a large Indian population, blacks and Indians worked side by side washing gold and in the associated food-producing activities. This was the case in Mexico, Chile and Peru, where the large indigenous population made it possible to form teams of Indians and blacks to work in the mines and agriculture.

With the disappearance in the second half of the sixteenth century of gold-washing plants, a second mining prospect opened up that was globally more important but in which labour yielded less. This new source of wealth was the silver mines, the largest of which were the mines at Zacatecas and San Luis in Mexico and Potosí in Bolivia.

Once it had been demonstrated that there were no large-scale economic advantages in the use of black slaves in silver production, Indians definitively replaced blacks as mine labourers, and this was made compulsory by the vice-regal decree of 1570 known as the *mita minera*. Blacks, who had been the auxiliaries of the Spaniards during the conquest, made their contribution to mining all through the colonial period as skilled workers rather than as labourers, acting as team leaders, supervisors, watchmen, etc. In some places their role was so important that they were given the special name of *saya payo* and their activities and functions were regulated by legislation.

In addition to being heavily concentrated in the silver mines, there were also blacks in the mining provinces and districts of Brazil, the gold mines of Ecuador and the copper mines of Cuba and Cocorote, in Venezuela. Generally speaking, many regions of the Americas constantly petitioned for slaves in order to use them as labour in newly discovered mines. This shared activity of slaves and Indians led to a transformation of the economic and social features of the population of mine workers: 'Throughout the second half of the seventeenth century and the following century ..., mining districts, such as Copiapó in Chile and Parral in Mexico, came to rely more and more on paid labour, so that the ethnic and racial distinctions became blurred among the miners. The black population, slave and free, together with a high percentage of black of mixed-descent, formed an important part of this new social group of workers.'[1]

As can be seen, many factors affected the gradual arrival of African slaves in the Americas to serve as a labour force. Their importation was closely associated with the development of new crops and industries, among which the sugar industry held pride of place. Sugar-cane growing developed in the islands, along the coasts and in the tropical regions of valleys, where European colonisation had led to the extermination of the indigenous population and the exhaustion of the mines. The combination of these two factors obliged the colonists to seek out an alternative source of wealth, and so they turned to producing a number of crops for which demand in Europe was high. Thus the Europeans established a new system of production, especially in regions where the indigenous population had diminished almost to the point of extinction, whereas in those areas where its numbers had held up, as in Paraguay, Bolivia, Peru, part of Central America and Mexico, very few blacks were brought in.

It was in the West Indies that sugar-cane growing began gradually to replace mining. Sugar-cane production grew to meet the demand of markets anxious to secure goods that could finance the cost of transporting slaves across the Atlantic and at the same time produce a profit. This led to the growing of maize, potatoes, oats, cocoa and cotton.

While cocoa, cotton, tobacco and colorants – all important for the colonial economy – were grown, sugar was far and away the typical plantation economy crop. In the sixteenth century the European powers attempted to diversify the American economy by creating, alongside mining, a craft industry connected with agriculture; they tried in particular to increase the production of cochineal and wax. But initially, the mainstay of the American economy was mining. Tobacco plantations worked by black slaves provided Holland and Portugal with trade goods as well as contraband goods. There are therefore grounds for believing that from the sixteenth century up to the second half of the nineteenth, tropical single-crop economies were almost wholly dependent on slave labour. Sugar was the most important product in this economy, as was reflected in the growth in the number of sugar refineries and the rising numbers of slaves employed. Hispaniola, for example, where the first sugar refineries (*ingenios*) were opened, had 21 refineries by 1540, with an equal number of mills, operated by some 30,000 African slaves. In Puerto Rico, the interdependence between black slaves and sugar production became strikingly clear when, in 1582, the 11 sugar refineries on the island produced only a tiny quantity of sugar because of the shortage of black labour, and their renovation was held up by the lack of resources of the colonists on the island.

In Cuba, large-scale importation of black slaves began in the early 1590s with the appearance of the first sugar mills. In Jamaica, because of the extermination of the Indians and the total absence of gold, sugar production using slave labour began as early as the second decade of the sixteenth century and grew considerably under English rule. In New Spain, in the areas with a warm climate such as Veracruz and the intermediate zones of the Mexico City valley, by the end of the sixteenth century there were some 30 sugar refineries and mills, the volume of production being close to that of Hispaniola. In 1599, the Crown prohibited the building of new sugar refineries in order to encourage mining and other products regarded as more profitable. In Venezuela, too, until the seventeenth century there was a demand for slave labour, which was assigned to agricultural work on the cocoa plantations in the valleys and regions in the centre. In 1780, farms in these areas had more than 36,000 black slaves.

The monopoly of the supply of slaves favoured the development of the Brazilian sugar industry which, by the eighteenth century, was the most highly developed in the New World. As in the Spanish possessions, sugar-cane growing in Brazil had first used indigenous labour after the opening of the first sugar mills between 1530 and 1535. But the development of the sugar industry and the extermination of the Indians led to the massive introduction of African slaves, of whom there were more than 20,000 by 1600. There were already 120 sugar refineries in 1584, and by 1628 there were 235.

In the French plantations of Guadeloupe, Martinique and Haiti, 400 sugar refineries were operating by 1700, with an annual production of a million and a half *arrobes* (18,750 short tons) of refined sugar. At the same time, in the English colonies, 800,000 slaves were producing about a million and a half *quintals* (165,345 short tons) of sugar.

Whereas in the Portuguese and Spanish colonies black slaves not only provided agricultural labour but were involved in other activities, in the Dutch, French and English colonies, they were used solely in the sugar industry, since the plantation system did not produce anything else. The Indians were not integrated into the colonies, the labour force being wholly of African origin.

The English market drew its supplies from its possessions in the Caribbean: in Barbados, for example, the tobacco-planting colonists farmed their plots with the help of English immigrants who formed a white labour force. In 1643, the lands were turned into sugar-cane plantations, which led to the immigration of whites, of whom there were 40,000 planters and servants at that date. From then on, Barbados's sugar production was wholly dependent on the importation of African slaves. In 1643 there were already 6,000 blacks, and, in 1655, 20,000. Their numbers continued to rise, reaching 40,000 in 1668, double the white population. By 1792, there were 65,000 blacks, and when slavery was abolished in 1835 there were almost 90,000 black slaves. It seems that blacks, being more adaptable, were more highly regarded than Indians.

Even when, in the mines, accessory jobs were reserved for blacks and indigenous labour was preferred, the limited number of the latter combined with climatic conditions compelled Europeans to use more and more labour brought in from Africa.

> It is beyond dispute that to work the mines preference was given to indigenous labour. But it is risky to generalize, since mining areas existed at a very early date.... For example, the copper mines in Cuba were constantly asking for special contracts (*asientos*)[2] giving them a monopoly on the importation of slaves; meanwhile, the gold and copper mines in Venezuela, or the washing plants of the New Kingdom, were dependent on blacks.... In fact, all the mining of these regions and the washing plants of the lowlands of Colombia were dependent on the work of blacks.... In the gold washing plants of the Bucaria valley, at Pamplona, 17 teams of blacks were employed, and, according to the governor of Cartagena, Pedro Buiral, the low yield of the mines at Zaragoza, Los Remedios and elsewhere was due to the poor relations between the miners and the slave dealers of Cartagena. In the gold mines in Tairona, Ramada and the Upar valley, and the silver mines of this region and Nueva Valencia, black slaves were sought after 1606.[3]

Blacks who had managed to acquire some skill in a few techniques were able to work as labour in businesses, as assistants or as domestics. This was the case in the Spanish colonies, but was even more so in the Dutch, French and English colonies, where the Indians had been decimated by the beginning of the seventeenth century and most of the consumer goods and manufactured items needed for the infrastructure of tropical single-crop economies was imported from Europe. It must be remembered that these colonies were dependent on home countries whose maritime technology and trade were more highly developed than those of Spain, so that, although limited in number, the slave population occupied in work outside tropical crop production was of some economic significance. In short, it can be said that anyone who owned some capital had slaves. And, provided that they could buy them, all – including the Indians – could have black slaves working for them.

After 1549, to operate the looms for weaving wool and cotton goods, the factories of New Spain were using male workers recruited among slaves, those condemned to forced labour or workers who had fallen into debt, all working in intolerable conditions of isolation.

During the colonial period, royal officials in almost all the American colonies purchased groups of slaves for such public works as the construction and maintenance of fortifications, work in military workshops, carrying heavy loads into remote areas, etc. In the few cases where Indians used black slaves, the latter were also used in the building of bridges, roads or churches.

Being colonial institutions, municipal hospitals and municipal councils also owned slaves who were, as they were everywhere, made to do the most arduous physical labour; a few, very few, were trained to become town criers, messengers or doormen.

Blacks in domestic service certainly enjoyed the most humane treatment. It is therefore quite natural that in that framework slaves should have shown a softer, more noble, even sometimes happy, face. As had been the case in Europe before the colonial period, for the white master the black domestic was a symbol of social success. Despite the education they received in their new 'host family', it was the black servants who were more successful than any others in ensuring the survival of a number of African cultural traits, and in doing so despite the dispersal of slaves belonging to the same ethnic groups as themselves, as was the rule.

Some authors criticise domestic slavery for being unproductive:

> Unproductive slavery and vagabondage are the features that have most contributed to characterizing many Indian cities socially, as made up of a large, inactive population, parasitic and idle.
>
> Unproductive slavery can also be analysed according to wholly different criteria. It raises such questions as how long slavery remained economical after Latin America developed from a mercantile system into that of modern capitalism, and what precise bearing uneconomical slavery had on the history of abolition.[4]

To understand fluctuations in the selling prices of slaves on the American continent, it is necessary to understand that after their delivery to the ports of entry, Cartagena and Veracruz, slaves still had to travel vast distances before reaching their final destination, which, of course, increased transport costs. The slave entrepôts were in the port towns where blacks arriving from Africa were landed. Traders took delivery of cargoes there and attended to their sale with the help of middlemen who either represented traders in the interior or were operating on their own behalf.

When it was necessary to take the routes into the interior, from Veracruz to Mexico, from Cartagena to Lima through Panama, and from Lima to other points in Ecuador, Chile or the rest of Peru, costs rose even higher. From Cartagena the slaves were redistributed to various parts of the Caribbean. In the course of this hazardous journey, the number of those dying rose, sometimes to as high a point as that in the middle passage.

In payment, silver metal or other goods that served as currency were used, the most highly prized being those transported by the Manila galleons. It is quite clear that the cumulative transport costs raised the price of slaves on the market.

Cost of moving a cargo from Cartagena to Lima in 1630

Cost of 189 slaves in Cartagena	73,680 pesos
Price of contract of sale to cover illegal entries	2,114 pesos
Expenses from Cartagena to Callao	11,287 pesos

Expenses in Lima (maintenance, freight charges, royal and municipal taxes, medical expenses, legal fees)	10,730 pesos
Freight charges on the silver carried to Cartagena	1,500 pesos
Miscellaneous	308 pesos
Total	99,619 pesos

Despite these high costs and the heavy losses, the trade was reliable because of the scale of the demand.[5]

On the coast of Africa, prices of slaves varied from one trading post to another and according to place of origin. Blacks from some regions were more highly prized than others: those from Cape Verde and Guinea, for example, were more highly valued than those from Angola. The former cost 250 pesos on a market in Cuba during the period of the *asientos* as compared with 200 pesos for a black from Angola.

Social Dimension of Slavery

Virtually all writers refer to the constant acts of rebellion by slaves, which ranged from individual escapes to organised resistance. The laws of the Portuguese Crown and the Council of the Indies demonstrated their determination to maintain rigid social control in order to achieve maximum economic benefit, but at the price of maintaining social divisions.

To deal with the legal situations resulting from slavery in the New World, royal officials relied on old provisions laid down in the Iberian kingdoms dating from several centuries earlier: they dealt with the purchase and sale of slaves, the various forms of emancipation and penalties for committing offences. But the particular situation of the colonies required the enactment of new laws or modifications of the old medieval ones. The purpose of these laws was to prohibit unions between blacks and whites or between blacks and Indians, who had been newly accepted as subjects of the Crown; to prevent running away and uprisings; to instruct and make the slaves productive; and to regulate inter-ethnic relations among blacks, Spaniards and Indians. Thus, in the Spanish colonies, the powers of lieutenant-governors, governors, *corregidores*, *alcaldes maiores*, royal courts of justice, municipal councils and viceroys were set out in legislation. Things were different in Brazil, where the laws governing relations among slaves, free men, blacks and whites were made by the chambers and *capitães-maiores*.[6] In fact, power was concentrated in the municipalities and was feudal-seigniorial in character, being exercised only indirectly by the planters and miners represented by the chambers and *capitães-maiores*.

Blacks who were successfully integrated in the process of European expansion in the early days (*ladinos*, who became the auxiliaries of Europeans in their work of conquest) or who fled had better chances of social integration than the slaves in the plantations and mines.

It is obvious that the conditions of slavery were determined by the way in which Europeans treated blacks. According to some authors, in Brazil, the patriarchal mentality of masters ensured protection for slaves and, when applicable, the fruits of their union, who enjoyed certain privileges: 'In Brazil, the children born of the union of a master and a slave enjoyed special treatment: they were trained as overseers of the sugar refineries and often sent to study in Portugal, at the University of Coimbra. There were also blacks who won their freedom and entered public life.'[7]

The arrival of slaves in the Americas was accompanied by laws governing their life in captivity, how they were to be used and the exercise by their masters of their right of ownership in them. Some legal provisions had some influence on American codifications: the *Code noir* (Black Code), for example, signed by the king of France in 1685, set out the punishments for runaway slaves (ears to be cut off, branding with the fleur-de-lys on the left shoulder and death for repeat offenders).

The *Siete Partidas*, as the Spanish medieval law is known, and the Roman laws of the *Fuero Juzgo* were the source of the *Leyes de Indias* (Laws of the Indies) which in turn incorporated French provisions into Spanish legislation enforced in the Americas. Under this legal regime, blacks as well as the castes descended from them had no rights and no access to free paid labour. The priesthood, of course, was closed to them. They were not given the least credit or respect, and they were looked down on because of their origins. They were also forbidden to bear arms or to use jewellery, clothes and other accessories solely reserved for whites. They could not move about freely in the cities, towns and villages, and were forbidden to marry anyone not of their own race.

But some illegal practices continued to exist, such as the branding, whipping or imprisoning of slaves, as was seen among certain European owners of sugar mills or cattle ranches in particular. Only intervention by the Church authorities could moderate the arbitrary behaviour of masters who had all too much of a tendency to replace the administrators of justice. The viceroys themselves often forbade the judicial authorities from following up complaints and accusations against the harshest masters.

By the beginning of the seventeenth century, the society of the Spanish colonies was divided into castes, reflecting the need for a rigid separation of social groups, based on racial differences, in order to justify Spanish rule over Indians, blacks, and, of course, the colonised lands. The definition of the castes that emerged from the intermixing of the three races – Spanish, aboriginal and black – involved the most contemptuous designations, which may be summarised thus:

> The names *ahí te estás* [stay there], *salta atrás* [jump backwards], *no te entiendo* [I don't understand you] and *tente en el aire* [stay in the air] expressed stagnation, regression, non-communication and the absence of support. *Ahí te estás* (the offspring of a coyote and a mestizo, himself descended from Spaniard, Indian woman, mulatress, *barcino*, black, *albarazado*, *cambujo*, *zambayo* or *zambaigo*, later, *tornatás*, *albino*, and *morisco*, among others); *salta atrás* (son of a *chino* and an Indian woman, grandson of a *morisco* and a Spanish woman, great-grandson of a Mulatto); *no te entiendo* (descendant of a *tente en el aire* and a mulatress, with an admixture of *calpa mulato*, *zambaigo* and *loba*, Indian and *salta atrás*); *tente en el*

aire (descendant of *cambujo* and *calpamulato*): the whole baroque world of racial discrimination and economic misfortune.[8]

Other forms of stratification, among the slaves, had to do with autonomy and learning: autonomy was measured by the degree of confidence that the master showed in the slave by entrusting him with tasks in which he exercised authority over other slaves; learning was measured by the knowledge that a slave possessed of African culture, while adapting himself to and becoming familiar with white culture. Being able to read and write the language of Europeans enabled slaves to understand the world and the reality of the masters; it guaranteed autonomy and a degree of participation in the privileges that were denied other slaves. All this gave them prestige in the eyes of the slaves themselves. Sorcerers and healers also enjoyed great prestige among the slaves, a prestige which implied, even if the masters did not acknowledge it, a knowledge of the supernatural which they feared and which they would sometimes seek out.

Familiarity with their original culture and the dominant culture sometimes enabled slaves to attain positions of command or, in the case of domestics, to act as cultural intermediaries. They were links between whites and blacks, and slaves who had been educated in their master's house enjoyed great ascendancy within the community.

Work was the be-all and end-all of the life of slaves, although some enjoyed less harsh living conditions than others. Slaves who were artisans in the coffee or sugar plantations enjoyed a degree of autonomy in their work and escaped the direct control of the overseer or their master. Others performed various tasks on the farms, which allowed them also to cultivate a piece of land for their own account. Finally, mention should be made of those whose skills enabled them to hire themselves out to engage in a variety of trades or craft activities. Because of its creativity, this category of slaves enjoyed a status close to freedom and a degree of superiority in relation to plantation slaves or domestics. But, paradoxically, the skills and talents of some craftworkers were such that their price was very high, making it even more difficult for them than for others to purchase their full freedom. The family unit was the form of social organisation most appreciated in the slave communities since, in particular when there was marriage, it promoted a balance which made life in a community easier. However, the rigid character of the division of society into castes encouraged concubinage, which prevailed in all social classes, even the highest class of whites. The majority of unions between slaves were not legalised even when, in the Catholic colonies, they had been blessed by the Church, in particular in plantations belonging to religious orders.

There are many difficulties in studying the slave family because of the variety of marriage practices to be found in the plantations, which reflected a wide range of models. Some authors point out that in the British West Indian colonies, adult slave fathers did not live with their wives, generally living in different plantations. Similarly, in the British-ruled sugar islands, in the late eighteenth and early nineteenth centuries, male slaves lived alone, households consisting of the mother and her children. In the plantations on the French islands, the family organisation of slaves was similar to that in the United States: the family unit was composed of both parents, but this model was undermined by sales and forced separations, which led to successive marriages and the birth of many children by different fathers.

The organisation of kinship ties survived in cases where several slave families that had established a stable union followed one another over several generations, thereby successfully forming genuine extended families; even if their members did not always live under the same roof, their relations conformed to certain rules borrowed from African or European tradition. Slave families can be said to have respected the universal taboo on sibling incest, which went beyond the prohibition on marriage between brothers and sisters and extended to marriage between collateral cousins. Members of extended families observed certain rules about residence – with the bride's or with the groom's parents – as well as the inheritance of goods and the custom of naming children after blood relatives on the father's or mother's side. In addition, in accordance with African custom, it was usual to address members of the family group by special names:

> A detailed study of several North American plantations in the eighteenth and nineteenth centuries has suggested from evidence on naming patterns that some United States slaves had a prohibition on cross-cousin marriage (a taboo not found among whites) and that naming of male children often involved the use of male ancestors several generations back. Similar studies have yet to be undertaken for any Caribbean or Latin American slave regions because of the lack of such family lists. On the basis of current evidence, it is difficult to make general statements about slave kinship practices, their origins and functions, or how they compare with the other classes in their respective societies.[9]

In Latin American societies a voluntary kinship pattern came into being known as *compadrazgo*, or godparenthood,[10] which existed in all social classes and was most widespread in the Caribbean. The Church helped to spread it through the sacrament of baptism which, while it legitimised births, bound adults in a spiritual relationship. Solidarity between parents and godparents was thereby further cemented, while at the same time a reciprocal obligation of mutual help was established.

Cohabitation between Indians and blacks in the Spanish-American communities was a common feature that the vice-regal authorities endeavoured – without total success – to control by decreeing laws aimed at protecting indigenous villages and communities from all contact, all abuse and all 'contamination'. Spanish officials endeavoured, using pretexts that were apparently religious and moral but in fact above all political, to prevent cohabitation between Indians and blacks at all costs. The need was pleaded to protect Indians against the abuses that some *ladino* and Creole blacks perpetrated in indigenous villages, and blacks were therefore forbidden to live in Indian villages. But it must not be forgotten that indigenous Indians had blacks in their service and that there were also some alliances between blacks and Indians.

Despite this protection, many villages remained surrounded by communities that included large numbers of mulattos, blacks and people of colour. Steps were also taken to prevent free blacks and mulattos from entering the great haciendas based on cattle or mixed agriculture. Yet this undesirable population was to be found there in the seventeenth and eighteenth centuries as new regions were opened up to agriculture and internal market systems developed. In this context, many free mulatto and black men became absorbed into the aboriginal communities and even married into them, thus acceding to the rights and privileges that members of those communities enjoyed. All these factors naturally favoured a mutual assimilation of the characteristics of family structure, and some of these men of colour even came to be aldermen and judges in the municipal councils of these villages. There can be no denying that in the Spanish possessions, cohabitation between blacks and Indians undermined efforts designed to prevent such contacts in the cities. In order to regulate cohabitation between the various ethnic groups, recourse was had *inter alia* to municipal councils; 'All the *cabildos* in America enacted similar regulations which were contained in various ordinances designed for law enforcement and in other ordinances described simply as being for negroes or slaves. The regulations prohibited slaves from carrying arms, wandering at night without permission of their owners, going into the Indian markets, entering private property, cutting down trees, and engaging in commerce.'[11]

In the Lesser Antilles, in the sixteenth century, unions between blacks and Caribbean Indians gave rise to the race known as *zamba*, black Caribs, among whom the physical characteristics of blacks prevailed but who spoke the indigenous language.

From the end of the sixteenth century, the colonial regime granted noble Indians the privilege of owning slaves, a privilege that was later extended to ordinary Indians and those living in cities. Ownership of black slaves by Indians had its counterpart, since blacks – *ladino* blacks, auxiliaries of the conquistadors – enslaved Indians. For that reason, royal decrees from 1541 to 1592 stipulated that blacks should not live in Indian villages, take Indians into their service or have business dealings with them.

What needs to be stressed here is that the opposition between blacks and Indians was further aggravated by laws forbidding intermarriage between them, since the resulting children would be born free. But nothing could halt the mutual attraction between the two races. Miscegenation went on continuously from the moment Europeans and Africans made their first contact with the Indians in the Americas.

From the very earliest days of the colonisation of the Americas, one of the principles favourable to blacks was manumission,[12] a form of emancipation much approved of by Christian doctrine and which has its roots in Roman law. In the slave societies it was practised from the very first days of colonisation. In every colony in Latin America a class of free men of colour came into being. Because of the prevailing racist criteria, these groups, whose numbers continued to grow throughout the sixteenth and seventeenth centuries, did not enjoy absolute freedom. In the eighteenth century, freedmen even had to fight against rejection by the authorities and the white population to be admitted into society, a rejection that flowed from the all-devouring racism of the American slave system, which regarded free blacks and mulattos as rivals of whites, economically and socially.

In every slave society in the Americas, economic, religious and cultural factors strongly influenced the social conditions that governed the acceptance of freedmen into society. Among these factors, racism was the most tenacious, opposing the acceptance of blacks and mulattos as free citizens. But reactions of acceptance or rejection differed in each of the areas ruled by the various European powers.

Racism has been said to be the consequence of slavery, although racism existed already in European nations before they began their expansion into the Americas. Spain and Portugal, for example, practised discrimination on the basis of religion, and, to a lesser extent, ethnic origin. This form of rejection of those seen as different was, in turn, the consequence of the cohabitation of Jews, Christians and Moors, marked by a long conflict which ended in the fifteenth century with the expulsion of the Jews from Portugal and Spain and the establishment of the principle of 'blood purity' imposing a distinction between 'Old Christians' and 'New Christians' at the expense, it goes without saying, of the newly converted Jews and Muslims. The policy of discrimination put into effect denied the latter the right to carry on certain trades and banned them from holding public or Church office, making them second-class citizens. Using this as a precedent, Europeans subjected Indians to similar treatment, some offices and trades being quite simply barred to them, which automatically placed them on a lower level than Europeans. The same criterion, even more radically interpreted, was applied to slaves and free persons of colour.

These latter also saw their rights limited by laws made in the home country or by local governments, which forbade them equality with the white population and put them on the same social footing as the 'New Christians' in Spain and Portugal, who could not prove their 'blood purity'. The Church was scarcely more generous to slaves or their descendants, forbidding them access to the priesthood and entry into the religious orders as well as access to high public office. Even if they were free, men of colour could not attend university, nor enter a profession. Free women of colour could not wear jewellery or certain clothes which only white women could wear. These restrictions were even extended to specialised occupations that might favour upward social mobility. All this was no more than the expression, in law and custom, of the racism at work in the Ibero-American colonies, in societies that were rigidly stratified. Thus, even when free, blacks and mulattos formed the lowest castes. The continued survival of the caste system which preserved white privileges was ensured by restrictions on free individuals of colour accumulating wealth or reward for their skills and talents: social mobility deriving from occupational mobility was thus closed to them.

Racism was not confined to the Ibero-American colonies; it affected the whole population of colour in the Americas. Nevertheless, the restrictions imposed on ex-slaves depended on the conditions attaching to their emancipation and the degree of freedom which freedmen enjoyed within a given economic and social order. In all colonies, at least at first, emancipation seems to have been quite common: many masters rewarded the loyalty of their slaves by granting them freedom and acknowledging children born of their relations with black women. Purchase of freedom and conditional emancipation (*coartación*) were also practised from the earliest days of colonisation. In the case of manumission, either the slave purchased his freedom, or it was paid for by a third party, whereas in the case of *coartación*, the slave made an agreement with his master on 'his price' and handed over his earnings until the agreed amount was reached. The traditional forms of emancipation were retained in the Iberian colonies, the practice of manumission developing as the number of freedmen grew.

The existence of restrictive legislation covering freedmen did not stop whites fearing that it was insufficient and that their privileges were at risk. Faced with the growing fear aroused by the increase in the free population of colour, the practice of manumission was resisted in some colonies. This was the case in North America, where it was subject to restrictions that bordered on a complete ban. The Iberian governments, on the other hand, legitimised the purchase of freedom. As a result, there continued to be few freedmen in areas where manumission was combated, and they were more numerous in the Iberian colonies.

The emergence of significant numbers of free blacks and mulattos began to raise doubts about the efficiency of the institution of slavery. In the French Caribbean, a number – a limited number, it is true – of individuals of colour even succeeded in building up sufficient power to threaten that of whites. For whereas in other areas, freedmen belonged to the lowest social classes, in the French possessions, once free, slaves turned themselves into planters and, as they prospered, began to compete with whites.

Generally speaking, the system of negotiated gradual purchase (*coartación*) enabled blacks from Africa to gain their freedom. As regards manumission granted by the master, it worked mainly to the advantage of mulattos and Creoles. The practice of free emancipation by masters led to a rise in the number of freed women and mulattos who consequently came to represent the biggest proportion of the free population of colour. As for the purchase of freedom, it seems that both men and women used that channel.

Emancipation could also be obtained through baptism, with the master recognising his bastard children; his word was sufficient for the newborn child to be declared free. All abandoned children, of whatever race, were also deemed free. Manumission was more common in the towns than in the countryside. In this connection, while urban slaves had a greater possibility of purchasing their freedom, especially if they were skilled, the fact of having a trade raised the price of their emancipation. In any event, slaves in towns often resorted to the courts and were more aware of their rights than slaves who remained isolated and under the control of timber firms, sugar refineries and plantations.

Most freedmen, destitute as they were, entered the lowest strata of society and had to fight to climb the social ladder. The freedman also had the heavy duty of freeing his family – his spouse and children – through his own labour. When a black was married to an Indian woman, the latter was quite easily freed, because her children were born free. In the French Caribbean, the bastard offspring of whites would often be freed, and even received some resources with which to begin their lives as free individuals.

The birth rate seems to have been higher among free people of colour than among the rest of the population, partly because the integration of free women into these communities raised their fertility rate. At the same time, the very high mortality and morbidity rate observed in this category of the population is to be explained by the conditions of extreme poverty in which these people lived, once freed from the state of slavery.

Military service being compulsory for freedmen, the latter formed the many companies of blacks and mulattos that existed in the Ibero-American colonies, which enabled the Crowns of Spain and Portugal not to maintain a standing army in the Americas but only a few professional officers at the head of militias. When a soldier of colour attained officer rank, he was entitled to demand all the benefits granted to whites of the same rank, resulting in countless disputes fought out between the military units made up of blacks and mulattos and the forces made up of whites.

Religion offered free individuals of colour some possibilities of social advancement which they put to good use: first, they would baptise their children and place them under the protection of godfathers chosen among people of high class from whom they could obtain favours and marks of interest. The institution of godfatherhood through godparentage made possible the establishment between godsons and godfathers of a moral relationship which ensured the advancement of the former. Furthermore, the Church encouraged the free population of colour to strengthen its links within fraternal and religious mutual self-help associations – the brotherhoods – in which priests placed slaves and freedmen under the protection of the saint of their choice. These associations were discriminatory in character and intent, their goal being to preserve the separation between whites and the lower castes. Nevertheless, they offered blacks and their castes a social and religious space which gave them the comforting feeling of belonging to a community.

> These black brotherhoods existed in every city and town which had a substantial population of free and slave blacks and mulattos. In most larger towns there were several such societies, and many of the brotherhoods admitted slaves as well. These organizations thus tended to maintain important ties between the two classes and counterbalanced the antagonisms which inevitably developed between those who had a firm stake in the status quo and those who inherently opposed it.[13]

It can therefore be said that if, once the system of kinship founded on the African lineage had been destroyed, the social organisation of blacks ceased to govern relations between Africans and their descendants, the brotherhoods gave them the cohesion and identity that any community needs.

In domestic service and some trades, former slaves found not simply a possibility of working but the relief of meeting less opposition from whites. In general, whites in the cities did little to oppose them working in domestic service, hawking and dock work. In the countryside, once they had won their freedom, blacks and mulattos became integrated into rural life as free peasants, although they had to occupy land illegally because they had no titles to property. Some urban centres indeed were supplied by the surpluses of these communities of colour.

In this way, although rejected and fought by the whites in ferocious rivalry, the former slaves become freedmen and integrated themselves into and multiplied within the slave regimes that had given them birth.

> They fought bitterly and sometimes successfully for the right to social and economic mobility and for the legal rights of full citizenship. This was the most difficult struggle of all and one that would go on long after the death of slavery. But it was this never-ending struggle of the freedmen for acceptance which ultimately prepared the way for the slaves to enter more successfully into free society after abolition was granted to all Africans and Afro-Americans [sic].[14]

Influence of Slavery in the Field of Culture

The process of transculturation that occurred in the Americas between Indians, Europeans and Africans led to a fairly significant modification of the three original cultures and the emergence of a new cultural reality. In its variety and complexity, this culture was defined not as the haphazard sum of the features of one or another culture, nor as a vague amalgam of customs, languages and other cultural products, but as an ongoing process composed of different interrelated branches, drawing on its own cultural roots. It was thus a culture of transition in which the three cultures that had given rise to it were represented, each expressing itself through new modes of knowing and feeling (collective representations), in which culture, regarded as a whole embracing the economy, social organisation and knowledge, gave a meaning to a new civilisation.

The captured men and women, reduced to slavery and embarked to be sold as so much merchandise by slave traders, belonged to advanced societies but ones whose military power was inferior to that of the Europeans. These beings, stolen from their homeland, carried with them their gods, their beliefs and the knowledge that they had acquired in the society in which they were born. From the beginning of their life as slaves, they put up fierce resistance, not only to the regime of forced labour but also to the system of values and beliefs that whites tried to impose on them by destroying their cultural heritage and depriving them of the possibility of reconstructing their folklore and customs – in short, their culture.

The existence in the Americas of remnants of African civilisation is not at all surprising, but we cannot claim that they have been so well preserved that they can be isolated from their environment. When some African cultural traits are manifest, it is because they have found a terrain capable of nurturing them despite the destructive grip of slavery. In the first phase of his life on foreign soil, the 'bozale' – the black freshly landed from Africa – was traumatised by the dispersal of his family, which meant a break in his lineage. Through sexual congress with other partners, he mixed his blood with that of foreigners, which had the consequence of the loss of another part of his heritage in his descendants. His way of life, his language and his customs disappeared and were replaced by those of his white master. Not only did he have to assimilate the culture of the white man whether he liked it or not, but he was marginalised and segregated. Blacks were denied integration, and so, in order to be able to survive in this social void, they remembered their ancestral heritage. Then, with their African past and their imposed present, they forged a mixed culture of elements drawn from African, European and indigenous traditions. This mixing was, in some regions, dominated by the African contribution, in others, by the Indian contribution; everywhere, the omnipresence of Europe was a sign of domination. But it is by no means possible to speak of absence of culture or cultural disintegration. Those who speak of black culture refer to a culture in which African survivals give life to the soul of communities. In fact, it is simply one and the same mixed and undeniable culture of which America was the crucible.

Interethnic relations among Europeans, Indians and Africans, and then among the descendants of these three strains, proceeded in the various regions of the New World, within different moral, religious and legal systems. The way in which the black individual and the slave were perceived and the possibilities of manumission, recourse to the law, marriage, etc., varied at different times and depending on the way of life of each colony. The upshot was a vast disparity in regard to the integration of slaves once their freedom had been won, and their future once they had been able to demonstrate their abilities. All these factors determined what we call the deculturation and acculturation of black populations as well as the various forms of cultural survivals and a wide range of syncretisms. But the vitality of the African personality resisted the attempts at reification and survived.

When the Americas ceased to be colonies dependent on Europe, then the manifestations of syncretism, which had been in gestation since the first years of slavery, took concrete form. The population of colour played an important role in the political, ideological and cultural domains right from the emergence of pro-independence movements. Freedom was demanded loud and clear in the *palenques*, the *quilombos*, the *mocambos* and all the other fortified enclaves where slaves rebelled against slavery from the very beginning. Once the colonial period was over, the African contributions to American culture, at the end of the process of transculturation, expressed their liberating message – in particular through music, dance and folklore.

It may be supposed that the very first communities of maroon slaves which succeeded in retaining their language, their systems of social and military control, their religious practices and their rituals were the places where African culture was best preserved. Unlike the first maroon slaves, the children born in the Americas in the enclaves of Creole maroons, who were converted to Christianity, underwent an acculturation which prevented them from handing down their culture of origin to their descendants. As Bastide writes: 'Thus, because of their heterogeneous ethnic origins, it frequently proved impossible for these bands to preserve their ancestral customs, or even to remodel them in their own way. At the same time their members found themselves obliged to come to terms with a new environment, to work out hitherto unknown methods of gaining a livelihood and organising their society. The result was a series of new civilisations: Negro certainly, but not in any genuine sense African.'[15]

Thus blacks born in the New World retained – doubtless thanks to oral tradition – only a few remnants of their African roots, but these were nevertheless sufficiently powerful to create a new syncretic system which facilitated the cohesion and unity of communities of African origin. Some of these communities developed to the point of constituting what were effectively free states. As well as being a movement of resistance to forced labour, *marronnage* was a movement of cultural resistance organised around (African) ethnic identity, while admitting indigenous participants with whom it reached an agreement to co-exist which did not imply the total assimilation of one group by the other. It gave rise to 'maroon culture', a model of the fusion of cultural elements and ways of life engendered by a syncretic process in semi-isolation. Actually, no community remained completely isolated; many of them maintained trading relations and remained in permanent contact with the rest of the colonial population by whom they were influenced. That is what explains the conservation among maroons of both old African cultural traits and a number of traits that derived from the slave system of colonial times – all elements that have now disappeared.

Afro-American folklore offers three levels, each highly recognisable by its own characteristics. The first is African folklore which was primarily preserved in religious survivals, present throughout the American continent. The most important of them, which have become genuine religions practised not only by Africans and their descendants but also by other population groups, are the cult of saints (*santería*), voodoo and *candomblé*. Religion has not been confined to conventional religious practices but has embraced all modes of everyday conduct and practices which have become a moral code governing the life of followers, offering them a mystical solution in times of crisis and acting as a palliative in the most trying circumstances. But, above all, it has been a link and the bedrock of their identity.

The second level of Afro-American folklore is what Bastide calls 'Creole' folklore: it was born in the Americas of relations between slaves and masters, the feelings of one group towards the other and the work of acculturating blacks undertaken by whites. In this folklore, the form remains African but the content makes room for the new realities of slave life: the plantation, forced submission, suffering, isolation. Among them are maroon slave rebellions which are expressed particularly in dance and narrative. It is spontaneous – whereas African folklore emerges from a heritage – and concerns every country in the Americas.

The third level is the 'artificial' folklore manufactured by the repressive sector of whites, which Bastide explains as follows:

> The first step was to make a selection of Negro dances, eliminating (for instance) the erotic ones, but keeping the war-dances. Negro drama would be encouraged, with great emphasis on the old African traditions of Bantu royalty, and ambassadors between kingdoms. Advantage was taken of the Negro passion for processions, bright-coloured costumes and music. In short, all these features of African culture could, by adroit manipulation, be exploited to the glory of God and the holy church.[16]

As is the case with all limited and restrictive patterns, artificial folklore was largely displaced by African folklore which, in the domain of religion, asserted itself despite the pressure it had to endure, and which has kept alive down to the present-day syncretic religions which have succeeded in preserving the music and dance, trances and liturgy of ceremonies. They were the bulwark that defended the heritage inherited by Creole blacks from their African ancestors. In the syncretic religions, speech is the password of African deities, the drum the listening language which consecrates the space of rituals, legitimises dance, Africanises the context and allows the sons of Africa, for the space of a rite, to return to the land of their ancestors. Elsewhere, however, artificial folklore succeeded in harming some African traditions.

The colonial government took note of the tendency of slaves to come together in ethnic groups to play or dance when they were relaxing and decided to institutionalise and hence give a permanent character to these regroupings by nation. They thought thereby to sharpen rivalries between the 'nations' living in the cities, in order to prevent them uniting and thus eliminate all possibility of rebellion. Such were the functions of the brotherhoods, the 'governments and councils' of black slaves. In the towns, the celebration of religious practices did not run into too many problems; the authorities who had observed that the blacks performed their rites at night did not authorise such practices but tolerated them because the faithful claimed that they were worshipping Catholic saints. In the countryside, the slaves had either to outwit the vigilance of overseers or involve them in their ceremonies. This was the case with *santería* in Cuba, voodoo in Haiti and *candomblé* in Brazil.

The division into 'nations', designed to stir up rivalries between blacks, helped conserve African languages as well as African beliefs and traditions: 'Here we come up against what is, for our purposes, the most important and basic fact of all. All these institutions tended to bring people from the same country together, in one single group, thus producing a close degree of solidarity between them. It was this that made possible the survival, on American soil, of African patterns of culture. The institutions and the cultural patterns were closely bound up together: when the former were abolished, the latter faded out.'[17]

This occurred when the colonial power discovered that the collective activities of blacks overlapped with those of African political organisations and that, in addition, slave rebellions and plots to escape were being hatched in them. By the time the ceremonies normally celebrated by these groups were suppressed, some had already broken out of ethnic limits and had become traditions for the whole of society: such was the case with carnival, celebrated throughout the hemisphere down to the present day. In Brazil, there are even some 'nations' and religious sects which still retain the names of their ethnic groups of origin.

The Africans did not bring to the New World any type of writing – not because they did not have any, since, in fact, systems of writing had been invented several times in Africa among peoples south of the Sahara – but because these scripts were used only on a small local scale and were not widely known. It is thought that in the absence of long-lasting materials such as papyrus, the oral tradition – which places the highest value on the spoken word and possesses a more lasting power than any written form – was adopted by black peoples as a means of communication. Alongside oral tradition, the peoples of Africa developed a unique and effective language: the drum. As Jahn explains:

> If we take the concept of 'writing' in a somewhat broader meaning than is contained in the word derived from the verb 'to write', and, as it comes more naturally to Europeans to do, understand the concept not by its method but by its purpose, as 'signs produced and employed by men for the purpose of making a communication', then the language of the drums is a kind of 'writing'. Looked at more closely, therefore, African culture is not a culture without writing. Both western and African culture possessed writing, one an alphabetical script, the other a drum script.[18]

The majority of Afro-American cultures have retained the use of the drum both in religious ceremonies and in secular celebrations. It was only in North America that blacks were deprived of it by their Protestant masters. Converted blacks replaced the instruments by stamping their feet and clapping their hands during religious services. Later, their musical creativity led to the return of the drums and the re-creation of various popular forms of band.

One last phenomenon should be mentioned: the institution that enabled the African woman to extend her motherhood to the children of her masters. Franco speaks in these terms: 'The mature black woman will become nurse and nanny, housekeeper to the family and governess to the children.... All her mistress's powers over the management of the house were delegated to her; she was responsible for keeping discipline among the domestic staff, and for giving them and their children religious education; in short, she was a "matron" whom everyone respected and honoured.'[19]

Notes

1. R. Mellafe, 1973, p. 97 (1975, p. 88).
2. *Asientos*: contracts between the Crown and an individual granting the latter a monopoly of the importation of slaves in a given area and for a set period (French translator's note).
3. See E. Vila Vilar, 1977, pp. 231–232.
4. See R. Mellafe, 1973, p. 109 (1975, pp. 96–97).
5. See E. Vila Vilar, 1977, p. 220.
6. The *capitães-maiores* were an authority responsible for enforcing laws or regulations (*ordenança*).
7. J.L. Franco et al., 1970, p. 37.
8. G. Castañon, 1990.
9. H.S. Klein, 1986, p. 173.
10. *Compadrazgo* is the relationship between the parents of a child and the child's godparents.
11. R. Mellafe, 1975, p. 104.
12. 'Manumission' is the legal emancipation of slaves.
13. H.S. Klein, 1986, pp. 233–234.
14. Ibid., pp. 240–241.
15. R. Bastide, 1967, p. 49.
16. Ibid., p. 181.
17. Ibid., p. 93.
18. J. Jahn, 1961, pp. 187–188.
19. J L. Franco, 1968, p. 14.

Bibliography

BASTIDE, R. 1967. *Les Amériques noires: les civilisations africaines dans le Nouveau Monde.* Paris, Payot. (Coll. Petite bibliothèque.) [Eng. tr., 1971. Green, P. *African Civilisations in the New World.* London, C. Hurst.]
CASTAÑON, G. 1990. *Asimilación e integración de los Africanos en la Nueva España durante los siglo XVI y XVII.* Mexico City. (Tesis de Maestría UNAM FF02.1991.)
FRANCO, J.L. 1968. *La presencia negra en el Neuvo Mundo.* Havana, Casa de las Américas.
FRANCO, J.L., et al. 1970. 'Facetas del esclavo africano'. In *Introducción a la cultura africana en América latina.* Paris, UNESCO.
JAHN, J. 1963. *Las culturas neoafricanas.* Mexico, Fondo de Cultura Económica. [Eng. tr., 1961. Greene, M. *Muntu: An Outline of Neo-African Culture.* London, Faber and Faber.]
KLEIN, H.S. 1986. *La esclavitud africana en América latina y el Caribe.* Madrid, Alianza Editorial. [American orig., 1986. *African Slavery in Latin America and the Caribbean.* New York, Oxford University Press.]
MELLAFE, R. 1973. *Breve historia de la esclavitud en América latina.* Mexico, SEP. [Am. tr., 1975. Judge, J.W.S. *Negro Slavery in Latin America.* Berkeley, University of California Press.]
VILA VILAR, E. 1977. *Hispanoamérica y el comercio de esclavos.* Seville, Bruguera Edición.

Part V

The Slave Trade and International Co-operation

Chapter 34

Towards the Pedagogy of the History of the Slave Trade

Jean-Michel Deveau

SHOULD WE TEACH PEOPLE about some of the bleakest episodes in the history of humanity, at the risk of creating feelings of hopelessness among the rising generations? This is something we have to ask ourselves before we decide whether the slave trade should be made a set subject in school curricula. It all depends on the attitudes of the people behind the idea.

If it is their intention to pave the way for co-operation between continents on the basis of a clear picture of the past and the truth that has hitherto been concealed – so that those whose task it will be to build the world can engage in disinterested action with all the facts in their possession – then it is essential for this mass deportation movement to be studied.

However, it is quite obvious that Europe, which has kept the written memory of this event locked up in its archives, cannot write this history all by itself. Africa, with its wealth of oral memories and its archaeological sites, holds the other half of the information needed. It will be possible to teach the true facts only after teachers on the two continents start working together in consultation and co-operation.

The purpose of this essay is to lay the basis for a dialogue. With that in mind, it does not claim to do any more than bring the partners together. It certainly does not set out to propose a model, even an educational one. The goal, in an attempt to spark off discussion, is to highlight the projects carried out at La Rochelle, France's second largest slave-trading port, in order to show what French schoolchildren can do and how French people nowadays visualise their education.

In other words, it is no more than the fruit of an experiment that is limited in both time and space but which is only waiting to be enriched or re-centred when the dialogue gets under way.

Objectives

Identifying the Slave Trade in Its Context

By definition, the slave trade, or deportation of slaves, cannot be dissociated from most of the slave-owning civilisations. It is necessary, therefore, to go beyond the narrow confines of the deportation episode itself and situate it in the context of transnational trade flows and the internal structure of the societies that lived through it. In the long-term view, the history of the Mediterranean and the Middle East from the very remotest past bears the traces of this shameful procession of victims torn from their homes and carried off as slave labour merely because other people were stronger than they were, like the blacks from sub-Saharan Africa who were immortalised on the stone columns erected by the Egyptians and Romans, or the 'Slaves' procured by the Greeks from the remote Caucasus whose supplications could still be heard all through the Middle Ages. There was an inexhaustible demand for labour among the peoples of classical antiquity and the Arabs who succeeded them in the southern and eastern Mediterranean.

Historians and legal scholars quibble over the victims and their status, over whether they were already slaves or were still only captives. Did the slave trade transport people who had been free or were they moveable goods that were already owned by other people? Did their change in status from one to the other occur before or after they were first sold? One thing is certain: most of them, although born free, sank into slavery because they were not strong enough in the face of the enemy or the slave-raiders, who both regarded the people they defeated as their property. They sold them or used them as they saw fit, and even exercised the power of life or death over them, since there was no law curbing the use of armed force. This may sound like a legal nicety, but it affords us an opportunity to grasp the fact that there was a switch from a legal void in which those who were strong could behave as they liked, without any restrictions, to a state of law, where the victims, once they had been sold, were hemmed in by a framework of laws which they had to respect to the letter without their opinion ever being sought. In the first stages of the slave trade, history goes hand in hand with civil instruction. This prompts us to give thought to the value of laws.

However that may be, legal scholars should step aside, so that the spotlight can be focused on the tragic predicament of the victims. Any last illusions they may have entertained were all too quickly swept away by the weight of their chains, the raucous bellowing of their gaolers and the savagery of the blows meted out to them. They would never again see their own countries or their own people, and only death would deliver them from slavery. It is this that accounts for the irrepressible urge to kill themselves felt by all those who were loaded on to the white man's slave ships.

Teaching about the slave trade means that we first have to convey this sense of despair and shed light on the experience undergone by the people who were deported. Any such attempt borders on presumption, since distress is something that cannot be shared. However, teaching, by its very nature, primarily addresses the intelligence and requires it to convey feelings at the risk of misrepresenting the main thing, which in the case of the slave trade was the monstrous emotional burden of the distress overwhelming the individual. In setting out to do the impossible, historians are stubbornly determined to make people understand. For that reason, they pinpoint problems in order to underscore their singularity. They accordingly start by identifying the component parts of the slave trade before linking them, on the upstream side, to the mechanisms that gave rise to the phenomenon and, on the downstream side, to those that it triggered off in its turn.

The slave trade, which is in itself very complex, can be grasped only when it is linked to all those things in agriculture, crafts and industry in Europe that were instrumental in preparing the journey and those in Africa that were likewise instrumental in rounding up the slaves. Thereafter, due account has to be taken of the situations in the Americas that acted rather like a suction pump in boosting or slowing down the rhythm of the voyages. It would be just as pointless to present the voyages of the slave trade without integrating them into the world system as it would be to try to explain the circulation of the blood without saying anything about the body which it keeps alive. However, the slave trade functioned with a logic of its own, and it is this singularity that has to be isolated in both time and space. The ocean voyage was radically different from the trans-Saharan trade or that of the Black Sea or the Mediterranean. The slave trade in the seventeenth and eighteenth centuries, when it was legally recognised and was dependent on specific maritime technologies, cannot in any case be confused with the trade in the nineteenth century, which was banned by law and profited from new clipper-ship designs. Similarly, the two Atlantic slave trades cannot be compared with the trade which deported Chinese across the Pacific to the Americas or sent Melanesians to Australia in the second half of the nineteenth century.

Although the drama is the same, its features vary in both time and space, and teachers are therefore compelled to 'freeze' them in a given space and at a given point in time, whereas it is only through continuity that economic processes are really meaningful. As a result, it is teaching that has to pay the price. At the risk of confusing the issue, it is necessary to use simplifying devices before the pieces of the puzzle can be put back together again. After doing this, it is possible to cover the second half of the journey, since photography is only a fixed snapshot, whereas the most important thing is movement. It will therefore still be necessary to explain the trajectories of the components which come into collision with one another. Events are no more than points of impact which are swallowed up by time and space and create other points that are just as short-lived. This is certainly the first and greatest difficulty in explaining a history that juggles with the centuries as it does the oceans.

Using the Past in the Service of Urgent Contemporary Issues

To Condemn Slave Trading and Slavery Which Have Still Not Disappeared Altogether. History can contribute to a better understanding of current affairs. In this respect, however, the history of the slave trade stands out because of its constantly rebounding after-effects. From time to time, the international press reports on dramatic incidents which may or may not be condemned by the United Nations or non-governmental humanitarian organisations. The last instances of the abolition of slavery date back to the 1970s, and Mauritania closed the list in 1980. However, we are only too aware of how wide a gap can exist between *de jure* and de facto situations.

The scandal lies less in those cases in which it still survives clandestinely in former slave-owning countries than in the resurgence of the practice in the heart of capital cities like Paris or London. Recently, a number of television programmes have alerted the public to this problem. Over the past 20 years, cases of slave trading similar in all respects to those of the eighteenth century have been exposed in the newspaper *Le Monde*. Deportations of labour still take Chinese to Arabia and Africans and Turks to Europe (to mention only the best-known cases) in a sordid state of clandestinity in which the individuals involved are treated no better than their predecessors who were shipped across the Atlantic. Brothels of all kinds are peopled by children sold in the Far East, and in Latin America the fortunes of criminal bosses are built on child labour.

This widespread contempt for the individual in the mid-twentieth century has sparked off indignant accusations from UNESCO. In schools, they have been echoed through UNESCO clubs or civic education courses. However, school curricula have not yet established the connections linking such outrageous occurrences from the time of antiquity right up to the present day. It is high time that we put an end to what is glossed over in the history of labour and of intercontinental relations.

Putting an End to the Law of Silence. The veil of silence shrouding the written history of the slave trade since the eighteenth century is only now starting to be lifted. The subject is brushed aside in Europe and Africa alike. School textbooks broach it with reluctance and continue to present hackneyed clichés without taking account of recent research findings. At the root of the taboo, we find complexes, false allegations of guilt and the embarrassment of tackling a past still oozing from the walls, covering people's determination to hush up the origins of present-day racist incidents or conflicts.

Europeans have adopted a scientific approach to studying the slave trade only in the past 20 years or so, and there are still very few specialists in the subject. France can claim only some 10 university theses on the subject plus two or three others recently being prepared – a paltry number!

The first exhibition on the subject was organised in Nantes in 1992. As a symbol of the way attitudes are changing, it is significant that France's leading slave-trading port should have participated in the exhibition, whose very title, 'Les Anneaux de Mémoire' (The Chains of Memory), clearly sets out to acknowledge past events which had hitherto been completely passed over in silence. Bordeaux has not yet said a word about its own part in those events, and La Rochelle pretends that it only recently realised that it occupied second place in the league-table of the country's slave-trading ports.

The list of those who have kept silent could be extended indefinitely. It would be equally easy to find the same attitude in Britain, for all that it prides itself on having instigated the abolition of slavery. It tends to forget that in the eighteenth century its shipowners beat the world all-comers record for crossings between Africa and the Americas. There are few publications on Liverpool, the world's No. 1 port in the trade, and there is only a vague 35-page brochure on Bristol, the second-largest British port. They have washed their hands of the subject rather too quickly. The Dutch, the Portuguese and the Danes are likewise afflicted with amnesia, as though they are afraid of the idea of having to account for the doings of ancestors who have been dead these past two centuries.

The sense of unease does not end there, however. The French in particular are bogged down in the contradictions of a history which prolongs the slave trade, while the country proclaims loud and clear that it now acts only in accordance with the principles of the Declaration of Human Rights. This discrepancy is compounded by the tragedy of the Second World War and the odour of complicity in the Nazi deportations, which adds to the sense of unease. Lastly, in order to show how closely all these complexes are intertwined, everything became bogged down in the colonial wars. Instead of drawing up curricula that take a clear look at the past, the events involved are dodged, portrayed in a biased manner or simply glossed over. However, since nobody is really unaware of what actually happened, schoolchildren accept these denials of the facts or half-confessions as if they were some shameful disease forming an integral part of the national heritage.

When we turn to Africa, the silence is scarcely any less eloquent. The entire history of this martyred continent has yet to be written. Since Africa was regarded throughout almost the entire colonial period as not having had a past of any interest, African historiography made scarcely any progress up to the 1960s. Since then, archaeologists have been uncovering whole areas of history on which oral sources can be expected to shed more light when more progress has been made in collecting them. In spite of the very effective work they have done, African historians have not yet had time to come to adequate conclusions enabling them to sketch out the internal history of the different forms of slave-trading. In the first instance, they have had to rid themselves of all the emotional inhibitions and complexes they have been bequeathed by colonialism. This has now been accomplished, and for the past 10 years this young school of historians has acknowledged that the continent bears a large share of the responsibility, although the idea is still not admitted everywhere. An immense area of research is being opened up.

What can we say about the United States of America, where the black problem is liable at any moment to set fire to interethnic relations? It is history in the present tense, in which the truth is not always compatible with people's emotional experiences – or indeed with living side by side in peace. We should not, therefore, be unduly surprised to find that the most recent publications deal more with the abolition of slavery than with the slave trade itself.

Thus, everybody changes the emphasis placed on history or is silent about it according to their particular interests at the time, driven as they are by their own neuroses or, worse still, by the prompting of the political authorities, who are inclined to manipulate the past for their own ends. How can teachers find their way in all this? How is it possible to teach when the subject being taught gives rise to such reservations and sometimes even disappears under whole areas of ignorance? Accordingly, it is not surprising that people go on repeating the same hackneyed and inaccurate clichés. It is a matter of urgency for all those who exercise some responsibility in education to get their facts straight and acquire an in-depth knowledge of the subject, and to demand that the slave trade be included in school curricula as one of the main chapters in the history of humanity. In this regard, international co-operation would not be out of place.

BRINGING CIVILISATIONS CLOSER. Although the slave trade is by definition violent, it represents one of those moments in time when history brings together continents embarking on an era of interdependence. Regardless of what forms they take, periods of contact are ideal moments to give children a perception of foreigners and to show them how outlooks on both sides can transform reality. European curricula, especially those in France, only broach the study of Africa in a very cursory manner. The slave trade would provide an opportunity for presenting the natural and climatic conditions under which it took place and the adaptation of everyday life, the outlines of the main philosophical and religious currents, and the evolution of political systems. This look at a real-life situation that is radically different from that experienced by European children would provide an opportunity for asking the question 'Why?'. This would then prompt them to understand rather than pass judgement.

At a time when systems and ideologies in the West are collapsing, school-children and students will accept these differences with greater tolerance than their predecessors, who basked in the pride of thinking they were right. In addition, it is not a bad thing for Western children caught up in technology to be confronted with different spiritual and artistic realities.

The study of the slave trade underscores the interdependence of a world system on the scale of four continents in which the responsibilities of each are watered down. The educational end-purpose will be neither to conceal those responsibilities nor to denounce them from the witness box before the judgement of opinion, but to make it understood how they could have occurred in defiance of the law of humankind and to show that there are circumstances conducive to liberation from all forms of perversity. Here we are at the very heart of the kind of education which goes to form the citizen, in other words the sort of education which shapes society and prevents it from lapsing into crime. Querying things in this way calls less for the finer sentiments than for the collaboration of researchers and teachers in establishing and conveying the truth over and above the differences existing between civilisations.

Finding the Themes

The World System

The idea is to define the interdependence of the four continents for the benefit of only one of them, since Europe, the point of departure and arrival, deliberately mobilised the wealth of Africa and the Americas. The first phase was the transportation of labour to perform unpaid work. The whole enterprise was organised in such a way that all Europe had to do was to spend the strict minimum on the food needed to keep the slaves alive. To get to that point, it was necessary to go through a phase in which genocide was committed against the peoples of the Americas, so that they could be replaced by other peoples who were completely subjugated. This was made possible by a deportation movement covering distances of thousands of kilometres. The victims, deprived of all hope of returning and without any possibility of organising themselves, could not readily see any possibility of escaping from the iron rule imposed on them. Psychological conditioning accordingly went hand in hand with the use of force, in respect of which the *Code noir* (Black Code), for example, stipulated different degrees of severity. In order to bring this about, the West reintroduced the condition of slavery at a time when it was tending to disappear altogether. The educational importance of this part of the study lies in conveying the idea of depersonalisation which makes it possible to manipulate individuals without allowing them the possibility of reacting.

The work demanded of the slaves was to produce exclusively luxury commodities, such as coffee, sugar, cocoa, cotton and spices, which Europe could have easily gone without. An interdisciplinary approach through the teaching of physical geography, botany and even agronomy would illustrate the need for controlling the region situated between the tropics, and parallels could therefore be drawn between the logic of production and colonisation, which at the same time would show the link between consumption and political system.

The choice of the Americas as an area of colonisation should be clarified in the light of the thinking of the seventeenth and eighteenth centuries. Why did the Europeans abandon Africa? The answer calls for very far-reaching research on the contacts between Europeans and Africans, about which very little is still known. The political organisation of the continent, which has still to be clarified in many respects, clearly seems to have discouraged any attempt at penetration. This is reflected in the European attitude which pretends to know nothing about it. Travellers and slave traders spoke of 'chiefs' and 'petty kings' and these stereotypes have been repeated right up to the present day. Did the whites think that they would save face and conceal their fears by turning the potential enemy into a caricature? Medical research could also clarify the concept of 'fevers' with which the slave traders said they were struck down. Were white people really incapable of adapting to the continent's climate or were they victims of a sense of terror that may have inhibited them to the extent that they became prone to psychosomatic illnesses? In the seventeenth and eighteenth centuries, the whites accordingly forged mental images of Africa and the Americas which, in turn, conditioned their attitudes.

Several questions come to mind: Why did Christopher Columbus, on discovering land in the Americas, describe it as the earthly paradise found again at last? Why did all those who followed him adopt the same view of things? Why did people speak so little about Africa (note how few books were published on the subject)? Why was it presented as the counter-image of the Americas, like a sort of hell? Should not these views also be related to those of China and Oceania put forward in the eighteenth century? On the basis of this, the teacher would show the strength of an attitude. In this case, the aim would be to put forward a justification for imperialist and colonialist policy, the first act of which consists of taking control of the world through the power of words.

The same work has to be done concerning the view which Africa had of white people. In this respect, some iconographic materials are significant – such as embroidered cloth from Benin, effigies of ships, anchors and rifles adopted in architectural or emblematic decoration by the kings of Abomey. The probably rich oral sources on this subject have still to be exploited, and it would be desirable for education authorities in Africa to start publishing extracts from them that would be accessible to schoolchildren and students.

Lastly, the triangular voyage ended in the American plantations. How profitable was the work done by the slaves? How did they adapt to the farming methods employed and to the world of white people? But also how did they go about rejecting them? What underground cultures enabled them to restructure their personalities and live under duress without the slightest hope? What place did Africa occupy in their mental universe? We still are finding the answers to all these questions.

On the other hand, we are on firmer ground when we come to study the economic system of the slave trade. The whole venture was based on a series of barter transactions. This makes it possible to identify where the European products came from that were essential for equipping the slave ships. The construction materials and the goods taken on board came from all over Europe. This would provide an opportunity for showing that industrial or commercial activity is not necessarily neutral but can also involve the people engaged in it in a sort of complicity which has all too often tended to be ascribed to the Atlantic ports alone. In Africa, although the system used for buying captives is more or less well known, we do not know what became of the goods exchanged in the slave trade and the area over which they were redistributed by the indigenous slave traders. The shipowners' accounts have been analysed in sufficient detail to make it possible to go as far as the resale of the slaves in the West Indies. After that, however, the payment for the return trips has never been completely elucidated. They need to be clearly described so as to make it understood that the reality of the profit was not based on the shipment of the slaves alone but on the entire system in which the bulk of the profit was generated by forced and unpaid labour.

In the eighteenth century, the problem was already being raised of how to maintain so complex a system. The danger of the crossings between Africa and the Americas posed it in unequivocal terms as more than 10 per cent of the officers and seamen lost their lives. This was slightly less than the 15 to 18 per cent of the blacks who died, but that was not a problem for the authorities, however. The loss of seamen deprived Europe's royal navies of their services in time of war. In addition, the security of the Atlantic routes cost a great deal, whereas it would have been simpler to produce the sugar or coffee in Africa. This is a key question which has to be asked when we start thinking about the economic aspects. Lastly, force of habit and the power of the capital invested and the networks established won the day against human sentiments and the fate of the slaves.

Maritime Travel and Technology

Such a world system can be readily understood from appropriate maps. Some charts of winds and currents illustrate the logic behind the maritime circuit. Other maps, with Europe at their centre, point to its complicity from the Baltic to the Mediterranean if one sees where the goods came from or where the insurance was arranged. Still others, centred on the companies that fitted out vessels and indicating their commercial and business networks, bear witness to the existence of slave-trade capitalism, which took no account of national borders in much the same way as the multinational corporations of the late twentieth century.

From a study of this kind emerges not only a picture of the slave trade but a picture of all the forms of trade that were needed for the slave trade to be possible. The sea appears to be the ineluctable link in the life of Europe, since everything converges towards it. It was from the ocean that the first international capital movement came into being in the sixteenth century, without which the triangular trade could not have existed.

Once this prerequisite has been established, it is then a good idea to make a close examination of the technical and human data of maritime life. Firstly, shipyards represented the largest industrial sector in the seventeenth and eighteenth centuries. The construction or refitting of ships and the manufacture of rigging and anchors take us into a technological world in which multidisciplinarity brings together history, technology and physics. Stress should be laid on the problems of friction and wear and tear on the rigging, the resistance of the timbers to shipworm and of the hulls to storms. The use of copper plating was not a panacea either (owing to the destruction of the iron nails through electrolysis, as well as other factors). Setting up the ribbing and sides of the vessel, making the masts and ensuring that the cargo holds are watertight are all complex problems. Some idea of what they involved can be obtained from the *Encyclopedia* of d'Alembert and Diderot. It is important to show pupils that these technologies governed the success or failure of the slave-trading expeditions. The same work can be undertaken on methods of navigation and the study of marine instruments and charts of the period.

It is through this that the technological era brings us back to people. A whole world emerges of craftsmen, workmen and sailors, with their own customs, apprenticeships and know-how. These people have all too often been left in the shade by historians, yet it was to defend their interests that Parliament refused to vote the abolition of the slave trade in 1789–90. The proposed alternative left the choice between continuing the trade or putting these skilled people out of work. This technological detour brings us to the very heart of the subject. Conversely, a picture can be obtained of the limits to the seamen's skills, since they could neither surf over sandbanks on the waves nor build suitable small boats. This gap in their technology meant that the whites had to depend on the Lapto, Krumen or Chamas boatmen, who could make them pay a high price. Even then, they regarded this as a more attractive proposition than making the investment needed to solve the problem.

The problems of nutrition were directly bound up with biology. How could food such as cereals, biscuits, salted meats, wine and so on be preserved on a sea voyage lasting for more than a year? What were the nutritional values and deficiencies? The significance of scurvy has to be gauged. The storage of drinking water was linked to the manufacture of barrels (and a cooper was specially embarked on the slave ships) but also to the risk of its being contaminated and to the existence of watering places on the coast of Africa. Reference would also have to be made to the origin of the food and an evaluation made of how much was sold by European agriculture and how much by African agriculture to slave traders and white people living in the ports on the coast of Africa. In this respect, the problem arises in a new way: was African agriculture disorganised or even ruined by the slave trade, or was it actually given a boost? What was the effect of the slave trade on the economy of the islands of Fernando Po and Principe, at which virtually all the slave ships called, since they knew that they could find 'victuals' there?

The period of the clandestine slave trade poses the problem in different terms if, as for the earlier period, we know nothing about how the caravans of slaves being brought down to the coast were supplied with food or, conversely, if we disregard the fact that the partners of the Mongos stimulated production in the coastal regions and they themselves kept up vast plantations which were often worked by the slaves before they were shipped to the Americas.

The problem of revictualling on the coast of Africa was also a cultural one. In fact, the whites seem to have been reluctant to take African produce. It has to be asked whether this was due to lack of habit or contempt for it.

Life as a Prisoner

A study of this aspect would make it possible to understand the attitude both of the gaolers, who had no experience of this kind of work to begin with, and of the innocent captives, who did not understand either why they were kept in chains in the unknown world of the slave ships or where fate was taking them.

A number of topics may be proposed for study. To begin with, a comparison could be made between the state of prostration of the captives when they were loaded onto the slave ships and their rage when they rose up in revolt. The following aspects would have to be stressed: the depersonalisation of the slaves (i.e. the fact that they were shackled, branded and prodded like animals when they were being purchased, and that their bodies were completely shaved) and the culture shocks to which they were subjected; in the case of most slaves, their discovery of the world of white people and the high seas, since they had been captured in the heart of the African continent; the fact of being torn from the continent forever, and hence from the land of their ancestors and from their lineage, and the impact which this had on human beings whose whole personality was structured by the ties binding them to land and lineage; hence their unrelenting desire to commit suicide.

The next thing to highlight could be the structuring of a new mental world based on the conditions in which the slaves were imprisoned. The fact that the prisoners were crowded together in dank holds was instrumental in creating bonds of solidarity between people who had not even known each other before. This created a sort of neutral world in which new ties could be formed. This community was united because it was set against the common enemy in the shape of the ship's crew. It was through this *esprit de corps,* this sense of togetherness, that they were able to restructure their personality.

A further subject for study would be the question of myths and fantasies: racist fears on both sides; the seamen's fear of revolts; the blacks' fear of being eaten by the bloodthirsty whites; the blacks' fear of being carried off to an unknown destination; fear of the sea of both slaves and sailors (storm, shipwreck, the doldrums, illness including scurvy, solitude and the impossibility of receiving any help); and the myth of sea monsters among the whites.

Next should come the study of slave uprisings: the rage of despair among the blacks, but also the first moves in a strategy based on observation of everyday life on the slave ships; the reaction of the whites torn between fear of dying and that of losing their stock-in-trade by killing or wounding the captives. Violence was much more common in general conditions of detention than in occasional instances of ill-treatment; even successful revolt was ultimately doomed to failure. Several cases in all respects similar to the one recounted by Mérimée in 'Tamango' are known: the wreck of the crippled ship or the impossibility of reaching land again without being recaptured by the inhabitants of the coast and again being sold as slaves.

Then there is the matter of everyday life on the voyage: discipline among the seamen and the captives; the regular nature of the daily schedule; highlights of the day, such as meal times, forced exercise on the deck, being chained in the hold at night; the fate of the seamen, including the officers; illness and the role of the ship's doctor; and death on both sides.

Africa and the Slave Trade

This aspect certainly calls for deeper thought, since it is based on recent historical advances which have scarcely begun to be used in teaching. Accurate tools have to be created to take into account the regional differences of a vast continent. Among Europeans in particular, the oversimplified and reductionist picture of Africa as being all the same from north to south and east to west has to be dismissed. This requires work by an international team of researchers and teachers who would: prepare a review of the state of knowledge of the history of Africa; determine the role played by Africans in the supply of slaves; plot a precise map of the areas raided and the slaving routes; specify the importance of the trans-Saharan trade and the exact impact it had on the Atlantic trade; clarify and evaluate the role of slavery in the internal workings of African societies, the overall economy of the continent and international relations on the continent; evaluate the real importance of the European presence in Africa from the sixteenth to the end of the eighteenth century; explain why the Europeans confined themselves to a policy of setting up permanent forts along the seaboard; explain how contacts came to be established between blacks and whites, and how they evolved (distinction should be made between occasional visits by whites, such as those by traders looking for slaves, and the presence of whites stationed in the forts; this should lead to more attention being focused on mixed-race societies, e.g. the Portuguese-speaking Africans, among others); ascertain the image fashioned by whites of African societies and the view which blacks may have had of whites; specify the nature of European rivalry for control of the African seaboard.

The Slave Trade and Demography

This should be approached by way of the actual situation on the four continents and still requires thorough research as far as Africa and the Americas are concerned.

In Africa, describing the regions supplying slaves raises the problem of the causes of and the forms that the slave trade took. Why did these regions not put up more resistance to the slave raids? Was it due to such factors as political weakness or inferior weapons technology? What was the precise relationship between the attackers and the peoples being attacked (a state of war, vassalage or tributary acts)? How did these regions react in population terms? Was there a decline in population or did population patterns adapt to the fact of the slave raids? How was it possible for everyday life to continue when deportations continued over so long a period? How was the economy able to adapt to such monstrous conditions? How many people really perished during the wars or the transportation of the captives to the coast or across the Sahara?

In the Americas, estimates of the number of people deported are still very imprecise. In particular, the period of the clandestine slave trade between 1815 and 1860 appears to have been significantly underestimated. English, Portuguese, Dutch and Danish historians have not yet made a voyage-by-voyage assessment of expeditions in the way that Mettas, Daget and Saugera have done in the case of France. On the basis of these findings, the population policy of the planters should be explained. Did they deliberately confine themselves merely to calculating profitability? After how many years' work was the investment made in purchasing slaves regarded as having been amortised? Was the slave trade activated by this need for replenishment? Was the mortality rate in the first year on the plantations looked upon with indifference, as if it were a necessary evil? Or did it have a considerable effect on the operating costs? Why were there not more births on the plantations? Were there not enough women? Or were the slaves determined not to have children? What means of contraception did they have? Were the colonists at the same time determined not to have to feed unproductive children and their mothers during pregnancy and the nursing period? On the other hand, were some people unsuccessful in managing to produce the future labour force *in situ*? The United States appears to have envisaged this type of response to the ending of the slave trade.

In Europe, if the example provided by the French is taken as a basis, it is easier to understand the mechanisms of a racist policy. Entries of blacks into France were so tightly controlled that the number recorded there was never more than a few hundred, whereas Portugal brought in thousands of blacks in the sixteenth century. A study of French legislation offers very eloquent material for teaching purposes, and it can be filled out by pictorial representations of blacks and a number of literary works. This makes it possible to grasp the consistency of governmental decisions and of public opinion in the eighteenth century.

The study of this ties in with the burning present-day issue of human rights in multiracial societies. Why not draw on the writings of Boris Vian when adopting an approach to interbreeding, in the same way as we draw on the press for looking at racial balances or conflicts in Brazil, the United States, Haiti or South Africa? Particularly close attention should be paid to language. Through the banality of the everyday expressions it employs, it is an extension of the myths and fantasies forged at the time of the slave trade. In this case, it would be desirable to seek the assistance of philosophers and psychoanalysts.

In the Americas, it is difficult not to look into the plantation system in order to understand the impetus given to the slave trade. It is proposed that the following teaching materials should be prepared for this purpose: maps of the areas where slave labour was exploited; a description of the population processes which take account of societies where interbreeding was high and those which had more racist attitudes; a description of the mechanisms of production by means of slave labour; an account relating the different stages in conquest and agricultural development to the different periods in the slave trade; an evaluation of the impact of slavery on political developments in the nineteenth and twentieth centuries; an assessment of the cultural contribution of the slaves; an attempt to present the real-life experience of the slaves and in particular the re-emergence of memories of Africa and nostalgia for the continent.

Doing Away with Caricatures and Stereotypes

An international team should, without delay, revise school and university textbooks which are still full of demeaning stereotypes or oversimplified pictures that often have no scientific basis but are very convenient for propping up ideologies. Prior to the work done in universities over the past 20 years, serial writers and popularisers used a few examples selected for their emotional impact or spectacular effect. Starting from there, they happily generalised, giving a completely distorted picture of the facts. All this is disappearing with the findings of studies based on time-series from which the anecdotal aspects have been deleted. However, there is advantage to be gained from deciphering the hidden meaning of such phrase and statements, a few of which are presented below.

> *Baubles*: Right up to the present day, even in such serious publications as *L'Histoire*, people still say that slaves were bought for a 'handful of baubles'. In actual fact, the term describes the goods that the officers were authorised to take with them so that they could trade on their own account. From being 'goods in small quantities', the term evolved into 'cheapjack goods'. This is tantamount to saying that slaves were bought for nothing and hence that the Africans let themselves be cheated. In other words, the white man's intelligence determined the outcome without any danger of competition. It is not necessary to delve very deeply into many archives to restore the truth, which seems to reverse the relationship and not ascribe the cleverer role to the white man.

> *Africans sold their families to the slave traders*: although this has been most vehemently denied by some people since the eighteenth century, this racist assertion is sometimes still repeated and tends to paint a picture of black people as being utterly lacking in the finer human sentiments.

> *Petty kings*: The 'petty kings' mentioned by the slave traders are likewise demeaning to African civilisation by giving the impression that it was impossible for any consistent political system to emerge on the continent. Up to now, all school textbooks have used this term which flies in the face of the reality of the great African kingdoms. Two caricatures have to be banished from this description – that of a society split into tribal groups and that of small drunken and bloodthirsty potentates. The terminology used by the Europeans is symptomatic of racist contempt but also of the fears which the blacks inspired in them, since they never dared to penetrate deeply into the African continent in the eighteenth century.

> *Racist caricatures*: What can we say of the caricatures that emerged in the eighteenth century and which persisted until almost the end of the twentieth century? The Negroes were branded as being lazy, drunken, thieving, shameless, animal-like in their sexual behaviour, and as having no feelings. We could go on adding to the list. No other continent has ever been described in such crude language. The time has come for it to be superseded by the language of humanism.

> *The profits of shipowners*: It was long claimed that these were enormous. By making exaggerated generalisations drawn from a handful of examples, people unhesitatingly spoke of profits of 100 per cent or more. Although there may have been some such cases, recent calculations based

on a whole century or on the career of a particular shipowner show actual figures of from 5 to 8 per cent, by no means insignificant when compared with the sums invested at the outset. This casts doubt on the argument that industrial capitalism in the nineteenth century was financed by the eighteenth-century slave trade. In the case of England, it does not appear to have provided more than 1 per cent of the seed capital.

These few examples show that the manner in which whole tracts of the history of the slave trade are presented in the textbooks must be reshaped. The advantage of setting up an international team is that its members would be made aware of the whole range of emotional and irrational factors that overload the language and distort the facts. It would be the ideal basis for presenting a historical account that brings together the movements of solidarity rather than accentuating the divisions.

Potential Teaching Approaches

It is not our purpose here to suggest what features should be included in the curriculum, but rather to point to a number of lines of inquiry that could spark off ideas. Nobody can lay down hard and fast rules in this area, since each continent and state reacts with its own culture and through the prism with which it views things. Through dialogue they will find ways and means of understanding other people better – and hence of explaining themselves better. The sole purpose of the comments made below is to put forward a set of working assumptions as visualised by a French person, in the context of his own culture, who knows about teaching through the school and university structures of his own country. We make absolutely no claim to be exporting a model. Our sole ambition is to foster the meeting of opinions and sometimes to contrast them, while continuing to hope that no one's sensibilities will be offended.

The experiments conducted in La Rochelle have introduced children – aged from 8 to 18 years old – to the problems of the slave trade. It is difficult to say whether one particular age-group has proved more receptive than another. They were all interested and moved by the problems, which gave rise to considerable indignation in every instance.

The compilation of a critical bibliography is an essential foundation for all research. Emphasis has to be placed both on published eye-witness accounts and those that may have been recorded on videocassette, by *griots* and praise-singers, for example. It would be an easy matter for a large team to update the bibliography every year and to prepare an accompanying press review.

Each age-group needs materials that are tailored to its requirements and accompanied by very full notes. If there are no such anthologies of materials, teachers will continue to come out with assertions that are inaccurate. The anthologies should also explain the reasons for and the ramifications of each assertion.

On the other hand, it does not seem desirable to write a specific text-book for teaching about the slave trade. It would be much too general and would overlook the key factor, which is that it should be adapted to the children's age-groups. Above all, it would be too cumbersome to update; printing costs would inhibit periodic publication of the latest scientific advances. For a long time now, the Departmental Teaching Documentation Centres (CDDP) and the National Institute of Educational Research (INRP) in France have been publishing brochures on different subjects. These are easy to handle in the classroom, are not very expensive to produce and can be readily changed. Adopting the same approach for instruction on the slave trade would prove expedient.

The nature of the materials presented would include: extracts from archives; engravings (although there are few iconographic examples); slides of African and American landscapes and of European ports; artefacts from teaching kits (slave irons, craft products, printed calico cloth, navigational instruments, etc.); old and modern maps; cassette recordings of tales and music and videos of dancing, television programmes, and so on.

The wealth of this material will depend on the number of people involved in collecting it. Their work should be carried further by evaluating the experiments according to the different age-groups and according to the countries agreeing to participate in them. The working tools could be adapted by holding annual meetings to compare findings.

Even so, if classes on the subject are confined to the national environment, the wealth of information to be gained from exchanging classes will be overlooked. One can well imagine the splendid work done in one and the same classroom with pupils from Benin and France reading the same documents side by side and each explaining them in the light of their own cultures. Such exchanges obviously depend on the initiative of individual teachers, but it would be desirable if UNESCO could urge governments to give favourable consideration to a proposal of this kind. If it is not possible to arrange travel on account of the cost involved, it is easy to visualise organising correspondence between schools, utilitising advances in technology to transmit images and documents over the Internet. Exchanges of work would be even more striking if video films were made of the children at work.

In La Rochelle, a wide variety of methods of approach have been used. Some of them started out from a topical news item, such as a serious racist incident, apartheid, or events in Africa or the Caribbean, or else from the simple wish to learn, through questions asked following a conversation, and so on. Teachers who adopt a more directive approach have deliberately introduced the subject by taking their pupils to places where there are local sources, such as visits to La Rochelle's New World Museum and port and to the museums of Rochefort. This is obviously possible only for children living in the main French, African or American ports. Regardless of the pupils' ages, approaches such as these can be adopted with the same degree of success, since the starting-point is always the pupils' own life experience. The impact of the event or the visit almost always triggers off the desire to learn more.

This move from the emotional aspect to the analytical is sometimes borne forward by the simple need to prepare for an examination. Studying for the *baccalauréat* in the last but one class in secondary school is stimulated by the materials included in the curriculum, and the indignation aroused by these materials prompts the students to envisage further study more relevant to the present day.

At every level, the study of the slave trade has led to work compiled from other studies or to creative work. In the French examination in France's last but one secondary grade, students are obliged to write a dissertation, but this does not prevent them from going on to study the ramifications of racism or the phenomena of deportation through the writings of contemporary authors. This can also come within the scope of civic education, especially in respect of human rights. In some cases, over a two-year period, the subject is covered through chapters on development in geography (in the top class of secondary school). All pupils remark on the similarity with the Nazi deportations already studied in the previous year. At this level, cutting across the different disciplines leads directly to the philosophy course in the top secondary class; this enables pupils to form their ideas on the human condition on the basis of precise facts, which are still most instructive to the minds of young people starting to deal in abstractions.

In both lower secondary and primary schools, freedom of action is no longer limited by the examination requirements. The curriculum for the third year of the lower secondary cycle covers the seventeenth and eighteenth centuries, in which the slave trade can be used to form a link with civic instruction and the study of human rights. This possibility also exists at primary school, through the study of France from its origins to the twentieth century in the intermediate primary classes (Cycle 3). In both cases, the discovery of archives and materials in museums, and reading the strip cartoon *Les Passagers du Vent* (1994) have proved to be excellent starting-points. Each type of information was adapted to the children's age-group. Thereafter, a stage in which the pupils go deeper into the subject has always been well received. The issues are raised by the pupils themselves on the basis of their initial findings. The teachers' role then consists in guiding them towards suitable sources of information, which entails a considerable amount of preparatory work by the teacher.

The natural sequel is a third, creative phase. The pupils variously organise exhibitions of drawings or photographs, map displays and compilations of materials, which they like to present in the form of a 'book' produced by themselves. Some pupils in intermediate primary classes have even drafted their texts on computer. Others prefer to produce a videocassette. All of this requires students to take a multidisciplinary approach, in which their interest in using one of these technologies goes hand in hand with scientific discovery.

One particular class chose to explain the findings of its work to a neighbouring class. This prompted the children to present certain documents and comment on them. The presentation was followed by a dialogue, which sparked off new questions that were the starting-point for even more far-reaching research.

It has been found in virtually every case that promoting children's awareness of the problems of the slave trade in this way extends into current affairs. The pupils talk about what they have seen on television or read about in the newspapers on similar present-day subjects. This provides a means of opening up the class to the world and of getting children to think for themselves.

It is interesting to note that, regardless of the age-group, the fundamental questions that arise are identical. The only factor that varies is the degree of complexity of the explanations given.

Creating an International Co-operative Teaching Body

It emerges from these few educational outlines that teaching about the slave trade and human rights is instrumental in fostering the formation of citizens from the intermediate primary school level right up to the end of secondary education. Although this chapter of history involving all the continents is still largely passed over in silence, it can be a building block in shaping universal awareness. It is not a page of history that has been turned forever, but rather a window opening wide onto the most burning issues of the present day, which should benefit in years to come from the rapid progress being made in historical research.

After a long period of silence, the veil now appears to have been lifted on a taboo subject, but a great deal still remains to be done. The drive imparted will work in two directions: the increased demand from teachers will stimulate researchers, and the progress the latter make in their research will be an incentive for teachers to go deeper into the subject. It is quite clear that collaboration between the two on an international level is essential. If it is not to cause even wider divisions, this subject, more than any other, calls for dialogue on a worldwide scale to bring people together in a desire for mutual understanding.

An international team of teachers and researchers should be set up under the auspices of UNESCO, the only organisation capable of amalgamating such an undertaking. The task of this team, subdivided into national groups, would be to furnish teaching materials tailored to the different pupil age-groups, together with an international bibliographical compendium; to establish a dialogue on the experiments conducted in the individual countries and engage in a comparison of the results; to organise regular symposia and meetings of classes leading to joint work carried out by exchange classes; to step up the exchange of correspondence between classes on the subject of the slave trade and human rights. Information technology should contribute significantly to the centralisation of the documentation compiled in different parts of the world.

In conclusion, why should we not set a date to recognise and commemorate internationally the suffering and inhumanity of the slave trade? One suitable date would be 8 February, for it was on this day in 1815 that all the nations attending the Congress of Vienna solemnly condemned the slave trade as repugnant to the principles of humanity and universal morality.

Bibliography

BOURGEON, F. 1994. *Les passagers du vent*. 5 vols. Paris, Casterman.

DAGET, S. 1990. *La traite des Noirs*. Rennes, Ouest-France.

DEVEAU, J.-M. 1990. *La traite rochelaise*. Paris, Karthala.

————. 1994. *La France au temps des négriers*. Paris, France-Empire.

DORIGNY, M. (ed.). 1995. *Les abolitions de l'esclavage; 1793, 1794, 1848*. Paris, UNESCO/Presses Universitaires de Vincennes.

RENAULT, F. 1989. *La traite des Noirs au Proche-Orient médiéval*. Paris, Geuthner.

RENAULT, F., and DAGET, S. 1985. *Les traites négrières en Afrique*. Paris, Karthala.

Société française d'histore d'outre-mer. 1990. *La dernière traite*. Paris, SFHOM.

————. 1988. *De la traite à l'esclavage*. 2 vols. Paris, SFHOM.

Chapter 35

Slavery, Genocide or Holocaust?

Roger Somé

> Will the advance of civilisation prevail over the disorders of communal living
> caused by humankind's aggressive and self-destructive urges? In connection with
> this question the present age is perhaps deserving of quite special attention. So far
> have today's people carried the mastery of natural forces that they are easily able
> to use them to exterminate one another until there is no one left.[1]

THE WORK IN QUESTION, which sought to take stock of the surge in science and
technology caused by the Industrial Revolution that started in the eighteenth
century, predates the term 'genocide' and comes after the era of the slave trade.
However, the passage quoted here contains beneath its surface the notions of
slavery, genocide and holocaust. As early as the fifteenth century, the forces of
nature were already sufficiently mastered, at least in Europe, for the continent
to be able to extend its will over the rest of the world. The European experience was to culminate in the colonisation of the American lands starting in the
fifteenth century, with its tragic massacre of the inhabitants; the enslavement
of increasing numbers of blacks in the seventeenth century;[2] and the colonisation of Africa in the late nineteenth century.

In the 1940s, 'humankind's aggressive and self-destructive urges' caused
the genocide of humankind, the Nazi project being based upon the perpetuation of the Aryan race alone. What I call the 'genocide of humankind' – the
deliberate denial by the Nazis of human status to any individual falling short
of their 'ideal person' by taking away his or her life – has, however, been
obscured to reveal only a specific genocide called the Jewish genocide, or the
Holocaust. People of the present generation, those spared the horrors of the
Second World War, those who today try to put themselves in the 'trenches' of
the 1940s via the press and the media, sometimes have the feeling that the aim
of the last war was to exterminate the Jews; the Gypsies are seldom referred
to, and homosexuals and Communists are completely overlooked. This feeling is strengthened by a glance at the titles of a great many works, particularly
in philosophy. At bottom, the Jewish genocide, or more generally speaking
'the Jewish question', has become the philosophico-political question of this

century, as if there were no other subjects worthy of consideration. Had there never been similar crimes or crimes that might be regarded as such in the world? Must it be supposed that the Jews were the only ones to pay the supreme price in the last war?

For when we nowadays talk about the victims of Nazism, there is automatic and insistent emphasis on the Jewish genocide, as though Hitler's plan concerned only the Jews. Could the Nazis conceivably spare 'niggers' while exterminating Jews? Did Hitler not leave the official tribune of the Berlin Olympics in 1936 to avoid shaking hands with Jesse Owens, the black American who had won the 100 metres sprint and four gold medals?

Given the media impact of the Jewish genocide, it is surely legitimate to ask why and how it is that the memory of the holocaust is still so vivid and close, while no less important events contemporary with it fade into a scarcely mentioned past. Who ever spoke of the martyrs of Oradour-sur-Glane, for example, before the celebration of the fiftieth anniversary of the 1944 Normandy landings? It is also hard to understand how it is that the memory of the black and Arab combatants who did so much to help recover Europe's freedom – and hence that of the Jews themselves – should be lost in a distant past, practically as distant as the memory of the 'triangular trade', the other genocide, which history ignores. True, the point can always be made that the Senegalese *tirailleurs* (infantrymen) and the Algerian spahis were soldiers, whereas the Jewish victims were civilians. But the argument would be rather simplistic, since the combatants concerned were – and remain today – sacrificed souls. Nevertheless, even if one concedes that the crimes committed under colonisation and the disappearance of numerous *tirailleurs*[3] are different, in a sense, from the Holocaust, can the same be said about slavery?

Is it legitimate, in the name of cultural values (freedom, for example) and ideological values (human dignity), to recognise the Holocaust as a genocide without adopting the same attitude to slavery or other massacres of populations? Is it because the term 'genocide' post-dates the massacre of American Indians and the slave trade? Is it because slavery has been regarded as a known practice of several civilisations in the world, and one of very long standing (among the Greeks, for example, it was practised as early as the seventh and sixth centuries BC)? In other words, is it possible not to see anything singular in slavery as opposed to the Holocaust?

With all this in mind, I shall attempt to establish a parallel between slavery, genocide and holocaust in a conceptual (rather than historical) analysis – even though this study may permit itself some statements of fact – with the aim of understanding why certain forms of genocide seem in my opinion to have been concealed by history.

Was Slavery a Genocide or a Holocaust? or Both?

Each of these three terms – slavery, genocide and holocaust – is used to pin down a fact. It may therefore be supposed that the advent of each coincided in time with the phenomenon it is supposed to define. It can thus be stated, beyond any risk of error, that slavery is a term that has been known since antiquity (it is used by Plato and Aristotle, for example), even though the French version dates only from the sixteenth century (1577). As to holocaust, it is also of fairly long standing, at least in its prime sense among the Jews of 'religious sacrifice in which the victim is entirely consumed by fire' (1170). Later, in the seventeenth century (1691), the term was to mean 'blood sacrifice of a religious character', which refers, for instance, to the crucifixion of Jesus. From 1958 onwards another sense came into being to refer to one of the occurrences of the Second World War. The notion, with the definite article 'the' and with or without a capital 'H', designates 'the massacre or extermination of the Jews by the Nazis'. The use of the article gives the event an absolute character. The word 'genocide' dates only from 1944 and means the massacre of a group of people on account of their belonging to a given race or ethnic group and, by extension, the 'massacre of a large group of people in a short time'.[4]

With regard to their historical status, then, these notions obviously do not belong to the same age. One might consequently be tempted to state that there is something anachronistic in attempting a parallel between them and everything they imply, since each denotes a specific historical occurrence. While such an affirmation seems plausible on the face of it, a more probing examination of the three notions points, on the contrary, to a semantic evolution that legitimates the drawing of such a parallel. Beyond this semantic evolution, it is interesting to note that certain historical facts pertaining to the semantics of these notions are not always as recent, at least in their general character. We know, for instance, that the persecution of the Jews goes back at least to the Renaissance. Who could also overlook the period of the discovery of the Americas and its consequences, namely the massacre of the Indians by Christopher Columbus's expedition and the subsequent subjection of the survivors to slavery? Could it be forgotten that on the very first Atlantic crossing by Columbus the expedition included black slaves, and that with the rapid disappearance of the Indians those blacks were to take over their not very viable places on the sugar-cane plantations? I could give many more examples. But let us call a halt to the nomenclature at this point and reformulate the original question: What racial destruction is there in slavery?

If one takes just the definition of the terms, there is nothing 'genocidal' in slavery. For what connection could there be between the methodical destruction of a population group and the subjection of one or more individuals? The connection becomes more tenuous still in the light of some of Aristotle's theses whereby slavery is the natural condition of certain beings – the slave is a 'being who by nature does not belong to himself or herself but to another', 'a living object of ownership', namely an 'instrument',[5] a 'machine' that a person controls. If we accept Aristotle's theses that subjection is a natural state, then logically there is nothing outrageous or tragic about slavery.

But if we go beyond definitions, meaning at this point an examination of the consequences of slavery, our quest becomes more far-reaching. The structure of the definition of the word 'genocide' rests upon two elements: method and deliberate intention. The perfect execution of a 'free' will and application of a method – the gassing of thousands of men, women and children with 'Zyklon B'[6] – was what created Auschwitz and was a part of the 'final solution'.

Working from this essential characteristic of genocide, one would seemingly be hard pressed not to see in slavery, on both sides of the Atlantic, an expression of genocide,[7] for the population of the island of Hispaniola, where Columbus landed, was largely destroyed by the battle against the invaders, forced labour in the mines of the West Indies and slavery. The indigenous population is thought to have dropped, in 20 or so years of Spanish occupation, from 300,000 to 50,000. Thus, as Jacques Attali sees it, 'an early genocide' took place in Hispaniola. He nevertheless considers the genocide in question to be 'involuntary, nobody standing to gain from this disappearance hastened on by the microbial invasion'[8]. It seems to us here that the author plays down what makes the Hispaniola tragedy a genocide. For it is less the number of victims (even if the figure advanced is the most conservative estimate) that determines this genocide than what ultimately gives rise to the casualties, namely the fact of denying the Indians human status, which quite logically leads to the lawful slavery proclaimed by Ferdinand of Aragon at Burgos in 1512.[9] Ferdinand of Aragon was over a century ahead of Louis XIV, who in turn was a century ahead of Charles III of Spain. As of the seventeenth century, the lawfulness of slavery was boosted with the drafting of the *Code noir* (1685), followed by the *Código negro carolino* (1784).

It is in the very existence and content of such legislation that the genocidal character of slavery is clearly evident. How is it comprehensible that European nations were able, lawfully, to permit slavery as a commercial activity (in which some Africans took part) intended to bring prosperity to Europe? Legislating on slavery contains in itself what determines genocide: namely, the way and the will to deny another's human dignity.

Although the object of slavery was not the physical destruction of the Indians and blacks, the triangular trade can at least be said to have caused large-scale slaughter. Furthermore, can one legitimately establish a specific, absolute difference between the fact of seeking to exterminate a population group on account of its racial affiliation and the fact of regarding human individuals as articles of commerce, knowing that in either case a great many lives were lost? Were not the blacks looked upon by the settlers of the West Indies and the Americas as 'spades'?[10] These 'spades' that had to dig the sugar-cane fields of Hispaniola and Santo Domingo were, in addition, considered assets subject to the rules of inheritance, as stated in Article 44 of the *Code noir* (Black Code): 'We declare slaves to be moveable property and, as such, to form part of the Joint estate, to be not mortgageable, to be equally shared among joint heirs....' Slaves were not people, despite the evangelisation that sought to make human beings of them (Articles 2–14 of the *Code noir*). They were nevertheless living beings over whom the king had the power of life and death (Article 43). Article 38 stipulates that 'a runaway slave who has been missing for a month or more ... shall have his or her ears cut off ... and, should he or she repeat the offence ..., he or she shall be hamstrung'; the penalty for fleeing a third time was execution. On closer consideration of the facts, we see that slaves were never human beings; they were merely essential 'tools' for the settlers, and that was the only reason for keeping them alive. How could it have been otherwise, seeing that the blacks had come to replace the Indians, who had been ravaged by harsh treatment and, more than anything else, the microbial invasion?

The equating of slavery with genocide is therefore based not just on the deaths of many individuals, the numbers being hard to assess today (many blacks were assassinated at the time of capture in Africa, and others were thrown to the sharks when revolts broke out aboard the slave ships), but above all on the fact that both blacks and Indians were denied their human status. Such denial is well borne out in the various articles of the French and Spanish *Codes noirs* that laid down the rules for the 'trade' and treatment of the 'products' purchased.

While slavery and the slave trade may be perceived as genocide in terms of the consequences, can one, on the basis of the notion of holocaust, implying as it does expiation or propitiation, establish an analogical parallel? During the Spanish-American war of independence, the United States of America chose to sacrifice the blacks in order to preserve the lives of their populations, for the very decree that abolished the slavery of the blacks dispatched them to the fronts. It was wholesale slaughter, but the event was regarded as something normal, for the emancipated blacks and had to pay the price of their freedom; it was therefore 'normal that by dint of their holocaust they should safeguard the population that was free' naturally.[11] Such a holocaust also occurred in Europe. One cannot help thinking of those thousands of Senegalese *tirailleurs* on whom the French general Bührer, adviser to Minister Georges Mandel, was counting when he said: 'Give me a million Senegalese and I'll break through the Siegfried line.'[12] One cannot help thinking of the 'black force', of our 'gallant *tirailleurs*',[13] who nevertheless served as cannon fodder and whose survivors were not even to have the opportunity of honouring the memory of their fallen comrades beside General de Gaulle as he descended the Champs Elysées on the occasion of the thirtieth anniversary of the liberation of Paris. There, too, those men who were 'naturally slaves' but legally free (France abolished slavery on 27 April 1848) were sacrificed so that 'naturally free' men might recover their lost freedom.

One cannot help thinking, too, of the 665,000 black victims of the Congo-Océan railway (1920–32), a tragedy that was subjected to the law of silence, despite the protests of the writer André Gide and the journalist Albert Londres.[14]

Generally speaking, slavery as practised by Europe, with the assistance of some Africans, from the sixteenth to the eighteenth centuries and, to a lesser extent, in the nineteenth century, is a forgotten genocide. And while genocide is regarded as the supreme evil, the tragedy of slavery and the colonial massacres hardly seem to be a matter of concern to historians, particularly French ones.

The Western Appropriation of History

Since the end of the Second World War we have witnessed a general 'credo' expressed in the well-known formula 'Never again!'. What set apart the Second World War was that it led to the genocide of millions of civilians. That is its distinctive feature, even though genocide is nothing new.

The question is often asked: 'How can one think after Auschwitz?'[15] Since Auschwitz, philosophical – and for that matter political – thinking has reached something of a turning-point. Theodor Adorno has written that Hitler imposed on humankind in its state of non-freedom a new categorical imperative: to think and act so that Auschwitz is not repeated, so that nothing similar can happen again.[16] The event is thus contemplated metaphysically. That even presupposes that no metaphysical thought can be envisaged outside the Auschwitz event. Adorno was to go still further in his reflection when he wrote that in place of the Kantian question concerning the theory of knowledge – asking how metaphysics is possible – there arises the philosophico-historical question as to whether a metaphysical experience is even still possible.[17] It is an irony of fate that, while the *Critique of Pure Reason* dates from 1781, the *Code noir* predates it by close to a century (1685) and the massacre of the Indians by three centuries. One wonders whether Kant knew about these.

The emergence of the 'philosophico-historical question' shows that 'the subject of philosophy' as a metaphysical question is no longer or should no longer be 'What is a human being?'. This subject should henceforth be 'Is it still metaphysically possible to ponder over human nature after Auschwitz?'. Or can one still consider that Auschwitz was the one and only tragedy of history? Yet 30 years earlier there was the Armenian genocide. This attitude reached such a pitch in 1987, at the time of the Barbie trial, that the press and other media tried to topple the last philosophical figure of this century, i.e. Heidegger. After attributing to Adorno something he did not say,[18] Maggiori wrote: 'What should we believe? What sensible propositions should be entertained regarding the humanity of humankind? Let me put it simply: how has the whole of modern thought, which has concentrated to the point of blindness on the horror of genocide, been able to make of a philosophy that has not uttered a single word on genocide the greatest philosophy of the century? A Nazi, Heidegger? Of course'.[19] That Heidegger went astray with his 1933 commitment to National Socialism or that he revealed a certain ambiguity in his thinking we can only deplore.[20]

How many philosophers of the sixteenth, seventeenth and, above all, eighteenth centuries condemned the slave trade and slavery? Did they not, on the contrary, encourage such doings? Who criticises seventeenth-century thinking (e.g. Descartes or Pascal), which was a decisive philosophy for the emergence of modern philosophy, for not saying a word about slavery and the colonisation of the Antilles and the Americas? Nobody. Who denounces the supposedly philanthropic thinking of the eighteenth century that merely accentuated the servitude of the blacks? At the time, no one, and today, but a few.[21] Who challenges the philosophical dimension of the thinking of Montesquieu, then shareholder of a slave-trading company, proposing a gradual emancipation – after the fashion of Condorcet – of the blacks, while acknowledging that 'sugar would be too expensive if the plant producing it was not cultivated by slaves'? And wasn't Voltaire a member of a *Compagnie des Indes* chiefly engaged in slave-trading?

If slavery as an institution was a genocide forgotten of history, it was because neither blacks nor Indians were perceived as human beings but rather as animals to be humanised. In any case, were blacks anything else but beings accustomed to suffering, subjected to 'despots who have the right to slit their throats'? Consequently, submitting them to slavery was surely the means of their deliverance from local tyrants.[22] Yet at the time of the *Code noir*, not only the European sovereign but also the mere subject (having become master of a slave) had the right of life or death over slaves, since he would automatically be pardoned if found guilty of murder, 'without the need to obtain from us [the Crown] letters of grace' (*Code noir*, Article 43).

Yet it was slaves – living tools, in the words of Aristotle – Indians and subsequently blacks, who were sacrificed for Europe's economic prosperity. It is no mere chance that even Danton, the most progressive of French revolutionaries, showed caution during the debate on the decree abolishing slavery when he suggested: 'Let us refer the matter back to the Committee of Public Safety and the Colonies, in order to devise means of rendering this decree useful to humankind without endangering it.'[23] However, the decree was inapplicable and was never implemented.

Whereas in the eighteenth century the slave trade and slavery existed for economic considerations, the reason for the sacrifice of black people in the twentieth century was the reconquest of freedom in Europe. In the two world wars, France called upon the Senegalese *tirailleurs*[24] and the Algerian spahis to liberate the so-called 'common territory', the empire, first from the German invasion and then from the Nazi occupation. At the end of each of the two wars, blacks and Arabs – to whom should be added Asians – were sent back to their countries of origin where they were kept in submission (examples are the massacre at Sétif, Algeria, in 1945; the repression in Madagascar in 1947 when whole trains were riddled with bullets to prevent the survival of any witness to the carnage; and that of Thiaroye, Senegal, in 1949).

Who would dare claim that the compulsory enlistment of the Senegalese *tirailleurs* in the two world wars was not a sacrifice? Of course one can always argue that sacrifice has a religious overtone which is absent in these cases. Yet let us not forget that the Holocaust, namely, the extermination of the Jews by the Nazis, had no religious connotation. Nor let us forget that the *tirailleurs* fought for a cause that was not theirs and from which they reaped no benefit. It could also be objected that in the forced enlistment of the *tirailleurs* there was no deliberate intention of sending them to their death. That is certainly true. But could people possibly have been oblivious of the fact that those men from the other side of the Mediterranean had no military training and were nothing but cannon fodder? What is most painful about how the massacres of black persons are viewed is not so much the forgetfulness surrounding these cruel events as the refusal to regard them as genocides. Which is exactly how the slave trade and slavery of the Indians and blacks is treated, not to mention the Armenian genocide of 1915.[25]

France is nowadays accused of suffering from a partial lapse of memory. In no other European country has there been this systematic bid to erase part of its recent history (with the exception of Turkey).[26] It is true that France finds it difficult to accept a certain collaborationist past during the Second World War. But we may well ask how France has come to terms with the deportation of thousands of blacks and Arabs who were killed in order to liberate it. How, too, has France come to terms with the slave trade and slavery of the blacks when it was the first nation (followed by Spain) to legislate on slavery and the black slave trade? Silence hovers over colonial France and its massacres (at Sétif, in Madagascar, Thiaroye or in Lobi country) or the French slave trade that ensured the prosperity of the ports of Bordeaux and Nantes.

And has Spain also acknowledged the wrong it did to the Indians and the blacks? At a time when it was expelling Jews from its territory in 1492, it was massacring Indians in America. In 1784, with the expulsion of Jews still in force, it legalised the black slave trade and slavery by means of the *Código negro*, deriving no doubt from its French forerunner. Yet in 1992, when Spain was apologising to the Jewish community, not a word was said about the Indians or the blacks who had been sacrificed on a massive scale and denied their human dignity for the economic prosperity of Spain.

It should be possible to account for such an attitude.

The reason perhaps lies in the fact that Nazism, in the words of Nancy, was a plan of destruction of Europe by Europe in which 'Westerners turned on themselves'.[27] This is what sets the Shoah apart. While such an interpretation seems to be justified, it is nevertheless still simplistic. For if the self-destruction of the Western subject entails expulsion of 'the non-self, of the wrong or unfit self', as Nancy (1994) puts it, it goes beyond the anti-Semitism argument and operates on the basis of difference. Just as the blacks, at the time of the slave trade, were regarded as individuals beyond the pale of humankind (they were moveable property, according to Article 44 of the *Code noir*), so the Jews were denied their human dignity. It scarcely needs restating that the *Code noir* ordered officers to 'expel from the Islands all Jews who have established their residence therein, whom, as declared enemies of the name of Christian, we command to leave within three months from the date of publication of these presents, on pain of arrest and dispossession' (Article 1). If the Jews had to leave the islands, it was because they were different from the Catholics.

Thus the expulsion of the Jew as a negative figure pertains to a general Western mind-set involving rejection of the other, of the unlike. Consequently, confining the Western rejection to a rejection of the Jew is – like a refusal of the self – a way of confining history or, if one prefers, an expression of the Western 'appropriation' of history.[28] By making the persecution and 'extermination' of the Jews a unique event in history, and on the grounds that Europe turned on itself, one is inevitably talking about difference. What is rejected is not assimilated, is not self; it is different. What Europe rejected was the part of itself that was not it or, at least, that it did not consider to be its own. When Europe attacks Europe there is a reaction. On the other hand, when Europe lets loose on other peoples, that concerns only the people in question (slavery and the slave trade being surely the best examples of this). When non-European peoples tear each other to pieces, in Africa for instance, the conflicts are regarded as tribal wars not deserving of special attention. How else can one account for the apathy of the West – which took prompt action at other times and in other places – when confronted with the genocide in Rwanda?[29]

To come back to the West's self-rejection as something based on identification rather than difference, Nancy states: 'The Christian Western subject is given as an infinite relation to self.' Can one exclude otherness from this subject? No. The 'Christian Western subject' seems to me to be also 'an infinite relation' to the other: 'Thou shalt love thy neighbour', says the Holy Scripture. In this relation of love with the other, there is one I in otherness, and another in the self. It is because the other is a subject like me that he is my neighbour and I must – in line with Western culture – love him. Love here is founded, in a sense, upon identity and not on difference. Neighbours are neighbours only because they are similar to me, and it is because they resemble me that I must love them. In that, the self-rejection of the subject indeed functions according to difference. The Indians or the blacks were rejected by the whites because they differed from the latter (as Jews differed from Catholics). To erase the difference in order that they might become fellow human beings, Indians and blacks had to be humanised through slavery and the gospel.

Furthermore, considering that evangelisation was in effect a colonial argument – as early as 1627 Richelieu declared that French colonisation must 'be exclusively Catholic and serve the purpose of missionary expansion'[30] – and that Christianity prevailed outside Europe, it is no longer possible to uphold the idea of a self-negation of the Western subject: it is a self-negation of the subject, because in Africa, for example, the non-Christians, those described as 'heathens', were regarded by the Church – and still are, for that matter – as Satan's offspring.

To regard the massacres perpetrated by Europe in Europe as singular because they represent Europe rising against itself – the Western subject taking root in its own negation – is to establish a de facto difference between such massacres and those occurring elsewhere or in another age. This difference is apparently due less to the nature of the massacres than to the geographical, cultural and historical affiliation of the victims and the perpetrators.

Personally, I consider that there is no such thing as exceptional and ordinary massacres, or exceptional and ordinary genocides. Any genocide possesses within itself its particular and singular nature. The difference between the various genocides of history is due less to the fact that the victims and actors occupy the same historical and cultural space than to the ways and means employed to commit them. Death is always distressing, whether it occurs in Goree, Dominica, the Euphrates, Auschwitz, Madagascar, Bosnia or Kigali.

Accordingly, regarding Auschwitz as a unique, incomparable event is, however justified, somewhat of an oversimplification despite the arguments put forward by Lacoue-Labarthe. That Auschwitz was a phenomenon which 'corresponds to no logic whatever' of a 'political, economic, social, military or other type'[31] may be admitted. That the extermination was unique in that it corresponded to no social dissension and that the means employed to kill were industrial ones may also be allowed. However, we are not convinced that this phenomenon was a revelation of the West 'in its true colours'. The black slave trade, too, was an event without precedent. If the unparalleled nature of 'the final solution' derives from the fact that the events at Auschwitz are without historical precedent, why should this uniqueness legitimised by the absence of a historical counterpoise not ordain the slave trade too? Has there ever been a trade in human beings on a scale comparable to that of the black slave trade throughout the history of humanity? And even if there had been such a trade, was it legalised and codified twice over, firstly by France and then by Spain, as was the black slave trade? Without going into the conditions in which slaves were taken in Africa, or their transport, or the manner in which they were treated before being embarked – at Ouidah (Benin), for instance, which was a slave port, there was a mass grave (now restored as a memorial) into which were thrown alive all slaves judged ill-fit to make the middle passage journey and/or work in the plantations – or the conditions of their enslavement in the West Indies and the Americas, the mere fact of the codification places the event in a bracket of its own.

Hence it may not be the extermination that holds the secret to Western being. Viewed from this angle, if Adorno's idea – in which he wonders whether 'a metaphysical experience is any longer possible' – has another meaning, it can only be sought in philosophical reflection. Why and how did humankind reproduce (produce) Auschwitz when it had known other tragedies in the course of history? Above and beyond Auschwitz and the revelation of Western being, it is the expression of human essence that is at issue and which history has not noticed or appears to notice even after the hiatus of Auschwitz. To regard Auschwitz as the demonstration of Western being would be a reductionist view of history. In this sense one could say not only that Heidegger failed to meet the challenge of the thought of the event of Auschwitz, but also that Western – not to say all – thought here failed in its duty to human thought.

One may well ask whether this thought has effectively analysed the familiar formula 'know thyself' that burdens human shoulders with all its weight. Has it sufficiently pondered the question 'What is man?', taken up by Kant followed by Cassirer and Heidegger. Taking this proposition from the hands of Cassirer, it would appear that this analysis still falls short, regardless of all that has already been said (see, for instance, Aristotle, Descartes, Rousseau, Dilthey or even Max Scheler), for our knowledge of man is still partial and fragmented. To know man means studying him both in his diversity and in his plurality. It means understanding the nature of each people, on the one hand, in its plural relationship to itself, namely as a cultural vector producing a culture network and, on the other, in its relationship to the other, namely as a being in relation, capable of continually becoming. From this viewpoint, the disclosure of the Western being cannot be restricted to an analysis of something that is regarded as a Western self-negation: Auschwitz. In other words, the West does not disclose itself, in terms of its being, solely in what Nancy terms 'Western self-rejection'. It is perhaps more so in its relations with others, for instance in its exclusion of others as not belonging to humanity, that its being displays itself. Why should the nature of the West be manifest in whatever it produces against itself, yet be absent from the phenomena that it perpetrates against the other? Even for purposes of a metaphysical analysis of technique as developed by Heidegger and explained by Lacoue-Labarthe (1986 and 1987), the perception of Western being cannot be confined to whatever is initiated and performed by the West within itself, because technique – in the old as well as the new sense – is, in terms of its effects, not peculiar to the West, all the more so in that its origins stretch beyond Western frontiers. Therefore, and in order to know and grasp Western being – knowledge that will contribute to that of man in general – we consider it essential and vital to give thought to the other dramas carried out by the West beyond its frontiers, not forgetting those that other peoples provoke at home or abroad at no matter what period.

Conclusion

The aim of the present chapter has been to bring together a body of views on a current topic that generally receives scant attention, being considered as of little importance. In our view, however, the subject could lead to problems of international co-operation between peoples when proper communication may well be the only solution. How else can the conditions for world peace be conceived if not by way of mutual acknowledgement of the different historic events experienced by humankind in all its diversity?

It might be thought that nothing can justify a comparative study aimed at drawing a parallel between different forms of historic tragedy and determining on what grounds the concept of genocide is possible. Yet such an approach could help to cool the debate, since it seeks to show, working from an analysis of ideas based on facts, that well before and even after 1944 there have been other cases of genocide about which little is ever said.

Comparing the repression of the Jews throughout history to slavery would certainly be of interest in view of a number of historical coincidences: for example, whereas at the time of the Inquisition, Jews were vermin to be eliminated, blacks were being captured and sold into slavery; and while Catholics were expelling Jews, the First Vatican Council was considering whether or not blacks should be evangelised. By what right did the Church – while recalling and deploring the curse of Shem – evangelise those whom God had excluded from His people? In order not to disobey the divine ruling, the Church turned to the Lord. An official prayer of the Congregation of Indulgences in 1784 went: 'Let us also pray for the very miserable Ethiopian peoples of central Africa who represent a tenth of humankind. May almighty God one day liberate their hearts from the curse of Shem, and may He bless them in Jesus Christ Our Lord.'[32]

Notes

1. Freud, 1971, p. 107.
2. Slavery was practised in Europe well before the seventeenth century, but I shall be dealing in particular with its official form endorsed by the *Code noir* (1685) and the *Código negro carolino* (1784). This will be covered later.
3. These men fought for a noble cause: freedom and human dignity. I cannot resist the temptation, however, of observing that defence of that for which they were enlisted was denied them for several centuries.
4. See *Le Robert*, 1989, pp. 116–117 for esclavage and derivatives, p. 880 for genocide and p. 214 for holocaust.
5. Aristotle, 1991, pp. 17–18.
6. L. Poliakov, 1973, p. 143.
7. For an author such as Louis Sala-Molins there is no doubt that slavery was a genocide. An author's subjective opinion, however, can never be substituted for recognition by history of a fact. We nowadays speak of 'a cloud hanging over the history of France' and cry out for the Vichy regime to be officially condemned, but that has not led to its condemnation.
8. J. Attali, 1991, p. 284.
9. L. Sala-Molins, 1987 and 1992b.
10. L. Sala-Molins, 1992b, p. 10. In this term 'spades', we find the old Aristotelian thesis of the slave as a 'living instrument'.
11. This passage, though formulated a little differently, echoes an idea of L. Sala-Molins, 1992b, p. 18, final paragraph.
12. J. Riesz, p. 216.
13. Ibid., p. 88.
14. R. Somé, 1993, pp. 225–248.
15. We borrow the expression from L. Sala-Molins, 1992a. But let us be clear about this: the author of books on the *French and Spanish* 'Black Codes' is absolutely convinced that slavery was a genocide that should be reflected upon. The expression borrowed from him is in fact part of a general context of indignation (op. cit., pp. 12–14 et seq.) which shows ironically that while the Jewish genocide is the subject of much reflection, the slave trade and the slavery of blacks constitute a run-of-the-mill event of history scarcely worth a second thought.
16. T. Adorno, 1992, p. 286.
17. Ibid., p. 291.
18. Adorno did not say 'How, after Auschwitz, is it possible to write poems?', as stated by Robert Maggiori (see note 15). Here is what Adorno in fact wrote: 'Endless suffering is as much entitled to expression as a tortured person is to scream; and so it may well have been wrong to affirm that after Auschwitz it is no longer possible to write poems.' (See T. Adorno, 1992, p. 284.) If, for Adorno, thought becomes problematical since the horror of Auschwitz, it is not in this idea that it must be sought. In this idea the author is still reserved; it is only in those of pages 286 and 291 (see above) that he specifies and radicalises his position.
19. R. Maggiori, 1987, p. 41.
20. Heidegger could be said to have explained his political commitment if one considers some of his affirmations. In the interview he gave *Der Spiegel* in 1966, which was published – at his request – after his death, he presents his debate with Nietzsche as an explanation addressed to National Socialism (see *Réponses et questions sur l'histoire et la politique*, p. 34). In the same interview, however, Heidegger

states that the *Rectorate Speech* (1933) is a sequel to the *Inaugural Lecture* (1929) (ibid., pp. 14–15 and 17–18). When questioned on the direction being taken by society and academic reform, in a televised interview with Richard Wisser in 1969, Heidegger refers him to the *Inaugural Lecture,* continued by the *Rectorate Speech,* and takes the same passage he cited in the 1966 interview, slightly modified, of the same *Lecture,* in reply to the question on academic reform *(Heidegger,* Cahier de L'Herne, Coll. Le Livre de poche, pp. 381–382). That suggests that the author remains true to his 1929 positions, which are to be found in the 1933 *Speech,* and he says as much himself: '... the greatness and magnificence of this start was my conviction' *(Réponses et questions ...,* p. 16). Furthermore, in *Nietzsche 1,* which is supposed to be 'an explanation addressed to national socialism', the argument of the quest for a German identity crops up again. 'In the form of this conflict [that of the Apollonian versus the Dionysian] Hölderlin and Nietzsche placed a question mark against the Germans' task of finding their historical essence. Will we understand the warning? One thing is clear. History will take its revenge on us if we do not understand it.' *(Nietzsche 1,* p. 100). The understanding of such a warning is what was to allow the birth of a German identity, the emergence of a German people, the 'metaphysical people' *par excellence (Introduction à la métaphysique,* p. 49, final paragraph). Understanding that warning is, for the Germans, wanting their people to fulfil its 'historic mission' (see *Discours de rectorat,* p. 22). This same idea, based on the 'angst' of the German people, namely the lack of a national figure as identifying German reality, is reaffirmed in 1946 in the *Lettre sur l'humanisme* (see Edition Aubier Montaigne, 1964, p. 99). Yet the course on Nietzsche, conducted 10 years before, is presented as an explanation. Still other passages could be cited, but one thing remains invariable: what Heidegger always sought to present as an explanation is never brought to a conclusion, for there are still features allowing doubt. It may be conceded that he provided an explanation, but on closer scrutiny of the material, the explanation remains questionable. Still, whether or not he properly clarified his political commitment, that in no way diminishes the greatness of his philosophy.

21. L. Sala-Molins (1987, 1992b, and in particular, 1992a) clearly shows how the philosophers of the Enlightenment helped aggravate the tragedy. Before him, W.B. Cohen had shown that the philosophers of that time were not explicitly opposed to slavery. In fact, their positions were rather ambivalent, sometimes due to the fact that some of them were paid naval ministry grants (see W.B. Cohen, 1981, chaps. 3 and 4 in particular).

22. P.-V. Malouet, 1775 (1981, p. 208 and footnote).

23. Speech delivered by Danton on 4 February 1794, in Jacques Hérissay, 1950, pp. 226–228.

24. Our thanks go to Jeanne-Marie Karabou-Ferrand, a specialist in colonial history who kindly provided documentation on the '*Tirailleurs Sénégalais*'.

25. H. Piralian, 1993, pp. 159–178.

26. T. Halier and J. Ramadier, 1993, pp. 95–110.

27. J.-L. Nancy, 1994, p.2.

28. Questioned by Michel Fennetaux on totalitarianism, and in answer to the question 'Do you consider totalitarianism to be one of the major symptoms of our time?', Jean-Toussaint Desanti (1976) limits totalitarianism to Nazism and Marxism of the ex-Soviet Union brand. Not a word on Western totalitarianism outside Europe. True, the expression 'our time' determines the answer to the question. Desanti is therefore at pains to define it as the period from the end of the Second

World War to the present. Such a definition highlights this Western appropriation of 'historical time', even though Desanti acknowledges that the use of 'our' points to 'a form of philosophical ... confusion'. For if the expression 'from 1940 to our day' refers to our time, why should there be no mention of colonialism as a form of totalitarianism?

29. However, while it is legitimate to criticise the Western attitude in the face of Rwanda's tragedy today, and of many others in Africa and elsewhere and in other periods, it is equally legitimate to castigate the scant interest taken by Africa itself in its own problems. For centuries Africans contributed to the deportation, orchestrated by Europe, of a great many of the sons and daughters of their continent. Yesterday it was (it still is) Ethiopia, Sudan and Somalia. While the major powers were contesting that so-called strategic part of the continent while causing numerous casualties under the cover of the 'right of humanitarian interference', no African voice was raised in protest. Yet 'fraternity' in Africa is perceived not solely as part of the terminology of kinship but more as a virtue covering a specific signification. This 'fraternity' could in fact be said to be to Africa what philanthropy was to the Western Enlightenment. At the time of the slave trade, some Africans were actors in the tragedy staged by Europe. During the conquest and throughout the years of colonial occupation, Europe set African against African, applying the law of 'divide and rule'. Does Africa escape that law today?

30. L. Sala-Molins, 1987, pp. 14 and 92.

31. P. Lacoue-Labarthe, 1987, pp. 33–40.

32. L. Sala-Molins, 1987, p. 40, note 22.

Bibliography

ADORNO, T. 1992. *Dialectique Négative*. Paris, Payot.

ARISTOTLE. 1991. *Politique I & II*. Paris, Les Belles Lettres.

ATTALI, J. 1991. *1492*. Paris, Fayard.

CESAIRE, A. 1973. *Discours sur le colonialisme*. Paris, Présence africaine.

COHEN, W.B. 1981. *Français et Africains. Les Noirs dans le regard des Blancs 1530–1880*. Paris, Gallimard. (Tr. by Camille Garnier.)

CONOMBO, J.I. 1989. *Souvenirs de guerre d'un 'Tirailleur Sénégalais'*. Paris, L'Harmattan.

DESANTI, J.-T. 1976. *Le philosophe et le pouvoir*. Paris, Calmann-Lévy.

FANON, F. 1991. *Les damnés de la terre*. Paris, Gallimard.

FREUD, S. 1971. *Malaise dans la Civilisation*. Paris, Presses Universitaires de France.

HALIER, T., and RAMADIER, J. 1993. 'Un trouble de mémoire sur la Gaule'. *Césure. Revue de la convention psychanalytique* (Paris), No. 4.

HERISSAY, J. 1950. *Les grands orateurs républicains*. Vol. 4. Monaco, Hemera.

KAMBOU-PERRAND, M. 1989. *Peuples voltaïques et conquête coloniale, 1885–1914*. Burkina Faso. Paris, L'Harmattan/ACCT.

LACOUE-LABARTHE, P. 1986. *L'imitation des Modernes*. Paris, Galilée.

———. 1987. *La fiction du politique*. Strasbourg, Association de publication près les Universités de Strasbourg.

LACOUE-LABARTHE, P., and NANCY, J.-L. 1987. *Le mythe nazi*. Paris, Editions de l'Aube.

Le Robert, Dictionnaire de la langue français. 1989. Paris, Le Robert.

LEVINAS, E. 1990. *Difficile liberté*. Paris, Albin Michel.

MAGGIORI, R. 1987. 'Heil Heidegger'. Paris, *Libération*.

MALOUET, P.-V. 1775 [1981]. 'Mémoire présenté au Ministère'. In Cohen, W.B. *Français et Africains. Les Noirs dans le regard des Blancs 1530–1880*. Paris, Gallimard. (Tr. by Camille Garnier.)

MARTIN, G. 1993. *Nantes au XVIIIe. L'ère des négriers 1714–1774*. Paris, Karthala.

NANCY, J.-L. 1994. 'Le procès Touvier est en cours depuis deux semaines. Quel sens un tel procès peut-il avoir?' Paris, *Le Monde*, 29 March (interview).

PIRALIAN, H. 1993. 'Le déni, un crime contre l'humanité'. *Césure. Revue de la convention psychanalytique* (Paris), No. 4.

POLIAKOV, L. 1973. *Les Juifs et notre histoire*. Paris, Flammarion.

RIESZ, J. 1993. *Images et Colonies (1880–1962)*. Paris, BDIC-ACHAC.

SALA-MOLINS, L. 1987. *Le code noir ou le calvaire de Canaan*. Paris, Presses Universitaires de France.

———. 1992a. *Les misères des lumières. Sous la raison, l'outrage*. Paris, Robert Laffont.

———. 1992b. *L'Afrique aux Amériques. Le code noir espagnol*. Paris, Presses Universitaires de France.

SOME, R. 1993. 'Afrique: une ruine d'âme'. *Césure. Revue de la convention psychanalytique* (Paris), No. 4.

Chapter 36

Diasporas, Multiculturalism and Solidarity in the Caribbean

Julie Lirus-Galap

> One morning the Caribbean was cut up
> by seven prime ministers who bought the sea in bolts –
> one thousand miles of aquamarine with lace trimmings,
> one million yards of lime-coloured silk,
> one mile of violet, leagues of cerulean satin –
> who sold it at a mark-up to the conglomerates,
> the same conglomerates who had rented the water spouts
> for ninety-nine years in exchange for fifty ships,
> who retailed it in turn to the ministers
> with only one bank account, who then resold it
> in ads for the Caribbean Economic Community,
> till everyone owned a little piece of the sea,
> from which some made saris, same made bandannas;
> the rest was offered on trays to white cruise ships
> taller than the post office; then the dogfights
> began in the cabinets as to who had first sold
> the archipelago for this chain store of islands.

Derek Walcott
Winner of the Nobel Prize for Literature, 1992

IN THIS CHAPTER I shall look at the range of cultural patterns in the Caribbean that derive initially from the various African and later Indian diasporas, in specific historical and economic contexts which determined their legal situations, varying from society to society and from territory to territory, thereby inaugurating, despite segregation, the era of cultural intermingling.

The particular pattern on which these societies developed has raised many questions. But, over and beyond the specific details of the origins of migrants – and their dispersal and the clashes – what emerges from this set of heterogeneous components is a sensation of harmony, as in a mosaic, that some might call 'unity'. This harmony has partly to do with geography but owes more to the historical, political and economic circumstances of the arrival of migrants in this region of plantations.

The Caribbean and Its Diasporas

It is not solely because the only migrants were Europeans and the diasporas African and Asian that these latter occupy a particular place in the Caribbean. It is also because they were the plaything of segregationist European colonial policies – might being right; because their migration was in fact a forced displacement of population, to serve as a docile labour force for mercantile capitalism; because, to achieve that objective, the slave trade became a state monopoly; because slavery became internationalised as a bargaining counter, as a mode of economic production, as a unique means of enrichment for the sole benefit of Europeans, wherever they were, in Europe or in the mainland of the Americas or in the islands of the Caribbean; because the Africans, like the Amerindians before them, were the victims of the discovery of the New World whose scars they still bear; because slavery or the destruction of the individual through enslavement and subjection constituted, for blacks, the reality of life from the fifteenth to the nineteenth century; because the immigration of Asians, Indians for the most part, followed the slavery of blacks and destabilised the white master/black slave relationship; and, finally, because all these immigrant populations – ethnically diverse, culturally and sociologically foreign to one another and foreign to their host environment – sought to legitimise their right to exist.

The islands that constitute the Caribbean archipelago stretch over an area of 240,000 square kilometres and have a population of over 30 million. What is special about the populations that live there, which are very diverse in origin, religion and culture, is rooted in an exceptional and virtually unique social and anthropological history.

The European Colonists

European colonists arrived in the Americas in 1492, and there they met autochthonous peoples – Tainos and Arawaks in some islands, Caribs in others – whom they exterminated.

These islands were ransacked and dispossessed of their original names, and their inhabitants were driven out or enslaved, deported to Europe or massacred. As Claude Lévi-Strauss writes: 'As we read the writings collected in *Chroniques d'une conquête*, we see more clearly that this conquest is not an event which can be assigned a date, that it did not even occur in the space of a few decades. Since the end of the fifteenth century, it has continued unabated, assuming varying forms in different places and different times, which, for the Amerindian peoples, were and still are reflected in physical and moral destruction and political, economic and religious oppression.'

The descendants of the survivals of this massacre today live on reservations on the islands of Dominica or St Vincent and, as a result, are set apart from the rest of the population. The celebration in 1992 of the Five-Hundredth Anniversary of the Encounter between Two Worlds was the occasion for the Carib Indians of those two Lesser Antilles islands and the French-speaking people of the Caribbean and French Guyana to organise a tribunal of history in Martinique, where Christopher Columbus, who imported the first black slaves on his second voyage, was put on trial; this was the subject of a solemn declaration which was brought to the attention of the United Nations in January 1994.[1] After the *tabula rasa* consequent upon the genocide of the autochthonous peoples, dehumanisation was the order of the day for Africans who experienced the slave trade and slavery: raiding, kidnapping, deportation, revolt, collective or individual suicide, infanticide or escape were the lot of blacks carried off from their homeland. This was the price that was paid for the Europeans' conquest of a new world which enabled them to feed the inhabitants of the old continent and enrich the cities and ports of the colonial powers.

The Deported Africans

The inhabitants who live in the Caribbean today are, for the most part, descendants of Africans deported by Spanish, Portuguese, French, English or Dutch Europeans. The African diaspora in the New World that was the result of the transatlantic slave trade, which continued long after its theoretical abolition by the Congress of Vienna in 1815, saw the deportation of millions of human beings scattered by force all over the Caribbean and the Americas. Exile was the firsthand experience of these African communities who, because of their deportation, were unable to participate in the creation of African states.

Countless works in English have attempted to identify the ethnic origins of the deported Africans. Today it is generally agreed that slave raiding involved not only the west coast of Africa but also the interior of the lands of enemy kingdoms. To people the islands from Cuba to Trinidad required the capture of more than 15 million Africans of all origins, along the Senegal, Niger and Volta rivers and their tributaries, seized from the Songhai empires, the Congo kingdoms, the Hausa, Mossi or Yoruba states, or carried off from the 'grain' (pepper) coast, the ivory coast or the slave coast (on the Gulf of Guinea), crowded into the slave depots on the islands of Gorée, Principe or São Tomé or the banana islands, branded and sold in the Portuguese, Dutch, English, French and Danish trading posts.

The *pièces d'Inde*, as fit young blacks in their prime were called, came from every corner of Africa: from Senegal, from Assini[2] – where the king of France, Louis XIV, had established his former musketeer, Aniaba, baptised by Bossuet to be the first heir of the kingdom of Assini – from the Bissagos islands, from Dahomey and so on.

Following are a few extracts taken from departmental archives in the *Répertoire des expéditions négrières*[3] on the ethnic origins of Africans loaded into the slave ships sailing out of Bordeaux: 'Cargo, Martinique, Guyana: 500 Congo blacks'; 'Cape: 123 Guinea blacks'; 'The blacks come from the coast of Juda [Ouidah]', destination not specified. In a letter (d'Orvilliers, 9 July 1751) we read: 'Ship coming from the coast of Angola, but Congos are not liked here, as they tend to run away and are ill-suited to labour.' 'A negro from Benin, taken on the coast of Guinea by the slaver *Le Vénus*, free, asks to leave France'

(Archives of La Rochelle, 6 June 1741); 'The vessel the *Imprévu* brings back a young black, 10 years old, not branded, of the Saint-Pol nation'; 'A negro, son of a prince on the coast of Juda, sold at Port-au-Prince in 1750, arrived from Guinea on the *Minerve* out of Bordeaux....'

On their arrival in the Caribbean, the slaves were sold to planters who recognised where they came from by some distinguishing features: '... from their soft-spoken manner of speaking, Calvaires from Cape Verde; from the scars on their faces, Bambaras; from the way their scars are stitched, Quiambas; from their harmonious speech, Mandingo; from their wart-like tattoos, Aradas from Dahomey; from their gaiety, Congos; from their odour, Angolas.'[4]

With the exception of Cuba, the Dominican Republic and Puerto Rico, Africans formed the bulk of the population of the Caribbean Islands where they arrived in two stages, first as slaves and then, from 1857 to 1864 as 'free workers': 'Hoeing the sugar cane, stripping indigo of the threads woven by caterpillars, topping tobacco, boiling sugar syrup, making rum in kill-devil furnaces and sky blue indigo in the indigo factories, such would be their harsh task, hurried along by the overseer's lash'.[5] The transatlantic slave trade helped develop and enrich the cities and great ports of Europe: Cadiz, Lisbon, Barcelona, Marseilles, Bordeaux, La Rochelle, Nantes, Rouen/Le Havre, Amsterdam, London, Bristol, Liverpool and Glasgow.

Europeans living in the Caribbean hardly formed a homogeneous community. There were 'great whites', aristocratic or bourgeois colonists, owners of large plantations thanks to the land they had stolen from the Amerindians; there were 'officials', representing the king, responsible for enforcing the monopoly on trade between the home country and its colonies; there were the *engagés* (indentured labourers), nicknamed the 'Thirty-Six Months', because they had signed on for three years, living in fairly dire conditions; there were those 'indentured by force', galley slaves or Protestant victims of the revocation of the Edict of Nantes; finally, there were soldiers and a few other nationals, Dutch Jews in particular.

In the Caribbean, the harsh realities of the plantation system combined with the cultural contributions of the various African peoples to shape a new human and ecological environment – for example, by introducing unusual plants and animals – thus altering the economy and production.[6] For centuries, in this superficially idyllic environment, Amerindians and Europeans, and later Africans, Europeans and Amerindians – the few that had managed to survive – mixed together even as they loathed one another. On the plantations, the loss of freedom and corporal punishments were countered by revolts and rebellions; bloodily suppressed revolts were met with *marronnage*, which in turn led to manhunts that often ended in death, but sometimes, too, in the slave winning his freedom at the risk of his life.

Resistance to this degrading system assumed various forms: suicide, which, depending on one's belief, enabled the soul to return to the land of the ancestors; for women, voluntary abortion, to spare their unborn children the yoke of slavery; the poisoning of masters with the aid of toxic plants; deliberate sabotage of work, which gave rise to the stereotype of the 'lazy nigger';

flight; uprisings and collective rebellions, the former making possible the liberation of the people of St-Domingue and the advent of the first republic of the African diaspora in the New World, led by General Toussaint L'Ouverture. This major historical event had enormous consequences, and Haiti has been paying the price for it ever since. In the other colonies, the slave system was reinforced, nipping in the bud any thoughts of liberation. But the aspiration to human dignity was such that, despite all the obstacles they encountered, slaves participated in the decrees abolishing slavery that were promulgated in the course of the nineteenth century.

The Indians

Immigration from India began after the abolition of slavery. The Indians had no desire to leave their lands. European colonists went and sought them out after the end of overt slavery (in 1834 in the British colonies, 1848 in the French colonies, 1863 in the Dutch colonies and 1880 in Cuba) to save the sugar economy. Between 1838 and 1917, more than 500,000 so-called 'indentured' Indians were brought to the colonised islands of the Caribbean. Most were recruited on contract, 'by persuasion', and were intended to replace the newly freed slaves.

On 24 December 1854, Guadeloupe welcomed the first 344 Indians. By 15 May 1885, more than 42,000 immigrants had arrived in the island, where upwards of 20,000 died in the sugar-cane fields. Only 8,000 returned to India. The rest made Guadeloupe their adopted home. Today there are large numbers of descendants of these Indians brought there virtually by force, especially in the English-speaking islands. British Guyana received 44 per cent of the total number of immigrants, Trinidad 27 per cent – where today Indians (Hindus and Muslims) account for almost 44 per cent of the total population of the island – Jamaica, Grenada, St Lucia and St Vincent received almost 50,000 Indians, Suriname about 35,000, French Guyana, 8,472, in 20 convoys (between 1855 and 1877) and Martinique, 25,509, who arrived on 20 ships (between 1854 and 1883).

There was no Indian immigration into islands where the plantation economy was impossible because the land was too dry or there was too little of it, or where there was abundant labour (Barbados, for example).

Other Immigrants

More recently, Malay or Chinese labourers from Southeast Asia have migrated to the islands that were formerly Dutch colonies, where they form small, self-contained minorities.

The last point to note is that the white population that arrived in the Caribbean was overwhelmingly male and that, despite the prohibition of sexual relations between blacks and whites, a class of free mulattos, made up of natural children set free and their descendants, came into being. This miscegenation – highlighted at the level of the collective self-image, although illegitimate –

helped to create social distinctions based on colour prejudice between blacks and mixed-race people.[7]

Disparities based on shades of skin colour – thus reproducing the racist view popularised by Gobineau in his *Treatise on the Inequality of the Human Races* – had serious consequences, for Haiti in particular, since in 1915 the mulatto ruling class of this country gave priority to its own interests over those of the majority black population by putting itself at the disposal of the Stars and Stripes of the United States.

Caribbean Panorama

Today the Caribbean comprises a disparate, predominantly Anglo-Saxon geographical, economic and political set of countries. Since most of these nations became independent in the 1960s, and since the disappearance of the Caribbean Economic Community which brought the colonial powers together, the Caribbean region has been made up of a mosaic of independent or associated states and entities with a special associated or dependent status watched over by the United States.

There are several ways of presenting the 30 or so countries dotted around the Caribbean. But the geographical criterion is scarcely relevant, since some states in the region (Mexico, Guatemala, Panama, Honduras, Nicaragua, Costa Rica or Colombia) have few or no direct relations with others, being more focused on North American problems, while others (Guyana, Suriname, French Guyana, and, to a lesser extent, the states of northern Brazil, Para and Amapa), strictly speaking situated outside the Caribbean, have features similar to those of the Caribbean. This criterion needs therefore to be supplemented by that of membership of regional organisations, such as the agreements between the European Union (EU) and the African Caribbean and Pacific (ACP) countries or the Caribbean Basin Initiative (CBI), or membership in international organisations – which favours a more geopolitical approach – or again linguistic proximity (Spanish-speaking, French-speaking, English-speaking, Dutch-speaking or Creole-speaking), which gives a more cultural picture.

Combining these various approaches yields five sets of countries: the British Commonwealth with the British West Indies (made up of five small territories with no more than 80,000 inhabitants) and the former 12 colonies, now independent, which have formed CARICOM since 1973 (the largest being Jamaica, 1962; Guyana, 1966; Trinidad and Tobago, 1962); a group of Dutch-ruled states (Aruba) and six Dutch Antilles territories with their 300,000 inhabitants; a series of territories under United States sovereignty (Puerto Rico and the American Virgin Islands, with a population of over 3 million); five major independent states, with Haiti on the one hand and the Dominican Republic on the other, with a population of around 6 million for the former and 7 million for the latter; the Republic of Cuba, with more than 10 million inhabitants, and, on the South American coast, Suriname, with a population of 400,000, and Venezuela, with a population of almost 20 million;

territories under French rule (Martinique, Guadeloupe and its archipelago, and French Guyana, with a total population of almost 900,000).

It was United States intervention in Cuba in 1898, under the cover of the Spanish-American War, that led to the emergence of a geopolitical dynamic peculiar to the Caribbean. From 1898 to 1960, the Caribbean was watched over by the United States since, according to the Monroe Doctrine, any outside intervention in the New World was regarded as a threat to the peace and security of the United States (whence the establishment of 40 navy and air force bases).

Castro's revolution in Cuba in 1959 led to intervention by the former USSR in the region. This was followed by the rise to power in Grenada in 1979 of a government led by Maurice Bishop. However, the spectacular invasion of the island by US forces in 1983 snuffed out this second socialist experiment in the Caribbean. More recently, in 1992, on the pretext of the globalisation of trade, a strategic battle erupted over the production and marketing of bananas, which enabled American firms to set up on the local market of the French Antilles.

In the Caribbean today, only a few territories dependent on a colonial power still subsist alongside the independent States: the Virgin Islands (United States, United Kingdom); Bermuda, Turks and Caicos Islands, Cayman Islands, Montserrat (United Kingdom); the Dutch Antilles (Curaçao, Aruba, Bonaire, Saba, St Eustatius and half of St Martin); Puerto Rico (United States); and the three French departments in America (Guadeloupe, Martinique and French Guyana).

After five centuries of conquest and European presence, the political heritage of colonisation still weighs very heavily, and many poets, dramatists and writers have denounced the situation of political subordination inherited from colonisation that makes it so difficult to establish relations of partnership between the islands, despite their common history. The transformation of the French colonies into overseas departments in 1946, for example, intensified their relationship with France and, today, with Europe, at the expense of closer ties with other Caribbean islands and active solidarity with the inhabitants of those islands.

What Are the Prospects of Economic Development for the Region?

Its situation makes the Caribbean a useful crossroads between North and South America, an area through which traffic between the east and west coasts of the United States and, above all, the Atlantic and the Pacific, has to pass, by means of the Panama Canal.

Over the decades, the strategic and economic importance of the region has grown continuously. The major trade networks start from the southern United States, since that is where the oil is to be found that constitutes the wealth of the coastal area, which explains the United States' and the world's growing interest in this region. The land beneath the Caribbean basin contains almost 10 per cent of total world oil supplies: Venezuela, with its 2,816 kilometres of Caribbean coastline, is a founding member of OPEC (Organisation of Petroleum-Exporting Countries); the islands of Trinidad and Tobago produce oil and natural gas, and are associated with the large refineries in the neighbouring Netherlands Antilles (Curaçao and Aruba); the refineries in the Caribbean also process petroleum from Alaska (routed through the Panama Canal), Saudi Arabia, Indonesia and Africa. The Caribbean region thus produces 25 per cent of oil imported by the United States, and also contains mineral resources such as bauxite, nickel, iron, copper, chromium and precious metals which supply regional industries and major trading networks.

And yet, despite all its potential, the Caribbean remains economically dependent and stagnant. For four centuries, the colonial system condemned the economies of the Caribbean to be producers of raw materials destined for the sole benefit of the industrialised colonial powers. These economies were essentially organised around a sugar monoculture and the production of coffee, bananas and a few other tropical crops (citrus fruits and spices). After the Second World War, the establishment of the Commonwealth Sugar Agreement in 1951, and then, in the 1960s, the diplomatic breach between Cuba and the United States opened up new markets for sugar from the Caribbean, although sugar production fell off in the early 1960s in both the English-speaking and the French-speaking West Indies, especially Guadeloupe and Martinique.

Despite the drive to economic individualism, regional unions were formed in the 1960s, such as the Central American Common Market. In the years that followed, there were several attempts to bring the countries of the Caribbean closer together, but even today they still do not go beyond agreements to co-operate in certain sectors.

In 1973, the move to unity was relaunched with the creation, chiefly in the English-speaking West Indies, of CARICOM (Caribbean Common Market). In 1975, the signing by the European Economic Community (EEC) of the Lomé Convention with the ACP (African-Caribbean-Pacific) countries opened up the European market to tropical produce from the Caribbean while at the same time making them face competition from African countries.

In 1981, through the voice of its president Ronald Reagan, the United States announced a number of measures including the creation of the Caribbean Basin Initiative (CBI) on the model of the Lomé Convention. CBI (Mexico, Belize, Nicaragua, Panama, Colombia, Venezuela, Guyana and Suriname) opened the American market to the free entry of goods from the Caribbean but, in reality, chiefly favoured the export to the United States of manufactured goods cheaply produced in the workshops of countries in the region.

In 1991–92, as the time drew near for the opening of the single European market, several American customs unions were formed: agreements between Mexico and Chile, the so-called MERCOSUR agreements (Argentina, Brazil, Paraguay and Uruguay), the revived Central American Common Market and the NAFTA agreements between Canada, Mexico and the United States.

On the fringes of these vast economic unions, the place of the Caribbean still remains to be defined, as does the question of the role of Martinique, Guadeloupe and French Guyana within the region.

In 1994, discussions were held to ensure that no one was left out because of the differing political statuses of the islands. Some countries, including

France, appeared to stand aside from these initiatives. Thus on 9 and 11 May 1994, in Santo Domingo, the second meeting of diplomats and senior officials was held that led to the establishment in Barbados in July 1994 of the Association of Caribbean States, designed to develop co-operation in the economic, cultural, health and communication fields between the sovereign and non-independent territories.

Multicultural Societies

The Caribbean societies are multiethnic and multicultural. With the exception of Puerto Rico, it can be said that there is a fairly close correspondence between social structures and 'racial' structures – the higher classes being white or mixed-race, the lower classes black or Indian. It goes without saying that the political exploitation of this situation generates imbalances and accentuates the underdevelopment of the region.

Balanced and controlled development of territories, structures and individuals requires that the cultural dimension be taken into account by a society at every stage of the drafting and implementation of economic, ecological, cultural and social programmes. This rule, which was the key idea of Unesco's World Decade for Cultural Development (1988–97), applies to the modern societies of the Caribbean – especially as individually and collectively they are a crossroads where the civilisations and cultures of Europe, Africa, Asia and America meet and combine in a process of cultural intermingling.

Music

The black literature of the Caribbean is well known; it has been much written about, and the great authors are today well known and win prizes: Aimé Césaire, Frantz Fanon, Edouard Glissant, Maryse Condé, Léon-Gontran Damas, René Maran, Alejo Carpentier, Jacques-Stéphen Alexis, Vidiadhar Surajprasad Naipaul, Wilson Harris, Derek Walcott, Patrick Chamoiseau, Xavier Orville and others.

Among the countries with a population of African descent, scattered by the history of conquest and colonisation all over the Western hemisphere, the Caribbean alone is home to more than 11 million African Americans. Some of its types of music, such as reggae, calypso or *zouk*, are known all over the world; others are less so and therefore need to be replaced in their own cultural context so as to be recognised as contributing to the universal heritage.

> Such recognition, which is of key importance to every human community, is vital for ours, a young emerging community, born of culture shocks that involved subordination, segregation and separation with the consequent conflicts between races and cultures; and even more for the African, the partial disappearance of the original institutions, the forgetting of ancestral cultures and the assimilation of new ones: in short, transculturation.[8]

The quest for identity of the peoples of the Caribbean is not over. Each day we understand a little more the importance that this collective process assumes in the movements of disalienation that are stirring in various societies. The new way in which researchers are looking at certain music-oriented events organised in the regions takes us on journeys through time and space, seeking to uncover processes of creation that still remain to be clarified, with the difficulties inherent in a diaspora scattered over a large number of islands where ethnic groups and cultures have for generations been confronting and cross-fertilising one another.

Music is the most powerful and popular means of expression of Caribbean groups. From slavery to the present day, it has always accompanied peoples in their sufferings and their advances. A Dan proverb tells us that 'the village without a musician is no place to live'. That shows what an important role music plays for Africans and people of African descent in the diaspora.

The slave dispossessed of his right to humanity found identity and dignity – at least in his own eyes – when he beat the drum to pour out his distress, his hopes and his desire to rebel. For slaves, music constituted the first area of freedom beyond the reach of their masters, the first *marronnage*, a new birth, the first historical wail of the men, women and children carried in chains to this unfinished archipelago.

This assertion of identity, beaten out on a goatskin, was to prepare the way for an irreversible evolution, marked by a rich variety of musical forms: work songs that accompanied forced labour in the sugar-cane fields; nursery rhymes of dull pain sung to children by wet nurses, godmothers, mothers, sisters and neighbours; wordless choruses, rising from constricted throats, to make them stronger and more determined; songs sung at wakes, satirical songs, songs born of everyday or political happenings. In short, songs pervaded by a musicality that came from the lips and from the heart, carrying within themselves the collective memory of a whole people.

That is how Caribbean music came into being, rich with a range of influences imposed by colonial history. First, there is the European influence, easily observed in the beguine and the quadrille; then the Asian influence with Indian music, somewhat marginal because of colonial divisions, but which was a constant presence; and finally the Amerindian influence in the use of the calabash so dear to the autochthonous population.

It goes without saying that this African-inspired musical wealth could not express itself unhindered. For a long time, this popular music was combated by the ideological apparatus of the dominant group (on this subject see Clarke's book [1991], which gives a good account of the survival of self-expression and the sheer creativity that that involved):

> Thus when the drum was beaten to entertain, communicate or for religious purposes, it threw the white slave-master into fear and apprehension. The drum was decried because it spoke the African's language. Consequently, the drum was banned and went underground for a while. The most emotional responses from the white overseer, slave-master or Christian missionary, were in relation to the drum.

It perhaps provided the terrifying reminder that the African, through all brutalities, had not lost his native tongue and could still 'speak' and thus communicate.... It went underground, became a subculture, and was distanced from popular acceptance (even after emancipation).... The black Christian, late of the slave world, thus emerged associating the drum with heathen or barbarian practices.[9]

The author gives a good account of how a process of alienation gets under way in a society, and distorts and perverts a tradition – in the sense that Igor Stravinsky gives it. 'A genuine tradition is not the testimony of a past that is dead and gone; it is a living force that inspires and informs the present' – to the point of rendering it illegitimate, as was the case in the Caribbean.

Present-day music, like all the cultural products that emerge from the mixing of many groups, is changing under the growing impact of urbanisation and the globalisation of trade.

The Caribbean Festival of Creative Arts, held for the first time in Georgetown (Guyana) in 1972, thanks to the determination of the progressive government of L. Forbes Burnham, itself constitutes a major political and cultural event for the region. For the first time, the main expressions of Caribbean culture came into contact, in Guyana in 1972, in Jamaica in 1976, and in Cuba for the second time in 1994. This last great gathering marked the end of isolation and demonstrated that Caribbean solidarity was possible.[10]

Indian Identity

Diversity is the hallmark of the origin – Indian, Chinese or Javanese – and status within each group to which Asian immigrants who have settled in the Caribbean belong. The Indians constitute the largest group within the Asian diaspora, in both French-speaking and English-speaking territories. The cultural future of these so-called 'indentured' Indians, in whatever island they settled, depends on several factors: the percentage of Hindus, from Tamilnadu in southern India, and Muslims, from Calcutta, on the island, or the time at which the immigration occurred, the colonial power to which the island they went to belonged, relations between European powers, etc.

There was also great diversity in the way the Asian immigrants were received and the work they were given to do. Some arrived on an island where the plantation system was very old and therefore well established, as in Martinique and Jamaica. They were mere replacements for the former slaves, and had no choice but to adapt to a pre-set mould. Only culturally specific features (certain aspects of domestic life, religious beliefs and music, for example) that were compatible with this system had any chance of surviving. Others migrated to places like Trinidad or Guyana, where the plantation economy was only just getting established. Especially if there were large numbers of them, such immigrants could retain their original culture. Between these two extremes, a whole range of cases were to be found in the host islands and territories.

Unlike the Africans, the Indians from India thus arrived in already fully formed hierarchical societies, on land that was more or less occupied, where slavery had been abolished. If they rebelled, or questioned the contract made with the colonists who had hired them, they would call down the wrath not only of these latter but also of the free Africans who occupied subordinate positions, especially as, being cheap labour, in the struggle between European planters and agricultural workers, they acted as strikebreakers and unfair competitors. The conflict-management strategies used and the adjustments that followed profoundly affected the culture and organisation of the communities from India. While there are numerous historical, demographic and socio-economic studies, works on the different cultures in contact in the Caribbean and their intermingling are few and far between.[11]

In Guadeloupe, despite the devastating effects of both European and Afro-West Indian assimilation, the majority of the Indian community remains attached to its customs, rituals and beliefs. Religious and mythical principles pervade the life of Indians and, in many Indian families, the turning points of life bear the imprint of Hinduism. Despite a measure of serenity that flows from a glorious past of which they are proud, the *vatialous* (Hindu priests) react to the demands of modernity with nostalgia. But the future worries them because they have been unable to construct the temple of Indian identity on the soil of Guadeloupe, despite maintaining some religious and mythical traditions.

'May Indian identity not be an epiphenomenon!'[12] The beginning of the new millennium should make it possible to complete the process of integrating Indians into the various societies of the Caribbean, socially and culturally: 'At a time when negroes and Indians, in the same boat, work their fingers to the bone in quest of daily bread for their children, and whites, negroes and Indians work the island and prepare for the future, each learning to love his homeland, brothers from every background, let us build the future of Guadeloupe and add our hibiscus or our lotus to the bouquet of the Caribbean.'[13]

The place, role and contribution of Indians in the construction of multicultural societies are evidence of the topicality and importance of this issue. Its consideration calls for an appreciation that rests on a bedrock of key values such as freedom for all and equal dignity for all individuals, whatever their ethnic, religious or cultural identity. That is the approach adopted by the anthropologist and sociologist Roger Bastide[14] in his study of intercultural relations in the Caribbean and black Americas.

The societies that emerged from the plantation economy are tending to 'explode' brutally as a result of the breakdown of the link between race and class, industrial diversification, trade globalisation, the end of old forms of dependence and attempts to organise heterogeneous cultural specificities – in other words, to decompartmentalise and 'de-ghettoise' the various diasporas. In the face of social, political, economic and cultural realignment on such a scale, what place is to be given to shared spiritual values and the shared sense of belonging? What bands of solidarity emerge from them? Will class solidarities, if they exist, be able to transcend ethnic barriers and make regroupings possible that are today unthinkable? Or shall we see, here and there (in the Caribbean, in Europe, in Africa, in the Americas or elsewhere), confrontations and clashes where class and ethnic antagonisms overlap?

Peoples United

Working Together for Better Understanding

Studies of the slave trade have shown the consequences of the crimes against humanity committed in the Caribbean between the fifteenth and the nineteenth centuries. These crimes were compounded by adherence to racist principles that sought to keep down particular types of individuals, make them inferior, alienate them from their culture and make them dependent beings.

The collective trauma is burned into memories, handed down and reactivated. The treatment and rehabilitation of the survivors, if it is to preserve the mental balance of their descendants, must take into account the totality of their history. The crime against humanity still continues, with its psychological consequences, and is affecting several successive generations.

The Amerindian peoples are still resisting, but live apart. The descendants of the African diasporas, for the most part of mixed race, are divided, either fighting one another or ignorant of one another, as are all who fight for power. What institutional solidarity can there be for the Caribbean? It is not surprising that, in a context of politically imposed and sustained division, there are few exchanges and co-operative twinnings. With the help of the Comité Français de la Fédération Mondiale des Cités-unies, three towns in Guadeloupe, one in Martinique and one in French Guyana have formed relations with Trinidad: between Port of Spain and Morne-à-l'Eau in Guadeloupe; and between San Fernando and Trinité in Martinique. The town of Cayenne (French Guyana) is twinned with two towns: Salvador in Brazil, and Thiès in Senegal. The town of Basse-Terre (Guadeloupe) is twinned with the town of Pondicherry in India. Pointe-à-Pitre (Guadeloupe) is twinned with Saint-Louis (Senegal).

The New Humanism

Societies are undergoing a process of internal transformation, a consequence of the brutal effects of globalisation. It is no longer enough simply to study phenomena: it has become urgent to combine such study with the search for a new humanism, based this time on freedom, which is inseparable from equality. To envisage our relations with others, each of us needs a system of plural values that makes it possible to appreciate and experience diversity within ourselves and with others. It is thus not simply a matter of a more ready understanding of the acceptance of others – in a relationship seen as unequal – but of achieving a real intertwining of interests that are of primary concern to all parties, none of which can be sure of reciprocity if it is exclusive.

History – in other words, people – has decided the fate of civilisations, nations and cultures. It is up to others to make equality between individuals effective. It is not simply a matter of knowing the other's culture so as to be able to understand and live alongside him or her despite the differences. It is also and above all a matter of distancing oneself from one's own ethnocentrism, remaining vigilant as to the use and dissemination of erroneous collective images that are hurtful for both individuals and nations, and pushing back the frontiers of ignorance so that prejudices erected into dogma that degrade the individual become a thing of the past. We need, therefore, to bring about a new state of mind so that the encounter with the other ceases to involve the suppression of differences and becomes enrichment through the acceptance of diversity. At the dawn of the twenty-first century, the major task is to grasp the concept of this new humanism, this new mode of communication, and to put forward legal, political, social, economic and cultural rules. As Aimé Césaire writes:[15]

> We know that the salvation of the world also depends upon us.
> That the world needs all and any of its sons.
> Even the most humble.
> The shadow advances ...
> Ah! We cannot face the century with too much hope!
> People of goodwill will create a new light for the world.

Notes

1. Organised by the Cercle Frantz Fanon at the municipal theatre in Fort-de-France.
2. A kingdom situated in the western part of the former Gold Coast, now part of Côte d'Ivoire. The French established a trading post there.
3. J. Mettas and S. Daget, 1984.
4. 'La France au-delà des mers', 1935.
5. Ibid.
6. 'Environnement africain. Environnement caraïbe', 1978.
7. See F. Fanon, 1950 (Eng. tr., 1968); H. Tolentino, 1984.
8. A. Carpentier, 1985.
9. S. Clarke, 1991 (Orig. Eng., 1980, pp. 25–26).
10. See E. Stephenson in J. Lirus-Galap, 1991.
11. J. Benoît, 1976; G.L. Etang, 1989; R. Thoumson, 1994.
12. E. Moutoussamy, 1987.
13. Ibid.
14. R. Bastide, 1967 (Eng. tr., 1971).
15. A. Césaire, 1941.

Bibliography

BASTIDE, R. 1967. *Les Amériques noires*. Paris, Payot. [Eng. tr., 1971. Green, P. *African Civilisations in the New World*. London, C. Hurst.]

BENOÎT, J. 1976. *Immigrants asiatiques dans l'Amérique des plantations*. Proceedings of the Forty-Second International Congress of Americanists.

CARPENTIER, A. 1985. *La musique à Cuba*. Paris, Gallimard.

CESAIRE, A. 1941. 'Présentation'. *Tropiques* (Fort-de-France), No. 1.

'Chroniques d'une conquête'. 1993. *Ethnies* (Paris), No. 14,

CLARKE, S. 1991. *Les racines du reggae*. Paris, Editions caribéennes. [Orig. Eng., 1980. *Jah Music: The Evolution of Popular Jamaican Song*. London, Heinemann Educational Books.]

DEREK, W. 1992. *Le royaume du fruit-étoile*. Paris, Circé.

'Environnement africain. Environnement caraïbe'. 1978. *Cahiers d'études du milieu et d'aménagement du territoire* (Montréal). Special issue. (Centre de recherches caraïbes.)

FANON, F. 1950. *Peaux noires et masques blancs*. Paris, Le Seuil. [Eng. tr., 1968. Markmann, C.L. *Black Skin, White Masks*. London, MacGibbon and Kee.]

L'ETANG, G.L. 1989. 'L'Inde en nous'. *Revue Carbet* (Fort de-France), N 9.

'La France au-delà des mers'. 1935. *L'Illustration*. Le Livre de Paris.

LIRUS-GALAP, J. 1987. *Identité antillaise*. 3rd ed. Paris, Editions caribéennes.

———. 1991. 'Communiquer la culture'. *Revue Mawon/Cedagr*.

METTAS, J., and DAGET, S. 1978 and 1984. *Répertoire des expéditions négrières françaises au XVIIIe siècle*. Nantes/Paris, Bibliothèque d'outre-mer.

MOUTOUSSAMY, E. 1987. *La Guadeloupe et son indianité*. Paris, Editions caribéennes.

THOUMSON, R. 1994. *Les Indes antillaises*. Paris, L'Harmattan.

WALCOTT, D. 1992. *Le royaume du fruit-étoile*. Paris, Circé. [Orig. Eng. ed., 1980. *The Star-Apple Kingdom*. London, Jonathan Cape.]

Chapter 37

The Slave Trade and Cultural Tourism

Clément Koudessa Lokossou

IT MAY SEEM ODD to include, among the studies in this historical pilgrimage to explore the most dramatic forced migration in history, one focused on a modern concept that epitomises the very opposite of stress – namely, tourism.

But even more astonishing is the ever broadening range of motives that drive present-day tourists to pay money for the most unusual cultural products. There are no longer any limits to exoticism. Is the period of standard tourist destinations evolving towards more rational choices, with present-day tourists deciding for themselves what they want to visit? Can the theme of the slave trade, with its organisation, structures, historical sites and monuments that remind us of that past, provide a response to that more rational outlook and engender a new type of tourism? Do the sites and monuments of the trade along the Slave Coast, and particularly in Benin, deserve the attention of researchers? Will they cease to be insignificant, nameless places and play a greater part in promoting the cultural, social, economic and touristic development and reputation of Benin and West Africa?

Can this new type of tourism, however odd it seems, bring people closer together and contribute to development and to world peace?

The Ingenuity of the Slave Trade

It has often been said that the slave trade was a meticulously organised enterprise on both sides of the Atlantic. A glance at how it was run will give a better grasp of its impact on tourism in the African countries that supplied slaves.

The maritime saga of the Portuguese, which started with the capture of Ceuta in 1415,[1] prompted the European nations to set about the conquest of other continents, including Africa. The reasons underlying the explorations of the Portuguese and other European states were well known: to find the kingdom of Prester John in the hope of making him an ally against the infidels, to reach the sources of gold production in the Sudan and, above all, to find a sea route to India and its silk and spice markets.

The capture of blacks – regarded as infidels – was not viewed as reprehensible. When, in 1441, Nuno Tristão, had the 'honour'[2] of bringing back the first blacks from the West African coast to the south of Cape Bojador,[3] and a royal edict of 1502 authorised the transporting of slaves to the New World, no one grasped the implication of such decisions, which would lead to the forced emigration of from 9 to 15 or 20 million blacks from Africa.[4]

The majority of European and American countries were involved in the trade, which was followed up by colonisation during the eighteenth and nineteenth centuries with the complicity of certain Africans. Beyond the involvement of Europeans and Americans, however, it is the sheer ingenuity of the structures developed for the capture, delivery to the coast, sequestration and transportation of slaves that makes it possible for the present-day tourism sector to utilise the slave trade for economic purposes.

As can be seen from the archives, the first form of slave-hunting – inherited from the European Middle Ages – was kidnapping or *filhamento*,[5] a surprise attack leaving no possibility for escape. The book *Roots* by Alex Haley provides a good description of the effectiveness of the kidnapping technique, in which slaves were caught in nets like fish. Wars, too, served as a pretext for procuring slaves and even became the most convenient method.[6] Thus it was that Ashanti and Dahomey[7] served as models when the slave trade became a quasi-monopoly of the state. The raids and round-ups, the purchase of slaves or the abductions organised by some influential people such as local chiefs constituted another source of supply of 'black gold'.

The sites of past combats and battles are therefore also relevant to the slave trade, even though the most meaningful and 'interesting' sites for the tourist industry are those relating to the assembly, sequestration and shipping of slaves.

A Few Slave-Trade Sites in Benin

The captive slaves intended for the Americas had to travel enormous distances to be assembled and dispatched to the ports of embarkation. Not all of them left at the same time or by the same boat. Many waited in transit areas – real death-traps – where living conditions were frightful.

The best known site in Benin is that of Zoungbodji at Ouidah. The memorial erected there by the government on the occasion of the first World Festival of Vodun Art and Culture, or 'Ouidah 92', triggered the transformation of a 'silent' and insignificant historic site into a vibrant spot of interest to tourists.

Sites Connected with the Slave Trade, Classified by Category[8]

Function of Site	Name of Locality	Present Status
Slave market	Godomey, Abomey-Calavi, Hêvié, Ganvié, Logozohè	Not developed as a slave-trade site
Slave transit points	Cotonou, Porto-Novo, Kétou, Avlékété, Ekpè, Sèmè, etc.	*Idem*
Sites where slaves were assembled	Allada, Abomey, Savi, Kétonou, etc.	*Idem*
Slave-sorting sites	Savalou, etc.	*Idem*
Entrepôts and embarkation sites	Ouidah, Agoué, Grand-Popo	Ouidah site partly developed

Other sites evocative of the tragedy of the slave trade – awaiting restoration and integration into the country's cultural heritage – are to be found in various parts of Benin.

Some Reminders of the Tragic Triangular Trade

There are in Benin a number of monuments directly related to the slave trade and others that owe their existence to the contacts between the Slave Coast and the Americas induced by that trade.

The first type of monument includes forts, trading posts, wrecks and many other objects linked to the slave trade. The French, English and Portuguese were given, by the kings of Ouidah (Juda), concessions of land situated at present-day Savi to put up strategically located buildings – forts or fortresses – to serve as living quarters for themselves and entrepôts for slaves. A description of one of these forts may be found in a narration by Père Labat:

> The French and the English each have a fort to the west of this village. The French one is further west; it is composed of four bastions with wide, deep ditches, but no covered way, glacis or palisade.... It has 30 cannons, some mounted on the bastions and others on the curtain walls.... The four main buildings, which form a large square, serve as storehouse, officers' quarters and garrison; that is what they call the place where the captives are held until the time for their embarkation.[9]

Even though these forts (built by the French, English, Danes and Portuguese) are not as celebrated as those on the Island of Gorée in Senegal or at St Jorge d'Elmina in Ghana – perhaps because it has not been possible to preserve all of them – they are a powerful reminder of the slaves who transited through them. Only the fort constructed by the Portuguese has survived; today it houses the Historical Museum of Ouidah, whose collections are essentially concerned with the history of the slave trade.

The trading posts have also disappeared. The one at Djêgbadji, on the coast – without doubt the most recent, and widely known as the 'customs house' – still exists and is awaiting renovation as a tourist attraction. Other indirect reminders of the slave trade, common in South Benin, are admired by tourists: among them are the remains of the Brazilian or Afro-American community of freed slaves who came back to the places from which their black ancestors had set out. The impact of this culture of return is easy to see in the towns of Ouidah, Porto-Novo and Agoué, living eco-museums of the most lively American traditions with their Brazilian-style architecture, cooking and cultural traditions, religious practices and Portuguese, French or English-sounding names.

Lastly, across the Atlantic Ocean, vestiges of the slave trade may increase Benin's attraction as a tourist destination. During the 'Ouidah 92' festival, for example, Benin was informed of the refloating of a ship bearing the inscription 'Whydah', discovered off the coast of Boston in the United States of America in 1982 and later transferred to Tampa (Florida) to join the collection of

Tampa's Museum of African Art. This ship, which served as a slave vessel before being taken over by pirates, was wrecked in 1717; plans were to turn it into a floating museum open to the public, located in a theme park. But, due to opposition from the black communities of Tampa and Boston, the project was cancelled. Might it be possible for Benin to recover this ship and make it a tourist attraction?

The monuments and sites of the slave trade are part and parcel of the culture of the country in which they are located. What are they? Places of shame or taboo? There is no need for reticence in facing up to history. These monuments and sites are primarily reminders of the past, however painful that past may be. They may, and should, be places of meditation and reflection for everyone, including tourists, in much the same way as are the Zoungbodji memorial, the statue of Toussaint L'Ouverture on the road from Allada, the Historical Museum of Ouidah and the various reminders scattered along the road leading from the town to the beach from which the slaves embarked.

Tourism, Development and Peace

Tourism, only yesterday seen as a form of relaxation for the privileged classes, has become a major facet of society, the most important economic activity in the world.[10] In 1994, there were more than 500 million tourists worldwide. Whatever the reasons for it, tourism constitutes an economic resource that could succeed in alleviating poverty, creating employment, increasing foreign currency holdings, resolving the problems of the rural world and encouraging the social and cultural development of local communities. And yet the concept of tourism is difficult to grasp and that of cultural tourism even more so.

Tourism opens up a wide variety of subjects: art as a means of expression, education, cultural activities and sport, town planning, industrialisation, infrastructure and technical progress, the environment, ecology and archaeology, holidays, gastronomy and entertainment, the craft industry, lifestyles and traditions, games for children and so forth – in short, life itself. Today tourism remains the ideal instrument for national and individual development. It is founded on the individual hunger for knowledge and understanding, on the desire to discover the world and fellow human beings, to explore nature and the human spirit – experiences most fully enjoyed when they are shared. The sharing of personal experience, of problems and hopes (in other words, 'communication') is the aim of the new approach to tourism.

Tourism is therefore a form of recreation away from the home. But it is also a state of mind shaped by the vast range of previous experiences. It is a way of understanding life and a theoretically harmonious means of enabling people today to fit into their environment. It thus becomes a fundamental component of human equilibrium. It helps one to relax, combat stress and 'recharge one's batteries', thus promoting individual fulfilment.[11] Of course, tourism takes a multitude of forms, as many forms as there are tourists. But business tourism does not exclude cultural tourism, which is not incompatible with recreational tourism, which in turn may overlap with sport-centred tourism.

On this basis, cultural tourism would therefore cover the various forms of tourism based on intellectual interests. Museums are visited for the works of art they contain, while historic monuments are valued for their architecture. Cultural sites are popular with tourists: the Alhambra, for example, the jewel of Islamic civilisation in Andalusia, draws more than 30 million visitors a year; the Taj Mahal, one of the wonders of the world, is a record-breaking attraction in India; in Paris, the Georges-Pompidou Centre attracts 8 million visitors a year and the Château de Versailles, 4 million,[12] Such historic monuments are of great architectural, cultural and touristic value. The so-called imperial cities of Rabat, Meknès and Marrakesh, with their palaces, mosques and fountains, are simply historic cities with a place in Morocco's past. Yet no sooner has one left them than one dreams of going back, for these cities are not only of cultural interest, but are tourist centres as well. In my opinion, St Jorge d'Elmina in Ghana or the Island of Gorée in Senegal fit perfectly into this context.

Besides sites and monuments, cultural events such as festivals, shows and carnivals are of great interest to tourists. The scope of cultural tourism is completed by nature parks and natural sites, and spiritual sites such as Lourdes or Mecca. One day perhaps the *vodun* sanctuaries, too, will become known all over the world. All these are places or events that encourage the mingling of populations and races, and reveal the similarity of behaviour, whatever the colour of an individual's skin. Is this not a pointer to mutual understanding and the promotion of world peace?

Everything we understand as cultural tourism is connected with a new interest that makes people want to travel, just as they travel on business, or for sport or recreation. Why should the slave trade, the biggest forced displacement of people in the history of humanity, and in consequence the sites and monuments engendered by it, not attract tourists? Why should the ardent desire of the descendants of the slaves, the blacks of the diaspora, to return in pilgrimage to the land of their ancestors not be considered a sufficient reason for renovating or rehabilitating a tangible and intangible heritage related to the slave trade? Would not that be enough to encourage the development of a form of cultural tourism?

The rehabilitation of sites and monuments related to the slave trade would help to bring the peoples of the world closer together, promote national development and create the conditions for greater mutual knowledge and understanding, the sole guarantees of world peace. We all realise that the better we know each other, the more we appreciate each other, and the more we respect each other, the more likely we are to engage in dialogue.

It would therefore be appropriate to stimulate reflection on themes that could lead to research projects for the development of slave-trade sites to receive visitors, including tourists. Such projects could focus on:

- archaeological research to rediscover and cast new light on the history of the old French, English and Dutch forts of Ouidah and the surrounding area, and an attempt to restore them for historical and touristic purposes (architecturally and in functional terms). The same approach could be used for the subregion and even for all other places in Africa connected with the trade;

- the revival of certain important slave-trade sites such as Allada, Ganvié and Kétou, where further studies could be carried out on the most interesting figures in the history of the trade. Tourist facilities, such as a 'Slave Route', could thus be organised for Afro-Americans;

- the transformation of Allada, in memory of Toussaint L'Ouverture, father of the Republic of Haiti, into a centre of pilgrimage for the blacks of the diaspora. A motel built in the purist Benin style (bricks in baked clay with natural vents) with organised activities on the theme of the slave trade (songs, dances, *vodun* cult and live entertainment) would cater for the tourists;

- integration of the segments of the Slave Route passing through Porto-Novo, Cotonou, Ganvié, Ouidah, Allada, Abomey and Kétou into the touristic Slave Route circuit linking up Cotonou, Ganvié, Porto-Novo, Kétou, Abomey, Allada and Ouidah (port of embarkation);

- production of a brochure containing historical and tourist information for visitors, and development of a web site that would encourage international tourism by disseminating information.

The slave trade, about which so many celebrated words have been written, has not yet revealed all of its numerous facets.

Through tourism, the Slave Route project could have immense repercussions. That is why everything should be done to make Benin a popular tourist destination for both specialists and amateurs eager to learn about Africa and its tragic history. Making use of a movement like the slave trade that had such a destructive impact on people and property would certainly be a highly unusual, even paradoxical, way of promoting national development.

Notes

1. G. Mbaye, 1986, p. 124.
2. Ibid.
3. *Ouidah, petite anthologie historique*, 1993.
4. It is impossible, in the present state of research, to give an exact figure for the number of Negroes affected by the slave trade. The most likely range lies between 9 and 15 million.
5. G. Mbaye, 1986, p. 124.
6. Ibid., p. 157.
7. 'Dahomey' was the name of one of the most powerful kingdoms on the Slave Coast before being used for the whole of the country at the time of the French conquest in 1894. The name of the People's Republic of Benin was adopted on 30 November 1975 and subsequently changed, on 1 March 1990, to Republic of Benin.

8. This classification by the author is based on the function of each site. The names used are those of localities in present-day Benin.
9. J.-B. Labat, 1728 (1993, p. 29). Labat was a member of the Order of Friars Preachers.
10. F. Vellas, 1992, p. 1.
11. *Nouvelles de l'OMT*, 1994, p. 1.
12. J.-P. Pasqualini and B. Jacquot, 1990, p. 8.

Bibliography

LABAT, J.-B. 1728 [1993]. 'Nouvelles relations de l'Afrique occidentale'. In *Ouidah: petite anthologie historique*. Cotonou, FIT Edition. .

LAHLOU, K. 1994. *La gazette du tourisme*, No. 19.

MBAYE, G. 1986. 'The slave trade within the African continent'. In *The African Slave Trade from the 15th to the 19th Century*. (General History of Africa: Studies and Documents 2.) Paris, UNESCO.

Nouvelles de l'OMT. 1994. (Geneva), No. 3, May–June, p. 1.

OFFICE NATIONAL MAROCAIN DU TOURISME. 1993. *Maroc, les villes impériales*. Rabat, ONMT.

ORSTOM. 1991. *Ouidah et son patrimoine*. Paris/Cotonou, ORSTOM.

Ouidah, petite anthologie historique. 1993. Cotonou, FIT Edition.

PASQUALINI, J.-P., and JACQUOT, B. 1990. *Tourismes: organisation, économie et actions touristiques*. Paris, Dunod.

UNESCO. 1981. *The African Slave Trade from the Fifteenth to the Nineteenth Century: Reports and Papers*. (General History of Africa). Paris, UNESCO.

———. 1994. 'Attention: Tourists at large!'. *Sources*, No. 55. (Paris, UNESCO.)

VELLAS, F. 1992. *Le tourisme*. Paris, Economica.

WTO. 1983. *New Concepts of Tourism's Role in Modern Society: Possible Development Models*. Geneva, WTO (A/5/12 Add., PG (IV) B.1.3 of 25 April 1983).

———. 1985. *Movements of Persons or the Facts about the Tourist Flows*. Geneva, WTO (SG/153 of January 1985).

Chapter 38

The Slave Route to the Río de la Plata: From the Slave Trade to the Contemporary Cultural Dialogue

Nilda Beatriz Anglarill

A DYNAMIC APPROACH to the relations among Africa, Europe and the Americas that emerged from the transatlantic slave trade is to inquire into the historical permanence of the links that exist today between the two shores of the Atlantic. Several meetings of experts have tackled the historiography of the slave trade and the mutual influences between Africa and the Americas. On the one hand, the abundant literature on these topics has taught us what was involved in procuring slaves, the life of blacks during the middle passage and the conditions of forced labour in the Americas. On the other hand, there has been much writing on the cultural contribution of blacks to the New World, especially in the areas of religion, music and language. Yet there have been very few analyses devoted to the contribution of slave revolts to the formation of the ideology of independence in the Americas or to the role of Afro-American cultures in contemporary relations between the two continents.

One of the reasons for this state of affairs has to do with the distinction made by Roger Bastide between the African contribution and the European contribution to the Americas, Europe having made a so-called 'noble' contribution in the form of political authority or economic and intellectual development.[1] In addition, co-operation between the independent countries in Africa and the Americas is today managed by state agencies and supranational organisations and not – or only marginally so – by members of the communities most directly concerned by relations between the two shores of the Atlantic.

Here I should like to look from a historical angle at the relations between Africa and the Americas deriving from the cultural dialogue that began in the period of the slave trade. What I have to say will be chiefly focused on the region of the Río de la Plata[2] during the colonial period and the independent states that emerged from Spanish rule. I shall start from an initial observation, namely, the lack of analyses of relations existing today between the countries of Africa and this region in the light of African contributions to the formation of American societies.

Four major types of research deal with the dialogue between the lands of the Río de la Plata and Africa. The most important, both quantitatively and qualitatively, are historical analyses of the slave trade and the integration of blacks into society, but the interpretation offered is more juridical than sociological. Most of these studies approach the question of the slave trade one-sidedly from the angle of the archives of Argentina and Uruguay, and they have only rarely been compared with African and European sources. They generally deal with the Spanish administrative organisation of the slave trade, the arrival of cargoes in the ports of the Río de la Plata and the legal status accorded blacks in colonial society. But the analysis – most of it legal analysis – of the social integration of Africans needs to be buttressed with work on racial miscegenation[3] or their absorption into the armies of independence, for the greater benefit of researchers working on the social dimension of the slave trade.

A second type of study stresses the cultural aspects of the slave trade during the period of slavery. But analyses of the African and *Afro-Rioplatense* cultures that came into being with the slaves chiefly describe folkloric aspects with few ethnographical references, or else are interpretative essays often tinged with exoticism. Most of these works give an image of the black person as an individual dominated by instinct, childlike and submissive by nature. These sources are interesting insofar as they describe not only cultural phenomena but also, and above all, the mentalities and intellectual attitudes of the time towards Africans. Unlike Brazil – where the resistance movements and cultural manifestations of slaves have attracted the attention of anthropologists and historians, in the Río de la Plata, cultural phenomena derived from Africa have been treated as a minor aspect of general analyses of slavery. Ethnic origin, festivals, dances and religion are dealt with briefly in a few chapters or paragraphs and are based on travellers' accounts or archives, but rarely on the evidence of those directly concerned.

A third type of study comprises anthropological monographs on manifestations of African culture such as it is being re-created today in the Río de la Plata and on new African phenomena. Anthropological research in Argentina, which is particularly rich as regards the study of indigenous cultures and rests on sound field-based information, has certainly had a methodological influence on the research that has been done on the population and cultural phenomena of African origin. In Uruguay, analyses of cultural manifestations of African origin follow on from the work of Ildefonso Pereda Valdés.[4] One of the favourite topics of researchers specialising in the study of *Afro-Rioplatense* culture is the origin of the *candomblé*, black music and dance that have survived down to the present day in Uruguay. The most widely studied Afro-American phenomenon today is the spread of Afro-Brazilian religions into Argentina and Uruguay, especially *umbanda* and *batuque*. The migration early in this century of Cape Verdeans to Argentina has been the subject of research on social organisation and the modes of integration into the host society. In them there is the beginnings of an analysis of the projection of these cultural phenomena onto relations between African countries and those of the Río de la Plata. Work on *umbanda* and Cape Verdean migrants in Argentina thus gives an outline of religious and social relations across the Atlantic.[5]

Finally, research on relations between the countries of the Río de la Plata and African countries[6] highlights above all the political dimension of co-operation. Work conducted in this framework has certainly delved further into analysis of the geopolitical problems of the South Atlantic region or some of the institutional aspects of existing relations between Argentina and independent African countries. But it has, above all, reproduced the popular myths and images of blacks that emerged from the transatlantic slave trade and the colonial period.[7]

It would therefore be interesting to consider the existence of a certain parallelism between the relations born of cultural influences resulting from the slave trade and the relations that the states of the Río de la Plata – and especially Argentina – maintain with African states. The fact is that inter-state relations cannot be separated from relations between communities. Conversely, the development of links between peoples constitutes one of the chief objects of international co-operation. Tying together these dynamics – those of communities and those of governments – will doubtless make it possible to point up gaps in existing studies and thus raise questions while identifying new lines of research to explore.

First Encounter in the Río de la Plata: The Invention of an African Culture in Exile

If there are gaps in the study of the slave trade in the Río de la Plata – which is the origin of the encounter with Africa – this is because of the long closure of the port of Santa María de los Buenos Aires to the slave trade and the scale of smuggling. For while Spanish *adelantados* and Portuguese traders in Brazil brought the first black slaves to the continent in 1530, the Spanish Crown authorised the trade only in 1587, and then banned it in 1604. In the course of the seventeenth century, only a few licences made it possible to breach the ban, which was finally lifted as a result of the *asiento* contracts allowing the sale of blacks in the Río de la Plata, signed with France in 1701 and England in 1713.

Certainly the scale of the smuggling of blacks, which was rife during the periods of both legal and illegal trade, makes it very difficult to assess the overall volume of the slave trade.[8] The only thing that can be said for sure is that the number of Africans legally entering American territory is but a small proportion of the actual number of blacks who entered through the port of Buenos Aires and over the Brazilian border. Portuguese ships bound for Brazil or Colonia del Sacramento, founded in 1680, French ships heading for the Southern Ocean and English ships seeking fresh supplies brought a whole range of goods into the Río de la Plata – including human beings brought from Africa. Some of these latter were sold to work in the mines of Potosí and Peru, with large profits for the traders who sold them at double their purchase price at Buenos Aires.[9]

In addition to the gaps as to the number of blacks brought into the Río de la Plata, there is our uncertainty as to their destination. The complacent view is that slaves providing domestic service in a subsistence economy society were better treated by their masters than plantation slaves. But the trade in blacks, especially active on the Buenos-Aires-Córdoba-Potosí route, and the conditions on the journey and in work in the mines prove that the reality was decidedly different.

Relatively little is known about the ethnic origin of blacks who landed on American soil, the African sources on the subject being inadequate. When the slave trade was legal, this origin was given as either the region where the purchase had taken place or the port of embarkation. Thus there are references to the 'Guinea ethnic group' or the 'Cabinda ethnic group' whereas many ethnic groups from the African coast or lands in the interior were involved. Conversely, little is known of the origin of blacks who were smuggled in, first because there was no register of the individuals so transported, and second because the blacks brought into the Americas illegally did not always come from a single cargo but from deals made between slave-traders even before their arrival at their destination.

In addition, there are uncertainties of other kinds, for example, when reference is made to notions of ethnic identity. This concept assumes acknowledgement of membership of a group, or nationality, and is misleading, since it brings in the notion of nation in the European sense of the term or refers to a status (that of a nation) which is not applicable to the slave, regarded as a 'thing'. This idea derives from the fact that blacks grouped themselves into 'nations'. Among the leading forms of association, there were the brotherhoods attached to churches, societies with name of the 'nation' to which its members belonged, and mutual aid organisations. In the Río de la Plata, the name of the 'nation' corresponded to that of the region from which the slave trade had set out (Angola, Guinea), the port of embarkation (Benguela, Mina) and, sometimes only, the ethnic group (Ashanti or Sante, Hausa or Ausa, Mandinka).[10]

The gaps in the sources that have just been mentioned chiefly pose problems when the survival or reproduction of 'identical' African traits is being sought, and is far less of a problem when a dynamic approach to these same phenomena is adopted. In contact with other cultures – African, European or indigenous – the blacks transplanted to the Río de la Plata invented a new culture of exile based on reinterpreting or re-creating elements in a different social context. As we all know, the concept of culture is not confined to musical and religious manifestations alone, but refers to a whole set of values, norms, ideas and symbols. It is therefore in this wider conceptual context that we shall examine the influence of African cultures in the formation of the society, ideologies and relations that the states of the Río de la Plata maintain today with those on the African continent.

The Integration of Blacks into the Society of the Río de la Plata

In Brazil, the integration of blacks into American societies has been the subject of interesting studies of the social, educational and economic discrimination against them and has revealed the precariousness of what was called a 'racial democracy'.[11] In the Río de la Plata, there has been virtually no calling into question of an allegedly humane treatment of blacks and their integration into a non-racist society, even in the most recent studies. We need therefore to look at the historiography of this region and the myth of the harmonious encounter of blacks, Spaniards and indigenous cultures.

One of the ways in which blacks could become integrated into the world of whites was to purchase their freedom (*manumisión*). According to Spanish law, from the time of the thirteenth century *Partidas*, *siervos* could purchase their freedom. But the Spanish *Code noir* (Black Code) of 1789 did not contain any general provisions on this point as regards the possessions in the Americas. Particular provisions of the Black Code concerning the 'Spanish Island', referring to anomalies in the purchase by slaves of their freedom, reintroduced the Roman rule on the acquisition of freedom in all its ancient harshness.[12] According to custom, the master was required to free his slave once the agreed sum was paid. But there again, in the Río de la Plata, some legal decisions demonstrate masters' unwillingness to free their slaves and variations in the legal criteria for the purchase of freedom against the will of the owners.[13] To obtain the money needed to buy their freedom, the slaves would work in addition to the obligations due to the masters or borrow from African associations or individuals to whom they would promise reimbursement in cash or through the provision of various services. Some slaves – very few, it is true – were lucky enough to become free by provisions in their masters' wills.

Slaves in the Río de la Plata could also gain their freedom by participating in the military campaigns to consolidate independence.[14] Many fought to defend Buenos Aires during the two British invasions of 1806 and 1807. But it was only after 1813 that, on the orders of the authorities of the independent government, they were enrolled in the militia in large numbers in return for the promise of freedom at the end of their service. However, as the date of freedom was repeatedly postponed and the conditions of military life were particularly harsh, many deserted. And the fact that a few former slaves or descendants of slaves were promoted to the rank of officer for valour does not constitute sufficient proof to say that prejudices regarding black inferiority had disappeared. More research needs to be done on this subject to know more about the situation of blacks enrolled in the militia, the attitudes of 'European' and *criollo* soldiers to a black military superior and the conditions in which black officers were promoted compared to white officers. The debate, of course, involves élite attitudes towards black social mobility and also the issue of the political role that these men played in the highly militarised society of the early days of independence.

How far were black, mulatto or *pardos* slaves integrated into the society of the time? What were their employment prospects? Did the freedmen have access to schools and universities? We know of the prejudices that prevented the promotion of black soldiers to the rank of general and the refusal at the end of the eighteenth century to award a degree to a student of the University of Córdoba whose grandparents were suspected of having black blood. Several general studies of blacks have suggested ways of closing the gaps[15] that have been found. Other research on blacks' standard of living, access to property and admission to the civil service might further enrich analysis of their social situation in the Río de la Plata.

The integration of Africans into the economy of this region also deserves close attention. The economic role of blacks has generally been analysed from three angles: the type of work done by slave labour, the trades exercised by freedmen and how blacks were treated by their masters. We have already indicated the limits of the arguments as to the good treatment that blacks are said to have received and have shown the need for a critical analysis of studies on the subject. Despite the works devoted to the trades exercised by blacks and the economic situation of the Río de la Plata provinces at the time of the slave trade, much still remains to be said on the role played by Africa and the Americas in the world economy as a result of the triangular trade and that played by the Río de la Plata in the balance of the Spanish economy. Buenos Aires – the port through which the silver from Potosí moved to the outside world and a supplier of leather, the 'poor relative' among the economies of the region – thus occupied an ideal position for redistributing goods involved in the smuggling trade. This question is sufficiently complex to extend the field of analysis and also to prompt a look at the rivalry between Portugal and Spain in South America and the balances and divisions of European power.

Questions need also to be asked about the participation of blacks in the political life of the region. We know, although patchily, the geographical distribution of blacks and their descendants on Argentine territory,[16] and also the 'blackening' of the population the further north one goes,[17] as well as some aspects of the black labour market.[18] Among possible research topics are the voluntary movements studied usually for their humanitarian aims but whose organisation and social and political demands are little known. We could even ask whether mutual aid societies did not aim to re-establish links between the Río de la Plata and its home communities, and even organise a return movement to 'mother Africa'.

In this context, we also need to ask whether the revolution led by Toussaint L'Ouverture in Haiti did or did not have an impact on the black slaves in the Río de la Plata. School textbooks have always taught us, when dealing with the 'events leading up to the May 1810 revolution', that four historical facts had helped to accelerate the breach with Spain: the independence of the United States of America, the French Revolution, the Tupac Amaru rebellion in Peru and Toussaint L'Ouverture's revolution in Haiti. Did the blacks hear about the black liberator of St-Domingue, either by word of mouth or by reading about him? Was there a link between the Haitian rebellion of 1791 and that of the 'Blacks and French' that occurred in Buenos Aires in 1793?[19] The reply to this question and study of the sources of other rebellions might open up new prospects for research on the existence or otherwise of a political culture among blacks.

Another question to be examined concerns how blacks participated in the electoral system of the region. Study of the electoral law since 1810 reveals an unexplored field: the fight waged by blacks for recognition of their political rights. The ordinance of 25 May 1810 had summoned 'the largest and healthiest part of the population',[20] and the general assembly that adopted the form of government of the new state decided that only 'free persons' who supported the American cause could be voters or could be elected as deputies,[21] which, on both counts, excluded blacks. One of the few electoral provisions devoted to blacks in 1817 established the right to vote for descendants of slaves (active vote) and, from the 'fourth degree' of descent, the possibility of voting and being elected (passive vote).[22] Since then, the question of black citizens has not been the subject of any separate provisions. A reductionist, legalistic approach might deduce from that an absence of political discrimination against blacks since the advent of the new state. Nevertheless, if we closely examine the social dynamic, we see that racial-type prejudices prevented the descendants of Africans from acceding to important political positions. Two individuals in political life at the beginning of the nineteenth century, Bernardino Rivadavia and Bernardo de Monteagudo, were suspected of being of mixed black blood although Rivadavia was entered as 'white' in the 1810 census. The 'whitening' of political figures and members of the local bourgeoisie, widespread in the last century, clearly shows the survival of prejudices in the area of 'colour' or 'purity of blood' imported by the Spanish.

The idealised, mythicised or denied character of the encounter between Africa and the Río de la Plata survives in the relations that the two regions still maintain today. A close examination of these three centuries of history, taking account of the actual intercultural relations – the achievements as well as the divergences – and drawing on the lessons of the past, would provide solid foundations for the construction of modern relations between states, faced as they are with the task of encouraging dialogue and solidarity among the various communities concerned.

Notes

1. R. Bastide, 1979, p. 54.
2. During the sixteenth and seventeenth centuries, Río de la Plata was the name of a vast area comprising the present-day republics of Argentina, Paraguay and Uruguay. The viceroyalty of the Río de la Plata, established in 1776 with Buenos Aires as its capital, extended the area with the inclusion of Cuyo and the silver-producing regions of La Paz, Oruro and Potosí in order to ensure the financial autonomy of the new administrative arrangements.
3. A. Rosenblat, 1954, pp. 127–167.
4. I. Pereda Valdés, 1965.
5. A. Frigerio, 1993, p. 92; M. Maffia, 1993, pp. 40–46.
6. Most monographs cover the co-operation between Argentina and African countries with some comparative analyses in relation to Brazil. The case of Uruguay is often dealt with in studies of the 'southern cone' subregion.
7. N.B. Anglarill, 1995.
8. For an assessment of the Spanish slave trade, see E. Vila Vilar, 1977, p. 209. The slave trade in the Río de la Plata has been studied more closely by E. de Studer, 1984.
9. On the arrival of the French vessel *L'Amphitrite* belonging to the Compagnie Royale de l'Assiento in 1705, two officers of the Spanish Crown purchased half the cargo (about 138 'heads', or 108 *pièces d'Inde*) at 270 pesos each, which were then resold in Lima for 600 pesos; *Archivo general de Indias* (Seville), 2,782; *Archivo general de la nación* (Buenos Aires) and *Acuerdos del extinguido cabildo*, 1705, p. 357.
10. The fact that the nations did not correspond to ethnic groups but rather to geographical names was pointed out in particular by I. Pereda Valdés, 1965, p. 89.
11. F. Fernandes, 1972; C. Hasembalg, 1977, pp. 7–33; and O. Ianni, 1962.
12. L. Sala-Molins, 1992, p. 73.
13. A. Levaggi, 1973, pp. 120–140; E. Petit Muñoz, E. Narancio and J. Traibel Nelcis, 1947, pp. 377 et seq.
14. G.R. Andrews, 1979, pp. 85–100.
15. G.R. Andrews, 1989.
16. N. Besio Moreno, 1939; E. Endrek, 1965; C. García Belsunce, 1976, pp. 83–92; and J.L. Masini, 1962.
17. Concolorcorvo, 1908; E. Endrek, 1966.
18. J.M. Urquijo, 1962, pp. 583–622.
19. J.L. Lanuza, 1946, pp. 151–152.
20. Act of 25 May 1810, p. 22.
21. 'Convocatoria a elecciones ...', 1811, p. 186.
22. 'Reglamento provisorio sancionado ...', 1817, p. 451.

Bibliography

Act of 25 May 1810. *Registro oficial de la República Argentina*, Vol. 1, p. 22.

Acuerdos del extinguido cabildo. 1705. Series 2, Vol. 1, Book 13 (13 July), p. 357.

ANDREWS, G.R. 1979. 'The Afro-Argentine officers of Buenos Aires province, 1800–1860'. *The Journal of Negro History* (Washington), Vol. 64, No. 2, pp. 85–100.

———. 1989. *Los afroargentinos de Buenos Aires*. Buenos Aires, Ed. de la Flor. [Eng. orig., 1980. *The Afro-Argentines of Buenos Aires, 1800–1900*. Madison, University of Wisconsin Press.]

ANGLARILL, N. B. 1994. 'El estudio de la población de origen africano en la Argentina'. Paper presented to the First International Symposium of Afro-Ibero-American Studies, Universidad de Alcalá de Henares/UNESCO.

———. 1995. 'Que pense l'Argentine de l'Afrique?'. In M'Bokolo, E. (ed.). *L'Afrique entre l'Europe et l'Amérique*. Paris, UNESCO.

———. 1996. *Las relaciones de Argentina con África: mitos y realidades de la cooperación entre países del Sur*. Buenos Aires, Universidad de Belgrano. (Working document, No. 2.)

BASTIDE, R. 1979. 'Historia del papel desempeñado por los africanos y sus descendientes en la evolución sociocultural de América latina'. In *Introducción a la cultura africana en América latina*. 2nd ed. Paris, UNESCO.

BESIO MORENO, N. 1939. *Buenos Aires, puerto del Río de la Plata, capital de la Argentina: estudio crítico de su población, 1536–1936*. Buenos Aires, Talleres Gráfico Taduri.

CONCOLORCORVO. 1908. *El Lazarillo de Ciegos Caminantes desde Buenos Aires hasta Lima 1773*. Buenos Aires, Compañia Sud-Americana.

'Convocatoria a elecciones para diputados a la Asamblea General'. 1811. *Registro Nacional*, Vol. 1 (24 October), p. 186.

ENDREK, E. 1965. 'El mestizaje en Tucumán, siglo XVIII, demografía comparada'. In *Cuadernos de historia del Instituto de estudios americanistas* (Córdoba), No. 35.

———. 1966. *El mestizaje en Córdoba: siglo XVIII y princípios del XIX*. Córdoba, Universidad nacional de Córdoba.

FERNANDES, F. 1972. *O Negro no mundo dos brancos*. São Paulo, Difusão Européia do Livro.

FONSECA, C. (ed.). 1993. *Fronteiras da cultura horizontes e territorios da antropologia na América Latina*. Porto Alegre, Universidade Federal do Rio Grande do Sul.

FRIGERIO, A. 1993. 'De la Umbanda al africanismo: identificación étnica y nacional en las religiones afro-brasileñas en la Argentina'. In Fonseca, C. (ed.). *Fronteiras da cultura horizontes e territorios da antropologia na América Latina*. Porto Alegre, Universidade Federal do Rio Grande do Sul.

GARCÍA BELSUNCE, C. 1976. *Buenos Aires, 1800–1830*. Buenos Aires, Compañia impresora Argentina.

HASEMBALG, C. 1977. 'Desigualdades raciais no Brasil'. *Dados* (Rio de Janeiro), No. 4, pp. 7–33.

IANNI, O. 1962. *As metamorfoses do escravo: apogen e crise do escravatura no Brasil meridional*. São Paulo, Difusão Européia do Livro.

LANUZA, J.L. 1946. *Morenada*. Buenos Aires, Emecé.

LEVAGGI, A. 1973. 'La condición jurídica del esclavo en la época hispánica'. *Revista de historia del derecho* (Buenos Aires), No. 1, pp. 120–140.

MAFFIA, M. 1993. 'Los inmigrantes caboverdeanos en la Argentina, una minoría invisible …'. *Museo* (La Plata), Vol. 1, No. 1, pp. 40–46.

MASINI, J.L. 1962. *La esclavitud negra en Mendoza; época independiente.* Mendoza, D'Accurzio.

M'BOKOLO, E. (ed.). 1995. *L'Afrique entre l'Europe et l'Amérique.* Paris, UNESCO.

PEREDA VALDÉS, I. 1965. 'El Negro en el Uruguay; pasado y presente'. *Revista del Instituto histórico y geográfico del Uruguay* (Montevideo), No. 25.

PETIT MUÑOZ, E., NARANCIO, E., and TRAIBEL NELCIS, J. 1947. *La condición jurídica, social, económica y política de los negros durante el coloniaje en la Banda Oriental.* Vol. 1. Montevideo, Facultad de Derecho y Ciencias Sociales.

'Reglamento provisorio sancionado por el Soberano Congreso de las Provincias Unidas de Sud-América'. 1817. *Registro Nacional*, Vol. 1 (3 December), p. 451.

ROSENBLAT, A. 1954. *La población indígena y el mestizaje en América.* Vol. 2: *El mestizaje y las castas coloniales.* Buenos Aires, Nova.

SALA-MOLINS, L. 1992. *L'Afrique aux Amériques: le Code noir espagnol.* Paris, Presses Universitaires de France.

STUDER, E. DE. 1984. *La trata de Negros en el Río de la Plata durante el siglo XVIII.* 2nd ed. Buenos Aires, Libros de Hispanoamérica.

URQUIJO, J.M. 1962. 'La mano de obra en la industria porteña (1810–1835)'. *Boletín de la Academia Nacional de la Historia* (Buenos Aires), A. 33, No. 2, pp. 583–622.

VILA VILAR, E. 1977. *Hispanoamérica y el comercio de esclavos.* Seville, Escuela de Estudios hispanoamericanos.

Notes on Contributors

Joseph C.E. Adande (Benin). Lecturer in the history of art at the Université Nationale du Bénin; is interested in 'traditional' arts and their contemporary transformations. He has published a number of articles on the subject in joint publications, in particular: 'Art et tensions sociales dans le sud du Bénin', in *Strategies for Survival Now* (Aica, Sweden, 1995), and 'Bocio, une sculpture de rien qui cache tout', in *Mélanges en l'honneur de Jean Pliya*, Cotonou, 1995.

Nilda Beatriz Anglarill (Argentina). Holds a doctorate from the École des Hautes Études en Sciences Sociales, Paris. Is currently a researcher with CONICET and teaches at the University of Belgrano, Buenos Aires. Member of the Institute of Public Law, Political Science and Sociology of the National Academy of Sciences, Buenos Aires, and of the Committee of African Affairs at the Argentine Council for International Relations. Author of numerous works on Africa, in particular, *África, teorías y prácticas de la cooperación económica*.

Dany Bébel-Gisler (Guadeloupe/France). Sociologist and linguist. Founder in 1979 of a Centre d'Education Populaire (Bwadoubout) where young people in difficulty receive a bilingual Creole/French education. Researcher at CNRS, author of numerous works and articles on the relations linking language, culture and power. Has been studying the survival of traits of African cultures and civilisations in the societies of the Caribbean for 10 years. In 1974, published the first scientific method of writing Creole (*Kèk prinsip pou ékri kréyòl*). His work *La langue créole, force jugulée* (1975) is the standard work in socio-linguistics. His other publications include: *Léonora, l'histoire enfouie de la Guadeloupe* and *Le défi culturel guadeloupéen. Devenir ce que nous sommes* (1989). In charge of teaching seminars in American universities. After secondment as professor at the Université des Antilles et de la Guyane (UAG), is currently preparing the second phase of the UNESCO Slave Route project.

Yolande Behanzin-Joseph-Noël (Benin). Born in Martinique, historian and researcher, *agrégée* of the Université de Paris-I La Sorbonne. Taught for 24 years at the Université de Conakry (Republic of Guinea) and has been teaching for 11 years at the Université Nationale du Bénin (Republic of Benin). Has published books and articles on French colonisation in Guinea and on the slave trade, the abolition of slavery and the African presence in the Caribbean.

Norbert Benoît. Career teacher. Was lecturer at the Institut Africain et Mauricien de Bilinguisme, and secondary school principal. Holds doctorate of letters, African studies option, from the Institut National des Langues et Civilisations Orientales, Paris (INALCO). Story-teller at CLE International, Paris; literary critic for Fernand Nathan. Has published a study on Loys Masson and introduced French-speaking Mauritian authors in the *Dictionnaire général des littératures*, published by PUF. He is a historian and has published, *inter alia*, a *Histoire du théâtre de Port-Louis, des origines à 1923* and *Les aventures de Jean-Baptiste Tabardin*, which are the memoirs of a pirate who was the son of a freedman. Author of numerous articles in the newspaper *Le Mauricien*. Currently cultural adviser.

Yves Bénot (France). Journalist (especially with *Lettres françaises*), teacher in Guinea and Ghana from 1959 to 1965; then in France, historian and essayist. Author of research works on Diderot, Raynal's *Histoire des deux Indes*, contemporary Africa (*Idéologies des indépendances africaines*) and colonial history (*La révolution française et la fin des colonies*; *La démence coloniale sous Napoléon*; *Massacres coloniaux, 1944–1950*). Chair of the Association pour l'Étude de la Colonisation Européenne, 1750–1850, Paris.

Bellarmin C. Codo (Benin). Beninese historian and researcher, lecturer in the faculty of arts and human sciences of the Université Nationale du Bénin, has participated in or organised numerous symposia and seminars, both national and international, at which he has presented papers. As Chair of the Scientific Committee of the Benin National Committee for the UNESCO Slave Route project, he organised the International Conference launching that project which was held in Ouidah (Benin) from 1 to 8 September 1994. He is the scientific editor of the journal *Mémoire du Bénin* published by the National Archives Division of the Republic of Benin.

Catherine Coquery-Vidrovitch (France). Historian of Africa, professor at the Université de Paris-VII Denis Diderot, former pupil at the Ecole Normale Supérieure, director of the Ph.D. course, 'Dynamiques comparées des sociétés en développement', member of the National Commission for UNESCO 1985–95. Her publications include *La découverte de l'Afrique des origines au XVIIIe siècle*; *L'Afrique noire de 1800 à nos jours*; *Afrique noire, permanences et ruptures*; *Histoire des villes d'Afrique noire des origines à la colonisation*, and *Les Africaines, histoire des femmes d'Afrique noire du XIXe au XXe siècle*.

Jean-Michel Deveau (France). Historian, currently lecturer at the Université de la Rochelle. Has published several works on the slave trade, including *Le commerce rochelais face à la Révolution* (1989); *La traite rochelaise* (1990) and *La France au temps des négriers* (1994). Vice-Chairperson of the International Scientific Committee of the UNESCO Slave Route project.

Marcel Dorigny (France). Historian, lecturer at the Université de Paris-VIII. Works on liberalism in the late eighteenth century and, more especially, in the time of the French Revolution and the Girondins. Member of the editorial committee of the journal *Dix-huitième siècle* and *Annales historiques de la révolution française*. Numerous publications on the economic, political and social thought of French liberalism in the eighteenth century. Ongoing research on the processes of abolishing slavery in colonial societies at the time of the revolutions, and publication, in association with UNESCO Publishing, of the proceedings of the February 1994 international seminar, *Les abolitions de l'esclavage, 1793–1794–1848. De L.F. Sonthonax à V. Schoelcher*. Published a work on the Société des Amis des Noirs in 1998.

Nina S. de Friedemann (Colombia). Anthropologist trained at the Colombian Institute of Anthropology, Hunter College and Emory University, Atlanta, United

States. Visiting professor at numerous American universities, winner of the Gabriela Mistral prize awarded by the Organization of American States. Edits the journal *América Negra* and participates in the *Expedición humana* research programme of the Universidad Javeriana, Bogotá. Has published numerous articles, works and papers on the Afro-Colombian communities, including *Ma Ngombe, guerriers et éleveurs à Palenque*; *Carnaval à Barranquilla*; *Criole, Criole Son del Pacifico Negro* and *Choco: magie et légende*.

Dieudonné Gnammankou (Benin). Philologist (Slav studies) and historian, trained in Moscow and Paris. Is researching the African presence in Russia in the eighteenth and nineteenth centuries. Foreign member of the Pushkin Society of Russia. Has published a number of works on the African origins of the Russian poet Pushkin. Author of a historical work published in Paris in 1996, entitled *Abraham Hannibal, l'aïeul noir de Pouchkine*.

Max Guérout (France). Retired naval officer. Founded, with a number of researchers, the Groupe de Recherche en Archéologie Navale, a society dedicated to history and naval archaeology. Since 1980, has managed excavation sites and underwater archaeological prospecting in France and abroad (Egypt, Senegal, Trinidad and Tobago). In 1986, at the request of UNESCO, he conducted surveys around the island of Gorée in Senegal and set up an underwater archaeological research programme on the slave trade which was incorporated into UNESCO's World Decade for Cultural Development programmes. In this context, he is organising an inventory of the underwater heritage of Martinique. Member of the Laboratoire d'Histoire et d'Archéologie Maritime à l'Epoque Moderne (a joint CNRS/Sorbonne/Musée de la Marine laboratory) and of the International Scientific Committee of the UNESCO Slave Route project.

Joseph E. Inikori (Nigeria). Professor of history in the History Department and Associate Director for Research and Curriculum at the Frederick Douglass Institute for African and Afro-American Studies of the University of Rochester. Previously taught at the University of Ibadan and Ahmadu Bello University, Nigeria. Was a scholar at the London School of Economics and the University of Birmingham in the United Kingdom. As a historian specialising in economics, he is particularly interested in international trade and development issues, and especially the transatlantic slave trade in the coastal regions bordering the Atlantic Ocean. He has published numerous articles, chapters in joint publications and books in his own right such as *The Chaining of a Continent: Export Demand for Captives and the History of Africa South of the Sahara, 1450–1870* (1992); *The Atlantic Slave Trade: Effects on Economies, Societies and Peoples in Africa, the Americas and Europe* (jointly with Stanley Engermann, 1992) and *Forced Migration: The Impact of the Export Slave Trade on African Societies* (1982) as editor.

Ibrahima Baba Kaké (Guinea) (deceased). Historian *agrégé* of the University, professor of history at the Centre de Recherches Africaines at the Sorbonne, and Lycée Jeanson de Sailly, Lycée Charlemagne, Lycée Henri Bergson and Lycée Turgot. Editor of the 'Grandes figures africaines' series. Author of several works of which the last, *Journal d'Afrique*, appeared in six volumes. Organiser and co-producer of the programme *Mémoire d'un continent* on Radio-France Internationale (RFI).

Joseph Ki-Zerbo (Burkina Faso). Specialist in the methodology of African history. Author of several works on Black Africa and its history. Director of the Centre d'E-tudes pour le Développement Africain (CEDA), Ouagadougou, Burkina Faso.

Hagen Kordes (Germany). Researcher-organiser trained in Paris, Benin and Malaysia. Professor at the Institute of Education Sciences of the University of Münster. Currently organises research-training groups on 'confrontations', on the one hand, between immigrants and 'majorities' (teaching of intercultural sociology) and, on the other, between those with folk/professional cultures and those with general/scientific cultures (integrative teaching approach). Author of numerous works, including *Das Aussonderungs-Experiment* (The experience of segregation); *Einander in der Befremdung begleiten* (Mutual assumption of strangeness); *Didaktik und Bildungsgang* (Didactics and human itinerary); and *Entwicklungsaufgabe und Bildungsgang* (Demands of development and human itinerary).

Clément Koudessa Lokossou (Benin). Historian trained at the Université de Paris-I La Sorbonne, diploma from the Centre d'Etudes Supérieures de Tourisme de Paris (Censier). Teaches at the Université Nationale du Bénin and is technical adviser to the ministry responsible for tourism, having held senior administrative posts there. Has taken part in a series of international meetings on tourism and has given several lectures on various topics in the field of history and tourism. Author of numerous writings on history and tourism, in particular: *La presse au Dahomey: évolution et réactions face à l'administration coloniale*; *Les Almoravides et le royaume du Ghana*; *La politique de développement du secteur du tourisme en République populaire du Bénin*; and *L'hôtellerie en Côte d'Ivoire*.

Robin Law (United Kingdom). Professor of African history at the University of Stirling (Scotland) and visiting professor in history at York University, Canada for 1996–97. Was joint editor of the *Journal of African History*, and author of: *The Oyo Empire, c. 1600–c. 1836* (1977); *The Horse in West African History* (1980); and *The Slave Coast of West Africa, 1550–1750* (1991); editor of *From the Slave Trade to 'Legitimate' Commerce: The Commercial Transition in Nineteenth-Century West Africa* (1995).

Hugues Liborel-Pochot (France). Professor of modern letters, former junior lecturer at the Universités de Paris-I and Paris-VII, assistant in the IUFM in the field of teacher training. Member of the Groupe de Recherches sur le Conte et l'Oralité at Paris-VII, organised by Professor Bernadette Bricout. Educational psychologist at the CEREP (day hospital for psychotic adolescents, Paris). Psychologist, psychoanalyst, member of the CEDAGR (Centre d'Etudes et d'Aide aux Antillais, Guyanais et Réunionnais). Has published *Métaphiles* and *Les fileuses, un mythe littéraire*.

Julie Lirus-Galap (Martinique/France). Social anthropologist, awarded a doctorate in 1977 from the Université René Descartes, Paris. Currently associate professor at the Université de Paris-VII Denis Diderot and member of the research laboratory Dynamiques des Sociétés en Développement (ex-Tiers Monde). Specialist in multidisciplinary research on the meeting of cultures, exchanges, processes of cultural intermingling and identity movements in contemporary societies in the Caribbean. Author of numerous studies on the components of Afro-American cultures and the work entitled: *Identité antillaise* (1982). Research officer at the Centre Roger

Bastide, then the Laboratoire Associé 220 of the CNRS. Publications editor of the journal *Mawon* on the social and cultural organisations of the Caribbean diaspora. Member of ministerial private office in France, 1988–93.

Francisco López Segrera (Cuba). Holds doctorates in law (University of Havana), historical sciences (Academy of Sciences, Moscow), and Hispanic and Latin American studies (Université de Paris-VIII La Sorbonne). Has given courses and lectures, as a visiting professor, on the history of Cuba, the Caribbean and Latin America in more than 20 universities in America, Europe and Africa, including: Johns Hopkins University (United States); the Norman Paterson School of International Affairs; Carleton University (Canada); the Mexico City College (Mexico); UNAM (Mexico); the Latin American Faculty of Social Sciences (FLACSO) (Costa Rica); the Latin American Social Sciences Council (CLACSO) (Argentina); the University of São Paulo (Brazil); Paris-VIII (France); the University of Santander (Spain); the Diplomatic Academy, Vienna (Austria); the Institute of Latin America (former USSR), and the University of Zimbabwe. Currently Regional Adviser in the social sciences at UNESCO in the Caracas Office. Has published numerous books and articles on contemporary aspects of the history of Cuba, the Caribbean and Latin America. Some of his studies have been translated and published in Brazil, Chile, Cuba, France, Italy, Japan, Mexico, the United States and Venezuela.

Paul E. Lovejoy (Canada). Distinguished Research Professor in African history at York University, Toronto, member of the Royal Society of Canada. Earned Ph.D. from the University of Wisconsin (1973). Author and editor of numerous works, including: *Caravans of Kola: The Hausa Kola Trade, 1700–1900*; *Transformations in Slavery: A History of Slavery in Africa*; *Salt of the Desert Sun: The History of Salt Production and Trade in the Central Sudan*; *Slow Death for Slavery: The Course of Abolition in Northern Nigeria, 1897–1936* (with J.S. Hogendorn); and *Unfree Labour in the Development of the Atlantic World* (with Nicholas Rogers).

Florence Omolara Mahoney (Gambia). Historian and specialist in educational sciences. Studied history at the University of London and education at the University of Oxford (United Kingdom). She has taught history at Gambia High School and Gambia College. Has written *Stories of Senegambia* for her students and *Gambian Creole Saga: The Emergence of the Liberated African in the Gambia in the Nineteenth Century* (unpublished), 1972–73: professor of African history at Spelman College, Atlanta, Georgia (United States); Earl Lecturer at the Pacific School of Religion, Berkeley, California (United States). Past Chair of the Executive Council of the All-Africa Conference of Churches, past Vice-Chair of the Faith and Order Commission of the World Council of Churches.

Patrick Manning (United States). Holder of a doctorate in history from the University of Wisconsin. Currently professor of history and Afro-American Studies and Director of the World History Center at Northeastern University. Author of *Slavery, Colonialism and Economic Growth in Dahomey, 1640–1960*; *Francophone Sub-Saharan Africa, 1880–1935*; *Slavery and African Life*; and numerous articles on the demography and history of the slave trade.

Luz María Martínez-Montiel (Mexico). Anthropologist and researcher, holder of D.Sc. from the Université René Descartes (Paris), diploma in Africanist research from the Centre d'Etudes Africaines (Paris), *agrégée* in Afro-American anthropology from the National Autonomous University of Mexico (UNAM). Conducts research at the National School of Anthropology and History of Mexico and coordinates the interdisciplinary and interregional programme *Afroamérica: Our Third Root* of the National Council for Culture and Arts of Mexico. Author of numerous works and articles on African and Afro-American cultures, is an advisory member of the African Diaspora Research Project of the University of Michigan (United States) and the International Scientific Committee of the UNESCO Slave Route project. Member of the Mexican Academy of Sciences.

Joseph C. Miller (United States). Historian of Africa, holder of Ph.D. from the University of Wisconsin (under the supervision of Professor Jan Vansina), specialist in the ancient history of Central Africa, the Atlantic slave trade and slavery worldwide. Currently professor of history at the University of Virginia (United States). Author of numerous studies on the political and economic history of Angola and oral traditions as historical sources, notably *Way of Death: Merchant Capitalism and the Angolan Slave Trade, 1730–1830*; joint editor of the *Journal of African History* (1990–1996); compiler since 1990 of the annual worldwide bibliography on slavery and the slave trade for the journal *Slavery and Abolition* (London, Cass); data recently collected in *Slavery and Slaving in World History: A Bibliography, 1900–1991*. Elected President of the American Historical Association in 1997.

Guérin C. Montilus (United States). Professor of cultural, religious and African anthropology at the Department of Anthropology, Wayne State University, Detroit (Michigan) since 1975. Founder and director of the African studies summer programme for American students in Benin in association with the Centre Béninois de Langues Etrangères (CEBELAE), Université Nationale du Bénin. Author of *Dieux en diaspora; Dompim: The Spirituality of African Peoples*; and numerous articles on Haitian and Benin Aja voodoo. Holder of diplomas from the University of Haiti, the Sorbonne, Université de Paris, Université Catholique de Paris and the Department of Anthropology of the University of Zurich.

Kazadi wa Mukuna (Zaire). Ethnomusicologist trained at the University of California (United States), where he obtained his doctorate in ethnomusicology. Also has doctorate in sociology from the University of São Paulo. Known particularly for his contribution to the study of African traditional music on the continent and in the Americas and urban music in Zaire and Brazil. Author of numerous works and articles, notably *The Characteristic Criteria in the Vocal Music of the Luba-Shankadi Children; Contribuição bantu na música popular brasileira; L'évolution de la musique urbaine au Zaïre durant les dix premières années de la Deuxième République (1965–1975); The Changing Role of the Guitar in the Music of Zaire*. Is currently associate professor in the Department of Music at Kent State University (United States).

Kabengele Munanga (Brazil). Holds doctorate in social anthropology; professor of anthropology and deputy director of the African Studies Centre at the University of São Paulo since 1980. Director of the Museum of Archaeology and Ethnology of the University of São Paulo from 1983 to 1989. Has taught at the Université Nationale du Zaïre (1969–75); the School of Sociology and Politics, São Paulo (Escola de Sociologia e Politica de São Paulo) (1977); the Candido Mendes University

-XVIIe *siècles* (1995); *Noirs et nouveaux maîtres dans les 'vallées sanglantes' de* ateur, 1778–1820 (1996); and *El negro en el Cuzco* (1996).

ie-Kouna Tondut-Sène (Senegal). Teacher of literature and researcher in the ian sciences. From 1969 to 1978, taught and worked with several cultural pub-:ions including the literary pages of the Dakar daily *Le Soleil*, the journal *Demb-Tey/Les cahiers du mythe* of the Centre d'Etude des Civilisations in the Ministry :ulture and the journal of Nouvelles Editions Africaines (NEA) and the Senghor undation, *Ethiopiques*. She also helped to draft the *Dictionnaire des littératures de igue française* (Bordas, 1984). She has lived in Geneva since 1978, where she is tive in various sociocultural circles linked to the United Nations system.

an-Norbert Vignondé (Benin). Holds doctorate in general and comparative litera-ire and diploma in African literatures and Third World civilisations; trained at the niversité de Paris-III La Sorbonne. Taught for many years in Benin, Togo and, prin-ipally, Gabon. Currently lives in France where, alongside his administrative post at .he Academic Inspectorate of the Gironde, he teaches the French-speaking literature of Black Africa at the Université de Bordeaux-III. Author of numerous articles in *Research in African Literature* (United States), *Notre Librairie* (Paris), etc., as well as a collection of Fon proverbs from Benin: *Lo* (1983), and an anthology of Negro-African criticism: *Le discours critique négro-africain de langue française* (1995).

Sheila S. Walker (United States). Director of the Center for African and African American Studies, Annabel Irion Worsham Centennial professor in letters and human sciences and professor of anthropology at the University of Texas in Austin. Holder of a Bachelor of Arts degree in political science from Bryn Mawr College and a Ph.D. in anthropology from the University of Chicago. She has taught at the Graduate School of Education and the Department of African-Amer-ican Studies of the University of California at Berkeley and at the Department of Anthropology of William and Mary College, Virginia. She has published both aca-demic and popular works and articles on Africa and the African diaspora, and has also participated in a number of nationally televised films.

Olabiyi B. Yai (Benin). Professor and director of the Department of the Lan-guages and Literatures of Africa and Asia at the University of Florida. Studied at the Sorbonne and the University of Ibadan. Has taught at the Université Nationale du Bénin, and the Universities of Ibadan, Ife, Bahia (Brazil) and Birm-ingham (United Kingdom).

(Conjunto Universitário Cândido Mendes), Rio de Janeiro (1... University of Rio Grande do Norte (Universidad Federal do R... (1979–80). Has published numerous works and articles on... African descent in Brazil, chiefly in the areas of race relations... black movements, etc., including *Negritude: usos e sentidos* (19... *políticas de combate à discriminação racial* (1996).

Alphonse Quenum (Benin). Holds doctorate in theology, histori... gist, specialist in the slave trade. Author of *Les églises chrétiennes et... tique de XVᵉ au XIXᵉ siècle* and numerous articles and works on soci... Africa and the world. Researcher and professor at the Catholic Inst... Africa. Writes for *La Croix* and *L'Evénement* (Paris).

Jacqueline Roumeguère-Eberhardt (France). Sociologist, film-make... director of research at the CNRS (project: totemic geography of Africa)... Roumeguère-Eberhardt received the teaching of the Venda and Magom... tion schools in Zimbabwe before broadening her outlook to include othe... in Africa and attendance at the Sorbonne, in Paris. She is privileged to... eral cultural identities: French, Venda and Masai. Author of numerous arti... works, including *Pensées et sociétés africaines: Essais sur une dialectique de... mentarité antagoniste chez les Bantu du Sud-Est* (1st ed., Mouton, 1963; 2... Publisud, 1986); *Le signe du début de Zimbabwe* (Publisud, 1982); *Quand le... se déroule* (Laffont, 1984); *Les hominidés non identifiés des forêts d'Afrique* (La... 1990); *La relativité culturelle* (editor) (Publisud, 1997).

Lluís Sala-Molins (France). Catalan, professor of political philosophy at the U... versité de Toulouse-II. Author of several works on distortions of the law and t... legal treatment of slavery. Has published *Code noir ou le calvaire de Canaan* (198... and *L'Afrique aux Amériques. Le Code noir espagnol* (1992). Member of the Inter... national Scientific Committee of the UNESCO Slave Route project.

Roger Somé (Burkina Faso/Italy). Holds doctorate in philosophy from the Uni- versité de Strasbourg, author of several articles on the arts and aesthetics of Black Africa and, in particular, a work, *Anthropologie, philosophie et art*, to be published by L'Harmattan. Is currently a member of the Management Board of the Musée de l'Homme's *Journal des africanistes*. He is also (in accordance with the French sys- tem for promoting researchers) on the qualifying list for the post of university lec- turer (section 18: arts, aesthetics, science of art) of the Muséum national d'histoire naturelle (section 20: anthropology, ethnology, prehistory), and organiser at the young workers' centre at Pontoise (France).

Jean-Pierre Tardieu (France). Holds D.Phil., professor of Hispanic American civil- isation at the Université de Clermont-Ferrand, member of the CIAEC of Sor- bonne-Nouvelle. Is working on the Spanish colonial mentality and, more especially, on blacks in the former Spanish possessions. Has published numerous articles and books on these topics, including: *Le destin des Noirs aux Indes de Castille* (1984); *Noirs et Indiens au Pérou. Histoire d'une politique ségrégationiste: XVIᵉ–XVIIᵉ siècles* (1990); *Le nouveau David et la réforme du Pérou* (1992); *Les Eglises et les Noirs au Pérou* (1993); *L'Inquisition de Lima et les hérétiques étrangers:*